BUSINESS AND GOVERNMENT IN CANADA

Partners for the Future

D. Wayne Taylor
McMaster University

Allan A. Warrack
University of Alberta

Mark C. Baetz
Wilfrid Laurier University

Prentice Hall Canada Inc.
Scarborough, Ontario

Canadian Cataloguing in Publication Data

Taylor, D. Wayne
    Business and government in Canada: partners for the future

Includes index.
ISBN 0-13-080716-8

1. Industrial policy — Canada. I. Warrack, Allan A. II. Baetz, Mark C. III. Title.

HD3616.C32T387 1999   338.971   C98-932215-7

ISBN 0-13-080716-8

Publisher: Patrick Ferrier
Acquisitions Editor: Mike Ryan
Associate Editor: Sherry Torchinsky
Senior Marketing Manager: Ann Byford
Production Editor: Nicole Mellow
Copy Editor: Mark Peranson
Production Coordinator: Deborah Starks
Permissions: Susan Wallace-Cox
Cover Image: PhotoDisc
Page Layout: Dave McKay

3 4 5 W 03

Printed and bound in Canada

Statistics Canada information is used with the permission of the Minister of Industry, as Minister responsible for Statistics Canada. Information on the availability of the wide range of data from Statistics Canada can be obtained from Statistics Canada's Regional Offices, its World Wide Web site at http://www.statcan.ca, and its toll-free access number 1-800-263-1136.

The cases in this book are written as a basis for class discussion rather than to illustrate either effective or ineffective handling of an administrative situation.

For permission to reprint copyrighted material, grateful acknowledgement is made to the following:

- *Canadian Public Administration* — "An Intepretive Understanding of the Non-fulfilment of Business-Government Relations" by D. Wayne Taylor, 30:3, and "An Interpretive Understanding of the Improvement of Business Government Relations," 35:2.

- *The International Journal of Public Sector Management* — "A Meso-level Understanding of Business Government Relations" by D. Wayne Taylor, 3:2.

- Schulich School of Business' Erivan K. Haub Program in Business and the Environment, York University — "Protected Areas and the Mining Industry in Canada."

- Robert Sexty, Faculty of Business Admininstration, Memorial University — "Benjamin Moore and Company Ltd. And the Government of British Columbia's Waste Paint Regulation."

- Paul Lachine for the cartoon in Chapter 5.

TO

Karen, Michelle, and Melissa Taylor

Jean, Lauren, James, and Daniel Warrack, and Alice Warrack

Jeanie, Kristin, and Julie Baetz

Plus ça change, plus c'est la même chose.

Alphonse Karr, 1808-90

A creditor is worse than a master; for a master owns only your person, a creditor owns your dignity, and can belabour that.

Victor Marie Hugo, 1802-85

Contents

Preface

Canada's most famous novel,
Two Solitudes,
talks about cultural isolation
of Anglophones and Francophones...
but another two solitudes exist —
business and government.

Pierre Elliott Trudeau, 1981

It should not be surprising that some degree of conflict exists between business and government. After all, government's task is to build a consensus from among an increasing number of competing interests and needs, and to provide strong leadership when no consensus exists. In a pluralist democracy such as Canada, the public interest can no longer be defined solely by business leaders or any other single interest group.

But are the halcyon days of C.D. Howe and elite accommodation really over? Do two new solitudes exist? What *is* the present state of business-government relations in Canada? Is there more to the subject than popular theories suggest? Until *Business and Government Relations: Partners in the 1990s* was written by D. Wayne Taylor in 1991 these questions had been largely neglected by Canadian social scientists and students of administrative studies. When Professor James Gillies started his research more than 15 years ago, almost every business-government study had been either conjecture, prescription-without-diagnosis, or anecdotal case study. The tools of social science had not been applied with much rigour. Most analyses of business-government relations since then have been primarily grounded in economics.

Building upon their earlier works, the team of Taylor, Warrack, and Baetz have collaborated to produce *Business and Government in Canada: Partners for the Future*, an up-to-date, practical guide to studying, understanding and strategically managing Canadian business-government relations. It is an empirically based examination of this integral variable in the strategic management of business and government enterprises today.

Students, no matter how well versed in management or government, need an understanding of the history and environmental framework of Canadian business-government relations. Only then can they interpret the present status of these relations and the constraints on modifying them. *Business and Government in Canada* provides such a background, as well as an up-to-date analysis.

To say the least, *Business and Government in Canada* should prove to be a controversial book. It has not been written in the normal textbook style because it is not a "normal" textbook. It is a book designed to inform student and practitioner, novice and expert alike about the uniquely Canadian underpinnings and manifestations of business-government relations.

Business and Government in Canada is also a book strong in its opinions. If the success or failure of Confederation is to determine the political future of Canada, the success or failure of business-government relations in the last years of this millennium will likewise determine Canada's economic future. Just as Canada can either remain a shining example of confederalism or become a victim of nationalist balkanization, so can it either remain a world industrial leader or retreat into the colonial backwaters of a new global order. The first will be decided by our 11 first ministers, the second by our business and government elites.

Instructors should use this book to provide background and a departure point for classroom debate. The opinions, conclusions, and generalizations of this work can spark, rouse, and even incite students not only to learn, but to think critically for themselves — the greatest gift an educator can bestow.

Business and Government in Canada covers *the* issues of the 1990s — debts and depression — as well as market and non-market business strategies. Chapter 7, Government in Canada, includes a discussion of all levels of government in Canada: federal, provincial, and local. Chapters have been included which consider privatization of Crown corporations, and trade, both international and intranational, with special emphasis on interprovincial trade barriers to intranational trade.

In addition, 11 cases have been included to assist the instructor in demonstrating the dynamics and outcomes of business-government relations. All of the cases have been carefully selected, not only to complement specific chapters of the book, but also to illustrate business-government relations (*i*) at different levels of government (federal, provincial, local, federal *and* provincial, and provincial *and* local); (*ii*) in different regions of the country (British Columbia, Alberta, Ontario, Quebec, Nova Scotia, and the Yukon Territory); (*iii*) in different directions (government directly helping business, government indirectly helping business, government impeding business, government helping *and* impeding business, government competing with business, and federal government opposing a provincial government with business stuck in the middle); (*iv*) conducted by business in different ways (reactive, proactive, and with business capitalizing upon government policy); and (*v*) conducted by government in opposite ways (nationalizing vs. privatizing).

Irksome to some may be the comparison of Canadian business-government relations to those of the United States. This comparison has not been done to ignore what is transpiring in the rest of the world, but to redress the injustice done to this field of study by the sometimes incorrect parallels drawn between these two quite different sets of business-government relations. In this management situation, we have more to learn from ourselves and our past than from others.

This book integrates practice with theory, using the following framework. It identifies what managers must know and do to improve their personal business-government relations and to help create a positive working partnership between the private and public sectors. However, borrowing from the contingency theory of business strategy formulation, what works for one firm may not work for another, given the same government and environment. If business strategists must avoid the trap of structuralist and reductionist thinking in developing their competitive, market strategies, so should they in developing government relations strategies. And likewise for government.

This book is concerned with the long-term survival of the private sector in Canada, the appropriate and most effective role of the state in post-industrial society, and the continuing survival of the Canadian economy in an increasingly challenging global commercial environment.

FIGURE P-1 **The Identification of Strategic Skill Requirements of Management: A Framework for Integrating Theory and Practice in Public and Business Policy Studies**

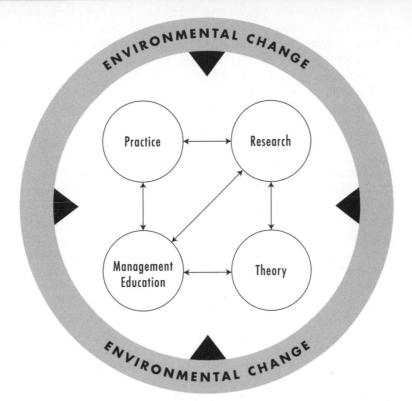

Above all, the book is written to make the reader *think*, to challenge you (and to have you challenge it), to encourage you to question conventional wisdom and popular reporting, and to scratch beneath the surface of public posturing and political rhetoric. We hope it does.

To the Instructor

Business and Government in Canada is accompanied by an Instructor's Resource Manual which contains case notes, sample test questions, and brief chapter outlines. This supplement is available for downloading on an FTP site. Please contact your local Prentice Hall sales representative for detailed information.

Acknowledgments

As in any endeavour of this nature, we would be remiss not to acknowledge those individuals and institutions who assisted us in our research and writing. First we would like to thank the McMaster University Arts Research Board, the University of Alberta Faculty of Business, and the Wilfrid Laurier University Research Grants Programme and The Laurier Institute for their financial and other support of our research and writing. We must also extend our gratitude to Dave Barrows, Peter Bartha, Sandy Borins, Mick Carney, Max Clarkson (now deceased), Bob Crothall, Jim Fleck, Craig Fleisher, Jim Gillies, Ken Hare, Vern Jones, Bill Jordan, George Lane, Rick Molz, John Mundie, Vic Murray, Robert Sexty, Bill Stanbury, Donald Thain, and Tom Wilson for their ideas, guidance, and wisdom over the years. We also appreciate the comments of reviewers Harvey Brown (Fanshawe College), Ken Rasmussen (University of Regina), and Howard R. Harmatz (University of Manitoba). Thanks also to all of the business and government managers who took time and had the interest to complete questionnaires, be interviewed and/or have cases written about them, as well as to suggest ways in which to improve business-government relations in Canada. Finally, special thanks for superb editing by Karen Taylor and Jean Warrack, Elsie Grogan, Karen Taylor, and Patti Wiebe for their almost endless hours of typing. Thank you.

D. Wayne Taylor
Allan A. Warrack
Mark C. Baetz

INTRODUCING BUSINESS-GOVERNMENT RELATIONS IN CANADA

Part 1

Closing in on the millennium, Canada is at a crossroads. The entire world is experiencing an economic and social paradigm shift the likes of which have not been experienced for some time. By way of introducing the topic of business-government relations in Canada the first chapter of this book takes both a retrospective and prospective look at Canada, its socioeconomic fabric, the roles business and government play in all of this, and the challenges lying ahead.

CHAPTER 1

Environmental Framework

ENVIRONMENTAL FRAMEWORK

He blunted us.

We had no shape.

Because he never took sides,

And no sides,

Because he never allowed them to take shape.

F.R. Scott, 1899-1985

Since the Great Depression of the 1930s, the governments of most industrialized nations have increased their involvement in the economies of these countries. As a result, nearly every sector of society has challenged the classic assumptions about the roles of both business and government in the economy. Among these are: the traditional role of business as provider of all goods and services of a collective nature; the ability of business to satisfy societal goals and needs; the efficacy of the market system; and the capacity or willingness of government to develop the economic climate required for private investment and growth.

Today, not only do governments fulfill their traditional roles by providing national defence, justice, and the protection of life and property, but they also regulate the actions of industry and, in some cases, provide actual goods and services.

In essence, the basic philosophy of capitalism has been modified worldwide into various concepts of collectivism. Societies once viewed as capitalist have, in fact, "mixed economies" today. Thus, most Western nations have public ownership of property, state-regulated markets, price allocation mechanisms other than consumer sovereignty, oligopolies, and state direction of enterprise.

The invisible hand of the marketplace has been transformed into the two *visible* hands of "rational" business management and state intervention. In the absence of a pure laissez-faire economy, private sector financial performance has been influenced as much by management's response to, and more important, use of government, as by its response to the marketplace.

BUSINESS-GOVERNMENT RELATIONS

No industry in Canada today is unaffected by the state. In 1996, government spending in Canada (federal, provincial, and municipal) comprised 41% of the country's Gross Domestic Product (GDP). About half of this was in the form of transfer payments and the redistribution of income. None of this is new for Canada. In fact, many have argued that Canada has had a mixed economy since the chartering of the Hudson's Bay Company in 1670. Business-government interaction, therefore, has been a reality for over three centuries. Borrowing from the lexicon of political science, one could describe the process by which Canada's business-government relations have been managed as "elite accommodation."

This process was particularly evident during the early 1950s when C.D. Howe, as Minister of Trade and Commerce, saw his role primarily as enforcing the "public interest." For him, this was ultimately business' interest. Ironically, those business managers who publicly display the strongest affection for the free market system are usually managers of firms with a fair degree of market power, thanks to their industry's particular structure. This situation often results from business' requests for and receipt of government assistance to close entry or control prices.

However, this is all changing. Academics, business leaders, and government officials all have reported the breakdown of elite accommodation and the overall deterioration of Canadian business-government relations since the 1970s. Much of the research on this theme has assumed a number of problems exist: that government intervention is emasculating the private sector; that business' interests are no longer synonymous with the "public interest;" *that what was once the workplace of a national socioeconomic partnership is now the battleground for two disparate solitudes, each growing increasingly antagonistic, mutually suspicious, and ignorant of the other.*

According to the press, the private sector regards cabinet ministers as political advantage-seekers and sees civil servants as paper-pushing, bumbling, irresponsible time-wasters. Civil servants, on the other hand, regard the private sector as people looking for a hand-out. Business calls for government to reduce its deficit and sell its state-owned enterprises so that jobs can be created. Even though the deficits remain, for the most part, and most state enterprises remain in the hands of the state, politicians say they have done *their* job and now it is up to business to create jobs. Both sides have described present business-government relations in Canada as futile, adversarial, prejudiced, and little more than a carnival sideshow. Beware the rhetoric — on both sides!

This book was written to provide an *interpretive* understanding of business-government relations in Canada. What does that mean? First, for business and government to interact more effectively *and* to their mutual benefit, a better understanding of each other's values, attitudes, beliefs, and perceptions is absolutely necessary. Second, this understanding can only be attained through increased interaction at the appropriate levels and at the appropriate times. Finally, both sides need to become fully aware of the historical and environmental backgrounds which will inevitably shape their relationship.

As the section headings of this book suggest, if the key actors in the Canadian economy first *understand* the historical and environmental backdrops to business-government relations in this country, and second *interpret* current events correctly within their proper context, they will then be able to constructively, cooperatively and strategically *manage* their interrelationships to meet the serious economic challenges which face them today. Or, to work backwards, business and government need to work cooperatively as partners to forge strategies that will guarantee Canada continued and sustainable economic prosperity, at less cost to the natural environment and within an increasingly turbulent and complex global order.

To become partners, both business and government must strategically manage their interface. Each side must: develop a full understanding of the values, attitudes, beliefs, and perceptions that the other possesses; learn how these variables are dependent upon the role and structure each has assumed in the Canadian polity; and see how the latter are grounded in over 300 years of neo-corporatist history and pragmatic culture.

Sounds simple, does it not? Then why do business and government continue to have problems? Perhaps common sense does not always prevail in business-government interactions, as we know it does not in most complex, long-standing relationships among people. Sometimes it takes a third party to reintroduce common sense into a long-time relationship. That is what this book hopes to accomplish.

For the purposes of this book, *business-government relations* shall refer to the entire gamut of interaction between business and government elites as it affects business strategy and/or government policy, rather than matters of a purely administrative, routine nature.

THE CANADIAN INHERITANCE

Why do Canadians elect governments that directly interfere with the economy? Why has Canada chosen a collectivist path rather than an individualistic route? Moreover, why does business not object philosophically to the size of government today?

The answers lie in a paraphrase of R. MacGregor Dawson, dean of Canadian government studies in the early 1900s. Professor Dawson maintained that if an individual's personality, traits, and characteristics were predetermined both genetically and through socialization, a nation's culture could form the same way. It would be affected by the heredity of its charter groups and its environment, including such situational variables as geography, climate, natural transportation networks, and human immigrations.

Canada's tendency towards an organic polity is thus deeply rooted in a lack of revolutionary tradition and a high tolerance for state intervention by the nation's founding, or charter, groups. Both "Tory" British loyalists, fleeing the republican anarchy of the United States, and pre-French Revolution Francophone settlers easily accepted a paternalistic state supporting their major economic institutions. *Thus, the early political, corporate, bureaucratic, and landed elites of our nation cast the mould for business-government relations for centuries to come — elitist, cooperative, and even collusive at times.*

For this reason, contradiction is the norm in Canadian politics and economics. The Conservative government of Prime Minister R.B. Bennett created the state media consortium of the Canadian Broadcasting Corporation (CBC). Similarly, the Progressive Conservative government of Prime Minister Brian Mulroney attempted to trim federal expenses by "privatizing" selected Crown corporations, just as the Liberals did after the war, while defending Canada's need to retain control of its state-owned national airline, Air Canada.

In the mid-1980s, Progressive Conservative Energy Minister Pat Carney told the House of Commons that the price of oil would not be lowered, nor would Petro-Canada, the country's state-owned oil conglomerate, be sold. These tax and operating revenues, she stated, help pay for a universal health insurance system, post-secondary education, and pensions. This is not right-wing ideology; this is Canadian pragmatism. It was equally pragmatic for the same government, as it became overburdened with debt, to sell shares in Petro-Canada to the public five years later and eventually sell off Air Canada.

Initially, the concerns of our United Empire Loyalist and French Canadian ancestors centred around protecting their beliefs and identities from the political, economic, and cultural expansionism of the United States. Never could they have realized the impact that their preserved values would have on modern-day Canada. *The British North America Act, 1867,* Canada's first constitutional document, included the Tory Loyalist values of social stability, hierarchy, order, and collective social action. These were manifested in the Act by the words, "peace, order and good government" — in stark contrast to the American Constitution's guarantee of individual rights to "life, liberty, and the pursuit of happiness."

The differences are clear. The United States was symbolized by Wyatt Earp — sometimes marshal, sometimes killer — his brothers, and Doc Holliday shooting it out with the Clanton Gang at the OK Corral for control of the territory. Canada, on the other hand, was symbolized by stiff and proper Superintendent James Walsh of the North West Mounted Police leading the exiled American Indian chief, Sitting Bull, to a peaceful new home north of the border. The American cowboy *tamed* the Wild West; the North West Mounted Police *settled* the Canadian West.

That is not to say that, in Canada, individualistic roots are trampled underfoot by a state monolith. Canadians are very individualistic. However, they temper their individualism with compassion for those in Canada less fortunate than themselves, who cannot exercise their rights as freely or as demonstratively. They manifest this compassion through the electoral and state policy apparatus.

With respect to business, there has never been a dogmatic, universal, liberal, free enterprise spirit in Canada as there is in the United States. Canada's founding fathers were immune to liberalism and capitalism, and to a large degree, so are their descendants.

These two founding nations produced the mercantilists of Canada's past and the Keynesian capitalists of Canada's present. Most illustrative of this influence is corporate concentration. As American industry consolidated in the late 1800s and reduced the level of competition in many industries, the United States government implemented a series of antitrust laws and regulations. It hoped to break up monopolies and oligopolies and restore a semblance of unfettered competition. In contrast, as Canada's industry consolidated during the late 1800s and the level of competition was reduced, the Canadian government did nothing. Thus, the state tacitly acknowledged and protected economic concentration in this country.

Historically, Canada has been, and still is, a public enterprise country, where business and government elites together direct and coordinate the economy. This has always been the case, and probably always will be. As a result of this heritage Canadians are, above all, pragmatic. Many critics say Canada has no national ideology because of this situation. They are wrong. Canada's ideology *is* pragmatism.

AN ECONOMIC CULTURE

Most social critics today, influenced by waning American hegemony, equate a society's cultural identity with its economic system. As a result, critics often mistakenly accuse Canada of not having a discernible cultural identity, since it has no distinguishable economy. Canadians appear as well-mannered Americans to the uncritical and untrained eye.

In fact, however, Canada's unique economic system is responsible for this nation's particular cultural identity. In keeping with the critic's form of analysis, the Canadian cultural identity *does* reflect its economic system. Both are grounded in two aspects of modern economic life. While not unique to Canada in form, they are certainly unique to Canada in the zeal and effectiveness with which each is applied: public enterprise and regional economic redistribution.

As evidenced later, Canadian public enterprise had its beginnings in the chartering of staple monopolies and the building of transportation and communication infrastructures for the growing Canadian economy. The latter commenced with the building of the Lachine Canal in 1821 along the St. Lawrence River to facilitate ease of passage for staple-bearing ships. Since then, public enterprise has provided the main stimulus to build a modern nation-state. Locks and canals, railways, public utilities, broadcasting, airlines, petroleum processing and marketing, and hundreds of other businesses have all worn the Crown in the name of uniting this vast land as Canada grew from sea, to sea, to sea.

For a labyrinth of political, economic, and cultural reasons, regional redistribution has been an equal force in this nation's building. The federal government has sought to keep geographically, socially, and economically disparate regions unified and as equal as possible in their standards of living, levels of health care, rates of employment, and opportunities for higher education. To facilitate regional equity, it has devised a number of complex financing arrangements and policy instruments. These have often been implemented through provincial agencies.

Canada's polity is continually reinforced by its *confederal* form of government. This is often erroneously labelled and compared to the *federal* form of government practised in the United States and elsewhere. A *confederation* by definition is a union of formerly independent political entities. It possesses a national government, as well as provincial or state governments. The national government is a first among equals, similar to the principle of the prime minister and his fellow ministers of the Crown in Cabinet. A *federation* is also a union, but clearly sets the national government supreme above the subordinate stable governments. In reality, despite a written constitution, the balance of power in a confederation fluctuates over time, often because of judicial or legislative interpretations and fiscal realities.

Canada appears federal in nature when the national government is strong with respect to the provinces collectively, as during the Government of Prime Minister Trudeau. It is in practice quite confederal when the national government is weaker with respect to the provinces collectively, as it is said to be today. Curiously, Sir John A. Macdonald's first preference was for a *unitary* form of union and government, as in the United Kingdom, where there would have been no provincial governments.

Thus Canada *does* have a cultural identity, grounded in the principles of public enterprise and regional parity, and complemented by the neo-corporatist values of state direction of the economy and state respect for and protection of private property.

A NEW CULTURE? — DEBT AND DEPRESSION

The same factors which gave Canada its economic cultural identity have also perpetrated a more visible, *social* cultural identity for Canada — one in which a publicly-funded (albeit increasingly with borrowed money) "social safety net" coupled with the duality of universal socialized health care and education sets the country apart from its industrialized peers. The benchmark manifestation of this social identity has been Canada's achievement of first place in the United Nations' Human Development Index three out of the four years preceding the writing of this book.

It is great for the collective ego to be considered "the best place in the word in which to live." But this 1990s accomplishment was achieved through *unsustainable* public expenditures at twice the rate of inflation on health care, education and social services throughout the 1970s and 1980s. This is unsustainable because Canada (and the rest of the First World) is now near the bottom of a 50-60 year Kondratieff economic/monetary/credit cycle, in other words, an economic *depression*.

Depression is a word shunned in the 1990s. There is plenty of discussion around the recent *recessions* — or inventory adjustments — of 1981-1982 and 1990-1991 in which the growth in GDP was negative for two or more successive quarters. But economies generally expand and contract in 50-60 year wavelike cycles. Recessions mark abrupt but relatively minor dips and rebounds along this greater wave of growth and slowdown. As economies "bottomout" along these 50-60 year cycles, there occurs a significant restructuring of these economies and societies. That is what is happening in the 1990s. Although a lot of business leaders, government officials, politicians, and economists are in denial over this, nonetheless it is reality.

Unlike the Great Depression of the 1930s in which hordes of individuals and businesses went bankrupt, this time governments are going bankrupt too (private bankruptcies doubled between 1993 and 1995). Although Canada's national current ratio of total assets to total liabilities was 2.2:1 in 1992, governments were not so well off. In 1988 the total liabilities of all governments (federal, provincial, territorial, regional, and local) in Canada exceeded their total assets. The Canadian public sector has been technically *bankrupt* ever since! The federal government on its own has been technically insolvent since 1977!

So what? In 1995-96 total government debt was 111% of its GDP. As government debts (the year-over-year accumulated net borrowings used to offset annual operating deficits) continue to exceed Canada's GDP in total dollars *and* continue to grow at a faster rate, public spending cannot sustain the nation's derived, social cultural identity. Thus, the federal government is ratcheting down its transfer payments to the provinces for education, health and social services. Thus, the provinces, in turn, are cutting programs (or off-loading them to municipalities or institutions which then perform the necessary surgery).

But why cut social programs that account for about two-thirds of most government budgets? Why not just raise taxes to cover the spread? Because most governments in Canada have "flattened out" in their taxing capabilities — or, even worse, are now experiencing "diminishing returns" as they increase the marginal tax rate. Tax revenues rise, peak, and then eventually fall, following an S-shaped curve (the Laffer curve) as the marginal tax rate is increased. If the marginal tax rate exceeds a given threshold, then individuals or firms go bankrupt, individuals become unemployed, burrow themselves into the cash economy, and/or leave the jurisdiction.[1] That is why governments everywhere are begetting gambling casinos and whatever other non-traditional tax generators they can.

And finally, as government debts mount, programs are slashed and revenues decline. Borrowing to pay off these debts, save programs, and offset revenue losses becomes more expensive. Gone are the days when Canada's bonds were rated AAA. Many of the provinces' bonds are A or BBB rated — with significant higher interest charges for each dropstep in rating.

The above does not do justice to the complexity of this issue. Many will gravely object to the simplicity of its analysis. Whether we view this issue negatively as a depression or positively as the fifth in a series of technological revolutions since the beginning of the Industrial Revolution, it is still cataclysmic. But the undeniable fact remains that Canada's economic *and* social culture as we have known it to date will be different — vastly different in the year 2025. *How and to what Canada evolves will depend largely upon how business and government grapple with the unsustainability of the status quo.* They will need to find new ways of both creating and distributing wealth.

IMPLICATIONS FOR MANAGEMENT

Canadians are a collectivist, politically pragmatic people strongly influenced by, but largely ignorant of, their past (remember Superintendent Walsh?). This is true of both the average individual's general historical awareness of Canada's roots, and of business' and governments' understanding of their beginnings in this country. Few Canadians truly understand the framework within which business-government relations were cast long ago and have operated ever since.

Most Canadians are also unaware of the historical, cultural, and socioeconomic differences between Canada and the United States. First, despite government protection of its cultural industries (including broadcasting, publishing, and the arts), Canadians are bombarded daily with modern American "culture." Second, and more important, Canada's social system and its novelties are less apparent to the naked eye and uninformed mind than are those of the United States.

Canadians have become masters in distributing wealth, whether as mercantilists or as enterprising, socially conscious public officials torn between liberalism's equality of opportunity and socialism's equality of condition. Such traits are well hidden in the superficial constructs of a western economy. Canada's roots in eighteenth-century Toryism have made twentieth-century democratic socialism quite acceptable — even by business — in many aspects of daily Canadian life. Business has even accepted publicly owned corporations which fill voids where private enterprise would not risk financial ruin in a country with a small population so widely and thinly dispersed.

Canada exhibits traditional views which can only be retained through slowly evolving social change. Revolution quickly kills old traditions and creates new ones. This is not to say that Canadians have not and are not changing; of course they are. During the 1970s, government's inability to curb rising inflation and unemployment severely undercut public confidence in, and traditional deference to, government. In the 1980s the pendulum began to swing back in favour of the provinces, again, at the expense of the federal government. As the microchip *glocalizes*[2] economic activity, individuals and firms look to either global or local opportunities and institutions for salvation, thus marginalizing national entities and polities. And now, in the 1990s, the whole Canadian inheritance is at risk.

Business managers in this country must remember that environmental influences are not always variables that can be internalized and controlled. They are fundamental to the very being of business and must be dealt with by chief executive officers head-on, with unblinkered vision, open minds, and all the negotiating and navigational skills they can muster. Of course, business can influence, and even control to some degree, its environment through advertising, vertical integration, cartelization, or other means. However, there are very real limits to what even the largest corporation can do, given the momentum of the Canadian governmental juggernaut, and more importantly, the paradigm shift the whole world is experiencing.

If anything, Canada is a practical country founded by practical people. Necessity truly has been the mother of invention, whether public enterprise has supplied public goods or regional income has been redistributed to overcome industrial and commercial disparities. These characteristics also represent the price Canada pays for independence, success in the world, and the unique benefits of a Canadian way of life. Canada's economy is definitely a public economy; Canada's culture, a public culture. The retaining of private property, promoting of state collectivism, and resolving of the conflict between the two are achieved through a process of elite accommodation.

Canadians have chosen to compete less against each other than against the odds of building a world-class country and economy where geographically such a feat was considered illogical and impossible. They both fear and envy the United States, but Canadians are not second-rate Americans. They are first-rate Canadians — a nation of creative, determined survivors.

Today Canada faces its greatest challenge since Confederation: surviving in a rapidly changing world economy in which the competitive advantages of yesterday will become the millstones of tomorrow. Business and government also face their greatest challenge: they must act in harmony as they have never done before. Only thus can they meet this external threat of global proportions when pressures are pulling them apart and when public esteem for both institutions has waned significantly.

To do this, as academic, politician, and corporate director James Gillies has advocated for some time, business and government must forge a truly "Canadian" approach to future interactions. For business, the economic imperative of long-term survival is identical to that of the Americans, Japanese, or Germans. All must maintain an adequate competitive advantage over existing and potential rivals and continually strive to produce an optimal balance among their environment, goals, strategies, structure, performance measures, and control and reward systems.

However, the political imperative of Canadian business is significantly different from its foreign counterparts, warranting an unprecedented approach to business-government relations. Not only has the Canadian government accommodated the economic needs of business throughout history, but Canadian business has been expected to provide the means through which government objectives are achieved. These include such areas as regional employment, security of domestic supply, and inter-provincial equity in prices and services. Of course, government has helped, but this co-agency of business and government is far more integral to the Canadian socioeconomic system than to the American system.

As Canada deindustrializes and follows the microchip into the even less labour intensive information age, the federal government's role in business-government relations will decline in proportion to that of the provinces and local governments. As Canada's economy is restructured, governments at all levels will have to "slash and burn" their way back to balanced benefits and sustainable public programs.[3] But many of those programs (health insurance, unemployment insurance, post-secondary education, welfare and public pensions, to name a few) also subsidize business tremendously. It is not surprising, therefore, that the largest critic of federal social program reform in the early 1990s was General Motors! The future — which is here now — poses monumental challenges to both business and government.

Canada's past must be the basis for its future, particularly with respect to business-government relations. This implies a uniquely Canadian approach to a uniquely Canadian problematic relationship. To this end, the nation must move forward if it is to remain the least imperfect country on earth. But business-government relations are not a reductionist function of management; they are contingent upon the times and circumstances. Human expectations (as well as those of business and government) are, more often than not, linear in nature. Yet these are definitely non-linear times. Canada survived the paradigmatic shift of the 1930s, but the 1990s are more complex. People (and businesses) are more dependent, less civil, less family and community oriented, and less accustomed to taking care of themselves.

SUGGESTED FURTHER READINGS

Bell, D.V.J., and L.J. Tepperman. 1979. *The Roots of Disunity: A Look at the Canadian Political Culture.* Toronto: McClelland and Stewart.

Blair, R.S., and J.T. McLeod, (eds). 1993. *The Canadian Political Tradition.* 2nd ed. Toronto: Nelson Canada.

Courchene, Thomas J. 1995. "Glocalization: The Regional/International Interface." *Canadian Journal of Regional Science,* 18:1.

Davidson, James Dale, and Lord William Rees-Magg. 1991. *The Great Reckoning: How the World Will Change in the Depression of the 1990s.* New York: Summit Books.

Grant, George. 1965. *Lament for a Nation.* Toronto: McClelland & Stewart.

Hardin, Herschel. 1974. *A Nation Unaware: The Canadian Economic Culture.* Vancouver: J.J. Douglas.

Hartz, L. 1963. *The Liberal Tradition in America.* New York: Harper and Row.

Horowitz, G. 1966. "Conservatism, Liberalism and Socialism in Canada: An Interpretation." *Canadian Journal of Economics and Political Science,* 32:2.

Lindblom, Charles E. 1977. *Politics and Markets: The World's Political-Economic Systems.* New York: Basic Books. (Especially Chapter 13)

Macpherson, C.B. 1976. *The Real World of Democracy.* Toronto: CBC Learning Systems.

Stewart, W. 1985. *True Blue: The Loyalist Legend.* Toronto: Collins.

NOTES

1. Although the average real family income rose from $52 500 in 1978 to $54 000 in 1994, after taxes it dropped from $45 000 to $43 500!

2. Glocalization is a term coined by economist Thomas J. Courchene to refer to economic power being transferred to both more local and global arenas.

3. Slashing and burning may not be all bad. As traumatic as it will be for those whose vested interests are gored, slashing and burning was agriculture's conventional method at refertilizing fields every nine years or so. Such refertilization may just work for government fields too.

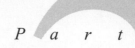

UNDERSTANDING BUSINESS-GOVERNMENT RELATIONS

To appreciate fully the problems and questions that business and government face, and the difficulties they have in facing them, one must first understand from where Canadian business and government come. The next three chapters respectively identify the history of business-government relations, the strategic problem facing management today, and the economic framework within which business and government interact.

CHAPTER 2

A Brief Historical Background

CHAPTER 3

A Changing Canada in a Changing World

CHAPTER 4

Economic Foundations for Business-Government Relations

A BRIEF HISTORICAL BACKGROUND

But what experience and history teach is this,
that peoples and governments have never
learned anything from history.

Georg Wilhelm Hegel, 1770-1831

Many historians, political scientists, and sociologists have concentrated on Canada's business-government relationship as affected by the country's economic development, social order, and cultural confusion. The one common thread through all these studies is the ease with which the state was accepted, at times even solicited, by the private sector as an economic partner — often a senior one. Canada's economic history clearly shows the reciprocal, almost symbiotic, relationship between public and private sectors. Thus national and private economic goals were achieved.

Because Canada has remained an open and relatively small economy, the United States has historically had significant potential influence on this country's pattern of economic development. Therefore, both political and business elites throughout Canada's history have regularly cooperated to develop a healthy, independent economic and political entity. In fact, businesses have frequently and consciously sought protection from American economic dominance. Consequently, the Canadian economic culture is different from the American economic culture against which Canadians often, and inappropriately, compare themselves. The government has always dominated the Canadian economy.

As Prime Minister Pierre Elliott Trudeau so succinctly noted in a 1976 speech to the Canadian Club in Ottawa:

> The free market system, in the true sense of that phrase, does not exist in Canada . . . the fact is that for over a hundred years, since the government stimulated the building of the CPR by giving it Crown land, we have not had a free market in Canada, but a mixed economy — a mixture of private enterprise and public enterprise.... Moreover, it has been with the support and encouragement of the business community that the government has continued to enter the marketplace to promote growth and stability. Among many examples are the creation of the Canadian Wheat Board, the negotiating of the Canada-United States Auto Pact and the government's heavy investment in Syncrude. [1]

THE EARLY YEARS: NATION-BUILDING OR EMPIRE-BUILDING?

Of course, the roots of Canadian business-government relations germinated long before the United States was a mighty economic power or Pierre Trudeau was prime minister.

The much heralded fur trade, for example, was a state-created monopoly. If not for the Crown's 1670 chartering and protection of the Hudson's Bay Company, and the colonial governing elites' involvement with the fur trade, so much wealth would never have been available to build the commercial empires which succeeded the fur trade.

Concurrently, the Canadian timber trade was a state-franchised oligopoly, again based upon the lease and/or sale of Crown land to geographically franchised monopolies. These seldom, if ever, had the inconvenience of competition imposed upon them. In fact, there was a succession of staple traders, each encouraged and protected by government. Each was dependent upon a more advanced, external economy for financing and markets; each business was an oligopoly or monopoly.

Canada's reliance upon its primary industries at the expense of its secondary (manufacturing) industries is not news to most Canadians. The preoccupation with the fur trade first by the French and then by British settlers represented the first and second commercial empires in Canada. The preoccupation with fish, grain, pulp and paper, minerals, and fossil fuels over the past century represents the third successful commercial empire in Canada. Each of these empires has been commercially, not industrially, based, and has been subservient in one form or another to a foreign, more advanced economy, whether French, British, or American.

Some historians believe that this reliance upon exporting staples and importing foreign investment has kept Canada in a permanent state of colonialism. Others argue that it was the only way such a geographically dispersed, thinly populated nation could have survived, let alone grow to be a member of the First World and the Organization for Economic Co-operation and Development (OECD). However, the facts remain: government intervention and business success worked hand-in-hand to build Canada.

In effect, Canada still is a colony.[2] With respect to industry, Canada is underdeveloped. As George Brown, one Father of Confederation, said as the new Dominion of Canada set its expansionist eyes on borders eastward, westward, and northward: "If Canada acquires this territory it will rise in a few years from a position of a small and weak province to be the greatest colony any country has ever possessed." History has proven George Brown right, although not in the way he would have hoped.

Colonialism implies that one group benefits from the exploitation of another. Therefore, being in an almost permanent colonial state is not all bad — at least the elites of the economies involved benefit. During the French regime — the first commercial empire of the North — native Canadians were exploited for their furs and the *coureurs de bois* were exploited for their labour, while the Montreal merchants grew rich.

Back in the seventeenth and eighteenth centuries, it was quite common to find Canada's founders or their heirs directing their conglomerates of monopolies and trading houses, sitting in the legislatures, and advising the heads of state as members of Cabinet. The local conservative merchant banks and insurance companies, which did their small part to finance and insure the trade of fish, furs, timber, and grain, were also owned by mercantilist-politicians. Seldom was a loan directly advanced to the manufacturing industry or to agriculture.

"Conflict of interest" was a concept yet to be advanced. There was no shame in being a merchant, banker, landowner, canal builder, and politician, all at the same time. Such was the closeness of business and government then; the public purse hung from the waistcoat of business.

With the *Treaty of Paris* in 1763, the French gave the British a virtual monopoly in Canada. This, combined with Britain's established monopoly in the Northwest, laid the foundation for modern-day Canadian business. Almost a century later, in 1844, the pattern of Canada's market structure was cast with the merger of the two largest land companies in the nation: the Canadian Company of Upper Canada, owned by Father of Confederation John Galt, and the British American Land Company of Lower Canada, owned by Peter McGill and George Moffat. Ironically, the new interlocked board of directors of the merged company also represented a large portion of the Executive Councils, or Cabinets, of these two provinces. This particular arrangement became known as the Family Compact, or *Château Clique* — the new elite of the second commercial empire of the North.

Business life was similar in the Maritimes. The merchant class had acquired wealth during the War of 1812, importing American goods and selling them to Britain, and importing British West Indian goods and selling them to the United States. This elite, led by Joseph Cunard, virtually controlled the timber, banking, shipping, and shipbuilding industries in Atlantic Canada.

Overall, there was low capital investment in pre-Confederation Canada, which relied almost solely upon labour-intensive harvesting of natural resources for its income. Local merchant capitalists, who dominated the business scene, were financed by British bankers, thus insuring that more money was sent to the mother country than remained in local coffers. As time passed, Canadian merchants pooled their capital into their own banks. It was natural for Canadian bankers, controlled by the land, fur, shipping, and timber companies, to allocate most of their loan capital to those involved in the trading of fish, fur, grain, and timber. Such investments were short-term and obviously with minimum risk. This was not so of agricultural or industrial development, which received very little in the way of loans.

During the late 1700s and early 1800s, Britain and the United States were beginning to invest in their own countries' industrial production. Growth of their respective manufacturing industries and saturation of their domestic markets required Britain and the US to find new markets for exports, and new and greater sources of raw materials. Canada offered both. But it would be government money that would build the infrastructure necessary in Canada to integrate the Canadian and American markets.

In 1826, the St. Lawrence canal system began. To this day, this system remains a prime example of a publicly financed work undertaken and still operated to reduce transportation time, to lower costs, and to benefit the coffers of Canadian commerce.[3]

In 1854, a fundamental shift in Canadian economic dependency began taking place. Canada initiated a policy of reciprocity (what we would today call "free trade") with the United States to develop this potential for trade. Railroads such as the Grand Trunk were built to penetrate the American midwest market and reach the ice-free ports of the East Coast. Americans built railroads and the Erie Canal across New York State to access Canadian raw materials and transport American manufactured goods to Canadian markets. Shippers of both countries soon preferred to use the American transportation network, since it was shorter and cheaper. Canadian business leaders began to look to the United States for financial opportunities and away from their parent, Great Britain.

In due course, however, the Grand Trunk and other Canadian railroads faced bankruptcy. Fortunately, John Galt, Minister of Revenue for the colony of Canada, was a member of the Grand Trunk Board. He proceeded to raise tariffs to protect his railroad; the United States retaliated, and reciprocity was scuttled. Canadian business-government relations were alive and well. Henry David Thoreau, poet, philosopher, and the United States' representative in the reciprocity negotiations concluded: "In Canada, you are reminded of government every day. It parades itself before you. It is not content to be servant, but will be master."

As the Union forces of the North emerged successful from the American Civil War in 1865, British investors in Canada, fearing Canadian annexation, clamoured for government protection of their assets. Canadian merchant capitalists also feared that, unless they were unified and protected, they would soon become American citizens. Sir John A. Macdonald and his allies provided the answer: political union of the British North American colonies and a tariff wall around the new dominion. As Macdonald argued:

> There are national considerations . . . that rise far higher than the mere question of trade advantage; there is prestige, national status, national dominion . . . and no great nation has ever arisen whose policy was Free Trade.

THE EVOLUTION OF A BUSINESS-NATION

Confederation, and Canada's evolution from a scattering of colonial autocracies to a unified, pluralist democracy, did nothing to change this business-government relationship. As Prime Minister Trudeau earlier indicated, the building of the Canadian Pacific Railway (CPR) was actually a joint venture between the private and public sectors. Sir John A. Macdonald's National Policy of 1879 was one of tariffs and quotas. It was intended to build domestic industry by assuring it the growing Canadian market and protecting its independence from the United States. Macdonald could not have said it better when, in 1878, he cried:

> We have no manufacturers here. We have no work-people, our work-people have gone off to the United States...these Canadian artisans are adding to the strength, to the power, and to the wealth of a foreign nation instead of adding to ours. Our work-people in this country, on the other hand, are suffering from want of employment...If these men cannot find an opportunity in their own country to develop the skill and genius with which God has gifted them, they will go to a country where their abilities can be employed, as they have gone from

Canada to the United States. If Canada had had a judicious system of taxation, they would be toiling and doing well in their own country. [4]

Thus was born the third commercial empire of the North — a mercantilist empire characterized by a strong and interventionist state, state protection of big business, tariff barriers, subsidies, and a positive trade balance. Strong corporate, elitist linkages were forged among merchant capitalists, landowners, financiers, transportation czars, and government leaders. The CPR replaced the Hudson's Bay Company as the favoured state-chartered monopoly. Tariff barriers protected small Canadian businesses, attracted foreign industrial capital (which was scarce in Canada), and discouraged potential emigrants from seeking opportunities elsewhere. Merchant capitalists grew richer without having to spend their own dollars; the state made sure of that.

Typical of the omnipresent businessmen-politicians of that era was Sir George-Etienne Cartier, a Father of Confederation and Quebec Lieutenant to Prime Minister Sir John A. Macdonald. Cartier's grandfather was a classic mercantilist, or intermediary in the flow of goods and services. He traded in fish, wheat, and salt; his father used the family fortune to establish the Bank of Montreal with Peter McGill of McGill University fame. Cartier himself was also intimately involved with the Grand Trunk syndicate, while serving as Macdonald's second-in-command.[5] His rhetoric underscores his beliefs: "In order that institutions may be stable and work harmoniously, there must be a power of resistance to the democratic element." As one of the French-Canadian elite, Cartier, along with Sir John A. Macdonald, would begin to accommodate the French-English elite in Canada. He also represented the elite accommodation of business and government.

A typical example of someone on the other side of the very low, unintimidating business-government fence was Donald Smith, later to become Lord Strathcona. Both preceding and following Confederation, he owned, controlled, or was a major shareholder in both the Hudson's Bay Company and its chief rival and eventual partner, the North-West Company. He also held shares in the Bank of Montreal, the Grand Trunk Railway, and the Canadian Pacific Railway. Strathcona also happened to own most of the land designated for the CPR and the urban settlements along its route, as well as most of the arable western land that the CPR would open up to settlers!

Canadian politicians and businessmen were quite willing to use the state to control and develop the economy in the name of nation-building, and to defy the lure of the south. If these well-meaning public servants and entrepreneurs happened to enrich themselves along the way and acquire their own personal financial empires, such was the reward for public mindedness. National goals were met, and personal wealth was accumulated. What a business-government relationship!

Another result of this interrelationship of Canadian merchant capital, British financial capital, mercantilistic zeal, and a sympathetic political establishment was the dearth of indigenous Canadian industrial capital and entrepreneurship. However, that could always be imported from the United States — for a price. Canada had everything it needed to drive a ribbon of steel across the northern half of the continent: money, labour, raw materials, and land. All it needed was know-how. It was no accident that William Van Horne, an American engineer, became responsible for the construction of the CPR.

The National Policy of 1879 may have protected Canadian industry but it also invited American industry to jump the tariff barriers and set up branch plants in Canada. These were of adequate size to serve Canada's small domestic market with neither mandate nor capacity to export. Macdonald's plan did create industry — American branch plant indus-try. Thus the growth of Canadian industrial entrepreneurism was further hindered, a situa-tion that continues today despite a freer and more liberal trade regime. True free-enterprisers would never have allowed such government "protection." They would have fought to the finish and died an honourable, glorious death.

The Canadian mercantilists of the nineteenth century were, in fact, the forebears of the service sector, now the largest single employing sector of our modern economy. More important, Canadian business has continued to solicit and receive government intervention and protection throughout the twentieth century.

Although debate about industrial strategies was rampant in the 1980s, economic planning and industrial policies are hardly new to the Canadian political economy. Sir John A. Macdonald's 1879 National Policy was an industrial strategy; it was a collection of measures to stimulate economic growth. The building of a transcontinental railroad, encouraging immigrant settlement of the west, and protecting Canadian industry with a tariff barrier, were all designed to boost the economy's performance. It was hoped that a secondary manu-facturing sector would develop in Ontario, the markets for which would be the Maritimes, the rest of central Canada, and the growing agriculturally-based prairie economy. Canada could be an economically selfsufficient, sovereign entity — or so it was planned by both busi-ness and government. Of course, the consequences of being an economic island are clear 120 years later; Canada has a tertiary sector-based economy, with a foreign-owned secondary sector and habitual reliance upon natural resources. Ironically, tariff and non-tariff barri-ers did not create high levels of economic concentration across the board, as was predicted. Some industries showed a direct positive correlation between protection and concentration; others demonstrated the opposite effect.

One unarguable benefit that emerged from the National Policy was the stimulation of east-west economic, political, and social activity. The National Policy accomplished its main goal — it built a nation!

The National Policy, in "protecting" Canadian industry, also led to the easy formation of cartels, oligopolies, and even monopolies. By the late 1880s, the exploitation of monop-oly power had become a political issue. In response, the Canadian Parliament passed its first anti-combines or competition policy in 1889 as part of the Criminal Code.

This policy sought to codify existing English common law on the subject, which had thus far been fairly ineffective. The Act was strewn with adjectives such as "unlawfully," "unduly," and "unreasonably," which meant that there was to be a *lawful* degree of collusion, that there was an *acceptable* level of aggregation, and that there was a *reasonable* level for price fixing. (Services were excluded.)

As a result, Canadian law became a matter for judicial interpretation, not administrative practice. Although penalties under the Criminal Code are generally greater than under the Civil Code, the costs of prosecution and the burden of proof under the Criminal Code are far greater. This makes it very difficult to enforce an act as vague as the *Anti-Combines Act*. Canada's policy was actually a non-policy — a toothless paper tiger.[6]

The obvious purposes of a competition policy are to reduce the inefficiencies of economic concentration and monopoly power and to guarantee fair play in the marketplace. *Historically, Canada's National Policy has never contained an effective competitive policy.* Aggregate and industrial concentration were considered necessary evils by government, and a desirable state of affairs by business. Should guaranteeing internal competition take precedence over being globally competitive? Should individual equity come before national economic survival? What is in the public interest here?

THE HALCYON DAYS OF C.D. HOWE: COME AND GONE

The Great Depression of the 1930s stimulated government intervention in the economy on an unprecedented scale. Keynesian economics, emphasizing government deficit spending in times of scarcity, took firm hold of the public policy fraternity. The National Policy was complemented by interventionist government monetary and fiscal policies. Keynesian economics took hold in Canada like nowhere else in the world! Unfortunately, most government policy makers soon forgot the other half of Keynes' prescription: for governments to save during times of economic prosperity!

Policies designed to stabilize or even control interest rates, inflation rates, liquidity levels, and unemployment rates have a major impact upon business' working environment. In effect, Keynesian macroeconomic policies are an attempt to stabilize the aggregate level of business activity. Monetary policies are used by the Bank of Canada to control the supply of dollars, market liquidity, investment and savings levels, and credit. Fiscal policies are represented by the annual and accumulated government budget surplus and/or deficit. If government chooses to have a "deficit budget," it must make ends meet by either borrowing or by printing money. If the latter, fiscal policies may influence monetary policies.

Stabilization policy is an adjunct to other government policies which address market failures, market inefficiencies, and market equity or fairness. Macroeconomic policy is really designed to address the net effect of cumulative microeconomic market problems. Keynesian policies have been used with varying degrees of success for 60 years simultaneously to create jobs, control inflation, and stimulate economic growth. But will they address the considerable structural problems which business and government must overcome, in order for Canada to compete in tomorrow's world markets?

Keynes' policies were originally a response to cyclical economic problems. When unemployment was high, government increased its spending. When inflation was high, government increased taxes. Keynesian economics affected demand. Industrial strategists recognize that Canada's problems today are centred more on the costs of production and supply, rather than on demand. The governments of Prime Minister Thatcher in the United Kingdom and President Reagan in the United States recognized this fact, and attempted to boost the supply side of the economy, again with varying degrees of success.

When Keynesian economic policies have failed, it is generally for one of three reasons. First, John Maynard Keynes was an aristocrat. He never understood that workers would demand more money than allotted them, that demand management inherently had potential for fuelling inflation. Second, Keynes believed that the United Kingdom's rising unemployment during the 1920s was the result of its stubborn allegiance to the gold standard. When Britain went off the gold standard in 1931, unemployment continued to rise. Third, Keynes urged government to increase its spending in bad times and borrow to finance part of it, and to bank its surpluses in good times for future borrowing needs. Of course, in times of surplus, governments have spent it and continued to increase spending when Keynes would have prescribed cutbacks. During the last 20 years of government borrowing, interest rates have risen and fallen, unemployment remains high, and inflation although never "wrestled to the ground," at times flirts with becoming *deflation*.

After the Depression, World War II produced a skilled federal bureaucracy reasonably in tune with, and partly recruited from, the business community. Businessmen, as "dollar-a-year-men," were conscripted into many of the major government positions under the leadership of American immigrant Clarence Decatur (C.D.) Howe.

C.D. Howe was in many ways the reincarnation of the nineteenth century mercantilist. He was a self-made millionaire from the grain trade and the consulting business, was blessed with sound intuition, and was a recognized leader of the national business community. He was also a minister of the Crown and a popular leader of the Liberal Party of Canada (the dominant political party in Canada throughout the twentieth century). Business' interest was solidly in the forefront of public policy.

During World War II, the federal government's economic policy increasingly reflected the influence of Keynes, and its budget became the major tool of economic reform. Business-government relations were considered by both sides to be very good and very important. Everyone agreed on the one clear, overriding objective — winning the war.

Under Howe's leadership, the Canadian GNP increased from $5.6 billion in 1939 to $11.9 billion in 1945. During the war, Canada was the fourth-largest Allied supplier of military goods and services. This industrial expansion was attained through Howe's generous loans, grants, tax write-offs, and accelerated depreciation. Canadian industry emerged from the war with world-class facilities fully financed by untaxed war profits. These firms had been primarily engaged in manufacturing small items to foreign design specifications and assembling offline manufactured parts.

Postwar business-government relations continued to be good. Although the 1945 *White Paper on Employment and Reconstruction*, a product of the public service, was a large step towards government direction of the economy, the business community generally accepted it. Government supported economic expansion, particularly in the basic industries, and semi-annual meetings were held for business and government economists. Fearing a postwar depression, the government extended its "temporary war-time measures" of assistance to business every year into the 1950s. Business, of course, did its share to cooperate. In fact, for over a decade after the war, Canada was regarded as one of the best countries in the world in which to invest.

Also after the war, Howe sold off many of the Crown corporations he had created for the war effort. He retained his strong belief in the concept of Canadian public enterprise, however, keeping Polymer Corporation Ltd. (the forerunner of Polysar) and Eldorado Mines (Eldorado Nuclear). He also protected the transnational monopoly of Trans-Canada Airlines (Air Canada).

Prime Minister William Lyon Mackenzie King had delegated so much authority to Howe during the 1940s and early 1950s that national economic and industrial policy had become his personal jurisdiction. If Sir John A. Macdonald had been the architect of the Dominion of Canada, C.D. Howe was the contractor who built it!

After the war, as in Confederation-era Canada, Howe's war-time "dollar-a-year-men" returned to the head offices of corporate Canada. They used their knowledge, contacts, and expertise to build and expand their empires and create huge fortunes. The epitome of these was E.P. Taylor, who amassed his empire under the name Argus Corporation.

Howe's greatest asset was his two-way channel of information from the boardrooms to the Cabinet table and back. His greatest skills were in intelligence-gathering and organization — and organize he did. Howe created the public enterprises to supply the Canadian war effort when the private sector could not respond quickly enough. He also helped put together the consortia that built the St. Lawrence Seaway and the Trans-Canada natural gas pipeline, and he encouraged the harvesting of Canada's vast natural resources — all, of course, with heavy government assistance.

Howe was the champion of megaprojects. He sincerely believed that the Canadian economy needed at least one megaproject on the go at all times. C.D. Howe did not believe in a competition policy just for the sake of having one. The key to Canadian prosperity, he believed, was low-cost, high-efficiency manufacturing. This meant large, workable business conglomerates with internal economies of scale, often oligopolies or monopolies, to offset the nation's natural diseconomies of scale.

Above all, Howe believed in Keynesian economics. He urged Canadians to believe that by carefully balancing government fiscal and monetary policies, economic growth would continue in perpetuity. The unabashedly pro-business Howe introduced to Parliament the 1948 *White Paper on Employment and Income*, the blueprint for Keynesian counter-cyclical government budgeting and government intervention.

To say the least, C.D. Howe was an enigma. He believed in private initiative; he believed in government protection of private initiative; he believed in government initiative. He certainly believed in the personal accumulation of power. Howe was conceptual and abstract in his thinking, yet he was pragmatic in his actions. Above all, he was typical of the era; he was truly "Canadian."

It was Howe who helped keep Mackenzie King in power longer than any other prime minister in the history of the British empire. But in 1957 it was Howe who was largely responsible for his government's downfall under Prime Minister Louis St. Laurent.

That year, the Liberals were defeated by the western populist Progressive Conservative leader, John Diefenbaker. The new prime minister decried the immorality of big business, big government, and the United States' collusion to build the Trans-Canada Pipeline. Howe, who had represented big business and big government, was also personal friends with American cabinet members and Texas oilmen supporting the project.

The Canadian electorate chose Diefenbaker's nationalistic rhetoric over Howe's continentalist pragmatism. Observers noted a gradual worsening of business-government relations with Diefenbaker's election. The process was rapidly accelerated under the successive Liberal governments of Lester Pearson and Pierre Trudeau.

One of Howe's projects, or "children of the war," was A.V. Roe Co (Avro), a manufacturer of warplanes for the Pacific theatre. Avro made its mark in the world of aviation with the production of its conventional jet fighter, the CF100 *Canuck*. With its cost-plus defence contracts and aircraft manufacturing profits, Avro purchased control of Atlantic Canada's steel and coal interests and diversified into a true conglomerate. As the *Canuck* aged, Avro unveiled plans for a successor — a supersonic, all-weather, state-of-the-art jet interceptor, the CF105 *Arrow*.

Cost projection overruns of 800% soon led to the Liberal government's secret plan to scrap the *Arrow* after the 1957 election, but the Liberals lost to the Progressive Conservatives. When Prime Minister Diefenbaker cancelled production of the *Arrow*, 14 000 jobs were lost at the Malton, Ontario, plant alone. Research engineers emigrated in droves to the United States, where a growing space program beckoned.

Prime Minister Diefenbaker's fortunes declined steadily thereafter, as did the state of business-government relations. Yet they should not have. The Progressive Conservative government's 1960 budget guaranteed that business would be preeminent among the growing number of pressure groups appealing to government for intervention. By reintroducing accelerated depreciation, investment tax credits, exemptions, and depletion allowances, government hoped to accelerate investment and economic growth and to postpone the feared postwar recession. Excise taxes, customs duties, and tariff rates were also increased to bolster government revenue to offset lost tax revenue. However, one effect of stimulating Canadian manufacturing and decreasing a reliance on imports would be negating the increase in nominal import tax rates. Business won again; private investment was again underwritten by an unwitting public.

C.D. Howe died in 1960 and was succeeded by Winnipeg economist Mitchell Sharp, who was both intellectual and personable. Sharp, too, had origins in the grain trade. He became Howe's speech writer, rose to become Deputy Minister of Trade and Commerce, eventually ran for Parliament, and was appointed to, among other posts, Minister of Industry, Trade and Commerce and Secretary of State for External Affairs. However, business-government relations were not the same as under Howe.

Later, under Pearson and Trudeau, decision making in Ottawa changed. It became collegial, centralized, and rationalized. Strong ministers were replaced with strong Cabinet committees; strong departments and their mandarins were replaced by strong central agencies — a new, inaccessible cabal accountable only to the prime minister.

Yet, as political economist, former cabinet minister, and successful businessman Eric Kierans noted:

> For the life of me, I cannot understand the hostility of the business community to the Trudeau government. It cannot be on the basis of what the federal government has done, for literally big business has never had it so good. With the exception of the United Kingdom, I doubt that any nation in the world has given its corporate 1000 a more handsome gift package of subsidies, tax allowances, two-year write-offs, deductibility of merger costs, cheap loans, export credits and insurance than our present Trudeau government. If this be socialism, business should cry for more. [7]

Ironically, these centralizing trends were not undone by Progressive Conservative Prime Minister Brian Mulroney, former president of the American-owned Iron Ore Company of Canada and self-described ideological ally of neo-conservatives Ronald Reagan and Margaret Thatcher. Every minister in his government was instructed to hire a chief of staff to coordinate the interaction among the minister, the minister's department, the minister's constituency, and the central agencies. This was continued under Liberal Prime Minister Jean Chretien in the 1990s. Rule-by-central-agency has become a given.

However, despite business' growing dissatisfaction with government, the two most significant reforms of the Canadian tax system since the 1930s Depression came from Liberal Finance Minister E.J. Benson in 1971, and Progressive Conservative Finance Minister Michael Wilson in 1988. These offered more provisions for big business to get bigger at the expense of the individual taxpayer.

From the 1960s through the 1980s, Canada experienced the birth and rapid growth of social security programs, federal-provincial transfer payments to finance them, social and economic regulations of every kind, and higher taxation to pay for all this. Canada also felt the effects of double digit inflation and unemployment, despite Keynesian interventions to control these. As government spending outstripped its tax revenues, government borrowing increased to cover off deficit budgets which in turn accumulated into a colossal government debt. Therefore, Canada's industrial strategy over the past 60 years from the 1930s to the 1990s — although never intentionally conceived, developed, and implemented as such — was a combination of tariffs, neo-laissez-faire market practices, and Keynesian-style voodoo economics. The mix served Canada well: it created a nation against all odds, raised it to be a middle economy and industrial power by the 1940s, and elevated it to membership in the G-7 by the 1970s. (G-7 is the acronym for the Group of Seven: United States, Japan, Germany, France, Britain, Italy, and Canada.) *Business and government cooperated as partners, mutually recognizing common goals.* Then things began to change.

Due to government's overwhelming complexity today in both decision making and program delivery, it is inconceivable to return to the halcyon days of C.D. Howe and the older, much simpler methods of business-government accommodation. The Howe days are over, never to return. But does it really matter?

IMPLICATIONS FOR MANAGEMENT

David Lewis, the one-time leader of the New Democratic Party (NDP), attacked Canada's "corporate welfare bums" in the 1968 federal election. But Lewis' targets for denunciation were not recent phenomena. Canada did not embark upon the road to a symbiosis of big business and big government with Brian Mulroney's election in 1984. Nor did it begin with C.D. Howe during the 1940s and 1950s, nor with the National Policy of 1879.

In fact, it began with the chartering of the Hudson's Bay Company in 1670. Since then, the government of Canada has been very supportive of business, particularly big business. It was true back in the days when Canada's national politicians were also Canada's business leaders, and when business' favourite son, C.D. Howe, was also controller of government policy levers. It remains true today.

Government's continuing economic support of business in this country has not eased the environment in which these two forces have coexisted. Misunderstandings and conflict abound. The tide of events influencing business-government relations has been running in the wrong direction. Of course, business people still work with government, but many are unhappy about its type of leadership. Nor has communication been as productive as might have been hoped. New initiatives have been tried and found wanting. Government has sought to legitimize labour organizations, whether or not they truly represented their sectors of society, or were interested in participating. *Government in Canada is slowly moving away from being the "broker of the public interest" to being a "facilitator of special interests." "Public consultation" is nothing but a killing field of vested interest — only one of which is business.*

With rare exceptions, the intimacy and obvious linkages between business and government of the 1950s, let alone of the nineteenth century, no longer exist. The few exceptions are challenged by charges of conflict of interest. In fact, business-government interaction today is very formal, with government acquiring information and advice through advisory boards and sectoral committees. Business offers its opinion when testifying before committees of the House of Commons or before royal commissions. One no longer "talks" to the deputy minister responsible for "whatever the industry-related ministry is called this week." Now industry-related policy decisions are taken by a committee of Cabinet advised by a general secretariat in the Privy Council Office.

Business' rhetoric criticizing government's intervention is both useless and hypocritical. The public does not buy it, nor government's rhetoric against big business. Both sides could better spend their time and energy reconstructing the linkages which have been broken — ironically, often as a result of government's trying to operate in a more business-like manner.

It is true that the federal government still solicits advice about business' needs at budget time, so appropriate changes to various tax statutes can be made. But is that enough? Can government alone construct the economic climate necessary for Canada to compete success-fully with the rest of the world? Can government alone forge the alliances which will best serve this nation's interest in waging that war? Can government alone carve out a niche for Canada within the global marketplace, after the dust of economic conflagration has settled? Most likely not. Business must be heard in Ottawa again, as it was ever so briefly in the shaping of Canada's negotiating position prior to signing the Canada-US Free Trade Agreement.

As celebrated political scientist Professor Alexander Brady has professed: "The role of the state in the economic life of Canada is really the modern history of Canada." There is no denying or escaping that fact. The only difference between today and the 1860s is that the Canadian mixed economy of Macdonald's era was dominated by business; today, govern-ment dominates it. Business must learn to live with this reality as best it can. Government and its economic intervention are not going to disappear overnight.

SUGGESTED FURTHER READINGS

Aitken, H.J.G. 1967. "Defensive Expansionism: The State and Economic Growth in Canada." In W.T. Easterbrooke and M.H. Watkins, (eds). *Approaches to Canadian Economic History*. Toronto: McClelland & Stewart.

Aitken, H.J.G. 1964. "Government and Business in Canada: An Interpretation." *Business History Review*, 28.

Bliss, M. 1987. *Northern Enterprise: Five Centuries of Canadian Business*. Toronto: McClelland & Stewart.

Bothwell, R., and William Kilbourn. 1979. *C.D. Howe: A Biography*. Toronto: McClelland & Stewart.

Brady, Alexander. 1980. "The State and Economic Life in Canada." In K.J. Rea and J.T. McLeod. (eds.), *Business and Government in Canada: Selected Readings*. 2nd ed. Toronto: Methuen.

Creighton, D.G. 1970. *The Commercial Empire of the St. Lawrence*. Toronto: Macmillan.

Creighton, D.G. 1956. *The Empire of the St. Lawrence*. Toronto: Macmillan.

Dean, W.G. 1993. *Historical Atlas of Canada*. (3 volumes). Toronto: University of Toronto Press.

Innis, H.A. 1956. *Essays in Canadian Economic History*. Toronto: University of Toronto Press.

Innis, H.A. 1930. *The Fur Trade in Canada*. Toronto: University of Toronto Press.

Innis, H.A. 1933. *Problems of Staple Production in Canada*. Toronto: Ryerson.

Lower, A. 1959. *Canadians in the Making*. Toronto: Macmillan.

Naylor, R.T. 1972. "The Rise and Fall of the Third Commercial Empire of the St. Lawrence." In Gary Teeple, (ed.), *Capitalism and the National Quest in Canada*. Toronto: University of Toronto Press.

Nelles, H.V. 1992. *The Politics of Development*. Toronto: Macmillan.

Taylor, G.D., and P.A. Baskerville. 1994. A *Concise History of Business in Canada*. Toronto: Oxford University Press.

Traves, T. 1979. *The State and Enterprise*. Toronto: University of Toronto Press.

NOTES

1. D. Wayne Taylor, *Business and Government Relations*: Partners in the 1990s. (Toronto: Gage Educational Publishing, 1991), 19.

2. This was confirmed yet one more time when Coca-Cola reorganized its world operations into six units in 1996 with the United States and Canada being one unit. The *Road to Avonlea*, Canada's number one television series from 1989-96 and a $30 million business is owned by Disney, although it was developed by a Canadian entrepreneur, financed by the federal government through Telefilm Canada, and produced by the CBC.

3. One hundred and seventy years later the Government of Canada decided to sell the St. Lawrence Seaway Authority to a consortium of nine companies which will operate it as a nonprofit corporation. The nine companies just happened to have been the Seaway's largest clients and users: steelmakers Dofasco Inc. and Stelco Inc.; grain merchants James Richardson and Sons Ltd., Cargill Ltd. and Groupe Immobilier Louis Dreyfus; shipping firms Upper Lakes Shipping Ltd., Canada Steamship Lines Ltd. and Algoma Central Corp.; and shipbuilder Canadian Shipbuilding and Engineering Ltd. Ironically, the United States, the bastion of free enterprise, opposed the sale.

4. Taylor, *Business and Government Relations,* 24.

5. Sir John A. Macdonald was later President of the Manufacturers Life Assurance Company.

6 It was not until 1986 that some parts of the *Anti-Combines Act* were removed from the Criminal Code and placed under the Civil Code as a new *Competition Act*. A Competition Tribunal was also established to handle such matters. The Director of the Bureau of Competition Policy can now investigate conspiracies to lessen competition, mergers and acquisitions, predatory pricing, price discrimination, price fixing, and misleading advertising and marketing practices. Banks, services, and Crown corporations are also included. The actual strength of the Act remains to be tested.

7 Taylor, *Business and Government Relations*, 28.

3

A CHANGING CANADA IN A CHANGING WORLD

He that goeth about to persuade
a multitude that they are not
so well governed as they ought to be,
shall never want attentive and favourable hearers.

Richard Hooker, 1554-1600

For the first 100 years of Confederation, Canada lived off its natural resources. For most of the past 25 years, Canada has lived off its credit! As **Chapter 7** will explain, the time of reckoning is upon us. That reckoning is both financial and political.

In the years immediately following World War II, Canada possessed the world's third-most robust economy and was the world's third-greatest military power. Wheat exports had doubled, and production of oil, iron ore, uranium ore, aluminum, and hydroelectric power had quadrupled. By 1958, the population had grown from 11 million to 17 million; now it has surpassed 30 million. Sir Wilfrid Laurier's dream of a world-class nation was being built by a flood of immigrants from the four corners of the world.

Canada was blessed with the best aspects of all worlds: the British tradition of government, the influences of French culture, and the dynamism of the American economy. Its only shortcoming was a small domestic market. In fact, it was far smaller than what economists would consider to be of minimum efficient size for industrial self-sufficiency at an affordable price.

But this, too, was turned to advantage. Canada became a trading nation[1] — one of the best in the world — with 25% growing to about 40% of the economy being trade-based.

However, not all of this continues to be the case. What has happened?

OURS IS A CHANGING WORLD

The world is a dynamic place. Nothing remains the same. The world's economy has undergone radical changes since World War II, and certainly since the Kennedy Round of the General Agreement on Tariffs and Trade (GATT) during the early 1960s. World trade has grown disproportionately compared with real growth in the world's GDP. A dramatic rise in exports due to fluctuating currencies, new natural resource discoveries, Third World development, and microchip technology are restructuring the global economy. A new world economic order is upon us — global competition!

These challenges are shared by the seven industrialized nations which, including Canada, have become known as the G-7. In the late 1980s and in the 1990s, the United States — formerly the engine of the economy of the non-communist world — faced a deteriorating trade balance position. In 1984, Americans enjoyed a surplus of over $110 billion; 10 years later they had a $130 billion trade deficit. Meanwhile Japan (which just 40 years ago was reeling from the devastation of the Second World War) holds a very large positive trade balance.

Who will drive the world's economy tomorrow? The United States, to regain its title, must drastically reduce its level of imports, probably increase taxes while reducing government services, and endure escalating prices. Not an enviable path to hegemony (i.e., predominant influence). To compound matters, the American dollar's value dropped substantially over the last decade, compared with the combined currencies of the other G-7 countries. At the same time, Japanese holdings of US paper debt have increased dramatically in the same time frame. However, Japan is not without difficulties. Formerly low manufacturing and production labour costs, once a powerful competitive advantage, have crept up towards the average American rate. Japanese consumption expectations and patterns may be overtaking their production advantages. To place all this in perspective, only a handful of countries have had strong real economic growth rates (greater than 5%) sustained over several years. All were totalitarian states. *On the face of it, pluralist democracies and industrial success no longer seem mutually congruous.*

There are also vast and forbidding differences among the G-7 nations themselves. One significant variation is in real rates of economic growth. During the early 1990s, Canada led the pack with annual increases in GDP averaging 4%. Germany, on the other hand, trailed behind the others with only a 1% average annual increase. Nor has inflation — or even standard of living — been consistent throughout the group. Italy's standard of living today is almost half that of the United States. But, to put all this into perspective, as **Figure 3–1** shows, Canada's growth in GDP is flattening out. Data for 1996 and forecasts for 1997 are encouraging but not assured as sustained improvement. What is for sure is that Canada cannot simply "grow out" of its fiscal problems.

A bright spot on the world economic horizon seems to be Asia, not only the "tigers" (especially Singapore, Hong Kong, Taiwan and South Korea) but India as well. Much investment and trade focus is on the Pacific Rim. Canada's "Team Canada" visits (each fall starting in 1994), including the prime minister and most premiers, are a response to a significantly changing world economic reality. A source of uncertainty was the Hong Kong governance change of 1997. Substantial Asian investment abroad, especially Chinese investment in

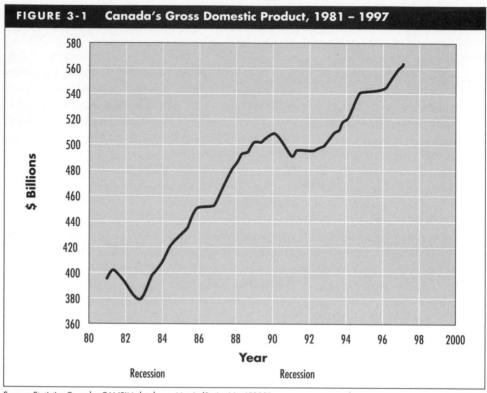

FIGURE 3-1   Canada's Gross Domestic Product, 1981 – 1997

Source: Statistics Canada, CANSIM database, Matrix/Series No. l53001.

Western Canada, is affecting economic activity and trade patterns for the future. The recent "Asian flu" has adversely affected the Canadian economy.

Ironically, Japan's star is beginning to fade as the Asian tigers get ready to pounce. In particular, Japan faces a serious credit crisis in the next few years given its banks' disproportionate exposure to the real estate market, which remains in the doldrums with no offsetting returns from other sources.[2] The shortening of the product life cycle in Japanese manufactures (thirty years for ships, ten years for cars, three years for software) and the falling natural resource and labour content of their products has also changed lending relations and opportunities.

As wealth and income gains begin to drop in Japan, unions will become militant, labour productivity will diminish, investment in education will decline, pressures on the middle class will rise, and income will be redistributed more extensively. Sound familiar? It seems unlikely that Japan will succeed the United States as the engine of the world. What was once a deliberate strategy for Japanese banks — to lend all their money with no credit-rating system in place to Japanese industry for an average return on assets of 0.44% — has come back to haunt them.

The Eastern Europe outlook is highly uncertain and likely will remain so for some time. Germany has achieved unification, facilitated by a special tax on Western Germany to finance reconstruction of the (formerly Communist) Eastern Germany, but unification has stalled Germany's quest for European (if not world) economic leadership.[3] Germany still has the potential to become an even greater economic power, but not for some time. Signs are more positive for South Africa, unlike only a few short years ago. Resources are rich across Africa with longer-term economic potentials. Latin and South America economies are spotty in their progress; likely it will be some time before "world economic driver" status can be bestowed on those regions.

Table 3–1 shows that economic growth is faster in *developing* economies than in developed economies such as Canada. Developing countries are accounting for a greater share of total world output than developed countries; however, in developing countries, populations are rising fastest. The crucial point is for *per capita* prosperity to be rising. Generally, the data show that it is. But this progress is vulnerable to variability and even reverse. For instance, when commodity demand is stronger so are the economies of developing countries; but these jurisdictions need sustaining gains in economic growth and prosperity. Recent economic research has identified sources variation in economic progress between developing countries.[4] Countries have advantages when on tidewater (*vs* landlocked), temperate climate (*vs* tropical), open economies (*vs* closed), fiscal prudence, and rule of law. Initial conditions of physical and social infrastructure matter, but if welladvanced the country is a developed rather than a developing one.

TABLE 3-1 Growth in World Output, 1981-1997

Annual % change	1981-90	1991	1992	1993	1994	1995	1996[2]	1997[3]
World[1]	2.8	0.8	1.8	1.3	3.0	2.4	3.0	3
Developed economies	2.9	0.8	1.6	0.7	2.6	1.9	2.4	2
Economies in transition[4]	1.7	-9.2	-13.6	-9.1	-4.4	-1.4	-0.9	2
Developing economies	2.4	3.3	5.2	5.2	5.5	4.6	5.7	6
Memorandum items								
Number of countries with rising per capita output	106	72	76	64	99	107	122	127
Number of countries in sample	127	127	141	142	142	142	142	142

1 Calculated as a weighted average of individual country growth rates of gross domestic product (GDP), where weights are based on GDP in 1988 prices and exchange rates.

2 Preliminary estimate.

3 Forecast based in part on Project LINK.

4 Based on reported GDP, which seriously underestimates activity in several countries.

Source: UN World Economic and Social Survey, 1997

But it may not even be nations which drive the world economy in the future. The 1990s has erased all doubt that the world has entered an era of monolithic, borderless corporations. Of the 100 largest economies in the world today, *47 of them are industrial corporations, not countries.*[5] The twentieth largest is General Motors, in between Austria and Finland. Six firms (GM, Ford, Exxon, Royal Dutch/Shell, IBM, and Toyota) are in the top 35. *More importantly*, the world's top companies are growing *faster* than nations.

Indicative of the service and information age the world is entering is the recent imbalance between world trade and currency transactions. For decades, world trade roughly equalled in dollars world currency transactions. However, in the mid-1980s, currency transactions began to pull ahead of trade. By the early 1990s currency transactions were four times the dollar value of world trade.

CANADA IN THE CHANGING WORLD

International

Where, then, does Canada fit into this gloomy picture for liberalist capitalism? According to the 1997 annual competitiveness scorecard by the Swiss-based World Economic Forum and International Institute for Management Development,[6] Canada recently ranked fourth (up from eighth in 1996 and 12th in 1995) out of 53 leading national economies in the world for overall competitiveness,[7] lagging behind only the United States, Singapore, and Hong Kong. Japan, Switzerland, Germany, Netherlands, New Zealand, Denmark, Norway, and Taiwan are contenders. Since 1988 Canada had gradually slid from fifth spot; its recovery primarily is due to fiscal improvements and freer trade.

Relative to other industrialized countries, Canada ranks amongst the highest in terms of both its human development record and its physical infrastructure. Human development included such measures as percentage of the population attaining higher education, advancement of women and visible minorities in society, health care, and social support services. Canada ranks high in quality of business management, integration into the world economy, and efficiency of financial markets. Our ranking was eighth for legal and social institutions necessary to support a competitive market economy. Canada fares rather poorly in labour (15th) and the role of the state (24th). Meanwhile, the level of Canadian public savings (about 9% in the past, half that of Japan) has fallen precipitously to less than 2% of disposable household income. Infrastructure includes such items as highways (which are crumbling), airports (which are overcrowded), telecommunications, electric power supply, and other tangible systems that link the country together, and the country to the world. Canada also ranked high in its ability to keep the level of inflation low, its availability of arable land, its improved terms of trade, its self-sufficiency in non-energy natural resources, and its receptivity to foreign investment.

At the other end of the scale, Canada ranked last in its diversification of export markets; over 80% of Canadian exports go to one market — the United States. By comparison, Germany's three largest export markets only accounted for about 30% of its exports. Canada also ranked 45th in air-borne pollution/greenhouse gas emissions. It was in the bottom quintile in savings as a percentage of GDP, personal income tax levels, volatility of exchange rate, productivity performance, on-the-job drug and alcohol abuse, and balance of trade in services (see **Figure 3–2**). Although Canada has a strong and improving trade surplus in goods traded, its huge chronic services deficit drags Canada's overall trade account into the red. Most surprising was Canada's poor performance in people productivity. In addition to the drug and alcohol problems, Canadians lost over 250 days/1000 employees/year during the decade 1985-94; employees have a low receptivity for retraining; employers have a low priority for training; and the educational system is not effective in teaching the skills required by the marketplace. This situation is ironic, given the money spent on education and the high participation rate. Canada ranked in the middle for its domestic economy, science and technology expenditures, management skills and GDP per employed person.

No surprise to most Canadians is the Forum's high ranking of the strength of our banking system. However, this sectoral strength has been, in part, achieved by charging some of the highest short-term interest rates among the countries ranked. This has, at times, made domestic, private borrowing by smaller Canadian enterprises almost prohibitive.

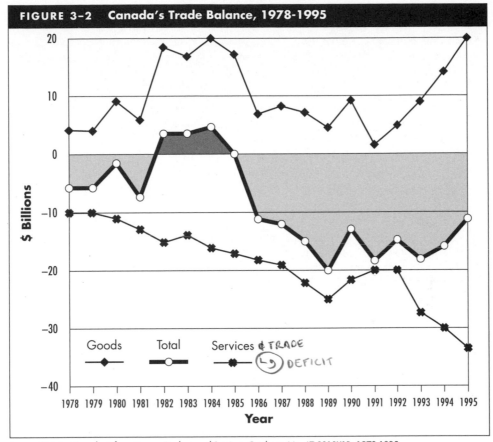

FIGURE 3-2   Canada's Trade Balance, 1978-1995

Source: Statistics Canada, Information on Products and Services, Catalogue No. 67-0010X1B, 1978-1995.

Most alarming, however, was Canada's drop from first place in 1988 to 19th place by 1995 in the role of government in not hindering private sector competition, despite trade liberalization (average tariff level of 4.8%) and low inflation (Consumer Price Index [CPI] of 0-2%) through the first half of the 1990s. The major culprit here was government's debt and deficits, the repayment of which has created a "fiscal drag" on investment in wealth-creating economic activities. This problem is compounded by the fact that this fiscal drag has taken effect at the same time (and for the same reason) as governments are reducing their program expenditures which support much of the non-wealth-creating activity that has kept Canada as high in the ratings as it is.

Despite the foregoing, Canada was ranked sixth in the world (and first among the G-7) on the Transparency International Corruption Perception Index for 1998. This index, based on the opinions of international business leaders, gauge which country's public officials are the least susceptible to offers of bribes, kickbacks, and pilfering public funds. Canada ran behind only New Zealand, Denmark, Sweden, Finland, and Iceland. The most corrupt governments were perceived to be those of Nigeria, Pakistan, Kenya, Bangladesh, and China. Canada may be broke but at least we are honest!

There is a significant structural weakness in all of this for Canada. Less than 15% of the labour force was engaged in manufacturing in 1996, as compared to 30% in Japan; 75% was employed in services, of which Canada is still a net importer. In 1993, Canada was a net *exporter* of forest products, minerals, energy, grain, fish, and automobiles, but a net *importer* of fruits, vegetables, textiles, clothing, chemicals, consumer durables, machinery, and equipment. The largest contributor to the deficit was the net outflow of investment income to foreign investors. Canadians remain "hewers of wood and drawers of water." Most economic growth has been, and will continue to be, in low value-added natural resources. Canada actually ranked at the bottom of the OECD countries in growth and investment in capital and industrial goods. More services, manufactured goods (80% of all imports in 1995), high value-added goods, and technology-based goods were imported than were exported. (Again, see **Figure 3–2**).

Most Canadian industries had 20% excess capacity in 1990-95. In general, Canada is a nation of low technology and high wages in an era when the competitive edge lies with high-technology and low-wages countries, such as the emerging industrializing bloc along the Pacific Rim of the Far East.

Many contend that Canada's exports, natural resources, have become the problem. What had been a competitive advantage since the days of the *coureurs de bois* in the 1600s and 1700s has become a competitive disadvantage. By definition, a supply of non-renewable resources means an eventual end to this source of prosperity, and escalating margins as the supply diminishes. Yet world prices for metals and minerals are at an all-time low. Stockpiles grow larger each day, thanks to Japan's strategy of financing natural resource development around the world. By offering unusually cheap loans, excess production was assured, along with lowest-cost inputs for Japan's manufacturing industries. Just as Canada's recoverable reserves were starting to show signs of depletion, substitutes were abounding everywhere.

Similar is the situation regarding renewable resources. Japanese-financed development of alternate sources of supply is springing up everywhere, providing lower-cost substitutes for Canadian renewable resources. Yet these are still being harvested in this country at a much greater rate than that of replenishment.

An important debate is underway regarding the economic prosperity linkage to freedoms enjoyed by the respective publics of countries. Are certain countries prosperous because of freedom? Or is freedom due to prosperity? Research does show economic well-being and freedom are linked.[8] There is agreement on the freedom-economy linkage; but is the linkage correlation or causality? If the latter, which causes the other? The right-wing logic would be that freer decision making is faster and based on economic value, so more value-added is generated by that free economy and adaptations to change are quicker and more assured (because not blocked or delayed by government). Cited as examples of the recent era are Britain, United States, Canada and West Germany. The contrary view is economic freedom does not cause prosperity, but rather that freedom is a side effect of wealth.[9] That is, if your economy is thriving you can afford to reduce the role of government because so much of government's work has been done and the economic prosperity is the evidence (see **Chapter 4**, Economic Functions of Government). Is Singapore an example? And Canada? Despite the "chicken and egg" nature of the debate, the issue warrants circumspect consideration within the context our study.

The world economy increasingly is global in nature; competitiveness is and will continue to be a must for Canada. Canada is a trading nation with one dominating trade partner, the United States. The Free Trade Agreement (FTA) came into effect January 1989. Then the FTA was expanded to include Mexico and became the North American Free Trade Agreement (NAFTA). Other Latin and South American countries (e.g., Chile) have expressed interest in an expanded NAFTA. Trade expansion will continue to be essential with the US, but also with Pacific Rim and European (Western and Eastern) countries. In 1994, the Asia Pacific Economic Cooperation (APEC) entity, similar to OECD, was formed with Canada as a founding member. In late 1997, APEC met in Vancouver.

⭐Domestic Economy

The economic health of the country is the dominating context for business-government relations. Canada's economic performance needs to be measured against a set of economic goals that can serve society, and policies are needed to meet such goals. A well-known and accepted set of economic goals for Canada are:

- Reasonable *price stability*
- Full *employment*
- A high rate of *economic growth*
- A viable *balance of payments*
- An equitable *distribution* of rising incomes. [10]

Goals are easy to state, difficult to quantify and even more difficult to achieve! Quantifying goals is likely to result in politics *vs* economics confrontations. Take full employment: choosing a percent goal for unemployment that is low enough to be politically acceptable is likely to be unrealistic economically, but a high enough target to be realistic (and operational) is likely to be unacceptable politically. Years ago Canada had a goal of "not exceeding three percent" unemployment. Such a goal is useless for practical policy purposes. In the current era Canada's unemployment has been in the range of nine to twelve percent, and never has been anywhere near three percent. Unemployment in Canada is too high. Being above some threshold, perhaps double-digit, is a social as well as an economic problem, but is not improved by goal statements that are unrealistic and thus ignored. Perhaps Canada should state this goal as seven to eight percent and leave "no stone unturned" in efforts to reach the goal and stay there!

The economic performance gap with respect to unemployment has been vast. Inflation has been minimized in recent years but arguably at a price of higher unemployment, especially when one realizes that CPI systematically overstates inflation. However, inflation was very serious in the late 1970s and early 1980s and could become so again. Economic growth has been sluggish for many years; stating a goal of five percent growth would be politically popular but not realistic on a sustained basis. For many reasons (outlined in the next chapter) economic growth is exceedingly important, not the least of which is assisting with DEBT/deficit problems in Canada. Again, we suggest that a realistic goal statement (say 4%) is more useful than an alternate goal that would be nice but is unattainable on a continuing basis.

Like high unemployment, high inflation imposes greater harm on individuals and families which already are disadvantaged. That adverse microeconomic effect has a macroeconomic companion — risk that dampens investment. Less investment means reduced job opportunity growth; this is called stagflation and is the "worst of all worlds." A protracted period of painful adjustment, such as that in Canada during the 1980s and early 1990s, must be endured to reestablish investor confidence in a country's currency and stability. Also, inflation erodes the *value* of money — which is great for debtors but not so great for holders of financial assets. In the post-industrial age, advanced economies have more financial assets than tangible ones; over half of Canada's assets are financial. Capital will *flee* a country with high inflation to other, more stable jurisdictions. A wise policy course is to maintain low-inflation policies to retain confidence and forestall inevitable harsh policies in the future. Although current politicians and policy advisors may not be around for the future pain, many ordinary citizens will be!

Economic growth is sought by governments of all jurisdictions and political stripes. There is a need to increase the "size of the economic pie" at least in pace with population growth, and the public seems to seek standard of living improvements that are feasible only with economic growth. As with all economic analysis, important aspects are debatable. Measurement issues are important as are environmental impacts and externalities. Another aspect is that Canada's assets, mostly physical in the past, now are at least half non-tangible. There are two crucial observations to be made here. One is that there has been, and continues to be, a substantial gap between Canada's economic growth performance and what is needed for economic and social reasons. The gap over time represents a significant lost opportunity. The second observation is that economic growth and full employment goals are linked strongly. A faster pace of growth provides needed employment expansion concurrent with business investment opportunities.

Prior reference has been made to the importance of international trade and payments balances. Details, such as currency valuation and capital flows, are complex and not pursued here. The important thing is to recognize importance itself. Distribution of income measures are available, but debatable in details. It is noted here that strong economic growth enhances the capacity of a country to afford successful distributional policies and also to improve its balance of payments position.

Problems and Prospects

A thesis of this book is that Canadian society should expect business and government to work as *partners* rather than coexist as separate and wary solitudes. Hence public problems and concerns for each, and prospects for the future, are jointly important and available. Problems of the latter 1990s should differ, if progress is being made, from the public problems and issues of earlier times. Progress should involve moving from larger problems to lesser ones as the larger ones are resolved. Progress has been made on major issues such as inflation control and enhanced international trade via GATT/FTA/NAFTA. Alas, many problems nag on and on and others become worse. A lesson is that *a new approach is needed*.

Unemployment remains seriously high, partly due to continuing sluggish economic growth. Youth unemployment is an especially critical issue. Unemployment again is emphasized not only because of its importance but because several of Canada's sapping problems constrain meeting employment objectives.

A trade opportunity continues to languish — inter-provincial trade freedom! Over a decade ago in the Macdonald Royal Commission Report,[11] major potential for improvement was identified and quantified. So little improvement was made that the "Clark Proposals" of September 1991 included Economic Union (EU) parameters for much freer trade within Canada's own boundaries. Estimates of economic values losses ($6 billion per year) are dealt with in **Chapter 14**. What could be more bizarre than that some items enjoy freer trade with a foreign country (US) than inside our own country? Certain provinces are pressing toward elimination of inter-provincial trade barriers.

Most modern governments of the world have pre-spent their respective futures. Hardships are being transferred into the future. Canada is no exception. With total government spending equal to nearly 45% of the GDP, the federal government alone spends $160 billion annually; barely 65% (and falling) of revenues is for program expenditures while 35% (and rising, even more so if interest rates rise for any reason) is interest on (not amortization of) the massive and growing debt.[12] The provincial, territorial, regional, and municipal govern-ments combined spend that much again, and some have been accumulating oppressive debts. According to the 1979 Report of the Royal Commission on Financial Management and Accountability (Lambert Commission) and successive annual reports of the Auditor General, Parliament has lost all financial accountability and management control of the public purse. (It is small comfort that the same had been said of Congress in the United States, where government spending as a percentage of GDP is much less than in Canada.)

What is the problem with increased government spending and, above all, increased government deficit spending? Is there a correlation between government upsurges in spend-ing and a country's poor economic performance? Does greater government intervention financed through foreign debt result in lower productivity, higher unemployment, higher costs and prices, and a poorer international competitive position? Or does government inter-vention actually lessen the blow of general economic fluctuations? The government cush-ion for the price of oil, for example, accomplished this throughout the 1970s after the Organization of Petroleum-Exporting Countries (OPEC) struck the West's economy in full force. Overall, the evidence is at best mixed. Sometimes government intervention works, and stimulates or protects the economy. Sometimes it actually makes matters worse, both over the short and long term, by masking the real problems which then go unaddressed.

Regional discontent is shaking the very foundations of contemporary Canada. To wit: the 1997 Federal Election results — *all* political parties now are regional! The most well-known region of grievance is Quebec, with its distinct history/civil law/language/culture.[13] But Western Canada feelings are strong and underlie the 1993 and 1997 Federal Election successes of the Reform Party of Canada. Canadians need to have ways to understand each other more fully. Across the language gulf, Quebeckers need to be able to understand citi-zens in other regions, and others need to understand why Canadian Francophones feel at risk.[14] The Quebec Referendum of October 1995 was a federalist result by the thinnest of margins. Hence, this segment of the future horizon is vitally uncertain and has mammoth social and economic implications.

How, then, can Canada expect a future of economic prosperity without sacrificing its democratic ideals? What is the role for business in achieving such a future? What new strategic management skills need business learn? Should the government provide lead-ership and direction? Can there be greater cooperation, consultation, and consensus between business and government, as in Japan and West Germany? How might busi-ness and government develop a greater appreciation for the growing interdependencies of the global economy?

These are among the challenging questions facing Canadian business and govern-ment leaders today. If many of the facts and figures have confused you, you have lots of company. The world is changing so fast and so unpredictably, it is almost impossible to have a thorough understanding of the global and national situations that matter to business-government relations. In the following pages, we will examine some of the factors that have created these situations.

THE STRATEGIC PROBLEM FOR BUSINESS AND GOVERNMENT

The amount of interaction between business and government has risen considerably in recent years. Business, to its credit, has exhibited growing concern about government's

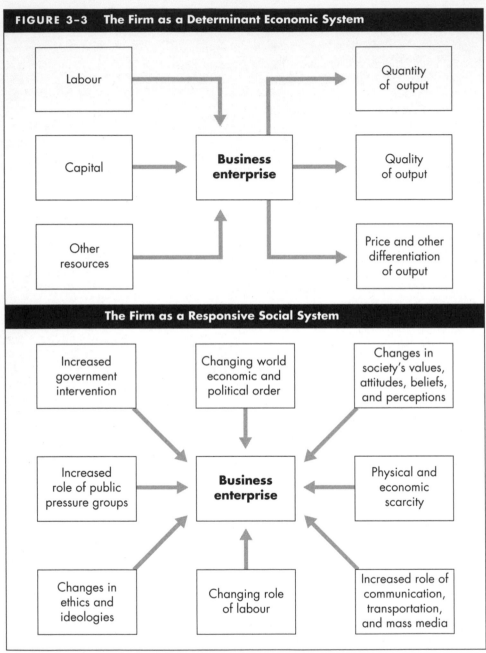

FIGURE 3-3   The Firm as a Determinant Economic System

Labour

Capital

Other resources

Business enterprise

Quantity of output

Quality of output

Price and other differentiation of output

The Firm as a Responsive Social System

Increased government intervention

Changing world economic and political order

Changes in society's values, attitudes, beliefs, and perceptions

Increased role of public pressure groups

Business enterprise

Physical and economic scarcity

Changes in ethics and ideologies

Changing role of labour

Increased role of communication, transportation, and mass media

Source: Based upon a concept found in Buchholz et al (1989: 26)

increasing role in economic affairs. The "consent doctrine" suggests that those who govern do so with the consent of those being governed, and those being governed (e.g., business) have a responsibility for active involvement and participation in the governance process.[15] However, the private sector remains reluctant to spend more money on the political process involved in shaping the role of government. It sees this as a long-term investment with no clear short-term benefits.

Business leaders may recognize that non-business interest groups are becoming more politicized, with greater success in getting their issues onto government's agenda. Yet, the private sector continues to be very reactive in nature, communicating its concerns to government *after* it discovers a threat, rather than before, by using the political process. In fact, most firms have no policy on political involvement, which underscores the low priority this subject has for business. Another distancing factor is management's disinterest in encouraging grass-roots political involvement among employees.

Therefore, the primary challenge for Canadian business lies not in managing its traditional tasks of production, marketing, or finance, but in relating individual firms to their ever-changing environments. Business must become particularly concerned about such non-economic factors as government policy, environmental uncertainty, global economics, and public pressure groups. As **Figure 3–3** illustrates, business has evolved from a determinant economic system to a responsive social system.

This may at times require business to defend its very legitimacy in a mixed economy in which government apparently holds the upper hand. Managers will once again have to demonstrate convincingly to the electorate, through compassion and superior economic performance, that the "public interest" is indeed being well served by industry and commerce. Above all, this must be accomplished while working with government on an on-going, proactive basis. Nothing will be gained by ignoring or working against government today. Business must adapt to this reality, as it must to free trade and other environmental changes.

To do this within a public forum, however, will not be easy. Beginning in the 1960s and continuing throughout the next three decades, public expectations of business have risen dramatically. During the 1970s and 1980s, business increasingly was viewed by the public with suspicion. Both its size, its sheer economic power, and its ability to slow the rate of innovation were contributing factors to this attitude. Business could refuse to expand capacity at times to create much-needed employment; it deliberately inflated prices when improved productivity reduced production costs. In the public's mind, as well, business polluted cities and harmed the environment. Business' interests no longer were endorsed blindly by the electorate as being in their own interest. In the 1990s, governments are increasingly viewed with suspicion; public cynicism may have reached dangerous levels. In fact, it appears that some in society helplessly feel ostracized from both business and government.

Government's economic involvement with business has increased in a way not always to business' liking. Regulations now affect almost everything, e.g., hazardous product labelling, foreign investment control, language requirements in Quebec, metric, pollution abatement, and so on. Public enterprise plugs market gaps to produce goods and services. Some firms have even been nationalized with the stated objective of better serving the public's interest. More recently, a strong trend to denationalization (i.e., privatization) is underway, as explained more fully in **Chapter 9**.

In effect, the price system no longer directs the Canadian economy; instead, society's value system does, one which measures success by means other than just profit. Social values are important to government today, and are eventually reflected in its policy. Public policy planners now concentrate on the net, as well as the gross, benefits of new business plans, proposals, investment, and requests.

The question of whether or not business has a corporate social responsibility is no longer debatable. Such arguments are akin to closing the barn doors after the horses have escaped. The voters have decided that business *does* have a social responsibility regarding job satisfaction, environmental protection, pay equity, community participation, and moral and ethical issues. The public looks to government, regardless of political stripe, to enforce this belief.

Why did this change occur in the public's attitude toward business? Some anti-business sentiment, sociologists would argue, is the result of Canada's inherent Judaeo-Christian suspicion of materialism. To many there are higher callings than selling wares and accumulating wealth.

However, there is another reason. At the same time the public was becoming critical of business' behaviour and government had begun encroaching on the private sector, business overtly started asking government for help. The economics of doing business were becoming more unfavourable to the risk-averse Canadian private sector. Therefore, government was asked for investment incentives, duty remissions, quota protection, loan guarantees, supply and price management mechanisms, and financial bailouts. Personal income tax rates — not corporate income tax rates — rose to cover these government expenditures. A new form of income redistribution was created: from the personal income taxpayer to the corporate income taxpayer, who often paid no tax at all!

Business is obviously reluctant to mobilize itself politically because there is no real advantage in doing so; in all probability, there is a great disadvantage. This is exemplified in a passage from a Sherlock Holmes story in which the intrepid detective described to his stalwart companion-in-arms, Dr. Watson, the unusual behaviour of a watchdog at the scene of a nocturnal murder. It was committed, as it turned out, by the dog's owner.

> Dr. Watson: Is there any point to which you would wish to show my attention?
> Sherlock Holmes: To the curious incident of the dog in the night-time.
> Dr. Watson: The dog did nothing in the night-time.
> Sherlock Holmes: That was the curious incident.

Moral of the story: Dogs do not bark at nor bite the hand that feeds them.

Where does government stand with all of this? Both business and government in Canada share the belief that it is in everyone's interest for Canada's economy to prosper and grow. Government obviously needs the tax revenue generated by economic growth to pay for all the social programs demanded by the electorate. Therefore, the Canadian government would be unlikely to stimulate competition through antitrust legislation and litigation, as in the United States. What's wrong with oligopolies, anyway, especially when one's small domestic market cannot support profitable and competitive businesses in many industries?

However, if you ask representatives of business and government to rank such economic issues as controlling inflation, ensuring full employment, stimulating real economic growth, reducing regional income disparities, and controlling foreign investment and ownership, you will receive many different opinions. *Although business and government agree on the ends, they disagree substantially on the means — and therein lies the strategic problem for business and government in Canada today.*

The ball is in business' court. The whole business-government issue is no longer a matter of garnering short-term benefits and assistance. It is now an issue of legitimacy and competence. Management must learn better to understand the players and processes of the public policy machine, the social, economic, and political goals of government, and the potential role of the private sector in government's formulation of macroeconomic policies within this changed environment. To accomplish this goal, management must reorganize its corporate structures and allocate resources, no matter how scarce, to this vital task. It must also concentrate on the long-term survival of the firm, its industry, and the entire private sector, rather than on short-term profits, quarterly returns, and annual growth rates.

Above all, business management must be consistent, both in language and behaviour. Its credibility suffers immensely when it first cries for less government intervention and defends "free enterprise," then accepts (demands?) government subsidies, tax breaks, and "corporate welfare."

Both public scrutiny of business and business' growing dependency on government have increased business-government interaction in frequency, if not in effectiveness. Yet, a wedge has been driven between business and government, of which we have seen only the thin edge. The government relations function for business has become a crucial, if under-utilized, function of corporate management.

Business is used to competing with other businesses in Canada. Now, it must get used to competing under a free trade regime with the United States and Mexico, and in a freer trade environment worldwide. The challenge remains for business to compete effectively with other legitimate interests to establish a solid position on government's agenda. Ironically, it must also learn how to compete with government itself in the marketplace.

IMPLICATIONS FOR MANAGEMENT

Successfully managing a business enterprise today requires an understanding of several environmental variables. These include technology, government, social values, demographics, organized labour, international competition, shifting trade relations, and the ability to adapt to change. In traditional graduate management education, business strategy or policy is a solution to a problem. The problem usually arises when a product or technology is mismatched with the market — a situation almost always precipitated by external change. The solution lies in adjusting that "fit" or developing a whole new interface.

Today, however, the business problem is as much a mismatch between its mission and its socio-political-economic environments as with the marketplace. Therefore, business' approach to strategy formulation, implementation, and management must change accordingly. Business must try to understand government and society just as it understands its markets, products, and technology.

The strategic question for business today should no longer be, "What is our role in society and how do we survive?" Nevertheless, management education and practice remain primarily market-oriented.

There is no denying the need for planning as resources become scarce everywhere and as the Western world's economic hegemony diminishes. Therefore, business-government relations today must be managed strategically for the long-term economic survival of both the firm and the country.

Given the environmental uncertainty of doing business anywhere in the world today, and given government's pervasive role in Canadian society, improving business-government relations can be illustrated (as in **Figure 3–4**) by an open-system model of change. This is responsive to environmental changes, is cyclical in nature, and is chock-full of interdependencies.

Government thrives because people want more of what it provides. Government in Canada has also grown partly because business has wanted it to grow. Today, Canada and

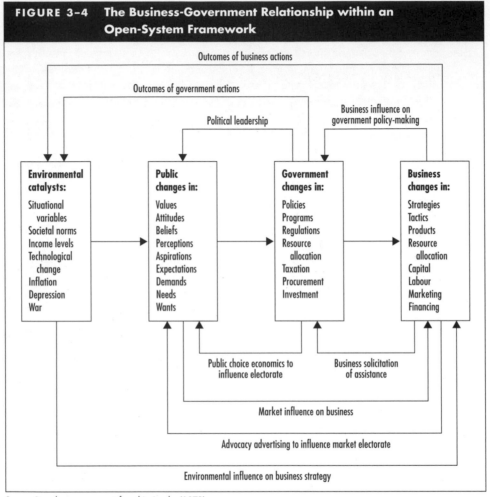

FIGURE 3-4   The Business-Government Relationship within an Open-System Framework

Outcomes of business actions

Outcomes of government actions

Political leadership

Business influence on government policy-making

Environmental catalysts:	Public changes in:	Government changes in:	Business changes in:
Situational variables	Values	Policies	Strategies
Societal norms	Attitudes	Programs	Tactics
Income levels	Beliefs	Regulations	Products
Technological change	Perceptions	Resource allocation	Resource allocation
Inflation	Aspirations	Taxation	Capital
Depression	Expectations	Procurement	Labour
War	Demands	Investment	Marketing
	Needs		Financing
	Wants		

Public choice economics to influence electorate

Business solicitation of assistance

Market influence on business

Advocacy advertising to influence market electorate

Environmental influence on business strategy

Source: Based upon a concept found in Jacoby (1973)

the world continue to change. For example, the US is a relatively declining world economic power. This decline may be temporary or permanent, but either way Canada has linked its future with that of the US — as the Free Trade Agreements (FTA and NAFTA) testify.

What role will Canada play in tomorrow's world economy? How long can this nation export its natural inheritance, while remaining grossly self-insufficient in manufactured and high-technology goods and services?

What role should business take in plotting Canada's future? What is the role of a chief executive officer? What responsibility should government take? How can business and government cooperate for the benefit of all Canadians? What are the odds for and against this happening?

Admittedly, this chapter has offered more questions than answers. However, without a clear view of the problems and questions to be faced, the next chapters would be far less meaningful.

The management of business-government relations is the greatest challenge to both business and government leaders today — whether in day-to-day management of the

Canadian political economy, or in bravely facing the new world together. *It is no longer adequate just to strive to do things right (i.e., efficiency). Today management, whether private or public, must strive to do the right things (i.e., effectiveness).*

SUGGESTED FURTHER READINGS

Buchholz, R.A. *et al* .1989. *Management Response to Public Issues*. 2nd ed. Toronto: Prentice Hall.

Caldwell, G.T. 1985. *Corporate Planning in Canada: An Overview*. Ottawa: The Conference Board of Canada.

Clark, Joe. 1994. *A Nation Too Good To Lose: Renewing The Purpose Of Canada*. Toronto: Key Porter Books.

Drucker, Peter F. 1969. *The Age of Discontinuity*. New York: Harper and Row.

Galbraith, J.K. 1971. *The New Industrial State*. Boston: Houghton-Mifflin.

Gibson, Gordon. 1995. *Thirty Million Musketeers*. Toronto: Key Porter Books.

Gillies, James. 1981. *Where Business Fails*. Montreal: Institute for Research on Public Policy.

Gwartney, James, Robert Lawson, and Walter Block. 1996. *Economic Freedom of the World, 1975-1995*. Vancouver: The Fraser Institute.

Gwyn, Richard. 1991. "Canada at Risk." In G. Bruce Doern and Bryne B. Purchase (eds.), *Canada At Risk? Canadian Public Policy in the 1990s*. Toronto: C.D. Howe Institute.

Jacoby, N.H. 1973. *Corporate Power and Social Responsibility*. New York: Macmillan.

Keynes, J.M. 1965. *The General Theory of Employment, Interest and Money*. New York: Harcourt Brace.

King, William L. Mackenzie. 1919. *Industry and Humanity*. Toronto: University of Toronto Press.

Macdonald, Donald. 1985. *Report of the Royal Commission on the Economic Union and Development Prospects of Canada*. Ottawa: Supply and Services Canada.

Murray, V.V. (ed). 1985. *Theories of Business-Government Relations*. Toronto: Trans-Canada Press.

Porter, Michael E. 1991. *Canada at the Crossroads: The Reality of a New Competitive Environment*. Ottawa: Business Council on National Issues and the Minister of Supply and Services.

Sachs, Jeffrey. 1997. "The Limits of Convergence: Nature, Nurture and Growth." *The Economist*. June 14.

Schumpeter, Joseph A. 1942. *Capitalism, Socialism and Democracy*. New York: Harper and Row.

Scott, Bruce R. 1997. "How Do Economies Grow?" *Harvard Business Review*, 75:3, May/June.

Sinclair, Gordon. 1996. "Look at Canadian History through Francophone Eyes." *Financial Post,* May 15.

Smith, Adam. 1937. *An Inquiry Into the Nature and Causes of the Wealth of Nations*. New York: Modern Library.

Stager, David. 1992. *Economic Analysis & Canadian Policy*. 7th ed. Toronto: Butterworths.

NOTES

1. A trading nation is simply one with lots of goods and services that other countries want. A nation of traders, however, is aggressive, always seeking out new opportunities, and works hard to exceed customer expectations.

2. Nine of the ten largest banks in the world are Japanese.

3. At the time of unification, the 16 million East Germans had a standard of living only 20% of that of West Germans.

4. Jeffrey Sachs, "The Limits of Convergence: Nature, Nurture, and Growth," *The Economist* (June 14, 1997).

5. Countries are ranked by GNP and corporations by total sales.

6. Non-profit, self-supporting research organizations conducting much of the research used by the OECD and the World Bank.

7. The World Economic Forum defines competitiveness as follows: the ability of a country to achieve sustained high rates of growth in GDP per capita.

8. James Gwartney, Robert Lawson, and Walter Block, *Economic Freedom of the World, 1975-1995* (Vancouver, The Fraser Institute, 1996).

9. Bruce R. Scott, "How Do Economies Grow," *Harvard Business Review*, 75:3 (1997).

10. David Stager, *Economic Analysis & Canadian Policy*, 7th ed. (Toronto: Butterworths, 1992), 89.

11. Donald Macdonald, *Report of the Royal Commission on the Economic Union and Development Prospects of Canada*, (Ottawa: Supply and Services Canada, 1985).

12. In addition to debt, there are unfunded pension liabilities and contingent guarantees (e.g., Crown corporations). Moreover, the population of Canada is aging and life expectancies have risen to 81 years for females and 75 for males.

13. Gorden Sinclair, "Look at Canadian History through Francophone Eyes," *Financial Post* (May 15, 1996), 15.

14. Richard Gwyn, "Canada at Risk," in G. Bruce Doern and Bryne B. Purchase (eds.), Canada At Risk? Canadian Public Policy in the 1990s (Toronto: C.D. Howe Institute, 1991), Ch. 8.

15 James Gillies, *Where Business Fails* (Montreal: Institute for Research on Public Policy, 1981), 17.

C h a p t e r

ECONOMIC FOUNDATIONS FOR BUSINESS-GOVERNMENT RELATIONS

Social progress is the point of economic progress.

Allan A. Warrack

In the beginning there was the market-capitalism model of philosopher/economist Adam Smith (1776), refined by David Ricardo early in the next century. This "invisible hand" or "laissez faire" model saw business giving focus to economic forces affecting the market, but being arms-length from social forces. Even this conception recognized that markets must have sufficient competition to preclude market control by private entities, and a role for government would be to ensure the "level playing field." Late in the last and early in this century the corporate form of business organization became important, and economic thinking and analysis began to take it into account.

ALTERED PERSPECTIVES

Economic thinking was altered sharply by the experience of the Great Depression. Economic cycles were not new, but the cycle severity in the "dirty thirties" was extreme and a question emerged as to whether governments could stand by idly in the midst of grave economic and social hardships. Keynesian Economics emerged on the thesis that government should include macrostability in its economic policy objectives; government could smooth the magnitude and speed of cycles through countercyclical spending/taxing patterns, thus relieving the hardships significantly. Keynesian fiscal policy would involve deficits in recessionary economic times and make up for it by generating surpluses in buoyant times (a point lost on most modern governments!), balancing out over the several business cycles that would constitute the longer term. The underlying logic is that the market "invisible hand" would have *failed* to assure macrostability and the "visible hand of government" would have a responsibility to interject the necessary correction.

Liberal economists of the 1960s and 1970s, for example Canadian John Kenneth Galbraith of Harvard University, extended the foregoing logic to other economic issues. Corporatism was in full flourish with attendant concerns about market power. Market power, the capacity for individual economic entities to influence outcomes such as price, were seen as violating the "invisible hand" and thus constituting the "visible hand of business" that needed to be countervailed by a "visible hand of government" on behalf of the public interest. The notion was that private market power of business could and should be neutralized by government market intervention. Thus a competitive market environment could be simulated. Wide acceptance of the idea meant that in Canada government participation/intervention/command of the economy expanded sharply. Transportation sectors (widely interpreted) were a focus of government economic policy due to inadequate competition; airlines, telecommunications, utilities, railways, pipelines, ports and trucking all became tightly regulated. This government intervention predominantly was microeconomic in nature, as distinct from Keynesian macrostability policies.

In a world of scarcity wherein choices must be made, economic analysis should contribute to understanding and to sensible choices. Each action taken has the consequence (opportunity cost) of the alternate action that is precluded. With enhanced economic affordability through economic growth or greater efficiencies in allocating public resources, more becomes possible. Public policies on behalf of society must be managed and led. A thesis of this book is that this is best achieved as a ***partnership*** of business and government, determining choices and implementing them on behalf of society.

⅄ TEN BASIC ECONOMICS MODULES

Economic affordability is vital to both business and government sectors so social goals can be advanced. Certain improvements are feasible without a government role, but many necessitate public sector infrastructure or services or regulation. Government economic functions are essential; so is business vitality, or the needed affordability will not be sustainable. Today in Canada that reality is much in evidence.

Economics
Economics is the science of choice and scarcity; it is the study of how people use limited productive resources toward human wants

- as a **physical/biological** science that deals with finite resources of nature.
- as a **social** science that deals with human behaviour and limitless wants.

This bipolar conception incorporates ***both*** SUPPLY (the first element) ***and*** DEMAND (the second) above. Their interplay determines not only price, but provides an economic metaphor to visualize the affordability issue for government as it tries to match public demands for programmes (e.g., services, subsidies) with its supplies of public funds through taxation and other revenue sources. In times of abundance (1960s to mid-1980s) greater economics research focus was on demand-side issues. But in more difficult times (mid-1980s into the new millennium) it is appropriate that greater attention is being paid to productivity supply-side issues of economics.

Managerial Economics

The **practical** use of economics concepts and analysis

- for decision making (including risk)
- for management processes (functions/people).

Managers in both business and government are assailed with information, data, and pressures. But they have shortages of budgets and time. In practice today's managers do not have the luxury of attention to things other than practical; they must sort and sift quickly for the subset of economics that is useful for solving the managerial problem on the agenda. Managerial economics intersects strongly with other disciplines such as accounting/finance, organizational analysis, and law. Management of business-government relations, from either of the perspectives, is dynamic and complex; it should be aided by common economic understanding and use.

Price

The payment for

- current (cash) commodity/service availability
- future (accrual) commodity/service availability.

The concept of price seems disarmingly simple — just balance supply and demand! Even those economically literate may substitute wishful thinking for **actions** that incorporate the "future" component of price. How else could all the major governmental jurisdictions in Canada weigh down future generations with fiscal debts? How else could a country like Canada have had an oil shortage? How else could similar Eastern Europe countries (e.g., East Germany) become so poor and environmentally decrepit adjacent to others (e.g., West Germany)? What good is it for downtown parking to be so cheap that you cannot get a place to park? When the price is wrong, much else goes wrong. Current Canadian issues abound: UI (now EI) policies, CPP funding, GST visibility/harmonization, privatization, and health funding. You can add countless examples. The overarching point is to disavow the economic naiveté that higher prices necessarily are bad, and lower prices necessarily good. Price theory posits that as the price of a commodity is lowered through subsidization, more such commodity is demanded; remember this the next time you read in the newspaper a story about overcrowding in your local hospital emergency room.

Interest Rate

The four interest rate components for the price/cost paid per dollar annually for the borrowing use of money are

- time preference = 2-3%
- risk = 2 ?? %
- inflation = 1-2% (1998)
- other/episodal = ?? % (e.g., separatism, exchange rate, civil uprisings).

Those who truly understand interest rates are those who have paid interest, and had this financial obligation impede cash flow for "meeting a payroll."[2] Adding the low ranges of the four interest rate components approximates the prime rate; commercial rates set by banks will be higher, especially according to risk and related assessments. Interest rates are low in Canada because of political stability, low inflation and tight monetary policies; in the early 1980s the prime rate exceeded 20%. It could happen again. Time preference is the logic that "good things are better sooner and bad things are better later" — so a borrower must pay for the deferral of good things that money could provide now. The primary source of interest rate variation is inflation variation; the nominal-vs-real value effect is direct, and there is the indirect effect that high inflation is confounded with higher risk. Clearly lower interest rates is in the calculations for more projects to proceed.

Inflation
A general and persistent rise in the average level of prices over time

• based on the CPI for a "basket" of goods applicable to a particular family size/income level and city size in Canada.

CPI overstates inflation by at least 2%;[3] three reasons are the substitution effect, the new goods effect, and goods quality improvement effect. Unless removed from CPI measurements, tax changes (that measure the price of government rather than the goods or services prices) can further distort results. This tax effect was an important source of confusion when the Goods and Services Tax (GST) was implemented; now that the GST clearly is here to stay, and especially if it is not visible, it is vital to understand the relationship between tax changes and inflation. As noted above, any inflation differentiates nominal and real interest rates. A lender must receive a level of interest that first offsets inflation, and only above that level receives an actual return for money lent. High inflation results in instability due to expectations of future inflation, and over some threshold confounds with risk driving towards even higher interest rates. Price instability through deflation is a severe risk; it can be argued that Canada's recent experience has been that, with a needlessly larger sacrifice through higher unemployment. Either way, economic growth is impeded. Re-establishing price stability has been a punishing experience for Canadians.

Consumers' Surplus
The difference between the value consumers place on ALL units (of a commodity/service) consumed and the payment that must be made to purchase an amount of it.

You will recall from economics principles that the DEMAND curve is a depiction of value, expressed as prices willingly paid for each level of quantity; for a small (scarce) amount, the demand curve depiction shows the extent that a higher price would be paid in the marketplace. As the quantity becomes larger the price falls. The key point is that the lower price is applicable to ALL units of commodity/service, albeit the purchaser would have been willing to pay more if fewer units were available. Visually, the payment is the rectangle framed by price and quantity within the quadrant, and the Consumers' Surplus (*CS*) is the triangle of value above the price line (see **Figure 4–1**).

Sellers with market power (and inelastic demand segment) will maximize profits by restricting supply so that price can be higher; the result is to retain an increment of *CS* for the producer rather than passing it along to the consumer. Monopoly utilities and agricultural marketing boards are classic examples applicable to this concept. The deviation from competitive pricing and resource allocations results in "deadweight loss" of economic value to society (see **Figure 4–2** later in chapter).

FIGURE 4-1   Depiction: Consumers' & Producers' Surpluses

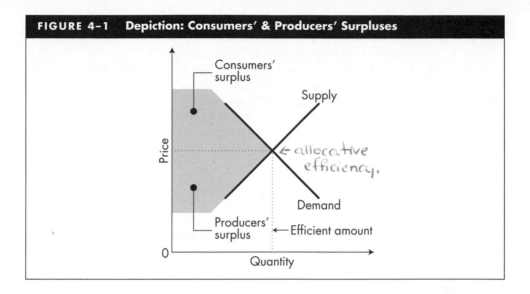

Producers' Surplus

The difference between the costs of production on ALL units (of a commodity/service) produced and the payment received for selling an amount of it.

Readers are reminded that the SUPPLY curve is the Marginal Cost function above the minimum point of its Average Variable Cost function. The supply curve is a depiction of value, expressed as costs willingly incurred to provide the commodity/service to the marketplace. As the quantity becomes larger the cost eventually increases. The key point is that the price received is applicable to ALL units of commodity/service, albeit the producer would have been willing to produce fewer units for each with lower costs. Visually, as with *CS* the payment rectangle is framed by price and quantity within the quadrant, but Producers' Surplus (*PS*) is the value between the Supply Curve and the price line (again, see **Figure 4–1**). The profit-maximizing firm with market power has scope for strategic decisions (e.g., quantity discounts) so that an increment of *PS* is retained rather than entirely passed along to the consumer. As with *CS, PS* deviations from competitive results impose "deadweight loss."

Markets

Where buyers and sellers transact goods and services within the intersection of market dimensions form, space, and time, and the

- product form incorporates quantity and quality features
- spatial location denotes geography
- timing of demand and supply must be reconciled.

Markets, from agricultural to industrial to services, facilitate the fulfilment of needs and wants. With sufficient competition in markets and reliable product standards self-imposed by suppliers or by government, fairness of results to the public can be reasonably assured. There are both products and factors (of production) markets. Effective market competition (or workable competition) creates and maintains economic pressures for: (*i*) lower costs of production and selling; and (*ii*) only necessary costs being reflected in the pricing structures applied to the marketplace. The ideal competitive market would serve the economic needs of a Canadian democratic society.

Market Failure

Market failure occurs when the freely operating market system fails to achieve efficiency of resource use and welfare maximization[4] due to one or more of five reasons

- monopoly
- market imperfections
- externalities
- public services
- common property.

There is little disagreement that private monopoly power must be regulated by counter-vailing government powers of public policy. Markets may have some but insufficient competition (e.g., oligopoly with very few dominant firms), so government must respond to the market failure. External costs imposed on other parties can be reduced by public policies such as "make the polluter pay." The provision of certain public services may be needed by society, but cannot be provided by other than the government on a collective basis; some infrastructure (e.g., historic linking from sea-to-sea by rail and road) and some services (e.g., defence) can be provided at much lower cost collectively. Common property, very difficult to price, may be publicly administered for practical reasons. Canada's vast and far-flung natural resources endowments, both within our boundaries (e.g., forests, minerals, hydrocarbons) and without (e.g., fisheries, undersea resources such as Hibernia and Sable Island) are common properties that hardly could be managed other than publicly. Canada's expansive geography and sparse demography combine to require that the government sectors do more than would be necessary if those physical and human features were different.

Market Intervention Choices

Government can exercise public policy on behalf of society with varied governing instruments, such as

- enhanced competition
- economic regulation
- direct ownership (see **Figures 7–3 and 7–4**).

Preferences within the stated range of governing instruments will be influenced significantly by political philosophy. Differences in views may be less in goals than in *means* to achieve them. Right-wing governments generally will favour enhancing competition, be reluctant to regulate, and only nationalize as a last resort or urgency. Left-wing governments will regulate and nationalize much more readily, but will aid and abet greater competition too. Saskatchewan's long history of farm cooperative enterprise was led by Co-operative Commonwealth Federation (CCF, later NDP) governments; rural areas across Canada emulated this policy approach. Numerous government programs, all across the land, are formulated and delivered to enhance competition in the relevant marketplace. Since its early history, Canada has had competition legislation. Later chapters deal with Crown Corporations in Canada (**Chapter 8**) and will address economic regulation (**Chapter 11**) more fully.

TEN BUSINESS-GOVERNMENT ECONOMICS MODULES

Keynesian Economics

Government increases spending in times of recession, often to the point of incurring deficits, and cuts back/builds surpluses in times of prosperity, accruing to balance over the longer term. Economic *in*stability has adverse distributional effects; severe economic cycles impose differential hardships on the disadvantaged in society. In depression the impact of unemployment hits harder those individuals, families, and communities which are less well-off. In boom times with high inflation, those with substantial assets can protect (or even gain) from inflation's impact. Stabilization is recognized as an economic goal, but it also is a social goal due to the above reasoning. To operationalize Keynesian theory, savings from previous surpluses would be utilized if they exist, but government would go into debt if it had to so that greater macrostability could be achieved. What is the problem? Careful examination of the data[5] for Canada reveals that deficit spending during recession is *not* the source of Canada's deficit/DEBT problem, the overlooking the second half of the Keynesian Economics concept is the problem — deficit spending during prosperity! The Government of Canada began to lose control of spending in the late 1960s, followed by being wildly beyond control in the 1970s, with monumental interest costs building up in the 1980s and retrenchment in the 1990s. Many provinces, soon after, fell into the similar "feel good" spending patterns that enfeebles Canadian budgetary capacities today.

Nevertheless there have been some Canadian examples of the savings side of Keynesian Economics. Both the Alberta and Saskatchewan governments established Heritage Savings Trust Funds, and Quebec is a major economic player through its Caisse de depot et placement entity. Alas, the Alberta and Saskatchewan funds have been overwhelmed by respective accumulated debts, so effectively they are gone.

Economic Functions of Government

A modern government undertakes

(*i*) the provision of public use goods and services

(*ii*) regulation

(*iii*) redistribution

(*iv*) stabilization

(*v*) infrastructure.

While there is debate about the level of services that should be provided and the way it should be done, it is clear that certain vital goods and services will be omitted if government is benign. Services can be provided direct by government departments, or quasi-direct by funding of arms-length bodies and boards (e.g., University Board of Governors) to ensure services availability. Another approach, one that has business opportunities, is government contracting (out) of services delivery. Regulation is targeted at fairness and a "level playing field." Many of Canada's policies have been geared to individual, business and regional distribution (e.g., equalization federal-to-provincial funding programs). Stability is conducive to greater economic growth through lower-risk investment prospects. Infrastructure lessens or deletes obstacles for economic development that is needed in Canada, its provinces, and territories. Infrastructure emplacement constitutes economic activity and employment in itself, often including a historical pattern of megaprojects in Canada. The Confederation Bridge, linking PEI to mainland Canada, is the 1997 example.

Economic Regulation

Government imposition of rules and controls which are designed to direct, restrict, or change the economic behaviour of individuals and business, and which are supported by penalties for non–compliance.[6] Regulation may be direct or indirect and takes many forms according to practical requirements, including monitoring of self-regulation by professions. Modifying economic behaviour is accomplished by a wide variety of administrative mechanisms ranging from government departments (e.g., food standards) to regulatory entities established by specific statutes (e.g., Workers' Compensation Board) to price-regulation commissions (e.g., utility rate-making). Over 25% of Canada's GNP is within the scope of regulation.[7] Benefits of regulation are indirect and exceedingly difficult to measure, but the costs are substantial. While there are administrative costs, compliance costs by industry are higher; a separate evaluation of regulation costs is presented in a later chapter.

Deficits/DEBTS

A public deficit is when government revenues are exceeded by the sum of program expenditures plus interest costs; a public DEBT is the net accumulation of deficits over time. The 1997-98 Government of Canada deficit was $17 billion, while the DEBT exceeds $600 billion. One-third of each revenue dollar goes for interest on the DEBT; Canadian all-government DEBT approaches a trillion dollars. The DEBT data does not include all pension nor contingent liabilities. An appropriate way to gauge the fiscal burden is to measure the proportion of the tax dollar that goes to service DEBT (money **not** available to fund services) in current budgets. For the federal government this calculation is 33 cents, for Ontario it is 19 cents, and even in Alberta it is 10 cents. Beyond these quantitative impacts, there are two other troubling aspects of public debt burden: (*i*) interest costs absolutely must be paid so any fiscal flexibility is forced totally onto programs; and (*ii*) substantial borrowing is foreign and the exchange rate risk must be borne. The good news is that most Canadian governments have balanced their most recent budgets; this situation is offset by the bad news. The first bad news is that each government carries substantial DEBT that forces interest payments instead of available monies for public services or tax reductions. The second bad news is that the "big three" governments (Canada, Ontario, Quebec), possessing jurisdiction over most of the people and economic activity in Canada, continue to have growing DEBT due to unrelenting annual deficits. The final bad news is that the DEBTS of the three biggest governments "cast a risk shadow" on credit ratings of all public and private sector borrowers in the country. There are only four options to reduce deficits, and thereby slow the pace of DEBT accumulation.[8] One is tax rate increases; Canadians appear to have "tax fatigue" and it seems unlikely to change soon. Another option is broadening the tax base, which has been happening (often in picayune ways), with limited scope for more of the same. Expenditure reductions is a third way and has been necessary for every government; Saskatchewan has charted a balanced course while Alberta has had only minor fee increases but deep cuts. Ontario is committed to tax reductions as well as expenditure cuts in their future provincial budgets. The fourth option, far less painful than the others, is economic growth and the government revenue increases that collate with economic growth; however, it is clear that economic growth alone *cannot* solve the problem. Research has identified the concept of sustainable debt to be 25-27% of GNP. Today that debt exceeds 70%; reducing it to a sustainable level will be a daunting task over time, and possible only with a strategy that includes financial retrenchment.[9]

Economic Growth

Increase in an economy's total real output of final goods and services, measured as GDP; more technically, it is the outward shift of an economy's production possibilities boundary. Public policy goals include the desire for a high and sustaining rate of economic growth. Three conventional reasons are

- population growth
- standard of living improvements
- income/wealth distribution.

It is easy to see that the level of prosperity will erode unless economic growth is in pace with increases in population, and it is equally easy to understand that economic growth must exceed that of population if standard of living improvements are to be possible. While there is the view that such improvements are not required in society, especially in view of environmental impacts, typical sources of this view are referring to **others**. Income and wealth distribution reasoning contains a direct and an abstract logic. The direct reason is that wealth (and income thereto) must have been created in the first place for there to be anything to distribute. However, the abstract reason is based on the logic that wealth/income holders are more willing to share new prosperity than share that which they already possess; thus economic growth lessens the zero-sum game difficulty regarding distribution goals of a modern society.[10] Beyond the conventional reasons for economic growth, economic restructuring and environmental retrofits can be achieved more readily in the context of rapid economic growth. Owners and workers can leave obsolete economic activities less painfully when there are vibrant economic alternatives to which they can turn. Expensive pollution abatement investments can be made more within the terms of economic feasibility when plant expansion investment can be made in conjunction with improvements to the older existing facilities. The deficit/DEBT straight-jacket of many Canadian governments compels very high priority for economic growth; as noted above, it is the only painless option for fiscal improvement. Today budgets are formulated with explicit economic growth assumptions. The 1997-98 federal budget assumes 3.2% growth; Ontario's 98-99 budget assumption is somewhat lower, and the Alberta budget assumption for economic growth is a bit higher. Even one percent stronger economic growth in every jurisdiction would help immensely due to the lock-step effect of higher government revenues; as well, higher economic growth reduces unemployment and lessens the expenditures side pressures on governments. A debate in economics is whether the multiplier effect is greater for private vs. public sector expenditures; if greater, then reduced government expenditures (thus more money in private hands) should enhance economic growth and concurrent government revenues.

Invisible Hand

Every individual entity, pursuing only own good, is led (as if by an invisible hand) to achieve the best for all (i.e., society). This fundamental idea has been referred to earlier in the book and earlier in this chapter; now it is stated explicitly. A thesis of this book is that government should do what only it can do, and do it with efficiency and economy; the argument is not so much for less government as it is for effective governance. Adam Smith and others to this day also are explicit that for the Invisible Hand conception of market economics to serve society, government must provide institutions and public works which contain a framework for commerce and sanctity of contracts.[11]

Visible Hand(s)

These forces have the power to alter outcomes of markets and influence the wealth and opportunity distribution in society. Three visible hands are

- market power by business — {**V(B)**}
- government policy and power — {**V(G)**}
- labour unions and professions — {**V(L)**}.

Private sector companies are expected to seek maximum profits; board members and managers have a shareholder responsibility to do so. Means to do so include technostructure decision making and market management to the extent that scope for the same exists. When market power exists (the first two market failures enumerated earlier), we expect {**V(B)**} to be exercised on behalf of the shareholders. As government renders its judgment on whether the result is acceptable to the society it serves, it must decide if countervailing {**V(G)**} policies are needed to protect the public interest. The relevant government can be at the federal, provincial, or municipal/civic level; some issues are intergovernmental in nature. Policy administration may be either direct (department) or quasi (e.g., Crown Corporations) where public funding prevails yet the operations are arms-length in nature. Another set of market power relationships exist when labour (or professions) are organized for member-bargaining purposes {**V(L)**}; in highly-regulated sectors a type of duopoly can emerge where {**V(B)**} and {**V(L)**} may reach accommodations serving both, but at the expense of the consumer. Again, {**V(G)**} may be needed to countervail the jointly-held market power. Over recent years public-sector unions in Canada have become prevalent in organized labour; thus the interaction of {**V(G)**} with {**V(L)**} becomes more complex as both policy bargaining and employee bargaining are intertwined.

Deadweight Loss

Inefficiency loss of economic value due to **in**correct quantity and price of a commodity/service. **Figure 4–1** earlier showed the "surplus" (consumer plus producer) created by the market; only at the intersection of SUPPLY and DEMAND does the marginal benefit of consuming one more unit exactly match the marginal cost of producing it. The "market clearing price" matches up the marginal benefit with the marginal cost. At this point the market is efficient because any deviation from that point results in losses, as depicted by the deadweight loss "triangles" in **Figure 4–2**. When the quantity is too little, both the Consumers' Surplus is less and the Producers' Surplus is less. The total together is deadweight loss, shown as the triangle to the left of the intersection point. When the quantity is too much, the additional cost of its production exceeds the additional benefit of its consumption and again the result is deadweight loss (triangle right of intersection). The gain in welfare, the point of efficiency, is maximized at the price that results in consumption quantity and production quantity matching precisely. A fundamental tenet of market economics, and government policies to foster same, is to facilitate economic efficiency.

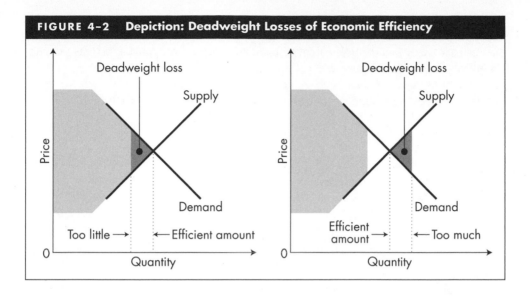

FIGURE 4-2   Depiction: Deadweight Losses of Economic Efficiency

Social Discount Rate

This rate is appropriate to society as a whole; and it is the minimum rate of return that a public investment must yield if it is to be worth undertaking on behalf of society, including both tangible and intangible benefits. The concept is an adaptation of the marginal efficiency of capital analysis; it holds that if expected cash flow and capital gains exceed financing costs, the investment in question will be profitable. If interest rates are lower, more potential investments will be profitable. Like commercial interest rates calculations, the social discount rate must be in real (not nominal) returns. To the extent that society's needs cannot be fully met (e.g., certain public services) on a commercial basis of the market interest rate, those unmet needs may be met on the basis of a lower (social discount) rate through actions of governments. [12] Distilling a vast economic literature on the subject, there are three reasons for the social discount rate to be lower: inter-generational equity, intra-generational equity, and risk pooling.

Who is to attend to the interests of the young and unborn? No one lives forever, so a fundamental inter-generational myopia seems plausible. While individual persons' and companies' actions might be otherwise, the collective will to preserve and even enhance future generations' prospects is a potential mission of government. Examples might be to harvest resources (especially non-renewable ones) less quickly, and insisting on environmental reclamation to a level at least as productive as before resource utilization. Who is to attend to the needs of those of a current generation unable to fend for themselves? A civil society will make provision at least to some rudimentary threshold; doing so necessitates public expenditure allocations apart from any conception of commercial market returns. Both the inter- and intra-generational arguments invoke a trade-off between economic efficiency and social equity. Either a commercial interest rate (see a previous module) or social discount rate can be lower if risk is lessened. The concept of risk pooling occurs when risks of individual or smaller groups are transferred to the largest pool in society — for which government decides. A common incidence of government policies is either to make direct contributions to a project or assist the project by indirect means such as loan guarantees; proper accounting requires that government financial statements show contingent liabilities for any risks that continue over time. Understanding the social discount rate notion will assist the business sector and the general public understand why governments do what they do. Careful use of social discount rate analysis (e.g., within Benefit Cost Analysis) will aid government to escape frequently fuzzy judgments and minimize the propensity for major mistakes. Canadian governments of all political stripes have made some dillies!

Pareto Optimum

There is no change which would make someone better off without making another worse off. Underlying this welfare concept is criteria for allocation efficiency (Pareto efficiency) where it is impossible to reallocate production and consumption activities to make improvements for some consumers and not simultaneously harm others. The criteria requires production and market conditions be fulfilled.[13] Four technical production conditions, predicated on achieving the lowest possible costs, are

- prices equal marginal costs of production
- firms make normal profits
- factors are paid according to contribution value
- factors fully employed.

Three market conditions, to reflect only necessary costs, require

- perfectly competitive marketplace
- absence of externalities
- divisibility of products and services.

The foregoing criteria are rigid constraints; the reality rarely reflects the ideal enumerated. But for *business* and *government* to seek the closest possible approximation, constantly striving for improvement will well serve the larger community. Pareto optimality/efficiency is a crucial "boilerplate" for the economic and social betterment of Canada. Business and government can be ***partners*** in this noble effort.

SOCIAL DIMENSIONS

Social progress is the point of economic progress. This chapter theme argues for interdependence of economic and social policies for Canada. Traditionally, Canadians and their governments have viewed them as separate policies. To be sure, much social advancement can be achieved without cost, and is often better distant from government. On the other hand, certain social advancement does require funding resources. But how much is affordable? Do we fund policies that actually are counterproductive — like outside Stage II of the production function? As well as issues related to these questions, the dynamics of technological and economic changes are proceeding at a dizzying pace. There are social dimensions to the economic state, and even more so when the economy of our country and regions is changing rapidly. Coming to grips with the impact of economic growth may be difficult, but vastly preferable to the risk of our economy collapsing. As economic foundations for business-government relations are set out, concurrently it is important to include a perspective of the social dimensions of economic change.[14]

Shorter term economic growth depends directly on financial investment. An existing base of other forms of capital stock may permit reasonably immediate success. Yet longer term growth and prosperity depends also on investments made in human and social capital; high quantitative and qualitative such investments, embodied in Canadians, should enhance the odds of citizenry resilience: then persons can reasonably be expected to be productive and prosperous. They should be able to fend for themselves in the "rough and tumble" of tumultuous changes, be they economic or social. They would be able and willing to make sacrifices now to improve opportunity for self and attendant families in the future. Hence, people would be resilient in adapting to change.

Self-reliance through individual effort has been a Canadian core value. Another has been compassion leading to collective responsibility. These core values are building blocks for success that should be fostered in Canadian society. Who would not favour moving to a stronger competitive position with more robust economic growth? Starting in the 1960s through to the mid-1980s, a regime of heavy government expenditure commitments, first from high-growth affordability but later supplemented by deficits and permissive inflation, cobbled together a complex and expensive social safety net. High interest rates driven by rising inflation was curtailed, a painful process beginning in the late 1980s. Competing on world markets became essential with freer trade in accordance with GATT, FTA, and eventually NAFTA changes. Meanwhile, Canada was fiscally irresponsible for a protracted period of years. Great resilience was needed if Canadians were not only to cope, but to harness these dramatic changes to their advantage. Did the enormity of the public expenditure, paid to individuals and companies and regions and other governments, put Canada into this advantageous position?

> The assumption was that the safety net designed for the high growth years of the 1960s and 1970s would be appropriate for the effects of the cold showers of the 1990s. That assumption has been clearly demonstrated to be wrong.[15]

Canada's future is endangered by economic and social polarization, a serious gap between the rich and the poor. What about Generation X, those born between the mid-1960s and the late 1970s?[16] Widening gulfs between citizens and generations and regions also is an ominous development; there is emerging despair. Employment opportunity and earnings divergence is widening. However total and average per person wealth may grow, there may be the danger of a disparate distribution of opportunity such that social cohesion is put at risk. Professional and technical skills are in high demand and highly compensated, but generally manual and clerical skills are in excess supply, and poorly paid with weak job security. To be blunt, there is the potential spectre of a trade-off between prosperity and security. "Gated" communities are common in the United States. Minimization, including by governments, may exacerbate the polarization. The plea here is for better *governance*, whether with smaller or larger governments.

Maxwell argues, and we concur, that it is essential to integrate social and economic programs. The longer-term view is necessary, not only to lessen waste but to frame expenditure commitments into a sustainable direction of investment in future economic growth and social cohesion. With trust and cooperation, the transaction costs of society are lower; the notion applies between individuals, between citizens and their governments, and between governments in Canada. Cynicism and mistrust is much in evidence today. In the new century Canada will have a stronger future as it builds four cornerstones of a resilient society:[17]

- a learning society, especially of the young
- a caring role for the family
- evaluation of outcomes, with focus on opportunity not universality
- collective action to nurture and protect its social capital.

One of Canada's most respected business leaders, Ted Newall, has spoken to the subject at hand. A key quote from his presentation includes the theme of this chapter:

> Our challenge, as Canadian business leaders, is to consciously strive to help create the highest possible quality of life for the greatest number of people in this country. We must work to enhance the quality of live for all Canadians if for no other reason than this is the best way to create the best possible climate for business. But how should quality of life be measured? I would answer that our most critical measure and *our most important challenges lie in the quality of life enjoyed by the least-advantaged 25 percent in our society.* [18]

USES AND ABUSES OF ECONOMICS

An analogy can be drawn between economics and the well-worn term "statistics and lies." As with many subjects, a little knowledge can be a dangerous thing. Economics interpretation often is the "truth but not the whole truth," whereupon "cherry picking" economics analysis and results can have handsome payoffs and thus are overwhelmingly tempting. Examples abound: *business* may plead for individual subsidies while ranting against subsidies in general; *labour* may cite inflation in collective bargaining despite there being no inflation; and *government* (e.g., Alberta) may repeatedly cite the economic reforms of New Zealand while disavowing the notion of sales tax (Value Added Tax [VAT] was the primary tax reform in New Zealand!).

Economics has turned itself into the superpower of the social sciences, exercising a powerful influence on the lives of ordinary people, yet economists are derided and accused of being irrelevant and wrong.[19] Why the paradox? Economists produce, analyze and present economics ideas, but other people use them. The present chapter has been about the uses of economics for business-government relations, but it is important to be alert to the abuses as well. The cited source suggests three prevalent abuses of economics: "one-sided coin," "shoot the messenger" and "allergy to change."

Economics may establish that two effects are necessarily different sides of the same coin. Politicians may take up only one side, pretending it as the only side; even more scary is the prospect of being purposefully unaware of the opposing dimension. Higher interest rates are good for lenders but seen as bad for borrowers. Higher exports are good but higher imports are bad! Government has been known to oppose (e.g., FTA) in opposition what they embrace after an election. Price increases nearly always are reported in the media as bad, but an earlier economics module argues to the contrary. Hype about one side of the two-sided economics coin, the myopic politicizing of economic realities, is not helpful to rational governance.

A second distortion "shoot the messenger" confuses consequences and causes. It is easier to blame financial "speculators and bigwigs" than acknowledge one's own fiscal policy frailty. Provincial elections in Canada have been won by "blaming Ottawa." Ottawa blames Washington (formerly London) and cities blame the provinces. And so it goes in both politics and economics — an awkward thing about the truth is that it remains after the messenger has been shot!

Perhaps "allergy to change" is the most dangerous of the three distortions; you will recognize it when someone claims that some basic rule in economics no longer applies. Competition from another country often mysteriously is seen as violating established law of economics. Cheaper labour of Asian countries, Mexico, or Haiti is somehow unfair! Belying a few centuries of evidence to the contrary, there are those who claim that new technology will destroy more jobs than it creates. Canada's examples are suspicion of American trade and barriers to inter-provincial trade (see **Chapter 14**). The American focus has been resistance to Japan and Mexico trade — remember "that giant sucking sound" phrase? Inertia resisting change, the tyranny of the status quo,[20] is the change allergy that impedes adjustment at the pace that is needed for the future of the succeeding generations of Canadians.

IMPLICATIONS FOR MANAGEMENT

Part II of this book has been written so as to help the reader better *understand* business and government, and the relationships between them. Therefore, in trying to understand business-government relations, it is important to keep in mind these key points derived from ideas, concepts and discourse on economics:

i.   The business of business is to create wealth;

ii.   Economics is about the creation and distribution of wealth;

iii.   Economic theories espoused by governments and applied as ideologies are drivers of social, economic and legislative change;

iv.   Business opportunities and trends are often the result of economic decision making (or the lack thereof);

v.   Strategic managers must incorporate local, national and global economic realities into their market analyses and planning; and

vi.   Economics, like business (and government), is really about people.

SUGGESTED FURTHER READINGS

Auditor-General for Canada. 1994. *Annual Report to Parliament, 1992*.

Boadway, Robin, Albert Breton, Neil Bruce, and Richard Musgrave. 1994. *Defining the Role of Government: Economic Perspectives on the State*. School of Policy Studies, Queen's University, Kingston, ON.

Canada West Foundation. 1998. *Red Ink IV — Back From the Brink?* Calgary, AB, January.

The Economist. 1995. "The Use and Abuse of Economics." November 25.

The Economist. 1996. "State and Market." February 17.

Friedman, Milton, and Rose. 1984. *Tyranny of the Status Quo*. New York: HBJ Publishers.

The Globe & Mail. 1996. "Generation X Faces A Barren Harvest." February 15.

Jackson, Mark. 1996. *MBA Economics*. Cambridge, MA: Blackwell.

Lipsey, Richard G. 1994. *Economic Growth and Debt Control*, Plenary Address, Pre-Budget

Consultation Conference (Federal Finance Ministry) and Canada West Foundation. Calgary, AB.

Luciani, Patrick. 1996. *Economic Myths: Making Sense of Canadian Policy Issues*. Don Mills, ON: Addison-Wesley.

Maxwell, Judith. 1996. *Social Dimensions of Economic Growth*. Hanson Memorial Lecture, Department of Economics, University of Alberta, Edmonton, AB.

Newall, J. Edward. 1996. "Sowing the Seeds of a Learning Culture." *The Edge*, Canadian Business Leader Awardee Presentation, Faculty of Business, University of Alberta, Edmonton AB, Spring.

Scarth, William. 1996. *Beyond the Deficit: Generation X and Sustainable Debt*. Toronto: C.D. Howe Fiscal Policy Commentary.

Strick, John C. 1994. *The Economics of Government Regulation: Theory and Practice*. Toronto: Thompson Educational Publishing.

Thompson, Arthur A., and John P. Formby. 1993. *Economics of the Firm: Theory and Practice*. Englewood Cliffs, NJ: Prentice-Hall.

Thurow, Lester C. 1981. *The Zero-Sum Society: Distribution and the Possibilities for Economic Change*. New York: Penguin.

Warrack, Allan A. 1993. *Megaproject Decision Making: Lessons and Strategies*. Western Centre for Economic Research Bulletin #16, University of Alberta, Edmonton, AB, November.

Weimer, David L. and Aidan R. Vining. 1992. *Policy Analysis: Concepts and Practice*. Englewood Cliffs, NJ: Prentice-Hall.

NOTES

1. Managerial Economics and Business Economics conventionally are used as interchangeable terms.

2. A handy calculation aid is the "Rule of 72." Divide the interest rate into the scalar number 72, the result is the years it takes for an amount of money to double; the calculation reverse also is valid and useful.

3. Patrick Luciani, *Economic Myths: Making Sense of Canadian Policy Issues* (Don Mills, ON: Addison-Wesley, 1996), , 180-1. The substitution effect is due to consumers altering their purchase patterns with changing relative prices; the new goods effect reflects that new goods do not enter the measured CPI basket without time delay; and quality improvements (e.g., wrist watches, tires, computers) can enhance value proportionately more than price increases. In late 1996, the Boskin Commission found that the USA CPI overstates cost of living changes by more than a percentage point per year. In times of high inflation the bias is even greater.

4. John C. Strick, *The Economics of Government Regulation: Theory and Practice* (Toronto: Thompson Educational Publishing, 1994), Ch. 2.

5. Auditor-General for Canada, *Annual Report to Parliament, 1992* (1994). Since Confederation, program spending has exceeded revenues by under $40 billion, only about 7% of the 1996-97 accumulated debt of about $600 billion (not including pension and contingent obligations). In an editorial, the Toronto *Globe and Mail* portrayed this result as "compound-interest hell."

6. Strick, *The Economics of Government Regulation: Theory and Practice*, 3.

7. *ibid*, 9.

8. Richard G. Lipsey, *Economic Growth and Debt Control* (Calgary, AB: Plenary Address, Pre-Budget Consultation Conference [Federal Finance Ministry] and Canada West Foundation, 1994).

9. William Scarth, *Beyond the Deficit: Generation X and Sustainable Debt* (Toronto: C.D. Howe Fiscal Policy Commentary, 1996).

10. Lester C. Thurow, *The Zero-Sum Society: Distribution and the Possibilities for Economic Change* (New York, Penguin, 1981). Since zero-sum changes are so difficult, the positive-sum strategy (e.g., economic growth) is more likely to succeed. Thurow notes that gains are distant, diffused and uncertain while sacrifices are immediate, specific, and certain. No wonder economic policy improvements are politically difficult.

11. Richard A. Musgrave, *"Fiscal Functions of the Public Sector."* In Defining the Role of Environment: Economic Perspectives on the State, by Bodway, Breton, Bruce, and Musgrave, p. 2. Kingston: School of Policy Studies, Queen's University.

12. See David L. Weimer & Adrian Vining, *Policy Analysis: Concepts and Practice* (Englewood Cliffs, NJ: Prentice-Hall, 1992), 304-6, for a fuller discussion.

13. Strick, *The Economics of Government Regulation: Theory and Practice*, 20-2.

14. Judith Maxwell, *Social Dimensions of Economic Growth* (Edmonton, AB: Hanson Memorial Lecture, Department of Economics, University of Alberta, Spring 1996). This section draws heavily on the publication of her lecture at the University of Alberta.

15. *ibid*, 5.

16. *The Globe & Mail*, "Generation X Faces A Barren Harvest," (February 15, 1996).

17. Maxwell, *Social Dimensions of Economic Growth* 17-8.

18. Ted Newall, "Sowing the Seeds of a Learning Culture," *The Edge* (Edmonton, AB: Canadian Business Leader Awardee Presentation, Faculty of Business, University of Alberta, Spring 1996). Mr. Newall is CEO of Nova Corporation and was awarded the 1996 Canadian Business Leader Award by the University of Alberta's Faculty of Business. In 1993 he was named Canada's CEO of the Year.

19. *The Economist*, "The Uses and Abuses of Economics," (November 25, 1995), 17.

20. Milton and Rose Friedman, *Tyranny of the Status Quo*. (New York: HBJ Publishers, 1984).

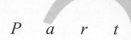

CASTING BUSINESS- GOVERNMENT RELATIONS

Having now developed an appreciation for the historical and cultural underpinnings of Canadian business-government relations, let us examine the nature of the key players — business and government. The next five chapters will show how Canada's past has shaped the respective roles and structures of business and the state, how these in turn influence their interrelationsips, and how these interrelationships are changing.

C h a p t e r

5

THE MYTH OF
A BUSINESS
IDEOLOGY

Here's the rule, for bargains:
"Do other men, for they would do you."
That's the true business precept.

Charles John Muffam Dickens, 1812-70

Any business-government relationship consists of social, political, economic, legal, and technological connections. The nature of these linkages reflects the prevailing ideology of a given business environment and vice versa. There are four such ideologies, each producing different connections between business and government: *libertarianism (or liberalism), egalitarianism (or socialism), environmentalism/humanism, and corporatism.*

Libertarians believe in the maximum freedom of the individual, in competition, and in government being limited to the courts, defence, and law enforcement. *Egalitarians* believe in economic and social equality among people within a society with state direction of economic affairs. *Environmentalists/humanists* seek to preserve the physical environment and promote the quality of human life above all else. This would obviously require close cooperation between business and government, and the responsible use of private property. *Corporatists* seek optimal economic growth, economic efficiency, and a high standard of living. Government supports the private sector by fostering efficiency and setting policies for economic growth to achieve this high standard of living.

Leo Panitch further defined corporatism as "a socio-political structure in which different centralized, hierarchical organizations interact and cooperate harmoniously at an elite level, and together control the masses."[1] Government in a corporatist state strongly urges private enterprise toward four goals: order, unity, nationalism, and economic success. Many regard corporatism as an integral quality of a post-industrial, anti-liberal, neo-mercantilist state.

Parts I and **II** of this book described an existing pattern of elitist mutual cooperation in Canada. The state has strongly emphasized corporatism's first three goals; consequently, the nation exhibits strong anti-liberalist tendencies. However, Canada does not fit the definition completely. Therefore, it is said to be a *neo-corporatist state*.

Potential relationships between business and government can also be categorized a different way using three models: *elite accommodation*, *market*, or *business ecology*.

The *elite accommodation* (or dominance) model is pyramid-shaped, depicting society as a hierarchy. Business and government elites create a privileged establishment which dominates the pyramid. Those with a Marxist orientation maintain that the state acts as the executive committee of the ruling class; thus, the business elite uses government for its own ends. Following this line of thought, economist John Kenneth Galbraith gave "socialism" an entirely new meaning in a 1980 interview with *The London Free Press*:

> Modern socialism comes not from socialists and not from liberal economists. Socialism comes when the heads of troubled corporations, pushed by unions, and urged by bankers, go to governments to be bailed out.

On the other hand, corporatists maintain that a dominant government elite uses private property to further its social goals, such as full employment. Galbraith contends that the business elite has become increasingly dominated by professional managers who are not owners of capital, and the government elite is influenced by decision-makers who have not been elected. The collusion between these two elites has created a *technostructure*, as Galbraith terms it. This dominates the whole of society and attempts to maintain a benign and stable environment for itself.

The *market* (or *market-capitalism*) model conceived by Adam Smith in 1776 and refined by David Ricardo in 1817, regards business as being at arms-length with social forces, and focuses on economic forces affecting the market. The market is seen as a self-contained system which buffers business from non-market, environmental forces such as church and interest groups. In this model, business managers concentrate on such market goals as profit, efficiency, and economic growth. Government, not business, ministers to social needs. The key elements of the market model are private property, economic incentives (the profit motive), a free market system, and political and economic freedom. These obviously hold strong appeal for libertarians.

Finally, the *business ecology* or *systems* model is concerned with the interrelationship of all the institutions and forces within the business environment. Firms are driven by a wide range of economic factors, as well as socio-political demands from government, pressure groups, and individuals.[2] Business is oriented towards self-preservation, maintaining its boundaries and increasing its control over forces acting upon it. In response to the cultural, economic, environmental, individual, political, social, and technological demands business makes on its environment, society makes new demands. It also chooses to increase or decrease its support of business, depending upon management's actions. Environmentalists/humanists work most effectively within a business ecology model.

ORIGINS OF THE BUSINESS IDEOLOGY

Business philosophy in Canada can best be understood by comparing it with parallel development in the United States — a country with similar antecedents and with whom we conduct nearly 80% of our trade. Some of the first American entrepreneurs believed that anyone could achieve economic success through hard work, thrift, prudence, foresight, and patriotism. They believed that government was inherently evil, to be limited to protecting life and property, administering justice, and defending the nation. Government intervention in the economy was considered a violation of "natural laws" that controlled the marketplace, resulting in lower output and less efficient production and distribution.

This early American business elite also considered government expensive, wasteful, inefficient, and prone to attract inferior workers. Government expenses were considered burdens on producers and consumers that diverted resources from better use, i.e., producing goods, services, and wealth. Government could best promote competition, they believed, by allowing the natural forces of supply and demand to operate freely. These leaders of industry and commerce were also generally opposed to subsidies and tariffs, although many did favour protecting their own industries. With this sole exception, these early capitalists were libertarians and followed the market model. This philosophy often is referred to as *the business ideology* — a clear statement of the ideals held by a business community.

CHALLENGES TO THE BUSINESS IDEOLOGY

The study of Canadian business-government relations reveals four premises which challenge the above ideology:

i. Competition in the marketplace is the preferred means to make business activities consistent with community need. Government involvement in business activities is justified only if there is a deficiency in the marketplace. In this case, government agencies take action: (a) to strengthen competition, such as by requiring a divestiture; or (b) to correct marketplace deficiencies by regulation, taxation/subsidization, or government ownership.

ii. There is and will continue to be a high level of government involvement in business. Government is now and will continue to be a primary force in business decision making. It is therefore vital that business managers learn how to work effectively with government to resolve business-government conflicts.

iii. Business has a legitimate role in the government decision-making process. Government needs feedback from business and other interest groups regarding the legislative and regulatory processes. These groups can provide information and even initiate legislation, as well as find ways to solve social problems.

iv. Cooperation among business, government, and labour is necessary to solve major national problems. Indeed, cooperation may be the key to coping with most of Canada's major public policy problems. In addition, as Japan and Western Europe have enjoyed a postwar economic renaissance and as nations in the Far East, Southern Asia, South America, and Eastern Europe have become more industrialized and competitive, international competition for world resources and markets has intensified. Canada's ability to compete will require effective working relations among business, government, and labour.

Today's business ideology actually has been very responsive to changes in the business environment during the twentieth century. The traditional view of business as a stable, predictable economic institution has changed. Business is now regarded as a more complicated economic and socio-political institution within a turbulent, rapidly changing environment.

A NEW MANAGERIAL IDEOLOGY

Business ideology in Canada is different from that of the United States for a fundamental reason, again rooted in their two respective pasts. The United States made a clean break from Britain in the late eighteenth century, whereas Canada preferred to remain within the British sphere of security well into the twentieth century. Americans in business had to take risks, and because of their revolutionary past were more inclined to do so. Canadians have remained risk-averse — a notion antithetical to a liberal, capitalist philosophy of doing business.

Modern business ideology is actually a *managerial ideology*. As large corporations grew even larger, management became separated from ownership and it became practical for managers to accept Keynesian economics. Resisting government intervention proved futile. It therefore made more sense to manage the situation than to continue to crusade for what was past. Over time, this separation created a professional managerial class which has accepted this modern managerial ideology. Today, many chief executives may affirm the virtues of, but do not necessarily practise, the liberal market model.

BUSINESS AND GOVERNMENT

In Canada, today's well-educated, professionally-trained manager is really no different from that of a hundred years ago. Both generations have recognized that Adam Smith's theory of capitalism was simply an intellectual construct to describe the nineteenth century's Industrial Revolution. The "natural laws" and organization of economic society into private property and competitive markets were really analytical tools, not laws.

Therefore, *Canadian business has no discernible ideology*. The current business-government relationship in Canada is actually a mixture of many shifting ideologies and perspectives. Consequently, each set of interactions — economic, social, technological, legal, and political — may lack ideological focus or at times be at cross-purposes. In fact, the whole business-government relationship may be unclear but most of the time it is pragmatic.

Due to this fluctuating ideological base, the nature of the relationship between business and government tends to change with prevailing conditions. In some situations, government actions may dominate business operations; in others, business may heavily influence the activities of government. Many contend that Canada's government is controlled by big business. Others hold that the public sector so dominates the economic activities of Canadian business enterprises that they are no longer competitive, either at home or abroad.

Some see the business-government relationship as adversarial, with business jealously guarding its territory from outside interference, claiming that any intrusion into market affairs could cause inefficiencies. Others argue that government is the uncooperative party, making arbitrary decisions that waste resources. Still others warn that it is actually better to keep business and government as adversaries, lest solidarity result in a tyrannical government-industrial complex.

In short, the business community holds no fundamental belief in the virtues of competition in Canada. Economic and political powers need not be separated for the good of free enterprise; in fact, Canadian business generally believes in the exact opposite. Canada has had no strong anti-combine policies compared to those in the United States, nor is there a natural, political constituency for private enterprise in this country. Competition is viewed as a destructive force to be avoided, not a constructive force to be sought.

This lack of a free-enterprise ideology among the Canadian business community was highlighted in the mid-1980s by Peter Pocklington, Alberta businessman and one-time aspiring leader of the Progressive Conservative Party. Pocklington requested government assistance to save his commercial empire from the heavy debt incurred from bad investments, high interest rates, and Alberta's economic downsizing at the time. Pocklington, a verbal proponent of free enterprise, managed to salvage most of his businesses by selling off his personal assets in 1982 to 1983, and accepting a $31 million helping hand from the Alberta Treasury Branches in 1984.

Once tasted, however, government largesse becomes addictive. In July 1987, Pocklington accepted a $100 million line of credit from the Treasury Branches for his Palm Dairies Ltd. operations; it was extended another $55 million in March, 1988. At that time, Pocklington also accepted a $12 million loan for his meat-packing company, Gainers Inc. In any other circumstances, this would qualify as a corporate "bailout." For Pocklington, despite his libertarian mantle, it was good business.

Business is largely ambivalent towards business-government relations. It wants to be free of government when it is doing well, and helped by government when it is doing poorly. For example, many firms in the 1960s and 1970s advocated international free trade policies. In the recessionary early 1980s, many of these firms wanted to retain, if not increase, tariff barriers to keep foreign goods from displacing domestic ones. Now that there is free trade within North American many of the firms which lobbied vociferously for it are clamouring for government protection and intervention once again.

Contemporary managers tend to regard government as a necessary evil. *Just as capitalism is now regarded as more theory than fact, an identifiable business ideology in Canada is more myth than reality.*

IDEOLOGY AND FREE TRADE

Today, Canadian business has become complacent. If a large firm faces bankruptcy due to its own inefficiencies, lack of strategic vision, and/or market forces, government will be there to assist (for as much and as long as it can) to save those jobs.

But soon, government will not be able to help. Renewable resources are being harvested faster than they can be replenished. Reserves of non-renewable resources are becoming scarce within Canada, while world supply exceeds demand. Inefficient manufacturing firms — even whole industries — hang on day-to-day under the regime of free trade. The huge tertiary sector of Canada distributes wealth and transforms it into services, while labour productivity is declining just when productivity is vital to compete in an essentially non-technological economy.

The century-old National Policy protected inefficient Canadian manufacturers by maintaining a tariff barrier to imports. Foreign direct investment has built branch plants in Canada to jump that barrier. As free trade dismantled that barrier, neither domestic nor foreign-owned secondary manufacturing industries could be protected. Success within a non-competitive environment does not herald success in a freer, much more competitive climate. Free trade is not about ideology; it is about Canadian manufacturing interests competing in tougher times. These times will require capital investment, rationalization, specialization, economies of scale, and a strong desire to win.

Certainly, Canada will export more of its finite supply of resources. There will even be competition in most segments of the service sector. However, in an age of global consolidation, successful Canadian resource and service firms will become prime candidates for takeover — both domestic and foreign. Foreign direct investment in manufacturing, on the other hand, has and may continue to decline as free trade makes it cheaper to export to Canadian buyers rather than produce in Canada. Also to be expected are a few high technology winners.

Overall, free trade does not promise less foreign investment or reduced economic concentration. If anything, probably the reverse will happen. History has shown that foreign investors have greater confidence in Canada's governments, social institutions, and resources than Canadian business leaders. This Canadian enigma is illustrated by the following political cartoon (**Figure 5-1**).

FIGURE 5-1

■ COUNTRIES THAT AGREE THAT CANADA IS THE BEST PLACE TO LIVE
□ COUNTRIES THAT DISAGREE THAT CANADA IS THE BEST PLACE TO LIVE

Source: Paul Lachine

Canada's corporate form of capitalism, oligopoly capitalism and administered pricing is not competitive capitalism. Free trade, however, is *all about* competition. As you read this page, a shift in the business-government-society paradigm is slowly occurring in Canada.

IMPLICATIONS FOR MANAGEMENT

This chapter has shown that the general Canadian business community, "big business" in particular, does not display the characteristics of classical, competitive free enterprise in which talented individuals seek and develop opportunities to secure wealth and status. The virtues of competition do not form the fundamental beliefs of Canada's private sector. This fact, combined with socially accepted large-scale government economic intervention to restrict potential entrants from joining the capitalist class, has put producer interests above those of the consumer.

Canada is clearly devoid of a free enterprise ideology. Simply observe the record of high tariffs, high levels of industrial and aggregate concentration, high levels of foreign ownership and foreign control of industry, recent Big Bank profits, production inefficiencies, and business' continuing solicitation of government assistance.

Is government a "crop" for business to "harvest?" A cynic might define a *Canadian entrepreneur* as "one who pushes his way to the front of the line to get a government subsidy." In truth, however, government's role in a classical free market situation is to help people become rich. In Canada, it appears that government's role is to protect those who are rich and to subsidize those who are not.

Business leaders will obviously publicly defend the merits of free enterprise, if only to retain their air of legitimacy in the eyes of their stakeholders. However, their actions — that restrict trade, invite "appropriate" government intervention, and contradict market theory — do not support their rhetoric. While bemoaning the level of concentration in industries with which they have to deal, they will strive vigorously to concentrate assets, capacity, and ownership within their own industries.

Does it really matter that Canadians are not really free enterprisers? Business is successful enough, and provides Canadians with one of the highest standards of living in the world. What should business management be doing differently? Why?

How should government policy makers respond? What should the role of government be in economic affairs? Why?

The remainder of this book should offer some insights into the above questions — and their answers. As to the "whys," the answer is simple. Canada's past cannot become its future if it wishes to retain a preferred standard of living. The forces of change will not allow the status quo to be maintained if long-term economic survival is Canada's goal.

Yet Canada's history of growth — through business and government working closely together to accomplish their goals — is the key to achieving a better future. After all, Canadian economic policy has always been pragmatic. Similarly, Canadian business has been pragmatic when dealing with government, its rivals, and its public. However, business has forfeited its former role in shaping the public interest by accepting the will of more aggressive, ideologically-driven governments over the past 30 years.

Changing ideologies will not solve the problem, however. Canadian business need not launch a defence of free enterprise; the Canadian public would never buy it. It is obvious that Northern Telecom, Seagram, and Canadian Pacific have moved into the United States *not* because Canada's government is socialist or anti-business, but because their abilities to grow in Canada were limited.

Canadian business must return to its pragmatic roots. Big business does much of its trade with government; it depends upon a publicly financed infrastructure. Business often goes to government for working capital in times of trouble. In return, the private sector must now act in the public interest to regain a privileged position in society.

Why is this so crucial today? Primarily, it is because business management in Canada lacks the global perspective necessary to survive in an increasingly integrated global marketplace. Although foreign trade accounts for over one-third of both Canada's GDP and Canadian employment, the nation's international business expertise is minimal. There are exceptions, but generally the skills demonstrated by Canada's business managers do not meet the standards required for international trade. Most success stories of Canadian exporters have had a helping hand from the federal government's soon-to-be-downsized trade commissioner service. However, government cannot do it all, nor can it move quickly enough.

If business and government are two solitudes, then academe is a third. Now, greater cooperation and improved understanding are needed among business, government, and the academic world. Business' needs must be met; but first, business should recognize its inexperience in negotiating successful business strategies within a freer global environment.

The dynamics of the world market will no longer allow business in Canada to retain its privileged position. If the functions of management are to plan, organize, direct, and control, then Canadian business managers must learn to plan in an era of uncertainty; to organize to achieve their objectives; to make things happen; and to provide leadership that will influence government and labour to accept this challenge and work with business, not against it. If financial security and growth have indeed replaced short-term profitability as the goals of Canadian business, then global competitiveness is the only means to achieve these ends. Resources will not provide long-term growth and services, but will only reinforce the status quo.

Managers must also recognize the necessity of real-time, integrated information systems and performance measurement systems so that corporate bureaucracies can shift in midstream when results do not match expectations. Mergers and acquisitions may provide growth for a firm, but they usually do nothing for the economy as a whole. Canada needs growth in the production of those goods the world demands.

Yet, business needs help to reach its goals. The tried but true bureaucratic symbiosis of business and government is ripe for revival to face a new challenge. If C.D. Howe was right in saying Canada always needs one megaproject on the go to remain prosperous, then here is the golden opportunity.

Canadian business can no longer afford to remain complacent. Today, business and the public share compelling interests: economic, social, and political survival!

SUGGESTED FURTHER READINGS

Andrain, C.F. 1980. *Politics and Economic Policy in Western Democracies*. Cambridge, MA: Dubury Press.

Aupperle, K.E. *et al* 1985. "An Empirical Examination of the Relationship Between Corporate Social Responsibility and Profitability." *Academy of Management Journal*, 28:2.

Bell, Daniel. 1976. *Cultural Contradictions of Capitalism*. New York: Basic Books.

Friedman, Milton. 1970. "The Social Responsibility of Business is to Increase Its Profits." *The New York Times Magazine*, September 13.

Galbraith, J.K. 1973. *Economics and the Public Purpose*. Boston: Houghton-Mifflin.

Galbraith, J.K. 1971. *The New Industrial State*. Boston: Houghton-Mifflin.

Kristol, Irving. 1978. *Two Cheers for Capitalism*. New York: Basic Books.

O'Toole, James. 1993. *The Executive's Compass: Business and the Good Society*. Toronto: Oxford University Press.

Panitch, Leo. 1977. *The Canadian State: Political Economy and Political Power*. Toronto: University of Toronto Press.

Panitch, Leo. 1973. "The Development of Corporatism in Liberal Democracies." *Comparative Political Studies*, 10:1.

Post, James E. 1978. *Corporate Behavior and Social Change*. Reston, VA.: Reston Publishing.

Preston, Lee E. (ed). 1978-82. *Research in Corporate and Social Performance and Policy*. Greenwich, CT: JAI Books.

Steiner, G.A., and J.F. 1994. *Business, Government and Society: A Managerial Perspective*. 7th ed. New York: McGraw-Hill.

NOTES

1. Leo Panitch, *The Canadian State: Political Economy and Political Power* (Toronto: University of Toronto Press, 1977), 66.
2. G.A. and J.F. Steiner, *Business, Government and Society: A Managerial Perspective*, 7th ed. (New York: McGraw-Hill, 1994).

6

BUSINESS IN CANADA

Markets are not created by God,

nature, or economic forces

but by businessmen.

Peter F. Drucker, 1909

Generally speaking, economies today are divided into three sectors, each of which is subdivided into a number of industries. The three economic sectors are: primary (agriculture, fishing, mining, oil and gas, and forestry); secondary (manufacturing, processing, and construction); and tertiary (wholesale/retail trade, finance, insurance, real estate, government services, transportation, communications, and utilities). In 1867, about 50% of Canada's GDP was in the primary sector, 30% was in the tertiary sector, and only 20% was in the secondary sector. By the early 1900s, those figures had changed to 40%, 30%, and 30% respectively. Today, less than 8% of Canada's GDP is from the primary sector, secondary industry now accounts for little more than 23%, and the tertiary sector, including all public administration, accounts for over 70% of the GDP.

Particularly important changes in the Canadian economy, and hence business opportunities, have taken place in the last four decades since World War II.[1] While we remain a small, open society and economy, Canadians have embraced much structural change and achieved significant economic growth. Growth was very strong into the early 1970s, but a painful era of stagflation (high inflation concurrent with high unemployment) followed. Public faith in economic management by government rose and fell accordingly.

OUR BUSINESS LEGACY

What legacy remains from Canada's three original commercial empires? How have they helped shape Canada's present business community? And what are the future prospects?

First, staples continue to play an important role in Canada's economy. Even though natural resources accounted for only 7% of GDP in 1995, they accounted for over 20% of the value of exports. Natural resources historically have been shipped from west to east, while manufactured goods flow from east to west.

Second, Canada remains a highly centralized economy. Ontario produces over half of all manufactured and technology-intensive exports. Toronto has displaced Montreal in becoming the commercial, financial, and trading capital of the nation, amassing its wealth in part from the natural resources of the rest of the country.

Third, nearly three-quarters of Canada's employment today is in the service sector, with less than 5% in agriculture and resources. This may be one reason why Canada's overall productivity has not increased dramatically of late, since most productivity-improving technology is used by the primary and secondary sectors. However, government is well aware of the service sector's importance to employment. For example, tourism is Ontario's second-largest industry. The American hotel magnate J. Willard Marriott, when in Toronto opening his 161st hotel worldwide, noted with envy the launch's enthusiastic reception from both provincial and regional governments.

> In the U.S., a Governor will fly to Japan immediately if there is a chance of getting an electronics plant in his state to employ 200 people; but propose to build a hotel, which will employ 600 people, and you get practically no response and certainly little incentive....Tourism is the main employer in 35 of our states, but our state and federal governments don't recognize it as an industry like they do here in Canada. [2]

Yet the Americans recognize that although service industries are labour-intensive, it is manufacturing that creates wealth, not hotels.

Fourth, there is a high degree of economic concentration within Canada today. This is particularly true of the insurance, banking, transportation, brewing, distilling, natural resource, and merchandise trading industries. In 1995 the top four firms in two-thirds of all industries accounted for over 50% of the total production in their respective industries. Increasingly, leaders of these industries are committing to foreign investment, thus becoming multinational corporations (MNCs). They have done so rather than support growth in their own country's secondary sector of manufacturing, processing, and construction.

Fifth, although Canada possesses a healthy supply of its own capital, foreign investment continues to pour into the country, while interest and dividend payments pour out. Today, the vast majority of foreign direct investment funds flow to and from the United States. Canada's economic metropole is no longer Great Britain, but the United States. Some would argue that American political influence is evident as well.

Sixth, Canada continues its tradition as a trading nation. During the last decade, with the signing of the FTA and NAFTA, Canada reaffirmed this focus. From Confederation to World War I, Canada imported manufactured goods from the United States and exported resources to Britain. However, by the outbreak of World War II, Canada had become much

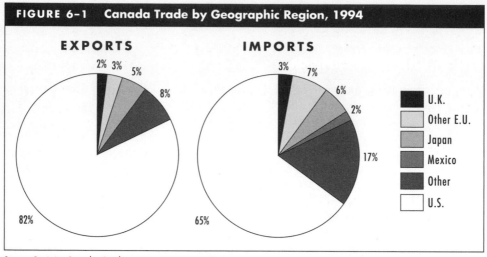

FIGURE 6-1   Canada Trade by Geographic Region, 1994

EXPORTS   IMPORTS

Source: Statistics Canada, Catalogue No. 65-0018, 1997

more reliant upon the United States as both a source of manufactured goods and a market for raw materials. As **Figure 6–1** shows, about 75% of all current Canadian trade (exports and imports) is with the United States.

Seventh, Canada has a very fragmented industrial relations system, with only about one-third of labour unionized. Active government involvement in social welfare has preempted the development of a strong, unified, politically active labour movement. However, Canada's labour costs are high because of both minimum wage legislation and pro-labour industrial relations legislation. In 1994, Canada had the ninth highest average industrial wage level in the world.

Eighth, Canada also has a chronically high rate of unemployment,[3] primarily because of a reliance upon seasonally operated resource industries such as fishing and logging. The temporarily unemployed are supported by government-financed schemes, in turn financed by taxation. This ultimately increases the costs of operating a Canadian business. Environmentalists, such as Barry Commoner (see **Chapter 15**), would argue that Canada's population has exceeded its economic carrying capacity in a post-industrial age given the country's economic structure and steady population growth.

Finally, Canada has a very strong state which, arguably except for labour rights, is both pro-business and pro-mercantilist. Canada's business community has grown, first through outside financial interests and later supported by a paternalistic state defending it from full competition of an expansionist United States.

Overall, Canada is a business nation. It is a country founded by business, and developed to further business' interests, all in the public interest. If the Fathers of Confederation were alive today, they probably would be pleased with the results of their initiatives; their objectives of a sovereign state with a mercantilist economy have been well met. Of course, there are some Canadians who are not as pleased with the current state of affairs as might be the Founding Fathers.

ECONOMIC CONCENTRATION: LOOKING BACK

Canada has a highly concentrated economy. In 1978, the Royal Commission on Corporate Concentration discovered that the volume of sales for the top 100 companies was equal to that of the rest of corporate Canada. More significantly, a mere one-eighth of 1% of all registered Canadian corporations controlled 58% of all Canada's private assets, produced 30% of all goods and services, and received 39% of total corporate profits. By 1990, these figures had climbed to 70%, 52%, and 60% respectively. *Taylor's 1994 survey of the top 500 firms in Canada further revealed that 70% were in industries where the top four firms serviced 50% or more of their respective markets.*

According to economic theory, the ownership of assets will be more concentrated than average within an economy in general, or a particular industry, when:

i. there is a sustained economic downturn;

ii. an industry has reached maturity and real growth is negligible;

iii. economies of scale are both desirable and achievable for the industry's long-term survival as competition intensifies;

iv. tariffs are used to protect domestic industry in a small domestic market; and/or

v. there is no government legislation to prevent it.

In Canada's case, explanations (*iii*) and (*v*) apply in almost all cases historically; explanation (*ii*) applies in some cases; explanation (*iv*) applied occasionally up until 1989; and explanation (*i*) has applied since 1992. Observant students of capitalism will readily admit that economic concentration is a natural objective for free market forces to pursue. Predator capitalists will attempt to diminish competition and increase their profitability through mergers and acquisitions. Monopolies or oligopolies make it much easier to control one's market.

In this sense, Canada is even more "capitalistic" (or at least more mature) than the United States. Thanks to a Tory-corporatist heritage, there has been little government interference in the concentration of wealth in the hands of a few. Canada has a "competition policy" which advocates a "reasonable" degree of competition for the economy. As a result, the rankings of Canada's largest companies usually change slowly. Few large firms ever go bankrupt. The United States, in contrast, has "antitrust" statutes which enable the government of that country to dismantle business giants such as Standard Oil and AT & T. The disadvantage of economic concentration is simple: there is an inefficient allocation of economic resources.[4] This results from the "waste" inherent in the "excess" profits from those companies that dominate an industry's production and ownership.

Historically, *aggregate economic concentration* — the percentage of economic activity accounted for by the very largest firms (usually four) — is lower today in Canada than it was at the turn of the century. In fact, it declined significantly from 1923 to 1966, remained about the same for the period 1966 to 1975, and has slowly increased since then. Furthermore, the average size of Canada's 100 largest non-financial, or 25 largest financial, firms is much smaller than their counterparts in other major industrialized countries. Yet Canadian aggregate concentration by assets is generally much higher than elsewhere, and about twice that in the United States. By 1992, the 10 biggest firms in Canada accounted for 30% of the total market.

However, Canada's level of *industrial* or *market concentration* — that within a particular industry — has been steadily increasing, particularly in the secondary sector, since 1948. Major booms occurred in the 1948-54 postwar period of C.D. Howe, and more recently during the 1980s and 1990s. Today, Canada's degree of industrial concentration is generally much greater than found in the United States.

On a global scale, most Canadian firms may seem small and inefficient, but within the home market they are giants! Top Canadian firms are, on average, 20% the size of their American counterparts but serve a domestic market only 10% the size. Only six Canadian corporations rank in the world's Top 100: Bell Canada Enterprises Inc., General Motors of Canada Ltd., Ford Motor Company of Canada, Chrysler Canada Ltd., The Seagram Co. Ltd., and George Weston Ltd. Yet, General Motors, Chrysler, and Ford are 100% American-owned. Weston's is 57% owned by the Weston family. The only Canadian-owned company with widely distributed ownership to make the Top 100 was BCE.

The actual level of concentration may be even greater than statistics show, given the level of private and family ownership of Canadian assets and a fluid definition of "control" (as opposed to outright ownership) of a firm. This effect is probably magnified by interlocking boards of directors, the relationship between holding companies and their subsidiaries, creditor relationships, pension fund investment strategies, public enterprise and state ownership of assets, and the personal influence of key individuals.

Holding companies and multidivisional conglomerates have enabled the *Financial Post 500* companies to maintain operating linkages with over 5000 other companies. The most important linkage of all, however, was through their boards of directors — a vast network of interconnecting points consisting of even fewer individuals. Members of a firm's board often include members of rival boards, its suppliers, major buyers, legal counsel, and most important, its bankers. Such formal contacts have helped to stifle "destructive" competition, improve financing capacity, improve communications within the industry, and lessen the overall risk of doing business.

The trend has been in the concentration of ownership of assets and not in control of sales. In fact, concentration on the basis of sales has dropped slightly over the last two decades as conglomerates diversified into unrelated product areas. On the basis of assets, 80% of the Toronto Stock Exchange 300 (TSE 300) is owned privately, compared to 20% of Standard and Poor's 500 in the United States. *A dozen families control 50% of the value of the TSE 300*! The only obvious exclusions from these tightly-held holdings were the banks, steel companies, Canadian Pacific, and BCE — all widely held stocks.

The 25 largest non-government companies in Canada were owned by 32 families and five corporate conglomerates. In turn, *these 25 firms* (as compared to 100 firms in the US) *owned 30% of Canada's $1.2 trillion worth of non-financial assets — this in a country in which there are over 900 000 businesses*! Out of the 100 leading firms by assets in Canada, 29 were family-controlled, 29 were controlled by conglomerates, 32 were foreign-owned and 10 were state enterprises. In fact, only 59 of the 500 largest companies in Canada had a wide distribution of ownership, as compared to over 400 in the United States.

These statistics for Canada do not include companies in which families/individuals may own only 20-30% of the equity but exert *de facto* control. Some of these families are household names to most Canadians. They are led by Lord Thomson with a net worth of $8.2 billion and the Irving brothers at $7.5 billion (as compared to the richest American, Bill Gates of Microsoft fame, reportedly worth US $12.9 billion). Following them are Charles

Bronfman with $2.9 billion and the Eaton, Rogers, and Weston families with $1.7, $1.4 & $1.3 billion respectively. Other billionaires are the McCains ($1.2 billion) and Paul Desmarais ($1 billion).

Whether the above are household names or not, the companies they control surely are. For example, Lord Thomson owns The Bay, Zellers (1997 disposed of), Thomson Travel, and more than 300 newspapers in the English-speaking world, including *The Globe and Mail*. Probably the farthest-flung empire is that of W. Galen Weston. His nearly 1000 companies in a dozen countries include: Loblaw Companies Ltd., Weston Bakeries Ltd., Bowes Company, Westfair Foods Ltd., Wm Neilson Ltd., EB Eddy Forest Products Ltd., British Columbia Packers Ltd., National Tea Company, Holt Renfrew, and Fortnum & Mason.

Of course, as mentioned earlier, two management-controlled conglomerates are not privately owned and are equally powerful: BCE Inc. and Canadian Pacific. BCE's holdings include: Northern Telecom, Bell Canada, Telesat Canada, Memotec Data, BCE Mobile Communications Ltd., Teleglobe Canada, NewTel Enterprises, Bruncor, Maritime Telephone and Telegraph, and 4.3% of the Bank of Nova Scotia. Canadian Pacific Inc. owns, among many others: AMCA International, Syracuse China, CP Hotels, Marathon Realty, CP Steamships, Soo Line, Arion Insurance, CP Express and Transport, CPR, CIP, Laidlaw Transportation, Great Lakes Forest Products, Unitel, Pan Canadian Petroleum Ltd., and Fording Coal Ltd. And these are only the tips of the mammoth commercial icebergs!

Economists would use a *concentration ratio* to describe the phenomenon of economic concentration. Most common is the CR_4. This indicates the weighted average percentage of the total production of a particular industry by the four largest companies in that industry. A *strong oligopoly* is said to exist when the four largest producers within an industry control more than 40% of their market. A *weak oligopoly* exists when the CR_4 is between 20% and 40%. When the four largest producers within an industry account for less than 20% of total industry sales within their market, *effective competition* is said to exist. For example, in 1994 the CR_4 for tobacco products was 0.908. This tells us that the four largest tobacco companies produced 90.8% of the total in that industry (see **Table 6–1**).

The industry concentration ratio for agriculture, on the other hand, is extremely low. This reflects the small, fragmented, family orientation of farming and the competitive nature of a commodity market structure. Another reason for the lack of large American-style agriculture-business in Canada is the reluctance of Canadian banks to give the high-risk, longer-term loans necessary to aggregate farming interests. However, agriculture is in large measure cartelized on the supply side, where federal or provincial marketing boards can set quotas. Supply management affects such products as eggs, broiler chickens, turkeys, milk, most fruit and vegetables, and wheat. Note that these arrangements impeded the flow of commodities between provinces, a point addressed in **Chapter 14**.

Over one-half of all manufacturing sub-industries have a CR_4 exceeding 0.50 because of oligopoly market structures. The other half has very low concentration ratios. As **Table 6–1** depicts, in general, the higher the technology-based, value-added component of the product, the higher the concentration ratio. The more labour-intensive a segment, the lower its CR_4.

Despite recent attempts at deregulation, Canada still has oligopolies in national air and rail transportation, telecommunications, television broadcasting, and newspapers. Government-owned or franchised monopolies provide electric energy (e.g., Ontario Hydro) and natural gas distribution (e.g., City of Medicine Hat).

TABLE 6-1	Selected Industrial Concentration Measures, 1994 Sales

Industry Ranking	CR$_4$
1. Tobacco products	90.7
2. Newspapers	75.9
3. Transport equipment	70.4
4. Petroleum/coal products	67.9
5. Communications	67.6
6. Rubber products	60.8
7. Primary metals	60.4
8. Transportation	47.1
9. Beverages	46.8
10. Metal mining	46.1
11. Textile mill	38.6
12. Electrical products	33.8
13. Non-metallic mineral products	27.0
14. Printing, publishing & allied products	25.2
15. Chemicals and chemical products	23.3
16. Knitting mills	18.8
17. Wood industries	18.4
18. Food	17.7
19. Machinery	16.1
20. Metal fabricating	13.7
21. Retail trade	11.1
22. Wholesale trade	9.5
23. Agriculture, forestry & fishing	4.3
24. Construction	4.1

Source: Statistics Canada

On the other hand, concentration in the retail and wholesale sectors is generally low. The one exception is fast food where the CR$_4$ is 0.61. However, within a particular product line, strong market control usually belongs to one or two companies. For example, Storkcraft makes 66% of all baby cribs sold in Canada; 75% of all baby food sold is made by Heinz; Kraft sells 65% of all cheese eaten in Canada; 35% of all detergent purchases are of Proctor and Gamble's Tide; 65% of all disposable lighters sold are by Bic; Inglis makes 40% of all the washing machines sold; and Proctor-Silex makes 46% of all toasters sold.

As to services, Budget and Tilden handle 56% of all car rentals; Conrad Black's Hollinger Inc. produces 42% of all newspapers read in Canada; and The Toronto Stock Exchange performs 74% of all stock trades.

Overall economic concentration in Canada is largely the result of three major periods of merger and acquisition since the turn of the century. *1909 to 1912* saw a shakeout in the steel, cement, and automobile industries worldwide, resulting in the formation of the oligopolies now common to those industries. From *1925 to 1930*, the processing industries such as pulp and paper, food products, and chemicals became much more concentrated through takeovers and expansion. More recently, the retail, land development, and resource industries were allowed to become heavily concentrated through mergers and takeovers between *1974 and 1984*; some of the large, diversified conglomerates congealed during this time were the ill-fated Olympia and York, the Thomson empire, and the non-Seagram Bronfman empire. *From 1974 to 1984 a staggering 4685 corporate takeovers were recorded, largely made possible by pension funds.*[5] *The total price: $235 billion — an amount equal to the national debt at the time!* Of that amount, only 6% or $14 billion left the country. Finally, during 1988-89, some of the biggest players in the biggest industries joined forces. Nova Corporation took over the federal government's privatized Polysar Energy and Chemical Corporation; Dofasco Inc. purchased Algoma Steel from Canadian Pacific; Imperial Oil Ltd. absorbed Texaco Canada; BCE Inc. took over Montreal Trust Inc. from Power Corporation; Wardair was acquired by Canadian Airlines International (formerly CPAir and Pacific Western Airlines); Molson Companies merged with Carling O'Keefe; and Noranda Inc. acquired Falconbridge Ltd. During these two years, Seagram went on an acquisition binge and purchased Tropicana Products of Florida, and Martell and Company of France. Of course, 1988-1989 is also infamous for some of the largest failed acquisitions in Canadian business history. It was during this brief period that the now-defunct Campeau Corporation ventured into the US and acquired Federated Department Stores, and Olympia and York Developments purchased Sante Fe Southern Pacific Corporation and Abitibi-Price Company.

ECONOMIC CONCENTRATION: LOOKING AHEAD

Today, Canada is in the throes of another takeover and merger binge. As a result of deregulation in the financial sector and the threat of foreign competition on Canadian soil, the major banks have each acquired a major stock brokerage firm already and are considering mergers amongst themselves. In today's global financial marketplace, Canada has too many banks for its population size. Even though their CR_4 is 0.53, the banks' productivity ratios are high.[6] Seagram Company Ltd. divested itself of EI duPont de Nemours and Co. in 1995 only to use the proceeds to acquire MCA Inc. Battle Mountain Gold Co. acquired Hemlo Gold Mines Inc.; Trans-Canada Pipelines Ltd. took over Alberta Natural Gas Co Ltd.; and Thomson Corp. purchased West Publishing in the US. In fact, over 50% of the mergers and acquisitions by Canadian companies since 1994 have been of American enterprises. Even the banks are looking outside of Canada for strategic acquisitions. In essence, the mid-1990s merger and acquisition binge has three characteristics: internationalization, building up core businesses, and/or divestment of previously acquired diversifications.

A benchmark to watch for will be the future of Bell Canada. As the traditional telephone business of the telecommunications giants of the world matures, growth and profit opportunities and prospects will flatten out. The fastest to merge will survive. Bell Canada — its parent being Canada's second largest industrial enterprise — is only the 25th largest telecommunications firm worldwide; it is one-seventh the size of the largest, NTT of Japan. To survive the tailend of the twentieth century, most firms in most industries will have to merge on a global scale, or find and secure proprietary market niches. *The future belongs to the big and the small. Being "stuck in the middle" is not an option.*

What does all this economic concentration mean for Canada? Is it good or bad for the consumer? For the nation?

Certainly, there are drawbacks to a highly concentrated economy. Readers should inform themselves about profit levels and CEO remuneration of the larger Canadian corporations and Big Banks.[7] We have an environment of oligopolistic industries and a country where government lacks initiative to force the private sector to compete. There will be higher and more stable prices than in a more competitive situation. If prices do change, they usually go in one direction — up. Economists call this *price leadership*: one firm within an industry decides to increase or lower prices, and the others swiftly follow. There may or may not be collusion involved; it just becomes accepted behaviour that the others will follow. Stelco has followed this practice for years in the steel industry; Black and Decker does this in the small household appliance trade.

As demand exceeds industry capacity, price leadership keeps new entrants out. The price leader, because of its size and its inherent economies of scale, will keep the price below a monopoly price level. It will also resist natural inflationary pressures to increase it, so that the leader and its few rivals can keep the lion's share of the industry in their own hands.

In the resource and resource processing industries, this practice is taken to an extreme where enormous barriers to entry and economies of scale exist. These arise from the control of the supply of raw materials and vertical integration. In resources, there is usually one very dominant firm, such as Alcan in aluminium and Inco in nickel.

When ownership of assets is concentrated in the hands of a few, with no specific firm dominant, and when products are homogeneous, a behaviour called *conscious parallelism* can also develop. Prices are never cut for fear of a devastating price war, and prices are seldom increased because of buyer resistance. When prices are increased, they rise simultaneously and to the same level because of their almost identical cost function. Such is the case of the oil companies and most industrial products. The results give the appearance of collusion, but are really the outcome of mutual interdependencies. Collusion is seldom necessary.

Finally, a common criticism levelled at big business is that economic concentration inhibits new job creation. Supposedly, the small, independent business sector,[8] not big business, creates employment. However, in Canada such is not completely the case. Since 1974 small business has generated 55% of all new jobs, while big business (employing 500 or more workers and usually part of an oligopoly) accounted for 40% of new employment opportunities. Overall, the effects of concentration for Canadians are:

- higher, yet more stable prices than under a more competitive regime;
- lower rates of entry, with less selection;
- excess capacity;
- lower rates of adapting technological innovation than in a more competitive situation; and
- gradually upward shifting cost curves following this inefficiency and lack of competition.

Yet, what does government do? Canada has had a competition policy of various sorts since 1889, but over 50% of its prosecutions occurred after 1970. (The entire service sector was excluded from the Act until 1976.) However, even though litigation has gone up, to date convictions remain few and penalties light. Why? Originally the *Competition Act* was wholly within the Criminal Code. Only since 1986 have salient portions been part of the Civil Code, thus making prosecution and the burden of evidence to prove guilt much more feasible. Moreover, the Competition Bureau was established with powers and independence to preassess whether proposed mergers are in the Canadian interest.

Canada's competition policy had always been little more than a grinning, toothless, paper tiger. Will the future be different? Business has been successful in arguing that stiff antitrust regulations are not "in the public interest," and government has agreed. For big business in today's competitive world, it is either grow, shrink, or die.

FOREIGN DIRECT INVESTMENT, OWNERSHIP, AND CONTROL

No other major industrialized nation in the world has the level of foreign direct investment, ownership, and control that Canada has. Foreign ownership of Canadian business peaked in 1973 at 37% of assets. By 1991, it had dropped to 28%, still twice the level as that of the United States, 26.8% of industrial assets, and 17.5% of financial assets. Foreigners controlled or owned 47% of all manufacturing businesses in Canada, 44% of the oil and natural gas industry, 31% of mining and smelting interests, 27% of transportation services, and 11% of the construction industry.

Before World War I, Britain was the major source of foreign capital and ownership in Canada. In 1900, for instance, 85% of all foreign investment in Canada came from Britain in the form of portfolio investment; a full 90% of British capital in Canada was invested in Canadian securities. Of particular appeal were government bonds, non-voting shares of banks and companies with monopoly or oligopolistic market control, and short-term loans. Thus Canada had the best of both worlds — foreign investment and domestic control.

Today, the proportion of foreign ownership of Canada's economy is about the same as it was in 1900. However, instead of Britain's 85% involvement, the United States accounts for 50% of total foreign investment. By the time the Statute of Westminster of 1931 formally severed Canada's last colonial ties to Britain, Americans accounted for 54% of foreign investment in Canada.

Most American investment is in Canadian branch plants as common voting equity or foreign direct investment (FDI). Today, Canada pays for its foreign investment by losing some control over its private sector. Originally, branch plants were built to produce and sell to the Canadian market without having to pay import tariffs. Since tariffs did not generally apply to "parts," most American branch plants were simply assembly operations, importing parts for assembly from elsewhere. As a result, these branch plants today are small, since they were established to serve only the Canadian domestic market. For the most part, they are in southern Ontario to minimize shipping costs from the United States' industrial heartland.

In 1978, the Royal Commission on Corporate Concentration revealed that foreign interests owned or controlled $100 billion worth of assets in Canada. Almost 75% of that was American-owned, a percentage first reached in 1959. Of that $75 billion, almost 60% was invested in secondary manufacturing, 30% in oil and gas production, and 10% in the mining industry. Clearly US capital has filled the gap left by the lack of Canadian industrial capital. In 1994 and 1995, FDI skyrocketed with foreign firms buying $6.6 billion and $125 billion worth of Canadian companies in 101 and 117 deals respectively. By the 1990s, though, American FDI had dropped to about 60-65% of the total. Growing sources of FDI were Japan and Hong Kong, the latter especially prevalent in British Columbia.

Historically, there has been a strong, positive correlation between FDI and concentration within the Canadian economy. The level of FDI is high in industries with both high concentration ratios and moderate-to-high barriers to entry, such as producers of automobiles, tobacco products, office equipment, petrochemicals, and pharmaceuticals. Americans in particular own a large proportion of these capital-intensive, highly profitable, manufacturing interests and non-renewable resource industries — the latter being Canada's historical competitive advantage. However, there is no valid evidence to suggest that FDI has added significantly to the high levels of economic concentration in this country.

Conversely, less FDI exists in industries with lower levels of ownership concentration. In fact, foreign investors (particularly Americans) are divesting themselves of assets and operations in unconcentrated industries. This is a result of the unacceptably low profit margins and intensifying domestic and international competition. Industries such as those producing clothing, beverages, furniture, and leather goods, as well as construction and wholesale merchandising — all heavily labour-intensive — have now become targets for foreign *divestment*.

Thanks to government policy and regulation, a low level of FDI is also found in industries of "national strategic significance," such as public utilities, transportation, communications, financial institutions, and broadcasting. Therefore, Canada has developed sufficient competitive advantages in these areas to acquire a foothold in world markets — at least for now.

In 1995, 171 of the top 500 corporations in Canada were at least 50% foreign-owned. Of these, 121 were completely foreign-owned. Another 31 of the top 500 were foreign-controlled.[9] Of these 202 companies (40% of Canada's top 500 corporations), 105 were American-owned or controlled.

Is FDI good or bad for Canada? As might be expected, there are advantages and disadvantages, depending on one's personal and political perspective. On the plus side, many argue that FDI provides:

- technology otherwise not available;
- management skills different or superior to our own;
- much needed industrial capital, either through initial investment or reinvestment of earnings;
- improved productivity through economies of scale;
- industrial growth;
- new markets for domestic goods and services;
- employment;
- more competition;
- more selection/better quality; and
- a higher standard of living.

Those who argue against FDI cite that it:

- restricts the amount of research and development (R&D) done in Canada, therefore decreasing Canadian innovativeness;

- retards even further Canadian industrial entrepreneurism;
- reduces Canada's exporting/trading capacity;
- reduces the opportunity to upgrade raw materials before exporting;
- increases the outflow of capital from the country in interest, principle, and dividend payments;
- infringes upon Canada's political sovereignty, since many multinationals place their home country's laws above those of their host country;
- reduces Canadian control over the Canadian economy;
- takes employment away from Canadians;
- reduces Canada's independent identity;
- forces consumers to pay higher prices while bearing much of the risk of foreign-owned business, while the rewards of doing business in Canada are exported;
- reduces Canada's real income and economic growth
- reduces Canadian participation in the economy; and
- impedes government from formulating and implementing economic and social policies designed in Canada's best interests.

Although the debate over FDI's advantages and disadvantages has raged on-again, off-again over the past 30 years, three truths have emerged from a number of studies. *First*, FDI has had no real effect on R&D or technological development in Canada. If Canadian investors owned the enterprises now in foreign hands, there is little evidence that they would have either the economies of scale or the retained earnings to conduct the same level of research and development as that of multinationals in their home countries. What little R&D does occur in Canada's foreign-owned or controlled multinational corporations probably equals what domestic companies could afford, given comparable Canadian spending patterns in this area. On the whole, foreign subsidiaries have contributed as much or more to new technology development in their industries as have their Canadian-owned competitors. The notable exceptions are such stars of Canadian R&D as Northern Telecom Ltd,, Bombardier Inc,, Newbridge Networks Corp., and Spar Aerospace. American investors of sizeable R&D funds in Canada are IBM Canada Ltd,, Digital Equipment of Canada Ltd,, and Xerox Canada Inc.

The *second* emergent fact about FDI is that Canadian-owned companies are estimated to be 19% less productive than foreign-owned or controlled subsidiaries. This is a direct result of the availability of capital to foreign multinational corporations. Other factors are production and marketing economies of scale, lower costs, advantages in production and information technology, and transfer pricing and internal trade capabilities.

Third, 98% of all new jobs since 1990 have been created by Canadian companies. FDI is no longer a driver of employment, if it ever was.

What has government's response been to foreign ownership and foreign control of Canadian business? Imperceptible. From 1974 to 1984, during the most nationalistic period of government screening of the foreign investment by the Foreign Review Agency, only 11% of all foreign investment proposals were denied. Since then, no foreign entry has been blocked. The Canadian government, regardless of political stripe, has accepted FDI as inevitable in a small, yet advanced, open economy where mercantilists have always prevailed

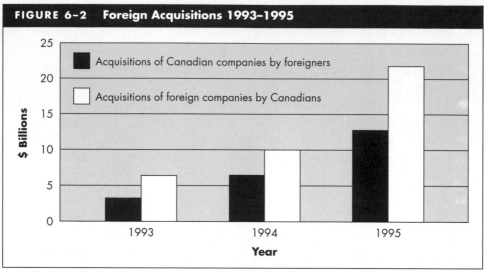

FIGURE 6-2   Foreign Acquisitions 1993–1995

Source: *The Financial Post and Crosbie & Co. Inc.*, March 23, 1996, p. 6.

over industrialists; 95% of foreign investments approved by government have been "compatible with national industrial and economic policies."

The irony of the foreign investment issue is that since 1973 FDI by Canadian companies abroad has grown at twice the rate as FDI in Canada. This shift accelerated in the 1990s (see **Figure 6–2**). However, Canada still had an FDI deficit at the end of 1995. Foreign investment in Canada totalled $673 billion and Canadian investment abroad totalled $333 billion — half the amount. But as a percentage of GDP it has declined to 43% from a peak of 45% in 1993. The gap is beginning to shrink.

Canadian FDI abroad has grown as Canada's weighted average manufacturing capacity utilization rate hovers around 80% or better. Eight of the twenty-two major secondary industries were posting rates of 90% or better. Growth like this demands either increased capital spending, diversification, or acquisition. The largest Canadian takeover in the past decade was Seagram's $18 billion acquisition of MCA Inc. in 1995. In fact, during the 1990s, Canadian firms have been investing twice as much in the US as American firms have been here. This is remarkable given that the US market is ten times bigger than Canada's. Of the 50 largest foreign takeovers during the last decade, 78% of the assets changing hands were foreign assets acquired by Canadian firms.

Foreign investment also changed form during the 1980s. Before the mid 1970s, half of foreign investment was direct; the other half was portfolio. Today, three-quarters of total outside investment is in the form of debt (as it was 100 years ago). The servicing of this foreign debt explains to a large extent Canada's growing trade deficit in services.

The future for successful Canadian businesses is not at home but **abroad**. As Canadian firms increasingly do unto others as others have done unto us, their "Canadianness" may get lost in the global shuffle.

SUGGESTED FURTHER READINGS

Bertrand, R. 1981. *Canada's Oil Monopoly*. Toronto: James Lorimer Publishers.

Bliss, Michael. 1974. *A Living Profit*. Toronto: McClelland & Stewart.

Crane, D. 1982. *Controlling Interest*. Toronto: McClelland & Stewart.

Financial Post 500 1996. Toronto: The Financial Post Company (1996 issue)

The Globe & Mail. 1997. "Fifty CEOs who made between $19.9m and $1.6m." April 12.

Levitt, K. 1970. *Silent Surrender*. Toronto: Macmillan.

Report of the Royal Commission on Corporate Concentration. 1978. Ottawa: Supply and Services Canada, March.

Slater, David W. 1997. "Setting the Scene: The Post-WWII Canadian Economy." *Canadian Business Economics*, 5: 2-3, Winter/Spring.

NOTES

1. David W. Slater, "Setting the Scene: The Post-WWII Canadian Economy," *Canadian Business Economics*, 5:2-3 (Winter/Spring 1997).
2. Taylor, *Business and Government Relations*, 44.
3. The average annual percentage of the labour force unemployed during 1980-1997 was 9.5%.
4. See the "deadweight loss" depiction in Chapter 4.
5. The top ten pension funds in 1996 had a total asset base of $183.7 billion of which $170.0 billion was invested by public sector employee groups.
6. Non-interest expenses as a percentage of total revenues were 0.633 for Canadian banks in 1994 but 0.585 for comparable American banks.
7. *Financial Post 500* (Toronto: The Financial Post Company, 1996); and *The Globe and Mail*, "Fifty CEOs who made between $19.9m and $1.6m" (April 12, 1997).
8. Small businesses with less than 100 employees account for 99% of all businesses in Canada, about one-third of the GDP and approximately one-half of the jobs in the private sector.
9. 20-49% ownership of voting equity represents the largest single block.

GOVERNMENT IN CANADA

The natural progress of things is for liberty to yield and government to gain ground.

Thomas Jefferson, 1743-1826

Democracy is the worst form of government, except for all the alternatives.

Winston Churchill, 1874-1965

Prior to the twentieth century, classical economists such as Adam Smith and David Ricardo believed that the role of government was to do what the market could not do for itself: to determine, arbitrate, and enforce the rules of the free enterprise game. During the Industrial Revolution of the 1800s, governments of capitalist democracies delegated to business the responsibility for developing and managing the economy. Government's priority was to "take care of business." The resultant economic growth would then help government attain its social policy goals, such as full employment. This would be achieved through "mutual adjustments" within a traditional bargaining process. Such is the case no longer in capitalist democracies, and certainly not in Canada.

GOVERNMENT INTERVENTION: ALL IN THE PUBLIC INTEREST

Adam Smith, the "prophet of capitalism," anticipated the deterioration of market capitalism once the pursuit of wealth began to conflict with the purposes and prerequisites of the system. Wealthy capitalists would obstruct the very economic mechanisms which had enabled them to succeed, thus preventing any of their wealth from falling into the hands of new entrants.

Competition begat concentration, rather than sustained competition. Economic progress, although democratically demanded, was not democratically achieved. As natural resources predictably dwindled, and as economic resources were increasingly owned by a few, government extended its influence over business. It chose to do this by a number of economic and social means, including:

- fiscal policy
- monetary policy
- subsidies
- the promotion of exports
- guaranteed loans
- the procurement of goods and services
- joint ventures
- the regulation of price and/or entry
- direct competition through state enterprise
- the regulation of disclosure, trade, labour, health, and safety practices
- environmental protection
- minimum wage legislation
- the restriction of political involvement
- suasion.

Some of these have been beneficial to business; others have been burdensome and costly.

The growth of the Canadian state and its interventions received strong impetus from the 1879 National Policy of tariff and non-tariff barriers — a state initiative planned and introduced 50 years or so before the impact of Keynesian intervention was realized in Canadian economic life.

Since World War II, business, too, has spurred the growth of government in Canada. Both federal and provincial policies toward business have moved slowly away from tariff protection and taxation policy, and toward transferring income from the public to the private sector. This shift helped advance such public policy goals as regional economic expansion, employment, exports, and industrial rationalization.

Canada has become one of the most Keynesian countries in the world. In fact, it became the epitome of John Kenneth Galbraith's "new industrial state," with high levels of corporate concentration, no real antitrust legislation, no free enterprise ethic *per se*, and government solutions to economic problems. The federal government has been quick to assist the private sector when it was confronted with economic crises and dysfunction. Despite current rhetoric, Canada's reality includes a dizzying array of programs and assistance (subsidies) by government for business. These subsidies are direct, indirect, and tax expenditures in typology.

Why has government intervened? Because it has been in the "public interest" to do so. What, then, *is* the public interest — and by whose interpretation?

Ideally, the *public interest* can be defined as the combining, weighing, and balancing of many special interests with those universal interests shared by the vast majority, such as fairness and equity. However, on a practical basis, the public interest often reflects whatever special interest wins government's support. In truth, the public interest reflects "where you stand depends on where you sit."

For example, the government performs direct economic regulation in the public interest to protect consumers from destructive competition, fraud, unsafe goods and services, or monopoly prices and profits. The prime beneficiaries, though, are the producers with their economic rents, oligopolies, and "polite" competition. Because regulation is promoted as "in the public interest," it is difficult to remove, even if it really only benefits a specific interest.

Government may also act in the public interest to address the unintended, usually negative impact of an individual's or group's actions upon others, such as pollution, littering, or traffic congestion. The wide-ranging government interventions in the marketplace are also intended to provide — or ensure that the private sector provides — certain "public goods." These include social security, education, defence, health care, telecommunications, utilities, and transportation.

Why must it be the state that intervenes? Primarily because most members of the public are self-utility maximizers following the dictates of public choice economics. Government, theoretically, can take a longer, societal view (i.e., the social discount rate discussed in **Chapter 4**) and assure that more people gain than lose. It can also, by redistribution or compromise, guarantee that the winners will compensate the losers.

The brokerage of special interests into a national public interest is no longer the responsibility of the elected official but of the appointed official, the public servant, operating within his or her own world of public choice economics. However, except where public servants have been given complete discretionary authority, the appointed official's interpretation of the public interest is almost always accredited to a political master. Ultimately, the appropriateness of all forms of government intervention in the public interest will be value judgments based on personal standards of legitimacy, expediency, and morality. However, it is seldom the public's judgment.

Political scientist Carolyn Tuohy coined the phrase "institutionalized ambivalence" to describe this brokerage of interests into moderation, compromise, and tolerance.[1] According to Tuohy, Canadian political (and many non-political) institutions have developed a distinctive competence in being able to "embody conflicting principles within structures ambiguous enough to allow for *ad-hoc* accommodations over time." As seen in **Chapter 1**, Canada has a highly developed sense of ambivalence toward the appropriate role of the state, the market, individualism and collectivism, federal and provincial governments, and political ideology. Canada's ambivalence in economic, social, and political affairs is, indeed, institutionalized — *Canadians are as ambivalent as they are pragmatic.*

THE LEGISLATIVE PROCESS

Canada's legislative process at the federal and provincial levels of government, is British Parliamentary (or Westminister) in nature. Municipal governance differs. In both federal and provincial governance the political system is dominated by organized political parties. Each party represented in Parliament will have a caucus. Each government's mandate is a maximum of five years, with the political party holding the most seats being assigned the responsibility for governance during the specified term; it is the governing caucus from which a cabinet is selected by the prime minister. The runner-up is the Loyal Opposition and generally is characterized as the "government in waiting." A difference between federal and provincial levels in Canada is that no province, any longer, has a Senate. Despite some important exceptions, the Liberal Party has dominated governance of Canada; from time-to-time the Conservatives have governed. Other parties have played important roles from time to time but none has governed the nation.

Provincial legislative processes are patterned on those for Canada. While jurisdictional prerogatives differ, some are shared, and the process is highly similar. Municipalities exist by provincial statutes and are governed by councils that generally are not politically partisan in nature (provinces and municipalities are discussed below).

Legislation

The fourteen steps outlined in **Figure 7–1** can be grouped into six stages: policy approval by Cabinet, legislative drafting, draft bill (a proposed new Act or an amendment to an existing Act) printing, Cabinet approval (or revision) of draft, Parliament/Legislature review, and regulations. Legislative review and approval is a path of four steps: (*i*) first reading is the public pronouncement of a bill's content and intentions; (*ii*) second reading is review/debate/approval in principle; (*iii*) third reading follows "approval in principle" and is detailed clause-by-clause study/debate/approval; and (*iv*) Royal Assent by Governor-General (Lieutenant Governor in provinces). If second reading fails (a rare event), the bill is not passed. From time-to-time a government may use its majority, if it has one, to force passage of a second reading. But the government may have misgivings stemming from the debate so it either withdraws the bill or lets it "die on the Order Paper" as the particular session prorogues. With major and controversial legislation, a government may introduce legislation and then withdraw it to engage political and public debate, so that improved legislation can be brought forward in the next legislative session.[2] Legislative change can come into force and effect immediately upon Royal Assent, according to a date specified in the bill, or by Order-In-Council; often a change in the law is delayed so that regulations can be prepared and ready for implementation concurrent with the legal change.

There are five basic sources that can drive legislative change:

- *Public*: requests from the public-at-large, often organized as an interest group, that are brought to the attention of their representatives and the government;

- *Government*: policy proposals emanating from political party conventions or policy conferences, caucus, commissioned reports, or policy review committees/forums that are invited to evaluate and recommend in a specified policy area;

- *Public Service*: recommendations based on administrative experience and programming so as to improve efficiency or practicality;

FIGURE 7-1   Overview of the Legislative Process

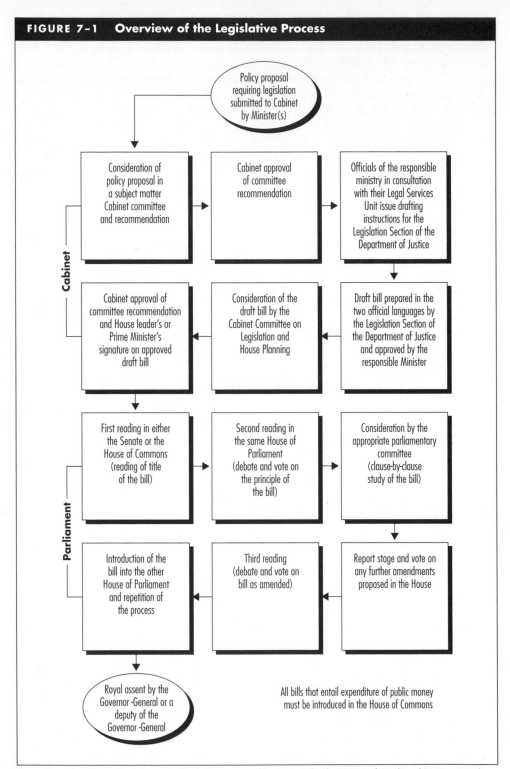

Policy proposal requiring legislation submitted to Cabinet by Minister(s)

Cabinet

Consideration of policy proposal in a subject matter Cabinet committee and recommendation

Cabinet approval of committee recommendation

Officials of the responsible ministry in consultation with their Legal Services Unit issue drafting instructions for the Legislation Section of the Department of Justice

Cabinet approval of committee recommendation and House leader's or Prime Minister's signature on approved draft bill

Consideration of the draft bill by the Cabinet Committee on Legislation and House Planning

Draft bill prepared in the two official languages by the Legislation Section of the Department of Justice and approved by the responsible Minister

Parliament

First reading in either the Senate or the House of Commons (reading of title of the bill)

Second reading in the same House of Parliament (debate and vote on the principle of the bill)

Consideration by the appropriate parliamentary committee (clause-by-clause study of the bill)

Introduction of the bill into the other House of Parliament and repetition of the process

Third reading (debate and vote on bill as amended)

Report stage and vote on any further amendments proposed in the House

Royal assent by the Governor-General or a deputy of the Governor-General

All bills that entail expenditure of public money must be introduced in the House of Commons

Source: Reproduced from materials provided by the Department of Justice Canada, The Minister of Supply and Services Canada.

- *Parliament/Legislature*: mandated standing or special committees may propose legislative change, as may private members or entities reporting (not to government) such as the ombudsman or auditor-general; and

- *Judiciary*: court decisions can determine results that differ from policy intent, so that remedial action is needed to align policy and the law (unless Parliament chooses to override the Judiciary as is its right).

Common in current rhetoric is that Canadian governments spend without accountability. Those paying little heed may be unaware of it, but *all* government expenditures must be and are provided for by legislative mandate. Some are after the fact, such as Special Warrants, but legal authority is a necessity. Many who "search for the devil" need only to look into the mirror! Some who are cynical about the size of the government trough are concurrently elbowing their way to that trough! Examples abound from the federal government's mid-1990s infrastructure program.

Regulations

Regulations are Cabinet Orders (Orders-in-Council): major pieces of legislation will need regulations, pursuant to provisions of the legislation, for practical implementation of the law. Regulations can be changed quickly but the law cannot. In governance environments where there is great uncertainty or rapid change, flexibility is essential; also, regulations no longer needed are much easier to expunge than the law. As experience is gained over time, provisions may become certain and secure enough that they should be written into law. There is a trade-off between accountability and flexibility. In certain circumstances, such as potential urgency, the law may provide for Ministerial Order action; an example is that forest fire fighting decisions may be needed in hours or faster, rather than waiting for a weekly Cabinet meeting. Where powers are draconian, there may be "sunset provisions" so that the power automatically lapses with time unless extended by a formal and reported decision process.

Timing

Politics is often described as the "Art of the Possible." We agree, but we add the corollary "and timing is its magic potion." Like the time dimension of a market (recall **Chapter 4**), and like the impeccable timing of great comedians, *timing* co-mingles items, events, and people so that it matters hugely. Hence, policy-making and legislative processes stall after and before *elections.* The window of time leading up to an election will be dominated by non-policy matters; not only does this include election preparation, but a risk-averse strategy to not encounter needless problems that could be unresolvable before the magic "E" date. A new (even if re-elected) government or city council will need time to get organized and familiarize themselves with issues and associated personalities and pressures. The menu of immediate issues is likely to be long. This situation occurs because of unattended matters in the run-up to the election, and because many "lost causes" from the past will be reintroduced with renewed hope and expectation. And some should be. The parliamentary time cycle is typically four years, and those in power get to choose the timing within the end-life constraint of five years. Little substantive policy is delivered in the first year, and short-term political considerations will dominate the legislative agenda for (at least) the last year. Bottom-line result: *there is no more than a two year "window" of each electoral cycle to achieve major* *changes in policy and legislation.* Business will be well-served to understand this reality about modern government in Canada.[3]

PROVINCIAL AND MUNICIPAL GOVERNANCE

Confederation

Canada has a confederal form of government distinct from a federation. A federation can be formed by a central government decentralizing regionally and assigning public service functions on pragmatic grounds, but a confederation is a union of formerly independent political entities. Canada as we know it was formed when four such entities came together in 1867: Nova Scotia, New Brunswick, Lower Canada (Quebec), and Upper Canada (Ontario). Over the next century, boundary adjustments and territorial expansions took place. Manitoba was next (1870) to join Canada followed by British Columbia (1871) and Prince Edward Island (1873). Alberta and Saskatchewan, formerly territories, became provinces in 1905 — becoming federated because they had not been independent entities. Newfoundland relinquished its former independence to join Canada in 1949. The Yukon and Northwest Territories, the eastern portion of the latter recently having become Nunavut, are part of the Government of Canada sphere rather than being provinces.

British North America Act (1867)

Canada's Constitution until 1982, the *BNA Act* set out jurisdiction for the federal government and for the provinces. Some functions were specified as joint between the two governing levels. Much dispute has ensued in various matters especially agriculture, resources, communications, immigration, and justice. First Nations people were "lost in the shuffle" and rarely accorded direct involvement opportunities. Despite living in provinces, so-called "Treaty Indians" remained a federal government responsibility. Really lost in the shuffle have been the Metis whose lineage (until more recent time "tracking" the male parent only) as First Nations citizens was lost; neither federal nor provincial levels of government fully embraced responsibility for these people.

Municipal Governments

Referred to as local government, cities/towns/villages, municipalities/counties/school boards — municipal governments are the governance that is closest to the people. It is much more important than available literature and research might suggest. Such governing entities are "creatures" of provincial legislation; that is, each province is a federation in the sense that its Municipal Government Act delegates and shares certain decision making. Governance in municipal jurisdictions is different, a "town hall" rather than parliamentary system of democracy. While interest groupings coalesce from time-to-time, partisan politics and caucuses are not the norm. Election times are fixed for shorter terms than is usual at the provincial and federal levels of Canadian government.

Always important, municipal/civic governments are becoming even more important in Canada for at least two reasons. The first reason is demographic — in most provinces the majority of the population lives in metropolitan city regions. In some provinces more than half of the people live in a couple of cities, or even one city such as Vancouver or Winnipeg; in all provinces this percentage is growing. The second reason is economic — the primary nodes of economic growth are located in Canada's metropolitan city regions. Meanwhile, the global competition is lessening the importance of governmental jurisdiction boundaries (glocalization). Perhaps Canada's future will mirror the medieval history of city states. Certainly as demographic patterns and economic systems change, so must government at the municipal level. Unlike the federal and provincial governments that have enfeebled themselves financially, local governments in Canada generally have been fiscally responsible: by law, municipalities must balance their budgets each year! Business and the Canadian public can expect a future where municipal/civic government will be relatively more important.

GOVERNMENT STRUCTURE AND THE POLICY-MAKING PROCESS

To influence government policy, in whatever direction, for whatever purpose, we must clearly understand how government operates. It is not as simple as most would believe. Canada is a constitutional monarchy with a parliamentary form of government. The federal government is comprised of three branches: the executive branch (Prime Minister, Cabinet, and public service), the legislative branch (House of Commons and Senate), and the judicial branch (Supreme Court of Canada and Federal Court of Canada). The judiciary operates at arms' length of both Parliament and the executive branch.

Inherent in the concept of Parliament are the two principles of *representative government* and *responsible government*. Representative government means that the people of Canada elect their governors to a legislative assembly, the House of Commons. Responsible government implies that the Cabinet, including the prime minister, sit in and are responsible to that legislative assembly. The political party winning a plurality of seats forms the government, with the leader of that party becoming prime minister.

Cabinet ministers are appointed and hold their offices "at the pleasure of the prime minister." There are ministers with portfolio (heads of traditional line departments with vertical constituencies, such as Agriculture and Labour); ministers without portfolio (Cabinet spokesmen for particular issues, usually with no departmental staff); and ministers of state (Canada's version of junior ministers who perform a staff function or oversee part of a larger department and may or may not be in Cabinet). Some ministers with portfolio have horizontal, coordinative functions (Justice, Foreign Affairs), or head up central agencies (Treasury Board, Finance) or co-coordinative, administrative departments (Revenue, Public Works, and Supply and Services).

Canadian cabinets operate under the principle of collective responsibility or cabinet solidarity; ministers never publicly disagree with government policy. Spending for existing programs is controlled by the statutory six-member committee of Cabinet known as the Treasury Board. Cabinet is supported by a *shadow committee* of deputy ministers headed by the Clerk of the Privy Council. Legislation and regulations generally emerge from one of the policy committees of Cabinet (Economic Union or Social Union), assisted by the public service and then introduced by a Cabinet Minister in the House of Commons for Parliamentary review and debate. In most cases, the latter is more ritual than substantive policy making. Only recently, committees of the House of Commons have been empowered to review issues other than those brought to the House by the Government. However, the funds given these committees are inadequate for their new formal responsibilities; thus, little investigation has transpired to date.

In such a system, the prime minister and his staff have an inordinate amount of power. A strong-willed prime minister with firm control of his party and a clear majority in the House is, for all intents and purposes today, the Government. The only sure check against tyranny is the formal executive or head of state, the Queen of Canada, as represented by the Governor-General. The Governor-General has the formal power to dissolve Parliament, appoint governments, and call elections. Rarely have any of these been done against the will of the prime minister.

Most regulations, guidelines, policies, and programs used to implement Parliamentary legislation appear as *Orders-in-Council*. These are executive fiats of the Cabinet and, due to their scope and technicality, are drafted by the public service.

In this system, the key to attaining political power is *votes*. One of the main keys to garnering at least a plurality of votes is the promise of *economic prosperity*, reflected primarily by full employment. However, the key to power within government is the *information* by which one can shape, create, or derail policy. Those with information have power. Those with power make policy. Revenue is a distant concern compared to votes, jobs, and information. (For more about the power of information, see **Chapters 12** and **13**).

Figure 7–2 shows a traditional, if skeletal, view of the structure of the Government of Canada. It also identifies four overlapping policy levels within this framework. Departmental policy is normally administered by directors-general and their subordinates. Yet departmental policy is produced by not just ministers and their deputies, but by assistant deputy ministers, directors-general, and sometimes even directors. Departmental priorities are set by ministers who consult with their deputies.

The Prime Minister's Office (PMO), personally appointed by the prime minister, provides the head of government with clerical, media relations, party relations, and constituency relations support. It is also the prime minister's major source of political advice. It is partisan and politically oriented, yet operationally sensitive. The PMO's staff of 100 or so is headed by a chief of staff, considered to be the closest person to the prime minister.

The Privy Council Office (PCO), comprised mostly of career public servants, and traditionally the secretariat for Cabinet and its committees, has evolved to become the 'department" of the prime minister. Over 200 staff members offer a full array of policy advice, and attempt to coordinate government policy and action. The PCO is non-partisan and operationally oriented, yet politically sensitive.

It prepares discussion papers for Cabinet under the prime minister's direction, and writes or critiques departmentally generated Memoranda to Cabinet. These memoranda are secret. They synthesize policy advice and recommendations and shape statutes, regulations, and government policy. The head of the PCO is the Clerk of the Privy Council/Secretary to the Cabinet, who also chairs the Committee of Deputy Ministers and recommends deputy minister appointees to the prime minister. The Clerk is arguably the most powerful person in government, except for the prime minister.

The PMO, PCO, the Treasury Board Secretariat, and the Ministry of Finance comprise the *Central Agencies* of the federal government. These departments are responsible for coordinating policy, allocating resources among competing government interests, and generally managing the policy process. These agencies have evolved from simply providing advice to making decisions, then actually controlling the decision-making process. While line departments give politicians technical data to make technical decisions, the Agencies provide the information politicians need to make political decisions. Further, the Privy Council

FIGURE 7-2   Management Organization of the Government of Canada

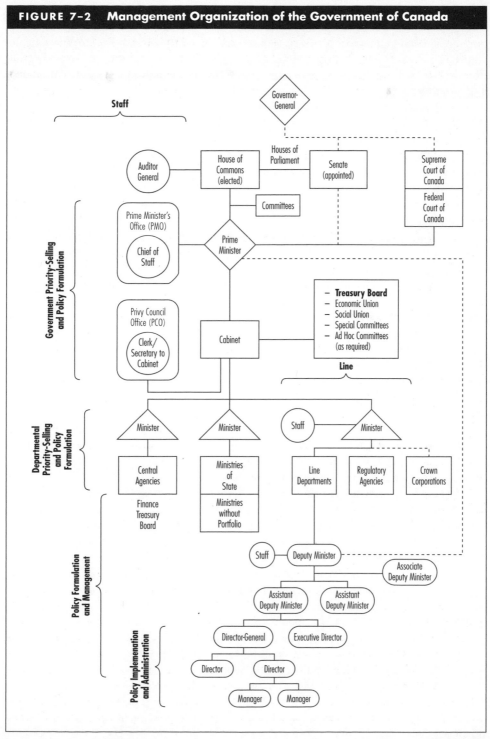

Office and Treasury Board Secretariat provide many of the fast-tracking senior management superstars in the federal government. These tend to be better educated than their peers, ambitious, loyal to the process of government, and have little or no business experience.

The days of swashbuckling Cabinet ministers who dominated their departments and policy areas are long gone at the federal level. Cabinet ministers today are marketers of government policy. In a majority government, government policy is usually the prime minister's policy. Canadians live at a time when the most important decisions are imposed on them by officials who need not face the consequences of those decisions. They are political managers as much as they are policy advisers.

Where is the true power in the government of Canada? Constitutionally, it is in Parliament, which under a majority government means the prime minister. Politically, it is with the leader of the governing party — the prime minister. Managerially, it is Cabinet — the executive branch of government — the members of which owe their appointments to the prime minister.

The prime minister, however, is hardly accessible. Even Cabinet ministers must make distant appointments to see him or her and wait in line like everyone else (except for the two or three ministers closest to the prime minister).

How, then, is policy made at the national level? The size and complexity of government prevent it from operating as a single entity. There are, however, obvious patterns of policy making in Ottawa that represent the government's decision-making process.

Before government entertains a public policy issue, a demand for action must be heard, whether from an interest group, a private individual, a Cabinet minister, backbenchers, or the public service. Increasingly, though, modern survey technology has helped the executive branch of government, especially the ever-growing PMO, to monitor public concerns and determine the country's political agenda. This process is ultimately controlled by the prime minister.

If the government believes and/or wishes an issue will just go away, a Task Force or Royal Commission may be appointed to study it into oblivion — paralysis by analysis! If the government is unsure what to do, it will issue a discussion paper for public debate, perhaps followed by a "round table" forum for feedback.

Once an agenda item is selected for action, the public service is instructed to develop specific proposals. (See **Figure 7–3**) These are sent to the appropriate Cabinet Committee for review. At this time, the PCO will either adapt these ideas into a more manageable form for the politicians (thus influencing the discussion through their editorializing), be asked to provide other options, relate the proposal to overall government priorities and existing programs, and/or negotiate with provincial officials, if necessary. At this time, the PMO will inform the Committee of the political ramifications of its proposal and give the prime minister's position, if one exists.

The Cabinet Committee will then report to Cabinet as a whole, where the proposed policy will be approved, amended, or rejected. Cabinet's action is then documented in a Record of Decision, of which the prime minister is the final arbiter. Cabinet, through the prime minister, will then inform the Government party's caucus and introduce the policy. It may take either the form of legislation to be passed in the House (a mere formality in a majority government situation), or an Order-In-Council (Cabinet fiat) under existing legislation. The final statute (law) or regulation will then be implemented and administered by the bureaucracy.

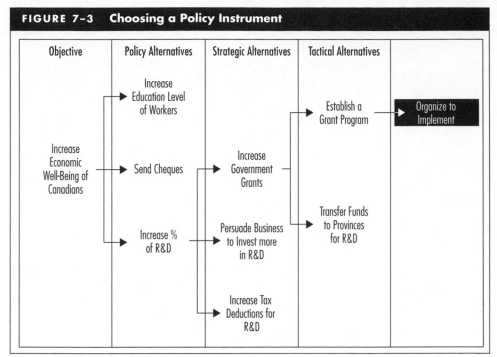

FIGURE 7-3   Choosing a Policy Instrument

Source: Excerpted from G.F. Osbaldeston, ("A Policy-Driven Process for Organizing"), *Organizing to Govern*, Volume One, by National Centre for Management Research and Development, Copyright © 1992.

In short, policy making is controlled and directed by the political executive and bureaucracy. It is hardly a creative process, as creativity emanates only from policy decisions made at the very top, such as the 1982 Constitution Act, the FTA or NAFTA. The federal government's policy-making process is at best the resolution of conflict, the result of a bargaining process, and incremental political change. The question for business is when and where to try to influence that process: at the issue identification stage, the policy formulation stage, or the Parliamentary debate stage? The answer to this question will depend on which policy instrument the government chooses.

INSTRUMENTS OF GOVERNMENT POLICY

Before an issue becomes part of government's policy agenda, there will be a gestation period characterized by cultural change or structural, social change. Only when a specific change challenges beliefs, values, or material wealth so drastically that "winners" and "losers" will result, does a phenomenon become a public issue. Groups will then mobilize, costs will be itemized in the media, and the public awareness level will be raised. Only then will an issue be politicized and government action demanded "in the public interest."

There are many types of policies available to government. Five economic functions of government were enumerated in **Chapter 4**. There are many ways to categorize types of policy, such as the following:

- *Distributive:* benefits are solicited by and awarded to specific persons or groups, while costs are distributed equally to the general population (e.g., tariffs, business subsidies, export incentives);

- *Regulatory:* economic and/or social behaviour of individuals or organizations is directly modified by sanction (e.g., environmental protection, price controls, control of entry);

- *Redistributive*: wealth is indirectly transferred from one segment of a population to another (e.g., progressive income taxation, Medicare, subsidized housing);

- *Constituent:* state management is facilitated; establishes the "rules of the game." Benefits and costs are widely dispersed (e.g., monetary policy, fiscal policy, enabling legislation for special-purpose bodies). [4]

Each policy type reflects a particular type of politics, policy arena, and set of public demands. *Distributive* policies are usually chosen when government responds to the needs of a single interest group or coalition of interest groups, using general government revenues as funding. *Regulatory* policies are the outcome of conflict between two parties, whether producer and consumer or two segments of the business community. The problems in resolving the conflict are passed on to ill-defined, special-purpose bodies, thus eliminating the need for politicians to act further. *Redistributive* policies, too, are usually the outcome of conflict between certain parties. Both regulatory and redistributive policies create winners and losers, further stimulating special interest groups to organize. *Constituent* policies are at best the compromises resulting from competing points of view within the government structure, as much as they are responses to the demands of the political environment. The development of these policies is an on-going process, only interrupted by economic or social crises, or less often by a philosophical change in the government's executive.

The type of government action chosen fully depends on the type of problem it is to address. Whether or not the political executive deals with the issue legislatively or through an Order-In-Council is unimportant. These are merely the vehicles by which decisions are transmitted. The crucial factor is to understand and appreciate the wide gamut of measures government can use to implement a decision or policy (see **Figure 7–4**).

Factors which shape government's choice of policy instrument include: (*i*) deciding how much coercion will be necessary to change behaviour; (*ii*) identifying who will benefit and who will pay the costs; (*iii*) deciding which publics must be considered; (*iv*) establishing whether the market deficiency or social problem is real or perceived; and (*v*) assessing how urgent the need is for government to be seen to be doing something.

A government's options are numerous if it intends to change private behaviour. It can lead by example; rely upon generally accepted, self-enforcing conventions (such as traffic signals); regulate; license; ration; charge user fees; prohibit the behaviour outright; or nationalize private assets. And a government can exercise (per)suasion (e.g., the V-chip issue). With the current Video Lottery Terminal (VLT) issue, churches and others seek to (per)suade government. If the intent is to provide public goods or services such as street lighting, fire protection, or telecommunications, government either will do so directly (public enterprise), contract out with an external party, command the private sector to do so (regulation), or give the private sector the means to do so profitably (incentives).

Inevitably, the problem of compliance arises. Minimal fines for pollution violations, for instance, are seen by some corporations as fees to pollute. Parking tickets have a simi-

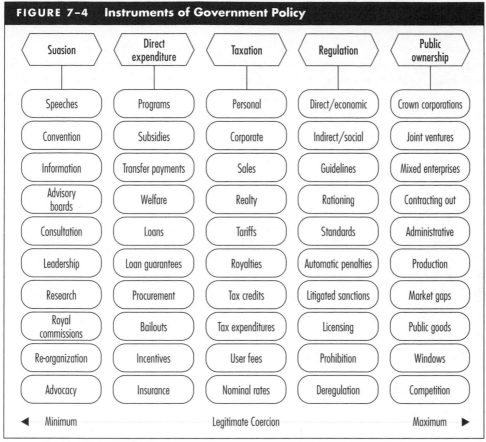

FIGURE 7-4   Instruments of Government Policy

Suasion	Direct expenditure	Taxation	Regulation	Public ownership
Speeches	Programs	Personal	Direct/economic	Crown corporations
Convention	Subsidies	Corporate	Indirect/social	Joint ventures
Information	Transfer payments	Sales	Guidelines	Mixed enterprises
Advisory boards	Welfare	Realty	Rationing	Contracting out
Consultation	Loans	Tariffs	Standards	Administrative
Leadership	Loan guarantees	Royalties	Automatic penalties	Production
Research	Procurement	Tax credits	Litigated sanctions	Market gaps
Royal commissions	Bailouts	Tax expenditures	Licensing	Public goods
Re-organization	Incentives	User fees	Prohibition	Windows
Advocacy	Insurance	Nominal rates	Deregulation	Competition

◄ Minimum ———————— Legitimate Coercion ———————— Maximum ►

Source: Adapted from Taylor (1991: 86)

lar effect. Desired outcomes are not always achieved, and behaviour is not always modified. *Even when there is full compliance, outcomes do not always equate with objectives.*

The choice of policy instrument and the type of policy will also determine whether government must push legislation through Parliament or use an Order-In-Council to deal with the problem under existing legislation. Similarly, government's choice will determine the structure and systems needed to carry out its decision.

A good example of this contingency approach to choosing government policy is the manner in which the federal government has treated FDI over the years. Basically, government has two choices to respond to the Canadian public's concern over the level of FDI in the country: *performance regulation* or *nationalization*. Performance regulation is designed to increase Canadian control over foreign-owned/controlled companies. This ensures that the company's net benefits contribute to the national economic well-being. The nationalization approach simply increases Canadian ownership. It offers no guarantee that Canadian business or government ownership will contribute any more than foreign companies would to the nation's welfare. Either way, government must be seen to be doing something. It is simply a question of how coercive it wants to be — and how effective.

FINANCING THE STATE

The story of our time is the shrinking of the State. With the advance of neo-conservatism in western industrialized societies the increasing involvement of the state has been seriously questioned. There has already been public (and political) resistance in many countries to the high level and intensity of state participation in the economy. Expectations of government rose too high. Government tried but was unable to meet those expectations, and became a target of dismay and cynicism. Market failure was explained in **Chapter 4**; in **Chapter 11** the concept of government failure is noted.

Canada has always been a government-centred society. Unlike in the United States, only a modest amount of serious debate arose about the appropriate role for, and the growth of, the public sector. Until the 1990s, Canada had put a higher priority on reforming and making more accountable its government structures and processes.

The Canadian federal government expenditure level (1998-99) exceeds $150 billion (see **Figure 7–5**). It represents about 22% of the country's GDP; this figure was up to nearly 26% in 1996-97, but only 18% in 1978! Over that two-decade period, the most significant increases in the first decade had been in a combination of financing the national debt, defence and funding statutory programs, entitlements and transfer payments such as Medicare, the Canada Pension Plan, and unemployment insurance. In the last decade, *program* expenditures have levelled off and now are decreasing, but the "compound-interest hell" of past fiscal follies is still increasing debt service charges. Nearly 30 cents of each tax loonie goes to pay interest on the national debt, up from about 20 cents a decade or so ago.

Corporations have carried less and less of the tax burden since 1970 despite tax reforms to achieve the opposite result. Corporate tax as a percentage of federal government revenues peaked at 26% in the mid-1970s and has dropped to approximately 12%.

The Deficits/DEBT discussion in **Chapter 4** identified the magnitude of the fiscal problem and the four options to address the fiscal monster. How did Canada, and many provinces, get into this untenable position? Two ways. The first was the continued violation of the second half of Keynesian economics. Between 1965 and 1985, the Canadian economy grew at a compound, real, annual rate of approximately 4%. Simultaneously, private capital formation grew at a slightly healthier pace of 5%, so the rich got richer. Federal expenditures rose 6% per year in real terms — at 150% the rate of the economy as a whole! Meanwhile, federal revenues barely kept up with general economic growth and grew at an annual rate of just under 4%. As a result, the net federal debt grew systemically by nearly 3% per year. In the 1970s, the Canada Pension Plan and other social programs were indexed to inflation so costs spiralled; meanwhile, the personal income tax system was deindexed so that real revenues fell in the most important source. Moreover, mid-1970s to mid-1980s high inflation forced higher interest rates on the rapidly increasing DEBT base. And Canadians have been saddled with the fiscal albatross ever since.

The second way severe fiscal impairment came about, for Canada and some provinces, especially Alberta, was by making "hard" expenditure commitments based on "soft" revenue streams. Hard expenditures are ones that are very difficult to reduce (e.g., entitlement expectations); hard revenues are those that can be counted on (say 95% probability) over the medium-to-longer term. Income taxes and sales taxes yield reliable revenue streams, but oil royalty revenues are subject to cycles and eventual decline because the resource base is non-renewable. As is now apparent, the glaring example of current soft revenue is *borrowing* against future generations; the folly is compounded when the money from deficit financ-

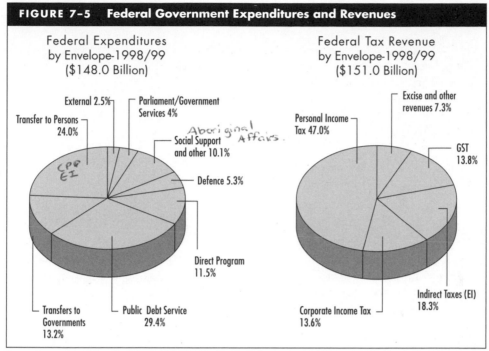

FIGURE 7-5   **Federal Government Expenditures and Revenues**

Federal Expenditures
by Envelope-1998/99
($148.0 Billion)

External 2.5%
Transfer to Persons 24.0%
Parliament/Government Services 4%
Aboriginal Affairs
Social Support and other 10.1%
CPP EI
Defence 5.3%
Direct Program 11.5%
Transfers to Governments 13.2%
Public Debt Service 29.4%

Federal Tax Revenue
by Envelope-1998/99
($151.0 Billion)

Excise and other revenues 7.3%
Personal Income Tax 47.0%
GST 13.8%
Indirect Taxes (EI) 18.3%
Corporate Income Tax 13.6%

Source: Government of Canada Budget, 1998-99. Reproduced with the permission of the Minister of Public Works and Government Services Canada, 1998

ing is used for current purposes rather than capital facilities that confer benefits to the public over time. Canada did both. Soft expenditures are one-time (e.g., 125-year celebration) or few-time commitments that lapse. **Figure 7–6** is a decision matrix that illustrates the matchups of hard/soft revenues/expenditures. There is a logical congruence to utilizing hard reliable revenues for public service purposes that are continuing, ones that are believed to be needed over a protracted time frame. There is similar congruence between soft unreliable revenues being used for one-time/few-time occasional budget allocations. What is absolutely unsustainable is hard continuing expenditures being initiated with no assurance of fundability in the future.

What about the handling of funds from soft sources? An emerging example might be lottery revenues. Endowment financial management is a method of converting current funds into future hard funds.[5] The fundamental methodology is to direct all soft-source funds into an endowment base; then the capital base purchasing power is maintained through time by reinvesting the portion of the yield that offsets inflation. The after-inflation yield is hard revenue available for either hard or soft expenditure budget priorities.

DEBT servicing costs represent monies unavailable for public services or tax reductions. Another problem is the rigidity imposed on government budgetary process: whatever fiscal flexibility needed for the whole budget must be compressed into the shrinking non-interest portion of it. The already grim spectre is worsened as larger proportions of borrowing is from foreign sources; this is because of exchange rate risk. As noted in **Chapter 4**, large federal government borrowings "crowd out" other governments and the private sector so they are forced into the disadvantages of more foreign borrowing activ-

FIGURE 7-6   Fiscal Strategy Decision Matrix

Expenditures

		Hard	Soft
Revenues	Hard	Yes	Yes
	Soft	No!	??

ity. In 1977, the federal government owed 10% of its debt to non-Canadians; by 1987 that figure climbed to 16%. Continuing to climb, the debt jumped to 27% by 1996 and alarmingly, for provinces, it reached 42%.[6]

To its credit, the federal government has tried and had some success in controlling its spending. But government is not a single entity. Ministers and Cabinet committees have been reduced in number. The number of federal departments has fallen, with a reduction of deputy ministers and assistant deputy ministers. A Chief Informatics Officer (CIO) was appointed to spearhead the harnessing of technology for administrative savings. Still, government budgets are the temporary culmination of multiple processes and competitions for funds. Federal budgeting has been characterized best as a game between *spenders* and *guardians*. Lower-level officials have little or no spending discretion. The middle-manager tries to meet all objectives within a budget while satisfying the requirements of Treasury Board. The "spenders" are the deputy ministers, who manage departmental resources. They are pitted against the "guardians" (also spenders in their own right) such as Finance, Treasury Board, and the Privy Council Office, whose job is to make the system work to meet the government's priorities.

A government budget is an expenditure budget: each expenditure item is specified. However, revenue (taxes, tariffs, user fees, Crown corporation dividends) is reported in an aggregate form as the Consolidated Revenue Fund. Universality, equity, and fairness in government policies override any incentive for cost recovery or net budgeting. Therefore, program and department budgets seldom balance; only the overall budget balances, thanks to deficit borrowing. Government budgets (and the budgets of organizations such as hospitals and universities which are government-funded) have tended historically to overestimate revenues and underestimate expenses, thus almost always ending up in budgeting shortfalls which could be blamed exogenously. Today, many governments are beginning to act a bit more business-like in conservatively estimating revenues and more accurately estimating and controlling costs (as opposed to expenses).

Ottawa plays a highly sophisticated level of budget gamesmanship. Federal bureaucrats are, above all, human, displaying human frailties encouraged by this environment. Public servants are budget maximizers. Since salaries for senior managers are lower than those of their counterparts in the private sector, government employees seek other rewards, such as information, "perks" (some of the most lavish executive offices are in Ottawa), and empire-building. Ottawa's mandarins are *lapsophobics* — they spend every penny of their annual budgets to justify increased funding in the following year.

In the late 1990s, most governments in Canada are coming to grips with their direct budget problems. Alas, the big black clouds of indirect financial liabilities must be recognized. The unfunded condition of pension plans and "insurance" schemes is more fiscal poison, especially with the federal government. The Canada Pension Plan evolved into more of a Ponzi scheme, coupled with non-pension payouts, than a responsible and reliable source of future income security. As we write, a belated struggle is underway to bring common sense policies and fiscal rationale to the Unemployment Insurance (now euphemistically Employment Insurance) failures.

As Pogo succinctly put it: "I have seen the enemy and he is us!"

A CHANGING JUDICIARY

In 1982, with the advent of the *Constitution Act* and *The Charter of Rights and Freedoms*, rights which were previously taken for granted, and in effect were only privileges under a constitutional monarchy, were guaranteed. Today, if individual rights are violated, the victim can ask the courts for retribution. Even if federal, provincial, or municipal laws violate most individual rights, with certain exceptions of national security, etc., the courts can now strike down those laws as unconstitutional. *Is Parliament no longer supreme*?

This is important for business because, in legal matters, the courts treat corporations as people. Firms now have rights which government cannot violate. Technically, companies could even challenge advertising restrictions under the fundamental right of freedom of speech. Inter-provincial trade barriers could be also challenged under the right to earn a living in any province. One could also defend one's right to as prompt a regulatory hearing as one could expect for a court trial or public trial.

Of course, every guaranteed right and freedom is "subject to such reasonable limits as can be demonstrably justified." Here, then, is where the interpretative, discretionary, and veto powers of the Supreme Court of Canada come into play.

The Charter is Canada's final, formal recognition that the United States is its model, not Britain. Protecting basic civil rights in a written constitution is an American phenomenon. Thus, we can expect Canadian interest groups to follow America's pattern rather than Britain's. Public court challenges of government actions will promote pressure group interests, mobilize public opinion, and perhaps even help restrain government.

Business should watch and learn. If Canada's system does evolve in this manner, a new window of opportunity for business will open. Business will have a legal avenue by which to reassert its claim as the engine of the economy deserving of a special place on the public agenda.

IMPLICATIONS FOR MANAGEMENT

In the *public choice* model of economic decision making, politicians and bureaucrats alike generally attain personal goals through the promotion of public policies ostensibly designed for another purpose. In particular, government tends to select policies which will benefit *marginal voters* — those groups, whether geographical or conceptual, to be won by narrow margins, because of Canada's FPTP (first-past-the-post) electoral system. Also attractive are well-organized, politically active interest groups. Costs of these policies will be dispersed as widely as possible over the remaining voters. Government will exaggerate the benefits of the policies and downplay their costs, which will be imposed early in a government's term of office. The benefits are released prior to elections.

Pareto optimality, where the greatest benefit is enjoyed by the greatest number, will remain an ideal in a pluralistic society and economy such as Canada's. Here, varied interest groups will vie for scarce resources, and politicians will adopt a planning horizon as far away as the next election. Although the structure and players of the 10 provincial and hundreds of regional and local governments are different, the principles are the same. Public choice economics is here to stay.

But that is not all bad for business. The private sector needs only to learn and apply the techniques already used by successful public pressure groups to win with government. Business needs to meet the full measure of the Consent Doctrine. Because business has more to offer, it can uniquely contribute to the formulation of national economic policy. This would be good for business, and if done well, could be good for Canada.

Business must try to side-step the trap into which most Canadians have fallen — that of "letting government do it." It must be willing to forgo some of government's largesse to achieve a more dynamic economy less burdened by government borrowing. Government itself will not take the initiative to forge a "Brave New Canada" if it means being turned out of office.

Business must also be willing to demonstrate to all Canadians that it can do without some assets the government has offered in the past. Government must get back to "governing" and business must get back to "creating wealth." This is probably as unappealing to one as it is to the other. It also will require skills not yet mastered and knowledge not yet acquired by business. But now is the time to learn — and to do.

The policy-making process in Ottawa is not impermeable or hostile to outsiders. It just needs to be understood in its proper context and worked with accordingly (more on this in **Chapter 12**). Remember, though, the bottom line to government is equity, redistribution, efficiency, information, revenue, jobs, and votes — all rolled into one.

Debt is the killer of activist government. Neo-conservatives may see this as a positive attribute of "less government in your face" due to the fiscal plight of our times. Others will worry whether government can meet its responsibilities in modern society, which certainly is getting more complex. There are Canadian political ebbs and flows, waves and attitudes that can change with surprising speed. Just as the late-1960s lurch to the political left sowed the seeds of fiscal impairment and a cynical public, a similar late-1990s lurch to the right may be the precursor to a future leftward swing of the political pendulum. Paradoxically, current sacrifices and efforts to correct the fiscal plight may make future voters and governments feel that renewed public sector growth is affordable and desirable!

Looking ahead to the new millennium, government will become more or less important according to financial capacity. This pragmatic dictum suggests that the federal government will become less relevant and local/civic governments will become more important. Provincial governments will be more or less important in the future depending on the extent with which they can deal effectively with their financial positions. Business will need to adapt to these changing realities. Business can retard the growth of government by performance that makes larger government less necessary. Business has a top-priority role to play for Canada by competing successfully in the global marketplace. Such success would be a convergence of business, public, and government interests.

SUGGESTED FURTHER READINGS

Allison, Graham T. 1971. *Essence of Decision: Explaining the Cuban Missile Crisis*. Boston: Little, Brown & Co.

Atkinson, Michael M., (ed). 1993. *Governing Canada: Institutions and Public Policy*. Toronto: Harcourt Brace Jovanovich Canada Inc.

Baetz, Reuben. 1993. "Reflections of a Long-Time Minister." In Mark C. Baetz, (ed.), *Readings and Canadian Cases in Business, Government & Society*. Toronto: Nelson.

Blakeney, Allan, and Sandford Borins. 1992. *Political Management in Canada*. Toronto: McGraw-Hill Ryerson.

Boadway, Robin, Albert Breton, Neil Bruce, and Richard Musgrave. 1994. *Defining the Role of Government: Economic Perspectives on the State*. Kingston, ON: Queen's University, School of Policy Studies.

Canada Supply & Services. 1993. "The Federal Legislative Process in Canada." In Mark C. Baetz, (ed.), *Readings and Canadian Cases in Business, Government & Society*. Toronto: Nelson.

Canada West Foundation. 1998. *Red Ink IV: Back From the Brink?* Calgary, AB: Canada West Foundation, January.

Clark, Joe. 1994. *A Nation Too Good To Lose: Renewing the Purpose of Canada*. Toronto: Key-Porter Books.

Coffey, William J. 1994. *The Evolution of Canada's Metropolitan Economies*. Montreal: Institute for Research on Public Policy.

Edelman, Murray. 1980. *The Symbolic Uses of Politics*. Chicago: University of Illinois Press.

Grubel, Herbert G., Douglas D. Purvis, and William M. Scarth. 1992. *Limits to Government: Controlling Deficits and Debt in Canada*. Toronto: C.D. Howe Institute.

Kernaghan, W.D.K. and, D. Siegel. 1995. *Public Administration in Canada*. 3rd ed. Toronto: Nelson.

Lowi, T.J. 1985. "The State in Politics: The Relation Between Policy and Administration." In R.G. Noll, (ed)., *Regulatory Policy and the Social Sciences*. Berkeley: University of California Press.

Maslove, Allan M., (ed). 1989. *Budgeting in the Provinces: Leadership and the Premiers*. Toronto: Institute of Public Administration of Canada, Canadian Public Administration Monograph 11.

McMillan, Melville L., and Allan A. Warrack. 1995. *Alberta's Fiscal Update: One-Track (Thinking) Towards Deficit Reduction*. Edmonton, AB: Western Centre for Economic Research Bulletin 28, University of Alberta, February.

McCallum, John S. 1994. "Managing in the Shadow of a Huge Foreign Debt." *Business Quarterly*, Summer.

Osbaldeston, Gordon F. 1992. *Organizing To Govern*. Volume 1. Toronto: McGraw-Hill.

Pal, Leslie A. 1992. *Public Policy Analysis: An Introduction*. Toronto: Nelson.

Plunkett, T.J. 1992. *City Management in Canada: The Role of the Chief Administrative Officer*. Toronto: Institute of Public Administration of Canada, Canadian Public Administration Monograph 13.

Sancton, Andrew. 1994. *Governing Canada's City-Regions: Adapting Form to Function*. Montreal: Institute for Research on Public Policy.

Sharp, Mitchell. 1982. "Neutral Superservants." *Policy Options*. Halifax: Institute for Research on Public Policy, November/December.

Taylor, D. Wayne. 1991. *Business and Government Relations: Partners in the 1990s*. Toronto: Gage Educational Publishing.

Tindal, C.R., and S.N. Tindal. 1995. *Local Government in Canada*. 4th ed. Toronto: McGraw-Hill Ryerson.

Trebilcock, M.J. *et al.* 1982. *The Choice of Governing Instrument*. Ottawa: Supply and Services Canada.

Tuohy, C.J. 1992. *Policy and Politics in Canada*. Philadelphia: Temple University Press.

Warrack, Allan A., and James Fleming. 1994. "Principles for University Endowment Management." *Treasury Journal*. Ottawa: Canadian Association of University Business Officers, February.

NOTES

1. Tuohy, *Policy and Politics in Canada*.
2. Two examples from Alberta are the *Alberta Heritage Savings Trust Fund Act* and the *Planning Act*.
3. For an insider's understanding of this subject, see the readings at the end of this chapter by former Prime Minister Joe Clark, former Saskatchewan Premier Allan Blakeney, former multi-portfolio federal Minister (and previously senior civil servant) Mitchell Sharp, former Ontario Cabinet Minister Reuben Baetz, and retired Clerk of the Privy Council/Secretary to Cabinet Gordon Osbaldeston.
4. Lowi, "The State in Politics."
5. Warrack and Fleming, Principles for University Endowment Management.
6. Canada West Foundation, *Red Ink IV*.

CANADIAN CROWN CORPORATIONS: NATIONALIZATION

Government, even in its best state, is but a necessary evil; in its worst state, an intolerable one.

Thomas Paine, 1737-1809

Public enterprise has been a major part of the Canadian political and economic fabric for many decades. The development of the Canadian economy has included the evolution of a "Canadian public enterprise culture" (Crown corporation/public enterprise/state enterprise are interchangeable terms). Indeed, some might say that one of Canada's greatest managerial strengths has been in public enterprises and management of same. Given Canada's geographic enormity, sparse population, inhospitable climate, and mercantilist capital base, commercially-oriented Crown corporations were a natural means by which government could intervene in the economy "to bind the nation (together), to develop and market its resources, and to retain some measure of the profits and rents."[1]

OMNIPRESENCE

Through Canada's economic history, numerous essential projects in Canada could only be financed, directly or indirectly, by one or some combination of governments. The omnipresence of public enterprise in Canada is readily exhibited by an examination of annual issues of major Canadian business publications.[2] Crown corporations comprise a significant proportion of the top 500 Canadian corporate firms. In 1995, of the top fifty firms ranked by revenue in Canada seven are Crown corporations, down from eight in the late 1980s. Petro-Canada and Canadian National Rail have been privatized, the former partially (80%) and the latter entirely. Seven of the top fifty financial institutions are state-owned. Ranked by employees, in 1995 state enterprises accounted for four (down from six) of the top fifty.

In fiscal 1992-93, federal Crown Corporations collectively had assets of $81 billion, employed 117 000 and lost $1.6 billion.[3] Crowns account for over 10% of corporate assets in the country, over 20% of all fixed assets, and nearly 10% of the GNP. Among the most visible federal public corporations are: Canada Post, CBC, CN Rail (until late 1995), VIA Rail, Petro-Canada (20% retained after three privatization disbursements), Atomic Energy of Canada, Canadian Mortgage and Housing Corporation, the Federal Business Development Bank, the Canadian Wheat Board, the Bank of Canada, and the Royal Canadian Mint. There are many others.

Despite privatizations over recent years, there remain in Canada over 300 federal and 100 provincial Crown corporations, and numerous Crown-like municipal business entities. Many of the corporate entities have one or more subsidiaries and other corporate interests such as partnerships and strategic alliances that include partial-ownership positions.

Many provincial utilities in Canada remain publicly-owned. Some examples are Ontario Hydro, Quebec Hydro, Manitoba Hydro, Saskatchewan Power, BC Hydro, and Saskatchewan Telephones. Virtually all of the water sanitation systems in Canadian cities and towns are owned and operated by their respective municipal governments. As well, several cities have their own public enterprises, including: Thunder Bay Telephone, Prince Rupert Telephone, Calgary Electric, Edmonton Power, and Medicine Hat Gas & Electric. Until 1990, the Province of Alberta owned and operated Alberta Government Telephones (AGT). In 1905 the City of Edmonton purchased its telephone system, continuing as a public enterprise until a 1995 sale to AGT/TELUS. Paradoxically, Alberta Treasury Branches remain 100% government-owned.

Adding to the confusion surrounding the role of government in Canada, however, is the changing behaviour of public enterprise. Given the background on business and government in Canada, the advent of Crown corporations is not surprising. However, many observers are puzzled by increasing evidence that public enterprise in Canada is often more concerned about getting a competitive rate of return on its investment than about the political imperative given to it by the government of the day. Also, like many private sector enterprises, Crown corporations have exhibited social responsibility only when required to stabilize their task environments, to routinize their procedures, or to escape from politics and surprise intervention; in short, to stay in business.

IN THE BEGINNING . . .

I know of no difference in the machinery of government in the old and new world that strikes a European more forcibly than the apparently undue importance which the business of constructing public works appears to occupy in American [Canadian] legislation....The provision which in Europe, the state makes for the protection of its citizens against foreign enemies, is in America required for...the 'war with the wilderness.' The defence of an important fortress, or the maintenance of a sufficient army or navy in exposed spots, is not more a matter of common concern to the European, than is the construction of the great communications to the American [Canadian] settler; and the state, very naturally, takes on itself the making of the works, which are a matter of concern to all alike.[4]

Historically, in Canada, public enterprise has arisen where there was little other prospect for profit. In the past, it was found predominantly in the transportation, communications, and utilities industries. As early as 1821, the government of Lower Canada built and operated the Lachine Canal as a "public work" to assist the fur trade of the Hudson's Bay Company.

Over the decades, until recently, little ideological resistance has greeted public ownership of assets and state operation of enterprise. No right-wing party had campaigned against public enterprise. Government ownership of railroads, airlines, electric power companies, the grain trade, and so on has always been a fact of Canadian political life. In fact, it was the Conservative government of R.B. Bennett that established the Canadian Radio Broadcasting Commission (predecessor of the CBC).

Canada may have lacked the industrial entrepreneurism of the United States, having inherited its financial entrepreneurism from Britain. But Canada's unique version of entrepreneurism has been reflected in the zeal with which public enterprise has been applied as a public policy instrument in this country.

According to Sandford Borins, nowhere was this pragmatism more evident than in the rapid growth of public enterprise under the leadership of C.D. Howe during World War II. [5] At that time, the overriding national goal was to win the war. Business-government cooperation was essential to this effort and the Liberal government found any form of "institutional innovation" justified. National security and security of supply were essential, and government needed a means to coordinate private activity with public policy; it needed a "window on the industry." Where regulation would not produce the desired results quickly enough, Crown corporations were used. It was as simple as that.

Some Crown corporations were incorporated to actually produce war-time goods and services, such as Eldorado Mining and Refining (1944) Ltd., Quebec Shipyards Ltd., Victory Aircraft Ltd., Small Arms Ltd., and Polymer Corporation Ltd. There were insufficient numbers of war-time suppliers and capacity needed to be increased dramatically and rapidly. Some suppliers were monopolies in the interests of security (e.g., Eldorado); others were "yardstick competitors" to monitor private companies and increase capacity (e.g., Victory).

Joint ventures with the private sector were equally common. Ambitious middle-managers were recruited from the private sector, and hoping for exclusive postwar opportunities, they performed meritoriously. It was clear that the private sector must produce, or the public sector would. Even private assets could be nationalized, if necessary. However, it was war; business trusted government, and government did not hesitate to act. History shows that Canada's public corporate suppliers of war-time needs enabled it to become the fourth-largest Allied supplier of war goods.

Other Crown corporations were created as simply administrative agencies. These included War-time Housing Ltd., War Supplies Ltd., War-time Oils Ltd., and Allied War Supplies Corp. They coordinated policy with private sector activities; they regulated and directed. C.D. Howe preferred the corporate form of organization to the departmental form because of lower costs and greater autonomy. These agencies were managed by successful business executives such as E.P. Taylor, who volunteered as "dollar-a-year men." Administrative Crown corporations were lean and mean.

After the war, many Crown corporations were terminated; most administrative corporations were terminated, and many production corporations were privatized or reprivatized. Others were retained in key sectors (weapons, housing, and uranium refining) or in areas where Howe perceived a promise of commercial viability. If a production Crown corpora-

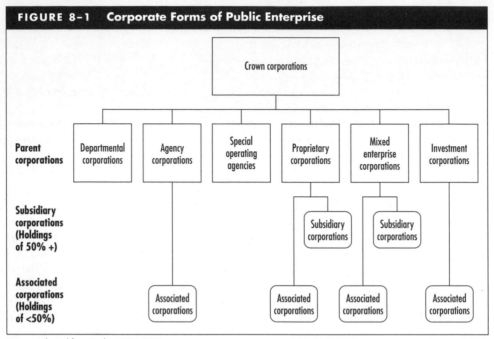

FIGURE 8–1   Corporate Forms of Public Enterprise

Source: Adapted from Taylor (1991: 101)

tion could survive after the war without protection from market forces, then it was retained. Howe was not ideologically opposed to public enterprise *per se*.

Some of Howe's personal decisions have helped shape Canada's economy as we know it today. He kept Polymer, which has grown into Polysar, one of the world's largest petrochemical companies. He sold Canada's merchant marine; in a matter of months, Canada went from one of the world's great naval powers to a dependent one. Howe privatized Canadair and A.V. Roe, but still used them as instruments of the government's policy goal of self-sufficiency in airframe production. He dismantled and sold Research Enterprises Ltd (REL), an optics research and production firm, because it was of no strategic interest to the government. This last decision heralded a major turning point in Canadian research and development and accelerated the "brain drain" of researchers to the United States.

TYPES OF PUBLIC ENTERPRISE

By 1951, there were only 56 federal Crown corporations left in Canada. Thirty years later, that figure had climbed to 464. Twenty-three were wholly-owned by the Government of Canada, 25 were *mixed* enterprises (or joint ventures with the private sector), 213 were subsidiaries, and the remaining 126 were administrative agencies.[6] (See **Figure 8–1** for a depiction of these federal Crown Corporations.) The Department of Finance reported in 1984 that since 1968, the federal government had created a new corporation at the rate of one every three months.

Technically, according to the *Financial Administration Act*, federal Crown corporations are "ultimately accountable, through a Minister to Parliament." In practice, however, where a share structure exists, the federal government's shares of a Crown corporation are held by a cabinet minister in trust. Shareholder rights and prerogatives are exercised by that minister on behalf of the government. Budgets and annual reports are tabled in Parliament for information only.

Today, Crown corporations can be classified within one of six categories of public enterprise listed in ascending order of managerial autonomy: departmental, agency, special operating agency, proprietary, mixed enterprise, or investment management.

Departmental Crown corporations are strictly administrative and do not produce any goods or services. The Atomic Energy Control Board, Economic Council of Canada (now disbanded), and National Research Council are examples of departmental corporations. They can regulate or advise, but are less autonomous than a special purpose body *per se*.

Agency corporations are more autonomous than departmental corporations, but are still only quasi-commercial. Although they operate as corporations, they are not considered profit centres. Examples of agency corporations are the Canadian Commercial Corporation (which exports Canadian public enterprise expertise), and the Canadian Film Development Corporation.

Special operating agencies (SOAs) are the most recent type of public enterprise and really represent the evolution of government departments into hybrid organizations. They are more commercial than agency corporations but less so than proprietary corporations and still retain some degree of *departmentality*. SOAs are former bureaus or offices that delivered goods or services to external clients that have been carved out of their government departments and set up as stand-alone, bottom-line, arms-length operational units with a customer-focus mandate. There are been several dozen SOAs including the Passport Office, Canada Communications Group (Queen's Printer), Consulting and Audit Canada, Intellectual Property Office, Canadian General Standards Board, and Canadian Grains Commission. The goals in setting up SOAs were: improved performance, increased management flexibility, greater autonomy, and enhanced public service and client satisfaction. But some things have not changed. Although seemingly autonomous, SOAs still operate within a departmental framework with their CEOs reporting to their respective deputy ministers. Further, CEOs are *not* on performance contracts but remain salaried, "tenured," civil servants. Although many are now operating on a full cost-recovery basis, those costs have been recovered primarily through exorbitant user fees being charged for their goods or services with no real business plan in place. One thing is for sure, though: SOA expenditures are now off the government's books.

Proprietary corporations are relatively few, but are the most common in the public's mind. They produce goods and/or services, operate at arms length from the government, and are completely commercial. Air Canada (now privatized), Petro-Canada and Cape Breton Development Corporation are well-known examples of this type of public enterprise. (More about privatization in **Chapter 9**).

Mixed enterprise simply refers to the popular joint ventures between state and business. Here, on the plus side, risk is shared by government and private investors; the corporation benefits from management expertise and technology from both sectors, and it has access to a larger, more diversified source of risk capital. However, mixed enterprise tends strongly to resist following non-commercial policy activities without appropriate compensation from government for losses incurred. Even then, it is less effective as an instrument of social policy than as a "window on the industry," or as a source of revenue. The now defunct Canada Development Corporation was probably the highest-profile example of this genre.

A very successful example of mixed enterprise is Telesat Canada, a world leader in satellite communications. In 1988 Air Canada shares were offered to the public; it was transformed from a wholly government-owned Crown corporation to a mixed-ownership enterprise, and later into a private sector business. More recent examples include Nav Canada (the quasi-privatization of the civil air navigation service) and the Confederation Bridge to Prince Edward Island.

Finally, *investment management corporations* have been established by both federal and provincial governments to manage public pension and insurance funds. Quite often, they possess vast and varied holdings in numerous private-sector corporations. This enables them to reap an above-average rate of return on their funds and generate investment income for other government programs. State investment management corporations are intended to be autonomous. Some, like the Caisse de dépôt et placement du Québec (Canada's largest, with well over $50 billion invested only 30 years after its creation), have made it clear that they are not passive investors, but have every intention of influencing the management of their companies for the betterment of the broader sector (e.g., Quebec). The Caisse is Canada's largest stockholder owning 10% or more of the voting rights in over 100 companies; it is legally classified as an "insider" in a substantial proportion of these companies. The Alberta Heritage Savings Trust Fund, begun in 1976, has financial assets of about $12 billion with little growth; management of the Heritage Fund has been passive compared to that of Quebec.

PRAGMATIC INSTRUMENT OF PUBLIC POLICY

There was a proliferation of Canadian Crown corporations during the 1960s and 1970s. Compared with the policy options of fostering competition or extending economic regulation, governments viewed public enterprise as having a distinct political advantage. A well-run public enterprise should result in wide dispersion of both benefits and costs, whereas with regulation only a small number receive the benefits, with costs spread broadly across the general population. Public enterprise has the capacity to maintain the basic political principle of equity.

Private-sector research and development has been limited in Canada for several reasons:

i. its conservative, mercantilist government policies;

ii. its limited, branch plant economy, wherein research and development is performed in parent companies' home countries;

iii. a lack of domestic risk capital from a conservative, mercantilist banking community; and

iv. a small, unprofitable domestic market.

When expenditures have been made, they have been in research, not commercial development. Governments have sought to bolster technological innovation, often with public enterprises.

Crown corporations therefore became a means to infuse risk capital into the economy and perform research and development. As a result, Canada has been a leader at one time or another in the development of railroad, hydroelectric, pulp and paper, nuclear, and petrochemical technologies. This stimulated Canadian enterprise where there was none previously, safeguarded key sectors of the economy, and earned foreign exchange by exporting these technologies.

Public enterprise has also secured supply and service continuity where the private sector could not profitably do so. For example, several years ago both the CNR's and CPR's tracks were covered by a snowslide in British Columbia's Fraser Canyon. CPR responded by following standard operating procedures — all very bureaucratic and cost-conscious. Government-owned CNR was much more flexible and quicker to respond. CNR's identification with the nation gave it the incentive to serve. When the emergency had passed, CNR had restored service more quickly than CPR, was operating just as efficiently, and had spent no more money than CPR to clear its tracks.

As mentioned earlier, public enterprise has also provided local industrial entrepreneurs with an opportunity to flex their muscles, create wealth, and command industrial companies which would never have been supported by the private sector. More than one disillusioned entrepreneur has moved from the risk-averse business community into the public sector. In fact, a major export of Crown corporations today is Canadian Commercial Corporation's sale of industrial/entrepreneurial management technology to foreign governments.

American competitors of Polymer/Polysar predicted its demise once the war was over. What they did not appreciate was its passive vertical integration and the strength it possessed in its ambitious, entrepreneurial managers. Polysar followed the American rules of business, grew, and became a self-sustaining success. *It may have been bureaucratic — any large organization by definition is going to be bureaucratic — but it was not bureaupathetic.*

Finally, public enterprise often has safeguarded the public's interest. In a small domestic market, monopolies are often more efficient than competition. The greater use of assets by monopolies can make a country more competitive internationally in global industries. Canada's general lack of ideological conflict has encouraged government monopolies in those areas requiring high levels of fixed capital investment, such as utilities, transportation, and communications.

However, problems do exist with this instrument of government policy. The most difficult of these to address is the mixture of objectives under which many Crown corporations are forced to operate. These problems involve the pursuit of commercial success while also pursuing public policies to create employment, provide public transportation, or protect the incomes of agricultural producers. Those Crown corporations that have been charged only with being commercially viable have fewer problems in this regard. But the vast majority remain inefficient by private-sector standards because of their mandate to meet government's social priorities.[7]

Given these mixed objectives, evaluating public enterprise's performance becomes very difficult. Business' benchmark of profit has little meaning when measuring a Crown corporation's effectiveness. Profitability is but one of many objectives of public enterprise.

Managerial control is another gray area. Government maintains nominal control of most Crown corporations as sole or major shareholder, with the power to appoint the board of directors and the chief executive officer. In some cases, Crown corporations also operate under legally binding government directives. However, business experience in general (let alone specific to an industry) is not always a prerequisite for appointment. Too often, board appointments are more often forms of patronage or regional representation rather than reflecting good business sense.

What happens, then, when the autonomous management of a Crown corporation with no overseeing body disobeys government? When a Petro-Canada becomes obsessed with becoming a retail giant with little exploration to its credit, despite a mandate to be much less ambitious and far more development-oriented? When a Canada Development Corporation has 80% of its portfolio in resource-related industries because that is where profits will be made, yet its mandate was to stimulate investment in less attractive secondary industries? How does government control its creations when profit takes precedence over social policy? The answer is, not very well.

Finally, financial control is an equally perplexing problem. Parliament grants Crown corporations global budgets by Parliament. Their capital budgets are dealt with separately from their operating budgets. Public enterprise is not required to operate under the same rules of disclosure as are private-sector counterparts. Of the very large number of Crown corporations in **Figure 8–1**, only a minority are clearly designated as such. These fall under the financial management and general accountability provisions of the *Financial Administration Act*, which attempts to control government finances. In short, there is no real financial control or accountability by Crown corporations to the Government of Canada.

Crown corporations have also begun to serve, unwittingly, another purpose. Like statutory regulatory agencies, they have become a target of public outcry against poorly conceived or carried out public policies. These corporations, and politicians, take the heat for government policy failures. However, one ought to be careful in criticizing the management of Crown corporations. For instance, Petro-Canada was sharply criticized by the business community for its grossly overpriced purchase of Petrofina in 1981. It is true that Petrofina was overpriced, but so was everything else. In early 1981, the Toronto Stock Exchange Industrial Index traded around 4400. Later that year, it rose to 5200. By mid-1982, it had dropped by almost 50%. Petro-Canada paid too much for Petrofina, the Bay paid too much for Simpsons, Dome Petroleum paid too much for Hudson Bay Oil and Gas and Cyprus Anvil Mine, Noranda paid too much for Macmillan Bloedel, and so on. In fact, of the $35 billion worth of takeovers in 1981, half was lost within a year of acquisition. Private industry should note that "those...in glass houses...."

POLICY DRIVERS — NATIONALIZATION

What are the imperatives that drive government policy? A subset of that very large question is to ask the question of government ownership of business (*nationalization*) and of government getting out of business (*privatization* — see **Chapter 9**). As they are enumerated, a surprise is that the drivers are so similar. A lesson (fully explored in the next chapter) will be to suggest that *the same drivers lead to opposite policies when the circumstances differ sufficiently*.

As noted earlier, public ownership of business activity can come about in several ways. *Nationalization* as a process would imply a change of ownership. Some examples are forced purchases of utilities by government, such as in some Provincial jurisdictions (e.g., BC Hydro) in Canada; other examples are commercial transactions either from a single private owner (e.g., Edmonton Telephones) or a widely held purchase of shares (e.g., PWA). Nationalization as a current state of ownership also can be the result of government ownership from inception (e.g., Edmonton Power, Atomic Energy of Canada). While not included in the meaning of nationalization, there have been many examples of partial public ownership: Syncrude and Alberta Energy Company are two.

Ideology

The body politic includes those that believe all business activities should be public ones; each and all engaged activities (including business) must be for social purposes rather than private profit. It is taken as self evident that public ownership, especially within a democracy, will serve society more effectively than the private sector alternative.

Today this thinking is in retreat. The "British disease" failure of democratic socialism, and more recently the monumental failure of undemocratic socialism (Communism) in Eastern Europe, have been revealing. But it must be noted that this ideology could again be a formidable force; its true believers often are zealots awaiting the next opportunity. In a democracy the true test is whether the moderate majority of a society can become convinced it is better. This ideology is best forestalled by socially responsible business sectors demonstrating fully and consistently that their societies are well served by private entrepreneurship. Seminars on this last point, by the Van Horne Institute and others, make a helpful contribution. But business needs to be ever vigilant. As always, actions speak louder than words.

Accountability

A very strong driver for public enterprise is the argument of accountability. The logic is that, with public ownership, there is assured accountability to the shareholder and to society as a tandem and that the "golden rule" is exercised on behalf of the public. This is a compelling argument, albeit it erodes with government using their board appointment prerogatives for political patronage. But what about business behaviour? Does anyone NOT know of some business abuses that would fail the "smell test," especially of public interest? Only a "squeaky clean" reality, that also is transparent can preempt the lure of an accountability driver toward public ownership.

Efficiency

Crown corporation proponents will argue that no efficiency losses are inherent. Rarely will anyone suggest greater efficiency as a driver. Business will normally press this issue, but the general public will have much less ardour. Efficiency will be higher on the public's agenda in difficult economic times such as the 1990s. The strategy of public ownership proponents will be to downplay economic efficiency aspects, and posit that any such losses (e.g., high union wages) are well worth it for the attendant social gains.

Financing

The financing of projects or enterprises incorporates risk-taking. (See the Edmonton Telephones [EDTEL] case as an example.) The general case is that there are many needs of society which MUST be accomplished whether they can be privately financed or not, that is, be provided despite risks that can mean the private sector cannot or will not provide the needed item. Megaprojects virtually never are built without some form of risk-sharing with government(s). However, most examples relate to infrastructure: railways, cross-country highways, tidewater ports, utility installations, shipping channels, bridges/tunnels, and airports. Due to Canada's geographic enormity and population sparsity, a higher proportion of infrastructure provision (e.g., compared with the US or Western Europe) is by government in Canada. The private/public joint financing arrangements can create feasibility for essential projects. Even though both business and government have abused these arrangements, the fundamental point remains. Among the range of other risk-sharing policy instruments (e.g., direct grants, interest rate concessions, guaranteed loans), often governments have decided instead on ownership. Nationalization is undertaken.

Episodal

There are empirical cases from world that do not fit any of the above drivers toward nationalization. There can be a particular circumstance that drives government ownership; indeed, it can occur despite the foregoing drivers. There may be many examples from various jurisdictions in Canada (WW II was mentioned earlier), but here are two Alberta examples.

PWA purchase/nationalization

This 1973 decision by the Alberta Government was NOT driven by any of the enumerated four above. The context was proactive policies for regional (i.e., Alberta) economic development, but the real driver was a threat. PWA was a growing regional airline centred in Calgary; its success had a spinoff benefit for Alberta's aspiration as Gateway to the North. The Progressive Conservative (PC) government of Alberta came to fear that the NDP government of British Columbia might purchase PWA, jeopardizing significant Alberta-based economic activity. The Alberta decision was to preempt the potential loss by an expeditious purchase of (nearly all) outstanding shares. The action was taken in contrast with the ideological philosophy of the governing PC party. In due course, the BC threat evaporated and PWA was privatized in 1983.

Syncrude

This megaproject was based on publicly-owned natural resources that became subject to the new resource policy as a driver by the new (1971) Alberta government. Initially an ownership position was taken to facilitate small Alberta investors having the opportunity of investing in the economic development of resources owned by them in the form of Crown lands. The indirect mechanism eventually became the Alberta Energy Company to whom the Alberta Government ownership position was assigned. A second driver emerged, the financing one noted above, when one of the four private sector partners dropped out. It did so because Syncrude project cost analysis and engineering was showing that costs were severely underestimated, so that risks and financing were jeopardized. The remaining three private companies felt they could not absorb their own higher costs and risks and also add the portion from the corporation leaving the consortium. Clearly the project would collapse unless rescued by Canadian government(s). Ownership positions were taken by the Alberta, federal and Ontario governments; in addition, Alberta agreed to provide convertible debentures of financial support. The Syncrude project was built during the 1970s and commissioned in 1978. Megaproject lessons and strategies include major public sector involvement and differ from conventional project requirements.

IMPLICATIONS FOR MANAGEMENT

The growth of government, by whatever means, restricts individual and collective freedoms. Yet, true to their heritage, Canadians seem little concerned.

A private-sector business in direct competition with a Crown corporation, however, does have reasons for concern. Public enterprise is not held accountable for its performance by its shareholders, usually pays no taxes, and enjoys easier access to risk capital than do many segments of the business community. Regulations are often skewed to favour Crown corporations or are waived altogether.

Yet, to date federal politicians have not favoured increasing the accountability of public enterprise to Parliament. This may be due to the implicit design of Crown corporations to distance elected officials from the implementation of public policy by public enterprise. In some cases, government-owned enterprise may actually enhance competitive market situations.

On the other hand, economists see private corporations, operating in a highly regulated environment, as less concerned with competition, their customers, productivity, efficiency, and managing technological change than their less-regulated peers. *Compared to regulated companies in regulated industries, some Crown corporations often appear downright aggressive and entrepreneurial.* While 80% of business success is based upon "doing the right things," such as meeting and beating the competition, most Crown corporations are preoccupied with "doing things right." They are sensitive to public scrutiny and criticism. They take their social policy mandates seriously. And given their efforts to achieve these social policy ends, they are efficient and productive.

As a result, public enterprise incorporates right-wing and left-wing political ideology into a pragmatic ethos which has won over public opinion time and time again. Canada's public enterprise culture reflects a collective, organic heritage and a passive desire for nominal, economic, and political independence.

Americans have had a genius for modern private enterprise; Canadians have had a genius for modern public enterprise. Canada *is* different, and it is futile to compare it to an American model to determine what works best.[8] *Canadian nationalism is concurrently the cause and the result of its public enterprise culture.*

If John Kenneth Galbraith is correct, ownership no longer matters. It is professional management that charts the course of enterprise today (recall the Visible Hand of Business from **Chapter 4**). And it is the behaviour of corporations, not its ownership, that has an impact upon Canadians' daily lives and national best interest. In that respect, government ownership is in the same category as foreign ownership. Public enterprise, like foreign-owned enterprise, is no more environmentally conscious than its Canadian-owned private-sector counterparts. Its research and development expenditures are no higher; prices are no lower, and so on. On the other hand, public enterprise, like foreign enterprise, fills market gaps with goods and services which local private capital is not interested in providing or cannot do so profitably.

The problem with all this is the **cost**. Billions of dollars are spent each year by the Government of Canada to subsidize most Crown corporations, commercial or not. If this expense were somehow eliminated, the federal government's so-called "deficit" would be considerably reduced. Theoretically, the costs of subsidizing Crown Corporations is more than offset by tax revenues collected from the economic activity generated by them. But, with a multiplier of 1.0 or 1.5 today, diminishing returns from rising tax rates and growing debt loads, the theory no longer works.

Can privatization be a successful public management strategy? Certainly, it was successful in the postwar years and from mid-1980s to 1996. Once privatized, Crown corporations can still remain instruments closely tied to government policy, such as the aircraft industry, both after the war and today.

It remains to be seen if there are any more Crown corporations of interest to the private sector. If so, privatization offers business an unique three-way opportunity. It will serve the nation, help government emerge from its crippling financial burden, and make a profit. Anything business can do to help government meet its economic and social policy goals will surely improve business-government relations in this country.

SUGGESTED FURTHER READINGS

Baumol, W.J., (ed). 1980. *Public and Private Enterprise in a Mixed Economy*. New York: St. Martin's Press.

Borins, Sandford F. 1982. "World War II Crown Corporations: Their War-time Role and Peacetime Privatization." *Canadian Public Administration*, 25:3.

Borins, Sandford F. 1982. *Investments in Failure*. Toronto: Methuen.

Brooks, Stephen. 1987. *Who's in Charge? The Mixed Ownership of Corporations in Canada*. Halifax: Institute for Research on Public Policy.

Butt, H.A., and D.R. Palmer. 1985. *Value for Money in the Public Sector*. New York: Basil Blackwell Inc.

Canada Government. 1984. *Treasury Report*. January.

Durham, Lord. 1839. *Report on the Affairs of North America*. Commission Report.

Economic Council of Canada. 1986. *Minding the Public's Business*. Ottawa: Supply and Services Canada.

Financial Post 500. 1997. Investor's Handbook, May.

The Globe & Mail. 1998. "Canada's Power Book." *Report on Business Magazine*, July.

Gordon, M. 1981. *Government in Business*. Montreal: C.D. Howe Institute.

Jenkins, K., K. Caines, and A. Jackson. 1988. *Improving Management in Government: The Next Steps*. London: Her Majesty's Stationery Office.

Kierens, Tom. 1984. "Commercial Crowns." *Policy Options*. Institute for Research on Public Policy, November.

Nankivell, Neville. 1994. "Crown corporations are at the Crossroads." *Financial Post*, January 25.

Nankivell, Neville. 1994. "Crown corporations in need of better boards." *Financial Post,* July 21.

Prichard, J.R.S., (ed). 1983. *Crown Corporations in Canada: The Calculus of Instrument Choice*. Toronto: Butterworths.

Strong, Maurice. 1984. "The Necessary Private-Public Mix." *Policy Options*, 5:6, November.

Tupper, A., and G. Bruce Doern, (eds). 1981. *Public Corporations and Public Policy in Canada*. Halifax: Institute for Research on Public Policy.

Warrack, Allan A. 1994. "Alberta Heritage Fund: Opportunity to Restructure Toward Sustainable Economic Development." in Sally F. Zerker (ed.), *Change and Impact: Essays in Canadian Social Sciences, International Canadian Studies Conference Proceedings*. Jerusalem: The Magnes Press, The Hebrew University.

NOTES

1. Tom Kierens,"Commercial Crowns," *Policy Options*, Institute for Research on Public Policy (November 1984).

2. *Financial Post 500*, Investor's Handbook (May 1997) and *The Globe & Mail*, "Canada's Power Book," *Report on Business Magazine* (July 1998).

3. Canada Government, *Treasury Report* (January 1994)

4. Lord Durham, *Report on the Affairs of North America*, Commission Report (1839).

5. Sandford F. Borins, "World War II Crown Corporations: Their Wartime Role and Peacetime Privatization," Canadian Public Administration, 25:3 (1982).

6. In 1980, the Comptroller-General of Canada prepared a comprehensive listing of federal enterprises. This had never been done before, nor since.

7. Note the sub-section "social discount rate" in **Chapter 4**.

8. It is only natural, though, for a colony to try to imitate the culture of its metropole.

Chapter

9

CANADIAN CROWN CORPORATIONS: PRIVATIZATION

"Markets are not perfect but the alternative is worse."

The Economist, October 7, 1995

Government has a gradient of public policy choices. The gradient ranges from the least-possible "softball" degree of influence to the fullest "hardball" exercise of government power. The pace of government action also can range from phasing to blunt change. And the consultation with those affected can be zero or extensive. Timing, relative to elections or other major events/issues, is always pivotal.

WHAT IS PRIVATIZATION?

Privatization is the undoing of previous *nationalization* whereupon Crown corporations were formed. The policy choice that is strongest or harshest for government to choose is the forced ownership disposition and thus nationalization of a business enterprise; this is how several of the provincial Crown utilities were formed. In other cases (e.g., Edmonton Telephones, PWA) market-based, commercial purchases were made from private shareholder(s). In other cases, Crown ownership was the basis upon which a public enterprise was initially formed. A softer version of public enterprise occurs when government ownership is partial ownership from inception; some examples are Alberta Gas Trunk Line (AGTL, now NOVA Corporation) and Alberta Energy Company (AEC). The point here is that ownership-by-government has proven to be a practical policy choice; that choice has been made by governments of all political stripes in virtually every major Canadian governance jurisdiction.

At the other end of the policy gradient from Crown enterprise is government efforts and programs to foster competition in the marketplace. Canada has had competition legislation under the Criminal Code since 1889; in 1986 the legislation was revised and important provisions were moved to the Civil Code. Beyond laws to prohibit "restraint of trade," all jurisdictions have competition-enhancing standards and programs to enhance the extent and effectiveness of market competition so that harsher measures by government are unnecessary. The notion of workable competition suggests that oligopoly markets of a few (five-nine) competitors are likely to deliver acceptably well on the foregoing economic objectives to serve the public interest. Reliance on market competition also has proven to be a practical policy choice of governments in various Canadian jurisdictions.

Between the policy choice extremes of Crown ownership and of fostering greater competition lies *economic regulation* (see **Chapter 11** for a more extensive discussion). Where natural monopoly exists, (e.g., utilities) competition is impractical, and virtually all agree such monopolies must be subject to government regulation. Much has been written about economic regulation in Canada comparing merits of Average and Marginal Cost Pricing; economic regulation bodies and processes must be diligent to keep up with dynamic complexities of modern business and new approaches such as price-cap regulation. Early enterprise nationalizations tended to be initiated as substitutes for regulation by government under the "golden rule" (who has the gold makes the rules). Over time an interesting phenomenon has developed whereupon public enterprise corporations became subject to similar regulatory requirements as private corporations. In these cases the result is *both* nationalization and economic regulation, surely an overextension of the visible hand of government *{V(G)}*. Current Canadian mainstream thinking has come to recognize that our modern economy is over-regulated in many ways and imposes an needlessly heavy burden on our ability to compete effectively in the global economy.

Each of the three policy choices of nationalization, competition, and regulation has been practical in most Canadian jurisdictions of governance. But the mix of these policies vary. Efforts are being made to reduce the costs and delays burdens of economic regulation; currently the pace of privatization actions greatly exceeds that of nationalization. Thus the mix of policies is changing significantly.

PRIVATIZATION OF PUBLIC ASSETS[1]

One of the additions to the vocabulary of public management during the 1980s was the term *privatization*. It refers to the transfer of activities and/or assets from the public to the private sector. Such transfers can take several forms. In Canada, privatization can refer to:

i.   *Liquidation*: government sale of a state-owned enterprise to the private sector, as was done with the Canada Development Corporation, de Havilland Aircraft of Canada Ltd., Canadair Ltd., Teleglobe Canada, Air Canada and Polysar;

ii. *Subsidization*: government provision of grants to non-profit organizations for public services, such as day care and home care;

iii. *Nation-building*: government franchising of a private company exclusively to provide a geographical area with a certain service, as was done with the provision of transportation services to the North; and *iv. Contracting-out*: government retention of responsibility for providing a service, but hiring a private contractor to deliver it, as with municipal waste collection and snow removal.

One answer to the problems inherent in public enterprise is to get rid of it — that is, to privatize Crown corporations. Strong arguments can be made for privatizing a state-owned business, although some may not apply in all cases. The first is *undercapitalization* of the public sector. As in the private sector, Crown corporations and government services require capital to modernize and expand. However, within government these enterprises must compete with other public services, as well as with government support of private business, for a limited amount of public funds. Second, the public sector is often *less efficient* in business because it is frequently protected by a monopoly position — whether natural or artificial — and thus lacks the incentive to operate efficiently. And its economic efficiency may be constrained by government imposing non-economic policies. Finally, public enterprise is often *unresponsive* to the market because its customers are a captured entity. Some Crown corporations became more like bureaucracy itself, immune to feedback but "tenured." Although many Crown corporations *are* profitable *and* meet their social obligations, collectively, federally owned Crown corporations have not been profitable since 1981. There are as many reasons for this as there are Crown corporations.

In 1985, eight Crown corporations were terminated.[2] During 1985-88, 24 more were privatized for a net total of $5 billion. Any effort to privatize a government service successfully will depend upon:

i.   establishing strong political leadership;

ii. assuring comprehensive advance planning, with clear criteria to weigh public benefits against public costs of choosing suitable candidates for privatization;

iii. involving business and organized labour in the process of privatization initiatives;

iv. encouraging employee ownership;

v.   including objective measurement of the level and cost of service before and after privatization; and

vi. beginning with companies or services that will make the easiest transition to the private sector so that the process will be constructive rather than disillusioning.

The federal government has not scored well on these points. A 1988 study by the Office of Privatization and Regulatory Affairs (OPRA) criticized the government for a "perceived lack of direction, control, and political will," with no one clearly in charge. The privatization process of 1985 to 1988 was plagued with long negotiating delays, poor communication between the government and employees of the companies sold, and a failure to sell the public on its ambitious and controversial scheme. The report also criticized several cabinet ministers for "spreading misinformation" and fumbling their public-relations role. Yet, despite these weaknesses, the same report claimed that "all companies report improved commercial potential, increased access to capital markets and product markets, and increased opportunity to compete aggressively." Quite revealing, given our earlier assumptions about the role and advantages of government ownership.

When the federal Cabinet met in Alberta in early 1988, its attitude towards privatization had changed. At that meeting, the Cabinet realized that the remaining 400 or so Crown corporations either:

i. were not at all profitable and therefore not saleable;

ii. had no commercial future and therefore were not saleable;

iii. provided government with much-needed revenue and therefore were too profitable to sell; *or*

iv. were well-liked by the public, which opposed their privatization.

Cabinet also was advised that divestment in the then bearish market would not be practical. The federal government also realized that the 315 or so commercial Crown corporations employed over 260 000 workers — more than the federal government's total departmental staff. As jobs would be lost with privatization, it would not occur if guaranteed, continued employment was a term of sale. And jobs mean votes.

In 1990, the federal privatization initiative resumed with the biggest sale yet — the incremental sell off of Petro-Canada. Political pragmatism (waiting for a bull market) prevailed once again. Meanwhile, remaining Crown corporations extended their reach into the national economy and acquired even more subsidiaries. *As a result, the net equity base of federal state enterprise under privatizing Prime Ministers Mulroney and Chretien actually has increased!*

Before the decision to privatize is made, it is vital to define success so as to measure the impact of privatization. A successful privatization strategy should result in at least the following:

i. a level of service at least as good, if not better than, that provided by government; and

ii. a lower cost of service than when the service was provided by government, with a discernible trend towards even lower costs.

Liberal Finance Minister Paul Martin has recognized Crown corporations' problems of accountability, misallocation of scarce capital, and that commercially-oriented Crown corporations inhibit the growth of Canadian private enterprise.[3] Current federal policies reflect the recognition of these problems and the role of the privatization process to relieve them. In 1996, AECL Theratronics International (maker of cancer therapy equipment) and federal shares of National Sea Products Ltd. of Halifax were put on the block. At the time of writing, the federal government was privatizing the national air navigation system (Nav Canada), federally-owned grain cars, major federally-owned airports, CN Rail (tranches in 1995 and 1996), CN Real Estate, some SOAs, and the St. Lawrence Seaway for a hoped-for total of $45 billion. (See footnote 3 in **Chapter 2**). Via Rail and Atomic Energy of Canada Ltd. (AECL) remain privatization candidates if valid buyers and prices manifest themselves.

Ontario was planning to sell the Liquor Control Board of Ontario, (the world's largest purchaser of beverage alcohol with 1995-96 *profits* of $680 million) as Alberta has done, Ontario Hydro (North America's largest electric utility), and TV Ontario for $40 billion or more. Manitoba was privatizing Manitoba Telephones for $750 million. And Alberta sold its investment in Syncrude Canada Ltd. for $352 million. While not strictly a Crown corporation, it is notable that Saskatchewan Wheat Pool is offering shares to the public.

Especially among electric utilities, there are many future privatization possibilities by provinces from Atlantic Canada to Quebec to the Prairies and British Columbia. Several sizeable municipal utilities continue as public enterprise such as North York Hydro, Winnipeg Hydro and Calgary Electric.

Table 9–1 lists, from among Canada's "Top 500" and "Next 250," those public enterprises (federal, provincial, and municipal) that could be privatized in the future. As well, there are significant Crown financial institutions. It is to be noted that this list is only from the largest 750 companies, so smaller public enterprises and subsidiaries are not included. An example is the Canada Lands Company Ltd., a Federal Crown Corporation which manages and/or disposes of certain surplus federal lands on behalf of the government.

TABLE 9–1   Potential Canada Privatizations

Top 750 Revenue Ranking	Federal	Provincial	Municipal
Top 50	4	3	Nil
51-100	Nil	2	Nil
101-150	Nil	1	Nil
151-200	1	3	1
201-250	Nil	3	Nil
251-300	2	1	3
301-350	2	2	3
351-400	Nil	1	Nil
401-450	1	Nil	Nil
451-500	Nil	Nil	1
501-550	Nil	1	Nil
551-600	Nil	1	2
601-650	2	1 (NWT)	Nil
651-700	Nil	1	Nil
701-750	Nil	Nil	1
TOTALS	12	20	11
Top Financial Institutions			
Top 50	4	3	Nil
51-100	Nil	1	Nil
GRAND TOTALS	16	24	11

Source: *The Financial Post 500*, May 1996.

The data yields two firm conclusions: there remains a vast potential in Canada for future privatization actions by government, and many of these are at the provincial and municipal/civic levels of government. Among the top 750 corporations as ranked by revenue and the top 100 financial institutions as ranked by assets, there are 16 federal, 24 provincial, and 11 local government enterprises that, theoretically, could be privatized.

If privatization is not a workable solution, an alternative should be sunset laws. (Any legislation incorporating a Crown corporation would require Parliament to review the need for such a corporation every five years or so.) In such a review, a no longer useful Crown corporation could be terminated. Moneylosers not serving a social need could be closed. Moneymakers could be sold, returning at least some of the public's investment. The rest? Well, that still requires a weighing of the public interest against the public cost.

PRACTICAL BUSINESS CONCEPTS

There are applicable business concepts with respect to privatization.[4] As well, it is essential to recognize that government policies can be instrumental in facilitating or thwarting a privatization initiative. Economics, finance, and business-government relations are all pivotal to the success or failure of privatization efforts.

Ownership Duality
Ownership includes not one but two dimensions. Property ownership and conferred benefits is a familiar component; the second component is risk(s) associated with the property. This business concept applies whether the property is an ordinary commodity, a physical structure, a professional credential, or an on-going business. Certainly it applies to a Crown enterprise. An inherent ownership responsibility is handling the risks, which may range from very small to very large, that are concurrent with any property ownership. Most of us have had cars that "nickel and dime" (now more like "hundred dollar") their owner, with attendant uncertainties of performance at critical times (like Canadian winter mornings). Many people change cars because the risk liabilities have come to outweigh the property benefits. Lots of common-sense examples can come to mind — like a remote lake cabin that always needs something fixed! Continued ownership may not be worth it.

Technological change is dynamic and is facilitating new competitive opportunities. Technology is embedded in capital facilities, so a competitive investment profile is imperative. Typically the needed profile is characterized by investments that are large, quick, clustered, and risky. An owner must be able to "step up to" the investment profile or lose market share to competitors who can. Most Canadian governments are in the financial straight-jacket of deficits/DEBTS, so they cannot meet the investment profile proscribed herein. If the private sector can, then why not the public sector?

Risk Commodity
Risk can be packaged, bought, and sold, like potatoes or any other commodity (even hockey players). Insurance transforms uncertainties into risks, for a price known as the premium. Often insurance risks are packaged and resold to insurance underwriters, again for a negotiated price. Like commodities, risks can be managed; few larger organizations today fail to have risk management as an integral operation. Risk mitigation strategies are vital in today's business or government. Risks can be identified and lessened through prudent management; some of the residual risks can be insured. Certain large risks, including business risks, may remain as liabilities beyond the capacity for owner(s) to sustain. Business may seek partners, or sell a property and concurrently remove the risk. The described actions supply risk to the commercial marketplace for risks.

But is there matching demand in the Canadian marketplace for more property ownership including its attendant risks? For privatization actions to succeed, the answer to this critical question must be *yes*. Investment bankers and potential purchasers assess this question for the relevant markets. Privatization can occur by direct purchase transaction or by an Initial

Public Offering (IPO). There are funds that manage savings of Canadians for longer-term gains needing more risk; attendant to the risk profile is the prospect for larger future gains, especially capital gains, in funds' portfolio value. A factor in the analysis is Canadian tax law wherein preferred tax treatment is allowable only if a threshold proportion of a fund's investments is Canadian. Privatization becomes a "deal" when a Crown business is worth less to its government owner than to a private sector purchaser.

Business-Government Relations

Inherent in any privatization is the intersection of public and private interests. Even though the business case may be there (according to the principles above), much more is necessary for a succesful completion of a privatization. The selling government must be capable of the disposition decision and in the applicable window of time; the purchasing private-sector entity (direct or partner or IPO) must be capable of the acquisition decision and in the same applicable window of time. As well as each managing internal decision making, the intersection of business-government decision making must be successful and timely. Typically at least two levels of government will be involved, even if only through respective provincial securities commissions. Then business-government relations with more than one government are involved in addition to government-government relations.

There are always more ways to resist change than to promote change. And no major change is devoid of disadvantages, at least in the eyes of some stakeholders and voters. *The importance of positive, cordial, and strategic business-government relations cannot be overstressed*. For the privatization process, it is a business principle. Even in the privatization of a midsized company, such as the ED TEL case in this book, the complexity of three levels of government intersected with at least eight business-government decisions.[5]

POLICY DRIVERS — PRIVATIZATION

As the preceding data demonstrates, a powerful pattern of privatization has developed in Canada. In part, this situation occurs because there is so much to privatize. Britain led the shift to privatization in the 1980s. Canada and some provincial governments undertook privatization initiatives starting in the 1980s and accelerating up to 1996. Inevitably political battles were the context for privatization decisions and implementation. Ontario is the new battleground. Full or partial federal privatizations into the commercial marketplace have included such venerable entities as Air Canada, Petro-Canada and CN Rail. Alberta has been aggressive; PWA, AGT, liquor distribution, and many and varied public services have been privatized. Other provinces and cities have been quietly disposing of Crown assets and activities. Why the privatization push?

Ideology

The body politic includes those that believe virtually all activities ought to be in the private sector "no matter what," conceding perhaps defence and policing. (Formerly this short list would include the post office!). It is taken as self-evident that superior wealth generation will include spinoffs that look after social needs to an acceptable level. A wide spectrum of the Canadian public may be concerned that "no matter what" can be unacceptably ugly. Ironically, American writers Osborne and Gaebler caution "Privatization is ONE answer, not THE answer;"[6] privatization is one arrow in the government's quiver, but should not be advocated on ideological grounds. Osborne and Gaebler note that business does some things better than government, but government does some things better than business.

Ideology is a powerful imperative toward privatization, usually seeking a substantial change in the mix of activities rather than extreme results. As we know, Canada is a mixed economy. Today the clear Canadian pattern is towards a change in that mix with fewer things being done by the public sector and more by the private sector, thus opening expanded business opportunities.

Accountability

This is the most difficult driver for privatization proponents. It is very hard to argue that private sector activity is more accountable to the public than government control. While public benevolence can be argued, it also must be recognized that shareholder interests must be the top priority; pragmatic considerations also should give higher priority to customers and employees. Accountability advantages of public ownership erodes when there is political abuse such as patronage appointments. Whether valid or not, there is understandable anxiety about undue influence in what should be commercial business decisions; are the Alberta Heritage Savings and Trust Fund and Alberta Treasury Branches examples? Notwithstanding these concerns, public perception may feel "calling to account" is more reliable with public rather than private ownership.

The key point on accountability is for private sector corporations and business to earn the trust and credibility of their public(s). An important aspect of this strategy is to avoid direct confrontations with government; when "push comes to shove" government is highly likely to win. Effective and positive business/government relations are vital. A further strategy is to recognize that the accountability driver contains risks; this driver should not be isolated, but rather bundled with winning drivers such as efficiency and financing.

Efficiency

This is a winning driver for privatization over nationalization. Despite the best of intentions, for many reasons public-sector decision making is slower, more risk averse, and less certain to decide. Bad intentions make it even worse. The advantage of private-sector decision making is magnified when decisions must be larger, quicker, and risk-laden to keep up with changes in the modern global economy. A further efficiency advantage of privatization is that when government has fewer things to do, it has the opportunity to do each and all of them better. Pursuing the strategy of bundling efficiency with accountability, a strong case can be made that society is better off when policy reality recognizes *both* considerations.

Financing

Financing was identified in **Chapter 8** as a driver towards a policy of nationalization; in this section financing is identified as a driver towards a policy of privatization. Why the apparent anomaly? The previous section noted that the financing of projects or enterprises incorporates risk taking, and that in the past some governments assisting with financing would choose outright ownership. Often the path to such nationalization would result from government having greater financial capacity than the private sector. But by the 1990s most Canadian governments had "pre-spent the future."[7]

Today governments' decision making in Canada are severely constrained by their debts and deficits. Overspending during the 1970s and 1980s has created "compound-interest hell" in Canada for the 1990s and beyond. Moreover, bond-rating services recognize that Crown corporation debt is guaranteed by the owner (government) and must be reflected as contingent liabilities on the balance sheets and in their credit-worthiness. Some publicly owned utilities have debt levels approaching 90% of capital structure. Governments in dire financial straits are not in a position to initiate nationalization steps. The essential point is that government intrusion into private sector activity is stalled if financing (usually more borrowing) is difficult to achieve or justify politically in the face of other expenditure pressures.

Privatization can offer some relief from government financial pressures. There are three financing drivers toward privatization. One is that the private sector may be in a stronger position than governments to finance projects/enterprises that should go forward in the larger interest of society. Another is that removal of contingent liabilities can improve credit rating and permit cheaper future financing. The final financing driver is that privatization, via whole or partial disposition of Crown-owned assets, can provide revenues to the cash-strapped public sector. Financing is an exceedingly strong driver toward privatization when governments are hard-pressed fiscally; just as government wealth, even if only perceived, is a driver toward nationalization.

The strong linkage of drivers #1, **Ideology** and #4, **Financing**, must be noted. A government that philosophically believes in a larger public sector will probably drive towards nationalization if it believes it can afford it. Often such a government is succeeded by one that philosophically believes in a smaller public sector, and its policy approach may also be constrained by an inheritance of fiscal problems due to overspending. Similarly, a fiscally prudent government can accumulate financial capacity (cash or "slack") and become a political target for a freer-spending alternative.

LESSONS AND ISSUES

In this century until the 1980s, Canadian commerce became more and more nationalized. This situation is especially true for the transportation sector of the economy. The trend has reversed toward privatization and it is instructive to analyze the reasons why. Is it a fad? Or are there substantive reasons that are reliable indicators for the future? **Table 9–2** depicts the nationalization and privatization drivers in an effort to reveal useful lessons from the Canadian experience to date. The suggested set of drivers are listed, and their likely impacts on privatization or nationalization are evaluated. It is important to recognize that applicable government policy is a mix of drivers weighed differently at different times and in differing circumstances.

Interpreting **Table 9–2**, it can be seen that *accountability* considerations will reliably favour nationalization. And *efficiency* will favour privatization. But the magnitude of each drive will likely vary, and is not likely to be offset in a given time frame. If corporations lose credibility with the public because of their actions/attitudes/behaviour/ethics, voters may insist that the government "do something" and questionable decisions can be the result. In difficult economic times such as the 1990s, the public is more likely to agree with economic competitiveness priorities and tolerate more accountability misgivings. A further interpretative point here is that a certain segment of society will always and more strongly demand nationalization on *ideology* grounds; even though the segment resisting it may be larger, it is not likely to have as strong and consistent an ideological thrust. Strong minority views can prevail, in ripe circumstances, when the larger but weaker majority views are not as vigilant. Both ideology drives will be omnipresent, but not with the same strength and consistency, so political results can differ in varying circumstances and time eras.

TABLE 9-2	Nationalization/Privatization Policy Drivers (1990s)		
Nationalization		**Privatization**	
Ideology	= (+ / −)	Ideology	= (− / +)
Accountability	= (+)	Accountability	= (−)
Efficiency	= (−)	Efficiency	= (+)
Financing	= (− ; formerly +)	Financing	= (+ ; formerly −)
Episodal	= (+)	Other	= (?)

The financing "driver" provides particularly intriguing analysis and results. It clearly seems to be the strongest impetus of all. **Table 9–3** is a decision matrix that examines the interface of financial strength and ideology. In that figure, the indication is that financially strong governments may initiate nationalizations. Nationalizations will occur under left-leaning governments if they can afford it; they may occur, usually in the context of some unusual circumstance, even if a government is right-leaning. The formation of the CBC and the PWA purchases were done by Conservative administrations; BC Hydro came about during a Social Credit era. Privatizations will not take place under left-leaning governments, despite financial difficulties. Privatizations under right-leaning political leadership are unlikely in times of financial strength but probable in periods of financial stringency; an initiative to privatize liquor distribution in Alberta failed during the booming 1970s but succeeded in the 1990s.

TABLE 9-3	Linkage of Financial Strength and Ideology		
	Nationalization(N)/Privatization(P)		
		Financial Strength	
		Strong	**Weak**
	Left	N = Yes	N = Maybe
		P = No	P = Unlikely
Ideology	**Right**	N = Maybe	N = No
		P = Unlikely	P = Yes

Scanning the financial strength vectors, one can readily see that fiscally weak governments are least likely to get involved in the commercial economy, and are most likely to extricate themselves from same. The analysis supports the body of thought that *the only way to keep a government from getting too large is to starve it financially*; those with egalitarian instincts will see the difficulty of that approach. There is commentary that suggests governments have not changed so much, but rather that their circumstances (especially financial) have changed and forced different patterns of behaviour and policy.[8] One must recognize that the empirical world does not divide so neatly for either ideology or finances. There are gradients between extremes of the ideology paradigm (Red Tories and Blue Liberals) and of financial strength.

The primary lesson about privatization is that circumstances, not the underlying philosophy, have changed. The circumstances are financial. A positive aspect of the dire financial circumstances of Canadian governments is that business is now paying attention; apathy and acquiescence cast a powerful shadow in the form of what happens while you are preoccupied with other matters. Business, especially sectors vulnerable to regulation and potential nationalizations pursuant to the "Consent Doctrine," must participate fully and continuously in the governance process.[9]

IMPLICATIONS FOR MANAGEMENT

Canada is a mixed economy. Today, the clear Canadian pattern is towards a change in the mix with fewer things being done by the public sector and more by the private sector, thus opening expanded business opportunities. There have been virtually *no* nationalizations over the last two decades. Yet governments in Canada now own and operate many public enterprises. The federal government still owns about 50 corporate entities that have over 100 subsidiaries and 80 other corporate interests and control or have equity in about 200 more enterprises, not to mention SOAs. As noted in this chapter, provinces and municipalities own literally thousands of entities that could be privatized. It is highly likely that future privatizations will take place federally and in certain provinces, especially Ontario and Alberta. Several Atlantic Canada privatization actions already have taken place. Business can look into the new century and expect few nationalization actions by Canadian governments, but privatization is likely to proceed in most jurisdictions.

Why is privatization in vogue? What are the advantages and disadvantages, and what are the issues that are likely to drive future outcomes? An effort has been made to address these matters, with some expected results and others that may be surprising. A conclusion is suggested that privatization is primarily a result of government *financial* circumstances in Canada, rather than a deeply imbedded change in philosophy. A change in the identified circumstance could stall the privatization process, and even permit future nationalizations in some jurisdictions.

Left-leaning governments will resist privatization strongly, but even right-leaning ones will be reluctant unless pressed by financial stringency. Even if a particular government prefers privatization, every agenda has a ranking of priorities and the top spots are highly competitive. The pace of change matters; unless a new government pursues privatization early in its mandate it can become stalled by the "iron triangle" of special interests/short-term political imperatives/bureaucracy.[10] Sufficient delay of alternatives is tantamount to acceptance of the status quo.

Due diligence is needed by business, especially sectors such as transportation, to forestall adverse government decisions. Impeccable performance, including both commercial and corporate citizenship results, is the best instrument to preempt nationalization. While ideology matters, and financial strength matters even more, accountability and efficiency matter too. Business needs to avoid gaffes that erode public credibility. Overcoming mistrust and contempt are very difficult and take time. Some corporations flaunt their power. Accountability to society needs continuous nurturing; when "push comes to shove," public understanding and sympathy can be absolutely vital. As suggested earlier, the accountability driver is a vulnerable one in the privatization/nationalization debate. Thus a great deal of attention in both the general public and governments is needed to prevent accountability from becoming an overriding issue.

Efficiency is a winning driver towards privatization. First, ensure that it is true, then transparently demonstrate the efficiency advantage. Economic efficiency is a basis for capital reinvestment, job opportunity growth, and community betterment. Whatever the government ideology and financial circumstance, the odds of privatization are improved greatly when efficiency is emphasized with positive results and the issues of accountability need not be a major concern to the public.

Surprises are minimized when working relationships between government and business are continuous and constructive. Even if a disagreeable government policy is forthcoming, positive consultation instead of cynicism can minimize problems and brighten the odds of change or even reversal. Effective business-government relations can lessen the odds of unhappy episodes and surprises. Business can assist government by supporting privatization policies both in general terms and in applicable specific cases. And don't overlook the Loyal Opposition. Certain Government of Canada privatizations are underway, but many more could be considered. Many privatizations could also be considered in each province and many municipalities. A clearer understanding of privatization principles and issues should enhance the future prospects of more extensive implementation in Canada.

Business in Canada should recognize the privatization trend as harbouring vast business opportunities. Enterprises run well by government should be run just as well by the private sector; among those not well-run, applying business principles and management techniques may achieve turnarounds. Privatization, changing a public-funded, government-run organization into a profit-motivated, private company, is not simple.[11] Major challenges await both government and business(es) involved, but with attractive opportunities as well. *Some of Canada's future business successes will be due to managing the privatization process well, and making good on delivery of private-sector energy and innovation for public good.*

Managing business-government relations goes in tandem with privatization activity. Even simply by way of the transaction, there is an interface. Often more than one level of government is involved. Moreover, it is usual for tax and regulatory provisions to require decisions by one or more levels of government. Managing the process successfully requires that *all* these decisions be achieved, and in the *same* time frame. Matching the vagaries of private market financing and government timely decision making is a challenge to the very best of managers and leaders.

SUGGESTED FURTHER READINGS

Canada West Foundation. 1995. *Red Ink III: Understanding Government Finances, 1990-95*. Calgary, AB, August.

Canada Statues. 1986. *The Competition Act, 1986*. Ottawa: Supply and Services Canada.

Dobni, Dawn, Brooke Painter, and Marvin Painter. 1996. "Navigating the Route to Privatization." *Business Quarterly*, 60:3, Spring.

The Economist. 1995. "The Myth of the Powerless State." October 7.

Financial Post. 1996. "FP 500: An Investors' Handbook of Canada's Largest Companies." May.

Friedman, Milton & Rose. 1984. *Tyranny of the Status Quo*. New York: HBJ Publishers.

Gillies, James. 1981. *Where Business Fails*. Halifax: Institute for Research on Public Policy.

Hardin, H. 1989. *The Privatization Putsch*. Halifax: The Institute for Research on Public Policy.

Martin, Paul E. 1984. "Why and How to Privatize." *Policy Options*, March/April, 5:2.

Osborne, David, and Ted Gaebler. 1992. *Reinventing Government*. Don Mills, ON: Addison-Wesley.

Richardson, J. (ed). 1990. *Privatisation and Deregulation in Canada and Britain*. Halifax: The Institute for Research on Public Policy.

Savas, E.S. 1985. *Privatization: The Key to Better Government*. Chatham, NJ: Chatham House Publishers Inc.

Taylor, D. Wayne. 1991. *Business and Government Relations: Partners in the 1990s*. Toronto: Gage Educational Publishing.

Tupper, A., and G.B. Doern, (eds). 1988. *Privatization, Public Policy and Public Corporations in Canada*. Halifax: The Institute for Research on Public Policy.

Warrack, Allan A. 1996. *Privatization Case: Edmonton Telephones*. Western Centre for Economic Research Bulletin 35, University of Alberta, February.

NOTES

1. Taylor, *Business and Government Relations*.

2. The terminated Crown corporations were: Canadian Sports Pool, Lotto Canada, Canagrex, Uranium Canada, Mingan Association, Societa San Sebastine, St. Anthony Fisheries Ltd., and CN (West Indies) Steamships.

3. Paul E. Martin, "Why and How to Privatize." *Policy Options*, 5.2 (March/April 1984). Mr. Martin was in the private sector when these remarks were made.

4. Allan A. Warrack, *Privatization Case: Edmonton Telephones*, Western Centre for Economic Research Bulletin 35, University of Alberta (1996).

5. These were city of Edmonton decisions as host, owner*, and regulator; provincial government as source of public-sector pensions* (Local Authorities Pension Plan) decision making; and the federal government sector as telecommunications regulator (CRTC), Revenue Canada* (tax credits), and Industry Canada* (partial integrality of directory operations), and Competition Bureau*. The asterisks "*" indicate "dealkillers;" any one (or more) of five out of eight business-government roles could have been fatal to the privatization decision, singularly or by the totality of lengthy delay.

6. David Osborne and Ted Gaebler, *Reinventing Government* (Don Mills, ON: Addison-Wesley, 1992), 45.

7. Canada West Foundation, *Red Ink III: Understanding Government Finances, 1990-95* (Calgary AB, August 1995).

8. *The Economist*, "The Myth of the Powerless State," (October 7, 1995).

9. Gillies, *Where Business Fails*.

10. Friedman and Friedman, *Tyranny of the Status Quo*.

11. Dawn Dobni, Brooke Painter, and Marvin Painter, "Navigating the Route to Privatization," *Business Quarterly* 60:3 (Spring 1996).

INTERPRETING BUSINESS-GOVERNMENT RELATIONS

In analysing business-government relations, it is not sufficient to understand only the past and the role of the key players in the relationship; one must be able to critically evaluate, or interpret, the present state of these relations. The next two empirically based chapters not only clarify the status of business-government relations in Canada, but also illustrate business' ambivalence towards the state. This section of the book completes the task of placing Canadian business and government in their proper contexts.

CHAPTER 10

The Current State of Business-Government Relations

CHAPTER 11

The Right Kind of Government Intervention

THE CURRENT STATE OF BUSINESS-GOVERNMENT RELATIONS[1]

Since the general or prevailing opinion on any subject is rarely or never the whole truth, it is only for the collision of adverse opinions that the remainder of the truth has any chance of being supplied.

John Stuart Mill, 1806-73

Nothing appears more surprising to those who consider human affairs with a philosophical eye, than the ease with which the many are governed by the few.

David Hume, 1711-76

Business-government relations in Canada are often said to be in poor shape. Some observers claim they are worse than those in the United States. Are some business-government relations better than others? If so, then why — and in what areas? If not, why have the above assumptions been accepted so uncritically? How has this perception evolved and why?

Much of the research on current business-government relations in Canada has assumed a problem exists: that government intervention is emasculating the private sector; that business interests are no longer synonymous with the public interest; *that what was once the workplace of a national socioeconomic partnership is now the battleground for two disparate solitudes.*

Most investigations have been largely issue-oriented case studies. Case studies generally provide specific information helpful in understanding a more generalized theory; they provide real life illustrations of hypotheticals, but on their own offer little else. Other publications on the topic have been commentaries, criticisms, and/or advocacies with little empirical research as a foundation. Much of the literature, both descriptive and prescriptive, available to Canadian scholars and practitioners, is American. Given the significant differences between Canada and the United States as identified in **Parts I** and **II** of this book, American material has little relevance to Canadian business-government relations.

THE INTERPRETIVE APPROACH

Prior to the 1984 federal election in Canada, there were cries from all sides for "improving" the relationship between business and government. Most critics sought to improve the means by which government made decisions on major economic policy issues. These reforms would have resulted in a stronger voice for certain preferred interest groups. It was hoped that, if the "right" people could be brought together at the "right" time with the "right" information, they might agree, or at least compromise, on crucial economic issues.

There are many possible reasons why behavioural and structural reforms are needed in the business-government dynamic. The "macro socio-political" school of thought blames deeply rooted economic, political, and social conditions prevalent throughout the Western world, conditions which cannot be changed easily. After all, as Davidson and Rees-Mogg have concluded "persons with the nearest access to the levers of power, who tend to benefit most from the status quo, are usually reluctant to undertake reforms whose first effects would be to whack their own pocketbooks." [2]

The "failure of business" school tends to emphasize more specific problems in the way business is organized to deal with government, while the "failure of government" school — a somewhat larger camp — concentrates on a variety of equally specific organizational problems within government. Yet another school offers an "interpretive approach;" this emphasizes the underlying values and beliefs that the parties hold about each other, their relationship, and the specific policy issue(s) under discussion. These subjective interpretations are believed to colour the actions of the parties, making accurate communication and collaboration virtually impossible. [3]

This interpretive approach to understanding business-government relations is predicated on several assumptions:

i.   in the case of large, complex economic, social, and political problems, it is not possible to *prove* what causes them or what will cure them by any of the usual tests of scientific rationality;

ii. in spite of (*i*), people interested in these problems form *beliefs* about their causes and cures;

iii. these *subjective interpretations of reality* influence and, along with situational variables, shape the actions of parties in dealing with one another; and

iv. changes in *behaviour* can only be achieved in conjunction with changes in related beliefs, attitudes, and values.

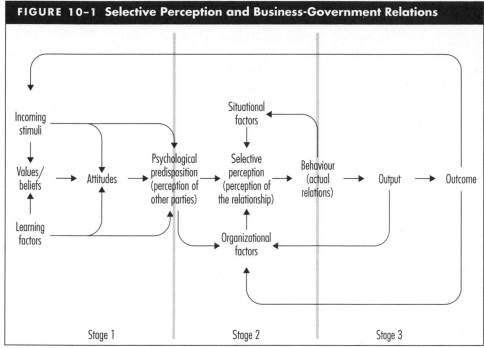

FIGURE 10-1 Selective Perception and Business-Government Relations

Source: Adapted from Taylor (1991: 117)

Figure 10–1 provides a sequential schematic interpretation of the relationship among values, attitudes, beliefs, perceptions, and actions with regards to business-government relations. First, any actor in a business-government relationship is bombarded with a complexity of incoming stimuli. These stimuli are filtered by his or her values, attitudes, beliefs, and sociological and hereditary learning factors into a manageable form. This, in turn, produces a *psychological predisposition* as illustrated in Stage 1 of the figure. Behaviour at this stage is highly predictable.

However, the influence of intervening *situational variables*, such as *social constraint*, can distort perception and reduce the predictability of behaviour. They can influence the individual to *selectively perceive* a given situation such as a business-government relationship. This selective perception (Stage 2 in **Figure 10–1**) provides the basis for one's choice of behaviour.

The combination of all actors' responses results in a particular strategic choice or policy output (Stage 3 in the figure). Outcomes then join incoming stimuli as feedback and the process may be reiterated.

Historically, there has been hardly any consideration given to sociological variables such as values, attitudes, beliefs, and perceptions to help define problems, interpret data, or formulate theories and/or recommendations about Canadian business-government relations. This is startling, given that perceptions are significant factors in understanding social relationships and organization. *Often, what people perceive to be real is real in its consequences for them; perception determines reality for the individual.*

It is important to understand this process of "selective perception," because while values may not change, attitudes can, given changes in situational variables. For example, a change in government leadership may alter a person's attitude towards government without affecting other values. As a result, one's perception of the business-government relationship may change even if the substance of the relationship does not.

When striving to improve business-government relations, it is extremely valuable to understand the subjective, interpretive elements that exist in the minds of business and government leaders. It is also important to explore what factors may shape the way these feelings are created and changed. Unfortunately, few studies have attempted to measure empirically some of these beliefs and values among the interested parties.

This section of the book will summarize the results of perhaps the most extensive series of studies ever conducted to determine these beliefs. It measured empirically how Canadian business and government elites perceived their overall relationship in 1984, 1988, and 1994, and why these perceptions changed like a pendulum swinging to and fro. It also tested the hypothesis that there is a similarity between the beliefs held by business and government elites about their relationship, and the perceptions they hold about themselves and each other. Before examining these findings, however, let us take a closer look at Canadian elites, and the role they play in Canada's socioeconomic drama.

THE ROLE OF ELITES

Every society has its elites. Tribal societies had their hereditary warrior chiefs; feudal societies had their noble and religious elites. Today's industrial societies have their economic and political elites. Canada is no exception: the existence, structure, and processes of Canada's elites has been documented extensively. In fact, since the publication of *The Vertical Mosaic*, John Porter's pathbreaking study of ethnic and socioeconomic elites, most Canadian social science research and commentary has concentrated on elites rather than on class.

For Canadian researchers, the elite group is a much more meaningful sociological grouping because less conflict exists between those who have power and those who do not, rather than between those who *already* have power. This country's powerful minority is composed of the leaders and primary decision makers within its numerous hierarchies. This is Canada's elite.

The great Italian economist Vilfredo Pareto was one of the first modern scholars to study the differences between elites and non-elites, or "the masses." Within an elite, he differentiated between the *governing elite* (the faction possessing real power) and the *non-governing elite* (the faction possessing wealth, learning, and position, but no power). Pareto also noted that each elite group, whether industrial, religious, political, or military, held consistent values, attitudes, and ideologies.

Twentieth-century studies have shown that a society's governing elite can contain its political elite as well as other elites; these groups could also affect political decisions. Specifically, industry's owners, managers, and the highest government officials have inherited roles once performed by the ruling class of feudal society. John Kenneth Galbraith, in his on-going analysis of the modern industrial state, has frequently referred to this group as a *technostructure*.

In this technostructure, elites not only compete for, but cooperate in, the exercise of power and influence to keep society running smoothly. Of course, cooperation and competition suggest periodic alterations to the status quo. These changes may be of an evolutionary or revolutionary nature. As change occurs, the relationship among elites also is altered.

New elites may rise and assume the positions of power vacated by graying elites. Political science refers to this whole process as *elite accommodation*. This process has much to offer in improving both the understanding and the conduct of Canadian business-government relations. Robert Presthus, Canada's dean of elite theorists, actually has proposed that elite accommodation is inherent in the process of democratic government today.[4] Business and government would do well to acknowledge this.

Elites are leaders of all bureaucracies in which power is concentrated at the top. Over time, these elites develop the means to maintain their positions, and to keep in check the power of other elites. Elites are less concerned with further subjugating those within their hierarchies and under their control. Certainly, this is true of business and government in Canada today.

In the 1960s and 1970s, Presthus identified a considerable degree of cohesion and frequent interaction between Canadian business elites and government elites. There were high levels of mutual interdependence between the private and public sectors, and an omnipresence of departmental-clientele relationships. To neo-corporatists, of course, this sort of convergence and even interpenetration was a symptom of the technocratic, corporatist state which they believe Canada to be.

In 1986, T.K. Das wrote a monograph about how strategic choices, corporate performance, and process outcomes partly were shaped by the backgrounds of an organization's senior managers. Found to be relevant were values, attitudes, beliefs, learning stimuli, demographics, and a host of situational variables. All these characteristics of business and government leaders help form their perceptions. A manager's understanding of a situation, along with his or her values, attitudes, and beliefs, provides the bases for choices and behaviour. Strategic management in both the private and public sectors can be improved by each understanding the vital values, attitudes, and beliefs of each other. *It is incumbent upon the key actors in both camps to be as familiar as possible with each other's qualities. Only then can they effectively influence and manage their business-government relations.*

Lacking this type of knowledge, business people often make two common errors when dealing with politicians or public servants. First, they believe that government is, or ought to be, run like business. Therefore, they expect that government behaviour can be predicted using business management processes as models. A recent article by Henry Mintzberg contests this model vigorously.[5] The second error is the belief that public officials, both elected and appointed, are completely different from their business counterparts, and operate in a world the latter can never comprehend. In reality, most senior bureaucrats plan and implement strategies in ways strikingly similar to senior managers in the private sector. They set goals, gather information, develop options from which they choose one, allocate resources, and set into motion an action plan.

However, theorists claim that *business elites* — the leaders of the major firms of a country — are not as hostile towards, and ignorant of, government as is business in general. Thanks to their companies' longer-term, broader perspectives, business elites recognize the benefits, as well as the costs, of government intervention. In fact, this inner group is likely to differ sharply from other members of the private sector when it comes to determining government's role in the economy. The elite recognizes the stability government offers society through its social and economic interventions, thus lessening the economic turbulence which plagues corporate managers. This suggests that chief executive officers in more frequent contact with government would espouse a political ideology more favourable to state intervention than might others.

It is a dangerous error on anyone's part to assume that business and government elites are internally homogeneous. Canada's business elites lack unity; in fact, a significant gulf has developed between the financial and industrial elites over the years. The adversity to risk demonstrated by Canadian chartered banks has often discouraged industrial entrepreneurs in this country. It is equally absurd to assume that all politicians and career public servants think and act the same way. Usually, a spectrum — no matter how small — of differing political, economic, and management thought will exist among the ranks of a government elite. To the untrained eye, such a spectrum is hidden from view due to party discipline, Cabinet and caucus solidarity, and a silent or silenced public service.

CHALLENGES TO THE CONVENTIONAL WISDOM

A recurring theme of modern business-government relations has been the changing dynamics between business and government. This resulted from the growth of Canada's government in both scope and in size during the last quarter century, and the resultant increasing complexity of its decision-making processes. From this awareness has come many proposed solutions to improve an apparently volatile, if not deteriorating, relationship. Contributing to the overall discord is business' failure to have a sufficient impact on the determination of the public interest, and government's failure to operate effectively.

Solutions proposed to improve the situation range from "mutual accommodation," issue management, and direct political involvement, to the more effective use of trade associations, public affairs consultants, and in-house government affairs staff. Many perceive a need for business to prove to society the value of an efficient and unencumbered private sector. As well, it is said, business must better understand factors behind government growth, as well as politicians' responses to the electorate's ever-increasing expectations and demands, and the apparent hypocrisy of the latter as governments attempt to downsize.

Business must also appreciate more fully changing social values and their impact on government's agenda, as well as the legitimate right for government to intervene in business' affairs. Most studies have agreed that problems exist on both sides of the Canadian business-government relationship, and that cultural, sociological, educational, and vocational gaps exist between them.

For the most part, reports about business-government relationships, whether anecdotal or case study, academic or practitioner-sourced, have supported one of the "failure of government" or "failure of business" schools. *They have sought to affix the blame rather than fix the problem.* But this conventional wisdom about business-government relations in Canada is no longer the whole truth. Empirical research supports the "interpretive school of thought" and clearly identifies both causes of and cures for business-government ills.

In the 1984 Taylor and Murray study of business and government elites' values, attitudes, beliefs and perceptions, it was found there were significant differences of opinions between business and government on the general state of the business-government relationship.[6] Business leaders saw relations as being fair, deteriorating, and worse than those in the US. Government leaders perceived relations to be good, stable but worse than those in the US. Each side blamed the other. However, given the rhetoric of government-bashing and business-bashing, relations in general were not all that bad. Both business and government recognized that previous structures and processes facilitating their interactions were inade-

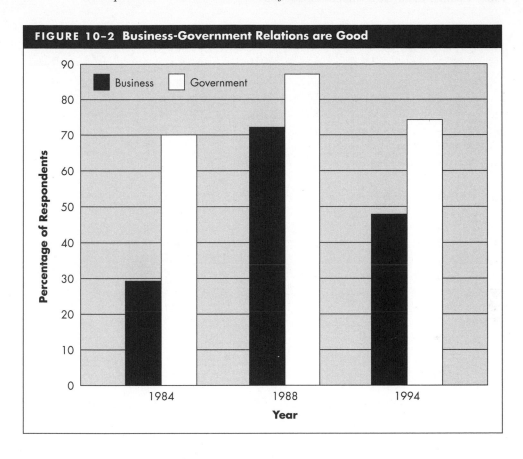

FIGURE 10-2 Business-Government Relations are Good

quate; improvement in business-government relations had to begin with the reform of their *mechanisms of interaction*.

The 1988 Taylor study found that both business and government believed business-government relations had improved significantly during the period 1984-88. Business, in particular, noted a marked improvement. The obvious explanation was the election of a Progressive Conservative government under Brian Mulroney after 16 years of Trudeau Liberal governments. But there was more to the shift than that. Attitudes and perceptions were now less role-specific. Each side had a clearer understanding of the others' role and constraints. Business made better use of consultants, lobbyists, and trade associations, such as the Business Council on National Issues (BCNI) and the Canadian Federation of Independent Business (CFIB). The federal government, in negotiating the FTA with the US, had consulted extensively with business through the Sectoral Advisory Groups on International Trade (SAGIT) and the International Trade Advisory Committee (ITAC). *Although much of the substance of business-government relations had not changed, situational factors (the party in power and the mechanisms of interaction used) influenced perceptions in a positive way*.

In his 1994 study, Taylor found some backsliding (see **Figure 10-2**). Although not perceived by either business or government as poorly as in 1984, the state of business-government relations had once again deteriorated since 1988. Some of the gains had been lost.

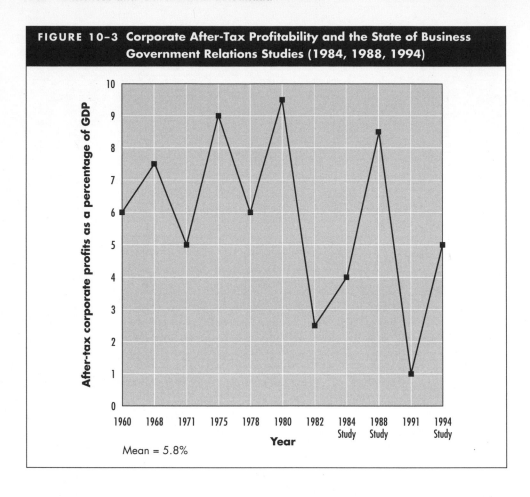

FIGURE 10-3 Corporate After-Tax Profitability and the State of Business Government Relations Studies (1984, 1988, 1994)

Mean = 5.8%

Again, a ready answer was that the Liberals were back in power. Further, now that the FTA and NAFTA were well underway to being implemented, the highly successful governmental mechanisms of interaction — SAGIT and ITAC — had been abandoned and business felt adrift once more. However, since 1988 massive investments by business in the use of rapidly spawning and growing lobbying/governmental consulting firms had been made — but apparently only to have little effect on improving business-government relations. Ironically, during much of the 1988-94 period the Mulroney Progressive Conservatives were actually the party in power. And during that time there was significant growth in the share of national assets that came under state ownership (refer back to **Chapter 8**) and in the membership numbers of the government elite as defined in these studies (see footnote #6). Despite freer trade and neo-conservative platitudes, the Mulroney years proved to be quite interventionist and government-centric. Business had not been fooled.

Is there any other explanation for the pendulum effect in the state of business-government relations? One hypothesis put forward by Taylor in 1991 was that *the perceived state of business-government relations was directly and positively affected by corporate after-tax prof-*

itability. Healthy profits were a proxy for good business-government relations, and all the rest was smoke and mirrors. Empirical evidence supports this hypothesis.

Overwhelmingly, business leaders choose *net after-tax profits* as the number one indicator of how well business is going. As **Figure 10–3** illustrates, survey results directly are reflected in corporate after-tax profitability. If profits are good, business is satisfied with government, and if business is satisfied, then government is satisfied. If profits are low, business' satisfaction with government drops, and if business is no longer satisfied, government is less satisfied as well.

Not surprising, in all three studies both elites' perceptions of the status of business-government relations reflected their political values and beliefs. If the business elite perceived government policies as ideologically "too far left," they went on to perceive business-government relations as "poor." If government policies were "just about right," the business elite tended to regard business-government relations as "good."

Most business respondents assessed their own company's specific relations with government as "good." On the government side, too, almost all judged their relations with specific businesses to be either "good" or "very good." Viewing their own relationships to be slightly better than relations overall is in keeping with general attribution theory.

All three studies also showed that certain groups in Canada have had more influence than others in the formulation of public policy, some have benefited more than others from public policy, and the distribution of influence among groups in Canada has changed over time. In 1994, the biggest gains in influence were considered to have been made by the media, the Prime Minister's Office, provincial governments, and special interest groups. Both business and government leaders considered these gains to have had a negative impact on business-government relations overall. There were not any significant differences in opinion between business and government on this issue; business simply felt stronger about this point than did government. Both felt labour was a less important player than in the past. Both also felt that *small* business has had a growing influence on policy and that it had been a positive experience for all. Interestingly, business leaders believed that regulatory agencies had *grown* in influence whereas government officials thought they had *less* influence than in the past. Very little had changed over the decade.

A factor analysis was conducted for a 26-part question which asked whether respondents agreed or disagreed with various explanations for the state of business-government relations in Canada. Four significant, underlying dimensions to the responses were discerned.

The first two dimensions that together summarized about one-third of a variation, supported the "failure of government school." This implied that the main reasons for ineffective business-government relations were due to various faults *within* government: faults of the politicians, the civil servants, or the structure and process for the making of policy decisions. The next two dimensions supported the "failure of business school." They suggested that the fault was primarily with business in the roles played by business leaders, and with ineffective organization for bringing the business point of view to government. When government responses were factored separately, the most significant dimension supported the "mechanisms of interaction" school. This group attributed the main cause of problems not to what goes on within the ranks of the two parties, but the mechanisms of interaction between the two: the details of who gets to see whom about what, plus when and how the interaction is conducted.

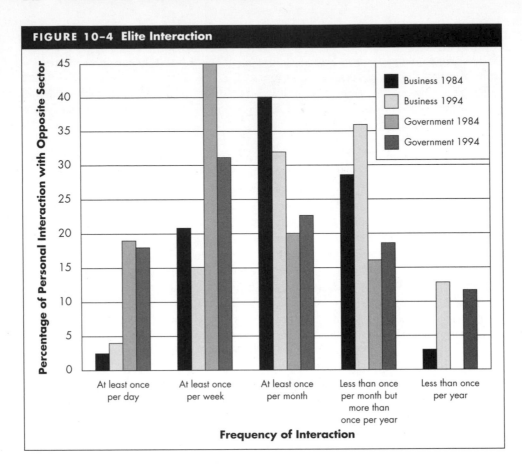

FIGURE 10-4 Elite Interaction

In essence, the business elite believed that **both** business and government were to blame for any problems between them, but that government shared a larger portion of that blame. Government, on the other hand, perceived the major problem to be the mechanisms of interaction between the two sectors, and then placed the blame on business and government respectively. These findings, of course, are in keeping with the first two principles of attribution theory: failure is externally blamed and success is internally credited.

Two external factors also had influence on business-government relations: the extent to which the electorate succumbed to the social value of entitlement (the feeling that the government must protect them against all misfortune), and the role of the media as biased reporter and editorializer in shaping public opinion. In both instances, each set of respondents agreed substantially that these were important factors.

The frequencies of personal interaction that members of one elite had with members of the other elite are displayed in **Figure 10–4**. Overall nearly 55% of the business respondents interacted with government one or more times per month (this was down from 70% in 1984); 22% interacted with a government official at least once per week. In 1984 almost two-thirds of those interactions were with the federal government; in 1994 they were evenly split between federal and provincial governments.

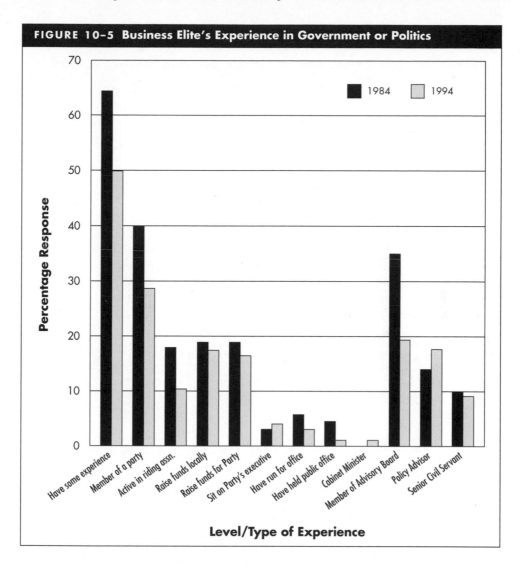

FIGURE 10-5 Business Elite's Experience in Government or Politics

Members of the government elite reported that they interacted with members of the business community even more frequently. In fact, almost 74% of the government respondents interacted with business one or more times per month (but this too was down from 84% in 1984); 51% interacted with business at least once per week.

Interestingly enough, though, there was no significant consistency in the pairing of business person and government official with respect to the frequency of their interaction. *This would clearly suggest that the days are gone in which a chief executive officer had a personal contact within government and in which government officials saw themselves as serving a specific business interest.*

The business elite was asked for their level of personal experience they had in government and/or politics while the government elite was asked for their level of business experience. Of the business elite, 50% had some sort of experience in either government or

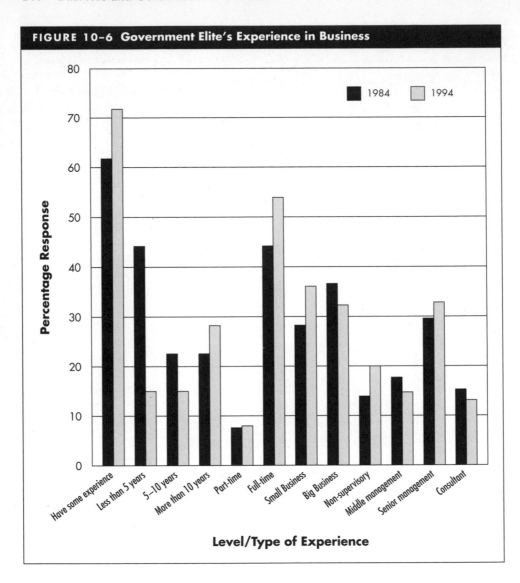

FIGURE 10-6 Government Elite's Experience in Business

politics. A third belonged to a political party, but only about one-half of that number was active in a riding association or in political fundraising. Three respondents had actually run for public office, with only one having won. Ten percent had been senior civil servants, while 20% had acted in some sort of formal advisory capacity to government (see **Figure 10–5**). All of these figures were down from 1984.

On the other hand, 72% of the government elite had some sort of experience in business with 52% having had full-time experience. Thirty-two percent had some or all of their experience in "big business" while 33% had been senior managers in the private sector (see **Figure 10–6**). These findings were higher than in 1984. Overall, both business and government elites tend to have more experience in the management of affairs "on the other side" and therefore understand the other side better than is commonly believed to be the case.

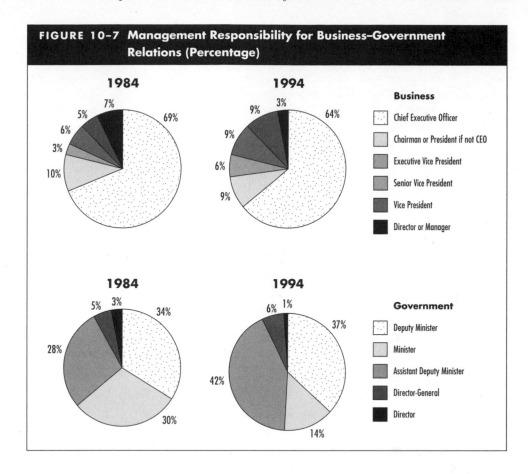

FIGURE 10-7 Management Responsibility for Business–Government Relations (Percentage)

Government, in particular, seems to value this a great deal. It is disturbing, though, to see business slowly regressing in this area.

Finally, **Figure 10–7** reveals that two-thirds of the time it was the chief executive officer who was a firm's most active person in formulating business-government policy (as it was in 1984). In the public sector, however, there has been a significant shift in responsibility for business relations *away from cabinet ministers to deputy ministers and, most markedly, to assistant deputy ministers*.

Within the business elite, individual CEOs and their companies had differing perceptions about a number of things. For example, the more senior the person responsible for government relations in a company, the better that company perceived business' relationship to be with government. For the firms which reported that their CEO was responsible for government relations, 41% reported that relations were good and 42% reported that they were fair. Of those companies, 58% thought that relations in Canada were worse than those in the United States. However, when the responsibility for government relations was delegated within a firm to an executive, senior, or ordinary Vice-President as part of a portfolio of responsibilities, business-government relations were more likely to be considered fair or poor. Similar results were found when the business elite was asked for their perception of the state of their organizations' specific relations with government. Firms with CEOs responsible for business-government relations were happier with their firms' relations with government than were those firms who delegated the responsibility for this function to a vice president responsible for a portfolio of responsibilities. *It was quite clear that the CEO, in most cases, could best manage their company's corporate relations with government.*

The relationship between industry concentration and perception was highly significant (see **Table 10–1**). The CEOs of firms in industries where four or fewer firms accounted for 100% of the industry's production reported less favourable perceptions of the state of business-government relations in Canada in 1994 than in 1984: 20% perceived relations to be good and 70% perceived them to be fair. For industries where the top four firms produced 80-99% of industry output, 61% perceived relations to be good or very good and 34% perceived them to be fair. When the top four firms of an industry accounted for less than 20% of industry output, 80% of the respondents answered that relations were fair. In effect, *oligopolies* with four or fewer firms have grown disenchanted with government because they either are being regulated more than ever, and to their disliking (e.g., tobacco products) or deregulated to allow entry and competition (e.g., telecommunications). The more competitive oligopolies remain quite pleased with the state of relations.

TABLE 10-1   Economic Concentration and Business-Government Relations

Percentage of Market Accounted for by Top Four Firms

1984	State of Business-Government Relations in Canada			
	Very Good	**Good**	**Fair**	**Poor**
100%	12.5%	25.0%	50.0%	12.2%
80-99%	6.7	26.7	63.3	3.3
60-79%	3.6	25.0	60.7	10.7
40-59%	—	23.1	61.5	15.4
20-39%	—	31.6	57.9	10.5
0-19%	—	—	100.0	—

Percentage of Market Accounted for by Top Four Firms

1994	State of Business-Government Relations in Canada			
	Very Good	**Good**	**Fair**	**Poor**
100%	—	20.0%	70.0%	10.0%
80-99%	11.6	50.0	34.6	3.8
60-79%	4.2	33.3	45.8	16.7
40-59%	10.6	45.0	40.0	5.0
20-39%	10.5	42.1	42.1	5.5
0-19%	—	20.0	60.0	20.0

TABLE 10-2 Business-Government Relations Over a Decade						
Year of Data Collection	State of Relations	Party in Power	After-Tax Profits (% GDP)	Major Issue of the Times	Mechanisms of Interaction	Key Players
1984	Fair	Liberals	4.0%	National Energy Programme (Nationalization; Interventionist)	Wrong People Wrong Time Wrong Information	CEOs & Deputy Ministers
1988	Good	Progressive Conservatives	8.4%	Free Trade (Most business in favour)	SAGIT/ITAC BCNI/CFIB	CEOs & Deputy Ministers
1994	Fair/Good	Liberals	5.0%	Debts & Depression (Most business critical)	Third Party Lobbyists & Consultants	CEOs & Assistant Deputy Ministers

However, there were exceptions when vested interests were involved. For example, all oil, gas, and chemical companies strongly disapproved of the federal government's investment in the off-shore Hibernia project except the firm in charge. All industries strongly opposed the bailout of corporations in trouble, except the electronics' firms which were split on the issue (see **Chapter 13** for a possible explanation). Manufacturers of metal products approved of current consumer protection legislation and government subsidies for job creation; manufacturers of nonmetal products did not. Why did this situation occur?

All industries approved of the Bank of Canada's support of the Canadian dollar — except the merchandising industry. Of course, a lower dollar would eliminate what little across-the-border shopping still exists — and that would be good for Canadian merchandisers. All industries did agree upon one item — whether the Liberals or Progressive Conservatives were in power federally; they saw no difference between the two parties' attitudes towards business.[7]

TOWARDS A NEW WISDOM

Given Canada's political and social history of collective pragmatism and consensus-seeking, it should not be surprising that conflict and confrontation are unpopular with both sides when seeking a middle ground. Collectivism in Canada has developed a popular value that society as a whole comes before the individual, and that government should be responsible for guaranteeing this. Here, collectivism does not translate into participative democracy beyond the ballot box. The state remains a very paternalistic force.

Canadian politics, as a result, tend to be *brokerage-style*, whereby compromises among various elite interests are negotiated. Along with the traditional English, French, federal, and provincial elites, there are now business and government elites — definable, recognizable, and effective.[8]

The basic aim of the foregoing surveys was to highlight a number of general concepts, beliefs, perceptions, and values held by leaders in business and government. These focused on attitudes towards each other and their relationships, since these subjective interpretations could have a significant impact on policy making as well as on the outcome of any interactions between them. Differences were apparent between the two parties in their interpretation of their situation.

Results of the 1994 survey of business and government elites in Canada showed that the business elite considered business-government relations to be average, to have deteriorated over the preceding six years, and to be worse than those in the United States. The government elite, on the other hand, assessed relations with business to be good, to have remained about the same, and to be about the same as those in the United States. (See **Table 10-2** for a summary of the three surveys' results).

More strikingly, the survey produced evidence that personal values, attitudes, beliefs, and perceptions correlated positively with elite perceptions of business-government relations. This supported the hypothesis that ideas about what is real can significantly affect the outcome of business-government interactive/consultative processes.

Specifically, statistical analysis of the above results showed that attitudes often arose from previous experiences by members of the business elite in government or politics. For example, those in the business elite with previous governmental or political experience often approved of government intervention, subsidies and regulation. Those with no such experience tended to disapprove. Furthermore, business leaders with political experience generally approved of state-owned enterprises and their activities. Those who had not been politically active did not approve.

Similarly, certain attitudes of government respondents reflected their levels of prior experience in the private sector. For example, those with prior business experience strongly disapproved of the government's participation in the Hibernia megaproject; those who had no such experience approved of Hibernia.

Further analysis showed that as members of the business and government elites interacted more often, their responses to government interventions became more similar. For example, those in the business elite who communicated with the government elite at least once daily (as opposed to the median frequency of once a month) approved of pay equity and employment equity, subsidies and the GST, while others disapproved and called for fewer such government initiatives. In another example, government leaders who had daily business with the private sector generally approved of existing competition legislation; those with less contact called for tougher, more exhaustive, competition legislation.

Situational variables also play a significant role in the shaping of perceptions. In a situation of high social constraint, both elites' leaders are strongly pressured from many sources to respond according to what they perceive their peers wish them to do (see **Figure 10–8**). For instance, business leaders must not be seen as having been compromised by government. They must maintain their legitimacy in the eyes of their shareholders and potential investors, regardless of how beneficial government policy may actually be for their firms. Thus, *business may take a public posture of not liking government, regardless of the reality of the situation*. Eventually, though, some participants may begin to believe their posturing and adjust their perceptions accordingly. This is when business-government relations really do start to deteriorate — all because of misperception and public posturing.

Furthermore, it is not unusual for survey respondents to report a high level of satisfaction with more general relationships from which they are somewhat removed. In response to a mail questionnaire, both elites reported a slightly higher level of satisfaction with their personal business-government relations than that for business-government relations in

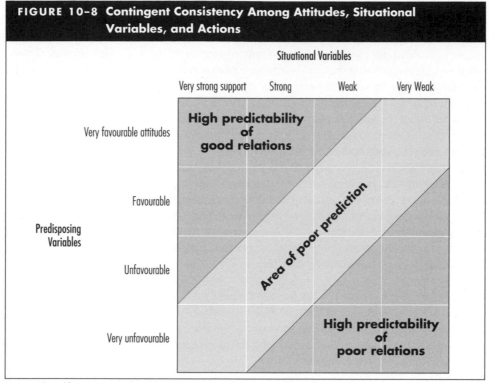

FIGURE 10–8 Contingent Consistency Among Attitudes, Situational Variables, and Actions

Source: Adapted from Warner and DeFleur (1969: 168) © With permission of the authors and the American Sociological Association

general. This response was consistent, whether the respondents chose not to admit that their own business-government relations were poor, or because they thought it was socially desirable to be seen to be dissatisfied with overall business-government relations.

In his seminal work on strategic crisis management, Graham Allison coined the phrase, "where you stand depends on where you sit."[9] According to Allison, a player's stance can be quite reliably predicted by observing his or her seat, or position, with respect to the others. Consistent with this theory was the finding that elite perceptions had been influenced by elite membership. Simply stated, chi-square tests showed that a respondent's perception of business-government relations was influenced by having been a member of a particular elite. Government respondents were more satisfied overall with business-government relations *because* they belonged to the government elite. Business respondents were less satisfied *because* they belonged to the business elite. The business elite was not expected to be happy with government, and of course, government was expected to think everything was just fine. Where they stood *did* depend upon where they sat.

However, as mentioned above, the business elite's response was internally inconsistent. As Pareto would have expected there were a number of attitudinal differences within the group. For example, there was a correlation between a CEO's industry and a positive or negative perception of the state of business-government relations. Also, the more senior the position of the person responsible for a firm's government relations, the better that company perceived its relationship to be with government. When a firm's CEO personally dealt with government, the firm was satisfied with government policy; when someone else did, the firm felt dissatisfied.

Business' ambivalence towards government intervention indicates "an elite within elites." The business elite resented government intervention when taxes eroded profits, when regulation curtailed freedom of economic behaviour, and when Crown corporations stimulated competition. Such competition, by an economist's definition, lowers industry profitability. On the other hand, the business elite liked government intervention when tax expenditures, grants, and subsidies lowered their start-up and/or operating costs, when direct economic regulation closed entry, raised profit levels and decreased competition, and when government provided markets for business' goods and services.

Surprisingly, the positive gradient relationship between industry concentration and satisfaction with business-government relations disappeared during 1984-94. Industries with a CR_4 of 1.00 were no longer very satisfied with business-government relations. Their once cozy existence, created and maintained by government policies — or the lack thereof — was now being challenged. Either interest groups, through government, were attacking them (in the case of tobacco), or government had changed the rules of the game and had eased entry to stimulate competition for whatever reasons. Firms in these industries perceived themselves betrayed!

The CEOs, boards of directors, and management teams of satisfied firms worked closely with government to secure preferential policy treatment from which they were benefiting. *Where business was satisfied with government policies, there was an identifiable "inner circle" of CEOs and state officials that worked together much more frequently than was the norm. There was also a high level of career crossover and interrecruitment.* As a result, the attitudes of these CEOs towards state intervention and business-government relations were closer to the government elite's attitudes than those of their business peers. They seemed to understand, appreciate, and respect the other side's point of view, the constraints the other side might have to endure, and the other side's public posturing that might not have reflected the reality of the situation.

IMPLICATIONS FOR MANAGEMENT

Based upon this analysis, a tentative conclusion can be reached. *Canadian business-government relations are not in an era of mutual mistrust and misunderstanding, as the popular press would have us believe, but in an era of selective elite accommodation.* If profits are considered a measure of satisfactory business-government relations, then the evidence supports this conclusion.

There is a significantly higher degree of career exchange between business and government elites than previously suspected. Members of the business elite who had once belonged to the government elite, and members of the government elite who had been part of the business elite, collectively formed a subset of the two elites. Business attitudes here were more sympathetic towards government policy, and government attitudes were more sympathetic towards business' needs.

A similar meeting of minds was evident where CEOs and their government counterparts communicated much more frequently than did their respective elites as a whole. Where firms and industries had secured favourable legislation and regulation, CEOs were much more supportive of government intervention than was the business elite at large. The business elite supported government intervention when an inner group of CEOs and government elite members interacted more frequently than normal, with numerous career crossovers and interrecruitment.

The lessons for management are clear. If CEOs want to improve their relations with government (or vice-versa) they need to:

(*i*)   *understand* the other side's role and constraints by being there and working there;

(*ii*) *interact* with their opposites more frequently;

(*iii*) *interact* in person **face-to-face** as often as possible; and

(*iv*) *ignore* what is reported in the **media**.

Business and government are not two disparate solitudes in Canada, nor are they united as a ruling class. An inner circle of business and government elites exists in Canada: a small fragment of the business elite is closely aligned — for practical, if not ideological, purposes — to sympathetic members of the government elite. Leading segments of Canada's business and government elites have embraced a set of relationships so as to accommodate the interests of both the private sector and the state.

SUGGESTED FURTHER READINGS

Allison, Graham T. 1971. *Essence of Decision: Explaining the Cuban Missile Crisis*. Boston: Little, Brown & Co.

Baetz, M.C. 1992. "Rethinking the government relations unit." *Canadian Journal of Administrative Sciences*, 9:4.

Bartha, Peter F. 1985. "Organizational competence in business-government relations: A Managerial Perspective." *Canadian Public Administration*, 28:2.

Das, T.K. 1986. *The Subjective Side of Strategy-Making*. New York: Praeger Publishers.

Davidson, J.D, and Lord Wm Rees-Mogg. 1991. *The Great Reckoning*. New York: Summit Books.

Henry, William A., III. 1994. *In Defense of Elitism*. New York: Doubleday.

Islam, Nasir, and Sadrudin A. Ahmed. 1984. "Business' Influence on Government: A Comparison of Public and Private Sector Perceptions." *Canadian Public Administration*, 27, Spring.

Mintzberg, Henry. 1996. "Managing Government; Governing Management." *Harvard Business Review*, May/June, 75:3.

Mintzberg, Henry. 1996. "The Myth of Society Inc." *The Globe & Mail, Report on Business Magazine*, October.

Murray, V.V., (ed). 1985. *Theories of Business-Government Relations*. Toronto: Trans Canada Press.

Murray, V.V., and C.J. McMillan. 1983. "Business-Government Relations in Canada: A Conceptual Map." *Canadian Public Administration*, 26:4, Winter.

Murray, V.V., and D. Wayne Taylor. 1986. "Towards Understanding Business-Government Relations at the Federal Level in Canada." In V.V. Murray, (ed), *The Consultative Process in Business-Government Relations*. North York, ON: York University.

Panitch, Leo. 1997. *The Canadian State: Political Economy and Political Power*. Toronto: University of Toronto Press.

Pareto, V. 1935. *The Mind and Society*. Volume III. London: Jonathan Cape.

Porter, John. 1965. *The Vertical Mosaic*. Toronto: University of Toronto Press.

Presthus, Robert. 1973. *Elite Accommodation in Canadian Politics*. Toronto: Macmillian.

Presthus, Robert. 1974. *Elites in the Policy Process*. Cambridge: Cambridge University Press.

Pross, A.P., (ed). 1992. *Group Politics and Public Policy*. 2nd ed. Toronto: Oxford University Press.

Taylor, D. Wayne. 1992. "An Interpretive Understanding of the Improvement of Business-Government Relations." *Canadian Public Administration*, 35:2, Summer.

Taylor, D. Wayne. 1991. *Business-Government Relations: Partners in the 1990s*. Toronto: Gage Educational Publishing.

Taylor, D. Wayne. 1990. "A Meso-level Understanding of Business-Government Relations." *The International Journal of Public Sector Management*, 3:2.

Taylor, D. Wayne. 1987. "An Interpretive Approach to Understanding Business-Government Relations." *Canadian Journal of Administrative Sciences*, 4:4, December.

Taylor, D. Wayne, and V.V. Murray. 1987. "An Interpretive Understanding of the Non-Fulfilment of Business-Government Relations." *Canadian Public Administration*, 30:3.

Thomas, W.I. 1966. *On Social Organizations and Social Responsibility*. Chicago: University of Chicago Press.

Warner, L.G., and M.L. DeFleur. 1989. "Attitude as an Interactional Concept: Social Constraint and Social Distinction as Intervening Variables Between Attitudes and Action." *American Sociological Review*, 34:2, April.

NOTES

1. Some of the material in this chapter originally appeared in articles by D. Wayne Taylor in *Canadian Public Administration, Canadian Journal of Administrative Sciences*, and the *International Journal of Public Sector Management.*

2. J.D. Davidson and Lord Wm. Rees-Mogg, *The Great Reckoning* (New York: Summit Books, 1991), 100-1.

3. (see).. V. V. Murray and C.J. McMillan, "Business-Government Relations in Canada: A Conceptual Map, " *Canadian Public Administration* 26:4 (Winter 1983).

4. Robert Presthus, *Elite Accomodation in Canadian Politics* (Toronto: Macmillan, 1973), 4.

5. Henry Mintzberg, "Managing Government: Governing Management," *Harvard Business Review* 75:3 (May/June 1996) and "The Myth of Society Inc." *The Globe and Mail, Report on Business Magazine* (October 1996).

6. Business elites are represented by the CEOs whose companies appear in *The Financial Post 500* listings. Government elites represented by federal government ministers, deputy ministers, associate deputy ministers, assistant deputy ministers, and equivalents. A 1998 study is planned.
Business: n = 635 (1984); 627 (1988); 654 (1994)
Government: n = 185 (1984); 350 (1988); 479 (1994)

7. With the makeup of the 1997 parliament, it will be interesting to see business' response in the next survey. Pursuant to Canada's "first-past-the-post" electoral system, ALL parties are now regional, with business support being split three ways.

8. Business and government elites have always existed in Canada; researchers and managers just never have considered them as such. This paradigm excludes organized labour. Unions represent only one-third of the work force, and are highly fragmented, job-conscious, and not class-conscious. Although each union bureaucracy and hierarchical labour congress has its leaders or elites, Canadian labour is not an elite by the Canadian definition in use.

9. Graham T. Allison, *Essence of Decision: Explaining the Cuban Missile Crisis* (Boston: Little, Brown & Co., 1971).

THE RIGHT KIND OF GOVERNMENT INTERVENTION

However much the Canadian taxpayer may favour a policy of strict economy in government in the abstract, he likes nothing so little as its application.

Sir Joseph Pope, 1854-1926

You cannot make the weak strong by making the strong weak.

Abraham Lincoln, 1809-65

In previous chapters, business' ambivalence towards government policy has been frequently referenced. Business likes government policies that help keep its bottom line healthy; business dislikes government policies that do not. In theoretical terms, different types of government policies were categorized and business was seen to favour those whose benefits accrued to business, but whose costs were indirectly borne by the masses. But, specifically, what kinds of government intervention are these, and at what cost to those non-beneficiaries are they implemented?

While researching this book, Taylor discovered that two-thirds of the business elite believed government economic policy to be "too far left," while two-thirds of the government elite thought it was "just about right." Twice as many business as government respondents thought there was too much government intervention overall. However, when pushed, both government and business leaders overwhelmingly agreed it was not a question of *degree* of government intervention, but of too much of the *wrong kind* of government intervention.

WHAT IS THE WRONG KIND?

In 1994, Taylor surveyed business and government elites to determine their attitudes about certain actual and proposed government policies and actions. This provided the opportunity to examine what the "wrong kind of government intervention" actually meant.

Business respondents generally disapproved of historical government equity investment, such as that manifested by Petro-Canada, Air Canada, CNR, and the CBC. An overwhelming 92% of the business elite approved the privatization of Petro-Canada and Air Canada as did 78% of the government elite. Their attitude towards the merger of the CNR with CPR was similar.[1] *Public enterprise is clearly the wrong kind of government economic intervention for both the business and government elites.* Business and government split, however, over the issue of some government departments re-establishing parts of themselves as SOAs. Of business leaders with an opinion, 65% disapproved of this trend and wanted to see no more SOAs created. On the other hand, over half of the government respondents approved of this form of quasi-privatization of government functions.

At the opposite end of the spectrum of interventionist activities, an impressive 85% of the business elite and 89% of the government elite opposed the government bailout of major corporations in financial difficulty. *Bailouts are another wrong kind of government intervention.*

Business and government elites generally approved of direct government assistance to business for enhancing export capabilities, but disapproved of government subsidies and incentives for new job creation. They split on the issue of government support of potential "high-tech winners." Business generally disapproved of this kind of support and wanted to see much less of it; government respondents believed in continuing such efforts.

Business and government leaders were united in strongly approving of deregulating industries in which there had been little competition historically (such as telecommunications); they supported as well dismantling marketing boards and other protectionistic anachronisms of the supply management era.[2] With respect to free trade, 96% of business approved of NAFTA and freer global trade as envisaged by The World Trade Organization (WTO). 84% of government interviewees approved.

Not surprisingly, business thought they were being taxed too much. Government respondents were split between thinking that existing corporate tax rates and policies were appropriate, and that firms should be taxed more. Both business and government approved of the GST and the Bank of Canada's support of the Canadian dollar.

Finally, both business and government elites approved of existing consumer protection legislation and competition policy; both disapproved of existing labour relations laws and preferred less government intervention and protection of unions. Business and government split though, with respect to pay and employment equity laws with government approving them and business disapproving of them.

Overall, both business and government elites *approved* of government financial assistance to business except for job creation. They also endorsed existing economic and social regulation of business, with the exception of labour relations laws.

Both sectors generally *disapproved* of, and wanted less of, government bail-outs of major firms in financial difficulty, and protection of labour-intensive industries. These policies were clearly the wrong kind of government economic intervention for *both* elites.

In essence, *competition was preferred over government regulation if it meant that the strong would get stronger and the big could get bigger. If not, then government intervention was acceptable, if not downright desired.*

Ironically, when public enterprise had the effect, whether deliberate or not, of stimulating competition, it was generally disliked by *both* business and government officials.

DETERMINANTS OF ELITE ATTITUDES: CAREER EXPERIENCE

Why do elites think and feel the way they do about various forms of government intervention? Survey and interview results showed that, once again, many of the above attitudes are rooted in the level of personal experience that members of the business elite previously had in government or politics, or the level of prior experience that members of the government elite had in the private sector.

As an example, those members of the business elite who had some form of experience in government or politics tended to approve of the maintenance of tariffs and quotas to protect labour-intensive industries. Those with no or little such experience tended to disapprove of them, and thought that the country needed freer trade even beyond NAFTA. Furthermore, business leaders who had held public office most definitely approved of tariffs, as opposed to those who had not been elected. Members of the business elite who had been involved in government or politics approved of government regulation of industries where there was little or no competition. The others, who had no government or political experience, generally disapproved of such regulation.

More specifically, business leaders who were members of a political party approved of the federal government's participation in megaprojects such as the Hibernia project. Those who did not belong to a political party did not approve of it. CEOs who were active in their respective riding associations tended to disapprove of Petro-Canada's privatization and generally approved of government equity investments. Those who were not active in this manner did not approve of such actions.

Those business leaders who sat on the executive of their political party disapproved of the dismantling of marketing boards; those who did not hold such a post approved of the WTO's demand that supply management be abolished in agriculture. Finally, business executives who had not been policy advisers or consultants to elected officials or senior civil servants strongly approved of current occupational health and safety regulations but disapproved of pay and employment equity measures. Those who had been such advisers or consultants thought that there was not enough occupational health and safety regulation and called for even more; they also tended to approve of pay and employment equity.

Some of the attitudes held by government leaders were similarly dependent upon members of the government elite having or not having experience in the private sector. Those government officials who had previous business experience in the private sector strongly favoured the establishment of SOAs, whereas those members of the government elite who had no such experience did not favour them. Ironically, public servants who had senior management experience in a large corporation did not favour SOAs being created. Government respondents who had business experience strongly disapproved of the government's participation in megaprojects such as Hibernia and support of potential high-tech winners, whereas those who had no such experience approved of the government's actions.

Finally, members of the government elite who had no experience in the private sector favoured current consumer protection legislation as well as pay and employment equity. Those who had been business executives actually called for more consumer protection legislation, but disapproved of pay and employment equity.

DETERMINANTS OF ELITE ATTITUDES: FREQUENCY OF INTERACTION

Another independent variable which had a significant influence on business' and government's attitudes towards government initiatives was *the individual's frequency of personal interaction with politicians and/or civil servants, or business executives respectively*. For example, those members of the business elite who interacted with members of the government elite the most frequently (at least once per day) completely approved government's support of potential high-tech winners and Hibernia, while the others disapproved and called for less such government intervention in the marketplace.

In a similar manner, the attitude of the government elite towards current competition policy was influenced by the frequency of the government respondents' personal interaction with those in the business sector. Those government leaders who interacted with business on a daily basis generally approved of existing competition legislation and corporate taxation levels. As the individual's frequency of interaction with business decreased, his or her level of disapproval of current competition policy and corporate taxation levels increased, as did the call for even tougher competition legislation and higher corporate taxes than presently existed.

One other variable interceded as well, but to a much lesser extent. CEOs who managed companies which were 100% Canadian owned tended to approve of the government's equity positions within the economy. The rest did not approve, instead wanting state enterprise growth halted.

ECONOMIC REGULATION AND DEREGULATION

Canadians spend an inordinate amount of time preoccupied with death and taxes. As Benjamin Franklin wrote in a letter to Jean Baptiste LeRoy in 1789, "...but in this world nothing can be said to be certain, except death and taxes." Today, we can add a third certainty to Ben's list — regulation. One-third of all federal and provincial legislation is regulatory in nature; over 55% of private economic activity is subject to regulation. There are innumerable examples, among them minimum wage and rent control regulations.[3] About half of all regulated activity is in the transportation field alone. When regulation does receive attention, it centres around two themes: there is too much regulation — or there is too little.

In **Chapter 4**, regulation was noted as one economic function of government, and then economic regulation was defined. As well, regulation was recognized as a policy choice *between* the "hardball" market intervention of government ownership and the "softball" alternative of policies to enhance competition in the marketplace. Economic regulation is intended to affect economic behaviour. To be effective regulations must: affect choices made by producers, distributors and consumers, be administered by an authority or agency, and include penalties to ensure compliance.] There are costs of regulation, while the benefits are usually indirect and thus very difficult to quantify. The fundamental basis for regulatory policies is to correct market failure. The objective is an optimal mix of market forces that may exist; government economic regulation should stimulate competition. The four technical efficiency conditions and the three market conditions were enumerated as Pareto Optimum in **Chapter 4**. If successful, the outcome of government economic regulation would be acceptably close to "Invisible Hand" results.

To date, there is no clear consensus on the optimal level of regulation, how to deregulate, or how to reform regulatory regimes. Worse still, there is little understanding of the cumulative effects of increasing regulation. Many theorists believe that ultimately there must be diminishing cost/benefit returns for a marginal rise in the level of regulation. However, few researchers have tackled the problem of how to measure the costs and benefits of regulation.[5] Cost categories include: direct administrative, industry compliance, political activity and induced inefficiencies.[6] Induced costs include efficiency and innovation losses and the diversion of capital and human resources to regulatory requirements rather than alternate productive uses. Moreover, industry structure may become biased toward larger companies because it can be so onerous for smaller businesses to meet government regulatory requirements.

Generally, business in Canada has adapted well to existing regulation, but dreads the cost of compliance future regulations might require. There is also general disagreement about the value of the level of discretion most special-purpose bodies (i.e., regulatory agencies) possess. The vagueness of enabling legislation — embodying the terms of reference for regulatory bodies — permits these agencies to regulate on a case-by-case basis, a controversial practice.

Most agree that there is redundancy in existing regulation. Overlapping regulations or their absence entirely may be blamed on the division of powers between the national and provincial governments. Regulations across the 10 provinces are often inconsistent, proving costly to business. There is a need for a set of rules and standards for securities regulations. Overlaps may exist within a single jurisdiction because of multiple regulations and regulatory agencies.

Interestingly, business in Canada generally does *not* support deregulation *per se*. It dislikes the uncertainty involved in a change of rules, and expects to be consulted about changes. Business usually demands *better* regulation based on equity, not efficiency.

Regulation is intended to alter the behaviour of individuals in the private sector. *Direct,* or, *economic* regulation tries to alter the private sector's economic behaviour. It is usually industry-specific and controls price levels and rates of return, entry, exit, and/or output. Economic regulation is almost always administered by a regulatory body or agency.

On the other hand, *indirect* or *social* regulation may not be industry-specific, and instead is designed to modify the social behaviour of the private sector. Areas covered include health and safety, environmental protection, fairness and equity in the workplace, consumer protection, and social and cultural values. Social regulation is often administered by either a government line department or a regulatory agency. Most new regulations since 1970 have been social regulations. Although certain regulations may be intended to *protect the consumer*, it seems ironic that most economic regulation is *requested by industry* and supplied in turn by government.

The impact of economic regulation can be measured in a number of ways. First, there are measurable direct costs of both providing and enforcing regulation. An estimated 2% of the federal budget and 6% of its labour force are allocated to regulatory matters.

Second, there are indirect costs, including production inefficiencies, lags in adopting technological innovation, and misallocation of resources. In a protected environment, there is also less impetus to remain competitive.

Third, economic regulation has winners and losers. Although the net effect upon national income is zero, income is redistributed within society. New rights and entitlements are created with regulation, and are threatened with deregulation. In most cases of economic regulation, wealth is transferred *from the consumer to the producer*. This results in higher prices that reflect higher operating costs due to inefficiencies and the higher capitalized costs of entry into a regulated industry.

Fourth, benefits accruing to certain parties are hard to measure, yet economic rents and capital gains upon exiting can be estimated in cases of economic regulation. However, it is harder to measure the values of less pollution, fewer deaths, reduced discrimination, and new employment opportunities from social regulation.

What are the composite effects of economic regulation?

i. Prices are usually higher and more stable.[7]

ii. Multi-part pricing is practised.

iii. Quantities produced can be increased or decreased.

iv. Demand can be shifted upwards or downwards.

v. Costs are usually higher.

vi. Producers tend to be price-searchers rather than price-takers.

vii. There tend to be fewer firms in an industry due to closed or restricted entry and/or exit.

viii. Firms tend to be larger than in an unregulated market of similar size.

ix. Profits tend to be higher.

x. Monopoly rents are accrued.

The objective of economic regulation ostensibly is to protect the consumer from the effects of "destructive competition:" poor quality, excess capacity, price-fixing, price wars, and withheld supply. However, the outcome is the protection of the producer from the effects of destructive competition: lower profits, greater instability, shake-outs, and fluctuating demand. *Little wonder that business demands to be regulated more often than not, and is wary about the idea of deregulation!*

In Canada, government has also initiated its fair share of regulation in the "public interest," justifying it as follows:

i. Market failure is the usual reasoning for government-initiated regulation: (a) to prevent or control natural monopolies; (b) to protect the consumer; (c) to prevent or ease negative results of private activity, such as pollution; and (d) to provide for the disclosure of information;

ii. Government wishes to redistribute income to a limited extent and sometimes uses regulation to do it;

iii. Social and cultural objectives are also met through regulation at times: (a) public goods, such, are provided to peripheral communities because of regulation and the internal subsidization it supports; (b) Canadian ownership is increased in key sectors; and

iv. Regulation is a means by which government does something when the public demands it. ("Taxation by regulation" gets votes!)

Special Purpose Bodies (SPBs) or *Statutory Regulatory Agencies* (SRAs) have a distinct purpose in all of this. Regulation is intended to create equity and fairness. SPBs relieve ministers of direct accountability in politically sensitive areas. For instance, most would agree that property rights should not be a political issue, but are a quasi-judicial matter. While not appropriate for departmental staff to handle, they do not warrant the costs of the courtroom either. Often specialized technical expertise is required, and can only be obtained by setting up a new agency.

For this reason, SPBs usually are not accountable to a minister. They are even able to enact "subordinate legislation" or regulations that might counter Cabinet or Parliament's intentions. For this reason, their often discretionary decisions can *sometimes* be appealed to the Federal Court of Canada, the Supreme Court of Canada, or even to the Cabinet. There are over 600 federal and provincial SPBs. There are literally *thousands* of municipal SPBs in Canada today.

The major disadvantage of SPBs lies in the *captive agency theory*. Simply put, when an industry is first regulated, its regulators need the industry's cooperation to garner the information required for their job. Over time, politicians lose interest in the SPB; the SPB's semi-judicial process becomes bureaucratic, and the SPB gradually becomes more concerned with equity than with policy. As a result, the SPB becomes preoccupied with protecting its industry from the effects of outside competition, rather than with the effects of the industry on the marketplace and the consumer. Thus, the SPB becomes a "captive" of the industry. Business and government become *partners* but, in some cases, not necessarily for the good of society.

Marketing boards are SPBs that enact a particular type of economic regulation, that which sanctions and supports cartels. Marketing boards inflate prices, close entry, and restrict output. Profits of large, efficient producers increase dramatically. Profits of small, inefficient producers rise only slightly. Additional capital gains are realized when excess profits are capitalized in the market value of the licence required to enter the industry. Therefore, early entrants benefit more than late entrants.

Today, as world prices for most commodities and exports are highly variable, excess capacity can result. Marketing boards often end up purchasing surpluses from producers. However, the call has not necessarily been to abolish marketing boards, but to *better* regulate them! Economic regulation demonstrates well the concept of Pareto optimality by violating it, always making one person, or one class of persons, better off at the expense of another. This trade-off is generally acceptable if ultimately in the public interest. But is it?

Some would counter that *deregulation* is in the public's best interest. During the early 1980s, the federal government proposed to deregulate the transportation sector, including the airline industry. Government-owned Air Canada opposed it, fearing competition on routes it had monopolized for decades, as well as the ensuing reduction of prices. Privately owned, much smaller CP Air was in favour. Eventually, CP Air convinced Air Canada that an orderly phasing-in of deregulation was good for them both. Deregulation of routes (entry) and prices began, and a host of small regional carriers entered the low end of the market. Pacific Western Airlines (PWA), a privatized Alberta Crown corporation, and Wardair

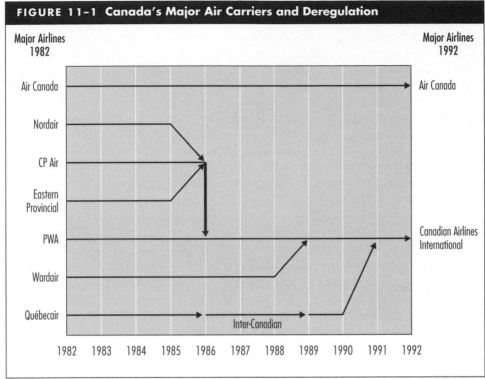

FIGURE 11-1 Canada's Major Air Carriers and Deregulation

Source: Aviation Statistics Centre, Air Transportation Association of Canada

began to challenge Air Canada's industry leadership. Prices plunged and competition intensified, requiring new, more efficient aircraft. Capital costs and corporate debts soared, and soon small carriers were being acquired by Air Canada, CP Air, and PWA. CP Air (now Canadian Airlines International) was bought by PWA, and Max Ward sold Wardair to PWA before Wardair crumbled under the weight of its debt (see **Figure 11–1**).

As a result of deregulation in the airline industry, concentration is greater and prices are higher than before. Ironically, one of the big losers was CP Air, not to mention the public. Yet, this experience could have been foretold if the American venture into deregulation several years earlier, in which 200 airlines went bankrupt, had been better understood. (Or maybe the ultimate outcomes of deregulation were very well understood.) Regulation held prices below the level of a natural cartel, yet above the level of free competition. Total deregulation likely would have eliminated all competition. Now Canada has a natural duopoly in airline transportation with a very small competitive fringe. If the American example is followed full circle, the industry will soon be calling for "better" regulation.

Self-regulation by industry is an alternative to government regulation of industry. Although successful in the medical, legal, and accounting professions, self-regulation for business seldom achieves the same ends. The tobacco industry is a case in point. During the early 1990s, the federal government passed legislation to prohibit tobacco manufacturers from advertising their products in any way, shape, or form. The tobacco manufacturers challenged these regulations in the Supreme Court of Canada alleging that they restricted their freedom of speech under the Charter of Rights and Freedoms. The Supreme Court agreed and nullified that part of the legislation. In return, as a show of good faith, presumably, the tobacco manufacturers agreed to self-regulate their advertising and established the Tobacco Advertising Supervisory Committee and a voluntary tobacco advertising code. In 1996, the tobacco industry admitted to multiple counts of violating its code by placing advertisements in stores that were within 200 metres of schools, and allowing promotional materials to be placed on shelves and counters without the appropriate health warnings.

Economic regulation is a tool of modern mercantilism. Regulations would not be proposed if someone important did not want them. Therefore, regulations transcend demo-cratic political ideologies. An industry will only change its support for a regulation if chang-ing conditions in the industry or market make that regulation disadvantageous.

Regulation creates other vested interests, as well, particularly those of the regulators. A proposal to do away with regulation means a loss of employment to those who regulate. Yet, the only sure constant is change. Industries have varying life cycles: some long, some short, and some rejuvenative. But none is static. A burning question is whether there is any normative justification for regulation. For some industries, regulation is as much an anachro-nism as are old-style labour unions; for others, it is the key to survival.

GOVERNMENT FAILURE AND REGULATORY REFORM

The shrinking of the Canadian state is *the* dominating trend of the 1990s. The scepticism and cynicism about government management, coupled with fiscal follies for a quarter century, could make an ordinary citizen feel that government has failed. The federal government taxed as much as it could, and borrowed as much as it could, so that expenditure levels became sadly overextended. The right kind of government is a solvent one; debt is a killer of activist government. The time of reckoning has arrived, for certain provinces as well. According to conventional economics literature, government regulation is predicated on the concept of *market failures*, and that governing policy correction and compensation results. But does it? Or does government fail?

There is widespread recognition, both in business and government, that economic regu-lation reforms are needed. This statement may also be true of other kinds of regulation in Canadian life. In the mid-1980s, the Government of Canada sought an economic renewal by initiating efforts to "redefine the role of government so that it provides a better framework for growth and job creation and less of an obstacle to change and innovation."[8] Four inno-vations and ten guiding principles were suggested for public policy consideration and deci-sion making.

The *first* was for a **priority-setting** "triage" exercise. This undertaking would facilitate a broad and linked view of regulations rather than each in isolation. Decision making on a "first things first" basis would be more sensible. Each department would submit their set of proposed new/changed/lessened regulations, with the prospective for same in the coming year. The purpose was to engage a planned process at both the department level and the govern-ment as a whole. Such an exercise was expected to result in more important actions being taken while holding off lesser priorities.

The *second* innovation was for regulatory impact analysis to be weighed in the deci-sion process. Benefit cost analysis (**BCA**) was recommended as being essential. Too often, regulations are decided without clear analytical guidance; devoid of hard analysis, benefits are too easily assumed and costs are too easily ignored.

The *third* innovation dealt with **timing**. An aspect of timing is advance notice. Another aspect is to reduce the length of the regulatory approval process; it is especially important to reduce risks by bringing stability and predictability to the process. The 1986 *Competition Act*, for example, specifies a timing protocol for the Competition Bureau. With major investment "on the bubble," lengthy delay can be the same as a negative decision.

The *fourth* innovation was for **systematic review** and evaluation of *all* regulatory programs over a continuous seven-year cycle. Such a periodic reassessment would identify no-longer-needed and obsolete regulations, so only necessary and relevant regulations would continue to be imposed.

A detailed framework for regulatory reform was set out in 10 guiding principles:

i.   recognition of the vital role of an efficient marketplace;

ii.   recognition that regulation should not impede the efficient operation of the market;

iii.   continued use of regulation to achieve social and economic objectives;

iv.   limit the overall rate of growth and proliferation of new regulations;

v.   evaluation of social and economic costs and benefits of new regulations, with explicit indication that benefits must exceed costs before proceeding;

vi.   greater control and review of regulation by Parliament;

vii.   increased public access and participation in the regulatory process;

viii. streamlining of the system to reduce costs, uncertainties, and delays;

ix.   greater cooperation with provincial governments on regulatory matters; and

x.   establishment of a new Office for Regulatory Affairs to be responsible for coordination and management of government regulatory policy and reform strategy.

The last of these guidelines has not been enacted, but the other nine are under review.

Pragmatically, it probably makes sense to tolerate some market failure in the knowledge that the cure might be worse than the disease.

IMPLICATIONS FOR MANAGEMENT

As one follows the development and growth of the federal government's economy involvement in **Parts I, II, and III**, it becomes clear that business often has solicited and benefited from government intervention. After all, who asked the federal government to set up agricultural marketing boards in the first place, to bail out Maislin, Chrysler, and Massey-Ferguson, to negotiate NAFTA, and participate in Hibernia?

However, business' rhetorical preference for free enterprise and its opposition to government involvement in the economy is not merely a form of role playing. It also indicates that business has clear preferences with respect to government policy and actions.

Both business and government approved of most government financial assistance to business, existing government direct economic regulation of business, and government social regulation of business. Both sectors, however, disapproved of government assistance in the form of bailouts. Nor did they want protection for labour-intensive industries.

A major change occurred in government respondents' attitudes towards government equity investment. In 1984, major disagreement existed. Business generally opposed the government's use of state enterprise to accomplish their goals, whereas government officials approved. By 1994, government leaders had swung over to business' position and no longer saw the value of state enterprise. They joined business in supporting privatization of Crown corporations. Although split in their perceptions in the mid-1980s, business and government both agreed by the mid-1990s that, in most cases, there was no need for or value in being an equity investor in the economy. Canada's centuries-long tradition of public enterprise was now in jeopardy. This was the only paradigmatic shift noted within a decade of investigating elite perceptions about business-government relations.

In short, the state of specific business-government relationships depended upon the type of government policy involved. Results also indicated that attitudes often depended on the *level of personal experience* that members of the business elite had had in government or politics. Similarly, the *frequency of interaction* by an executive with a counterpart in the opposite sector influenced his or her attitudes.

As interest in the business-government *problematique* has heightened, normative works either have addressed the subject with a *macro*, policy-making model of elite accommodation, or a *micro*, firm-level model of issues management. The macro approach assumes that business-government relations are singular in substance; that one political model can easily fulfill the needs of all organizations experiencing difficulty with "the other side." Common sense, of course, tells us that in reality there is a myriad of different, simultaneous business-government relationships: firm-specific, sector-specific, cross-sector, national, provincial, local, issue-oriented, administrative, ideological, and so on. Business-government relations, therefore, with the exception of learning how national economic strategies are developed (of which there are few cases in Canadian history) cannot be studied meaningfully using such a reductionist approach.

On the other hand, the micro approach assumes that managing business-government relations is simply a task for a skilled, competent public affairs/government relations department or lobbyist. If that were true, then the growing importance of the public affairs and/or government relations function in business should have contributed to an improved relationship. In 1988, 26% of the firms studied had government relations units (GRUs); by 1994, 34% had GRUs. Yet those firms with GRUs did not perceive business-government relations (either in general or theirs specifically) to be significantly better than those without GRUs. Likewise, there was no significant difference between those who had developed GRUs within the six-year period and those who have had them since before 1988. Likewise, neither firms with or without GRUs perceived relations to have improved. Also, similar results were found for firms extensively using registered lobbyists and those not using registered lobbyists at all. Business-government relations is not as simple as issues management advocates would have you believe.

To overcome this conceptual gap in business-government theory, the findings reported in this and the preceding chapter would suggest that a middle-ground approach would be more useful in helping managers to better handle their business-government relationships. (A multiple approach would be best, but is not always practical.) In fact, this interaction can best be studied at the level of the public-policy type. Thus, if public policies are grouped by type, each with its own identifiable policy network and set of dynamics, at least an equal number of generic types of business-government relations would exist, each with its own set of characteristics. "Reinventing the wheel" thus would be avoided each time a fracture occurred in a firm's relationship with government or vice-versa.

By definition, business-government relations are political relations; a specific business-government relationship is a political relationship. Each relationship is determined by the type

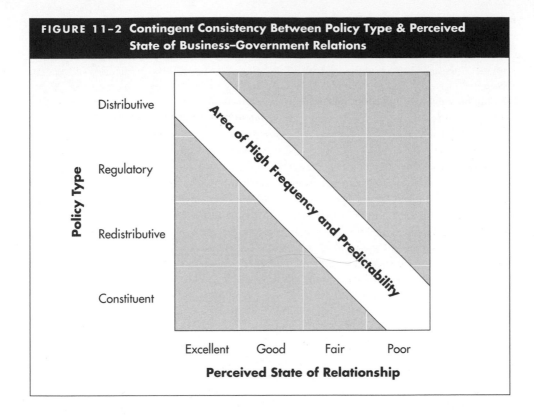

FIGURE 11-2 Contingent Consistency Between Policy Type & Perceived State of Business–Government Relations

of policy at stake, as every type of policy is likely to call for a distinctive type of political relationship. Since each of the four types of public policy — *distributive, regulatory, redistributive,* and *constituent* — has a distinct nature, so too will the relationships involved in each type. (Refer to **Chapter 7** for a discussion of policy types).

There will also be a direct correlation between policy type and business' satisfaction with business-government relations. For example, a firm whose largest percentage of time spent interacting with government is within a policy network that yields benefits concentrated on its particular industry and whose costs are widely dispersed predictably will have satisfactory relations with government. Such a firm will also perceive the overall state of business-government relations to be good.

Conversely, a firm whose industry does not benefit from a specific distributive policy will not be as satisfied with business-government relations, and will perceive them to be "fair" or "poor." Further, a firm that spends most of its time relating within a policy network from which it does not directly benefit, and for which it perceives itself as paying a progressive share of the costs, will be less satisfied with government. In fact, it will assess the relationship as "poor." Between these two extremes there will be a close correlation between policy type and the perceived state of a business-government relationship (see **Figure 11–2**).

Based upon the research findings contained in this book, both business and government elites generally approved of distributive-type government policies, except for tariffs and quotas. In fact, business respondents overwhelmingly approved of them when they directly benefited the respondents' industries. *Those sectors which benefited most from various distributive policies were the most satisfied with their relations with government and perceived overall business-government relations to be excellent.* Politicians elected or seeking election much preferred the high visibility of handing out money to business rather than the much more low-key approach of enacting/changing laws to encourage investment, innovation, or whatever. Hand-outs cast politicians as "doing something;" fiscal policies have less vote-getting/fundraising appeal, in their opinion.

Next, when questioned about direct, economic regulatory policies, the government elite consistently approved existing and proposed regulatory policies; business was ambivalent. Respondents from highly market-competitive industries disapproved of regulation much more than those from the least market-competitive (and most heavily concentrated) industries. *The majority of those in highly regulated (highly concentrated) industries generally were satisfied with business-government relations.* After all, regulatory regimes generally inhibit entry to newcomers, which award early entrants into these sectors with economic profit.

Referring again to **Figure 11–2**, the next order of public policy examined was redistributive policy. Again, a strong 79% of business leaders disapproved of the government's attempt to redistribute wealth through progressive income taxation and various forms of social insurance. However, 70% of the government elite approved of such redistributive policies.

Finally, when the question turned to constituent-type policies ("rules of the game") an overwhelming 83% of the business respondents were dissatisfied. The business elite generally did not approve of the federal government's fiscal policies. Instead, they called for less government equity investment in the economy, less government spending, and lowering of government debt. The business elite strongly disapproved of government spending money to create jobs and other such policy initiatives. On the other hand, government respondents were ambivalent. They approved of the government's constituent policies by a narrow margin. They approved of most fiscal policies but generally disapproved of state enterprise and job creation programs.

There is a clear consistency and predictability that exists between policy types and business perceptions of business-government relations. It also affects the respondents' sense of satisfaction with their organization's specific relations with government. Various public policies can affect the perceptions held by different industries. This depends, of course, upon which types of policies are important to a firm, and how a firm is primarily affected by them. Based on this, business' satisfaction with government will range from being poor to very good.

CEOs will usually approve of distributive policies if they benefit the respondent's firm. If a CEO was immersed in a distributive policy network, feelings about the state of business-government relations were good. Most regulatory policies also meet with business' approval — especially when directly affected by them. Such approval, however, is slightly lower than for distributive policies, and deregulation is favoured only when it is the "right kind."

In short, businesses most affected by either a distributive policy network or a regulatory policy regime are most satisfied with business-government relations. They approve of said policies which tax the general public to give business an economic advantage. However, businesses most affected by either redistributive or constituent policies, or which are not beneficiaries of distributive or regulatory policies, are displeased with the state of business-government relations in Canada.

Therefore, to understand and improve upon this relationship, a much more interpretive, middle-ground approach is needed than has been previously used. This does not imply that other methods have no merit. To the contrary, these pioneering works have gained for business-government relations a lot of ground and attention.

Now, business-government studies can be meaningfully broken down or combined into policy fields, each with its own set of characteristics and dynamics. Some business-government relations have been found to be healthy; others are not. Some need work; others do not. Common threads run through heretofore isolated instances, and there are boundaries between discrete sets of interactions. This approach to business-government relations provides the opportunity to generalize more than through case studies, yet is more pragmatic than universal systems theory.

Business and government are not two isolated, disparate solitudes as former Prime Minister Trudeau proclaimed in 1981; nor are they fragmented beyond redemption. They simply need to be identified as they actually exist — as an array of differentiated clusters and networks, each centred around a generic type of public policy, and each with its own set of variables.

Business-government relations in Canada are no longer an illustration of mutual political accommodation. Nor have they disintegrated to a state of mutual misunderstanding and distrust, as often suggested in the popular press. Rather, they exhibit characteristics of mutual dependency.

However, business management in Canada does not seem to see it that way, or at least is not willing to admit it. There is a long way to go.

SUGGESTED FURTHER READINGS

Boadway, Robin, Albert Breton, Neil Bruce, and Richard Musgrave. 1994. *Defining the Role of Government: Economic Perspectives on the State*. Kingston, ON: School of Policy Studies, Queen's University.

Canada Government. 1988. *Regulatory Reform: Making It Work*. Ottawa: Office of Privatization and Regulatory Affairs.

Carlton, D.W., and J.M. Purloff. 1994. *Modern Industrial Organization*. New York: Harper Collins.

Gillies, James. 1986. *Facing Reality: Consultation, Consensus and Making Economic Policy for the 21st Century*. Montreal: Institute for Research on Public Policy.

Green, C. 1990. *Canadian Industrial Organization and Policy*. 3rd ed. Toronto: McGraw-Hill Ryerson.

Greene, Ian, and David P. Shugarman. 1997. *Honest Politics: Seeking Integrity in Canadian Public Life*. Toronto: James Lorimer & Co.

Jordan, William A. 1972. "Producer Protection, Price Market Structure and the Effects of Government Regulation." *The Journal of Law and Economics*; 15:1.

Lenihan, Donald G., Gordon Robertson, and Roger Tasser. 1994. *Reclaiming the Middle Ground*. Montreal: Institute for Research on Public Policy.

Lindblom, C.E. 1977. *Politics and Markets: The World's Political-Economic Systems*. New York: Basic Books. (Especially Chapter 13.)

Luciani, Patrick. 1996. *Economic Myths: Making Sense of Canadian Policy Issues*. 2nd ed. Don Mills, ON: Addison-Wesley.

Maxwell, Judith. 1996. "Governing Canada's Social Union." *Canadian Business Economics*. 5:1, Fall.

Osborne, David, and Ted Gaebler. 1992. *Reinventing Government*. Don Mills, ON: Addison-Wesley.

Purchase, Bryne, and Ronald Hirshhorn. 1994. *Searching for Good Governance*. Kingston, ON: School of Policy Studies, Queen's University.

Putnam, Robert D. 1997. "The Decline of Civil Society: How Come? So What?" The 1996 John L. Manion Lecture. *Optimum, The Journal of Public Sector Management*, 27:1, April.

Seidle, F. Leslie, (ed). 1993. *Rethinking Government: Reform or Reinvention?* Montreal: Institute for Research on Public Policy.

Strick, John C. 1994. *The Economics of Government Regulation: Theory and Canadian Practice*. 2nd ed. Toronto: Thompson Educational Publishing.

Taylor, D. Wayne. 1989. "The Economic Effects of the Direct Regulation of the Taxicab Industry in Metropolitan Toronto." *The Logistics and Transportation Review*, 25: 2, June.

Trebilcock, Michael J. 1994. *The Prospects for Reinventing Government*. Toronto: C.D. Howe Institute.

Viscusi, W.K., J.M. Vernon, and J.E. Harrington. 1992. *Economics of Regulation and Antitrust*. Toronto: D.C. Heath and Co.

World Bank. 1997. *The State in a Changing World*. Annual Development Report, June.

NOTES

1. The CEO of the CNR is former Secretary to Cabinet Paul Tellier.

2. In a survey reported in the *Financial Post* (August 8, 1995:4) the majority of Western grain farmers opposed internal and external trade barriers but favoured retaining subsidies and the Canada Wheat Board. On the other hand, cattle ranchers opposed marketing boards.

3. Luciani, *Economic Myths*.

4. Strick, *The Economics of Government Regulation*.

5. For a case example see Taylor, "The Economic Effects of the Direct Regulation of the Taxicab Industry in Metropolitan Toronto."

6. Strick, *The Economics of Government Regulation*, Ch. 6.

7. A 1983 study by Statistics Canada showed that regulated prices do not respond to changes in market conditions as quickly as non-regulated prices. This is one reason it took longer for inflation in Canada to come down than in the United States.

8. Canada Government, *Regulatory Reform: Making It Work,* (Ottawa: Office of Privatization and Regulatory Reform Affairs, 1988), 7.

9. Economic profits on goods sold are the difference between revenues received from the sale and the opportunity cost of the resources used to make them. The opportunity cost includes charges required to use the firm's capital, and to take risk.

MANAGING BUSINESS-GOVERNMENT RELATIONS

With a fuller understanding of past and present business-government relations and the variables which have shaped them, managers can now address the question of how best to manage them in the future. As with strategic planning, there is no one best choice, but an array of techniques and mechanisms of interaction the choice from which will be contingent upon business' and/or government's objectives, needs, and circumstances.

CHAPTER 12

Business Dealing with Government

CHAPTER 13

Government Dealing with Business

CHAPTER 12: BUSINESS DEALING WITH GOVERNMENT

Government and cooperation are in all things the laws of life;
anarchy and competition, the laws of death.

John Ruskin, 1819–1900

Government in Canada (and the federal government, in particular) has been called a *mono-lith* and a *leviathan.*[1] These words imply not only that government is big and totalitarian, but that everyone in government thinks identically, behaves identically, and seeks to achieve identical goals. Yet, nothing could be further from the truth! *The biggest mistake that those outside government make is believing in a "single player" theory of government.*

In fact, there are as many government points of view on any subject as there are outside of it. Nowhere else do we expect two people to be exactly the same, so why should government be an exception? In fact, there are myriad opportunities to win support over a policy issue; one must simply find the right person at the right time. Who is the right person? That depends on the issue. When is the right time? It's usually before the issue becomes an issue!

To illustrate the principle, one needs only look at business' greatest triumphs in its recent dealings with Ottawa. For decades, Boeing Aircraft of Seattle and McDonnell Douglas of St. Louis supplied Air Canada with its fleet of commercial aircraft. However, since 1990, Canada's national airline has been acquiring its aircraft from Airbus Industrie of Europe. Why? Because Airbus hired a consulting firm headed by Frank Moores, former Progressive Conservative Premier of Newfoundland, to represent it in the corridors of Parliament Hill. Brian Mulroney was Prime Minister and the Tories had a majority in Ottawa. The other two manufacturers worked through the trade service of the United States' State Department. Did Moores open doors and push buttons? Probably not; more likely he simply showed Airbus which doors to open and which buttons to push.

Another victory was the Canadian Brewers' Association's success in excluding the beer industry from the terms of the FTA and then again from NAFTA even though wine and distilled spirits were included in both. The federal government saved the beer industry from its own diseconomies of scale, its price maintenance ritual, and the provinces' outdated barriers to inter-provincial trade. The ante: thousands of jobs. The price: the probable loss of the much smaller, mass-production segment of the Canadian wine industry. After all, Hockey Night in Canada without Molson's would be inconceivable.

Not to be overlooked is how effective Canada's lawyers and accountants can be in getting their own way. During the term of then-Finance Minister Michael Wilson, a Value Added Tax was proposed. The legal and accounting professions, fearing client revolt at higher prices for the same level of service, convinced the minister that a national sales tax would be a better idea — at least for them. So, Canada got the GST instead.

Even neighbourhood grocers have Ottawa's ear these days. This has been largely due to the Grocery Products Manufacturers of Canada, who developed an information system that impresses upon local MPs the number of jobs and other economic benefits the grocery trade provides in every riding. The association's success in doing this almost rivals that of the consistently recognized dairy farmers and their provincial marketing boards.

Last but not least are Canada's venerable banks and their cousins, the insurance firms and automobile leasing companies. As matters stand now, the federal government is preparing a range of reforms to Canada's financial institutions,[2] the most revolutionary of which include: *i*) allowing banks to sell insurance; *ii*) allowing banks to offer automobile leases; and *iii*) allowing foreign banks to open branches more easily. Historically, the bank's expansion into new fields has lowered prices, increased volumes, and produced greater product variety. Canada's insurance distribution system at the time was 20% less productive than the OECD average. Auto leasing was a virtual cartel of the auto manufacturers. Greater entry of foreign banks into domestic banking circles promised the same gains as allowing banks into insurance and auto leasing. But the lobbying became fierce. The banks and auto companies lobbied in their own self-interests; the banks and insurance companies did likewise; and the banks also fired upon those foreigners. In the end, Ottawa caved in to the pressure and confusion, watered down its plans for a White Paper (see **Chapter 13** about coloured papers) and decided to have a panel of "non-government experts" study the three proposals, much to the consternation of the troops in the Department of Finance.

Parliament Hill has become a killing field for the vested interests of big business. But what about small business? Let alone the average Canadian on the street! Of small business, 92% do not think the big banks have improved their treatment of their small-business clients; 75% do not think that governments represent small business' best interests in its policies. But perhaps Ottawa should start by defining what type of banking system we need before getting caught in the crossfire again.[3]

There are also several CEOs who devote so much of their time to dealing with government, it eventually pays off. Paul Desmarais of Power Corporation probably is the "best connected" of the lot, having also deftly transcended political dynasties. Former Prime Minister Mulroney used to be on his payroll, as did Finance Minister Paul Martin, and so too is former Ontario Premier Bob Rae's brother. Desmarais is also father-in-law to Prime Minister Chretien's daughter! Talk about being "in the loop!"

MARKET AND NON-MARKET STRATEGIES

In the study of strategic management, students are taught to examine their *internal* environments for organizational strengths and weaknesses and their *external* environments for opportunities and threats. The optimal combination of these internal strengths and weaknesses with the coexistent external opportunities and threats is the objective of formulating and implementing corporate strategy. The external environment of business is comprised of both *market* and *non-market* systems, the integration of which is also required for a corporate strategy to be successful.[4]

The market system of the external environment is economically-driven, based upon voluntary transactions and private exchanges of property. The non-market environment is both political and public; non-market interactions can be either voluntary or involuntary. Any firm, to survive and grow, needs to balance its market activities with its non-market activities and responses. Thus, not only will a firm improve its economic performance within its market but also improve the environment in which it has to compete. Just as market tactics are the responsibility of line managers, so should be non-market tactics (with the appropriate assistance of staff specialized in external relations of various kinds — governmental, legal, regulatory, public and international).

Most management strategists today agree that firms need to develop an offense *and* a defence to deal with the five market forces: rivalry among existing firms, threat of new entry, threat of substitution, and the bargaining power of business, and of suppliers. If modern, competitive strategy needs to be tailored to the realities of the marketplace and to capitalize upon firm-specific competitive advantages, then they also need to be tailored to non-market realities and a firm's distinctive competencies in dealing with the non-market environment.

The non-market, external environment can be divided further into social, political, and legal segments that interact with each other as well as with the market. Of course, the biggest potential opportunity *and* threat to business within the non-market is government.

This non-market environment also can be characterized by the four *i*'s: issues, institutions, interests, and information. *Issues* are exactly what non-market strategies should address — issues such as regulation, free trade, or labour rights. Many non-market issues naturally arise from market activities. *Institutions* refer to government departments, agencies, boards, committees, and so on as appropriate for each issue. *Interests* are simply individuals, groups, or organizations, such as unions, consumers, the media, subcontractors, investors, and competing firms, with a vested stake in an issue. Finally, *information* includes what the above interests, you, and government know, believe, feel, and perceive about an issue and the circumstances enveloping it. Successful management of non-market strategies requires a mastering of all four (issues, institutions, interests and information) but the most important of these is information (as discussed later in this chapter).

The idea of a firm successfully formulating and implementing a fully integrated market and non-market strategy (see **Figure 12–1**) advances one step further the notion presented in **Chapter 3** of the firm as a responsive social system to one of the firm being a legitimate player in the non-market realm. Yes, it is better to respond to government, society, and the public-at-large than to ignore them like an ostrich with its head in the sand, but it is *best* to attempt to influence (if not control) non-market dynamics — such as the rules for market competition — as they affect you and your firm or industry. Non-market strategies can be used to defend a firm against the five forces of the market, just as much as market strategies.

As seen in **Chapters 7, 8,** and **11**, even market opportunities/threats can be either market

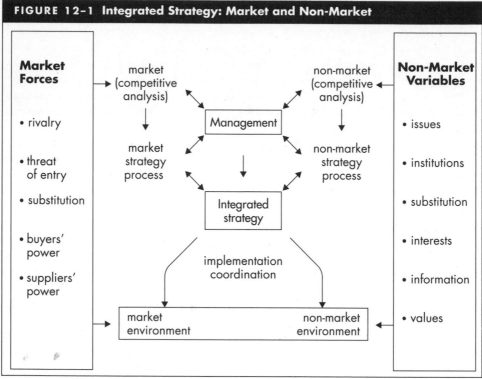

FIGURE 12-1 Integrated Strategy: Market and Non-Market

Market Forces			Non-Market Variables
• rivalry	market (competitive analysis) → Management ← non-market (competitive analysis)		• issues
• threat of entry	market strategy process ↔ ↕ ↔ non-market strategy process		• institutions
• substitution	Integrated strategy		• substitution
• buyers' power	implementation coordination		• interests
• suppliers' power			• information
	market environment ← → non-market environment		• values

Source: Adapted from Baron (1995: 49). Copyright © 1995, by The Regents of the University of California. Reprinted from the California Management Review. Vol. 37, No. 2. By permission of the Regents.

controlled or government controlled, the latter through one or a combination of legislation, regulation, and/or state enterprise. Similarly, the importance of urgency of specific non-market issues and strategies will vary firm by firm, industry by industry, country by country, and over time. Therefore, there is a *contingent* relationship between non-market strategies and opportunities just like there is for market strategies and opportunities (see **Figure 12–2**). In other words, a firm's overall strategy (market and non-market components combined) will depend upon the circumstances. A successful corporate strategy will be congruent with the capabilities of a firm and both the market and non-market characteristics of the environment for any given time period. In a mixed economy such as Canada's, the non-market component of a strategy is just as crucial as — and can even *influence* — the market component. *As with a market strategy, there is no best way to deal with the non-market. But there are some wrong ways!* There are far more failures than successes when talking about business dealings with government.

BLUNDERS, BLUNDERS, BLUNDERS

When dealing with political and governmental issues, business managers continue to perform poorly more often than not. They cry out against government intervention (except when it benefits them), unaware that Canadians are highly tolerant of state involvement in most aspects of their lives. In all, there are seven fundamental errors that business makes when dealing with government.

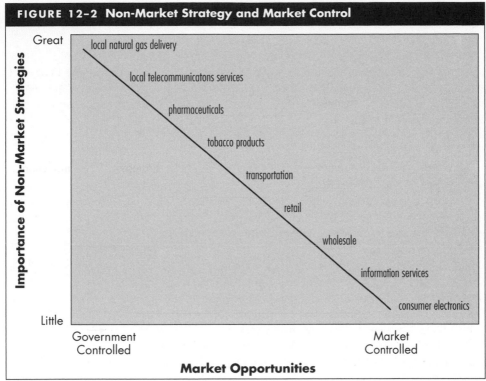

FIGURE 12-2 Non-Market Strategy and Market Control

Great — local natural gas delivery

local telecommunicatons services

pharmaceuticals

tobacco products

transportation

retail

wholesale

information services

consumer electronics

Little

Importance of Non-Market Strategies

Government Controlled

Market Controlled

Market Opportunities

Source: Adapted from Baron (1995: 50) Copyright © 1995, by The Regents of the University of California. Reprinted from the California Management Review. Vol. 37, No. 2. By permission of the Regents.

First, politicians come and they go, but the bureaucracy and the acolytes who dwell therein change far more slowly. (This is the case, even though deputy ministers now change jobs almost as frequently as ministers do.) *Still, private sector senior managers, especially CEOs, continue to disdain the public service and demand to deal with the minister.* Yet, it is often the middle manager of a department or central agency who can best assist an outsider. A political quick fix is rare; beware anyone selling the promise of a quick fix. Furthermore, it is the politician's job and nature to be open, friendly, and sympathetic; such appearances, though, are sometimes calculated to be deceiving.

Second, *business loves to prepare comprehensive briefs at great expense to its organization and shareholders.* These are presented to the appropriate public forum — a committee of the House of Commons, a committee of the Senate, or a government task force.[5] By then, however, it often is too late. When a government goes public with a policy, it is committed to its adoption. The best a company can hope for is to dilute, slow down, or change the policy's packaging. Briefs are devoured by the information-*hungry* bureaucracy, but are largely ignored by the information-*overloaded* politician. Too little, too late.

Third, *some businesses still believe that economic power emanates totally from their boardrooms.* Yet, in the past quarter century, a shift has taken place. Equal if not greater economic clout now emanates from the Prime Minister's Office, the Privy Council Office, and the shadowy bowels of line departments. CEOs ignore at their peril the fact that they are only additional players in a pluralist, political system, wherein government must appease numerous competing interests. Business' concerns are not necessarily the public's, at least not so far as the public (a government's shareholder's) is concerned.

Fourth, *business fails to deal with government in a business-like manner.* The basic tasks for business managers are gathering and analyzing data, identifying and solving problems, formulating and implementing strategies, making decisions, organizing, and motivating. All these require reasoning. Yet, when business deals with government, passion — vs. reason? — comes to the fore. Business leaders plead cases of self-interest, rather than offer to help government analyze, organize, decide, and solve problems. Demands are often unsupported by evidence, options may not be suggested, and the competition is often ignored.

Fifth, *despite that business' intentions are good, its approach to government is all wrong.* Often, businesses approach the wrong people with the wrong information at the wrong time; they have failed to analyze and understand government's organizational dynamics, as well as the institutional setting of political problems. They may ignore potential allies and miss potential antagonists. Worse still, they fail to see that the machinery of government evolves over time, as do appropriate pressure points within it.

Sixth, *business goes to government in a state of disarray.* Often, there is no agreement within an industry, let alone a sector of the economy or the business community as a whole. Government then faces the same dilemma as when facing the electorate. Its only two options are to provide for the majority as reflected in public opinion, or to do what it thinks is best, regardless of public opinion. Disarray is vulnerable to a government response of playing some off against others. Unless a company pleads an exceptional case, going solo is unlikely to bring positive changes in government policy. Nor is business adroit in identifying a political constituency it could mobilize for support. Strange, considering that government is politics and politics is government.

Seventh, *business generally lacks a commitment to successful on-going business-government relations.* There are relatively few cases of significant resources being allocated for this purpose within organizations. Whether these resources be financial, human, attitudinal, or specific expertise, the key is commitment from the top. And that takes the rarest resource of all — a CEO's time.

PLURALISM AND CONSTITUENCIES

Although **Parts I** and **II** of this book revealed that Canada is hardly a true pluralist democracy, it does possess three of its characteristics: political parties, an unfettered media, and numerous interest or pressure groups vying for public attention and government largesse. Each of these factors can either impede or expedite business' dealings with government.

Political Parties

These play a minimal role in Canadian public policy; they simply select and help elect members of Parliament or legislative assemblies. Political parties in Canada fail to aggregate and articulate particular viewpoints along the political spectrum, as do those in Europe.[6] With the advent of executive federalism in the mid-1960s, parties have become even more irrelevant to the governing of the nation and to business' interests. Therefore, they are not likely targets for business' lobbying efforts, with one exception. The leader of a political party not in power today may become the First Minister tomorrow.

Media

Since the 1960s, media's intensified coverage of current events has increased the pressure for short-term "quick fixes" to social and economic problems. These ready solutions often result in new budgets, new spending initiatives, or more regulation. In the extreme, an election will be called to cloud the issue with euphoria and promises, later found to be too expensive. Acting as intermediary between government and its public is the media, which channels public opinion to government decision makers and sells (whether wittingly or unwittingly) government programs to the electorate.

This has a profound effect on public policy. Theoretically, the media is neutral. However, this assumption has been repeatedly challenged as the concentration of ownership in the media increases.[7] Not only can the media report public opinion — it also has the potential to filter, shape, and distort both public opinion and government policy. As a result, the prime minister is a "media junkie," (as are most premiers and mayors of major cities); their staff read every major newspaper and watch the network newscasts before breakfast and before retiring. News-clipping and monitoring services are a major growth item in most federal government departments. Two new sections even were added to the form for a Memorandum to Cabinet (the policy summary document reviewed by Cabinet before making a policy decision) entitled, "Possible Best Headline" and "Possible Worst Headline."

Canadian journalism has lost its strong investigative past; its present strength lies in the editorial boardrooms. Therefore, a public servant's main task today is to keep his or her minister out of trouble with the media. Business can learn from the media what government is thinking, or at least is considering, when making policy. Also, business has a powerful potential weapon in the media, but one which could turn and attack it just as quickly. Public opinion and the media are exogenous non-market variables in a business-government relationship and corporate strategy: they can strongly influence government, but themselves are very difficult to influence.

Interest or Pressure Groups

Almost every organization in Canadian society has been an interest or pressure group at one time or another; it has tried to influence in its favour the output of the political system. Unlike Europe and the United States, however, formal, full-time interest groups in Canada have not aligned themselves with political parties. As a result, business must first compete for government's attention; then, for its favour. This makes the government relations function and non-market strategies all the more crucial to business' long-term survival.

Although Canada seeks to be a pluralist democracy, it is not a highly developed participatory democracy. Party politics are split between federal and provincial levels, and are not significant at either level outside of the legislature. The media, on the other hand, is concentrated but not terribly aggressive. Interest groups are numerous, but not politically active in a partisan sense. Nor are there signs of any of this changing. If anything, parties will become increasingly splintered and less relevant in the technocratic age, as the media is becoming more concentrated, and interest groups are more numerous.

Business must develop a continuing and effective relationship with government or be swept aside as just another voice in the din. Political parties will help little; the media is as much a threat as an opportunity, and business is not alone in courting government's favour.

Two key ingredients for any **successful** business-government relationship are: (*i*) identifying the most influential *target(s)* within government; and (*ii*) choosing the most effective *tactic(s)* by which to approach and influence those targets.

What, then, are business' targets? Whom in government should business approach? When? And for what? With alliances? How?

GOVERNMENT TARGETS — TECHNOCRATS, CENTRAL AGENTS, AND POLITICAL ADMINISTRATORS

It should now be clear that if business' concerns are truly of national importance (however defined by the politicians or media of the day), the key player, i.e., target, should be the prime minister (or premier if a provincial matter). Even though the vast majority of a prime minister's cabinet could have grave reservations about particular policy initiatives, those initiatives will be primary agenda items for a government if the prime minister wills it so. (And vice versa). The prime minister's opinion counts. When it comes to national or international issues of great urgency, sometimes *only* his opinion counts. Given the centralized nature of decision making in Ottawa today, this would be true regardless of who held the office. Former Prime Minister Mulroney appears to have exemplified this role of being the "first amongst equals." So too current Prime Minister Chretien, albeit having earlier opposing the GST, Canada-US free trade (now extended to Mexico as NAFTA), and the prohibition of tobacco advertising — Canada got all three. Why? Because the Prime Minister apparently changed his mind and fought for them, even though there was fierce lobbying on all three issues.

Obviously today's Prime Minister of Canada cannot be accessible to most citizens or stakeholders. He represents the whole nation; at best there will be time to meet with large, national organizations. But the PM's key advisers and *their* advisers *are* accessible. These include staff of the Prime Minister's Office, Privy Council Office (the *central agents*), assistant deputy ministers, directors-general and directors (the *technocrats*).

Other interest groups who always seem to get their way with government have known this for years. As ministers and their deputies get shuffled around every 18 months or so, only the second-rank bureaucrats — the assistant deputy ministers, directors-general, and directors — have a real grip on the reins of power and the information base by which to use them. That is why assistant deputy ministers in current business-government research are considered the equivalent of CEOs in the private sector. *If chief executive officers like talking to their counterparts, they had best forget about ministers and get used to talking with assistant deputy ministers and their immediate subordinates.*

Nowhere is the contingency theory of management more applicable than here. *Whom you target depends on what you want.* Generally, the more detailed and routine a matter, the lower down the hierarchy business should go; the more abstract and singularly unique an issue, the higher.[8] Correspondingly, the higher the government official, the more imperative it is that the CEO be involved; the lower the government official, the more practical it is to involve someone closer to the technicality of the issue. Either way, business has to take the initiative.

In addition to these central agents and technocrats is one often overlooked target — the growing class of *political administrators*. These include the chief of staff who controls a minister's agenda, the chief of staff who controls a deputy minister's agenda, executive assistants, special assistants, speech writers, and policy advisers. No longer are all these players young men and women hot off a campaign trail embarking on new careers. Instead, they will likely be professional people, often in mid-career, sometimes co-opted from the public or private sectors, and capable of influencing their political masters. However, even in the Prime Minister's Office, there are only about three key staff who really have the prime minister's ear. There are many political administrators but only a **few** who count. Find them!

Ministers and deputy ministers have been omitted from this list of targets. They have little more time than the prime minister does (except for those rare business concerns of national importance), and prefer to meet with coalitions or sectoral representatives to conserve their time. In essence, a policy must be well-developed by outside interests, with due consideration given to its political ramifications, before a minister or deputy minister will take it seriously. Ministers and deputy ministers will most often be courteous if accessed but that is all. After all, both owe their positions to the prime minister, and therefore will likely defer to "the government." There will be exceptions, but they will be few and far between.

Despite the case for approaching central agents, technocrats, and political administrators, there is still one to be made for approaching ministers, MPs and the Opposition. These approaches should not be aimed at achieving one's ends, but should rather be courteous in nature. One day, one of those ministers may become prime minister; some of those back-benchers will become ministers; and the Opposition could become the government. Consider this contact an investment in the future. And when approaching these individuals, provide them with whatever information is available to other policy-making contacts that is not confidential, of national importance, or relating to corporate security. This approach has worked well for some. By working with government continuously they have been able to create a sense that their cause(s) should take priority.

Even here, however, things could be changing. Under the new procedures of the House of Commons, committees of the House now have increased investigative and policy review powers. So far, only the Finance Committee has flexed its muscles though with little effect. The point is that processes can change, and it is wise to keep abreast of them and even exert influence.

Working with people in the Prime Minister's Office, Privy Council Office, and line departments, and educating members of the Cabinet, backbenchers, and Opposition may appear to require considerable time and resources. It certainly does not seem a logical continuation of the concept of *targeting*, or focusing one's efforts. But in fact, it is. This is not a shotgun approach which dissipates business' efforts to no avail. It is not a "minister only" approach, which is also likely doomed to futility. *It is a concentrated, all-out effort to persuade those key players who do, or perhaps will, influence the making of policy.*

The first thing to be done by any CEO not yet plugged into Ottawa's pulse is to purchase the latest edition of the Government of Canada Telephone Directory for the National Capital Region. Here, one will find the key players. A good consultant can help and more will be said on this later. The more important an issue, the more research needs to be done before meetings take place.

As **Chapter 7** explained, decision-making power has become increasingly centralized even within the central agencies. In essence, the prime minister, the Prime Minister's Office, the Privy Council Office, and a very small number of ministers and deputy ministers run the show. This increased centralization of decision making and the politicization of deputy ministers has pushed the real nuts-and-bolts of policy making down into the middle levels of line departments and central agencies. The same group is also responsible for implementing policy. (See **Figure 12–3** for a continuum of government targets.)

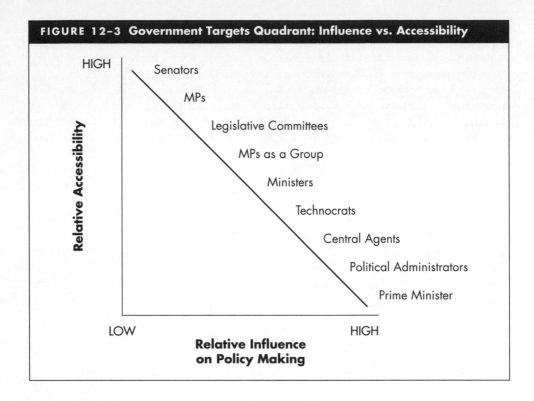

FIGURE 12-3 Government Targets Quadrant: Influence vs. Accessibility

Of course, budget time is where the gamble will always lie; another unknown is what priority the prime minister, the deputy prime minister, the minister of finance, and the president of the Treasury Board will place on a request.

Here is where *tactics* become important. *The key* is to reach one's targeted policy makers *before* a policy is made, or needed.

REACTIVE BUSINESS TACTICS: THE ADVERSARIAL MODEL

Business has two classes of tactics with which to consult with, influence, or otherwise interact with government: *reactive* and *proactive*. As the names imply, business can either react to government's initiatives after the fact, or can develop a relationship giving it input into government's policy-making process before decisions are made or program changes are announced.

As can readily be seen, proactive interaction offers business more significant, longer-term benefits. It also allows business to present its case within a public interest framework — something very difficult to do later, when it must take a defensive mode.

The reactive method will at best provide only short-term solutions to immediate problems, and presents business as acting only in its self-interest. It is usually issue-oriented and intended to prevent a change in policy after government has made its decision to go ahead. *Surprisingly, according to the surveys conducted by Taylor, 85% of today's business-government dealings are still of a reactive nature.* Although each reactive tactic described below has its place in a firm's non-market armoury, *there is a clear opportunity for business to improve its rela-*

tions with government by shifting its reliance upon reactive tactics to more proactive tactics and strategies.

Reactive-type tactics cover a wide spectrum, but can be grouped as follows, from shortest-term to longest-term; from most reactive to least reactive;[9] from simplest to most complex:

- Issues Management;
- Government Relations Function;
- Consultants (Lobbyists);
- Trade Associations;
- Sector Associations (Coalitions);
- Advocacy Advertising;
- Political Mobilization.

Issues Management

The past and current practice of most businesses has been to fight government's increasing involvement in economic affairs on an issue-by-issue basis. This should not be surprising, given business' pragmatism and conservative ideology. In fact, this method of dealing with government was prescribed by texts for years — *texts written in the United States for an American audience.*

Thus being of American origin, issues management assumes that policy development in the federal government moves from the bottom up (that is, generally speaking, incorrect in Canada), and is based upon the art of persuasion rather than a position of strength. Issues management also erroneously assumes the private sector's unchallenged legitimacy in the eyes of both government and the public. Managing business-government relations on an issue-related basis is difficult at best, given the ever-evolving nature, decision-making process, and priorities of government and its key players. However, to manage these relations with no full-time staff dedicated to the task is not to manage them at all.

For some companies, this may be an optimal strategy; there may be little else they can afford or need to do. However, this is not true for all Canadian businesses. With the passing of C.D. Howe and the halcyon days of the 1950s, so went the use of issues management as the primary means by which to deal with government. But it should not be forgotten, nor ignored, nor should it be relied upon too heavily.

Government Relations Function

During the OPEC oil crisis of the early 1970s, both business and government were completely taken off guard by the actions of the Arab oil-producers and several of the world's largest oil conglomerates. Since then, strategic management theorists have urged the addition of environmental scanning, strategic planning, and government-relations functions to corporate organizational processes at the highest level. These were expected to help corporations survive by easing their adaptation to externally driven change. The intent was to monitor and anticipate both public opinion and government actions, plans, legislation, and regulations, and prepare a company for possible government change.

Ideally, the head of a government relations department would know exactly how government operates and what government needs. This individual would play an integral role in corporate strategy making and senior management decision making. Reporting would be done directly to the CEO, with high levels of respect from within the organization as well as in the halls of Ottawa. In essence, improving government relations could be a new form of intelligence function.

This option was widely prescribed by well-meaning but naive Canadian academics, consultants, and practitioners during the early 1980s. However, for the most part, companies with a government-relations department do not benefit from it. Most companies view government relations as a staff function to be tolerated, not a line function of importance. For all the resources Imperial Oil had spent on government affairs (one of the leaders in this field at that time), it was still humiliated by the late 1970s by the *Bertrand Report*, which alleged that Imperial and other oil companies had "ripped off" the public by $12.1 billion.

In 1994, only one-third of the *Financial Post 500* corporations had a government relations unit. Very few directly reported to the CEO. Such a unit costs money and most Canadian businesses were too parsimonious to oblige. Those who did represented the most concentrated and regulated industries. The government-relations function is doomed to failure unless CEOs assume responsibility for the political impact of their corporations' actions, and rise to the challenge of defending Canada's private sector.

Consultants (Lobbyists)

Consultants in business-government relations may be paid consultants or paid third-party lobbyists. *Lobbying,* which simply means influencing the powers-that-be to change legislation or policy, involves a series of learnable skills. These include: defining one's goals; identifying who has the power to shape a policy to fulfill those goals; doing one's research; finding allies, if possible; packaging one's message; and communicating it in a positive manner.

Some consultants provide the early warning advice; others help companies develop policy position papers and briefs. Still others will help companies identify key players on government's side, and educate business managers about the intricacies of government policy making. Of course, some will do all three. Unfortunately, a large number will actually plead business' cases, rather than help them do it themselves. Hiring such firms often proves a waste of a company's money. A busy assistant deputy minister or director-general would much rather meet with a CEO in a candid conversation than speak to a go-between.

CEOs and companies successful in dealing with government may hire consultants to help them research and prepare for the task, but they always deal with government personally. Consultants who promote their own influence with Ottawa and their ability to "get things done" tend to be the snake-oil salesmen of today. In the long run (when they have long packed up and left town) these influence peddlers can do a firm more harm than good. CEO and company reputation and trustworthiness are very important.

The legitimate consulting firm has a valuable role to play: strategic advice. Most of these firms are staffed by knowledgeable former cabinet ministers, government technocrats, mandarins, leadership campaign managers, or political administrators. When hiring a consultant, note what is promised and compare this with the firm's track record. Generally, the "one-man shops" have currency valuable for two to three years after they leave government. The larger companies tend to have a *revolving door,* which keeps their personnel fresh and in touch with current issues, key players, and processes. But reputation alone does not assume success. Good government-relations consultants should have solid experience in the business world.

Lobbying Canadian-style has become big business: Canada's largest firms in the field, The Capital Hill Group, GPC Government Policy Consultants, and Hill & Knowlton Canada Ltd., have around 75 clients each. Several hundreds of millions of dollars are spent annually on consultant lobbyists. The business is also rapidly becoming more professional. Increasingly, lobbyists and consultants in Ottawa hold graduate degrees in economics or political science. Large multinational communications and advertising firms have also entered the industry by acquiring smaller Canadian firms.

In 1989, the federal government introduced the *Lobbyists Registration Act* requiring anyone being paid to influence federal decisions to register their names, the names of their clients, and general areas of activity with the Lobby Registry. In 1996, the Act was amended to define three types of lobbyists: consultant lobbyists (of which there are over 1000), in-house corporate lobbyists, and in-house association/non-profit organization lobbyists (the latter two totalling over 1700). The amendments also require lobbyists to disclose specific laws, regulations, policies, and/or contracts they are seeking to influence; identify the lobbying techniques used in a specific assignment; list their employer's and/or client's subsidiaries and parent company; and any government grants or other non-repayable funding received by their employers and/or clients. Despite these amendments, lobbyists successfully lobbied not to have their fees disclosed, and to return full tax-deductibility for their clients of these fees.

Smart companies will use consultants to complement, rather than replace, in-house expertise. Each individual lobbyist is far more influential than any one government or opposition backbencher; collectively lobbyists are more influential than all backbenchers combined. *The best government consultants will not only help resolve a current problem, but will also help devise a strategy to avoid future ones.* As one advertisement for a major government affairs consulting firm said, "There's a lot more to government relations than opening doors."

Trade Associations

This term refers to industry associations, product associations, professional associations, vertical trade associations, horizontal trade associations, and so on. All of these represent a group of companies with similar interests. Theoretically, trade associations are designed to exchange information within an industry, trade, or group and to promote their members' views to outsiders, particularly to government. They tend to monitor (with varying success and in varying proportions) government actions and plans, develop consensus within their specific business communities, and promote their members' needs. Over 300 trade associations are at work in Ottawa, employing over 2000 people and spending hundreds of millions of dollars annually.

Government officials like these associations for two reasons. First, they save the harried minister or bureaucrat a lot of meeting time. Second, they provide a forum in which to reach a consensus rather than leaving it to government. However, different associations have varying success in influencing government. Either they cannot develop that elusive consensus among their members or, if they do, they may be unable to offer the government practical, detailed proposals. National, broad-based associations such as the Canadian Manufacturers Association (CMA) and the Canadian Chamber of Commerce (CCC) historically have had limited effect in Ottawa. Reading one of their position papers is like listening to a politician's speech; there's plenty of hyperbole but often little substance. However, the CMA has been able to position itself better, with a lessening of the fragmentation of business' voice. In early 1996 the 2500 member CMA merged with the 1000 member Canadian Exporters' Association to form

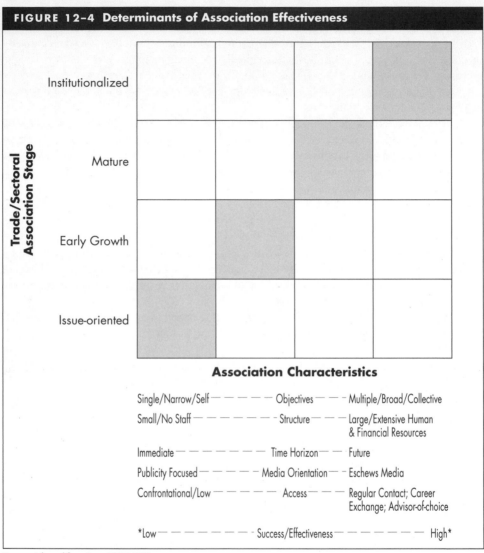

FIGURE 12-4 Determinants of Association Effectiveness

Trade/Sectoral Association Stage

Institutionalized

Mature

Early Growth

Issue-oriented

Association Characteristics

Single/Narrow/Self — — — — — Objectives — — Multiple/Broad/Collective

Small/No Staff — — — — — — Structure — — Large/Extensive Human & Financial Resources

Immediate — — — — — — Time Horizon — — Future

Publicity Focused — — — — Media Orientation — — Eschews Media

Confrontational/Low — — — — — Access — — Regular Contact; Career Exchange; Advisor-of-choice

Low — — — — — — — Success/Effectiveness — — — — — — High

Source: Adapted from Pross (1990:290)

the Alliance of Manufacturers and Exporters Canada (AMEC). AMEC staff will concentrate on trade issues in Ottawa and labour issues at the provincial level.

Two very significant groups today are the Business Council on National Issues (BCNI) and the Canadian Federation of Independent Business (CFIB). Both arose when ministers no longer catered to specific business constituencies on a one-to-one basis. The BCNI has succeeded in influencing government policy because it represents the 150 largest corporations (private-sector employers) in Canada. It also develops timely, well-balanced research papers providing new information on issues of importance to both government and business. The BCNI is led by Tom D'Aquino, an assistant to former Prime Minister Trudeau, university roommate of former Prime Minister Clark, and husband of Susan Peterson, ADM in the Finance Department.

The CFIB has been very effective on behalf of small business in Canada. It directly represents 85 000 independent businesses that account for nearly 1 000 000 voters, and has been relentless in its pursuit of its mission. It was founded by John Bullock, a successful second-generation Toronto small businessman. CFIB spends $14 million annually and employs over 200 people. Recent CFIB lobbying successes include a lower corporate tax rate for small business, decreases in unemployment insurance premiums, and simpler GST regulations.

Even though these two trade associations appear opposite in all of their characteristics, they are successful for the same reasons: hard work, knowledge of the government system and actors, consistency, openness, good information and forthrightness (see **Figure 12–4**). They do not always win, but they do well in a city not known for succumbing easily to lobbyists. Both have won the confidence of decision makers in Ottawa.

Sector Associations (Coalitions)

A special subset of trade associations worth separate mention is *sector associations*. These represent the manufacturers/processors/producers, buyers, suppliers, labour, investors, and creditors of sectors of the economy. They are not national, all-embracing associations like the AMEC or CCC, nor are they as specific in their membership as an industry association such as the Canadian Carpet Institute. They are cross-sectoral, not unlike the BCNI and CFIB, representing varying interests within the same economic grouping.

Successful sector associations exchange and promote information like any other trade association. They also develop a consensus which includes labour, thus representing a true political constituency. Smart associations never call for increased government spending unless they can identify where government can save elsewhere in the same sector. Unlike many of their industry counterparts, they promote job creation and court the Opposition and backbenchers for the long haul. Their approach is to accommodate, not to confront.

The best example of a sector association at work is not a formal association at all, but rather a coalition of interests representing the auto industry. This is comprised of vehicle manufacturers, auto parts manufacturers, and the Canadian Auto Workers' Union (CAW). These three mutually interdependent groups who often find themselves in fundamental disagreement have put aside their differences more than once. Their objective: to work with government to agree on a policy direction in which everyone — big business, small business, labour, government, and the public — wins. A win-win proposal to government will seldom be turned aside.

A promising new model for getting business expertise into the policy-making process along the lines of a sector association is the New Directions Group. Several dozen CEOs and heads of public interest groups have come together to produce sensible solutions to environmental problems. Participants include such divergent vested interests as Dow Chemical Canada Ltd., Noranda Forest Inc., Pollution Probe, and Friends of the Earth. Environment Canada takes the Group seriously because New Directions' members: *i*) recognized that polarized confrontation between industry and environmental groups was counterproductive; *ii*) were willing to break ranks with their peers; *iii*) believed that progressive leaders could rise above the crowd; and *iv*) were determined to move beyond rhetoric to action. Key to their success has been the Group's willingness to eschew the spotlight, keep a low profile, set specific goals, and work toward deadlines. It has no budget, staff or hired lobbyists — this is cheap but effective.

Good business groups, whether formal associations or ad-hoc coalitions, also recognize that not everyone in Ottawa wants to see them. The Prime Minister's Office likes associations if they truly represent a consensus. Middle-level managers of line departments like them because they can offer at least information and often solutions for their policy dilemmas. *Sector associations succeed because they are partnerships bonded together for one common purpose — survival!*

Advocacy Advertising

Simply defined, *advocacy advertising* is designed to promote opinion, not sell goods or services, through paid media advertising. It is aimed at influencing the public's political, economic, or social behaviour, not its purchasing behaviour. The most successful type of advocacy advertising (for its paid sponsors) is directed at influencing public policy choice rather than improving one's image or appeal.

Regardless of the type employed, advocacy advertising is aimed at a company's employees as much as at the external public. It hopes to boost management and labour morale where, in fact, it is often more successful than in shaping public opinion. Advocacy advertising stops being propaganda when the audience agrees with the opinions being expressed. However, this is difficult to measure. The public's understanding of information and how well it receives it are two different phenomena.

However, business is no longer a spectator sport, and advocacy advertising has a deserved place in the private sector's arsenal. Like any other weapon, it should be treated with respect. It is expensive and often a gamble. It can also backfire as easily as it can succeed.

Business is slowly beginning to recognize that winning over the public means winning over the government. If business can shape public opinion to its favour, then government will be hard-pressed to ignore business' case. Political parties and governments engage in various forms of advocacy advertising all the time. They call it "campaigning" and "informing the public."

Successful advocacy advertising avoids posturing and belligerence, but focuses on a short-term issue with long-term consequences, presented objectively and credibly in its audience's best interests. Objectives must be clear; target audiences must be precisely defined; messages must be unambiguous; and the right media must be chosen for the circumstances. Successful advocacy advertising will present an on-going case for its argument spanning several months.

Advocacy advertising came of age in Canada during the 1980s. Voters saw an overwhelmingly successful $5.2 million, pro-free trade campaign by the Canadian Alliance for Trade and Job Opportunities. This was actually a coalition of the CFIB, BCNI, CMA, CCC, CEA, Consumers' Association of Canada, and 19 other trade associations and interest groups. During the 1990s and into the new millennium, advocacy advertising will have a major impact. The issues and times change but the concept continues intact.

Political Mobilization

The least attractive option to business is that of political mobilization and direct involvement in the political process.[10] This option assumes that business minds think ideologically, that business deserves special status within the political bargaining forum, and that there is an open, public policy arena in which economic power is distributed and benefits are conferred. All three of these assumptions, as we have seen earlier, can be easily challenged. Political mobilization is more of an American concept. However, it does have some merit for business in Canada.

Many researchers still urge CEOs to run for public office and represent business' interests in Ottawa. Someone must carry business' message to Ottawa, and Ottawa claims it would benefit from proven management skills, whether in caucus, Cabinet, or the public service. As we know, a successfully elected former CEO would have to represent many diverse interests, not just personal ones. As a member of the government party, one would have no choice but to follow party discipline and government policy. These would be good lessons for a CEO to learn, as well as the fact that power no longer resides in the House of Commons or even in the Cabinet as a whole; government is too busy just to accommodate business. Listening, the new MP would learn, does not necessarily mean agreement, and action does not necessarily follow consultation.

Naturally, the CEO would want to be in Cabinet, but the odds of becoming a Cabinet minister are not high. This would depend on the region represented by the CEO and his sex, religion, ethnicity, and age — not just merit.

Worse still, if one does make minister, an authoritarian business executive used to a formal, rational, directive decision-making structure will not feel at all comfortable — let alone excel in — Ottawa's much more fluid, intellectual, social decision-making process. Dynamic, achievement-oriented business leaders are often quite frustrated in government's cumbersome management environment.

Finally, the $64 400 salary of an MP or even $100 000+ for a minister will be a far cry from the salary, stock options, bonuses, pensions, and perks received as a CEO or senior executive. Besides the low pay, business executives running for office could impose personal and family sacrifice on themselves — like the politicians they relish criticizing! Poor incomes may lead one into that ill-defined territory of conflict-of-interest problems; this has happened before.

Political mobilization means more than just CEOs seeking public office. *It means business developing consistent positions, identifying allied constituencies, and mobilizing votes as do labour unions*. Speeches to one's peers will change nothing. Bashing government from time-to-time plays right into someone else's hands.

Delivering or denying votes, though, gets results directly in proportion to the number of votes at stake. Witness Quebec's success at the federal-provincial bargaining table over the last 30 years, regardless of the political colour of the governments in Ottawa or in Quebec City.

Unfortunately, there is no natural political constituency for business in Canada today. There is much work to be done in this regard, and it will take time. Business must also be prepared to play to win; anything goes in the political arena. Politicians and bureaucrats seldom get angry in public, but they can and do get even!

Whether reactive or proactive, the complexity of government is immense. **Figure 12–5** illustrates the decision process of the Government of Canada.

PROACTIVE BUSINESS TACTICS: THE ACCOMMODATION MODEL

There should remain little doubt that, in business' present environment, modern business management must learn to monitor environmental change. Business must interpret these

FIGURE 12-5 The Decision Process of the Federal Government

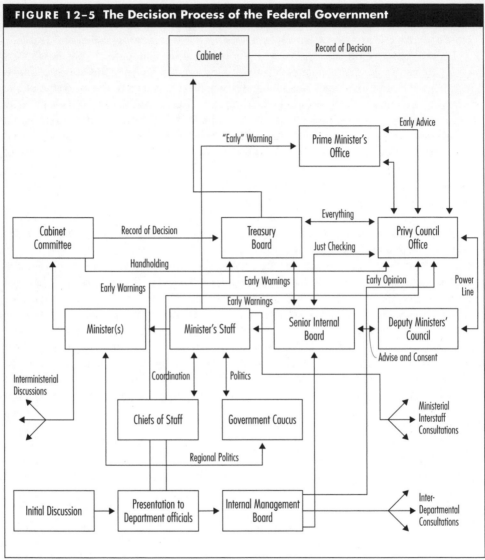

Source: Updated from McIlroy (1993:14). Les McIlroy, author of *The Manager's Mentor*

changes, adapt where practical, be flexible, innovate, overcome, and anticipate future change. However, most importantly, business management must understand the need, and develop the capability, to influence public policy rather than managing its effects once passed. This will require hiring personnel with significant understanding of government, giving them adequate resources to do their jobs, and having them directly accountable to the CEO who must take charge of dealing with government. After all, this is a question of survival — and the CEO is charged with the survival of the firm.

Business, not government, must take the initiative to restore the old government department-clientele relationships, once the cornerstone of early Canadian business-government relations.

Of course, many such linkages still exist at the routine, technical, administrative level. It is at the general policy-making, senior management levels that they must be reestablished.

In other words, business must be proactive. It must objectively, professionally, and discretely demonstrate to the real powers that form government policy how vital business enterprise is in Canada's economy. Business must provide policy makers with accurate, complete information *before* policy options are eliminated, decisions taken, and a government department drafts its memorandum to Cabinet. Above all, business must actually do the above *in the public interest*.

In effect, business must interact more often with government to enhance mutual understanding. This requires a strategy, whether at the firm or sector level, to identify the right people and the right time in government. The **CEO** must take the lead in all of this. After all, *decision makers want to deal with decision makers* in any bargaining arena. By doing so, business will be able to prevent as well as initiate change.

Such a proactive stance would return business and government to an era of mutual accommodation and cooperative planning. It would narrow the perceptual gap between business and government, and once again develop shared beliefs in how national goals could best be achieved, perhaps help decide even what those goals ought to be. Above all, it would restore trust between these two solitudes and forge a national partnership. Business-government relations are not in desperate disrepair; it is just that the challenges facing business and government today are so awesome.

This is not to be construed as lobbying. This is having *input* before decisions are made. It is an exchange of information and cooperation for favourable legislation and regulation. It is business offering to implement government policy through the mechanisms of the marketplace, as well as showing government why business needs it to redress the imbalances in that marketplace from time-to-time. It is integrating market and non-marketing strategies into a purposeful whole.

The answers to business-government misunderstandings do not lie in Parliamentary reform nor improved reactive tactics, but in business showing government and the public that a healthy private sector is in the best interests of the nation. Going to government with a ready-made consensus, within part or all of the business community, would be Utopia for both business and government.

What are the rules for proactive government relations?

i. Business' policy recommendations must be sound, reasonable, legal, and specific; do not ask for the impossible, nor succumb to hyperbole — that is the politicians' job in selling policy.

ii. Business should avoid the discussion of specific benefits and the need to disperse costs, as government will assume as much; business must go to government with an action plan, not more problems for government.

iii. Business will not always win, losing gracefully is a must; it should be prepared to play a long game for that all-important big win someday.

iv. It must deal with the *real* decision makers, and deal with their very real problems; business must understand the needs and goals of government and its policy engineers (as well as their own).

v. Business must support its brief oral submissions with completely documented written verification and research.

vi. Be patient. The wheels of government move cautiously and slowly, and that is not all bad; there is no single channel of authority for any one matter.

vii. Being bilingual will certainly help in Ottawa and Quebec City; having a sense of humour will help everywhere.

viii. Business must be aware of the political ramifications of its proposals or information, and be able to offer intelligent, informed advice about them. This does not mean that its advice will be taken, but it will show that business is sympathetic to the constraints upon government policy makers. For example, business should understand that in "bad times" government must be seen to be "doing something."

The CEO of a firm (or one who chairs a sector association) should do all of this.[11] Here are some characteristics of a successful CEO dealing with government. The individual should be:

i. Articulate, well-informed, and consistent in presenting a case;

ii. Frank, candid, positive, and sensitive;

iii. Competent and popular in the business community;

iv. Not overly extroverted, aggressive, or strident;

v. An "organization person," self-confident and socially adept; and

vi. Ethical (and appear to be so as well).

Efforts must be conducted on an on-going basis, but without being overly persistent. (This raises government's suspicions, and rightly so, wasting time and goodwill). Although these efforts likely have little impact upon quarterly profits and market share, they have great bearing on a company's, industry's, or sector's long-term prospects for survival. The overall process is more important than the immediate outcome.

Reactive confrontation produces a lose/lose situation at worst. Compromise is still a lose/lose situation, but of less consequence all around (that is why most erroneously view compromise as a win/win situation). Only proactive cooperation and consultation can produce a true win/win situation. Canadian business may not be able to shape world economic trends, but it does have the potential to again influence domestic economic policy. *Information is the key and it is results that count.*

IMPLICATIONS FOR MANAGEMENT

Business no longer has (if it ever did) a monopoly on relations with government. Government now meets with, and sometimes even listens to, a large number of very diversified interest groups. Yet business has not clearly recognized or understood this fact and has not learned to adapt.

To compound this situation, the private sector lacks coordinated and hence effective leadership. The Canadian business community has not been united in its efforts to influence public policy making and implementation. Different business interests often talk at cross-purposes, which allows government to play one segment against the other. This diminishes the impact business might have had on public policy. In this respect, business' rivals may actually be their best friends. Banded together, there would be a cohesiveness and strength in numbers never experienced by business when dealing with government.

Even though individual interest groups, including segments of the business community, have sometimes succeeded with short-term, reactive issue management, they have as

FIGURE 12-6 Generic Strategies For Business to Deal with Government

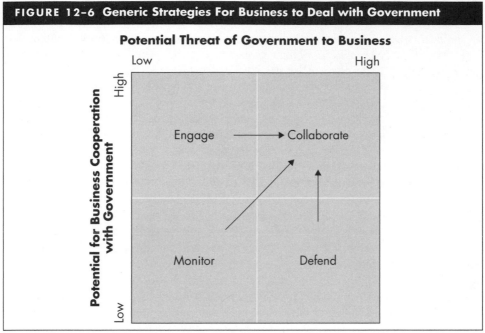

Source: Reprinted with permission of Academy of Management, P.O. Box 3020, Briar Cliff Manor, NY 10510-8020. "Generic Strategies for Business to Deal with Government" from Strategies for Assessing and Managing Organizational Stakeholders, Academy of Management Executive, 5:2. Reproduced by permission of the publisher via Copyright Clearance Center, Inc.

often failed to promote their own interests in the longer term and over a broader spectrum of public policy issues. Cross-business compromise and cooperation would probably lessen much of the short-term individual gain, but would achieve a greater collective gain overall.

In Japan, business makes the tough economic decisions and government implements them. This works in a homogeneous society, but Canada is very much a pluralist society. To expect the CEOs of the *Financial Post 500* to agree unanimously on all government policies would be unrealistic. However, CEOs must accept business-government relations as an important addition to their mandate. Being responsible for strategically managing their enterprises, they should realize that often *there is nothing more vital to the survival of their firms than government and its collective impact upon them.*

Chief executive officers must also adopt a much broader perspective when approaching or dealing with government. At the very least, they should envelop their parochial interests in a greater national interest, fine-tuning them to more closely match the national interest — however defined by the government of the day. Working with and through sector associations that include buyers, suppliers, and labour, and taking a more personal role in the leadership of these associations, would expose CEOs to the consensus-building mode of decision making so vital for effective public policy.

Business leaders often are dismayed to discover that government operates by the principles of political science. Business should therefore strive to understand government's convoluted agenda and processes (again noting **Figure 12–5**). Hiring senior line managers or lobbyists from senior government ranks is one way to do this. Maintaining an office in Ottawa with staff directly responsible for improving contact with appropriate government staff is a second option.

Improving the quality of trade associations, working through them more often, and developing them as training schools for executives is a third option. The Business Council on National Issues type of association appears to be an ideal candidate for the latter. It has the support of many key players within the business elite, has been fairly effective in lobbying and working with government, has demonstrated that it knows how and why government works as it does, and is respected by many in government circles. Such organizations would contribute substantially to improving business' understanding of government if it assumed the role of an academy designated to train senior business executives in the art and principles of political science. *Business leaders would then learn that in the short-term, it is the process that counts; in the longer term, it is the results that count.*

In short, business should move beyond firm-specific, individual efforts to more collective, representative, cross-sectoral approaches to government (see **Figure 12–6**). Business should concentrate more on the *real* decision makers in government and less on the public figureheads. Business must concentrate less on *ad-hoc* responses to announced government policy and become more proactive in influencing government policy. It needs to stop opposing automatically every government program it does not like, and address economic issues before they become political issues. [12]

All of these recommendations require an increased allocation of resources to the business-government function, not necessarily in the form of a department, but in recognition of the fact that a CEO needs advice, research, contacts, support, and time to do the job. Although this practice may erode short-term profits slightly, it will improve substantially business' longer-term position within the economy. Canada and Canadians need business to get more involved in the public policy process.

SUGGESTED FURTHER READINGS

Baron, David P. 1995. "Integrated Strategy: Market and Non-Market Components", *California Management Review*. 37:2.

Baetz, Mark C. 1993. "Rethinking the Government Relations Unit." In Mark C. Baetz, (ed), *Readings and Canadian Cases in Business, Government & Society*. Scarborough, ON: Nelson Canada.

Bartha, Peter F. 1990. "Issues Management: Theory and Practice." *Gestion-Revue Internationale de Gestion* (Ecole des Hautes Etudes Commerciales de Montreal), 15:5.

Bartha, Peter F. 1985. "Organizational Competence in Business-Government Relations: A Managerial Perspective." *Canadian Public Administration*, 28: 2.

Bregha, F. 1981. *Bob Blair's Pipeline: The Business and Politics of National Energy Development Projects*. 2nd ed. Toronto: James Lorimer Publishers.

Coleman, W.D. 1988. *Business and Politics: A Study of Collective Action*. Montreal: McGill-Queen's University Press.

Fleischmann, G. 1993. "Lobbying Governments: Who, How and Why." *Business Quarterly*, 58:2, Winter.

Gillies, James. 1981. *Where Business Fails*. Montreal: Institute for Research on Public Policy.

Lermer, George, (ed). 1984. *Probing Leviathan: An Investigation of Government in the Economy*. Vancouver: The Fraser Institute.

Lyon, J. 1983. *Dome: The Rise and Fall of the House that Jack Built*. Toronto: Macmillan.

McIlroy, L. 1993. *Marketing Your Message To Government, Your Ideas Are A Product — Government Is A Consumer*. Ottawa: Public Policy Forum.

Pross, A. Paul. 1990. "Pressure Groups: Talking Chameleons." In: M.S. Whittington and G. Williams, (eds), *Canadian Politics in the 1990s*. 3rd ed. Toronto: Nelson.

Savage, Grant, Timothy Nix, Carlton Whitehead, and John Blair. 1991. "Strategies For Assessing and Managing Organizational Stakeholders." *Academy of Management Executive*. 5:2

Sawatsky, John. 1987. *The Insiders: Government, Business and the Lobbyists*. Toronto: McClelland & Stewart.

NOTES

1. George Lermer, (ed). *Probing Leviathan: An Investigation of Government in the Economy*. (Vancouver: The Fraser Institute, 1984).

2. The federal government was required by law to complete a review of the 1992 *Bank Act* by March 1997. It has been delayed, but the mid-1997 Royal Bank of Canada purchase offer for London Life might prod the government into action.

3. To this end, the federal government set up *two* task forces to report within 18 months. For government, non-action is always a legitimate option.

4. For a more complete review of market and non-market strategies see David P. Baron. "Integrated Strategy: Market and Non-Market Components," *California Management Review*. 37:2. (1995).

5. Royal Commissions are not listed because they are more often used to defuse an issue rather than to develop a policy or make a decision.

6. In Europe, unlike Canada, the electoral method is predominantly PR (proportional representation).

7. Canada has a near-duopoly in national private television and the six largest newspaper conglomerates account for 90% of the market.

8. Another way of looking at this strategy is: the larger the number of jobs potentially affected, the higher up one should go within government.

9. In fact, the potential proactive capacity of these tactics increases for each one as you go down the list.

10. This excludes financial contributions to political parties, since these are now limited by the *Election Expenses Act* and similar Provincial Acts.

11. Chief executive officers of large Japanese firms spend almost all of their time dealing with government, at home and abroad.

12. For a strategic perspective on managing government relations is particular, and stakeholder relations in general (which also expands on the framework identified in **Figure 12–6**), see Grant Savage, Timothy Nix, Carlton Whitehead, and John Blair, "Strategies For Assessing and Managing Organizational Stakeholders," *Academy of Management Executive*, 5:2 (1991).

GOVERNMENT DEALING WITH BUSINESS

He that would govern others, first should be the master of himself.

Philip Massinger, 1583-1640

The federal government of Canada has traditionally sought public input in the policy-making process *after* it has drafted its policy intentions. This history is not unique to the federal government in Canada. More recently, due to vigorous interventions of stakeholders, governments have genuinely started to seek public input. Business, in particular, has been consulted before the details of a policy are finalized. The rounds of business-government consultation while the Canada-US Free Trade Agreement was being negotiated best demonstrates government's newer proactive stance. Might this be the trend for the future of business-government relations, or is it an aberration in how government deals with business? What more should government be doing?

These questions and more form much of the substance of this chapter on how government deals with business. But first, it should be recognized that government can be just as reactive as is business. The best, most glaring case of its reactive approach to business' needs is the 1970s and 1980s bailing out of firms in deep financial trouble, or *corporate welfare bums*, an enduring term coined by then-NDP leader David Lewis in the 1968 general federal election.

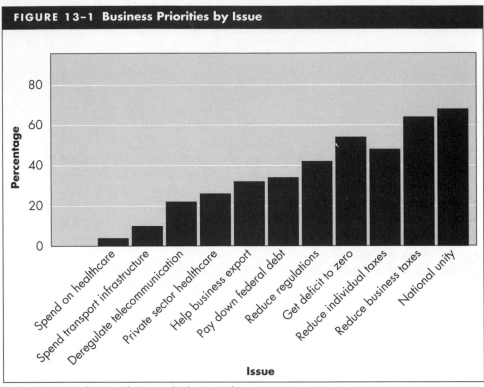

FIGURE 13–1 **Business Priorities by Issue**

Source: COMPAS Market Research. Appeared in the *Financial Post* on May 24, 1997.

CURRENT BUSINESS ISSUES

In the preceding chapter the dominant theme was the need for business to understand the responsibilities and processes of government. This chapter begins with the counter theme — the need for government to understand the needs of business. If business and government thinking converge rather than diverge, business could better meet society's needs and less government would be necessary.

In June 1997, a federal election was held. Besides the decision that the Liberals will rule for the coming period, this election proved a laboratory of society's thinking and perceptions exist on a range of important issues. About mid-campaign, a detailed business survey was conducted and its results are depicted in **Figure 13–1**. While these results are a May 1997 snapshot in time, it seems likely that many of the issues are sustaining ones. Depending on the progress Canada makes on these issues into the millennium, some of them will be longer term in nature, but hopefully some will pass into history.

By far the dominant business priority was national unity. Unfortunately the issue simmers still and the danger of separation is very real, perhaps even probable. There can be no doubt that the high priority reflects how deeply business persons, like most others across the land, care about Canada being whole. Beyond profound sentiment, the separation threat is a source of commercial risk. Investment is repelled by risk. This increment of business risk is not welcome anywhere in Canada, but it has particularly punished business opportunities in Quebec.

The next priority was to cut taxes, even ahead of deficit reduction and regulation relief. Of particular concern are taxes on payroll and income levels that are high enough to dampen employment, savings, and investment incentives. Capital, both financial and human, is increasingly mobile in the globalized economy; both types are ever more readily able to shift from a higher to a lower tax jurisdiction.[1] A significant domestic way for disappearance is the underground economy. A recent study by the Fraser Institute estimates the underground economy size at 20%,[2] while the "official" Statistics Canada estimate is 3-5%. Some countries, most recently New Zealand, have shifted the tax base from income to consumption and property (taxes which are immobile and difficult to hide).

Worthy of note in **Figure 13–1** is that business purports a vital role of government in business exports; in the global competition ahead, that priority likely will prove to be correct. While little social infrastructure came out the survey being reported, transport infrastructure spending is supported. This fits with the economics functions listing provided in **Chapter 4**. Notably absent is any priority to bailouts or other subsidies of business by government. In each election each party seems to come out firmly against business subsidies. So why does the issue continue to be relevant? Nobody favours them, but everyone wants them.

BAILOUTS AND CORPORATE WELFARE

Government financial assistance to business (aside from regional and employment development initiatives) usually takes one of three forms: loans or loan guarantees; bailouts, or the last-minute infusion of funds, either of a debt or equity nature; or grants, a more common, less reactive form of direct subsidization.

During the Great Depression of the 1930s, government *loans and loan guarantees* to failing businesses represented up to 14% of the GNP. By the time of the postwar economic boom of the 1950s and 1960s, that figure had dropped to an average of 4.3%. Now throughout the 1980s and into the 1990s the figure has risen again to nearly 20% of the GNP!

The vast majority of this amount comes from the federal government.[3] In fact, Ottawa is the fourth-largest lender to the business community. About 40 federal agencies lend money or guarantee loans for business, with about 60% of that money in the housing market. Another 15% supports other forms of domestic business (primarily resource upgrading); 10% encourages exports; and 10% goes to the agricultural sector.[4]

Nearly all export financing today is done by the Export Development Corporation (EDC), and over half of all mortgage insurance is through the Canada Mortgage and Housing Corporation (CMHC). Indeed, the CMHC has become the 13th-largest financial institution in Canada, with assets of $6 billion. The farm community receives 30% of all its credit from government loans and loan guarantees.

And government does not discriminate between borrowers. Take the case of Peter Pocklington and the Government of Alberta. He had been an outspoken defendant of free enterprise who unsuccessfully ran for the federal PC leadership in the early 1980s. The platform was to minimize the role of government. In fact, he was totally opposed to all government support for business. In a regular Alberta newspaper column on March 6, 1988, he censured "government funded movements of the liberal-left." On March 10, however, he accepted a $12 million loan from Alberta's Treasury Branches for his meat-packing company, Gainers Inc., and a $55 million loan guarantee.[5] Why the sudden shift in philosophy? Because the "free enterpriser" needed the money to compete with Fletcher's Fine Foods (a government-controlled enterprise) in central Alberta, where he planned to build a new plant and modernize his existing one. Nor was this the first time that Pocklington had fed at the government trough. In 1984, he accepted a $31 million loan from Alberta, and in July, 1987, received a $100 million line of credit for his Palm Dairies, Ltd.

Of course, this was not a bailout, and Pocklington opposed bailouts. During 1976-1983 the federal government bailed out ten major firms: six of these subsequently went under, one turned around, and three remain in limbo. This spate of corporate welfare occurred when "anti-business" Pierre Trudeau had been prime minister for all but nine months. In 1976, 49% of the equity of Consolidated Computer was purchased by the federal government for $30 million. It was later sold for $100 000, with the government losing $119 million overall on the deal. On the other hand, Ottawa poured $15 million into Electrohome, was paid back by 1980, and made $10 million.

In 1979, CCM received $22 million from the federal government and went bankrupt in 1982. Taxpayers lost $16 million. In 1981, $13 million was given to White Farm Equipment, which went bankrupt in 1983. Also in 1981, Massey-Ferguson received $125 million from Ottawa and another $75 million from the Ontario government to save its combine manufacturing operations. By 1988, this division of the now-renamed Varity Corporation was in receivership, with the federal government writing off previous loans totalling $226.3 million.

1982 was a watershed year for business. Maislin received $33 million from Ottawa in 1982 and went bankrupt in 1983. The Lake Group received $13 million and lost $23 million in 1983 alone. The East Coast fish-processing industry was nationalized, and subsequently partially reprivatized at untold costs to the taxpayers. Co-op Implements received $13 million. Bailouts ceased by 1983, with Petromont of Quebec receiving $25 million that year. Chrysler Canada and Dome Petroleum both negotiated rescues by the federal government but both refused the government's terms. Chrysler succeeded; Dome failed.

Bailouts are a total waste of time and money. They are usually "too little, too late." Most of the companies bailed out had exhausted every other form of government largesse. Corporate welfare fosters inefficiency, dependency, and misallocation of resources, *but it does save jobs*, although usually temporarily.

The only difference between a subsidy and a bailout (both are essentially free money) is that *bailouts are for losers, and subsidies are for winners*. The rich get richer at the public's expense in order to increase capacity, relocate, open a new plant, or create jobs. For example, the auto industry is continually being subsidized by the federal, Ontario, and Quebec governments for one reason or another.

In 1994, business grants and subsidies totalled $6.2 billion or 1% of our GDP. The forest products industry, Canada's number one industry in certain regions, is continually being subsidized for machinery, jobs, reforestation, infrastructure, exports, and so on. Normick, Perron and Forex's $400 million newsprint mill in Quebec was heavily subsidized by that province's government. The company sold out to American interests. Daishawa Paper of Japan, when building its $500 million pulp mill in Alberta, received $65 million from the province and $10 million from Ottawa. Why? Not because the company needed it (as they admitted) but because they tried "to follow the Canadian way of doing things." Agriculture, industry's number one beneficiary of this type of government largesse, received $1.3 billion from the federal government in 1994, an amount equal to 8% of total production and about 70% of net income.

Is government subsidization of business dangerous? It can be. Overcapacity already exists in both the auto and forest products industries, and in both industries, the firms are subsidized. Government subsidization drives industry profits down further, creating a vicious circle. Overcapacity reduces profitability, which means lay-offs, so government subsidizes new capacity to create jobs. This new capacity reduces profits, and so on.

Why do governments loan money to business as a lender of last resort, bail out losers, and subsidize excess capacity? There are nine generally acknowledged reasons:

i. *Jobs, Jobs, Jobs*: Votes, votes, votes;

ii. *Market Failure*: The private sector cannot profitably or does not want to provide a public good or service;

iii. *Instrument of Public Policy*: This is relatively rare, an example being the East Coast fish-processing industry;

iv. *"Favoured Son"* : This is for purely political reasons, as some critics claim Maislin and Petromont were because of their Quebec location. Other examples include the fishing case; the Massey, White and Co-op cases (for the farmers' sake); and the Electrohome case because of its location in that bastion of Liberalism, Kitchener-Waterloo;

v. *Regional Development*: Pressure is felt from provincial governments especially Quebec, the East Coast, and the Prairies;

vi. *Key Sectors*: Forestry, oil and gas, agriculture, mining, and fishing are heavily capitalized and have huge unemployment, and have a major share of the GNP. Six out of the ten bailouts above were in key sectors;

vii. *Promote/Retain Canadian Ownership*;

viii. *Save Sources of Future Corporate Tax Revenues*; and

ix. *Promote/Retain Reasonable Levels of Competition within an Industry*.

But what is the cost when government deals with business in this way? To begin with, there is greater industrial inefficiency, higher prices, and higher taxes. Unfortunately, these actions neither address nor cure the root problems. Worse still, government simply raised others' expectations that they, too, were entitled to funds. *Business joined the age of entitlement!*

How does government decide whether business failure is due to outside variables or to mismanagement? Is such support of business an unfair trade practice under the terms of the WTO? Surely there must be a more sensible approach for government to deal with business than to transfer 25% or more of the nation's wealth from the consumer/taxpayer to the producer? An alternative is for business to get involved in government policy making. This would enable it to develop an economic climate that would avoid failure. But to what extent should government get business involved?

NORMATIVE LEVELS OF BUSINESS INFLUENCE

In the study discussed previously, business and government elites were asked whether they believed that business should have more, less, or the same amount of influence as they had in forming these government policies:

- monetary policy
- fiscal/taxation policy
- competition policy
- government spending
- foreign investment
- tariffs and trade policy
- development/location incentives
- bailouts of financially troubled companies
- government investment in or ownership of business
- labour legislation
- environmental regulation.

The majority of business leaders thought that business should have more influence in shaping all the above-listed policies. Specifically, respondents felt strongest about having more influence in creating the following policies. They are listed in descending order of importance to the respondents:

- government spending
- fiscal/taxation policy
- labour legislation
- tariffs and trade policy.

Interestingly, a strong inverse relationship exists between a business leader's level of satisfaction with business-government relations and the wish for greater influence in the making of public policy. In other words, *the more satisfied one was with business-government relations, the less interest there was in having more influence.* In fact, those who perceived business-government relations to be in very good shape actually thought that business should have less influence. On the other hand, *those who were less satisfied thought business should have more influence.*

The government elite generally was in agreement. It was satisfied overall with current levels of business input but was open to greater input. There was only one exception and that was social regulation; government thought that the business community should have less influence on labour and environmental regulations.

An earlier survey revealed that fully half of central agents — those powerful, if shadowy, decision makers in the Prime Minister's Office, Privy Council Office, Treasury Board Secretariat, and Ministry of Finance — actually consulted with business leaders for policy advice. [6] In the United States the response was 75% and in the United Kingdom, 81%. More striking, though, was the fact that out of the 16 groups most often consulted, business was considered the most reliable, tied with provincial government officials.

In short, both business and government see the benefit of greater business involvement in the public policy-making process. Each must see and understand each other as they set and pursue their strategic agendas. [7] How, then, can government facilitate this most effectively?

COLOURED PAPERS AND TRADITIONAL CONSULTATION

A most time-honoured mechanism by which business and the general public can have policy-making input in a parliamentary democracy is through Green and White Papers. A *Green Paper* is usually a collection of propositions about a subject, released by government for public debate and discussion; it is not actual government policy. These papers are released at the very earliest stages of the policy process, usually when government is genuinely unclear about a new area of public concern. There are generally few precedents to follow, or the subject may be a very difficult one involving many irreconcilable differences and vested interests. A Green Paper usually precedes a Royal Commission, Task Force of Inquiry, or a White Paper.

A *White Paper* is a government document outlining intended government policy about a specific issue or policy. It usually describes planned legislation and the scope of any necessary accompanying regulation. Its contents are more refined and directed than are those found in a Green Paper which may have preceded it. If a Green Paper debated options, a White Paper will expand upon the chosen option. White Papers are usually only issued after government has decided what to do but is still interested in business' (and/or public) reaction to its proposals. Often White Papers will follow the deliberations of a Royal Commission or Task Force of Inquiry. The advantage of a White Paper for government is that if its proposals are unpopular, they can be withdrawn more easily than if they had been tabled in Parliament.

Today, the federal Liberal government refers to its policy documents as *red* papers. In recognition of the dominant colour of the party's logo, PCs often refer to *blue* papers. Regardless of this change in terminology, the types of papers remain two: general discussion, or proposed policy. Their purpose is to gain feedback from outside the government before policy decisions and public commitments are made, either in Parliament or in the media.

The Liberal governments of Prime Minister Trudeau discovered from their frequent use of Green and White papers that, although it did open up the policy-making process somewhat, only elites actually took advantage of it. Business elites unfortunately rarely did. Like most things in life, Green and White Papers are not fully appreciated until they are absent from the scene. For example, the Liberals' National Energy Program (NEP) of the early 1980s offered no warnings — not even the customary phone calls by the deputy minister or assistant deputy minister to the industry the night before the announcements were made. Nor had there been a Green or White Paper on repatriation, socialization, nationalization, or self-reliance in energy supplies and capitalization capacity within the oil and gas industry. All hell broke loose! Later even Liberal governments acknowledge that the NEP was a costly failure, and especially in the West it became a lightning rod of mistrusting Ottawa.

Business has a responsibility to respond to Green or White Papers. The private sector should take every opportunity to know its government counterparts better, and to have each others' opinions heard. However, even if business does not accept government's offer to get involved in this way, these coloured papers offer business an early warning of things to come.[8] If a firm or industry is conscientiously monitoring its non-market environment for threats and opportunities, the messages contained in these papers can often prepare it for one or the other.

TRIPARTISM

Many of the economic and social problems facing this country over the past quarter century have arisen from high inflation, low productivity, commodity shortages or surpluses, and high unemployment. All these are set against a backdrop of rising expectations, although less so in recent years. To address fully these national problems, government must view them in both a global context and one in which both business and labour can assist in resolving them.

This level of consultation, cooperation, and consensus building among government, business and labour has become known as *tripartism*. This concept has actually become an institution in Austria, Denmark, Germany, Norway, Sweden, Holland, and Belgium; alas, such has not been the case in Canada. However, the process holds great promise for the future.

Given the environmental challenges identified in **Parts I** and **II** of this book, neither the classical, political model of interest brokerage nor the traditional, management-labour model of problem solving works well. *Tripartism is an admission that the process of decision making is more important in achieving desired economic or social outcomes today than is rigid adherence to outdated economic formulas or political ideologies.*

Tripartism is not a panacea. Consensus is difficult to reach at the best of times. It has not always been reached in the six countries mentioned above, and the few tripartite experiments in Canada have had mixed results. It also excludes environmental and consumer interests.

Tripartism will only work if government is actually willing to bargain with business and labour, and then follow through on its agreements. Traditionally, government has balked at this, claiming that the supremacy of Parliament must never be eroded. The real opposition has come from the federal bureaucracy. The public service enjoys a very privileged position, serving elected officials both as policy advisers and policy administrators. Tripartism threatens that privileged position. Over the past 25 years, central agencies have usurped much of the policy-making role of line departments. Now, business and labour could do the same.

The very logistics of tripartism are staggering. Who represents business? The AMEC?[9] CCC? BCNI? CFIB? Who represents labour? The CLC? CFL?

A very realistic drawback to tripartism is the belief that neither self-interested business nor labour can approach or deal with the range of socioeconomic policies which government must address every time a major issue arises. Nothing can be handled by government without compounding some other situation; otherwise, it would not be in government's lap in the first place. Business and labour think *unidirectionally*; government by necessity thinks *circuitously*.

But the greatest drawback to tripartism is government's preference for selling prearranged policy initiatives rather than working towards a three-way consensus. In two familiar cases of tripartism described below, the Canadian government took the initiative both times. One case met with mixed reviews; the other was a resounding success. Neither would have occurred if government had not taken the lead.

The genuine attempt at tripartism has come to be known as *Tier I/ Tier II*; it is a useful "for-instance" experience from which to learn. Jean Chretien had been appointed Minister of Industry, Trade and Commerce (ITC) in 1976. His mandate was to improve relations with business by listening to it, and to develop an industrial strategy. Chretien's deputy minister proposed an interdepartmental committee to prepare sectoral profiles based upon business, federal, and provincial input. When Jack Horner was appointed as the next Minister of ITC in 1977, he included labour in what was to become a tripartite (with continued provincial involvement) study of these 23 sectoral profiles. Meetings would be chaired by business, with committees staffed by public servants. All 23 studies would be published as Tier I. Each sector then set up a Tier II committee with six representatives from business (including the chairman), five from labour, and one academic. These would determine the appropriate government policy for that sector. The whole exercise took one-and-a-half years and cost $25 million.

Labour cried foul throughout the process, claiming its participation was an afterthought and that it lacked the staff resources to compete with business and government. In fact, the CLC refused to participate until after the task forces had actually begun to meet. Eight sector reports were unanimous, with labour dissenting in another eleven. Over 600 recommendations were made in the energy, transportation, and research and development fields alone; government responded to every one. (Coincidentally, there were slightly over 600 participants in all.) Not surprisingly, there was neither agreement nor government action taken on taxes or tariffs at that time. For six years afterwards, the federal government continued to consult with sectoral task forces but on a smaller scale.

Research conducted by Baetz showed that the outcomes of Tier I/Tier II were important. One was that differences among segments of the private sector were clearly seen to be greater than was the traditionally assumed gulf between business and government, or business and labour. Another outcome was that the levels of appreciation, understanding, and rapport with the "other side" markedly improved. A third outcome — government wanted information, and got lots of it. Finally and very positively, 58% of participants said they learned something substantive and 53% indicated having made new, lasting contacts. Yet Tier I/Tier II *failed*, primarily for two reasons. First, business thought this tripartite body would forge an industrial strategy; meanwhile, government simply sought information with which to develop an industrial strategy. Second, sectoral task forces were asked to address problems which were not sector-specific. Thus, little real consensus was ever formed or even possible.

The second example of tripartism in Canada was truly a success. In the early 1980s, the Canada-United States Auto Pact became more favourable on a net basis to Canada than it was to the United States. Successful renewal of the pact meant tough negotiations from a position of strength for the Canadian government. This led then-ITC Minister Ed Lumley to create a sector task force which included the presidents of the three major auto manufacturers, representatives of the auto parts manufacturers, and representatives of the auto workers' union. The President of the Automotive Parts Manufacturing Association of Canada, Pat Lavelle, and the President of the Canadian Autoworkers, Bob White, were co-chairmen. It worked.

The final, unanimous conclusion of this task force was that producers of imported vehicles should have to invest in the countries in which they sold their cars. This meant that foreign cars produced in Canada would be exempted from Canadian import duties provided 60% of the vehicle content was Canadian. The same applied to the United States. This kept domestic producers price-competitive and meant more business for the parts manufacturers. New plants also meant new jobs. Although ITC's Lumley did not accept the task force's recommendations as government policy, it gave the government much-needed ammunition to negotiate hard with the Japanese and save the Auto Pact with the Americans. They could invest in Canada or face higher barriers to trade. The rest is history.

The conclusion is that, although relatively untried in this country compared with Europe, tripartism holds much promise. It needs to be initiated by government in good faith.[10] Experience suggests following this set of guidelines or rules:

i. concentrate on longer-term issues (e.g., five years);

ii. concentrate on sector-specific issues;

iii. include business, government, and labour from the start;

iv. set ground rules at the beginning, which are agreed upon and understood, with clear objectives;

v. keep expectations realistic;

vi. start with and limit initiatives to sectors predisposed to tripartism success, when one or two are successful the others will follow; and

vii. have business and labour share the cost with government, inasmuch as they will share the benefit, and have more reason to take the process seriously.

Conventionally government has been sheltered from, and immune to, many business world realities. Consultation — tripartism — is therefore a necessary educational process. However, business is even more ignorant of the realities and constraints of government. Business also needs to work on developing a consensus within (the segment of) its community, *before* participating. Labour definitely will show up united.

Finally, government must realize that effective consultation and consensus-building among business, labour, and government cannot be done in public, where posturing overtakes substance. Tripartite meetings must be held behind closed doors, so that when one party concedes and changes its position it need not lose face. After all, that is why most inter-governmental federal-provincial conferences fail.

FREE TRADE AND THE NEW CONSULTATION

The Government of Canada learned well from the Tier I/Tier II exercise of 1977-1979 (that failed) and the Auto Task Force exercise of 1982-1983 (that worked). The lesson: it *pays for government to consult with — not just to listen to — business.*

For the first time since World War II, business and government had begun to collaborate on current issues. The most prominent example case of this closeness was in negotiating the Canada-United States Free Trade Agreement (FTA), subsequently extended to Mexico (NAFTA).

The government developed a relatively elaborate system to consult with business and develop an agreement to benefit Canada on a long-term net basis. In 1986, an advisory group of business leaders was appointed for each of the 15 major sectors of the economy.[11] These were collectively called the Sectoral Advisory Groups on International Trade (SAGIT). The chairs of these groups reported through the International Trade Advisory Committee (ITAC) to the Minister of International Trade; ITAC advised regarding bilateral and multilateral (GATT) trade negotiations. Both levels were staffed with government officials and supported by academics and consultants. While very little has been made public about the dynamics and impact SAGIT and ITAC had on the free trade agreement, both the business community and the federal government have glowed over the success of the process. Business communicated its concerns to government, and government priorities were influenced by those concerns. The success of SAGIT and ITAC rested on two inherent characteristics of the bilateral free trade talks. First, there was a clear deadline for both Prime Minister Mulroney and US President Reagan to establish a free trade treaty, which had to be met by both nego-tiating teams. Working a timeline backwards placed the consultation process in a very compressed and urgent time frame. Second, the issue at hand was one of survival for Canadian business and for Canada as an economically prosperous polity, given the alternative of increased US protectionism. Trade is a strategic priority for Canada.

But SAGIT and ITAC worked for another reason, as well. The process was created by and supported by the prime minister of Canada. He set goals; consultation developed the poli-cies. Prime Minister Mulroney dismissed parliament, parliamentary reform, and executive federalism as totally ineffective means by which to accomplish those goals. Given the Canadian Labour Congress' vocal, rigid opposition to free trade before the consultation process began, he also established the option of any tripartite approach to the issue.

Mulroney's free trade agreement was a major accomplishment. Perhaps it is a modern parallel to the creation of the National Policy by Sir John A. Macdonald. As then, and as in Japan today, it was business rather than government that implicitly chose which industries were winners and which were losers. This had been a tough but important lesson for govern-ment to learn: sometimes business *does* have a better idea.

This is a stark contrast in government technique from the mishap of the National Energy Program. Time will tell whether or not SAGIT and ITAC signal the beginning of an era of more cooperative, effective government consultation with business. If so, business had best be prepared to accept every opportunity government offers it to become more involved in the making of public policy.

An extension to coloured papers are government-initiated, sit-down consulation exercises often referred to as "roundtables" or "forums." In the mid-1990s, Premier Klein's Alberta Government used this method of public consultation. The federal government has taken this one step further to become consensus conferences (e.g., budget) with not just business at the table, but all significant stakeholders. One rule is clear: if these meetings are public, hence open to the media, then hard results may be elusive. If they are behind closed doors, then hard results actually may be achieved, but not to everyone's liking.

The key to successful consultation between business and government is that the process address a strategic priority for both parties. That is, something both urgent and important that threatens their very existence. Only then will a true consensus emerge, and public policy in the best interests of the nation be created.

IMPLICATIONS FOR MANAGEMENT

Government must act if business-government relations in Canada are to improve. In **Chapter 12**, it was recommended that business attempt to better understand government's agenda. To help business accomplish this, government must set clear ground rules and terms of refer-ence for any consultative or interactive process. It must also clearly communicate its objec-tives to business for specific consultations or interactions. Government should thus tell business whether it is only in search of information or that it wishes to make a deal. This would prevent business from becoming unduly disappointed and wasting resources.[12]

As a show of good faith, and in its own fact-finding interest, government should consult with business on a continuing basis, not just in crisis situations or before elections.

Government could clearly identify whether it was offering a proactive, maintenance type of consultation, or a reactive, crisis-management one. The first would be designed to reach an agreement with business on certain facts and to diminish the differences between their viewpoints. The latter would respond to a perceived problem.

Second, government should provide more opportunities and incentives for business-government executive interchange. (On business' part, of course, it must be willing, and be seen by government to be willing, to capitalize upon such opportunities). The area of most agreement by both elites was a desire for more crossover in careers between business leaders and senior civil servants and political office holders. A career in either sector in Canada was expected to be more of a lifelong commitment than it was in the United States, where mid-career crossovers and even re-crossovers have been much more prevalent.

If one's belief about society is tied into one's position in society, then senior managers in both private and public sectors must learn to cross-pollinate with the opposite sector. Only thus will they understand the values, attitudes, beliefs, and ideas of the other side. As a result, they can begin to forge common links, goals, and avenues to achieve mutual understanding — an objective obviously in the best interests of the nation.

Executive exchanges promise to help weld together the two elites. Here, senior executives from one sector visit the opposite sector to take up a similar position for a year or two. This can help close what has become known as the "personal and personnel gap" between the two sectors, but more is needed. Senior civil servants should be trained and more fully experienced in the intricacies and imperatives of competitive strategic management in the private sector. Not only will they better understand their private sector counterparts, but they will learn to formulate more effective economic and industrial policies. Similarly, chief executive officers in the private sector should be trained in the complexities of both political process and political economy. Only thus will they fully appreciate the temporal and political constraints which political leaders must face.[13]

The objective would not be to compromise one side or the other but to promote a better understanding of the other side. Having said that, one-year or two-year executive changes are not really adequate. Strong incentives must be developed to encourage and support senior executives from both sides to switch careers, preferably along sectoral lines, in order to close that perceptual gap which exists between them. The evidence in this book clearly suggests that this interchange would be successful. *It is government's place to facilitate such an endeavour*.

Finally, government needs to realize that for consensus to exist among industries, and between business and government on major economic issues, there must be some form of compensation for the "losers." In any major change of the Canadian economic system, some industries will gain, while others will lose. Government itself should not pick winners and losers, but let technological and economic trends identified by business determine them. This was done in 1989 in the free trade agreement with the United States. As in Japan, and to a lesser extent in other countries, government should assist those "losing" businesses in changing their products, financing, or even their industries. The funds used for this assistance should appropriately come from marginal taxation of the winners.

Political will remains an absolute necessity for any recipe of consultation or interaction to be successful. Economic gloom makes people more willing to accept the need for change. However, sometimes the political will not to get involved is greater than that required to get involved.

SUGGESTED FURTHER READINGS

Baetz, Mark C. 1985. "Sector Strategy: How to get effective input from industry into public policy formulation." *Policy Options*, 26:1.

Baron, David P. 1995. "Integrated Strategy: Market and Non-market Components." *California Management Review*, 37:2.

Bartha, Peter. 1995. "Preventing a High-Cost Crisis." *Business Quarterly*, 60:2.

Blair, Cassandra. 1984. *Forging Links of Co-operation: The Task Force Approach to Consultation*. Ottawa: Conference Board in Canada.

Bon, D.L., and K.D. Hart. 1983. *Linking Canada's New Solitudes: The Executive Interchange Programme and Business-Government Relations*. Ottawa: Conference Board in Canada.

Cameron, Dan. 1997. "Interest Based Bargaining in the Public Service of Saskatchewan," *Policy Options*, 28:5.

Campbell, Colin, and George Szablowski. 1979. *The Superbureaucrats: Structure and Behaviour in Central Agencies*. Toronto: Macmillan.

Canada West Foundation. 1995. *Toward Affordable Government*. Calgary: Canada West Foundation, October.

Courchene, Thomas J. 1994. *Social Canada in the Millennium: Reform Imperatives and Restructuring Principles*. Toronto: C.D. Howe Institute.

The Economist. 1997. "The Disappearing Taxpayer." May 31.

Gibson, J.D. 1981. "The Flow of Policy Ideas Between Business and Government." In D.C. Smith, (ed)., *Economic Policy Advising in Canada*. Montreal: C.D. Howe Institute.

Gillies, James. 1986. *Facing Reality: Consultation Consensus and Making Economic Policy for the 21st Century*. Montreal: Institute for Research on Public Policy.

Government of Canada. 1993. *Consultation Guidelines for Managers in the Federal Public Service*. Ottawa: Privy Council Office.

Lippert, Owen, and Michael Walker, (eds). 1997. *The Underground Economy: Global Evidence of Its Impact*. Vancouver: The Fraser Institute.

Luciani, Patrick. 1996. "Part 3. Myths about the Role of Government." In *Economic Myths: Making Sense of Canadian Policy Issues*. 2nd ed. Don Mills, ON: Addison-Wesley.

McCallum, John S. 1996. "The Corporation Can Only Take So Much." *Business Quarterly*, 60:4.

Murray, V.V. (ed). 1987. *The Consultative Process in Business-Government Relations*. Toronto: The Max Bell Business-Government Studies Program, York University.

Rugman, A.M., and A. Anderson. 1987. "Business and Trade Policy: The Structure of Canada's New Private Sector Advising System." *Canadian Journal of Administrative Sciences*, 4:4, December.

Thain, Donald H. 1993. "Managing the Strategic Agenda." *Business Quarterly*, 57:3, Spring.

NOTES

1. *The Economist*, "The Disappearing Taxpayer." (May 31, 1997).

2. Owen Lippert and Michael Walker (eds). *The Underground Economy : Global Evidence of Its Impact* (Vancouver: The Fraser Institute, 1997).

3. Many loans are never repaid because companies meet mutually agreed-upon sales projections.

4. Farm income rose from $1.3 billion in 1970 to a high of $4.3 billion in 1988; by 1994 it had crashed to $4 billion.

5. Eventually Pocklington defaulted in 1989; the cost to the Alberta public totalled $209 million.

6. Colin Campbell and George Szablowski, *The Superbureaucrats: Structure and Behaviour in Central Agencies* (Toronto: Macmillan, 1979).

7. Donald H. Thain, "Managing the Strategic Agenda," *Business Quarterly* 60:2 (1995).

8. Peter Bartha, "Preventing a High-Cost Crisis," *Business Quarterly* 60:2 (1995).

9. In 1996, the Alliance of Manufacturers and Exports of Canada (AMEC) was formed by the merger of the Canadian Manufacturers' Association and the Canadian Exporters' Association.

10. In practise this has come to mean "principled" (i.e., based on principles) or interest-based negotiation. See Dan Cameron, "Interest Based Bargaining in the Public Service of Saskatchewan," *Policy Options* 28:5 1997).

11. Nine groups had representation from labour.

12. John S. McCallum, "The Corporation Can Only Take So Much," *Business Quarterly* 60:4 (1996).

13. D.L. Bon and K.D. Hart, *Linking Canada's New Solitudes: The Executive Interchange Programme and Business-Government Relations* (Ottawa: Conference Board in Canada, 1983).

Part

6

CHALLENGING BUSINESS-GOVERNMENT RELATIONS

To meet the challenge of developing a sustainable, national economic strategy that will secure a place of leadership for this country in the new evolving world order while safeguarding the integrity of Canada's natural environment, business and government need to work together as partners. Effectively managing business-government relations in the future is a national strategic imperative. To do this requires understanding, awareness, honesty, trust, and, above all, political will.

CHAPTER 14

Canada Trades: Global to Local

CHAPTER 15

Business as Moral Agent — A Note

CHAPTER 16

Not the Conclusion — But Beginning Anew

CANADA TRADES: GLOBAL TO LOCAL

"All articles of the growth, produce or manufacture of any one of the provinces shall, from and after the Union, be admitted free into each of the other provinces."

Article 121, British North America (BNA) Act, 1867

When Canada was founded, policy intentions for internal trade hardly could be clearer than the above. More than 150 years later, barriers to trade between Canadian provinces remain numerous, complex, and costly.

Trade is a word that makes most people think of exchanging goods and services between countries. As earlier chapters have pointed out, Canada's economic history begins and continues to be strongly identified with trade. Trade patterns have evolved, rapidly so in more recent decades. Canada has been a vigorous participant in trade arrangements, policy discussions, and negotiations; Canada has dealt with the dynamics of world trade in a proactive fashion. *There is a perverse disparity between Canada's commitment towards freer international trade, and its maintenance of protectionism and balkanization of trade between its own provinces.*

A TRADING COUNTRY: HISTORIC TRADE POLICY

Canada's earliest trade strategy stems from Europe and Britain of the 1800s. It was the doctrine of mercantilism: a country is better off if it exports more than it imports. Since gold was instrumental for payments, it was accumulated with successful mercantilism policies. Three specific policies emerged: (*i*) exports would be promoted; (*ii*) imports would be restricted by tariffs and the like; and (*iii*) trade flows could be taxed (by Kings/Queens and later by governments).

Eventually, the problems of mercantilism became recognized. For one thing, not all countries concurrently could have exports exceed imports. For another, holding gold (apart from speculation) was undesirable because gold is not a productive asset and thus has no yield. As the net effect of restrictive trade policies (protectionism) evolved, economic prosperity gains from comparative advantage potential were foregone. Nations experienced slower economic growth and had lower standards of living than available resources and technology could have permitted.

Throughout Canada's economic history, trade with the United States has been vital. Over two centuries, American trade policies have swung wildly and have driven Canada's economic fate and prosperity into even steeper cycles. Protectionism was the strategy from 1879-1990.

In 1905, Alberta and Saskatchewan joined British Columbia and Manitoba as provinces. With strong support from Western Canada, in 1911 the Government of Canada negotiated a free trade agreement with the United States. Before being passed into law, the government of the day was forced to call an election which it then lost. Also lost was the proposed US free trade agreement.

The Depression period of the 1930s was one of high tariffs. Despite Canada-Britain reciprocal trade preferential arrangements, trade policies remained about the same as 50 years earlier. Manufacturing was fostered in Central Canada (Ontario and Quebec), mainly of smaller branch plants under a protective tariff umbrella; the structure was not conducive to the economies of scale necessary to be competitive on world markets. Outer Canada (the West and the Atlantic) had to pay higher prices. Linked by expensive transportation systems, this economic structure sowed seeds of future stresses and strains regarding Canadian unity.

Canada is a trading nation. Thus policies have evolved that facilitate trade, with institutions to execute the policies. At the world level, Canada is a member of the OECD and is a G-7 country. Canada plays an active role in the Asia-Pacific Economic Co-operation (APEC), the International Monetary Fund (IMF), and the World Bank. Internal Canadian trade financing and marketing policies are carried forward by Trade Commissions, External Affairs, the Export Development Corporation, and the Canadian Commercial Corporation. The Bank of Canada is responsible for monetary policy, including currency exchange rate determinations.

POST-WORLD WAR II TRADE LIBERALIZATION

GATT and WTO

After World War II, high tariffs on industrial goods were reduced. The General Agreement on Tariffs and Trade (GATT) was signed by 23 countries in 1947, and can be viewed primarily as a reaction to the costly trade wars of the 1930s. GATT was the basis for our current multination trading system. Countries that cooperated in the war effort found they also could cooperate for mutual gains in trading goods. Canada was a founder and is an active member of GATT.

GATT provides three basic functions: (*i*) a common set of rules for the conduct of international trade; (*ii*) an independent forum for the monitoring, discussion, and settlement of trade disputes; and (*iii*) a sponsor for multilateral negotiations on trade policy. Disputes are not resolved by enforcement, but by the mediation role based on moral authority. Eight multilateral "rounds" of trade negotiations have been sponsored by GATT. The first two rounds were between 1949 and 1951. Trade liberalization has been generic to each round, resulting in significantly lower tariffs. More recent rounds have added other vital aspects of multilateral world trade. Moreover, the scope of trade has expanded from commodities to include services, intellectual property, and financial flows.

Two other notable rounds were the Tokyo (1973-79) and Kennedy (1964-67) Rounds. The latter round succeeded in across-the-board tariff cuts for manufacturing industries; this marked the end of Canada's policy of trade protectionism for manufacturing. The Tokyo Round made additional reductions in manufacturing tariffs, but its main objective was to reduce or restrict the use of non-tariff barriers to trade. Much earlier progress with tariff reductions had been offset by less formal but insidious and effective other barriers.

The Uruguay Round (1986-94) was the most recent; its twin focus was on non-discrimination and trade liberalization. Non-discrimination means that each country should have a unified structure of tariffs with respect to all other GATT countries. Trade in agriculture issues were divisive, specifically due to subsidies (especially in the European Union and US) whereas domestic subsidies would distort prices in export markets. There were other issues such as intellectual property rights and trade in services. As the Uruguay Round concluded, GATT had 125 members.

The Uruguay Round Agreement created a new international organization, the World Trade Organization (WTO). WTO is now the pertinent institution for multilateral world trade. GATT has become an agreement, within the broader aegis of WTO as an institution for world trade. These changes took effect January 1, 1995.[1]

FTA and NAFTA

The Canada-US Free Trade Agreement (FTA) went into effect January 1, 1989. It built upon the highly successful 1965 Auto Pact, a bilateral and sector-specific free trade of wholesale-level automobiles and parts agreement between the same two countries. This special agreement, and another for textiles, was sanctioned by GATT.

FTA negotiations were concluded in 1987 and approved by respective leaders of governments in early 1988. US Congressional ratification was straightforward, but Parliament's approval was tortuous. An oddity was that FTA was opposed by many who had benefited so handsomely from the Auto Pact! In business-government relations, matters rarely are simple. Canada's House of Commons approved FTA, but the non-elected Senate resisted the legally-necessary ratification. Thus Canada's Parliament failed to ratify. An election was called for November 1988, fought predominantly on the free trade issue, with the re-election of the government. The Senate then bent to the will of the Canadian public and ratified FTA.

As a side note, Canadian free trade debates and elections have provided a lesson for students of business-government relations — political "flip flops!" Former PC leader Brian

Mulroney used vitriolic language to oppose free trade while in Opposition, only to embrace FTA after becoming prime minister. Prime Minister Chretien, when in Opposition, said he would "tear up the free trade agreement," but as prime minister he signed NAFTA.

The arguments for and against free trade have changed very little over the last century. Proponents of free trade envision accelerated economic growth, with attendant employment and prosperity opportunities. Opponents fear loss of cultural identity, sovereignty, and jobs. Each argument has merit. Proponents of free trade did not see the choice being between free trade and the status quo, but between free trade and increased US protectionism. The view was amplified in 1986 when the US placed a 22% across-the-board tariff on all imports. A significant portion of Canada's late-1990s economic growth is trade-driven, especially with the largest affluent market in world history. So, Canada has hitched its wagon to the United States' falling star.

Mexico initiated interest in what became the North American Free Trade Agreement (NAFTA). It built on FTA provisions and was negotiated during 1991-92. Learning from the FTA experience at the political level, 1993 was left as the ratification window for the three countries; but in both Canada and United States new governments took office. In Canada the outgoing government (which lost the election of October 1993) already had approved NAFTA, and the new government had to decide whether to reaffirm or withdraw approval. The new government and the Senate decided to proceed. The new American Congress exhibited much hesitation about NAFTA. Additional negotiations ensued, resulting in side agreements on several issues, with US approval then forthcoming. Mexico ratified the agreement and NAFTA came into effect on January 1, 1994. At the time NAFTA came on stream, Canada's exports to and imports from Mexico were very small; while each is growing, our imports are growing more rapidly than exports so the gap between them is widening.

Academic, business, and labour-sponsored evaluations are underway. Some of the research is "no matter what" in nature — seeking to substantiate predetermined yes or no positions. But more and more objective evidence is becoming available. Looking ahead to the millennium, there is little evidence that FTA and NAFTA will be reversed as Canadian policy. Indeed there have been discussions (most notably with Chile) about NAFTA extensions into Latin and South America.

FTA and NAFTA are examples of regional trade agreements. There are others in the world that matter to Canada. Examples are: Mercosur (a customs union between Argentina, Brazil, Paraguay, and Uruguay), the European Union (EU), a Central European Free-Trade Area, and APEC. Proponents say regional trade arrangements can be struck more quickly and flexibly while results are consistent with WTO/GATT principles of freer trade and prosperity.

INTER-PROVINCIAL TRADE

Now to the important matter of trade *within* Canada. There is extensive and vital trade between provincial jurisdictions; this trade equals about 25% of our GNP, with only Ontario and Quebec having surpluses. The lead quote of this chapter would make one think that goods and services move freely within our country. Not so.

The Government of Canada clearly is responsible for international trade policies. But provincial governments pursue policies that affect trade, both inter-provincial and international. Provinces use regulatory and administrative barriers to impede the flow of goods and services; virtually all provinces exercise some degree of preferential procurement policy. These barriers discriminate against producers from other jurisdictions so that local producers and labour can be favoured. On occasion such barriers lead to nasty spats among Canadians; an example was the 1993 dispute between Ontario and Quebec regarding preferential hiring practices for public sector construction projects.

The concept and analysis of comparative advantage will be familiar to students of policy and practitioners of business. They are not repeated here, but are standard components of economics texts. However, the deadweight loss analysis module of our earlier **Chapter 4** demonstrates how economic value is wasted by resources allocation by means other than price. The mid-1980s Macdonald Commission concluded that Canadians could enjoy a permanent 1.0-1.5% increase in income by removing internal trade barriers. In this decade, the Canadian Manufacturer's Association calculated the economic efficiency loss as $6.5 billion. As well as the indicated efficiency gains, there may be a very large benefit from an improved climate for business created by free internal trade.[2]

So why do inter-provincial trade barriers persist to this moment? Let us examine the history, economics, and politics of the issue.

INTER-PROVINCIAL TRADE BARRIERS

The BNA Act, as expressed in Article 121, left little doubt of the original intention. Beyond strictly sentiment, the economics of trade and comparative advantage were strong then as now.

History

For most of its first century Canada was a trading nation in spite of itself. Despite resources endowment and geography that would compel free trade, since Confederation trade issues in Canada have been labourious. Canada was formed by Confederation (i.e., a union of formerly independent entities), and despite agreement on wording such as BNA Act Article 121, it is not surprising that behaviour and deeds differed. Indeed, other BNA Act provisions have been used to justify inter-provincial trade barriers. Section 92 gives provinces the governance of non-renewable resources/forestry resources/electricity, and Section 36 requires that both provincial and federal governments commit to "economic development to reduce disparities in opportunities."

As manufacturing was protected, primarily in Central Canada, areas of outer Canada had to pay more. Transportation costs added to the burden. Meanwhile, exports such as forestry, grains, and hydrocarbons were subject to federal government policies. In the context of this history, not surprisingly, provincial jurisdictions sought to control their economic destinies wherever they could do so. Sophisticated and substantial internal trade barriers evolved, especially in: government procurement, liquor, agriculture supply management, and industrial subsidies.[3] In the 1960s and 1970s an inter-provincial trade economic gain of at least 1% may not have seemed badly needed, but in the last 10 years of economic difficulty for Canada it seems vital. Most (but not all) provinces have embraced a freer-trade perspective. A hidden cost of protective measures is that they shield provinces from the worldwide economy when Canada needs to be prepared for the onslaught of global competition. FTA and NAFTA results may be opening Canadian minds to the potential gains that can be added with reductions and eventual elimination of internal trade barriers.

Change vs. Inertia

As identified by a range and variety of studies, there are hundreds of barriers to trade between provinces. Some are overt, but others are insidious. Once barriers exist, business and farmers invest accordingly and losses are incurred with rule changes. The removal of barriers would have gainers and losers. *Losses* will be specific, certain, and soon; but *gains* are likely to be diffuse, uncertain, and distant. Political voices that mirror the described reality make policy decisions for change very difficult. Protected producers (especially if demand is inelastic) will be better off because of trade barriers and usually are well-organized and politically influential. Consumers' higher costs will be spread thinly and they generally have limited and diffused influence. The fundamentals of Pareto Optimum come into play with a resulting inertia; sometimes the inertia can be overcome by compensation (of losers by gainers), phasing (over time or segments), and grandfathering (of persons or investments). The pace of change is accelerated if gains distribution can be broadly based and losses can be minimized. In short, inertia can more readily be overcome if the prevailing environment for change is a positive-sum rather than zero-sum context.

The *prisoner's dilemma* may explain why provinces are tempted to establish and retain trade barriers to each other. If no province had barriers, all would be better off. But each has an incentive to establish barriers, so long as others do not have them. However, when a province succumbs to temptation, the best that other provinces can do is to respond similarly with protectionist policies of their own. From time to time there are bound to be episodes of severe political pressure to erect barriers, irrespective of political party philosophies. Not all such philosophies harbour belief in free trade. Squabbles (even if for unrelated reasons) between provinces do not help. As we have seen, once the barriers are in place they are very difficult to erase.

From the comments above, one might infer that the inter-provincial trade barrier problem is strictly that of the provinces in Canada. Inadvertent or not, certain federal government policies have reinforced the establishment or continuing of internal trade barriers that are economically harmful. Labour mobility within Canada has been constrained by federal government policies. Social policy money and rules have weakened incentives for Canadians to move to jurisdictions with stronger employment opportunities. Government policy-induced "10-42," especially well known in Maritime Canada, has used precious public funds and stunted adjustment toward future opportunities.[4]

Many years and designs of "regional economic development" programs have impeded economic adjustment and adaptation. Every federal government since Confederation has, in its own way, tried to close the gap (measured by comparing per capita income and/or unemployment rates) between "have" and "have not" provinces, rather than concentrating on lessening the gap between existing and potential economic development of each region.[5] Each has failed. Regional economic disparities persist to this day (and always will, although their magnitude and patterns may change over time). Another danger has been taking from the poor of "have" regions and transferring to the rich of "have not" ones. The real effects regional economic development initiatives have had are: (*i*) the institutionalization of disparity and associated relief; (*ii*) the further fragmentation and compartmentalization of the nation's internal market; and (*iii*) the delay of inevitable change in the face of global economic realities.

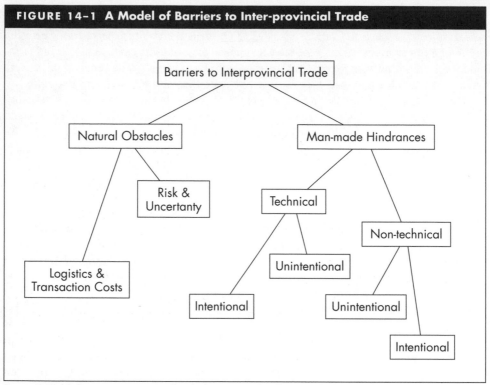

FIGURE 14–1 A Model of Barriers to Inter-provincial Trade

Source: "A Model of Barriers to Interprovincial Trade" from *Provincial Trade Wars: Why the Blockade Must End* by Filip Palda (ed.)
With permission from The Fraser Institute.

Models and Forms

It will be helpful to visualize a model of barriers to inter-provincial trade. **Figure 14–1** depicts a conceptual model or "tree" breakout of each general type of inter-provincial trade barrier.[6] While taken from a focus on agricultural trade, the concept map is generic to the overall internal trade barrier issue.

There are barriers that are "natural" obstacles, requiring policies and expenditures (e.g., transportation) to overcome. Such obstacles may be overcome by incurring actual costs of marketing and delivery so that "external" markets can be penetrated and served.

Natural barriers can be formidable. There are logistics costs with selling products in distant markets, whether in the same country or a foreign one. These include transportation, packaging, storage, inventory shrinkage, control, and financing; each tends to be more difficult with greater differences, either physical or cultural. Transactions costs can range across not only distance (e.g., field sales staff), but also linguistic needs along with foreign currency exchange and telecommunication challenges. In addition, and much more difficult to estimate, are the business risks of conducting external trade. The inherent risks/uncertainties constitute an intangible barrier to trade.

But the issue here is man-made hindrances. As forbidding as natural obstacles can be, man-made impediments often are added in the form of government programs and regulations that impose higher trade costs. While international-type barriers like tariffs are highly visible, most inter-provincial ones are disguised in subtle ways that discriminate against external suppliers relative to local producers. While local producers have proximity-to-market cost advantages, natural barriers may be easier to overcome because they are stable and predictable. But man-made blockages may be met by an external competitor, only to have new regulations and licenses imposed, so that there is the risk of continuous policy discrimination. Potential competitors may be unwilling to take these risks. Thus local suppliers can provide higher-cost goods and services, with attendant higher prices, to the consumers of the jurisdiction (i.e., province) being protected.

As an example, **Table 14–1** is a matrix of agricultural trade inter-provincial barriers; the forms noted are generally applicable to most industries. The typology of barrier forms includes technical or non-technical, and intentional or unintentional types. There can be no doubt that food industry regulations are essential to protect public health and safety. However, certain technical requirements can be imposed where the real motive is trade blockage. An example was when margarine producers were not allowed to colour their product the same as butter. Product wrapping and labelling requirements are other often used gambits. Higher costs, including losses of economies of scale, are imposed and must be passed along in the form of higher prices to consumers.

TABLE 14-1	Inter-provincial Barriers to Agricultural Trade	
Type	**Technical Impediments**	**Non-technical Impediments**
Intentional Barriers	Cost-increasing Product Regulations	Monopolistic Product Marketing Agencies
Unintentional Barriers	Health, Safety & Consumer Information Regulations	Farm Support and Adjustment Measures

Source: "Interprovincial Barriers to Agricultural Trade" from *Provincial Trade Wars: Why the Blockade Must End* by Filip Palda (ed.) With permission from The Fraser Institute.

As denoted in **Table 14–1** there are non-technical impediments to Canadian internal trade that are devised as intentional barriers. Supply management by farm product marketing agencies are examples that are utilized extensively; they are afforded within-province monopoly powers by provincial law. Some product movement (notably poultry and dairy) is also restricted by national legislation. Even where supply control may not be sanctioned by statute, significant impediments to free movements can be imposed by product groups. Rudimentary economic analysis underlies the payoff to producers for curtailing levels of supply. Agriculture products' demand is inelastic, so supply restrictions have the net effect of increasing revenues (i.e., the increment of revenues due to higher prices more than offsets the decrement of revenues due to lesser supply quantities).

Frequently public policies aimed at certain worthy goals have the incidental effect of impeding trade flows of commodities or services. A classic case is the "Crow Rate" policy affecting prairie grain movement to export ports; this policy has a century-long history. The point here is to recognize that subsidizing grain export transportation costs will distort and impede the flow of grain for domestic uses such as feedstuffs for meat production.

While agriculture provides useful illustrative examples, there are many other examples of technical/non-technical barriers to commodities/services flows between provinces. Professions such as law, medicine, dentistry, and accounting have provincial requirements that restrict movement. Professional standards are essential for public protection and likely are better done by the professions themselves than by governments. But beyond some point of public protection, are the barriers between provinces intended or unintended impediments? Many are intended.

Finally, one last example shows how inter-provincial trade barriers have reduced Canadian firms to operating plants greatly below the minimum efficient size. Brewing companies, in order to sell their beer in a province, have had to build a brewery there. Why? Jobs! So until recently Canada's two major brewers had plants in every province except Prince Edward Island, fully realizing that the *excess capacity* of one plant of a large American brewer could supply the entire Canadian market. Little wonder Canadian beer costs more in Canada than American beer does in the US. Moreover, there is higher alcohol taxation in Canada.

INTER-PROVINCIAL TRADE BARRIERS REDUCTION

Until the 1970s, efforts to remove Canadian inter-provincial trade barriers were limited and occasional. As early as 1937, the Rowell-Sirois Royal Commission recognized the negative impact of these trade barriers and advised that they should be removed. But, as has become Canadian custom with Royal Commission advice, nothing came of it. During the decade of the 1970s, debate regarding trade (both international and domestic) heated up and certain proactive governments in Canada began pressing for liberalization of both types of trade. Much of the debate was focused within the larger issues of Canada's Constitution decisions. In 1979, the Pepin-Robarts Report included a specific recommendation: "Section 121 of the BNA Act should be clarified in order to guarantee more effectively free trade between the provinces for all produce and manufactured goods, and be extended to include services."[7]

In the 1980s, the Macdonald Commission was established with specific terms of reference to Canada's economic prospects and development.[8] Two particular features of Commission recommendations were compelling: (*i*) reaffirmation of Canadian unity issues related to economic conduct; and (*ii*) measuring the economic losses associated with restricted internal trade. The first feature agreed with the Pepin-Robarts conclusion and was influential on the public policy debate; the second feature was that the magnitude of losses was substantial and warranted expeditious policy attention. Macdonald, formerly a federal finance minister, concluded that a Code of Economic Conduct should be established for the purpose of reducing barriers to movement of goods and services across provincial boundaries. Under the Code, provinces impeding trade would be required to justify their actions publicly. Suasion and moral authority would be the instruments of policy implementation.

Constitution

Since the late 1960s, efforts have been made to formulate a made-in-Canada constitution. The patriation took place in 1982 with two enactments.[9] The **Canada Act** accomplished the transfer and the separate **Constitution Act** encompassing the substance, including Part III dealing with economic opportunities and essential public services. Part V deals with future amendments, and a lengthy agenda remained to be resolved as "the devil is in the details;" while unfinished economic business remains, the intent of the constitutional provisions was clear. Inter-provincial trade barriers should go.

The 1987 **Meech Lake Accord** between the prime minister and Canada's premiers attempted to get Quebec's signature on the Constitution; the objective was to bring Quebec fully into Confederation. The Accord was subject to ratification of Parliament and each provincial Legislature within three years. The Accord was not ratified by all provinces and died in 1990. Urgent and renewed effort by the government of Canada followed, led by former Prime Minister Joe Clark. In late 1991, the **Clark Proposals** were submitted to Parliament.[10] A primary component of the submission was to strengthen the Canadian economic union. "The common market clause...would be modernized to strengthen the four economic freedoms — the free movement of people, goods, services and capital within the Canadian common market." Conferences were held in regions of Canada, each with a particular priority focus of policy; the Economic Union Conference was held in Montreal. The results of this intensive and lengthy process became the **Charlottetown Accord**. On October 26, 1992, a national referendum on it was held. It lost. The constitution-based drive toward liberalized inter-provincial trade was lost along with the rest of the package of proposals.

Non-Constitution Initiatives

Certain public policy think-tanks in Canada (e.g., Canada West Foundation, C.D. Howe Institute, and the Fraser Institute) long have advocated freer internal trade, and contended that much could be accomplished by mutual agreement. Beyond constitutional debates, the early 1990s saw efforts by governments of Canada and provinces/territories to negotiate an *Agreement on Internal Trade*. It was signed in July 1994 to take effect on July 1, 1995. There are 10 chapters.[11] It is a "rules-based," stronger than "principles-based," agreement. The six rules are:

i.   *Non-discrimination*: Provinces agree to treat residents, goods, services or investments of any other province no less favourably than they treat their own. For the federal government it means it cannot favour one part of the country over another part of the country;

ii. *Right of entry and exit*: No import or export controls by provinces;

iii. *No unnecessary obstacles*: Any measure adopted or maintained must not operate so as to create an obstacle to trade;.

iv. *Legitimate objectives*: A measure can be inconsistent with rules *i*, *ii*, and *iii* if the objective is to protect health, safety, the environment and consumers, and the measure is carried out in the least trade restrictive way;

v.   *Reconciliation of standards*: Through harmonization, mutual recognition, or other means; and

vi. *Transparency*: Measures must be visible and made readily accessible.

There are detailed rules for each chapter that can be characterized as "positive integration" (promoting the harmonization of policies and regulations to facilitate more open trade) and "negative integration" (telling members what they cannot do to each other's citizens). The first applicability of the Agreement is procurement by the governments themselves; later extensions would include Crown Corporations and the respective MASH sectors (Municipalities, Advanced Education entities, Schools and Hospitals). Major issues regarding agriculture and energy are outstanding, but have agreed deadlines for future resolution. There is a dispute settlement mechanism. A secretariat for the Agreement on Internal Trade is in Winnipeg.

IMPLICATIONS FOR MANAGEMENT

Certain conclusions stand out and provide an important context for future business-government relations in Canada. Since its beginning, Canada has been a nation that trades, but for about a century it was in spite of itself. Canada prospered from trade but was hesitant about it. Despite protectionism policies over most of the time, Canada's trade grew and grew due to the compulsion of economic forces.

Canada's assets, though not designed for international trade, formed a basis for great trading advantages. Canada is endowed with vast and rich resources. Canada's physical infrastructure, largely provided by government for other purposes, can hardly be matched anywhere in the world. Our human infrastructure, people who are well-educated, healthy, honest, and hard-working, is a jewel. Canada is located on both Atlantic and Pacific tidewaters, with a water shipping system that penetrates to the upper Great Lakes. With political stability to date and a respected financial system, Canada stands out as a low-risk investment jurisdiction. By various measures by various bodies, competitiveness of Canada is good (though not great) but **is improving**. Whether Canada really wished to be a trader or not, it was bound to happen. A conclusion is that, in Canada's first century and a quarter, we became a nation dependent on trade despite passive public policies toward trade.

By the late 1980s, Canada made up its mind **to be a trading nation**. The watershed decision was that of the FTA with the United States, absolutely the largest and most affluent market in the world ever. Corollary decisions needed to be made so that there would be flesh on the bones of the agreement. Some of these decisions were painful and ultimately damaging politically. Two examples were: replacing the Manufacturer's Sales Tax (MST) with GST, and curbing inflation with policies that inevitably were accompanied by high and persistent unemployment levels. The MST was exceedingly damaging to Canada's competitive position, and high inflation drove interest rates to levels that seriously constrained investment. A few years later FTA was extended to NAFTA by including Mexico. Other Central and Latin American countries may be admitted in the future.[12] Canada is actively engaged in the markets of India and the Asian "tigers." In the foreseeable future, Canada should be able to do business in Eastern Europe beyond what could have been imagined only a decade ago. We conclude that Canada **must and will pursue policies that are proactive, the policies of a trading nation**. The business opportunities, from all regions of Canada and cutting across a broad range of sectors, will magnify the importance of business-government relations in the millennium. Unless Canada "blows it" from within, there should be great prospects for economic prosperity and social affordability.

Progress on inter-provincial trade is uncertain, and perhaps bleak. In spite of many research results showing the economic benefits of eliminating provincial trade barriers, so far shorter-term and regional politics has staved off longer-term and larger economic rationale. The logic of inter-provincial trade mirrors that of international trade: major gains are possible from scale economies of longer production runs and there are low-productivity costs of shielding provinces and sectors from worldwide competitive realities. Labour mobility constraints are harmful and consumers bear the brunt of deadweight economic losses where prices exceed what is necessary.

Two dramatic examples should help to make the point. If a province separates from Canada (Quebec and British Columbia seem the most likely candidates), by joining NAFTA that province-turned-country could trade more readily from **out**side Canada than **in**side Canada. Second example: a foreign investor (e.g., Japan) strategically should establish its business in the US rather than Canada because it could then serve Canadian customers in various provinces more readily than by locating in some province within Canada.

To date Canada's prosperity is hobbled, because we hurt ourselves economically in many ways with trade barriers. Among the most major are:

- capital flow restrictions, including the lack of a national securities exchange;
- labour mobility constraints. Some are restrictions but others are insidious status quo incentives;
- professions such as law, medicine, accountancy, trades, and teaching; and
- preferential purchasing requirements.

What kind of economic union of a country is it when **Canadian** businesses face fewer barriers to trade with the US than they do within Canada? There is a danger, after protracted discussions drone on, that the issue may sink into obscurity. Or worse, it could become a source of cynicism and scorn like that evoked in the 1990s by the "C word" (Constitution). *Urgent and strong efforts are needed by both business and government.* While devolution of certain governmental functions in the country makes sense for some, it does not for all. *The inter-provincial trade issue is precisely where federal government leadership is needed,* or the opportunity may escape Canada's grasp.

Globalization and international trade obligations have an impact on inter-provincial as well as international trade. Globalized regulation is a trend for some trade sectors (e.g., food safety); this could prod the provinces into cooperating with the federal government to develop national standards that reflect emerging international market requirements. In fact, in such cases the pattern is for these global trade requirements to transcend the federal and provincial governments — the economic market link would be between the local node of economic activity and the international market. The Winnipeg or Sherbrooke or Halifax supplier would link specifications to the respective European or American or Asian market demand. Referred to as glocalization, the noted tendency is for economic power to shift both to global and local levels of human settlements. Perhaps the medieval paradigm of city-states is in our Canadian future; a conclusion is that *economic power is being transferred upward, downward and outward from nation-states.*

As surely as all old ideas were once new ideas, Canada's future will differ from its past. One thing has not changed — our national goal of survival.

SUGGESTED FURTHER READINGS

Appleton, Barry. 1994. *Navigating NAFTA*. Scarborough, ON: Carswell.

Bowker, Marjorie. 1991. *Canada's Constitutional Crisis: Making Sense of it All*. Edmonton, AB: Lone Pine Publishing.

Canada Government. 1979. *A Future Together: Observations and Recommendations*. Ottawa: The Task Force on Canadian Unity (Pepin-Robarts Report).

Canada Government. 1985. *Royal Commission on the Economic Union and Development Prospects for Canada*. Ottawa: Macdonald Report.

Canada Government. 1991. *Shaping Canada's Future Together: Proposals*, and *Canadian Federalism and Economic Union: Partnership for Prosperity*. Ottawa: Clark Report.

Canada West Foundation. 1994. *Internal Trade and Economic Cooperation: Down to the Wire on an Internal Trade Agreement*. Calgary, AB: June.

Canadian Chamber of Commerce. 1996. *The Agreement on Internal Trade and Inter-provincial Trade Flows: Building a Strong United Canada*. Ottawa: September.

Canadian Manufacturer's Association. 1991. *Canada 1993: A Plan for the Creation of A Single Economic Market in Canada*. Toronto.

Carlson, Cynthia R. 1992. "Inter-provincial Trade Barriers and the Economic Union Proposals." *Economic Union and Constitutional Change*. Calgary: Canada West Foundation, January.

Conference Board of Canada. 1992. *Barriers To Inter-provincial Trade: Implications For Business (Fifty Case Studies)*. Toronto.

Courchene, Thomas J. 1995. "Glocalization: The Regional/International Interface." *Canadian Journal of Regional Science*, 18:1, Spring.

Howse, Robert. 1996. "Securing the Canadian Economic Union: Legal and Constitutional Options for the Federal Government." C.D. Howe Institute *Commentary*, 81, June.

Janzen, S.S., and Chambers, E.J. 1996. *Alberta, Western Canada and the FTA/NAFTA: 198895*. Edmonton, AB: Western Centre for Economic Research and Centre for International Business Studies Bulletin #38, University of Alberta, June.

Lenihan, D.G., G. Robertson, and R. Tasse. 1994. *Canada: Reclaiming The Middle Ground*. Montreal: Institute for Research on Public Policy.

Palda, Filip (ed). 1994. *Provincial Trade Wars: Why the Blockade Must End*. Vancouver: The Fraser Institute.

Prentice, Barry E. 1994. "Inter-provincial Barriers to Agricultural Trade." In Filip Palda (ed.), *Provincial Trade Wars: Why the Blockade Must End*. Vancouver: The Fraser Institute.

Rosenbluth, Gideon. 1996. "Inter-provincial Migration and the Efficiency of Provincial Job Creation Policies." *Canadian Business Economics*, 4:2, Winter.

Trebilcock, Michael J., and Daniel Schwanen (eds). 1995. *Getting There: An Assessment of the Agreement on Internal Trade*. C.D. Howe Institute Policy Study, 26.

NOTES

1. At the time of writing the members of the OECD were negotiating the Multilateral Agreement on Investment (MAI) to provide countries with a level playing field in the international marketplace for investment and to reduce barriers to asset mobility.

2. Filip Palda (ed). *Provincial Trade Wars: Why the Blockade Must End*, (Vancouver: the Fraser Institute, 1994).

3. Cynthia R. Carlson, "Interprovincial Trade Barriers and the Economic Union Proposals," *Economic Union and Constitutional Change* (Calgary: Canada West Foundation, January 1992).

4. "10-42" means working for 10 weeks so as to qualify for government "insurance" payments the remaining 42 weeks of a year.

5. For fuller coverage, see Taylor, *Business and Government Relations*, Ch. 12.

6. Barry E. Prentice, "Interprovincial Barriers to Agricultural Trade," in Filip Palda (ed), *Provincial Trade Wars: Why the Blockade Must End.*

7. Canada Government, *A Future Together: Observations and Recommendations* (Ottawa: The Task Force on Canadian Unity, 1979), 123.

8. Donald Macdonald, *Report of the Royal Commission on the Economic Union and Development Prospects of Canada.*

9. Marjorie Bowker, *Canada's Constitutional Crisis: Making Sense of it All* (Edmonton, AB: Lone Pine Publishing, 1991).

10. Canada Government, *Shaping Canada's Future Together: Proposals* (Ottawa: Clark Report, 1991).

11. The 10 chapters are: procurement, investment, labour mobility, consumer-related measures and standards, agricultural and food products, alcoholic beverages, natural resources processing, communications, transportation, and environmental protection.

12. In July 1997, Canada signed a bilateral trade agreement with Chile.

BUSINESS AS MORAL AGENT - A NOTE

Liberty means responsibility. That is why most men dread it.

George Bernard Shaw, 1856-1950

Power without responsibility – the prerogative of the harlot throughout the ages.

Rudyard Kipling, 1865-1936

It has been four decades since John Kenneth Galbraith wrote his controversial, yet seminal, *The Affluent Society*, in which he documented the "dependence effect" in microeconomics. Essentially, Galbraith posited that as a society becomes increasingly affluent, its members' base wants are increasingly satisfied and replaced by new wants. He predicted greater government investment to provide the services not offered by business in this increasingly materialistic society. He also called upon business to be less preoccupied with economics and more socially responsible.

Social responsibility was easy for business when the self-interest of the corporation and the public were compatible. Today, they are not. Both sectors' ideologies, philosophies, underlying beliefs and values are mutually exclusive. The corporate sector emphasizes productivity, efficiency, economy, and accumulation of wealth; the public sector focuses on social values such as cooperation, inclusiveness, altruism, community, self-gratification, and compassion. Leaders of both business and government have assigned varying weights to, and different responsibilities for, these two sets of values or goals. Consequently, there are tensions and conflicts between these groups.

The concept of efficiency, whether that of the economist or the engineer, directly conflicts with the public sector's primary concern for equity. As the gulf between these two concepts widens, *it is only a matter of time before government(s) in Canada shift the burden of a firm's social costs back onto that firm*. Government cannot do much more without forfeiting, through deficit borrowing, its future generations' birthright.

The future of business-government relations must depend somewhat upon business' interpretation of its social responsibility. Specifically, the private sector must accept its share of the responsibility to the community. Also to the natural environment and the moral fabric of the nation. Today's public demands that business expand its responsibility to the community beyond the payment of taxes. Moreover, the environment cannot be treated as a "free good" any longer.

Business is no longer value-neutral. Although there are no ready-made solutions to these challenges, it must begin to make more of its decisions from a societal viewpoint. If business is willing to take from government, then in its own interest it had best recognize that its mandate now requires going beyond economic and material satisfaction.

CORPORATE GOVERNANCE

Corporate governance is the process whereby companies organize the interactive roles and responsibilities of their directors and executive management to protect stakeholder interests. Effective corporate governance ensures that long-term strategic objectives and plans are established, and that the proper management and management structure are in place to achieve those objectives. As well, such governance would ensure the maintaining of integrity, reputation, and accountability to its relevant constituencies. Consensus statements are the easy part. But it is what actually happens, performance, that counts. **Chapters 8** and **9** included comments and concerns about Crown corporation governance and accountability. Generally the private sector elite has joined in this chorus of criticism, often with relish. But what about private corporations?

The 1990s have borne witness to rumblings about corporate governance, presumably leading to future changes. Why? Our horizon scan suggests three reasons. First, Canada has been forced to "go global" and be competitive on a world market basis rather than get by within its protected small economic fiefdom. No one denies the link between corporate governance and competitiveness, so governance matters more than it did before. A second reason is that government fiscal impairment has brought an end to the undeclared business strategy of "government as insurance broker." Bailouts, so prevalent with the federal and several provincial governments (e.g., Alberta), are at an end and the consequences of management mistakes will need to be internalized. The results will be jeopardy of cash flow and arresting of capital gains — no wonder investors are paying attention! A third reason is an increasing demand for transparency. Ontario legislation (with purview over the Toronto Stock Exchange) has forced greater disclosure of matters such as corporate board and executive compensation. The concept of ethical investments has materialized.[1] Ethical investments might exclude tobacco and alcohol from portfolios, and possibly investment markets believed to harbour human rights abuses, nuclear arms, or other factors.

In 1992, the Cadbury Report was issued in the United Kingdom. Its thrust was toward a "code of best practice" for corporate governance, and UK public companies are now required to report publicly on their compliance with this code, with auditors to confirm the factual correctness of such reports. The Toronto Stock Exchange commissioned an assessment, and its report was issued in December 1994; it suggested a variety of changes to corporate governance systems for all TSE-listed companies. Meanwhile, extensive academic work and commentary has been undertaken to analyze corporate governance in Canada.[2] Others were calling for changes, including the renown investment manager and minority-shareholder rights activist Stephen Jarislowsky.

Following issuance of its report in January 1995, the TSE adopted a set of guidelines designed to enhance corporate governance in Canada. The adoption of these guidelines marked the beginning of a new era in corporate governance with increased public attention to the roles and responsibilities of boards of directors. By June 30 that year all corporations listed on the TSE were required to report on their governance structures with respect to these guidelines as part of their annual reporting to shareholders. The Conference Board conducted a survey of 205 Canadian companies and found actual practices to differ sharply from TSE guidelines; the study concluded that directors focus on a narrow range of financial responsibilities and are less involved in strategic planning or assessing managers.[3] Beyond the Statement of Corporate Governance Practices reporting and administrative guidelines, certain substantive changes were recommended:

- boards should be smaller;
- a majority of directors should be independent;
- the board chair and the CEO should be separate persons; and
- a committee of outside directors should nominate new directors and assess the board's performance.

There were various other recommendations too, including the director liabilities issue.

Predictably, reaction was diverse. With about 75% of TSE companies having controlling shareholders, there was immediate and strong negative reaction to the independence recommendation. Not surprisingly, persons holding board chair/CEO positions questioned the separation recommendation. And so forth. As always, there is powerful and well-meaning resistance to changing the status quo. Others felt strongly that the TSE guidelines did not go far enough. Despite boardroom resistance, in 1996 the potpourri of corporate governance issues were receiving a "going over" by the Senate committee on banking, trade, and commerce. The legislative focus was the Canada Business Corporation Act. Like it or not, change is brewing.[5]

CORPORATE SOCIAL RESPONSIBILITY REVISITED

As mentioned in **Chapter 5**, the Canadian business community has not embraced Milton Friedman's definition of social responsibility, simply stated, for business to everincrease its profits. Given Canada's neo-corporatist background the evidence clearly shows that business accepts the role of political mechanisms, as well as market mechanisms, in the allocation of scarce resources. For Canadian enterprise, this is not socialism, as Friedman would suggest, but pragmatism.

Nor has Canada embraced the opposite view: that a company's primary responsibility is to its stakeholders, principally its employees. Championed by famous management gurus like Peter Drucker and Charles Handy, who argue that stakeholding attention makes commercial sense, the approach has been adopted as stakeholder capitalism in Germany and Japan.[6] Just as the paradigm is coming into question in these countries due to sluggish productivity, the approach is being promoted by re-elected American President Bill Clinton and new British Labour Party Prime Minister Tony Blair. Again, Canadians have found the pragmatic middle between the extremes.

Those who agree that business' only responsibility is to its shareholders, as well as those who argue that business should pay to clean up the world, miss an important point. Profit does not exist except for true monopoly surplus. There are only costs of labour, raw materials, technology, capital, and those associated with future risks and uncertainty. The so-called profit reported in financial statements should really be interpreted as the cost of capital and risk, the latter including the costs associated with tomorrow's jobs.

Not to earn at least the cost of capital is to operate at a loss. For an entire business community not to earn at least the cost of capital is to impoverish the economy, and eventually the larger society. Despite all of government's recent borrowing, the largest single source of capital with which to finance tomorrow's jobs remains with business, in the form of earnings.

In Canada, net jobs have been lost in the textile, furniture and footwear industries under free trade and a worldwide more liberal trading regime. Jobs will be lost in at least a dozen other sectors and industries as well. The new jobs of tomorrow will be in environmental protection, waste management, renewable energy, health care and social support for an aging population, alternate food production, and services. Government alone, however, cannot pay for the transition.

Government compensating workers laid off by free trade is not the answer. It would be difficult to conclude whether job losses were a result of regional free trade, GATT, poor management, the Depression, or something else. Training and retraining laid-off workers is an answer, however, and that should be a business responsibility. If government were to assist business in retraining workers through tax incentives, grants and revised labour legislation, the cost to taxpayers would be at least $300 million.

Any firm that cannot cover its own operating costs, cost of capital, and costs of tomorrow's jobs, cannot cover its own costs of doing business and society's costs of that firm doing business. While these additional costs are not as easy to determine as the cost of goods sold, they are as vital as other costs or depreciation amounts known to cost accountants.

In short, there are the costs of *doing* business and the costs of *staying in* business — the costs of *surviving*. And for the private sector to survive in this country, it had best learn this fact of economic life. Business' enemy is not government, but itself and its lack of credibility in the eyes of the public. In a poll conducted by Decima Research (a subsidiary of the lobbying firm of Hill and Knowlton), 76% thought that government, not business, best protected consumers; 83% thought that government best protected the national interest. The public was split on who could do more to promote economic growth, government or business.

This is not social responsibility in the standard sense, as in product content disclosure, constructive employee relations, or support of local culture. What is being discussed here is *societal responsibility* (see **Figure 15–1**). Business has a responsibility to operate efficiently

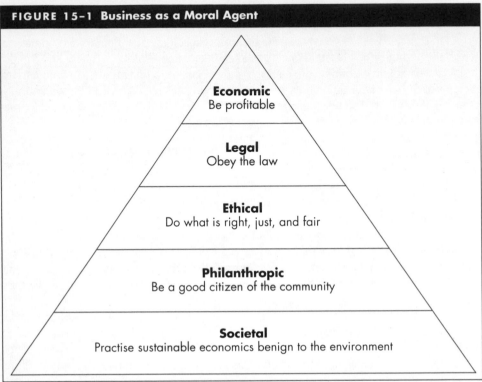

FIGURE 15-1 Business as a Moral Agent

Economic
Be profitable

Legal
Obey the law

Ethical
Do what is right, just, and fair

Philanthropic
Be a good citizen of the community

Societal
Practise sustainable economics benign to the environment

Adapted from: A Carroll. (1991: 42). From "The Pyramid of Corporate Social Responsibility: Toward the Moral Management of Organizational Stakeholders" *Business Horizons* 34:4 July/August. With the permission of the publisher JAI Press, Stanford, CT and London, England.

and be able to cover costs beyond externalities such as pollution; it must also pay what is required to maintain Canada's standard of living, Canada's position within the world, and its collective future.

Business and government must cooperate to solve society's problems. Honest and open communication between them is necessary for business to know how to help the social and economic entity known as Canada survive and prosper in the years ahead. Performing socially responsible activities in the short run will earn business profits in the long run. A key is to link shorter-term tactics to longer-term strategy. Above all, business should be around to enjoy those profits.

Business and government must redefine their interdependent social contract for the future. It is no longer, "What is good for business is good for Canada." Now it is, *"What is good for Canada is good for business."*

BUSINESS AND THE NATURAL ENVIRONMENT

Deserving special attention in this discussion of business as moral agent is the natural environment. Business, like all of us, owes its very existence to the environment. But no longer can we separate the economy from the environment.

Every day the media reports the latest ecological calamities: marine oil spills, acid rain, ozone depletion, deforestation, soil erosion, the Greenhouse Effect, species extinction, famine, disease, nuclear meltdowns, and growing deserts. In recent years, many newscasts have carried items on economic growth and the need to increase prosperity. Hardly ever do broadcasts or articles link the two seemingly disparate phenomena of economy and environment.

Yet, there is a vital connection. Scientific evidence is both ample and conclusive in documenting the link between economic activities and environmental deterioration. Of course, this is a global problem; but no matter how comparatively small Canada, its government and business community may be, both can take decisive steps to improve localized ecological imbalances and take international leadership where none exists. We question that Canada can be proud of its record here.

Since the beginning of the Industrial Revolution, environmental concerns have taken a back seat to economic ones. But scientists insist that the climatic global warming trend is upon the world. If this continues, rising food prices and scarcity will threaten our standard of living, as well as the very stability of a world growing by 80 million people per year. The world already has nearly 6 billion inhabitants; another billion is added each generation. *Every significant economic decision from today onwards must be subject to an ecological imperative*. If the affluent minority of the world does not take the lead, what can we expect of those persons, families and societies that can barely survive?

According to Barry Commoner, one of the early and most respected environmentalists, nothing short of a total redesign of the production of goods will suffice. Production processes must be re-engineered from benign linear to become cyclical. The world's population increase needs to be tempered. Pollution and biospheric rape can only be halted if business and government *together* change their values, attitudes, and beliefs. Political and corporate leaders need to adopt, soon, a shared vision of economic growth without environmental deterioration. As the United Nations' World Commission on Environment and Development phrased it: *sustainable development* is required — meeting the needs of the present without compromising the ability of future generations to meet their own needs.

The World Bank, in an attempt to quantify the total wealth per capita per nation, has chosen a measure which includes "produced assets" (goods and services), "natural bounty" (land, water, and natural resources), and "people power" (health and educational levels). The average score for the world in 1995 was US$86 000. Canada ranked second in the world with US$704 000. [7] At the same time, the National Centre for Economic Alternatives in Washington, D.C. ranked Canada as the second *worst* polluter in the industrialized world (only France was worse still). The main reasons for this abysmal record was our huge reliance upon inorganic fertilizers and pesticides, our growing municipal waste, our severe loss of wetland habitats, and our wasteful energy and water practices. We have a lot to protect, gain, and share by following Commoner's advice and the World Commission's recommendations.

Earlier, it was clearly stated that business must intersect its own interest to that of the public so as to win the ear of government. Putting shorter-term self-interest aside, business can show government it deserves a say in public policy matters by taking environmentally safe action. Nor need this strain business' bottom line, especially when viewed from an accrual perspective. Just a decade ago, urban recycling proved unprofitable for the private sector and even too costly for local government. Today business is discovering that millions can be made in helping to clean up the environment and reducing industry's impact on it. It is a business opportunity.

In 1992, the Earth Summit was held in Rio de Janeiro. Several commitments were made; 108 heads of state or government attended, including Canada. One commitment was a five-year accountability checkup. In December 1997, the follow-up "Earth Summit + 5" took place in Kyoto, Japan. The results were disappointing, and Canada's performance was hardly reassuring. Countries have not lived up to their environmental promises. Richer countries impact the environment the most (e.g., 75% of carbon emissions spewed into the atmosphere) yet, ironically, can best afford to provide leadership by both policies and actual performance.

To place all of the onus on business would be unfair. Governments pollute and destroy the environment as much as business. Eastern Europe, under strict socialism, was environmentally brutal. But not only should government clean up its act; it needs to take the lead in weaning both business and the public from their bad habits, whether burning fossil fuels, using fluorocarbons, wastefully using paper products,[8] or accepting convenience over biodegradability.

For example, Canada's energy policy is an ecological disaster waiting to happen. There is no serious development of alternate, renewable, clean fuel sources in Canada today. The federal and Newfoundland governments continue to support developing the Hibernia and other North Atlantic oil fields in the vicinity of the precious Grand Banks. When these come on stream they will produce the world's most expensive oil in some of the world's most dangerous waters. These are uneconomic **and** environmentally hazardous megaprojects.

No longer can economic growth be viewed as a trade-off for a healthy environment. Economic development and the private sector must assist governments in harnessing the means and mechanisms by which to achieve a healthier and safer environment. It is not a question of economic survival; in time, it is a question of *survival*, period. Canada needs more conservation, research on benign forms of energy and food production, and a massive reduction in toxic emissions and effluents. To achieve these, government must provide leadership. *Business must take the steps to master twenty-first century technology*, rather than settle for being custodians of last-century technology.

Government's role must be to provide an economic climate in which environmentalism is not only altruistic, but profitable. This requires major institutional reform now before it is too late. If business and government working together could once build a nation-state against all prevailing logic, then it must surely be able to work together towards saving this corner of the planet.

These are tall orders, but surely not beyond the capacity of humans. A true test for business and government in the future is to turn a real threat into a real *opportunity*.

BUSINESS ETHICS: DO THE ENDS JUSTIFY THE MEANS?

The Harvard Business School claims that its case method of pedagogy is ethically neutral. However, the "right" solution to a management problem may not necessarily be ethical. Which leads us to examine whether or not the ends *do* justify the means. If one accepts the above arguments for business' wider role in societal and environmental affairs, then modern business enterprise can no longer afford to be managed in an ethically neutral manner.

Today, business no longer commands an esteemed position in Canadian society. The public no longer perceives it as the sole, legitimate channel of economic growth and prosperity. If the private sector wants to regain its former preeminent position, or even be accepted as an equal partner with government, it must be ethically clean.

Like government, business must lead by example. If long-term economic prosperity, full employment, and ecological preservation are the public's concerns, then business must address these issues constructively and ethically. A corporation's ethics will be only as good as those of its leadership. Therefore CEOs, senior managers, and corporate directors must resist peer group pressure to conform to neutral management technique. If a "bad" law exists business should pursue getting it changed, not break it. Boards of directors should be diligent in ensuring that ask all laws are being followed and hold management and operations fully accountable. Corporate responsibility should not, however, end with the law.

Ethical behaviour does not stop with good public relations. McDonald's and Dofasco have great public images; yet Dofasco continues to pollute the environment, and McDonald's (despite recent progress) continues to use large quantities of chlorine-bleached paper and petroleum-based, non-recyclable materials. Corporate Canada must practise what it preaches.

For one company to act ethically on all fronts could place it at a cost disadvantage with its domestic and foreign competitors. Yet, if business' full purchasing power were used to convert to environmentally safer processes and materials, economies of scale would be obtained. When business works together to improve its ethical conduct the public will reward it, once again, with the legitimacy needed to enhance their markets and to influence public policy.

Ethics need also to be imbedded in business' internal operations. For example, if a company issues stock options to senior managers as a performance reward, and then its share price plummets shortly thereafter, the company should not call in those options and reissue new ones at a lower price. Another example might be is when a Canadian-born chief executive officer of a foreign-owned Canadian subsidiary obtains a 15% tax concession for increasing its upstream investment in Canada — should he or she object if the foreign owner transfers the saved tax money to itself without investing a cent in Canada?

Public policy must be ethical too. Is affirmative action (or so-called employment equity) attempting to redress old discriminatory imbalances? Or is this reverse discrimination ignoring the value of merit? Should the government award contracts on the basis of whether a bidder subscribes to affirmative action or not? Is it ethical for government policy to evolve from assuring equal opportunity to assuring equal results or even equal conditions? Ethics is essential to public policy.

Should Atomic Energy Canada sell CANDU reactors to nations it has reason to believe will use the materials and technology to create nuclear weapons? Even though it may be common and generally accepted practice in foreign countries, should a Canadian Crown corporation bribe foreign officials through a third-party agency to get a sale

On the human rights issue, should Canadians sell mainland Chinese products? Is Canada's position consistent with the former "high ground" of dealing with South Africa? Is the "level of the ground" determined by moral principles or by commercial potential? Should Canada do business with off-shore sweatshops? If not, what about all the other right-wing or left-wing countries which do not share Canada's regard for human rights? If Canadian companies should avoid dealing with countries which violate basic human rights, then Canadian business interaction will be reduced to far fewer (mostly Western) nations. Is it more ethical to boycott a nation or to establish business relations in that country, raise the expectations of the oppressed, and indirectly assist evolutionary change from within?

Regardless of business' answer to these problems, it must clearly be able to defend its behaviour on ethical grounds just as easily as it can on economic grounds. Only then might relations with government, and the publics to whom they are accountable, improve. Both government and business need to face these and similar questions, preferably together.

IMPLICATIONS FOR MANAGEMENT

Unfortunately this chapter has raised more questions than it has answers. However, its intent was not to provide a formal framework for social responsibility, to prescribe remedies for every environmental ill, or to define what is ethical in business and what is not. Instead, we wish to raise consciousness. Our sole purpose is to make you *think*, so you can ask yourself this private question: *would the child you were be proud of the adult you are?*

For the most part, this book has dealt with the concrete, the practical, and the absolute. But business-government relations are not as straightforward as one might have assumed from the previous chapters of this book. For that reason, this chapter has indulged in the more abstract.

The arguments for and against business as a moral agent are clear. Those who oppose the concept of business as a moral agent believe that the capitalist system (such as it is) will not survive if firms introduce non-economic values into the equation of their corporate decision making. Those who favour the concept argue that if business, especially big business, does not assume its proper societal, environmental, and ethical responsibilities, society will be much the poorer and could eventually perish.

The answer to this debate is simple. It is in the private sector's *enlightened self-interest* to create a social and physical environment that allows it to stay in business. Being an executive in either the private or public sector today is not an easy task. However, executives sometimes complicate their lives by dwelling on the immediate and the inconsequential, rather than on what really matters in longer horizon of life. This short chapter is intended to lift the content of this book out of the realm of the immediate, and place it in its true perspective.

SUGGESTED FURTHER READINGS

Carroll, A. 1991. "The Pyramid of Corporate Social Responsibility: Toward the Moral Management of Organizational Stakeholders." *Business Horizons*, 34:4, July/August.

Catherwood, Robert. 1994. "The Revolution in Corporate Governance." *Policy Options*. Montreal: Institute for Research on Public Policy, April.

Conner, Carolyn. 1995. *Canadian Directorship Practices 1995*. Ottawa: Conference Board of Canada, September.

Commoner, B. 1990. *Making Peace With the Planet*. New York: Pantheon Books.

Dorfman, Robert and Nancy S. (eds). 1993. *Economics of the Environment*. 3rd ed. New York: W.W. Norton and Co.

The Economist. 1996. "Stakeholder Capitalism." February 10.

Financial Post. 1996. "In The Line Of Fire..." Three-part series on Corporate Governance: May 4, 11, and 18.

Finlay, J. Richard. 1995. "Business Ethics Is Not A 'Soft' Issue, It's A Matter Of Survival." *Financial Post*, March 11.

Galbraith, J.K. 1958. *The Affluent Society*. Boston: Houghton-Mifflin.

Gillies, James, and Daniela Morra. 1997. "Does Corporate Governance Matter?" *Business Quarterly*, 61:3, Spring.

Malthus, R.R. 1990. *An Essay on the Principle of Population*. New York: Oxford University Press.

Mishan, E.J. (ed). 1993. *The Costs of Economic Growth Revised*. London: Weidenfeld and Nicolson.

Pearce, D.W., G.D. Atkinson, and W.R. Dubourg. 1994. "The Economics of Sustainable Development." *Annual Review Energy Environment*.

Thain, Donald H., and David S.R. Leighton. 1997. *Making Boards Work: What Directors Must Do To Make Canadian Boards Effective*. Toronto: McGraw-Hill Ryerson Ltd.

Thain, Donald H. 1994. "The TSE Corporate Governance Report: Disappointing." *Business Quarterly*, Autumn.

Toronto Stock Exchange. 1994. *Where Were The Directors? — Guidelines For Improved Corporate Governance in Canada*. Toronto: TSE Report, December.

World Commission on Environment and Development. 1990. *Our Common Future*. New York: Oxford University Press.

NOTES

1. In fact, Credit Unions in Canada have formed a group of Ethical Mutual Funds to incorporate concerns such as those listed.

2. Donald H. Thain and David S.R. Leighton, *Making Boards Work: What Directors Must Do To Make Canadian Boards Effective* (Toronto: McGraw-Hill Ryerson Ltd., 1997); James Gillies and Daniela Morra, "Does Corporate Governance Matter," *Business Quarterly* 61:3 (Spring 1997).

3. Carolyn Conner, *Canadian Directorship Practices 1995* (Ottawa: Conference Board of Canada, September 1995).

4. Donald H. Thain, "The TSE Corporate Governance Report: Disappointing," *Business Quarterly* (Autumn 1994); J. Richard Finlay, "Business Ethics Is Not A 'Soft' Issue, It's A Matter of Survival," *Financial Post* (March 11, 1995).

5. Robert Catherwood, "The Revolution in Corporate Governance," *Policy Options* (Montreal: Institute for Research on Public Policy, April 1994).

6. *The Economist*, "Stakeholder Capitalism" (February 10, 1996).

7. Australia was 1st; the US was 12th.

8. Ironically, computers (which were to have led us to "paperless offices") have led us to use more paper in the workplace and at home than ever before.

NOT THE CONCLUSION — BUT BEGINNING ANEW

16

Come, my friends, 'Tis not too late to seek a newer world.

Lord Alfred Tennyson, 1809–92

The solutions to problems are not necessarily found in new and brilliant ideas. They are sometimes discovered by making the old, proven ideas work.

D. Wayne Taylor

This book is written with eyes on Canada's future.

Sir Wilfrid Laurier claimed that the twentieth century belonged to Canada. Did his dream come true? Or did it not? What was, and was not, accomplished in this century was in large part a result of the actions taken by business and government under the rubric of a "National Policy." Similarly, what the twenty-first century will hold for Canada largely depends on the options that business and government choose today. Can one suggest that the next century will belong to Canada? Our relative market share in many sectors is declining; real growth in exports is increasing but at a diminishing rate. Our exports are growing, but partly because of a cheap Canadian dollar. A predominant portion of our prosperity and exports is based on resources endowment; Canada is as not competitive now as it will need to be. But there is hope that Canada will still have a place in the First World 10 and 20 years from now.

For the fourth straight year the United Nations has reported that Canada is among the wealthiest of nations. Canada tops the UN Human Development Index, a well-being measure based on income levels, educational attainment, and life expectancy. As good as this sounds, is there a basis to be smug or complacent? No! Canada is beset with current problems that could "take the bloom off the rose." The fissure of Canada, as Quebec contemplates its future, looms as a black cloud on the horizon. Youth unemployment is a ticking time bomb. We have an alarming proportion of Canadians who are poor, and in contrast with "politically correct" statements, the poor are not so much seniors as young persons in Canada.[2]

The World Bank concludes that successful economies are predicated on effective governmental administration. There are two more ingredients for success: (*i*) a vibrant and progressive business community is vital to Canada's success; and (*ii*) a positive synergy between business and government is needed for Canada to be all that it can be in the future. [1]

STRATEGICALLY MANAGING THE BUSINESS-GOVERNMENT INTERFACE IN THE TWENTY-FIRST CENTURY — BACK TO FIRST PRINCIPLES

Time will tell about the health of business-government relations under current governments; but we can learn from the recent past. Much of the Canadian business-government literature has assumed that prior to the election of neo-conservative President Ronald Reagan, the state of business-government relations in Canada was similar to that south of the border. That is: relations were adversarial; interests of business and government were antagonistic; and each side lacked insight into the role, motivations, problems, and modes of action of the other. Although such was hardly the case in Canada before the early 1970s, Canadian business-government relations did deteriorate thereafter, but hardly to the extent portrayed.

Why was this so? Some blamed business. They claimed that ineffective business leadership at a national level produced fragmentation and a lack of consensus within the business community. Each sector offered its own self-serving option on economic and industrial policies and programs. Other critics cited the dearth of effective consultation and coordination processes between the private and public sectors. This was seen as compromising the health of business-government relations. Because democratic governments tend to be risk-averse, Ottawa has been slow to take the initiative in business-government consultation when business has lacked enthusiasm for the idea. Still others noted that because of their geographic location, some federal politicians and public servants became isolated from the world of business in Toronto, Montreal, Vancouver, or Calgary.

Overall, there is little evidence to substantiate many of the negative claims made about Canadian business-government relations. In fact, contrary to popular opinion, the most recent empirical research showed that business and government do not perceive their interrelations to be all that bad, but admit there is plenty of room for improvement.

An informed student of Canadian business-government relations would have expected this. *If one understands the socioeconomic underpinnings of business-government relations in this country and its key players, and interprets data with an eye to context and circumstance, then one becomes aware of how to manage this interrelationship constructively and effectively. As partners who understand and respect each other, business and government can turn the economic challenges of the twenty-first century into victories.*

Business can take the first step by voluntarily and aggressively offering its advice to government. This must be accurate, objective, and well-documented. Business must also be willing to wait for government's reaction, and to return again and again, if necessary, to get it.

Furthermore, business must show interest in having an impact on policy decisions and being helpful to the decision makers, rather than just having its own point of view publicized. It must know what it wants, and go after it as professionally as it professes to manage its internal operations. Business must visibly perform well its traditional role of wealth creation, and show that it is serving the public interest, however defined by the public policy makers of the day.

Conversely, government must provide greater access for business and be willing to listen to and digest business' input. Government-line departments, which once acted as Ottawa's listening posts for business, no longer influence the policy-making process as much as they once did. Through the last quarter-century to the present, the centralization of decision making in Ottawa has reduced departments to one of many players in the policy arena today. This centralization of decision-making authority within the federal government has had a severe, negative impact on business-government relations. There has been a gradual movement away from the mutually dependent department-client relationships which were built up during the 1940s through the 1960s. Today, a less approachable and less comprehensible government-by-central-agency has left most industries and businesses without readily accessible contacts in government who can influence government policy. Cabinet ministers and deputy ministers are now being moved around much more frequently than ever before. This compounds the problem of business' losing touch with government, and government with business.

There is no doubt that Canada is overgoverned: one national government, ten provincial, two territorial and thousands of regional, county, district, municipal, and local governments, councils, agencies, boards and commissions — all for thirty million people (the population of California!). No wonder the overall government sector is so costly and debt-ridden. If reversing so-called entitlements to individuals, groups and businesses is difficult for governments to do, imagine the (un)likelihood of substantive change being made to governing jurisdictions and their fiefdoms. But as the world becomes more glocalized, business must understand and partner with these other levels of government more so each passing year. As fiscal burdens are devolved from Ottawa to the provinces, and from the provinces to local governance entities, the loci of business-government interaction will likewise shift. Perhaps this will provide the impetus needed to eliminate inter-provincial trade barriers.

The governmental role must change too. Before World War I the role of the state was analogous to that of a night watchman: providing defence, law and order, and a stable currency. Since the 1960s, the state has become a first assault force, trying to do everything imaginable to alleviate poverty, provide "essential" goods and services, and correct market failures. As the year 2000 approaches and then becomes history, the role of the state needs to return to that of a nightwatchman — but with a difference. This time government needs to be a state-of-the-art security guard equipped with the latest in hardware, software, and human resource training. Government expenditures on many social programmes, let alone in producing consumable goods and services, are irrelevant as the government spending multiplier nears a unitary value (i.e., one).[3]

Despite the foregoing concerns, comparing across the world, Canada still has effective and honest government at all three levels. This is valuable infrastructure. Business people who deal with governments in other countries appreciate the assets: social stability, public service competence and continuity, and a lack of corruption. Nonetheless, there is urgent need for bold reform of government in Canada.

The state's role is not to be *in* business or even be *pro* business, but to be pro-market. Individual *choice* needs be reinstituted as the way of life; the state does not know best. Vested interests need to be shown for being just that and not allowed to sway or control the public agenda. And again, as the world "glocalizes" and companies become footloose nomads with less and less national attachment, all governments will need to reach out to business more than they ever have.

If the principal function of economic policy is to create wealth, and the principal function of political policy is to protect and redistribute it, (even though most of the redistribution is from one middle-class constituency to another), differences are bound to arise between business and government. However, a herculean task awaits them. Government must listen to *and* hear business. Business must get its story straight, both to government and the public, and behave accordingly. A company or corporation cannot, in one breath, call for reduced government spending, deficits and debts and then in the next breath plead for government help or even rescue. Society must formulate a political-economic framework which balances the *creation* of wealth and *distribution* of wealth in a way that both sides and the public can accept.

The prime requisite for success is *political will*. The will to work with business, to induce business to do what Canada needs it to do, and to do so in an environmentally sustainable manner. Economic issues need to be recoupled with socio-political issues.

Although business in Canada does not want government on its back, it does need government by its side.

THE FUTURE OF CANADIAN BUSINESS-GOVERNMENT RELATIONS — TWO SOLITUDES OR A NATIONAL PARTNERSHIP?

Above all Canada has always been, still is, and will continue to be a trading nation. With the advancement of freer trade around the world and the triangulation of economic power among the Americas, Europe, and Southeast Asia, Canadian productivity and competitiveness will become very important to this nation of producers, consumers, governors, traders, and tax-collectors. Becoming more competitive has been helped by Canada's sustained period of low inflation and attendant relatively low interest rates. Gains in productivity may be offset in the short term by expected deflation and a low Canadian dollar. Management has two choices: to be less generous on the wage front (a stopgap measure at best), or to improve technological productivity dramatically.

But Ottawa tends to complicate things even further. At present there appears to be no coherent federal government strategy to manage the economy, cope with federal accumulated debt, or help business emerge from the 1990s depression. Coherent policy will require imagination as well as practicality. One thing that the twentieth century has taught managers the world over is that centralized economic state forecasting, planning, and management does not work. *What Canada needs is consistency and congruency between its economic and social goals and the actions of both business and government.*

Academe also has a role to play. Human resources, especially capacity for adaptation, remain the key to productivity and change management. Both management and labour must work more smartly to compete in a freer trade environment, and in an age of rapid techno-logical change. The ability of people to develop, adjust, utilize, manage, and work alongside new technologies will be critical. Schools of management need to develop problem solvers, leaders, strategic thinkers, and change agents as much as marketers, policy analysts, and financial whiz kids.

Innovative organizations will survive turbulent times, but they need change agents and leadership. Change is not to be feared, but exploited. The Japanese believe that the differ-ence between how Easterners and Westerners manage change reflects the different ways the two metacultures view death. In the East, death is a part of living not to be resisted. In the West, people resist death with every ounce of their strength and guile. As a society, Canadians resist rapid industrial and socioeconomic evolution as they do death — fighting it every step of the way. Japan's ability to manage rapid industrial and socioeconomic evolu-tion is similarly grounded in its beliefs about death — something to look forward to, not resist. It is *not* ironic that as Japanese society has become more Westernized, its ability to change with the economic times has diminished.

Canada has a lot to learn, and so little time in which to apply that knowledge. Simplistic, structural, reductionist solutions will not work. How can Canada escape being tossed upon the scrap heap of economic history?

As the Japanese realized over the last quarter century or so, the key to a successful economic future is productivity. Canada can improve its productivity by effectively combining and integrating technology, capital, labour, management skills, and educa-tion. It must increase its expenditures on research and development, loosen the reins on its ultra-conservative and risk-averse banking community, include labour in the national policy agenda, and improve its management expertise. There is a great need to instill a new sense of pride in the educational system, with a commitment to quality and a heightened degree of competitiveness.

Greater emphasis on product-specific, plant-level economies of scale ultimately will lead to a rationalization of assets within an industry. This will increase economic concentration and decrease internal competition. The costs and unemployment associated with this process will be high. For how long can we tolerate about a tenth of our population being idle? The costs associated with coaxing and retraining workers from one industry to another to increase competitive advantages are substantial. If it is not recognized already, policy makers and indus-trialists alike soon will have to admit that a twenty-first century Canada will need *less* people not more. More importantly, Canada will need well-educated, vocationally adept, hard-working, self-supporting citizens with realistic expectations of government, business, and soci-ety. And most importantly, Canadians need to return to a state of harmony with their natural environment. It is not the high cost of living (inflation) that is jeopardizing our future as the "most desirable country in which to live," but our costs of high living. Canada is a *wasteful* nation.

We are wasteful, and conspicuous, consumers. The average personal savings rate, which peaked at 18% in the early 1980s, now is closer to zero. In the 1950s, the average worker earned 30¢ per hour and gasoline cost 5¢ per litre. So, an hour's work bought six litres of gas. In the 1990s, the *minimum* wage is nearing $7.00 and gasoline costs 60¢ or more per litre. One hour's work buys 12 litres — and we buy it! It is no wonder that Toronto is in a yellow haze from June to September each year. Canadians need to find peace once again with their corner of the planet.

Business must recognize change, plan for it, and be willing and able to cover its costs. Government must financially support and encourage an educational system that will produce the scientific management and labour skills needed to compete in the global technological arenas. This may well be the greatest challenge facing educators, business, and government in the next decade. It will not be easy, as governments at all levels have cut back on educational funding. But one thing is sure: our educational system leaves *much* to be desired. From pre-school to post-graduate, our educational institutions and programs must once again become standards-based and results-oriented. *Damn the process if the results are incongruent with the nation's needs.*

Above all, Canadians, their elites, and institutions, must become and remain flexible. Retirements will not be like anything previously imagined; the paths between youth and retirement will be completely unpredictable in the next millennium. This is compounded by the federal government's high-risk fiscal policy. The timeframe required to accomplish even a slight reduction in the nation's debt is too long. Significant debt reduction will not be achieved before the government has to respond to the social spending pressures created by the aging, retiring baby-boom generation. Unrealistic expectations by baby boomers will collide forcefully with economic reality. But will prudence prevail?

Over a 100 years ago, business and government working as partners built a nation out of a wilderness, and kept it from becoming part of the American union. It was a question of survival. Today, business and government must again become partners to rebuild this nation, protect its sovereignty, and secure for its children a leadership position on the world stage. *It is still a question of survival — both for business and for Canada.*

⤷ Authors Bio

It is now the moment when by common consent we pause to become conscious of our national life and to rejoice in it, to recall what our country has done for each of us, and to ask ourselves what we can do for our country in return.

Oliver Wendell Holmes, Jr.
1809–94

SUGGESTED FURTHER READINGS

Davidson, J.D., and Lord Wm. Rees-Mogg. 1997. *The Sovereign Individual*. New York: Summit Books.

Jerome-Forget, Monique. 1997. "Human Capital: Investing for the Long Term." *Financial Post*, June 28.

Reid, Angus. 1996. *Shakedown*. Toronto: Doubleday Canada Ltd.

NOTES

1. Monique Jerome-Forget, "Human Capital: Investing for the Long Term," *Financial Post* (June 28, 1997).
2. Statistics Canada data show that twice as many young people (16%) as seniors (8%) are poor; of course, seniors vote and young people generally do not. The government income support level for seniors is a level upon which young working Canadians must pay income tax.
3. In the nineteenth century the multiplier was around 2.5. Today, with a high marginal tax rate and marginal propensity to import, the multiplier is much lower.

Part

7

CASES

AUTOMOBILE INSURANCE IN ONTARIO

In October, 1990 Andrew Rogacki, president of Progressive Casualty Insurance Company of Canada (PCICC), was wondering what to do next with an economic study PCICC commissioned following the totally unexpected victory of the New Democratic Party (NDP) in the Ontario election of September 6, 1990. The study commissioned by PCICC predicted widespread damage to the Ontario and Canadian economies if there was government takeover of the automobile insurance business in Ontario.

BACKGROUND ON THE AUTO INSURANCE INDUSTRY

Ontario auto insurance represented a full one-quarter of the $12 billion in premiums collected by general insurers in Canada in 1989. (General insurance included automobile, property, and liability). Premiums and return on equity in the insurance industry followed a roller coaster pattern. When premiums rose and profitability increased, the result was more competition in the market which, in turn, lead to rate stability or reductions. Competition then lessened to an extent and premiums subsequently rose again. Traditionally insurance companies depended on the underwriting function of their business to provide the major portion of their earnings. However, investment income reaped huge returns while the underwriting resulted in a loss in every year from 1979 to 1989. (Exhibit 1).

One of the major on-going challenges for the industry was to devise criteria which were perceived as fair and equitable for determining premiums. While Ontario auto insurers were under pressure from human rights groups to remove age, sex, and marital status as the criteria for rate classifications, the industry argued in court cases that these criteria formed the foundation of actuarial estimates of an insurance company's future liabilities so that the policy-holders which generated the largest claims would be required to pay the highest premiums, otherwise "one class would be forced to subsidize the other."

Another on-going challenge for the industry was the pressure on costs because of the changing legislative environment. For example, the Family Law Reform Act in 1975 made it possible for husbands and wives to bring civil actions against one another and for children to sue their parents, thereby increasing the number of potential claims which could arise out of any one accident. A section of the Act was later added allowing extended family members to claim for loss. In 1977, the Highway Traffic Act was amended so that passengers could sue the drivers and owners of vehicles for negligence without having to prove gross negligence, thereby increasing the number of accident claims. In 1980, the Ontario government made third party liability auto insurance mandatory and third party liability policies had to provide accident benefits for occupants of the insured vehicle. (Third party is the claimant under liability insurance and is so called because s/he is not one of the two main parties—insured and insurer—who enter into the insurance contract which pays the claim.)

INSURANCE BUREAU OF CANADA

The Insurance Bureau of Canada (IBC) the "official voice of the general insurance industry" had a staff of approximately 150, and its members provided "approximately 80 percent of the automobile, property and casualty insurance written by private insurers in Canada." The IBC communicated with the public, the media and the government on behalf of its members. It gathered and processed statistical information and monitored the environment. In the late 1980s, the IBC described its objectives as to: (*i*) "secure the business we have from further government takeover," (*ii*) "retrieve those parts lost to government in B.C., Saskatchewan, Manitoba, and Quebec," and (*iii*) "make the auto insurance business profitable again." In their 1987/88 Annual Review, the Bureau outlined their strategy in Ontario: "Our approach has been to debate quietly with government in private, rather than to confront it noisily in public."

The vast majority of general insurance companies considered the IBC to be their voice. Most of the company executives preferred to run their companies and let the IBC do the monitoring and lobbying for them. Some individual executives took a more active role but collaborated closely with the IBC. When the IBC required speakers for public meetings or call-in programs, these individuals volunteered their services.

The IBC represented a diverse group of more than 100 company groups representing more than 85 percent of total premiums for the private insurance industry; large and small; direct-writing companies and companies selling through brokers; regional and national companies; Canadian and foreign firms. More than 60 percent of the non-life insurance business in Canada was foreign-owned. The diversity of the membership of the IBC made it difficult to reach consensus on all issues or to formulate a strategy for just one segment of the membership such as the auto insurers in Ontario. The Vice President of one IBC member company noted: "All member companies do not always agree with the lobbying efforts of the IBC. A lack of cohesiveness has long been a problem in the auto insurance industry — it is a very competitive industry."

THE SLATER REPORT

Following concern about the shortages and increased cost of liability insurance, the Ontario government (under Liberal premier David Peterson) appointed David Slater, in January, 1986, to head The Ontario Task Force on Insurance (hereafter Slater Report). In its report in May 1986, Slater urged a move to no-fault auto insurance but rejected government-run auto insurance. At the time, Ontario had in place a liability auto insurance system based on the tort system. (Tort is defined as any act or omission that may give rise to an action in damages.) The compensation under the system was regarded by critics as a lottery where the awards did not match the needs of the injured, and legal costs seriously detracted from compensation. In a tort case only 40 cents on the dollar found its way to the accident victim, the rest went to running the system. Indeed, legal fees accounted for greater than 30 percent of claims payments resulting from injuries in automobile accidents. Furthermore, studies had shown that it took an average of four years for the courts to settle tort cases.

The Slater Report's recommendation for a move to a no-fault auto insurance system pleased the insurance companies since they had been advocating this system since the 1970s. A pure no-fault system would remove an injured party's right to sue and replace it with a guaranteed fixed compensation. All injured parties would receive compensation regardless of their fault in causing the accident, however the party at fault would be subject to resultant higher premiums. Proponents of no-fault insurance proclaimed that it would settle cases much more quickly than under the tort system and reduce costs. On the issue of soaring liability insurance premiums, the Slater Report noted that the courts were responding to the greater needs and demands for personal injury compensation arising from a society increasingly exposed to risk. The Report concluded it was time for a new personal injury compensation program to be legislated by the government and delivered by the industry. The Slater Report also criticized the industry for failing to provide timely notification to policy-holders for changes in price, coverage, exclusions, and nonrenewal.

AUTO INSURANCE AS AN ELECTION ISSUE

In the spring of 1986, the NDP organized a series of public hearings at 15 different centres around Ontario following public outrage about the increases in auto insurance premiums, which had increased nearly 40 percent over a two-year period. In the spring of 1987, in anticipation of the upcoming election, the NDP promoted their "driver-owned" government-run auto insurance system, with the right to sue under certain circumstances. The system aimed to address three problems with the current system: (*i*) the high cost of premiums, (*ii*) unjust discrimination among different classes of drivers, (*iii*) industry's failure to provide a decent level of compensation to everyone. In various public forums, NDP representatives claimed that a switch to government-run auto insurance would save Ontario drivers between 20 and 75 percent of present premium costs depending on age and driving habits for a total of $750 million because of lower legal and administrative costs.

In early 1987, both the IBC and IBC member companies undertook campaigns to respond to worsening public opinion about the industry. An IBC-commissioned survey discovered that the ratio of those preferring private auto insurance to public auto insurance was 2.5:1 in 1972, while in 1986 it was less than 2:1. The IBC hired a government relations consultant, S.A. Murray Consulting, Inc., who recommended the development of a "consensus on a solution." Following from this recommendation, and to distinguish from the NDP's no-fault proposals, the IBC proposed a "Smart no-fault" insurance system whereby injured parties would retain the right to sue if their injuries were serious or permanent. The IBC pointed out that during 1986 only eight percent of all claims involved serious injuries or fatalities, the other 92 percent were for relatively minor fender benders which could be handled by an arbitrator without the financial burden of costly lawyers. In March 1987, the IBC launched a six-week television and newspaper ad campaign outlining their "Smart no-fault" plan and denouncing a government-run system. Full page ads claimed that insurance companies had little control over costs (see Exhibit 2). These ads were run on CTV and Global but were considered to be so controversial that the CBC network refused to run them.

At the same time as the IBC campaign, individual company executives undertook their own campaigns. A "Grass Roots" campaign funded and encouraged by the IBC was under-taken by one IBC member company, The Personal Insurance Co., to educate the public about the industry and its proposals for correcting shortcomings, to establish closer relations with the Liberals and PCs, and to formulate a strategy to deal with the NDP. As part of this campaign, interviews and TV appearances were accepted as often as possible, employee education programs were initiated, and presentations were made to the key leaders and caucuses of both the Conservative and Liberal parties.

Another company campaign, known as Project Action, was created by The Co-operators, Ontario's largest automobile insurer. The catalyst for this campaign was a statement by Premier Peterson that he would be in favour of government-run auto insurance if it could be run without public money. This statement was seen as a reversal of the Premier's earlier positions. In this campaign, the Co-operators ran full-page advertisements in 40 daily newspapers (see Exhibit 3) and received over 8000 return coupons. In addition, a company Vice-President was made available to the media and special interest groups. The company also sent a letter to its 2300 employees urging them and their friends to write to Ontario MPPs to "express your support for retaining a competitive auto-insurance industry in the province and your opposition to a Government monopoly." The letter contained 14 potential arguments that could be used in the letters. Unlike other parts of the Co-operators' campaign, this move had some unexpected backlash. Mel Swart, the NDP insurance critic, immediately attacked the letter as "unscrupulous and dishonest." There were also some employee complaints about the letter. As a result of these criticisms, the company sent another letter stating that no one was required to write to MPPs.

At the time of the corporate and industry campaigns, NDP critic Mel Swart toured the province to hear complaints about the current auto insurance system and to mobilize support for the NDP cause through hearings, speeches, and media interviews. Swart emphasized the excessive profits of the industry, backed by Stats Canada numbers, the administrative savings potential (greater than 50 percent) under a government plan, and criticized the industry for unfair tactics. Swart also pointed out that private industry had unlimited amounts to spend on advertising while the NDP was confined to a campaign budget.

The Consumers Association of Canada (CAC) got involved by advocating a modified no-fault system and the elimination of age, sex, and marital status as criteria for setting premiums. The CAC rejected an immediate switch to public insurance (i.e., government-run) since the CAC had a policy of rejecting government takeover of any enterprise that could be run successfully by private industry. The legal community viewed no-fault as a threat. The Canadian Bar Association opposed no-fault auto insurance using the argument that eliminating the right to sue would violate the fundamental freedoms enshrined in the Charter of Rights.

In April 1987, the insurance industry was embarrassed with the revelation of a $1 billion profit for 1986. The profit levels were from investment income due to the booming stock market, and the underwriting loss was only half of 1985's record amount.

THE GOVERNMENT STEPS IN

On April 23, 1987, the insurance industry was hit with devastating news from Monte Kwinter, Minister of Financial Institutions, the overseer of the insurance industry. Kwinter said:

> We have repeatedly urged the [insurance] industry to voluntarily improve their practices but their response has been inadequate....We have urged the industry to prepare for non-discriminatory rating practices. Nothing has been delivered. In fact much energy has been expended by the industry in defending current practices.

Kwinter froze most auto insurance rates effective immediately and did not rule out a government-run system even though he added that "our preference is not to be in the insurance business." The rate freeze came in the industry cycle where competition was strong and premiums were low. The Liberal government also planned to establish a permanent board to review and set auto insurance rates, and to regulate auto repair shops.

The IBC quickly responded to Kwinter's criticisms by noting that auto insurers lost about $100 million in 1986 and Kwinter's moves would force some automobile insurers out of the province. Jack Lyndon, IBC president, claimed that a no-fault plan would save 20 percent in administrative costs while providing better benefits. The NDP reiterated their claims for a government-run auto insurance system, singling out the Manitoba, Saskatchewan, and British Columbia systems as cases in point. In these provinces the NDP set up government-run auto insurance systems which were not disbanded when opposition parties regained power. (None of the government-run systems were no-fault.) Also cited were various examples comparing the premiums of an Ontario resident to a western counterpart with a similar car and insurance policy but under the government-run insurance system. The insurance industry vehemently denounced all such comparisons as invalid since there was a greater population density, more roads and major highways, and more vehicles on the roads in Ontario. Also, government-run insurance systems had been shown to be subsidized by provincial gasoline taxes and license assessments. Nevertheless, Ontario residents typically had insurance rates that were 20-50% higher, a fact that was not lost to the public, especially the male under 25 years of age who was paying thousands in annual premiums for being in a high-risk category.

On the last day of the 1987 spring session of the Legislature, the minority Liberal government introduced a bill that proposed to set up the review board and regulate auto repair shops. However, the bill died on the order paper with the adjournment of the House. Although no enforcing legislation was passed, insurance companies complied voluntarily to caps on insurance rates.

THE LIBERAL PROMISE

The provincial election was set for September 1987. A two-year coalition agreement between the Liberals and NDP expired in June, 1987 and the Liberals, buoyed by increasing popularity, were convinced they could obtain a majority government and be freed of the NDP's direct involvement in government policy.

Automobile insurance was the main election issue. The Liberals promised an auto insurance review board to lower insurance rates. The NDP suffered from some problems of credibility during the campaign when NDP leader Bob Rae was found using inaccurate data about the insurance industry resulting in the departure of an NDP researcher. Advocacy advertisements were sponsored by industry groups such as The Insurance Brokers of Waterloo Region (Exhibit 4). On election night the Liberals swept to a crushing win (garnering 95 seats of 130). The NDP became the Official Opposition for the first time in Ontario history with 19 seats, claiming that the results would have been even worse for the NDP if it had not been such a strong advocate of auto insurance reforms. The PCs, long aligned with big business, suffered their worst showing ever. The 120 insurance companies that wrote auto insurance in Ontario claimed that Ontarians' votes showed that they do not want a government-run auto insurance industry.

Throughout the previous months and especially during the election, the IBC was well mobilized, lobbying on three fronts to counter the fact that the insurance industry was vastly misunderstood by politicians and by the public. The first prong of the lobby effort involved an IBC-organized industry network which became known as the Political Action Committee (PAC) involving eight regional advisory committees across the province. As part of PAC, an industry representative, such as a local company employee or broker, in each of the 130 ridings talked to the MPP in order that they might better understand issues confronting the insurance industry and to correct any misinformation before it became too widespread. On a second front, the IBC pursued public education using radio, television, and print media. Speakers were made available from either the local insurance industry or the IBC. The IBC found that the news media needed to be educated on auto insurance and thus went to great lengths to explain the workings of the industry. The third lobbying front involved meetings between the IBC president and board, and bureaucrats and politicians at Queen's Park. Individual insurance company lobbying was discouraged in order that the IBC could present a united front for the industry.

To the relief of the insurance industry, in the November Throne Speech, the Liberals backed away from their earlier promise to cap auto insurance rates because it trusted insurance companies not to gouge the public. This prompted the NDP to claim that the Liberals and insurance industry were in liaison.

In February 1988, the Ontario Automobile Insurance Board (OAIB) Act was passed. The OAIB, an independent review board, was given the power to determine, after holding industry-wide hearings, rates or ranges that must be charged by insurance companies in accordance with a new uniform classification system that did not discriminate on the basis of age, sex, and marital status. At this point, virtually all companies were basing premiums on age and sex (for drivers under 25) along with other criteria such as driving experience, car type and use, accident history, and geography. Furthermore, there was some variation among the companies in terms of the specific criteria used. It was apparent the government was proposing not only to eliminate age and sex as criteria but also to eliminate any variation among the companies.

In April 1988, Justice Osborne, who had been commissioned by the Peterson government, released his report, Inquiry into Motor Vehicle Accident Compensation in Ontario. The report rejected both a government-run system and a private no-fault system but instead recommended fine-tuning the current tort system to increase limited no-fault benefits to discourage lawsuits, while retaining the right of accident victims to sue for damages. The industry was pleased that the report recommended against public auto insurance with the following rationale:

> The modest potential for cost savings particularly in the area of business acquisition costs (mainly broker commissions) would be offset in the short run by the substantial start-up costs of a public plan and would be completely eroded in the longer term by other cost-based considerations, particularly the elimination of the potential for lower premiums derived from competition.

In July, the OAIB announced it would be holding a series of four public hearings to consider the following topics: (*i*) Classification system and data availability regarding age, sex and marital status system; (*ii*) Actuarial rate making; (*iii*) Rate of return standards; (*iv*) Rate setting using results of three previous hearings, rates to be effective June 1, 1989. Exhibit 5 contains an illustration of the type of cost and premium data supplied by the IBC to the OAIB during the third set of hearings. In November, the OAIB, which operated independently of the government, ruled to allow the auto insurance industry to earn 12.5% return on equity on car insurance in 1989. As a result, the province's drivers were told by the media not to expect rate cuts.

In December 1988, a report commissioned by the OAIB and prepared by a consulting firm, William M. Mercer Ltd., recommended that auto insurance premiums be hiked by 35-40% in anticipation of the Board's rates due to be set early the next year. Murray Elston, the new minister of Financial Institutions, was forced to defend heavy criticism from Peter Kormos, the new, maverick NDP insurance critic, who took over from the retired Mel Swart. Most auto insurers recognized that the large increase advocated by the Mercer report would generate a public outcry and quickly stated that they would not increase their rates by 35 to 40% even though these increases were in line with what the industry felt was needed. Premiums had been so low that the Co-operators Insurance Co. announced the previous October it would not be accepting any new auto insurance customers in Metro Toronto. Many other companies were effectively closed for new business and some were not renewing clients who incurred accidents or convictions. In January 1989, Mercer Ltd. recalculated its controversial car insurance rate proposal, based on different insurance reserve values and came up with 13-21% increases instead. However, Mercer's actuaries stated that they were still recommending increases of about 35 percent as justified by industry losses.

In February 1989, Elston asked the OAIB to hold public hearings on alternative forms of car insurance, including no-fault. Two alternatives were to be considered: threshold no-fault and freedom of choice where the insured was to have a choice between no-fault and liability (tort) insurance. Threshold no-fault insurance would not allow any injured party to sue for damages unless the injury was greater than a certain "threshold" injury, such as serious and permanent injury or death. The party would only be allowed compensation as granted according to fixed compensation rates. At the hearings, the IBC recommended a "choice" proposal, which related to bodily injury insurance only and would permit the consumer to select either a no-fault plan or one retaining the right to sue. Ralph Nader, US consumer advocate, appeared before the Board and like the Canadian Bar Association of Ontario (CBAO) condemned no-fault in any form.

After receiving 1000 written submissions from the public and various experts, the OAIB announced in February that it was permitting insurance companies to raise their premium rates by an average 7.6 percent effective March 15, to the end of 1989 and that use of age, sex, or marital status in rate-setting would be forbidden when the OAIB plan came into effect. Furthermore, companies would be allowed to raise their premiums by up to 16.6% or lower them as much as 12.4% without seeking approval from the OAIB. At that time the premiums had been frozen for 22 months, with only 4.5% increases allowed in January and August, 1988. It was expected the insurers would take full advantage of the 16.6% maximum.

In April 1989, Elston announced that insurance premium increases would be capped at 7.6 percent for all drivers by June 1 because it was becoming clear the insurance industry was just going to take advantage of the maximum allowable rate even though the government could dictate the rate. As a result, the insurance industry was now confused with the government's agenda and was upset since the industry had wasted much good time and money complying with the government's requirements. Insurance companies claimed the 7.6 percent cap was woefully inadequate in an industry that lost about $400 million on auto insurance during the previous year. Some companies decided to leave the auto insurance business.

In June, the Ontario government changed the legislation governing the OAIB so that OAIB decisions could now be overruled by the government. In July 1989 the OAIB released its report on the various types of auto insurance studied. The report was not enthusiastic about pure or threshold no-fault systems because savings for the consumer were not apparent, but preferred the threshold version to the pure version. Also, the OAIB was clear on the need to oversee the insurance industry's payment of benefits, which OAIB chairman Kruger called "abysmal." In response to the apparent move toward a no-fault system, a lobby group called FAIR (The Committee for Fair Action in Insurance Reform), a loose coalition of litigation lawyers, placed a half-page ad in the *The Globe and Mail* claiming that no-fault insurance was not the answer for Ontario drivers. FAIR contended that a no-fault plan would not deter drivers from irresponsible behaviour which could threaten the safety of other drivers. Overall, FAIR was concerned that no-fault would greatly reduce the benefits received by accident victims.

BILL 68: THRESHOLD NO-FAULT AUTO INSURANCE IS PROPOSED

In September 1989, the Peterson government tabled Bill 68, known as the Ontario Motorist Protection Plan (OMPP) which involved a threshold no-fault system. The major changes proposed in Bill 68 were: (*i*) virtually everyone injured in a traffic accident without regard to fault is entitled to prompt compensation for economic losses such as lost income and rehabilitation expenses at a level much higher than before, (*ii*) the opportunity to sue other drivers for additional compensation is only limited to cases involving death, "permanent serious disfigurement," or "permanent serious impairment of an important bodily function caused by continuing injury which is physical in nature." Collision coverage would still be optional and if not purchased, the driver's insurance company would pay for repairs to the extent the driver was not at fault.

An IBC spokesperson claimed that Bill 68 was acceptable to the insurance industry but savings would be greater under a pure no-fault plan. Critics declared the insurance industry the big winner under the scheme and lawyers the big losers, since the insurers' legal expenses would be largely eliminated while their premium income would remain unaltered.

The government estimated it would take three to five years to work out the legal implications of the threshold limits through court decisions. Indeed the "threshold" definition in

Bill 68 was very vague and invited court challenges to provide a clear definition. The government estimated 90 percent of claims would avoid court action and be paid by the no-fault system. The other 10 percent could still sue. A representative of the Canadian Bar Association said that only 10 percent of claims made it to court under the present tort system, but also the courts would see even more cases as threshold limits for the plan would be tested.

Critics of Bill 68 further charged that motorists would pay higher premiums but get little in return for giving up their right to court access. The average driver in the city was told that he could expect rate increases of eight percent per year while the rural driver would suffer no rate increase, thus proving to Ontarians that David Peterson broke his campaign promise for lower rates. Also, opponents claimed that the government was subsidizing the insurance industry by paying $48 million the insurance companies had paid to the provincial health insurance system (OHIP) and another $95 million by eliminating taxes levied on premiums. It was clear the government was attempting to moderate insurance premium increases by changing OHIP and premium taxes. NDP leader Bob Rae, the most vocal critic, added that the new no-fault insurance plan would penalize victims with emotional and psychological trauma since only physical injuries would receive compensation.

In October, the government followed through by introducing legislation to have a tough commissioner as regulator to review underwriting practices. The Ontario Insurance Commission (OIC), replacing the OAIB, would have broad powers of intervention and enforcement, essentially having the same mandate as the OAIB. It would regulate rates and be responsible for ensuring that accident victims received prompt compensation. By this point the OAIB directive to eliminate age, sex, and marital status in rate-setting had not been implemented. The government apparently was responding to the concerns of not only the industry but also various groups such as seniors and younger women who were opposed to sudden and dramatic insurance premium increases. As a result, virtually all companies continued to base premiums at least partly on age and sex for drivers under 25. There also continued to be variation in the criteria used among the companies, that is, a uniform classification system had not been implemented.

SECOND READING AND PUBLIC HEARINGS

In December 1989, Bill 68 passed a second reading in the Legislature. The matter then went to a legislative committee, which held public hearings around the province starting in January, 1990.

Bill 68 was given exceptionally harsh treatment by health care and legal community lobbyists. An ad-hoc anti-no-fault lobby group, BATFIV (Better Auto Accident Treatment for Injured Victims in Ontario), composed of 150 members, wanted to see the bill changed especially as it related to the definition of the injury "threshold." The Canadian Paraplegics Association claimed Bill 68 would force victims into institutions since injury compensation was insufficient. The group also claimed that although the government plan would pay victims $500 000 in long term disability payments, this compensation would be doled out by insurance companies at a rate of $1500/month ($50/day) for 27 years — an inadequate amount for proper home health care. The Advocacy Resource Centre for the Handicapped (ARCH) supported no-fault to a certain extent but attacked the proposed $1500 per month limit on the benefits available for long-term care. An Angus Reid telephone survey in February, 1990 revealed more opposition than support for Bill 68 (Exhibit 6).

At the hearings the Canadian Bar Association claimed that the proposed revisions to auto insurance would only provide new work for lawyers trying to help victims obtain benefits from insurance companies. The Ontario Federation of Labor suggested that the government's promise of major savings in legal costs was largely illusory. The Consumers Association of Canada warned that the proposed limits on the type of victim allowed to sue would result in years of new litigation as the courts ruled on the new law. The CAC now preferred a government-run, pure no-fault system. The Canadian Federation of Independent Business (CFIB) argued that under Bill 68 independent business owners, if temporarily injured, would not be able to run their businesses and would not be able to sue for economic losses. Another complaint was that accident victims must use up company disability benefits and sick leave plans before the no-fault benefits would kick in, shifting more of the burden to workers and their employers. In addition, anyone making more than $30 000/year would need extra coverage to cover lost wages if injured, thereby driving up their premiums anyway. It was also noted that the loss benefits were based solely on the income being earned at the time of the accident and did not take future prospects into account, a problem for certain groups such as students, individuals starting up a new business, and housewives planning to return to the workforce.

During the hearings, the IBC continued its three-pronged lobbying efforts. For example, it placed a large advocacy ad in newspapers claiming that personal injury lawyers collect more than $500 million in fees and disbursements a year from the current car insurance system, some 30 percent of the total amount paid out in claims for personal injuries. In addition, the IBC set up a toll-free number to handle the public's queries about no-fault auto insurance as well as distributing two booklets through supermarket stands that explained the new system.

Even though many lobby groups inundated the committee hearings not much of the legislation was expected to change. Indeed, after an NDP filibuster in April led by Peter Kormos held up passage of the bill for weeks, Bill 68 passed third reading on May 28, and was due to take effect on June 22, 1990. The changes that were implemented included raising the lost income compensation from $450/week to $600/week and raising the disability payments from $1500/month to $3000/month. As a result of the implementation of Bill 68 a government study revealed the insurance industry would save $800 million in legal costs each year.

AN (UNNECESSARY) ELECTION CALL

The Peterson government, with two years of its mandate left, decided to call an early election, to renew the mandate before the expected recession caused voter dissatisfaction and before a court ruling was due on a scandal involving Liberal party fund raising. The election was set for September 6, 1990.

During the election, the absence of high premiums was taking the sting out of insurance as an election issue. The insurance industry, while very active during the 1987 campaign, decided to take a lower profile during the 1990 election although the PAC continued to monitor the political campaigns in each riding. When the NDP scored an incredible totally unexpected majority win, there was an obvious immediate threat that the new NDP government would take over car insurance as occurred in British Columbia 16 years earlier and Manitoba 21 years earlier. It was well known that some form of public auto insurance was central to the NDP party platform originating in a 1954 party resolution.

NDP MAJORITY AND A PROMISE KEPT

The insurance industry's worst fears were realized when Premier-elect Rae pledged to move quickly to set up a government-run car insurance scheme. Insurance industry executives responded that the no-fault system was working out well with Ontarians and should be given a chance to prove itself. Furthermore, the industry had undergone great effort and expense to implement the threshold no-fault system. Nevertheless, an alternate proposal seen as acceptable by some industry executives was a hybrid plan as in Quebec whereby the government would insure drivers for personal injury policies and private firms would cover property damage policies.

The insurance industry suffered another setback when the insurance industry's toughest critic, Peter Kormos, was put in charge of their industry as Minister of Financial Institutions. Kormos, a 38-year old criminal lawyer, was described as a "hard-headed, fast-tongued, anti-business grand-stander." Kormos' disdain for the insurance industry was displayed during the Bill 68 committee hearings when he called insurance officials "sleazy and slimy" and was subsequently reprimanded by Rae for unparliamentary behaviour. In the Legislature, Kormos stood out by wearing cowboy boots and no tie with his suit.

Kormos' insurance system of choice would strongly reflect the British Columbia system, incorporating the following aspects: (*i*) government-run, (*ii*) drivers can sue, (*iii*) independent brokers would sell the government auto insurance, (*iv*) the rates would be based on type of vehicle, whether it is used for business or pleasure, and geography, (*v*) no penalty for new drivers, (*vi*) good drivers would receive a 10 percent reduction for every claimfree year (up to 40 percent), whereas bad drivers would face surcharges, (*vii*) non-profit, any profits made would go to reducing the premiums the following year, (*viii*) no-fault system if a single vehicle accident or while a lawsuit is making its way through courts, and (*ix*) $200 per week disability compensation, up to $150 000 for rehabilitation, plus various death benefits. Kormos claimed such a system would reduce premiums but the IBC contended that such a system could not reduce costs.

As of 1990, the entire general insurance industry employed about 44 000 people in Ontario (approximately two-thirds were women) and over half these jobs related directly to auto insurance. Under a government-run scheme there would be: (*i*) fewer brokers/agents (insurance sales people) as there would be a single provider of auto insurance and commission levels would likely decrease, as occurred in British Columbia, (*ii*) less insurance company staff as a single entity would eliminate operational/administrative duplication, and (*iii*) less adjusting/appraising staff (i.e., those establishing fault and the value of claims) again eliminating duplication.

PROGRESSIVE CASUALTY INSURANCE COMPANY OF CANADA

The president of Progressive Casualty Insurance Company of Canada (PCICC), Andrew Rogacki, was stunned by the NDP victory and immediately commissioned DRI Canada

Ltd., an economic forecasting and consulting company, to assess the impact of the NDP's takeover proposal. PCICC was a subsidiary of Progressive Corporation of Cleveland, Ohio, which had 1989 revenues of $1.4 billion and outperformed the industry in the US in terms of return on equity and premium growth. In Canada, PCICC was a relatively small company focusing on certain niches such as drivers rejected by other companies and fleets of heavy commercial vehicles.

The DRI study was based on an econometric model with several assumptions supplied by Progressive Casualty. The assumptions were as follows:

i.   The entire foreign-owned capital that supports the writing of auto insurance in Ontario will leave Canada and not return. Sixty percent of the total capital was foreign-owned representing $1.8 billion in 1989 dollars. The pullout from other markets — whether other lines of insurance or other provinces — would take at least a further $500 million from Canada. In total, $2.3 billion would leave Canada of which 50 percent would be long-term bonds, 25 percent money-market instruments, and 25 percent equity. Since the marginal investor is foreign, this would require that an additional $2.3 billion would have to be attracted from abroad through higher short and long-term interest rates.

ii. The Ontario government would have to raise a further $500 million in the capital markets to start up and provide capital to an insurance company.

iii. International investors would become more averse to holding Canadian investments and therefore would require an increase in long-term bond yields for 18 months of an additional 25 basis points (a basis point is one-hundredth of a percent).

iv. Direct employment in the auto insurance industry would decline by 10 000 representing net employment loss after accounting for the staffing-up of the new Crown Corporation. Of the 10 000 jobs lost, 5000 would be from various functions in the insurance companies. The remainder work for brokers whose commissions would be cut in half as happened when the government-run system was created in British Columbia.

v.   Output (or value added) by the auto insurance industry in Ontario would decline by an amount proportional to the decline in employment in the industry.

vi. The exchange rate would be unchanged assuming perfectly offsetting capital flows.

vii. The new government run scheme would begin January 1, 1992 and all 1989 dollar values were inflated to 1992 values using seven percent per annum.

Using the above assumptions, the DRI macro model, which contained approximately 550 endogenous equations, projected the following results:

i.   The outflow of $2.6 billion (in 1992) forces short-term rates to rise by approximately 89 basis points while long-term rates rise by about 94 basis points. These interest rate increases have the usual decelerating effect on the economy by raising the cost of capital for corporations and the cost of borrowing for consumers. As a result, investment and durable goods consumption are both lower.

ii. Over the four-year period, the federal government deficit increases by a cumulative $6.3 billion and the Ontario government deficit increases by a cumulative $3.9 billion. These increased deficits are a result of the higher cost of servicing the debt, the impact of the slower economy and the increase in provincial government expenditures of $572 million by 1992.

iii. Ontario output drops an average of 0.3 percent over a four year period, while output for the entire Canadian economy drops 0.2 percent. This decline in output translates into a decline of 15 000 jobs in Ontario, including 10 000 jobs directly in auto insurance, in the first year of the new scheme. By 1995, there would be 23 000 fewer jobs in Ontario. As a result, total disposable income in Ontario declines by a cumulative $1.1 billion over the four-year period, 25 300 people would move to other provinces, and Ontario housing starts fall by almost 14 000 units. The rest of the country would gain as follows: total disposable income rises by $1.3 billion, housing starts rise by 2000.

Rogacki was surprised by the magnitude of the effects projected in the DRI study. At the same time, Rogacki was aware that government-run schemes in other provinces were working well and well-liked by many people in those provinces. Supporters of those public schemes felt that the premiums were lower because there was no need to earn a profit, and administration costs were lower given the lack of duplication of overhead costs and services.

THE NEXT MOVE

Among the options facing Rogacki in publicizing the DRI study were: (*i*) Release the study to IBC member companies and hope to develop an IBC-sponsored campaign publicizing the study; (*ii*) Send the study on a confidential basis with a covering letter to Premier Rae and/or his Minister of Financial Institutions, Peter Kormos; (*iii*) Request a meeting with Rae and/or Kormos to discuss the study and possibly request the government to do its own simulation of the economic impact of government takeover; and, (*iv*) Release the study in a press conference so that the media would publicize the study results.

In reviewing these options, Rogacki thought back to the various interactions of his company with the Ontario government up to this point. Progressive had been an active participant in the various government-sponsored hearings on the industry. At these hearings the company presented what Rogacki regarded as well-documented studies and positions, and the DRI study was a natural extension of this earlier work. At the same time, Rogacki was one of the industry people who Kormos challenged during the Bill 68 Committee hearings, so it was difficult to determine how Kormos would react to the DRI study. Overall, Rogacki hoped to change the arena for discussing the possible government takeover of the industry from a public arena where politicians such as Kormos could utilize their strong public speaking abilities to the arena of "facts and figures." One important fact was that Ontario auto insurers had been experiencing losses in recent years (Exhibit 7) but expected that Bill 68 would improve their financial performance.

EXHIBIT 1	Net Income for General Insurers in Canada			
YEAR	UNDERWRITING INCOME (LOSS)	INVESTMENT INCOME	NET INCOME AFTER TAX	RETURN ON EQUITY
	(Dollars in Millions)			
1978	$ 28	$ 582	$ 443	16.04%
1979	(193)	701	400	12.65
1980	(572)	783	212	6.12
1981	(889)	937	160	4.32
1982	(562)	1054	456	11.30
1983	(328)	1119	741	15.06
1984	(917)	1255	362	6.86
1985	(1260)	1350	383	6.88
1986	(555)	1509	1004	15.49
1987	(535)	1707	1165	14.90
1988	(774)	1927	1042	12.05
1989	(1369)	2130	919	9.90

Note: Net income is after federal tax.

SOURCE: IBC Facts, 1989; compiled from Statistics Canada.

No-fault auto insurance.
What you should know if you drive in Ontario:

There has been a lot of talk recently about bringing a no-fault auto insurance system to Ontario. You've heard about how it can reduce premiums, how some Canadian provinces have government no-fault in place, and how no-fault works to the driver's advantage.

But along with the news about no-fault, there's been a lot of confusion. Some people actually believe that no-fault means government insurance, and the New Democratic Party would have you believe that the only no-fault plans in Canada are the government-run plans in some Western provinces. This is not so. Your present policy in Ontario, provided by private insurance companies, already contains similar no-fault benefits.

In this advertisement, your private insurance companies want to explain why we believe in "Smart" no-fault, and why we were working on such a plan long before it became a political issue.

Why we need a change.

Insurance costs have gone up in Ontario. Many people believe that insurance companies are entirely to blame for this.

But in fact, we have limited control over the cost of insurance legislation under which we must operate has been introduced in recent years, often to achieve desirable social objectives. However, it has a hefty price tag attached to it: the Family Law Reform Act, for example, costs insurance buyers of Ontario hundreds of thousands of dollars each year. The insurance industry has to respond to the amounts that are awarded by the courts, and these, of course, influence the majority of cases that are settled out of court.

Insurance companies make convenient scapegoats when you're looking for someone to blame for rising insurance rates, but the truth is that we're as concerned as you are. We're professionals, trying to establish an insurance system that makes sense, at a sensible cost to our customers. The system has, basically, been a good one. But in recent years, changes beyond our control have weakened it, and it's time to do something about it.

"Smart" no-fault: a better way.

Your private insurance companies have developed a form of no-fault auto insurance that works. But to fully understand our "Smart" no-fault, you must first understand no-fault in general.

To begin with, pure no-fault auto insurance means that if you are injured in a car accident, you cannot sue the at-fault driver. Instead you recover specified benefits from your own insurer, and the at-fault driver recovers benefits from his insurer. Such a pure no-fault system can also extend to property damage.

Ontario's private insurance companies believe that it is going too far to take away your right to sue entirely. We believe the right to sue should be maintained for losses that exceed specified policy benefits, and for pain and suffering in cases involving death and serious permanent injury. As well, the benefits currently payable under your present coverage will be considerably enriched with ample provision for rehabilitation of accident victims.

We call this a "Smart" no-fault system, backed by the more than 40 000 men and women who operate this province's private insurance system. We know more about insurance than the government does because it's our area of expertise. We believe "Smart" no-fault will help make premiums more realistic for us all by doing away with the need to determine fault and assess damages in all but the really serious cases.

Let's all get Smart.

No-fault insurance is we believe, a viable alternative to a system that has become more and more expensive.

But keeping premiums down is only part of the solution. The system must also work. That's why "Smart" no-fault, administered by insurance professionals, makes more sense than the other schemes you've been hearing about.

If Ontario allows itself to fall victim to government monopoly car insurance, you'll lose your right to choose who you want to handle your insurance policy. It will be the government's way or no way. Freedom of choice versus no choice at all.

Let's all get Smart. Write to Insurance Bureau of Canada at 181 University Avenue, Toronto, Ontario M5H 3M7 for more information about "Smart" no-fault auto insurance that could reduce your premiums, speed up payments and improve your protection.

The smart way.

Insurance Bureau of Canada
Private Insurance Companies.

A change for the better.

EXHIBIT 3

Now is the time to do something positive about auto insurance in Ontario

What's Wrong

According to many people, quite a bit.
Consumers are unhappy with premiums and service.
Some politicians suggest that a government monopoly may be the solution.
Insurers find that the present legal system is responsible for escalating premiums and delaying settlement of claims.

The Co-operators Believes:

- our mission is to be responsible and responsive to effectively meet the needs of the families we serve.

- consumers have good reason to be concerned about premium increases over the past year, the high rates for young and newly licensed drivers, and the service they sometimes receive.

- the present Ontario legal system is a major cause of high insurance costs and is in urgent need of reform.

- government monopolies do not reduce costs. They can hide or transfer costs among taxpayers, but they are not known for efficiency. Nor do they have a record of providing satisfactory service.

- the interests of Ontario motorists will best be served by a competitive auto insurance marketplace.

- insurers, lawyers and the provincial government should work together to improve the present system.

We Urge:

The Ontario government to show the kind of leadership that it demonstrated during the "liability crisis" last year. It should now work with the insurance industry to make necessary corrections to enable the competitive market to meet consumer needs. And work in the legislature to make changes to the legal system that will reduce waste of time and money in providing compensation to victims of auto accidents.

Insurers to become more responsive to consumers and do a better job of explaining the basis for rates charged. Rapid steps are needed to correct problems. For example: stop charging drivers higher rates than their experience, vehicle use, and accident/conviction records warrant; stop arbitrarily cancelling agreements with agents and brokers which leaves them with no source of coverage for customers; and stop assigning to the higher-rated "facility" plan drivers who do not represent a higher risk.

You to think seriously about how well Ontario drivers would be served by a govern-

ment-run auto insurance monopoly in Ontario. Consider the service you get from other government institutions. Add your voice to the call for the government to change the legal system so a competitive insurance industry can do a better and more cost-effective job of serving you.

To Do Our Part, We At The Co-operators Will:

- set rates based on financial results necessary for us to continue in business and serve our customers, and credit to our policyholders any excess revenues.

- establish an independent appeal system to which customers may refer decisions which they feel are not fair.

- not cancel or refuse to renew any auto insurance policy except in the case of misrepresentation or fraud.

- not put in the "high risk" plan newly licensed drivers or under-age-25 drivers who have a clean record.

- provide auto insurance for any Ontario private passenger car drivers who wish us to insure them.

- provide six months auto coverage for the customers of any agent or broker unable to arrange coverage with their present insurers. (We normally operate only through our own offices and exclusive sales representatives, but we are prepared to temporarily accept other business in order to ensure that Ontario drivers have somewhere to turn while the industry sorts out problems.)

- continue to work with industry associations and the government to press for reform in the legal system and improvements in the way the industry serves its customers.

- commit to reducing premiums for bodily injury and liability coverage if the government implements a no-fault insurance plan similar to that proposed by the Insurance Bureau of Canada.

Who We Are

The Co-operators is the leading home and auto insurer in Canada (we also write life, commercial and other lines of insurance). In Ontario we insure over 500 000 cars (one in every nine) through a network of service offices and sales representatives across the province. We employ some 2 300 people in Ontario.

We are Canadian, owned by 35 co-operative, credit union, farm and trade union organizations across Canada. Cooperatives are seen as a third sector—an alternative to traditional shareholder-oriented business and to big

government. Our mission is to provide excellent service to our customers at a fair price, and we operate in all provinces and territories except Quebec.

We're proud of our record of service for the past 40 years. In 1985 we received a Canada Award for productivity. Our expense ratio—the portion of policyholder money we spend operating our business—is among the best in our industry.

It's our view that, to overcome problems in Ontario auto insurance, the industry and government must work together to improve the present system to better serve the needs of their publics, who are both policy-holders and taxpayers.

Do Something Positive

If you're an Ontario driver, we urge that you:

- complete and send to us the coupon below adding your support to the call for the industry and the government to work together to resolve consumer concerns about auto insurance.

- write, phone or visit your local MPP to express your views on this subject.

We will report your views to government and the insurance industry and continue to work for reform and improvement of the auto insurance market in Ontario.

Return Coupon

❑ I agree that Ontario motorists would be served best by a competitive insurance industry and that the Ontario government should work with the insurers to urgently correct problems in the auto insurance market in Ontario.

❑ I would like more information on no-fault insurance.

❑ Other comments:

Send to: Bill Weafer
Vice-President, Ontario Division
The Co-operators, Priory Square
Guelph, Ontario
N1H 6P8

Name: _____

Address: _____

City: _____

Postal Code: _____ Phone Number: _____

The Co-operators Insurance Services

Source: *The Globe and Mail*, March 7, 1987

EXHIBIT 4

Auto Insurance:
LET'S GET THE FACTS STRAIGHT

MYTH:

A government "driver-owned" auto insurance plan would be cheaper.

TRUTH:
CHEAP GOVERNMENT INSURANCE IS A MYTH — LIKE "CHEAP" POSTAL SERVICE. THE COST OF REPAIRING CARS, PAYING MEDICAL COSTS AND SETTLING LAWSUITS ARE THE SAME IN ANY PLAN — PRIVATE OR GOVERNMENT. AN INDEPENDENT 1984 STUDY OF B.C.'S GOVERNMENT AUTO INSURANCE PLAN SHOWS THAT DRIVERS WERE PAYING MORE THAN THEY WOULD UNDER A COMPETITIVE SYSTEM.

MYTH:

A government-run auto insurance plan would be more efficient.

TRUTH:
GOVERNMENT-RUN OPERATIONS HAVE A TRACK RECORD OF LOW EFFICIENCY, POOR SERVICE, AND BAD MORALE. WHO WOULD WANT THE "EFFICIENCY" OF CANADA POST WHERE COSTS KEEP GOING UP AND SERVICE KEEPS GOING DOWN?

MYTH:

A "driver-owned" (government) plan would be fairer.

TRUTH:
THE PROPOSED GOVERNMENT PLAN MEANS THAT THOSE DRIVERS WHO HAVE EARNED LOW RATES WILL HAVE TO PAY MORE SO THAT OTHER DRIVERS CAN PAY LESS. IS THIS FAIR?

MYTH:

Government auto insurance would pay its own way.

TRUTH:
NOT ONE OF THE GOVERNMENT-RUN AUTO INSURANCE PLANS IN CANADA HAS PAID ITS OWN WAY. <u>MANITOBA PUBLIC INSURANCE</u> CORP'S AUTOMOBILE DIVISION HAS LOST AT LEAST $18 MILLION DURING THE FIRST SIX MONTHS OF THE CURRENT FISCAL YEAR. WHAT YOU DON'T PAY IN PREMIUM, YOU WILL PAY IN TAXES.

MYTH:

There is public support for government auto insurance.

TRUTH:
SURVEYS SAY THIS SIMPLY ISN'T SO. A 1986 STUDY BY CONTEMPORARY RESEARCH FOUND THAT CANADA-WIDE ONLY 12% OF CANADIANS FAVOUR GOVERNMENT INSURANCE. IN ONTARIO NEARLY 60% PREFER PRIVATE AUTO INSURANCE.

LOCAL ECONOMIC BENEFITS
Our area is called the insurance capital of Canada. Each year millions of dollars comes into Kitchener, Waterloo, Cambridge, and Guelph from across Canada.

In fact, a $30 million payroll is reinvested in our local communities, a major contribution to the economic strength of our region.

WE'RE PROUD TO SERVE YOU
We know our products and more importantly, we talk to you every day so we know what you want.
We also know that as long as we do our job right you'll keep on using our services.
We also realize that if we don't do our job right, you have the choice to go somewhere else.
The auto insurance question boils down to a matter of choice.
Proponents of Government Auto Insurance do not believe you have the right to choose for yourself.
We think you do.
On election day, vote for the candidate who gives you a choice.

SPONSORED BY THE INSURANCE BROKERS OF WATERLOO REGION.

Source: *Kitchener-Waterloo Record,* September 5, 1987.

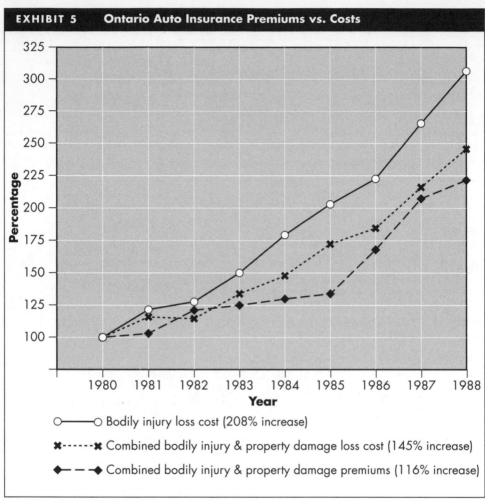

EXHIBIT 5   Ontario Auto Insurance Premiums vs. Costs

○———○ Bodily injury loss cost (208% increase)

✖------✖ Combined bodily injury & property damage loss cost (145% increase)

◆— —◆ Combined bodily injury & property damage premiums (116% increase)

Source: "Green Book" of Automobile Insurance Experience compiled by Insurance Bureau of Canada.

EXHIBIT 6

FAIR ACTION IN INSURANCE REFORM (FAIR) COMMITTEE
SUMMARY OF POLL RESULTS

1. Overall, based on what you have seen or heard about the Ontario government's proposed no-fault insurance program, are you in favour of or opposed to the proposed system?

OPPOSE	strongly	34%
	moderately	20%
	moderately	21%
FAVOUR	strongly	6%
	undecided	18%

(of those with an opinion 2/3 opposed the Bill)

2. Under the proposed no-fault system, unless your injury is serious and permanent, you would not be able to sue for compensation, regardless of how the accident occurred or who is to blame. Instead you would receive a predetermined amount of money based on your injury. Do you think this is fair or unfair?

UNFAIR	**FAIR**	
59%	31%	
	undecided	10%

(of those with an opinion 2/3 consider Bill 68 unfair)

3. When no-fault insurance was first proposed, the government said that insurance premiums would increase by no more than 8 percent. The government has now stated that an unspecified number of Ontarians could pay up to 40 to 50 percent more in insurance premiums, depending on things like the type of car they drive, their income and their driving record. Does this make you feel more positive about the no-fault insurance proposal, does it make you feel more negative, or does it make no difference in how you feel about this proposal?

MORE NEGATIVE	**MORE POSITIVE**	**NO DIFFERENCE**
64%	8%	18%
	undecided	10%

(70% of decided respondents feel more negative)

Source: Angus Reid Group, February 1990.

EXHIBIT 7

ONTARIO AUTO INSURANCE ESTIMATED RESULTS

($ millions)

	1986	1987	1988	1989	1990 (1st 6 months)
Net Premiums Earned	2 598	3 078	3 337	3 636	1 992
Net Claims	2 574	2 875	3 365	3 582	1 822
Operating Expenses	685	730	817	855	465
Underwriting Gain (Loss)	(661)	(527)	(845)	(801)	(295)
Investment Income	334	389	449	518	285
Net Pretax Income (Loss)	(327)	(138)	(396)	(283)	(10)

Source: Based on IBC Members Quarterly Survey Samples

NOTE

This case was written by Mark C. Baetz with assistance from Peter Kuttenkeuler and Margaret Klatt. It was written as a basis for class discussion rather than to illustrate either effective or ineffective handling of an administrative situation. © Mark C. Baetz and Petter Kuttenkeuler, 1991. Revised 04/93. Distributed through the LAURIER INSTITUTE,School of Business and Economics, Wilfrid Laurier University, Waterloo, Ontario, Canada, N2L 3C5. No part of this case may be reproduced, stored in a retrieval system, or transmitted in any form or by any means — electronic, mechanical, photocopying, recording, or otherwise — without the permission of The Laurier Institute, School of Business and Economics, Wilfrid Laurier University.

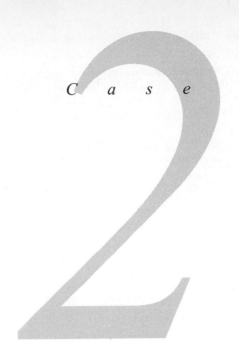

Case

B.C. FOREST ALLIANCE

In July, 1991, Gary Ley, Executive Director of the newly-formed B.C. Forest Alliance was preparing for a meeting of the Alliance's Executive Committee to discuss media coverage of Alliance activities. Ley felt that *The Vancouver Sun*, Vancouver's largest daily newspaper, was unfair in its description of the role and organization of the Alliance and Ley wanted the Executive Committee to determine how to respond to the Sun's apparent attempts to discredit the Alliance.

ORIGINS OF ALLIANCE

The Alliance described its origins as follows:

> In the past several years, there has been growing public awareness and media attention given to the level of timber harvesting and harvesting practices taking place in British Columbia. There has been a concurrent growing concern amongst the senior executives of a number of the province's forest product companies that the media attention given to these matters is unfair, that public perception with respect to these matters does not reflect what is actually taking place and that the activities of certain groups or individuals results in the public being misinformed.

> The forest industry views this as a serious problem, creating public pressure which could have disastrous implications, not only for the environment but for the industry and accordingly, for the provincial economy as a whole.

> As a result, the CEOs of 13 of the largest forest products companies in the province decided that they should seek professional advice on how to address this problem. After exploring

several alternatives (including an aggressive, confrontational approach marked by intense and negative advertising), they retained the services of Burson-Marsteller (B-M) to provide them with advice in this regard. (B-M was the world's largest public relations consultancy. Its Vancouver office opened in 1982.)

After careful consideration, B-M developed a program which included *as a component*, the creation of a broad-based, grass roots coalition (or "Alliance") to work towards a common sense resolution of forest and environmental issues. The 13 CEOs accepted B-M's recommendation of an Alliance and gave B-M the mandate to create the Alliance.

On April 10, 1991 the formation of the Alliance was publicly announced. The Alliance was to have a Citizens Advisory Board chaired by Jack Munro, long-time president of the International Woodworkers of America (IWA), the largest union in the B.C. forest industry. The Alliance's first press release read as follows:

Saying the "time has come for all British Columbians to get on with the job of shaping wise environmental decisions," IWA-Canada President Jack Munro today announced the formation of the B.C. Forest Alliance — "British Columbians for shared environmental responsibility."

Munro is Chairman of a Citizens Advisory Board established as a cornerstone of the new organization. He is joined on the Board by Vancouver Mayor Gordon Campbell, UBC professor Hamish Kimmins, SFU professor John Borden, Prince George physician Dr. Brian Taylor, and professional forester and educator Melissa Hadley of Halfmoon Bay. An additional nine members of the Advisory Board were named. The Board will expand to 30 members in coming weeks.

"We've got to find the common ground of a healthy natural environment and a healthy industry," says Munro. "And the answers to the tough questions aren't going to come from politicians. The answers must come from all of us as individuals....That's why the B.C. Forest Alliance has been established."

All British Columbians will have the opportunity to join the Alliance through individual memberships. The organization will undertake specific activities such as a regular TV report on forest environmental issues. The Alliance, with a staff of seven, will also produce research reports, newsletters, fact sheets, and sponsor fact-finding missions to Sweden and other areas.

Munro says that initial funding has been provided by business and labour. He points out that while some forest product companies have provided funds for the Alliance to be established they will be held accountable through a code of environmental practice that the Citizens Advisory Board will develop...

What was not discussed in the literature announcing the Alliance was that the industry association, the Council of Forest Industries, had undertaken a $1 million ad campaign entitled "Forests Forever" which failed to sway public opinion. Discouraged by this, the CEOs of the 13 companies involved in the Alliance had bypassed their public affairs managers (who were instrumental in the "Forests Forever" campaign) and approached B-M directly. Before the official launch of the Alliance, a survey was carried out for the Alliance based on telephone interviews with 500 randomly selected adult residents of British Columbia. The key findings of the survey were as follows:

- Concern about the environment and forestry practice is high among British Columbia residents. Five in ten say they are "very concerned" about these issues. Harvesting methods and pollution from pulp mills are most frequently the source of these concerns.

- Six in ten residents think the industry is working "very hard" or "somewhat hard" to protect the environment. Residents of the province are aware of some action the industry has taken, but they see a lot of work yet to be done.

- British Columbia residents do not see economic problems as a reason for slowing environmental improvement. They appreciate the economic importance of the forest industry, but see environmental protection as something which ensures the long-term strength of the industry — not as something which undermines the industry. In fact, 90 percent believe that a strong forest industry *and* a healthy natural environment can coexist.

- The European boycott of British Columbia forest products that some environmentalists are encouraging is not acceptable to most residents. Seven in ten oppose the boycott. However, British Columbians do see a citizens' coalition as holding considerable promise. Residents were asked about a proposal to set up a citizens' organization to monitor the forest industry's environmental performance and to ensure that a balance between environmental protection and economic stability is maintained. The proposal is strongly supported across the province by almost nine in ten residents (49% strongly support, 37% somewhat support).

The reference to a European boycott related to reports in early 1991 that environmental groups, such as the Western Canada Wilderness Committee (WCWC), Greenpeace, and the US based Sierra Club, and Green Party members in Europe were pushing their governments and consumers of B.C. forest products to boycott B.C. forest products because of such practices as clearcutting and pulp mill effluent. Environmental groups like the Sierra Club escorted foreign journalists, environmentalists, politicians, and TV crews to Vancouver Island clearcuts and supplied footage of clearcuts to German television which ultimately portrayed Canada as "the Brazil of the north." (Brazil had been heavily criticized for clearcutting vast areas of forest without any reforestation.)

Clearcutting is the practice of removing all the trees in a particular area, leaving only the tree stumps. Robert Findlay, the president of MacMillan Bloedel, a main logger of B.C.'s coastal forests, justified clearcutting as follows:

> We see it as a form of harvesting like a cornfield. We cannot log areas as large as we have to log in Canada economically, efficiently and safely without clearcut logging. That is how it is done in Sweden and Germany — they log more volume in Germany than we do on the coast of British Columbia.[1]

However, critics of clearcutting were concerned about the following: (*i*) "junk forest" may grow over the clearcut sections if the land is not properly treated after cutting, (*ii*) if a clearcut is too close to a stream or river, siltation may effect the marine life, and in particular the salmon spawning beds, (*iii*) the logging roads necessary for clearcutting disturb the soil/water ratio, and may impede regeneration of the clearcut area, (*iv*) too much volume of timber is taken out at once threatening supply without immediate reforestation. The industry responded to such criticism with clearcuts which were smaller, less visible from roads and communities, and better contoured to the land and prevailing wind for better protection of the remaining forest, fish, and wildlife. Other improvements included enhanced stream protection measures and better road building. Despite these actions, one company attitude survey suggested that the industry still needed to get its story across (Exhibit 1).

On the issue of supply, a survey of 2362 government, industry, and private professional foresters commissioned by the federal government in the fall of 1990 found "widespread concern" about the sustainability of harvestable wood. Some of the survey findings, as reported on April 10, 1991, were:

- Among the one-third of respondents from B.C. almost half believe the prospects of sustaining the current supply of harvestable wood is "poor," and 72% say the B.C. government's annual allowable cut is either definitely or likely too high. Both B.C. figures led the nation.

- There is broad belief that forestry practices have improved over the past decade particularly in the area of reforestation. B.C. foresters led the nation in praising reforestation in their province with 77 percent giving it a positive rating. 80 percent of harvested areas were renewed through natural regeneration or reforestation in 1988 compared to 61 percent in 1975. However, it is still uncertain whether wood from managed forests will replace the high quality wood in areas like coastal B.C.

- Canada's national timber supply appears sustainable within the next 30 to 60 years but the outlook in the longer term is less clear, depending on more intensively managed forests. Canada's productive forest land shrunk two percent over the past decade due to logging, urbanization, forest preservation, fire, insects, and disease. The overall softwood supply utilization situation suggests that there may be real risks to Canada's industrial economy if timber resources are removed from the commercial forest for reasons such as Aboriginal land claims, water quality, and recreation.

- 90 percent of B.C. foresters disagree with the argument that clearcutting is a poor practice, compared to 79 percent across Canada. However, 46 percent of Canadian foresters believe clearcutting is used too widely today. No B.C. figures were provided.

- Overall, the forester's perspective on forest management in Canada is not the bright one portrayed by the industry nor the gloomy one espoused by environmental and conservation interests.

In reacting to the survey, the federal forestry minister, Frank Oberle, said the results would help him fight against Canadian environmentalists promoting an international boycott of Canadian forest products. Export markets were critical to the B.C. forest products industry, and therefore any threat of a boycott was of great concern. Exports to the EEC from B.C. in 1989 amounted to nine percent (by value) of all wood products produced in the province and 26 percent of all pulp and paper products. MacMillan Bloedel was particularly concerned about boycotts in Europe given that about 12 percent of the company's total sales and more than half its pulp sales in 1991 went to Europe.

In their campaigns, some environmental groups employed illegal tactics such as pouring sand into bulldozers' fuel tanks, stringing heavyduty fishing line between trees to trip loggers, stuffing rocks and logs into drainage culverts, tree-spiking (i.e., hammering spikes into trees to shatter a chainsaw or cause big millsaws to explode into deadly shrapnel), foam-coring (i.e., inserting a styrofoam cup into a tree to prevent the chemical reaction that turns pulp into paper), and blockading logging roads. Different environmental groups followed different positions on the issue of civil disobedience. The WCWC formed in 1980, declared in 1985 that it would not condone acts of civil disobedience, Greenpeace had "an unwritten code that roughly translates into civil disobedience if necessary, but not necessarily civil disobedience," and the Valhalla Society issued a policy statement that "there is a time when people of conscience have no choice but to be lawbreakers."[2]

REACTION TO FORMATION OF ALLIANCE

In the weeks following the launch of the Alliance there was extensive media coverage. Some of the positive coverage made points such as the following:

> ... the action-oriented Alliance has been created to find common ground solutions to disputes relating to land use and the environment. Improving the industry's image will only occur through improved industry logging practices.[3]

> Credibility of the Alliance depends on its willingness to present all sides of the argument, and not just pay lip-service to views which may run counter to what the industry and its employees perceive to be in their best interest.[4]

> Environmentalists...must not only have a role in the Alliance, they must be seen to have both a role and a proper degree of participation. This is what balance is all about. If it turns out the group has imbalance then the work of the Alliance will be impeded by fighting and squabbling...[5]

The negative media coverage focused on several aspects of the Alliance. First, the role of Burson-Marsteller (B-M) became contentious. B-M, with worldwide revenues of $215 million and 60 offices in 25 countries, was a New York-based public relations firm which had been retained to help manage corporate crises such as the Exxon-Valdez Alaskan oil spill, tampering of Johnson and Johnson's Tylenol, Union Carbide's Bhopal poison gas disaster, and Perrier's benzene contamination. B-M had also been retained by the Argentina government in the late 1970s to try to attract investment to the country after the military government had suspended parliament, exiled, jailed or murdered opposition senators, systematically intimidated or killed critical journalists, and begun a state-run terror campaign. In fact, B-M was hired well before the junta's human rights atrocities were known and B-M reasoned that because the United States, Canada, and the European nations continued to deal with Argentina in a normal way, its role was proper. Nevertheless, there was negative media reaction and even some members from the Council of Forest Industries, the industry association representing more than 100 companies and associations, questioned the propriety of an "independent citizens' group," taking direction from a PR firm. Concern about B-M's role was described in media coverage as follows:

> No matter how professional a job B-M does for its clients, perceptions of the firm are colored by its association with a few disasters. In fact, directing attention to such links is a technique for detracting from an organization's credibility. This is not intended as a defence of B-M which can look after itself. The point is it would be unfair to saddle the Alliance with Argentina. The Alliance signed up B-M for services peculiar to itself, not for a lot of former client's baggage.

> Early on, B-M told the companies an advertising campaign would be a waste of money, that they would have to deal with the substance of the issues, not the surface. Again, good advice. It was also good advice to involve a group of citizens prickly enough to resist loudly if the

companies try to dictate to them. People like Jack Munro, Patrick Moore and Gordon Campbell. But why does the industry need a PR firm to tell them these things? The environmental groups don't insert a layer of spin doctors between them and the public. And they are the ones the public trusts, not the industry.[6]

Representatives of B-M and the Alliance responded to the concerns by noting the following: B-M was "merely channelling the campaign, not determining its content;" when representatives of several companies came to B-M, "we gave them three pieces of advice: first, tell the truth, second, improve your practices, three, create an independent group to oversee it all;"[7] B-M generated the idea of the Alliance, "brought it to life," and have been retained to keep things going; the selection of B-M was based on its reputation for swift, quality results and not disaster-management; the industry felt it had a story to tell and professional help was needed to assist in getting the message out.

A second area of criticism concerned the composition of the Citizen's Advisory Board. It was pointed out that the Board lacked a representative of B.C.'s native community, a "spokeswoman from any of the firmly established environmental organizations," and an "ordinary Joe, a taxpayer who isn't slave to either industry or environmentalism, but whose day-to-day life is subtly influenced by what goes on in our woods."[8] A representative of the WCWC noted that the WCWC had not been invited to participate on the Board and concluded that it was part of a general "stratagem of the forestry lobby to co-opt the environmental position." The idea was to make the real environmentalists look like extremists. "This idea of a middle ground is an impediment."[9]

The Board was also described as "top heavy with people with a vested interest in chopping down trees...their careers and/or communities are at risk."[10] Another article noted: "the business and academic affiliations of many members show they really represent the vested interests of big business and big labour."[11] Alliance spokesmen responded to such concerns with the following points:

- Board members were chosen in consultation with the 13 forest companies involved in setting up the Alliance, and certain environmental groups (Sierra Club, WCWC, Greenpeace, Thompson Watershed Coalition) will not be invited to join because "we ask people (who) have an open mind about the value of the forest industry and the environment ... some of these people do not."[12] Nevertheless, interested environmental groups could make their views known through presentations to the board. Furthermore, the Board does include a native leader as well as Dr. Patrick Moore, with a Ph.D. in forest ecology and one of the co-founders of Greenpeace in 1970.

- Only five of the 30 people on the Board are "directly related" to the industry and "none of them is going to be part of anything that's a blind mouthpiece, or a toady for the forest industry."[13]

- "We've got well-known and respected people who, as a team, have the skills and experience to look at the problem from all perspectives province-wide including the environmental, the people, the financial, resource management, and the industry. Other sectors of our economy such as ranching and tourism are also represented on the board."[14]

A third area of criticism concerned the role, positions and style of Jack Munro. In terms of his role, Munro was described as having a conflict of interest in his dual roles of union leader (president of the largest union in the B.C. forest industry) and part-time chairman of the Alliance. This conflict became apparent when the executive of a local of IWA passed a motion rejecting support of the Alliance, even though Munro was president of IWA-Canada. The local was mainly concerned about the connection between the Alliance which was planning to develop a code of good practices, and B-M which "doesn't seem to have the right kind of record by being involved in 'sleazy' past deals." Other articles noted:

- Senior officers with five (IWA) locals (representing almost half of IWA's 35 000 B.C. workers) say they weren't consulted by Munro before his decision. The union only voted to help fund the Alliance after considerable debate at a national executive board meeting chaired by Munro in Vancouver on May 28, seven weeks after the Alliance was formed, they said...Those opposing Munro's decision say by chairing the Alliance he is undermining the IWA's own solutions to forestry disputes. For instance, the IWA has called for B.C. to enact a tough Forest Practices Act to be administered by an expanded provincial ministry of forests. Yet Munro now sits on the Alliance's forest practices committee, helping develop a code of ethics and practices that may not have the teeth a legislated act would.[15]

- "It's simplistic to blame the problems of the forest industry on the environmentalists. The IWA needs leadership in tackling the real problems in the forest industry. The solution is to promote a united front of the three major forest unions: IWA-Canada, the CPU and the PPWC. Such an alliance needs direction...The way not to defend the interests of B.C.'s forest workers is for Munro to involve himself with the corporate agenda represented by organizations like the Alliance. That's the road to ruin, both for trade unionism in the forest industry, and for the province's economic base as well."[16]

- "All the polling that's being done shows the industry has no credibility with the people in Canada but the IWA has...So they got Jack Munro and they have instant credibility. But it's going to be at the expense of the IWA."[17]

There was also criticism of Munro's positions as follows:

- "Jack Munro accuses natives and environmentalists of taking jobs away from his union, yet the volume of wood cut in B.C. has doubled in the last decade while jobs have decreased by over a third. He accepts the loss of jobs through modernization and automation as a necessary price of global competition, yet Switzerland cuts only a tenth of the volume of wood B.C. does and still has the same sized forest workforce. Who is betraying B.C. loggers?"[18]

- "Munro represents one trend in forest unions today. The other, a growing voice of anger, wants real action from the union to fight the real causes of the current round of job losses — modernization or technological change, free trade, the overcutting of our forests, the corporate control of our forest base, and the lack of a value-added industry in B.C."[19]

Munro did not see any conflict of interest in his dual roles noting that: "the Alliance is about jobs in the forest industry, and as a trade unionist, jobs are my concern."[20] Further he noted he "supports a legislated code of ethics, which is what the union wants."[21]

Another aspect of the Alliance receiving criticism was that the initial funding came from industry resulting in the charge: "This Alliance (is) paid for by the industry to make the industry look good."[22] Alliance representatives responded:

The Alliance is an independent group...Just because industry is providing the funding doesn't mean it's calling the shots, especially when you consider some of the people on the board[23]...Yes, seed money did come from our member forest companies and IWA-Canada – we're very open about this. We believe the forestry industry has the most to gain, but also the most to lose in the forest/environment debate. But we are seeking additional funds from our membership drive (see Exhibit 2) as well as from other companies and organizations throughout the province. Our goal is to have thousands of British Columbians become members.[24]

While the Alliance was open about the sources of its funding it decided to keep confidential the actual budget, the fees to B-M and the specific cost of Alliance activities.

A final aspect of the Alliance which drew criticism related to its goals which were announced as follows:

i.   Monitor the forest industry's environmental performance and build public confidence in the industry's actions;

ii. Provide British Columbians with the true picture of what is occurring in the forests;

iii. Conduct educational programs, seminars, and special projects which will get the citizens of B.C. actively involved in reforestation; and

iv. Create a broad-based membership of people who support saving the environment, the industry and B.C.'s economic stability.

The following concerns were noted about the Alliance goals:

- One Alliance goal is "to provide a monitoring service over the industry's environmental performance" and to provide "the true picture" of what is happening in B.C.'s forests...The federal and provincial governments are charged with the responsibility of seeing that the industry supposedly lives up to those laws now in effect and those commitments undertaken by the industry. If that is not now working then what clout can the Alliance bring to the equation?[25]

- The only way to resolve the long-running battle for the forest of B.C. is through negotiations but the Alliance is not set up to mediate or negotiate and the Alliance's Executive Director said "he could not judge whether a public relations executive like himself is likely to be seen as a fair mediator."[26]

The above concerns about the Alliance's potential impact raised questions about the role of the government in the industry. In fact, in early May 1991, the B.C. Forest Resources Commission released its two-year $3 million report which recommended major changes in the role of government in the forest industry. Specifically, the report recommended the creation of a Crown corporation to oversee forest management in B.C. including the administration of an open log market (forcing forest companies to buy at least half of the timber cut each year on an open market), payment for forest renewal and borrowing money in bad economic times to continue looking after the forests. The report also recommended the creation of a new Ministry of Renewable Natural Resources that would draw together the ministries currently responsible for forestry, fish and wildlife, and water management.

The commission based its recommendations on the following conclusions: (*i*) stumpage payments made by the forest companies holding licenses to cut vast tracts of Crown land were not capturing the full value of the resource over time (nearly 90 percent of the commercial forests in B.C. were on Crown land); (*ii*) there was no open and competitive market for logs since 85 to 90 percent of the wood cut involved long-term licenses by the top 20 companies and 75 percent of the cut involved the top 10 companies (currently, the forest companies bought some wood on the open market); (*iii*) in many cases, the forest companies had not met the legal requirements of their licenses, i.e., commitments for silviculture and forest management; (*iv*) the government had not committed sufficient funds to forest renewal (the latest provincial budget for forest renewal was down 22.4 percent); (*v*) the Ministry of Forests, currently playing the lead role in land use planning through the awarding of cutting licenses to forest companies was not integrating its planning power with other lead ministries so that there was a lack of integrated management of the public forests for their full range of values.

In mid-May, the provincial Auditor General (AG) echoed some of the commission's findings by criticizing the forests ministry for lack of planning, staffing, and vision so that it was not able to properly monitor the performance and obligations of the forest companies, particularly the large ones. The Forests Minister agreed with most of the AG's conclusions and noted that many of the tasks the ministry once performed were now the responsibility of the licensees but the ministry had not yet determined how to deal with the change. In the last 10 years, field staff levels were reduced almost 40 percent, partially due to privatization.

INITIAL ALLIANCE ACTIVITIES

From April to July, the Alliance undertook or announced several initiatives. Some of these initiatives sparked criticism, as noted in the following sections.

1. TV Programs

The first three of a series of seven 30-minute TV programs was aired (April 15, June 9, July 14) on Sundays on BCTV reaching most of B.C. The estimated number of viewers for the Alliance programs was about 200 000.[27] With the theme "The Forest and the People," the programs addressed such issues as the environmental consequences of clearcuts, the potential effects of a boycott, the economic impact of the forest industry, and the impact of the decision in the United States to ban logging to protect the spotted owl.

In a progress report, the Alliance described the impact of the TV programs as follows:

> Response to the first two programs has been excellent. While the first drew some negative public comment from environmentalists, the second did not. BCTV received five mildly negative calls after each broadcast considered to be a very low complaint level.

The environmentalists reacted to the programs as follows:

- The first program depicted environmentalists, not as well-spoken people but "wild haired lunatics." Tapes of protests included only segments in which protesters were thrashing against police officers or padlocked to a truck.[28]

- "At a time when the forest companies are losing millions of dollars (one report predicted a loss of $1 billion for 1991 due to such factors as global oversupply of pulp and high Canadian dollar) and throwing hundreds of long-time workers on to the bread lines, Jack Munro and his boys manage to come up with enough money to make a half-hour TV show designed to take the wind out of the sails of the environment movement."[29]

- "Docuverts (also known as "infomercials") are those sneaky TV shows that look like real documentaries and talk shows but actually try to sell miracle baldness cures, get-rich quick schemes — and forest industry viewpoints."[30]
- "In an age of ecological limits, the real problem facing B.C. and Canada is an intransigent and increasingly manipulative forest industry. The hiring of a New York-based PR firm to concoct a phony public interest group...and then buy entire TV shows to promote its one-sided message is a dangerous example of this anti-democratic manipulation."[31]
- "The program implied environmentalists are demanding a complete shutdown of forestry when in fact we are simply calling for a restructuring of it...It also side-stepped many concerns shared by Greenpeace and loggers, such as the critical issue of creating value-added products to raise the value of our logged wood."[32]
- "The program's concern for jobs was especially ironic, since automation in B.C.'s pulp mills has cut the workforce by about a third in the last dozen years."[33]

One report noted that if the reaction to the initial broadcast was any indication, the Alliance "seemed to have little chance of persuading ardent environmental groups to understand industry views."[34]

2. Advertising

The Alliance used limited advertising such as bus signs in Vancouver and newspaper ads in all B.C. dailies to promote its TV programs and recruit members.

3. Government Relations

Meetings were held with provincial and federal officials to make them aware of the Alliance and ask for their support, but no government funds were requested. Lobbying was specifically prohibited under the Alliance constitution and by-laws.

4. Media Relations

Discussions were held with media outlets both in and outside B.C. including CBC's The Journal, German TV, Time, Reader's Digest, and ABC TV Prime Time Live. The Alliance "aggressively corrected" errors found in the media either by phoning the reporter directly, or through letters to the editor or setting up interviews for Alliance staff and board members or taking reporters on industry tours.

5. Membership

As of July 1, 1991, the Alliance had 400 members. As a result of this encouraging support, within just three months of the Alliance's formation, a direct mail campaign was created involving 20 000 B.C. households.

6. Economic Impact Study

In cooperation with the Vancouver Board of Trade, the Alliance commissioned a study of the forest industry's economic impact on the Vancouver area. The study released in July concluded that: (*i*) one in five people employed in Greater Vancouver owe their livelihood to the forest industry, and (*ii*) without the forest industry, the provincial and local municipal governments would have $1.4 billion less in tax revenues to spend in Greater Vancouver which means local taxes would likely have to increase $1000 per person to maintain services. Munro said the report fulfills one of the Alliance's key roles by giving the public new information to consider in weighing the consequences of any decisions we make regarding the forest industry. Other Alliance representatives noted that the study indicated that the forest industry has a significant impact not only on the hundreds of logging towns in B.C. but also on the large metropolitan areas like Vancouver. A representative of the WCWC stated that the study was "fallacious because it was premised on the damage done if the whole industry were abolished, or if the cutting of old growth were taken away (but) the WCWC was against clearcutting not the logging of old growth."[35]

7. Speeches/Presentations

From April to July, Alliance staff spoke to 35 groups in 13 communities in order to "broaden the reach of (the Alliance) message to community leaders and decision makers." This activity was expected to increase.

8. European Trip

Because of the on-going suggestions that European forestry practices were more environmentally sensitive than in B.C., the Alliance planned to sponsor an intensive 12 day tour of European mills and forests by a group of 20 Alliance members, staff, television crew, and members of the media. The purpose was to gain impressions about European forest practices from a layperson's perspective, and compare them to present-day forest practices in B.C. The trip was to be the basis for the September TV program.

9. Code of Ethics/Practices

In mid-May, the Alliance announced it would begin developing a code of ethics and practices through a process of fact-finding trips, hearing submissions from special interest groups and reviews of related research. The need for such a code was described as follows:

> Much of the public's confusion over what is or isn't good forestry can be traced to the fact that there is no universal code of practice that covers all aspects of harvesting and silviculture. The Forest Act, for instance, requires "environmentally sound practices," but doesn't spell out in detail what that means. The Professional Foresters Act establishes standards of conduct for foresters, but specifically precludes them from timber harvesting and road construction (since forestry is just one factor in harvesting and road building as economics and operational engineering skills outside forestry are involved). Those words come from the report of the Forest Resources Commission, which goes on to recommend that a single, all-encompassing code of forest practices — setting minimum standards of forest management — be established through introduction of a new, stand-alone, Forest Practices Act.[36]

While the code developed by the Alliance would apply only to the companies in the Alliance, the Alliance board planned to put pressure on segments of the industry if they did not conform to the code although the Alliance felt that all forest companies would adhere to the code without coercion because of the weight of public opinion.

RESPONDING TO NEGATIVE MEDIA COVERAGE

Among the toughest challenges facing the Alliance was how to deal with negative media coverage. In early July, Alliance representatives criticized a two-page *Time* magazine article for comparing clearcut logging in B.C. to internationally condemned deforestation in Brazil. The article failed to point out the extensive tree-planting programs in B.C. and also failed to note that the practices in Brazil and Canada are not comparable because in Brazil they were cutting away tropical forest with no intention of restoring it.

One article in *The Vancouver Sun* particularly concerned the Alliance. This article discussed B-M's role as the PR firm that worked on behalf of the military junta in Argentina. Ley took the following position on the article:

> The Alliance is going to be around for a long time and if the media wanted to write about its ties to B-M that was its prerogative. All we ask for is fair coverage. I'm not from New York. So if *The Sun* insists on referring to B-M as New York-based then when they talk about the Sierra Club, they should call them "San Francisco-based." They talk about our $1 million budget, but should talk about the WCWC $2 million budget. They talk about B-M's ties to Argentina. I know nothing about Argentina. They could point out that B-M also works for the Children's Hospital.

Another Alliance member Patrick Moore was particularly distressed by *The Sun* stories which continually referred to the Alliance as a "public relations campaign" or a "lobby group." Moore noted:

> The Alliance's citizens board is the industry's attempt to reach out into the greater community of B.C. to seek out people interested in helping solve the problem of a crisis in public confidence in the industry. The Alliance is not a lobby group or PR group. It is now a duly registered non-profit society under the B.C. Societies Act and it is composed of people from very diverse geographical and occupational backgrounds in B.C.

Munro described his feelings as follows:

> Is it *The Sun*'s view that we're unacceptable, or that we should be discredited? Why is every story a third of what we're talking about and the rest is explaining to the people that B-M is in *The Sun*'s view a bunch of bastards who advised industry to do this? Furthermore we're not here as salesmen for the God damned industry. But we can't have an industry survive if we constantly feed them through the media stories about what a bunch of bastards are in the industry. Or what a bunch of bastards the industry is when they try to do something right — when we're going to smaller clearcuts, planting more trees and spending a lot more money on silviculture.

The issue for the Alliance's Executive Committee was how to respond to *The Sun*. One alternative being considered was a meeting with *The Sun's* editorial board.

EXHIBIT 1	Attitudes Toward MacMillan Bloedel (M-B)		

| | | Percentages | |
		1987	1991
Favourability Toward M-B			
Very/somewhat favourable		61	71
Very/somewhat unfavourable		35	26
In agreement			
M-B spends time and money in forest management research		81	72
M-B consults with many agencies on other forest resources		75	67
M-B is planning forest management for the next 100 years		72	67
M-B is as concerned about BC's forests as I am		61	56
M-B is as concerned about the environment as it is about profit		39	45

Source: Poll of 778 residents of coastal BC where M-B operates.

B.C. FOREST ALLIANCE

JACK MUNRO
Chairman

ANNE CLARKE
Deputy Chairman

Melissa Hadley

Daniel Johnston

Patrick Moore

Ray Smith

Dr. John Borden

Gordon Cameron

Gordon Campbell

Graham Clarke

Geoff Day

Bert Gayle

Iain Harris

John C. Kerr

Dr. Hamish Kimmins

Stuart Lang

Charles Lasser

Michael MacCallum

Abbie Milavsky

Ted Moffat

Ed Moul

Frank Ney

Barbara Rae

Les Reed

Guy Rose

Dr. Brian Taylor

Gillian Trumper

Jack Webster

Ray Woods

Dear Friend:

The forest industry is facing challenging times in British Columbia today, as it strives to protect a healthy environment, jobs and a renewable supply of harvestable timber.

The future of this province cannot be reduced to a senseless tug-of-war, fought tree by tree and valley by valley. There has to be a common sense, middle-ground approach that seeks B.C.based answers, enabling both our environment and economy to prosper.

Your company has taken steps to ensure forests, jobs, and the environment are protected. It has put its support behind the B.C. Forest Alliance, a new group composed of citizens from various backgrounds and political beliefs from throughout the province who share a desire to strike a balance between environment and economy. A Citizen's Board made up of 29 well-known and respected individuals from many regions of the province will direct the actions of the Alliance. IWA-Canada President Jack Munro is our voluntary chairman. Legendary broadcaster Jack Webster, Greenpeace co-founder Patrick Moore and Vancouver Mayor Gordon Campbell have also joined the Alliance as board members.

A monthly B.C. Forest Alliance television program will examine the good and the bad in current forest practices. The Alliance is also developing a code to monitor the forest industry's performance, a code which will be signed and adhered to by all member companies, including yours. The Alliance has a monthly newsletter, publishes forest fact sheets and will compare forest practices in B.C. to those in the US, Sweden and Germany.

We need the support of all British Columbians. The Alliance will be holding local events and encouraging citizen participation in our activities. This is where you come in. Your membership fee will help carry out the activities of the Alliance. It will help make sense of some very serious issues. And it will help the Alliance educate the citizens of B.C. about some of the more controversial forest practices, such as clearcutting.

Please fill out the enclosed form and mail it with your cheque or money order to the B.C. Forest Alliance. Your membership in this new organization is the first step toward resolving the heated controversy facing B.C. today. The Alliance is presently being incorporated under the B.C. Society Act, and we hope financial contributions will soon be tax-deductible.

Thank you in advance for your participation.

Yours truly,

Gary Ley
Executive Director

P.S. You may have heard about the proposed European boycott of B.C. forest products. This would have serious consequences for British Columbia. Though it is unlikely this boycott would ever happen, the Alliance is working actively to prevent it.

210 1100 MELVILLE STREET VANCOUVER, B.C. V6E 4A6
TEL: (604) 685-7507 FAX: (604) 685-5373 TOLL-FREE: 1-800-567-TREE

NOTES

1. *The Globe and Mail*, July 8, 1991, B3.
2. *The Globe and Mail*, January 5, 1991, D1.
3. *North Island Gazette*, May 29, 1991, (Port Hardy, B.C.).
4. *Capital News*, April 12, 1991, (Kelowna, B.C.).
5. *Nanaimo Daily Free Press*, April, 1991.
6. *The Vancouver Sun*, July 20, 1991.
7. *British Columbia Report*, August 19, 1991, 24.
8. *Nanaimo Times*, April 11, 1991.
9. *ibid.*
10. *Capital News*, April 12, 1991.
11. *Vernon Daily News*, April 17, 1991.
12. *The Globe and Mail*, July 8, 1991, B3.
13. *Times Colonist*, July 10, 1991.
14. *The Vancouver Sun*, July 18, 1991, E1.
15. *North Island Gazette*, May 15, 1991.
16. *Pacific Tribune*, April 29, 1991.
17. *The Vancouver Sun*, July 18, 1991, E1.
18. *The Vancouver Sun*, May 21, 1991.
19. *Pacific Tribune*, April 29, 1991.
20. *The Province*, July 21, 1991.
21. *ibid.*
22. *The Globe and Mail*, July 8, 1991, B3.
23. *The Vancouver Sun*, July 22, 1991, D9.
24. *Interior News*, July 3, 1991.
25. *Vernon Daily News*, April 17, 1991.
26. *The Globe and Mail*, July 8, 1991, B3.
27. (Stanbury).
28. *The Globe and Mail*, July 8, 1991, B3.
29. *British Columbia Report*, May 13, 1991.
30. Publication unknown.
31. July 9, 1991 (publication unknown).
32. *British Columbia Report*, April 29, 1991, 20.
33. *The Vancouver Sun*, April 16, 1991.
34. *Powell River News*, April 17, 1991.
35. *Peace River Block News*, July 16, 1991 (Dawson Creek).
36. *Province*, June 16, 1991.

BENJAMIN MOORE & CO. LTD. AND THE GOVERNMENT OF BRITISH COLUMBIA'S WASTE PAINT REGULATION

INTRODUCTION

Joe Sobie, president of the Canadian division of Benjamin Moore & Co. Ltd., was preparing for a meeting with the Canadian Paint & Coatings Association (CPCA) on June 24, 1994. The main item on the agenda was a new environmental regulation introduced by the Government of British Columbia (B.C.) that would impact all paint sellers in the province.

As president of Benjamin Moore, Sobie had overall responsibility for spearheading the corporation's response to the new law. As immediate past president of the CPCA, he also had to play an active role in the industry's response to the regulation. The government action was not a complete surprise to him, but the timeframe for implementation was a matter of concern. As Sobie reviewed the legislation, he reflected on how the company and the CPCA should be approaching the issues.

ENVIRONMENTAL REGULATION

Public awareness of environmental issues is at an all time high. As the awareness increased, so have demands for government and business to acknowledge the severity of the problems and to do something about them. In Canada, the national focus for environmental regulation has been on sustainable development, which maintains that economic development is linked to environmental protection. The move toward sustainable development plays a critical role in improving the efficiency and environmental performance of companies in the traditional manufacturing and process sectors. Environmental regulation now exists at four levels.

Generic Regulation The first attempt by government is often at a general level by enacting broad legislation supporting ideas such as its sustainable development policies. In this case, responsibility rests with government to develop programs to support these policies.

Regulations Targeting Industry The next level of regulation is the stewardship level, an example being the current legislation facing the British Columbia paint industry. Product stewardship is a concept that delegates cradle to grave responsibility to industry for its products and processes. This shifts responsibility for waste from the public to the private sector, raising concerns over the protection of both the consumer and the public interest.

Regulations Targeting Consumers What is also emerging is a third type of environmental regulation with emphasis at the consumer level. An example is charging consumers for each bag of garbage that is collected from their home. In this case, government is shifting responsibility to the ultimate user, the consumer.

Regulations Targeting Both Consumers and Industry At this level, legislation involves both consumer and manufacturer and the parties share responsibility. An example might be soft drink bottle recycling where industry is legislated to recycle the bottles and consumers are charged for the bottles through a deposit/refund system.

It is in this regulatory climate that the paint industry must respond to the impact of its products on the environment and the possibility of government regulation. Paint products are purchased by virtually all Canadians, and there is usually unused or waste paint remaining after the consumer finishes the painting project. An environmental concern for the industry and government is how consumers dispose of this waste.

BACKGROUND ON THE REGULATION

The B.C. environment ministry estimates that paint makes up 70 percent of Household Hazardous Waste (HHW), and the ministry has made several attempts to manage the HHW issue over the past decade. First, there was the B.C. Hazardous Waste Management Corporation that operated for several years and tried to address the problem of HHW before being disbanded. Then there was a program which funded eight regional HHW depots which was abandoned in April, 1994 after three years. It was estimated that these depots collected only one to eight per cent of the province's household hazardous wastes. The provincial government realized that a more comprehensive program was needed.

During 1993, a special report, "Greener Homes — Cleaner Communities," was prepared by the Waste Reduction Commission and submitted to B.C.'s Minister of the Environment in January 1994. The report recommended that the province shift the HHW management burden from the government and the provincial taxpayers to the producers and consumers of hazardous waste products. In particular, an active role for industry was recommended, with a transitional timeframe of three years. An industry-funded organization was recommended to administer the program.

THE REGULATION

On June 23, 1994 the B.C. Government introduced the first regulation under the Waste Management Act called the "Post-Consumer Paint Stewardship Program Regulation." This law placed significant new requirements on "brand-owners" to establish a "stewardship program." The term brand-owner essentially means manufacturers and distributors of paint but potentially includes paint retailers as well. The regulation defines a stewardship program as an initiative that:

i.   establishes a process for collection, transportation, and final treatment of post consumer paint, regardless of the original brand-owner or seller of that consumer paint product; and

ii. incorporates the principles of pollution prevention through the implementation of the pollution prevention hierarchy by moving progressively from treatment or containment to recovering of energy, recycling, or reuse.

What this means is that the paint industry will be responsible for left-over product in consumer possession.

The regulation states that this stewardship program seeks to establish three objectives: environmental protection, consumer convenience, and cost efficiency. The effect of this program is to divert left-over paint from landfills, sewers, and waterways. This can be achieved through the collection of left-over paint and also through encouraging consumers to reuse paint and to buy only the paint they require. Industrial markets can also be sought so that some paint can be recycled or used as an energy source.

In order to encourage consumer participation in the program, the regulation requires that consumers must be able to return their left-over paint at reasonably convenient locations and times. This should include a no-charge drop-off collection service for household consumers, reasonable hours and repetition of available collections, one-stop collection for future HHW where possible, paint exchange opportunities where possible, and safe and well-marked collection locations. The intention should be to find the most cost-effective process to administer the program.

The regulation means that retailers and wholesalers of paints, stains, and wall coatings will be required to accept for recycling or disposal all brands of paint and paint containers. If retailers prefer not to accept waste paint at their stores, they can designate a return collection facility to serve the same function. The regulation defines a return collection facility as "... a convenient and environmentally sound place for the return and short term storage or treatment of post-consumer paint for the purpose of the stewardship program." The retailers can also contract with a person who operates a fixed site return collection facility, or a mobile return collection facility. The facility must be located not more than four kilometres from the seller's premises in an urban area, or not more than ten kilometres from the seller's premises in a rural area. This means that there would have to be the establishment of ten used paint collection centres in the greater Vancouver Regional district, five in the Capital Regional district, and one for each of the remaining twenty-eight regional districts by September 1, 1994.

In a press release dated July 14, 1994, Environment Minister Moe Sihota announced:

> Because these collection facilities will likely be located at existing recycling centres and municipal sites, the phase-in schedule allows industry time to develop necessary contracts with recycling groups, municipalities, and other agencies.

Once collected, the regulation stipulates that the brand-owner must treat or contain, recover energy from, recycle, or reuse all post-consumer paint within six months after receiving the left-over paint at the return collection facility.

The ministry favoured an aggressive stance and required submission of plans for a permanent system by December 1, 1994, with the program fully operational by January 1, 1995. The regulation also requires brand-owners to submit annual reports to the ministry outlining the specifics of the brand-owners' stewardship programs, including financial statements, to ensure that the program is effective and accountable. Manufacturers that do not comply with the regulation face fines of up to $200 000 per offence and could be prohibited from selling paint in the province.

When the regulation was introduced, officials of the Ministry of Environment, Lands and Parks encouraged paint manufacturers to form an industry funded organization in order to comply with the terms of the regulation. It was expected from the beginning that most funding would be provided by the industry.

CHALLENGES FACING THE B.C. PAINT INDUSTRY

The paint industry faces an enormous challenge, made more difficult by the speed with which the regulation was developed and the short timeframe for implementation. The regulation was announced on June 23, 1994, an interim solution had to be developed by September 1, 1994, and a complete program had to be in place by January 1, 1995.

It will also be very difficult for the paint manufacturers to question the government's environmental position. British Columbia is one of the more progressive provinces in Canada when it comes to the environment, with very vocal debates regarding forestry practices and other environmental issues. The Ministry of the Environment bases its policies on a precautionary approach, whereby action is undertaken prior to conclusive proof of environmental damage (i.e., they would sooner be safe than sorry). This has resulted in the toughest pulp mill emission standards in Canada and with the government turning down construction projects because of their possible negative implications for the environment.

Although collective action by the industry is the preferred response for Benjamin Moore and the CPCA, it will be very difficult for a B.C. based industry group to drive the actions of all the brand-owners. Many of these manufacturers, wholesalers, and retailers are based outside of British Columbia and have only a cursory understanding of its legislations. There are approximately 130 paint manufacturing plants in North America, and of these, only a handful operate in British Columbia. However, many of these manufacturers sell their products to B.C. retailers.

The retail consumer in Canada typically buys paint through the following outlets: department stores such as Sears; hardware stores such as Home Hardware; decorating outlets which might be franchised, such as Color Your World; or independent small businesses. Both Color Your World and Home Hardware manufacture the paint that is sold in their stores. Other retail stores sell national brand paints such as Pittsburgh, Sherwin-Williams, or Benjamin Moore Paints. Some paint manufacturers also private-label their products for larger companies such as hardware stores or retail chains. The CPCA estimates that there are about 60 paint "brand-owners" in B.C. who are affected by the new regulation. All companies, from manufacturers to retailers, are now expected to set aside their differences as competitors and work together to create North America's first industry-operated paint recycling program.

BENJAMIN MOORE — COMPANY BACKGROUND

Benjamin Moore and his brother founded a partnership in the United States in 1883 under the name "Moore Brothers." These early pioneers of the company built the business on the principles of profitability, intelligence, and integrity, and established this reputation upon practices which were morally correct and socially responsible. These principles remain as the guiding philosophy behind Benjamin Moore's corporate policies today. It remains a privately held company with active family member involvement, and is the largest independent paint manufacturer in North America.

In 1906, Benjamin Moore & Co. Ltd. began operations in Canada when it opened its first plant in Toronto. Today there are also plants in Vancouver and Montreal, seven warehouses across the country, and 285 employees. Joe Sobie joined Benjamin Moore in Winnipeg in 1955 and became President of the company in 1983. He has been actively involved in the Canadian Decorating Products Association as well as the CPCA for many years, including serving as president of the latter group.

Benjamin Moore is generally viewed as a market leader and has built a reputation for a superior paint product. Business operations are conducted in accordance with the company's "Declaration of Policy" presented in Exhibit 1. It was founded on a policy of selling only to independent dealers and the company has made a decision to continue with that strategy. In recent years, the changing market conditions have caused most other manufacturers either to sell through company owned stores or to sell their products to mass merchandisers and direct contractors. As well, sales in the paint industry have declined mainly due to the movement away from painted exteriors and towards vinyl or other types of siding. Despite this industry trend, Benjamin Moore has continued to show gains in market share and sales. The company believes that one of the main reasons for this success is its continued support for the wide distribution network of independent dealers. Another reason for its success is the shift by consumers away from poor performing "bargain-brand" paints and a movement towards quality products, like those manufactured by Benjamin Moore.

ENVIRONMENTAL EFFORTS IN THE PAINT INDUSTRY

The national paint industry has undertaken a voluntary initiative since 1992 aimed at educating paint dealers and consumers on proper paint use and disposal. This program is known as "BUD," which encourages paint customers to Buy only the paint they actually need, Use all the paint that they buy, and Dispose of all left-over paint safely and properly. Exhibit 2 is a copy of the brochure describing this program.

About the same time, Environment Canada launched an "Environmental Choice" Program where it certified various paint manufacturer's products with an "EcoLogo" if they met specific environmental standards. This program is overseen by an independent body which sets environmental criteria for products, and conducts follow-up inspections on certified products to ensure compliance. Companies voluntarily submit their products for scrutiny, pay for inspection and testing, and pay an annual fee based on sales of the licensed products. The guidelines are evolving and will become tougher. Even when a company earns the right to display the EcoLogo on its products, they likely will have to requalify against even more rigorous criteria when standards are revised every three years.

Benjamin Moore's commitment to the environment and the licensing of its products by the Environmental Choice Program is described in Exhibit 3.

Because of Benjamin Moore's high sales volume, the EcoLogo is an expensive program for them and the benefits are difficult to measure. Since most major manufacturers have products that offer this designation, Benjamin Moore feels that they need the designation to remain competitive. Other manufacturers received the EcoLogo designation only on specific products within their product line, and often after changing product composition. Benjamin Moore was the first paint company to have carte blanche approval for use of the EcoLogo on all of its latex paint products, without instituting any change to the product composition. They are also continuing research into eliminating the use of volatile organic compounds (VOCs). VOCs allow paint to freeze and thaw during transportation without breaking down, but, they contribute to chemical smog.

While the EcoLogo indicates that Benjamin Moore's products are environmental friendly, the problem of disposing left-over paint remains for all producers in the industry. Exhibit 4 presents an overview of the paint recycling process. Current research on paint recycling shows that the solvent in oil-based paints can be used as an alternative fuel through incineration. Latex paint can be used in a remanufacturing process to create recycled Latex paint. Technology exists to recycle about 50 to 60 percent of all paint, but at present only 10 to 20 percent is recycled. Another form of recycling is a paint exchange program where consumers exchange left-over paint with other consumers. Even though the B.C. government has banned all paints from landfills, the industry contends that latex paint can be allowed to solidify and be disposed of harmlessly in landfills because it does not leach toxins once it has hardened. This position is upheld by the Environmental Choice Program, and about 70 percent of the paints sold in B.C. are water-based, non-toxic latex paints.

One problem with old oil-based paint is that it often contains toxins such as lead and PCBs, which makes recycling impossible. As well, research from previous recycling efforts has shown that consumers often dump other chemicals into paint cans brought in for collection. This requires testing of the paint waste product before a decision can be made on how to dispose of it. These problems present challenges for an industry environmental program.

OTHER SOLUTIONS TO HOUSEHOLD HAZARDOUS WASTE (HHW) EFFORTS

British Columbia is not alone in dealing with the problem of HHW. The province of Alberta and the state of Washington both provide examples of sustainably managed HHW programs. These programs rely heavily on the participation of local governments due to their considerable waste management infrastructures and awareness of community needs. Alberta's comprehensive program for the collection and treatment of all HHW cost $1.7 million 1993. Washington State's largely mobile program for all HHW cost a similar amount of money, plus about $1 million to operate two fixed sites.

Based on HHW programs elsewhere, the government expects the B.C. program to cost approximately $2 million annually. The projected amount is within the parameters of its own past HHW program, where approximately $1.4 million was spent annually.

THE CPCA MEETING

At the CPCA meeting, discussion immediately turned to the industry's situation. There seemed to be three areas where decisions needed to be made. First, the group needed to decide whether they should ignore the legislation, postpone action through lobbying efforts, or meet the requirements of the regulation. Second, if they decided that action should be taken to support the regulation, they needed to develop a transition plan and a long-term comprehensive stewardship program. Third, if they were to try and meet the regulation, then they needed to decide what process would be used to achieve the objectives of the program. The regulation offered two different ways for collecting and managing waste paint, either return-to-retail or the establishment of other return collection sites. Return collection facilities could include a mobile collection system, temporary round-up collection sites, or permanent collection sites. The industry could consider establishing their own collection system, which might be contracted out to a private enterprise, and/or working with recycling groups and local governments to use existing recycling centres and municipal sites.

It was rumoured at the meeting that some of the major players in the B.C. paint industry were interested in finding a joint solution. These manufacturers and retailers included Pittsburgh, Para, Pratt & Lambert, Flecto, International, Sico, Color Your World, and St. Clair. It was also rumoured that some national retailers, such as Home Hardware stores and Sherwin Williams & Co. stores, were not interested in joining an industry group. It seemed likely that these two companies would be pursuing their own solutions based on a return-to-retail collection method.

As Sobie listened to the discussion, many questions were racing through his mind related to Benjamin Moore & Co. Ltd. As president of a manufacturer with dealers across the country, he was struck by the magnitude of the situation and its implications for the company. Because many Benjamin Moore dealers also carried other manufacturers' products, Sobie felt that most of their dealers would want to find an industry-based solution. He wondered which of his competitors would be willing to work with him to develop a fair solution to the regulation. He also questioned exactly what social responsibility the company had towards the community.

As a CPCA director, Mr. Sobie had another set of questions. He wondered whether lobbying against this type of regulation would be a futile effort. He also reflected on how the independent dealers and manufacturers with a small market share would respond. How could he ensure a united industry response to this situation? If the industry had to implement some kind of solution, who would pay for it? How should the industry position be presented to the government?

Joe Sobie reflected that this regulation was the first of its kind in Canada and would likely be used as a model for the rest of the country. He also knew that the other CPCA directors would be looking to him for leadership because of his many years of experience, his interest in environmental issues, and his background of active participation in industry initiatives. Mr. Sobie felt that both Benjamin Moore and the B.C. paint industry had several important decisions to make, and time was not on their side.

EXHIBIT 1   Benjamin Moore's Declaration of Policy

Declaration Of Policy

To protect the Independent Paint Dealer by maintaining policies that afford opportunities for profit and business growth in a highly competitive market.

To support the efforts of the Independent Paint Dealer to increase paint sales to consumers, painting contractors and industry within the dealer's service area.

To maintain product quality, service and price at levels competitively advantageous to the Independent Paint Dealer.

To respect the Independent Paint Dealer's rightful opportunity to operate without direct selling competition from the supplier.

Today, thousands of independent paint dealers selling Benjamin Moore & Co.'s products in the United States and Canada know from experience that the Company's Strict adherence to these policies is the dealer's assurance of a business relationship that fosters continuing growth and prosperity.

EXHIBIT 2   The "BUD" Program

When buying or using paint remember...

"BUD"

Buy no more than you need

Use all the paint that you buy

Dispose of all leftover paint safely and properly

*B*uying more paint than you need costs you money. It also creates the problem of disposing of leftover paint. Do yourself, and the environment, a favour by buying the right amount for the job. Ask your paint dealer for help.

*U*se all the paint that you buy. An extra coat will give more protection. Or share your leftovers with a neighbour who has a small area that needs painting.

*D*on't pour leftover paint down the drain. Save it for your "Household Hazardous Waste" collection day, or if your community has a permanent Hazardous Household Waste Depot, take it there. Properly collected, paint and paint cans can be recycled. Check with your local government or municipality for details.

How to handle leftover paint for recycling

Empty Cans
Once you have used all the paint in the can dry it by leaving the lid off. Make sure that the can is out of reach of children and animals, and in a well-ventilated area. Completely dry cans are easier to collect for recycling.

Don't Put Oils or Other Wastes in Paint or Paint Cans
This can make it difficult, or even impossible, to recycle the leftover paint.

Leave the Label On
It makes it easier to recycle the paint if the label is still on the can.

Don't Mix Leftover Paints
Don't mix two incompatible paints (for example, one alkyd with one latex). If you do, that mixture cannot be recycled.

Bring your paint in safely

When bringing the paint in, there are a few simple, but important, things to remember.

Make Sure the Lids on the Cans Containing Paints Are On Tightly

You don't want a spill in the trunk of your car. If you cannot close the lid properly, and the can still has liquid paint in it, you may want to put it in a box which won't tip over, or secure it in the trunk so that it can't be overturned and leak.

Don't Leave the Paint Cans in the Trunk for a Long Period of Time...

...particularly if it's a sunny or hot day. This could cause the solvent in the alkyd paint to evaporate and, for both alkyd and latex, prolonged exposure to heat could cause a pressure build-up in the partially full container. It is suggested that you load up the paint in the car and come directly to the collection site.

A few pointers on re-using wash solvent

Store the Dirty Wash Solvent in a Properly Labelled Closed Container

Do this after you have washed your brushes and rollers in paint thinner, mineral spirits, or turpentine. In a few days, the paint particles will settle to the bottom, leaving usable solvent at the top.

Carefully Pour the Clean Solvent into Another Container

Label and seal it, then put it away safely for future use. Reseal the original container and save it for your "Household Hazardous Waste" collection.

Published by:
The Canadian Paint and Coatings Association
9900 Cavendish Boulevard, Suite 103
Montreal, Quebec, Canada H4M 2V2
Telephone (514) 745-2611

RECYCLED PAPER

EXHIBIT 3   Press Release

Moore Concerned About the Environment

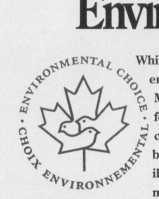

Low pollution water-based paint
Peinture à d'eau, peu polluante

While 'green' may be the colour of environment friendly, Benjamin Moore is pleased to announce that for them, environment friendly comes in all colours of the rainbow - from Forest Green to Hamilton Blue - and has done so for many years.

Benjamin Moore's interior and exterior latex paints are certified by the *Environmental Choice** to be a reduced pollution water-based paint. To be able to carry this *EcoLogo**, Benjamin Moore had to meet exacting standards set by the *Environmental Choice** program. Over two hundred Benjamin Moore interior and exterior latex paints in a variety of colours and finishes have been labelled with the *EcoLogo**.

You can be assured that when you buy Benjamin Moore paints, you are dealing with a company that shares your environmental concerns.

Benjamin Moore PAINTS

*The words *"Environmental Choice"* and *"EcoLogo"* are official marks of Environment Canada.

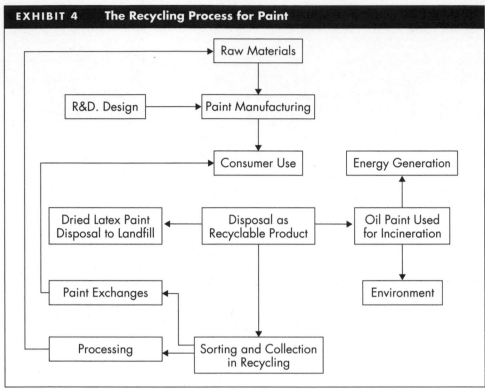

EXHIBIT 4   The Recycling Process for Paint

Source: Adapted from Figure 18–1, "The Recycling Process," Robert W. Sexty, *Canadian Business and Society: Understanding Social and Ethical Challenges*, 1995, p.389

NOTE

THE BOARD
OF PWA CORP.

In August, 1992, Rhys Eyton (pronounced "Rees Eaton"), chairman of the board and CEO of PWA Corporation (hereafter PWA) had to decide how to respond to an apparent split in his board over the issue of the role of the federal government in the affairs of PWA. Prime Minister Mulroney had just revealed publicly that Ronald Southern a director of PWA had indicated to Mulroney that the federal government had not interfered with PWA's possible alliance with American Airlines but was simply trying to help. However, in Eyton's view the events which transpired suggested that the federal government had indeed interfered with PWA's attempts to form an alliance with American. Mulroney called on the board of PWA to clear up the "falsehoods" being told about the merger talks between PWA and Air Canada. Eyton now had to decide how to respond to the Prime Minister's calls to clear the air. Before reviewing the events preceding August 1992, this case will outline the history of PWA and Air Canada (AC).

HISTORY OF PWA

Pacific Western Airlines Ltd. was formed in 1953 when it changed its name from Central British Columbia Airways Ltd., which operated charter and contract flights in B.C.'s interior. The airline expanded through acquisition during the 1950s and 1960s. In 1974, the Alberta government purchased the company and its head office was moved from Vancouver to Calgary. In 1983 Pacific Western Airlines Corp. was created as a holding company to purchase the airline's shares from the Alberta government. The airline went public through an offering of 10 million shares. Growth continued through investment in other smaller airlines, alliances with other carriers such as Air France and Lufthansa, and two major acquisitions. In 1987, Canadian Pacific Airlines was acquired from Canadian Pacific Ltd. for $300 million; the two airlines were combined under the name Canadian Airlines International Ltd. (hereafter CDN) and the holding company name was changed to PWA Corporation. With this acquisition, CDN was now competing directly with AC.

PWA's other major acquisition was Wardair Inc., acquired in 1989 for $250 million and then amalgamated with CDN. Through its takeover of Wardair, CDN gained access to all of AC's high density, high yield markets in the North Atlantic. The federal Bureau of Competition Policy did not oppose the deal with Wardair because it determined that Wardair would have failed (thanks to a vicious fare war) if the merger did not proceed and when Wardair was asked to find alternative purchasers, none came forward. Under the Competition Act, even if mergers cause a substantial lessening of competition they can be approved if one of the companies is heading toward insolvency.

The mission of PWA was described as "to be a leading global airline." As of August, 1992, CDN was the only Canadian carrier authorized to fly between Canada and Japan, the fastest-growing Canadian air route over the previous decade. Since 1988 AC had made seven written requests to the Canadian government for designation to serve Japan but the government deferred a decision in every case. (Competition on all international routes was controlled by bilateral agreements between governments). CDN argued against AC's request for designation in the Pacific on the basis that it developed the Japanese market over more than 40 years and it had arranged a joint service with Japan Airlines out of Toronto to increase the capacity of the market. Furthermore, CDN noted that AC had been designated to serve Korea and Singapore but withdrew from Singapore and chose not to serve Korea. Overall, neither AC nor CDN were satisfied with the Canadian government's "divide the skies" policy on international routes. AC was frustrated by its inability to serve Japan and CDN was frustrated by AC's historical dominance on US routes. In terms of expansion into the United States, Rhys Eyton noted the following:

> The Canadian and U.S. governments are currently renegotiating the bilateral air services agreement between our two countries. We believe that there are promising opportunities for expansion of services into the United States and we support increased liberalization of the agreement. We have made it very clear, however, that Canadian air carriers cannot compete effectively, particularly due to the onerous government charges placed upon us. Federal and provincial charges and taxes now take approximately 20% of an average domestic fare, whereas in the United States the government's share is significantly lower at 13%. Since airline operating margins have seldom exceeded 7% even in the industry's strongest years, it is difficult for us to achieve adequate margins when the government is taking such a large share.[1]

One study concluded that the bilateral air service negotiations between Canada and the United States were likely to result in "the early continentalization of the North American market and much more intense competition," necessitating airlines to restructure their network, routing systems and affiliations."[2]

In mid-1992, PWA was a holding company with investments primarily in the airline industry. About 80 percent of PWA revenues were represented by CDN. The remainder of the revenues were represented by the company's regional commuter partners, Canadian Regional Airlines Ltd., the leisure travel tour business, the computer reservation system business, the leasing of aircraft to other airlines, and the provision of services to other carriers such as aircraft and engine overhaul and maintenance, passenger and cargo handling, flight simulator and equipment rentals, employee training programs, and airline computer software products.

HISTORY OF AIR CANADA

AC was first known as Trans-Canada Air Lines which was created by the federal government in 1937. The name was changed to Air Canada in 1965. The airline grew through investments in several airlines but sometimes divested certain parts of its operation. For example, in 1979, it acquired Nordair, a regional airline in eastern Canada but then sold it in 1984. En Route Card Inc. was established to manage travel-card operations but it was sold for $300 million in 1992 to Citibank Canada. In 1989, the federal government completed its privatization of AC. The divestiture legislation restricted individual ownership to 10 percent and cumulative ownership by foreigners to 25 percent of the total outstanding shares. As of August, 1992, the stock of both AC and PWA was widely held. The president of AC in 1992 was Hollis Harris, an American who had been president of Continental Airlines in the United States when it declared bankruptcy for the second time.

Until the mid-1970s, AC was given preferred regulatory treatment so that regulatory decisions involving other carriers were made to ensure other carriers complemented, not competed with, the crown carrier. Beginning in the mid 1970s, regulatory policy was gradually liberalized increasing other carriers' ability to compete with AC. In 1984, airline regulation was substantially liberalized for southern Canada (e.g., unlimited entry into the round-trip charter market, freedom to reduce prices, freedom of exit from market when faced with new entry). In 1988, formal deregulation for southern Canada was announced (e.g., complete elimination of price and entry controls). The United States had moved to complete deregulation in 1978, 10 years earlier leading to the entry of many new airlines and the decline and sometimes failure of many major US carriers.

AC's long-term objective was to "build a network of international alliances that span the globe." In this regard, AC announced alliances with Air France and United Airlines, the second largest air carrier in the United States. AC had also announced in 1991 an alliance with US Air, the fifth largest carrier in the United States, but the two airlines could not agree on the terms of the alliance. In July, 1992, US Air "apparently gave up" on AC and chose instead to sell a large portion of its equity to British Airways (BA) to the dismay of US airline executives who argued that the deal threatened the future of international aviation by US carriers. One executive noted that the deal gives BA its own airline in the United States while US carriers are denied similar opportunities abroad because of international accords. Nevertheless, US law forbid foreign companies from owning more than 49 percent of an airline's stock and 25 percent of its voting shares. Globally, in response to the pressures of trade liberalization and air transport deregulation, the trend in the airline industry was consolidation of carriers into five or six mega-systems competing in the major markets of Europe, North America and Asia. In 1992, only the United States and Japan had more than one major airline. Many large carriers in the world continued to be owned at least partially by government, although a few (e.g., BA) had been privatized.

MERGER TALKS BETWEEN PWA AND AIR CANADA

In February 1991, PWA invited AC to open discussions on alternatives available to Canada's two national carriers. PWA first suggested that AC buy out CDN in its entirety. AC's response, and very much its first choice, was the consolidation of international operations under AC, with PWA compensated in cash for its international operations. Only when PWA rejected this concept was the possibility of a full merger considered. In May 1991, the federal Minister of Transport indicated the government's position on merging AC and PWA:

> The continuing imperative of our airline policies must be to enhance competitiveness. Merging Canada's biggest airlines would not make the remaining entity more competitive. It would not produce a mega-carrier big enough to dominate markets occupied by giants like United and British Airways. But if the assumed benefits of a merger don't come from a more competitive company which wins its battles in the marketplace, then inevitably these benefits must come directly from the consumer pockets in the form of less competition, higher fares, and a guaranteed return for the airline. Higher levels of debt, the destruction of thousands of jobs and reregulation of the airline sector are three other likely products of a merger between our two major carriers.

During on-again, off-again talks with AC, PWA was also talking to other carriers. In March 1992, PWA decided to negotiate exclusively with American Airlines (AMR), the world's largest airline (American's parent was AMR Corp. based in Fort Worth). However, there had been some support among board members for merging with AC. Directors who were reported as favouring a merger were Ronald Southern, a Calgary businessman who controlled ATCO, a large construction company, Peter Lougheed, a former Alberta Premier, Arthur Mauro, a Winnipeg businessman, Harry Steele, a Newfoundland publisher, and Max Ward, former owner of Wardair.[3] Exhibit 1 lists the Board of Directors. Ultimately, Rhys Eyton reportedly persuaded the majority of the directors that an alliance with AMR was preferable since it would preserve more jobs, including those of senior managers and maintain a strong Western Canadian presence. (PWA was the largest private sector employer in B.C. and a major employer in Alberta.)

STRIKING A DEAL WITH AMERICAN

From March to July, 1992 AMR and PWA held on-going discussions. AMR hoped to increase the return on its investment in its sophisticated hosting services system, called Sabre, widely recognized as one of the world's most sophisticated systems for processing reservations, tickets and boarding passes. It was also noted that AMR was interested in gaining access to CDN's Pacific routes since AMR had been granted only limited access under US bilateral agreements. The following deal was beginning to take shape:

i.   AMR would pay PWA $246 million for a 25 percent voting stake and 33.9 percent economic stake in PWA; in addition, for the $246 million, non-voting preferred shares were to be included in order to keep AMR under the 25 percent foreign ownership restriction in the airline industry; the deal valued PWA shares at $7.50 (the shares traded in the $5 range at the time, trading as high as $6.37 within the last year and historically were above $28); there were clauses allowing AMR to force PWA to buy back its shares at a predetermined price; AMR's investment would be structured through a holding company;

ii. PWA would retain six seats on the board of directors, and AMR would have two seats, exactly proportional to AMR's voting interest in PWA;

iii. As noted in a shareholder's agreement, majority board approval was required for PWA's annual business plans, major capital expenditures, changes to PWA's operations required by AMR, any declaration of dividends, and the appointment or removal of independent auditors; approval would be required by at least one of the two AMR-designated board members in certain areas including the appointment or termination of the company's chief executive, PWA's annual capital plan, capital expenditures unrelated to the airline business, such as real estate transactions, and any amendments to company by-laws; third party arbitration would take place where there was a major disagreement among members of the board;

iv. As noted in a 20-year services agreement, for a fee AMR would provide CDN with computer-based information and management support systems which AMR had developed to administer its global airline network. (The services agreement was seen as matching CDN's need for low-cost but sophisticated support systems with AMR's skills and resources. Because of its economies of scale, AMR could make systems available to CDN at a price lower than CDN could achieve on its own.) CDN was to retain full management control and decision-making authority under the services arrangement which covered the following activities: accounting, capacity planning, data processing and communications, (e.g., frequent flier program), food and beverage systems, operations in certain cities outside Canada and the United States, operations planning and support (e.g., aircraft performance monitoring), passenger services procedures, yield management (i.e., systems to maximize revenues and minimize costs by making best use of discount fares and setting booking levels to reduce the costs of no-shows), and reservations calls originating in the United States. Because these various information systems were closely integrated with AMR's Sabre hosting system (which stored the master inventory of data on flights, fares and passenger bookings), AMR's provision of these services depended on CDN's internal computer systems residing within Sabre. In addition, the AMR frequent-flier programs would be linked. In terms of employment, it was calculated that 1500 to 2000 jobs would be exported from Canada, largely in the areas of accounting, fare setting and capacity planning.

In order to transfer to AMR's Sabre system, CDN would have to remove its internal system (known as Pegasus) from a partnership of three companies known as the Gemini Group based in Toronto. PWA's director of corporate affairs and two senior vice presidents of CDN were on the board of the Gemini Group. The partnership, equally-owned by PWA, AC, and Covia, a US-based company primarily owned by United Airlines, had been created in 1987 for two purposes: (*i*) to promote a computerized reservation system (CRS) for Canadian travel agents using its branded product — Apollo by Gemini, a system owned by United and others, and located in Denver, Colorado, (*ii*) to manage the internal computer systems of CDN (Pegasus) and AC (Reservac). The Bureau of Competition Policy had backed off its earlier efforts to dissolve Gemini when the carriers agreed in a consent order in 1989 not to use their joint operation as a means of discriminating against other airlines. There were five years remaining on a contract involving Gemini's management of Pegasus and Gemini's president believed Gemini could not survive without CDN's continuing involvement. Gemini lost more money than forecast in 1990 and 1991. The management of

Pegasus represented about $30 million per year or 20 percent of Gemini's total revenues. Gemini employed 700, of which 400 were in Western Canada. CDN predicted a loss of 140 jobs with the removal of Pegasus from the partnership and a loss in income to Gemini of about $2 million per annum. Gemini had 65 percent of the Canadian travel agency CRS market and AMR, through its Sabre Travel Information Network division, had about 35 percent of the market. CDN and AMR expected Sabre to gain fewer than 10 percentage points of market share if PWA moved over to Sabre.

A key element of both the survival of PWA and a potential merger with AMR was third-party maintenance work. By merging with AMR, PWA could specialize in such maintenance work and there was significant potential to expand third-party contract work in the United States and Asia. In fact, earlier in 1992, because of its competitiveness in terms of cost and quality, PWA was successful in obtaining a $24 million (US), five-year US Air Force contract at the expense of GE. More of this work would reduce the cost of PWA's maintenance operation (estimated to be $265 million in 1992), improve efficiency and make its B.C. operations more competitive with US rivals. The airline's maintenance and engineering division had about 2000 workers at the Richmond, B.C. headquarters and the merger talks between PWA and AMR did not include moving this division to the United States. These jobs were regarded as "prized, high-skill jobs that the provincial NDP government desperately wants to protect." It was also observed that AMR had a new maintenance facility in Texas and might eventually want to shift PWA's maintenance needs to this new facility. Nevertheless, a deal with AMR was seen as ensuring a greater number of jobs overall compared to a deal with AC. AMR had the continent's largest fleet of about 600 planes thereby offering the most options, including specialization in maintaining certain aircraft types. In contrast, AC's fleet was largely incompatible with the PWA fleet.

During the first week of July, American specified four conditions before it would agree to close the deal with PWA: (*i*) PWA was to raise an additional $195 million in equity to help survive the long process of government approval required to complete the deal (acquisition of a 25 percent stake in PWA by AMR would have to be screened by the Bureau of Competition Policy); (*ii*) PWA would transfer to the SABRE system as soon as possible; (*iii*) certain loan covenants would be renegotiated with PWA's banks in Europe, Japan and Canada; (*iv*) four-year contracts would be signed with PWA's unions, including no-strike clauses and wage freezes.

THE JULY 15 BOARD MEETING

At the board meeting on July 15, PWA had expected to ratify the strategic alliance with AMR but with AMR's closing conditions more time was clearly needed. However, the company's financial condition was deteriorating rapidly. At the July 15 board meeting, directors learned that PWA had no more than $80 million cash in hand — about $150 million less than AMR had been told. Moreover, about half the cash was earmarked for the directors' liability trust fund. Some directors were reportedly distraught with the news about the company's financial situation and asked about the company's liability insurance. The directors' concerns were exacerbated by the news that the directors of Westar Mining, which was in bankruptcy protection, had resigned over concerns that they could be personally liable for claims from company employees.

The directors of PWA were justifiably concerned about their exposure since directors of Canadian companies could be held personally liable for their company's obligations if it should fail. Such obligations could include unpaid goods and services tax (GST), unpaid Canadian pension plan and unemployment insurance contributions, and under the employment standards legislation in most provinces, they could be liable for wages, vacation, and severance pay. By some estimates, there were more than 100 federal and provincial statutes that imposed liability on directors. Directors could also be held legally accountable for business decisions made to escape their liability. One lawyer noted:

> Every year, there's been another layer of liabilities added ... flowing through to individuals ... so that it's almost prohibitive to be a director. They can wipe out everything you've worked for all your life. A person has to really be in the business to make it worthwhile. You can't get outside directors unless the company is truly blue chip. The risks aren't worth it. People are fleeing from directorships.[4]

Even resignations did not necessarily eliminate director liability. Legislation such as the GST Act could hold directors liable even after they resigned.

On July 18, the PWA board learned that the company's liability insurance coverage was only $10 million — a fraction of their potential $105 million liability. Immediately, Ronald Southern received a mandate from the board to seek assistance from federal and provincial governments. Southern was described as "the wealthiest member of PWA's board and one of the West's most influential business leaders (who) stood to lose the most if claims were made on the directors' personal fortunes."[5] Southern was also described as having very high credibility. As one industry source put it — "If Ron Southern believes this company is nearly out of business, then they are nearly out of business."[6] Along with two other directors, Southern met with Deputy Prime Minister Donald Mazankowski, "who became so alarmed by the spectre of a PWA failure — including stranded passengers, screaming shareholders and directors on the hook — that he made a 10 p.m. phone call to Mr. Mulroney."[7]

On July 21, Southern and two other directors, including Eyton, met with senior representatives from four different governments: federal deputy ministers of finance and transportation, B.C. finance minister and his deputy, the head of the B.C. Trade Development Corp., the Alberta treasurer and his deputy, and Ontario's deputy ministers of the ministry of treasury and economics, and industry. The meeting was described as follows:

> It was Mr. Southern's show. The meeting was held in the boardroom of one of his companies and he did most of the talking, describing a corporate disaster in the making. Mr. Eyton would have tempered Mr. Southern's remarks if he had the chance, but he wasn't in on the entire meeting. He was brought in only to answer specific questions. By this time, some directors were suggesting the company could fail as early as July 25 ...[8]

> Mr. Southern spoke frankly. He told the government officials that PWA was close to completing its deal with American but needed $150 million in loan guarantees for which it was willing to put up collateral, largely real estate. The company was bleeding badly from a fare war initiated by Air Canada and needed to buy time to complete several conditions laid down by American before the deal could close. Moreover, the company needed a government guarantee for a proposed $195-million share issue. Investment dealers thought the issue would fly with investors but balked at a delay that could last six months while the deal was scrutinized by the National Transportation Agency....Directors were particularly worried about their personal

liabilities if the company should fail. Mr. Southern told the meeting they had already resigned from the boards of PWA subsidiaries, including Canadian Airlines, to escape possible claims for wages, severance and vacation pay, as well as for government remittances such as the goods and services tax.[9]

At the meeting, PWA asked for $150 million in loan guarantees and government share guarantees of $50 million each from B.C., Alberta, and Ontario, and $65 million from the federal government, totalling $195 million. The government's role would be to pick up any stock which could not be sold. In making this request PWA argued that PWA's employees generated $200 million in income taxes each year and another $500 million in other kinds of taxes. It was observed that such an argument implied that PWA employees could all become unemployed which was highly unlikely given that 70 percent of the traffic would still be there.

Within a day, all four governments responded that they would not provide the requested financial support and suggested that PWA examine all their options, including a merger with AC. The provinces also replied that Ottawa should handle the problem since the airline's plight could be traced to the federal government's deregulation of the airline industry. It was also reported that the Ontario government decided against the loan and share guarantees because it feared that the proposed alliance with AMR would eventually force AC to seek a similar deal with a US carrier. In that event, Canada would have two national carriers that would be junior partners of US airlines and if those carriers gained a high degree of influence over their Canadian affiliates they might shift operations out of Canadian cities to the United States.

The Deputy Minister of Finance, Fred Gorbet, responded that Ottawa's involvement would be "limited to a previously negotiated purchase from PWA (by the Defence Department) of three A-310 passenger jets for $150 million and a vague promise to improve the conditions under which PWA and AC competed."[10] The subsequent events were reported as follows:

> Mr. Southern reiterated (to Gorbet) that the outlook for PWA was desperate. The only remaining options, he said, were bankruptcy or some kind of government help in reaching a merger with Air Canada. Mr. Mazankowski had apparently been hearing the same message. On July 23, he detailed PWA's troubles — as outlined to him by Mr. Southern — to Mr. Mulroney over lunch. They discussed the urgency of rethinking the nation's air policy and the effects of deregulation. At the same time they were aware that Air Canada had been rejected once before in a merger attempt with PWA. Air Canada needed to know that it was not merely the bait in a PWA game to draw American into an eleventh hour agreement. Simple enough, it seemed. With a little Ottawa leverage, the two could be brought to the altar and everyone would be happy.

> The task fell to Glen Shortliffe, Clerk of the Privy Council. A few hours later, at 5:05 p.m., Ottawa time, he called Mr. Eyton and delivered the government's message: It would purchase the A-310s, but only if PWA halted talks with American and began merger discussions with Air Canada ...[11] Then rather abruptly, he told Mr. Eyton: "There's no time like the present to start these talks. Mr. Shortliffe said Air Canada chairman, Claude Taylor, was waiting in his anteroom and pressed Mr. Eyton to speak to him then and there. Mr. Eyton would not...[12]

Eyton's reaction to Shortliffe's call was described as follows:

Mr. Eyton was flabbergasted. He did not believe merger was the only option available, and he was stunned to learn the government was interfering in a private business transaction. He didn't understand that most of the government's thinking was a product of Mr. Southern's doomsday scenario...[13]

At their July 25 meeting, the board decided to break off talks with AMR and resume its negotiations with AC. It was clear that without government financial support, PWA could not meet AMR's closing conditions.

ATTEMPTING TO STRIKE A DEAL WITH AIR CANADA

On July 27, PWA publicly announced it had broken off talks with AMR and would resume its negotiations with AC. In heavy trading, PWA shares lost nearly 25 percent of their value. There were reports of immediate shock and opposition to a PWA-AC merger from the unions of both airlines. Further there was deep anti-AC sentiments among PWA employees who adopted an unofficial slogan — "Better dead than red" — a reference to AC's colour. One later report explained the feelings as follows:

> The perception, at least among many Canadian Airlines employees and industry analysts, is that Canadian is the much more entrepreneurial carrier and that Air Canada, with its history as a Crown corporation, is much more bureaucratic. Many Canadian employees are furious over what they believe to be the government's preferential treatment of Air Canada. As the sources of their rancor, they cite massive debt write-offs when Air Canada was privatized in 1988, and less than even-handed distribution of lucrative international routes... "My work performance will go down if I'm made to work with people who don't care about their jobs as much" said one Canadian ramp worker who made it clear that he doesn't believe Air Canada employees measure up to their Canadian counterparts. He cited the unloading of baggage from planes as an example. "When we unload an aircraft, we use three-person crews. Air Canada uses anywhere from six to 10 people for one aircraft, or more if it's a 747... There are more people to do one person's job, which is typical of most Crown corporations."[14]

In fact it was well known in the industry that AC had been slow to reduce its costs following privatization.

On July 30, the front page headline of *The Globe and Mail* read: "Cabinet killed airline deal." The events of the previous weeks were now made public. In particular, the article reported that the federal government was "instrumental in scotching Canadian's planned alliance with American and with persuading it to restart talks with Air Canada."[15] The phone call by Shortliffe to PWA was also reported ("Ottawa would not buy the planes unless they broke off talks with AMR and reopened negotiations with Air Canada"). The article noted that, "a merger with Air Canada is expected to result in at least 10 000 lay-offs, whereas the deal with American, according to industry sources, would have meant fewer than 2000 job losses."[16]

The July 30 article "touched off a storm" among politicians in Ottawa. Opposition critics demanded to know if government interfered with the crossborder deal for political purposes saying that a merger of PWA and AC would likely protect jobs in Quebec at the expense of several thousand jobs in Ontario and Western Canada. It was noted that "the move was seen as proof of the federal government's anti-West, pro-Quebec bias." One opposition critic noted that Defence Minister Marcel Masse, who has been widely criticized for favouring Quebec in this defence-procurement decisions, might be "shaping airline policy ... through the back door!" The Transport Minister Jean Corbeil denied that Ottawa had interfered to influence the fate of PWA noting "the government assumed its role of giving its best advice to people that come to it." Nevertheless, there was speculation that the federal government had been influenced by public opinion polls indicating widespread opposition to a US airline taking over one of the two national airlines. One lobbyist noted: "Canadians want to see a Canadian flag on the tail of their airplanes."

While the federal government was being accused of supporting a deal which would move jobs away from Western Canada, other observers had a different assessment. For example, Tae Oum of the University of British Columbia and two other academics from Queen's University and the University of Victoria found in a study commissioned by AC that Vancouver would probably lose some jobs within six months of a merger between PWA and AC, but more jobs would have been lost in the long term if the deal with AMR had gone ahead. PWA was one of the largest private sector employers in Vancouver with jobs in the following categories: 1150 flight attendants and 650 pilots operating out of Vancouver, 1500 maintenance workers overhauling wide-body planes, 850 employees at airport counters and on ramps, 250 in reservations and 750 in accounting. Overall about 6700 PWA employees lived in B.C. and 2500 were based in Alberta with three-quarters in Calgary.

The study by Oum et al. concluded that 35 000 jobs would be lost and economic output would increase by $5.8 billion if AC and PWA each became controlled by a US mega-carrier but only 1300 jobs would be lost and economic output would increase by $10.4 billion if AC and PWA merged and formed a strong alliance with US Air. The study concluded that a combination of PWA and AMR was preferable in terms of consumer welfare given the likely lower prices in the short term on domestic and international flights. Overall, the study concluded that an AC-PWA merger combined with a strong alliance with US Air was "clearly better" because of the following longer term benefits: (*i*) positioning the Canadian carrier in preparation for globalization of the industry and the eventual North American open skies regime, (*ii*) relatively higher economic output in Canada, (*iii*) relatively higher employment in Canada, and (*iv*) increased availability to Canadian consumers of nonstop and direct flights to more international destinations.[17] This study was sent by AC to all federal and provincial politicians in Canada and to the mayors of all cities into which Air Canada flew.

Observers of a possible PWA-AC merger were not only predicting job losses but other consequences such as an end to discounted tickets, fewer flight departures and the deterioration of frequent-flier programs. It was noted that the airline was likely to award points only for international destinations, since there would be no competitive reason to offer such incentives at home. It was also suggested that air terminals across Canada could shut down as the number of aircraft they serviced declined and passenger volumes dropped. It was also predicted that travel agents could expect a 20 percent drop in commission rates since the monopoly could dictate terms. Finally, a group representing about 500 pilots working for Transport Canada suggested that safety could be compromised by a merger because of the following:

> The main concern comes from integrating two separate groups accustomed to different operation procedures, with one group having to adjust the procedures of the other. It's very difficult for anyone, pilots included, to adopt new procedures without ever reverting to old habits, especially in an emergency. The probability of a pilot reverting to old procedures is very high and the consequences could be very serious.[18]

Despite these reported concerns about safety, it was observed that PWA was itself the product of an amalgamation of a number of airlines and safety had not proven to be a problem.

In early August, the federal Transport minister Jean Corbeil stated the following publicly:

- While the federal government favours a merger of PWA's and AC's international routes, it would prefer to see PWA remain in business to provide competition on domestic routes, possibly with the help of a US partner. "I would encourage them (Canadian) to seek an alliance with American. It would result in better fares and improved service for Canadians. Our major concern is domestic service. We're not concerned for international travel and this is why only the domestic aspect of the service will have to be subject to examination by the competition bureau." (A merger of AC and PWA would lead to a single airline carrying 96 percent of the domestic scheduled airline passengers in the top 205 city pair markets in Canada and accounting for 90 percent of all domestic scheduled traffic. Charter services carried 3.7 percent of all domestic passengers in 1991 and there were many restrictions with charter services such as advance purchase or non-refundability making charter services a poor substitute for scheduled services for most business travel. Nevertheless, a merger of PWA and AC presented opportunities to charter companies such as Nationair or Canada 3000. First, there was likely to be less competition in the charter market as happened when PWA acquired Wardair. Before the acquisition, PWA and Wardair had about 49 percent of the charter market, and after the acquisition, their market share dropped to 33 percent. Second, the charter carriers could enter the scheduled service segment of the market. Overall, the president of AC argued that with a merger of PWA and AC domestic fares would be kept in line by competition from charter companies, regional airlines, including the regional partners of AC and PWA which might be spun off to provide some competition, and new carriers jumping into the best markets, such as the Ottawa-Montreal-Toronto triangle. In fact, there were plans to launch at least three new airlines but those associated with these plans apparently wanted some assurances from government that a merged AC-PWA will not be allowed to simply crush any new competitors.)

- To encourage a PWA-AMR alliance, the government might amend the legislation restricting foreign ownership to 25 percent.[19]

- The federal government will not provide any financing to assist a merger of PWA and AC. However, the government is helping PWA by accelerating plans to buy three aircraft for about $150 million for the defence department.

- In regard to job losses associated with a merger, existing government programs for worker adjustment and retraining will be available to laid off employees. No special adjustment assistance will be provided by the federal government.

- "There are many ways to ensure the Canadian travelling public — the domestic market — will have full competition." (Corbeil did not want to speculate whether one of the government's options is the possibility of allowing foreign air carriers to operate more extensively in the Canadian market.[20] In fact, during the bilateral negotiations between Canada and the United States, the issue of cabotage, i.e., allowing US airlines to carry passengers between Canadian cities as a way of encouraging more domestic competition was dropped off the table at the first negotiating session and the Canadian government did not intend to bring it back for future negotiations.)

A spokesman for the Reform Party reacted to the government's position by noting the following:

- The governing Conservatives are manipulating the merger talks between PWA and AC by first refusing loan guarantees that forced PWA into the talks, and then insisting the headquarters for a national airline remain in Montreal. (The Transport Minister had stated that AC must keep its head office in Montreal under legislation that privatized the former Crown corporation.) "What if Montreal is not the best city from a business point of view? They shouldn't be bound by that."

- The federal government is in a conflict of interest. "On one hand we have a government that is supposedly committed to deregulation and privatization. On the other hand, we have evidence that the federal government intervened to prevent one of the airlines from taking steps that might have enabled it to survive as an independent carrier."

- The federal government's role should be strictly neutral and not be manipulating the merger talks to influence the business decisions of private corporations and to bring about any particular outcome. 'The government's chief concern should be protecting the interests of the Canadian travelling public." Ottawa should be telling Canadians how it intends to keep air fares reasonable and encourage competition should the airlines merge.[21]

At its August 6 board meeting, PWA directors considered an offer from AC which involved the following elements: (*i*) a share swap giving AC shareholders 65 percent of the merged company, (*ii*) equal board representation in the new firm, (*iii*) a commitment to maintain significant operations and employment in Western and Eastern Canada, (*iv*) creation of an equally-balanced Merger Committee to recommend the appointment of senior management, selection of new board members, a corporate name and headquarters location. A number of uncertainties needed to be resolved before a deal could be struck:

i.   Determining the headquarters location was complicated by the fact that the Air Canada Act required the airline to be headquartered in Montreal and required maintenance facilities to be maintained in Winnipeg, Mississauga, and Montreal and Alberta's PWA Act required that the company's headquarters be maintained in that province.

ii.   Financing the new company would be challenging given the large debts involved. The new company would be saddled with $4.5 billion in debt and another $3 billion in long-term aircraft leasing obligations. Against this, it would have only $500 million in equity, leaving it with a debt to equity ratio of 15:1 compared to a ratio of 3:1 for AMR. Analysts concluded the new company would need to raise about $1 billion of new capital to be competitive but it was not clear where this capital would come from, especially in the face of the significant losses both airlines were experiencing (Exhibit 2). One analyst expected the two airlines to lose nearly $600 million between them in 1992 and another $500 million in their first year as a combined entity and not make money until 1995. One report noted that investors would be "largely unwilling" to invest in a merged company until the following occurred: (a) a federal-provincial fund was created to minimize the new airline's severance payments to the estimated 10 000 employees expected to lose their jobs; severance costs could exceed $100 million; (b) the federal government agreed not to provide foreign airlines with "too quick and too brutal access to the Canadian market;"

(c) a European or Asian airline invested several hundred million dollars in exchange for 10 to 15% of the equity in the new company.[22]

Observers noted that AC was bargaining from both strength and weakness in its dealings with PWA. It was seen as being able to make such a one-sided proposal — more like a takeover of PWA — because of PWA's precarious financial position. Furthermore AC was seen as enjoying political support in Ottawa for a merger; the AC offer referred to the "federal government's policy preference for a made-in-Canada solution." Finally, AC was able to generate more cash than PWA through the sale of assets and draining down existing lines of credit. The company had about $150 million in cash and believed it could generate another $450 million through the sale and leaseback of planes and by other means. Because of its financial position, AC was better able to withstand the costly price war dragging down both airlines. In fact, this price war was of such concern to PWA employees that they considered filing a complaint with the Bureau of Competition Policy alleging that AC had adopted predatory pricing which was a criminal offence punishable by jail sentences of up to two years. In addition, PWA employees were dismayed with reports that AC had increased its inventory of seats by at least 10 percent. In fact, from 1989 to 1992 both AC and PWA had increased domestic capacity by about 10 percent and other smaller Canadian carriers such as Nationair and Canada 3000 tripled their domestic capacity. It was estimated by one analyst that there was 25 to 30 percent overcapacity in the domestic industry.

AC was also seen as weaker than PWA in some respects. PWA was seen as more cost effective, spending about 15 percent less than AC for each passenger mile. PWA also appeared to be gaining on AC in the marketplace and "controlled the most coveted asset of either airline — access to the fast-growing Pacific Rim region, particularly Japan." AC was also suffering greater losses — $1.8 million a day compared to 800 000 a day for PWA.

On August 6, the PWA board unanimously rejected AC's offer "largely because they were unhappy with the minority ownership that PWA shareholders would have in the merged airline." PWA asked for a second offer.

In the meantime there were several new developments that the PWA board needed to consider. First, Alberta's Treasurer Dick Johnston suggested that the Alberta government might move to block the sale of PWA shares if its proposed merger with AC went against Alberta's interests. Under legislation amended in 1991, no person other than the province of Alberta could own directly, indirectly or beneficially more than 10 percent of the shares of PWA. Prior to 1991, the limit was four percent. Johnston said that the government could enforce the legislation if, for example, attempts were made to remove completely from Alberta the headquarters functions of the newly merged entity. PWA had taken the position that the 10 percent rule did not apply because the merger would apply to CDN, rather than its parent company. However, observers noted that even in that case, a merger could contravene the spirit of the legislation since CDN accounted for so much of PWA's operating revenues. Nevertheless, the Alberta Treasurer also suggested the Alberta government would participate in a financial rescue package if it received strong support from other interested parties, but it would not take the lead.

A second development involved the employees. A retired PWA vice president, Sidney Fattedad, led a group seeking the commitment of Canadian employees to offer cash, loans, or foregone wages to invest in an employee share purchase which would raise a portion of the $195 million additional equity required to conclude negotiations with AMR. It had been reported that AMR was "extremely surprised and angered by the breakdown of its negotiations with Canadian" and was still interested in a deal with PWA. Fattedad suggested that an employee investment would be used to leverage additional funds from investment bankers. A representative of the Calgary Economic Development Authority supported the Fattedad initiative noting that the loss of PWA's Calgary head office and the attendant jobs, not to mention the loss of domestic air links to smaller centres, would devastate Calgary. B.C. premier Michael Harcourt also supported the Fattedad plan, by writing the federal Transport minister requesting Ottawa withhold approval of any merger "until the Canadian employee groups are given every opportunity to participate in a deal to maintain the integrity of their airline."

It was reported on August 12 that five of the six unions at PWA agreed to develop the idea of a payroll deduction scheme to block the proposed merger. One union leader noted: "We hopefully can come up with between $150 and $200 million, and if all the promises from the Alberta government are true, that it will match that dollar for dollar, that will put us back at the table." However, Alberta premier Getty responded that there was no such funding arrangement struck with the employees. Furthermore, the leader of the CAW, the union representing 3 200 Canadian ticket agents and strongly opposing the plan noted that "the employees are not responsible for the massive billion dollar debt" and "wage cuts would not make a dent in the debt that is bogging down both airlines." Furthermore, the CAW did not believe the data existed to determine which deal — either a merger with AC or alliance with AMR — preserved more jobs at PWA. The previous fall, most of the unions representing airline employees had rejected a request by PWA that they forego scheduled wage increases. One explanation given for the rejection was that it was not believed that concessions would save jobs. Union members were also aware of the history of Eastern Airlines once the largest US carrier, which ultimately folded despite a series of employee wage cuts.

RESPONDING TO THE PRIME MINISTER

A third development confronting the PWA board was a lashing out by Prime Minister Mulroney concerning the silence of the board about the government's role in the affairs of PWA. Over a two day period, as reported in the media in August 13 and 14, the Prime Minister "lashed out at PWA Corp. and the media for not clearing up what he called 'the falsehoods' being told about the government's role in merger talks between PWA and Air Canada." The Prime Minister blamed the media for leaving the impression that Ottawa was favouring Quebec over the West by pushing for a merger of Montreal-based AC with Calgary-based PWA. Mulroney noted:

> To have people in Alberta encouraged to believe that we would take an action to favour Quebec as opposed to Alberta in this thing is damaging in the extreme. It's false and it's cheap as hell...
>
> This was a bloody outrage when they (PWA) came knocking at our door asking for help. Rather than let the market decide, that Saturday (July 25) we were told they were going under (causing) extraordinary damage with 1 000 000 tickets having been sold and $200 million worth of bookings in the middle of the summer sitting in the computer....The PWA board of directors expressed serious concerns about the financial viability of the corporation and their own personal liability as directors, which was explained to us to be in excess of $100 million...we intervened at the request of the board of directors to help PWA. And now, by God in Alberta we've got people suggesting that we intervened to help Air Canada. We got involved

specifically at the request of the board of directors of PWA. I'm waiting for some of the directors of PWA to stand up in Alberta and indicate exactly what happened.[23]

The media coverage[24] of the Prime Minister's comments made the following points:

- Mulroney clearly wanted to make a statement on the airline issue. "He was anxious to get the line out," a government official said. "This has been bothering us." The issue had stirred up regional tensions and angered Mulroney's influential Alberta caucus which issued a statement opposing any merger of the two airlines. Western Canadian MPs were deluged with angry calls from Canadian employees convinced that Ottawa was favouring Air Canada over Canadian. The chairman of the Alberta caucus noted: "This is the most volatile issue ... it goes to the heart of Western Canadian pride and aspirations."

- "While many of the points made by the Prime Minister were consistent with previously published reports, he made no mention of the assertion of certain sources that Ottawa pushed Canadian to the table with Air Canada by making a Department of Defence purchase of three airplanes from Canadian contingent on (Canadian) dropping out of talks with American and entering talks with Air Canada."

- Mulroney said that Ottawa doesn't favour "any specific outcome" other than the fact it wants a private-sector solution. But he also noted he was "heartened that other options are being developed, including the employee initiative." Another government official further noted: "We're not opposed to an American Airlines-Canadian linkup. The law is clear that they can buy 25 percent." But he indicated that "A merger has been seen in bureaucratic circles (the civil service) as the way to go."

- Mulroney referred to Ottawa's "help" for PWA but it is unclear exactly how Ottawa has aided the airline given that it turned down requests for loan guarantees.

- The consumer and corporate affairs and government operations committee scheduled televised hearings on the proposed merger for August 14, with officials from the airlines slated to be the first witnesses.

THE NEXT STEP

Rhys Eyton had to decide if he would respond to the Prime Minister's call to "indicate exactly what happened." One of the members of his board, Ron Southern had just sent a handwritten fax to the Prime Minister from New Zealand where Southern was on unrelated business. Southern indicated in the fax that the federal government was simply trying to help and had not killed PWA's deal with AMR as suggested in the media. However, Eyton was contemplating sending his own letter to the Prime Minister informing the Prime Minister that Southern's version of events was inaccurate.

EXHIBIT 1   Board of Directors: PWA Corporation and Canadian Airlines International

* R.T. Eyton, Chairman, President and CEO, PWA Corporation; Chairman and CEO, Canadian Airlines International Ltd.

* A.F. Campney, President, Vanley Agencies

Senator C. Castonguay, Chairman of the Board, Laurentian Bank of Canada

K.J. Jenkins, President, Canadian Airlines International Ltd.

The Hon. Peter Lougheed, P.C., C.C., Q.C., Senior Partner, Bennett Jones Verchere

A.V. Mauro, C.M., Q.C., Chairman, President and CEO, The Investors Group Inc.

* R.R. McDaniel, Chairman, McDaniel and Associates Consultants Ltd., Chairman, Canadian Regional Airlines Ltd.

H.C. Pinder, Jr., President, Goal Management Group

* J.H. Robertson, President, Mack Travel Ltd.

M. Sigler, President and CEO, Canadian Regional Airlines Ltd.

* R.D. Southern, C.M., M.B.E., Chairman, President and CEO, ATCO Ltd.

* H.R. Steele, President and CEO, Newfoundland Capital Corporation Ltd.

B.C. Steers, Former Canadian Ambassador to Japan; Consultant and Lecturer, U.W.O. School of Business

W.W. Stinson, Chairman and CEO, Canadian Pacific Ltd.

A.S. Wakim, Q.C., Associate, Weir and Foulds

* M.W. Ward, Retired (former Chairman and CEO, Wardair Inc.)

* Member, Executive Committee

EXHIBIT 2   Positions of AC and PWA

	AC	PWA
Revenue, 1991	$3.6 billion	$2.9 billion
Revenue, first 6 months of 1992	$1.7 billion	$1.4 billion
Loss, 1991	$218 million	$162 million
Loss, first 6 months of 1992	$293 million	$108 million
Fleet size (aircraft in service)	102	88
Passenger km, 1991	20.3 billion	18.8 billion
World rank by revenues (1991)	19	23
Yield per revenue passenger mile	17.3 cents	16.9 cents
Employees (1992)	20 600	16 350
Load factor (1991)	68.4%	64.1%
International Routes	United States, Caribbean, part of Europe, Middle East, Africa, Venezuela, part of Asia.	The Pacific (to Japan, India), part of Europe, Mexico, Central and South America (except Venezuela), Australia, New Zealand, part of Asia.

NOTES

This case was prepared from public sources by Mark C. Baetz as a basis for class discussion rather than to illustrate either effective or ineffective handling of an administrative situation. Copyright © Mark C. Baetz, 1992. Revised 03/93. Distributed through the LAURIER INSTITUTE, School of Business and Economics, Wilfrid Laurier University, Waterloo, Ontario, Canada, N2L 3C5. No part of this case may be reproduced, stored in a retrieval system, or transmitted in any form or by any means — electronic, mechanical, photocopying, recording, or otherwise — without the permission of The Laurier Institute, School of Business and Economics, Wilfrid Laurier University.

1. PWA Corporation, *1991 Annual Report*, 5.

2. Oum Tae, A.J. Taylor, and Anming Zhang, *Canadian Aviation at the Crossroads: Policy Choices for the New Global Environment*. (Faculty of Commerce and Business Administration, University of British Columbia, 1992.)

3. *The Globe and Mail*, September 5, 1992, 4.

4. *The Globe and Mail*, August 15, 1992, B3.

5. *The Globe and Mail*, September 5, 1992, 4.

6. *ibid*.

7. *ibid*.

8. *ibid*.

9. *The Globe and Mail*, August 24, 1992, A9.

10. *The Globe and Mail*, September 5, 1992, 4.

11. *ibid*.

12. *The Globe and Mail*, August 24, 1992, A9.

13. *The Globe and Mail*, September 5, 1992, 4.

14. *The Globe and Mail*, October 13, 1992, B17.

15. *The Globe and Mail*, July 30, 1992, 9.

16. *ibid*.

17. Oum, et al., *op. cit*.

18. *The Globe and Mail*, July 30, B1.

19. *Kitchener-Waterloo Record*, August 5, 1992, B7.

20. *Financial Post*, August 3, 1992, 4.

21. *Kitchener-Waterloo Record*, August 5, 1992, B7.

22. *Financial Post*, August 3, 1992, 4.

23. *The Globe and Mail*, August 13, 1992, B14.

24. *The Globe and Mail*, August 13 and August 14, 1992.

THE CITY OF CAMBRIDGE AND ADULT VIDEOS

In May 1994, the Administration Committee of the Council for the City of Cambridge, Ontario had to decide what to do about a recently-enacted by-law regulating the sale, rental and exchange of adult videos. This case will review the background to the by-law.

REGULATIONS GOVERNING ADULT VIDEOS

The adult entertainment industry involved several different media forms including print (e.g., books, magazines, playing cards) audio/visual (e.g., cassette and videotape), sexually-created goods (e.g., sex aids), services (e.g., adult entertainers) and computers (e.g., software and bulletin board exchanges). The various media forms were controlled and regulated by three levels of government: federal, provincial, and municipal.

1. Federal Jurisdiction

At the federal level, Section 163 of the Criminal Code dealt with "offenses tending to corrupt morals" which made it illegal to circulate "obscene" material. A publication was deemed to be "obscene" if a dominant characteristic of it was the "undue exploitation of sex, or of sex and any one or more of...crime, horror, cruelty and violence." Section 163 was criticized because the test used by the police, prosecutors, judges, and juries as to whether material unduly exploited sex was that of "community standards" which varied across Canada. The federal Parliament had tried over a number of years but failed to replace the definition of obscenity with one more explicit. For example, one proposal in 1987 containing a list of specific acts deemed unacceptable was severely criticized for being too restrictive. Furthermore, it was felt such a list could not keep up with changing public attitudes.

One of the issues raised by Section 163 was that it potentially infringed on the freedom of expression in the Charter of Rights and Freedoms. A landmark Supreme Court decision in 1992, sometimes referred to as the "Butler decision," acknowledged that Section 163 infringed the Charter but that its objective of avoiding harm to society warranted a restriction on individual freedom. The decision was significant for providing a new definition of obscenity based on the harm any material could cause. Parts of the decision noted the following:

> The portrayal of sex coupled with violence will almost always constitute the undue exploitation of sex. Explicit sex which is degrading or dehumanizing may be undue if the risk of harm is substantial. Explicit sex that is not violent and neither degrading nor dehumanizing is generally tolerated in our society and will not qualify as the undue exploitation of sex unless it employs children in its production. While a direct link between obscenity and harm to society may be difficult, if not impossible to establish, it is reasonable to presume that exposures to images bears a causal relationship to changes in attitudes and beliefs.

As a result of the decision, the court ordered a new trial for Donald Butler, the owner of a Winnipeg adult video store who had appealed more than 200 obscenity charges leading to the Supreme Court decision.

The 1992 Supreme Court ruling played a role in future court rulings. For example, in late 1993 an Ontario Court of Appeal ruling concluded that explicit non-violent sex scenes between consenting adults cannot automatically be considered obscene. With this ruling, a number of video operators were acquitted of obscenity charges.

2. Provincial Jurisdiction

At the provincial level, legislation enabled film review boards to classify and approve films publicly exhibited and distributed in each province. In Ontario, the Ontario Film Review Board (OFRB) was given the mandate of classifying films into one of four categories under the Theatres Act enforced by the Ontario Ministry of Consumer and Commercial Relations. The four categories were: (*i*) family, (*ii*) parental guidance advised, (*iii*) adult accompaniment required under age 14, and (*iv*) admittance restricted to persons 18 years of age or over. Using standards set out in the regulations of the Theatres Act, board members could choose not to approve a film in its entirety, or require certain eliminations before the film was approved for distribution. The OFRB classifications were expected to reflect societal attitudes and community standards throughout the Province of Ontario. As a result, OFRB was expected to change its classification standards with changes in community standards.

A major change in the standards occurred in 1990. The process for the change was described as follows:

> The Ontario board has long had a reputation for being one of the most conservative in the country. In the latter half of the 1980s, the board...would only allow soft-core films containing simulated sexual activity. Everywhere else in the country, provincial film boards were lowering or eliminating restrictions to allow people to watch sexually explicit films. Robert Payne, a freelance Toronto journalist and then chairman of the Ontario board, decided in the fall of 1990 that the province's film classification system needed an overhaul.

Payne organized a weekend retreat for board members, and after two days of debate and discussion, they decided that Ontario was ready for sexually explicit films. "Each member was asked what they could not possibly abide," recalls Payne. "Explicitness was not a problem. Some people in Ontario felt this was a rather revolutionary move, but in the broader context of Canadian society, we were more or less catching up."[1]

The change in 1990 had a major impact by creating a "bonanza" for distributors and retailers of hard-core pornography. The president of one of the country's largest distribution companies noted: "There was a pipeline that had to be filled."[2] The impact in the video stores in Ontario was quite dramatic. One store owner noted: "Overnight my stock of 3000 adult movies was worthless. My customers wanted the more explicit material."

In 1993, the OFRB decided to change the classification rules again, (e.g., bondage and the insertion of foreign (non-injurious) objects were to be permitted if not in a context that is verbally or physically coercive and does not cause physical harm.) There was significant opposition to the new rules leading the OFRB to review its decision. The media covered the issue as follows:

After receiving hundreds of letters of protest, the (OFRB) postponed putting into place the May 6 decision to loosen its sex film guidelines. Instead the board decided to review not only sex film rules, but all its film guidelines. "It's very tumultuous and it's a very emotional issue," board chairperson Dorothy Christian said in an interview. "They (board members) weren't comfortable with rescinding (the May 6 sex film rules) in their totality"...(board members) "want to deal with the violence issue (by reviewing existing guidelines on permissible depictions of violence) and take a stand on violence"...but she wondered if the public is also aware of the role that computers and "other available technology" play in passing on violent visual images. "Violence can be portrayed in many forms and levels," Christian said. "It's a far deeper issue than the...little part the OFRB plays."[3]

Christian's comments were described in one editorial as "disturbingly defensive and defeatist...about the board's role in dealing with unacceptable violent images."[4] In any case, the OFRB was encouraged to hold public hearings as part of its process for reviewing the film guidelines. To this suggestion, Christian noted:

Consultation with the community now happens when groups visit the panel monthly to see how films are classified....As well, groups address the board and board members are encouraged to go out in the community and speak to citizens....The province has tried to address the community standards issue by appointing 30 community members to the board from across Ontario...."I don't know whether or not it's meeting community standards or people's expectations of community standards."[5]

One group which decided to make a presentation to the OFRB about its guidelines was the Coalition for the Safety of Our Daughters which was particularly alarmed at the growing body of evidence linking the increased distribution of pornography to increases in sexual assaults against women and children.[6] Other individuals or groups made their feelings known through comments to the media. For example, Waterloo Regional Police Sgt. Bob Gooding, who investigated pornography complaints, noted that if the new OFRB classification (e.g., bondage now permitted) was implemented, "we're certainly going to receive more complaints about it (and) rightfully so (given the Criminal Code)." Gooding further commented: "I don't think that's what this community tolerates....I would be surprised if that is the case."[7] The comments by Gooding reflected the fact that criminal charges under the

Criminal Code could still be laid for circulating a film approved by the OFRB. An interest group, Canadians for Decency, assessed the situation as follows: "Now many approved videos will not be legal. This means more tax money will be spent by the police to investigate approved videos resulting in more expensive court cases. Haven't we been hearing about government cutbacks?"

To add to the possible inconsistency between the implementation of federal and provincial legislation, there was the issue of enforcement. Randy Jorgensen, the president of Adults Only Video (AOV), the largest adult video chain in Canada, complained to the Ministry of Consumer and Commercial Relations and the police that as many as half of Ontario adult film distributors (rivals of AOV) were bypassing the OFRB, knowing there was little enforcement of the law. Jorgensen believed there was only one inspector handling complaints for all of Ontario and he had never heard of any charges being laid. In fact, Det. Sgt. Bob Matthews of Project P, the joint OPP and Metro Toronto anti-pornography police team, said police don't have the mandate to lay charges just because a film was unapproved. Jorgensen contended that bypassing the OFRB meant that thousands of movies were being distributed that were not approved. A spokesperson for the ministry admitted there were not enough investigators and more were needed. Christian, chair of the OFRB agreed that the lack of enforcement was undercutting the OFRB's credibility "almost rendering us meaningless" leading the province to consider a "sticker" system for OFRB-approved films, a move advocated by Jorgensen.

3. Municipal Jurisdiction

Municipalities could use the Municipal Act to pass by-laws regulating certain aspects of stores selling adult videos, e.g., licensing, regulating, classifying and inspecting, but not prohibiting.

DEALING WITH THE REGULATIONS: THE CASE OF ADULT ONLY VIDEOS

After completing high school in a small Saskatchewan town, Randy Jorgensen was involved in a number of businesses including a muffler shop, industrial tools franchise, hotels, and wholesale cars. In 1986, he met a Saskatoon video store owner who was selling his inventory of about 1000 soft-core movies, i.e., cablevision tapes containing simulated, not explicit sex. At the time, many video store owners were moving to the more explicit material because of customer demand. Jorgensen became involved in a partnership which bought these tapes for 50 cents each, with the rationale that even if the contents of the tapes were erased, the blank tapes could be resold for a profit. Jorgensen described the subsequent events as follows:

> Nobody wanted the tapes since they didn't think they could tape over them leaving us with a dead product. So the partnership brainstormed and decided to put the videos out for rent from an exclusive adults store as there hadn't been anything like it in Saskatchewan. We opened the store in a plaza where the landlord was having trouble renting so we got a good deal on the lease.
>
> As soon as we opened, we were told by all the distributors who handled the product and the customers that the cablevision material was not good enough, that we should be offering more explicit material. We then discovered a niche market. While we thought initially we

would get the business up and running and then sell it, we found it was a viable business which could grow. It was an easy business to manage — just leave the staff and manage externally. We took on partners in different cities in the West. It was like franchising, but it was a partnership where we recruited friends and relatives to manage and finance each store. They were very successful. The recession at the time made things easier since landlords and property-owners were not able to pick and choose their tenants.

Jorgensen described some of the keys to the success of the chain as follows:

In order not to offend the public, we discovered we could segregate the store by covering the windows with opaque. It made it a little more acceptable. A lot of the Western mentality is that no one is forcing you and if you don't agree with it that's fine...whether I agree with it or not, I'd sooner have the choice than not have the choice. We created customer confidence by learning how to make customers comfortable to discuss their sex lives in public.

AOV attempted to make the shopping experience as comfortable as possible first by locating the stores in middle-class neighbourhood strip malls with respectable neighbours such as dry cleaners and convenience stores. In addition, the stores were kept clean and well lit, and the company used radio, print and television advertising (see Exhibit 1). Jorgensen noted:

Most people think of adult video stores as sleazy, dark, back alley, run-down operations patronized by dirty old men in trench coats. But image is very important to us. Many of our customers are well-educated people with lots of disposable income. Our stores are designed to make them feel comfortable. Our objective is to make people not feel as though they are doing something wrong.

According to a 1992 customer survey, it was found that couples were the largest part of AOV's market. While 80% of those renting the movies were male, 56% of the customers indicated they watched the movie with a partner.

In Manitoba the first major resistance to corporate expansion of AOV occurred. In 1990, the RCMP seized 8000 movies in AOV stores in Manitoba and then laid a record of 1091 obscenity charges against Jorgensen. If convicted and given maximum fines, Jorgensen faced 1626 years in prison and $3 million in fines. Ultimately the Crown apologized for the police action and withdrew all the charges. Nevertheless, Jorgensen and other adult video store owners were forced to close their stores in Manitoba following a Manitoba Court of Appeal ruling which made sexually explicit videos illegal. (Subsequently, AOV reopened in Manitoba following the 1992 Supreme Court decision.)

AOV moved to Ontario in 1990 when the OFRB classification standards changed. While Jorgensen had been told he would be "put in jail" if he entered Ontario, he hoped that prosecuting attorneys in Ontario would conclude AOV should not be convicted given : (*i*) AOV never handled illegitimate material, only OFRB-approved material, (e.g., no violence and no children involved), (*ii*) AOV did not import any product directly, but bought it from legitimate distributors, and (*iii*) AOV stores were segregated from people under the age of 18. (Signs on the door warned customers that no one under 18 was allowed to enter and AOV memberships were restricted to only those 18 and over.) The strategy and results in Ontario were described as follows:

In less than three years, Jorgensen opened 59 stores across the province, hitting the small and secondary cities before moving on to Metro Toronto and its suburbs. The strategy was simple: get in before city officials could pass laws to keep him out. "Smaller centres can react faster than big cities with by-laws and licensing regulations," said Jorgensen. "I was up and running a year before any by-laws were changed." Several Ontario municipalities, including Mississauga, Burlington, and Hamilton, have since passed stringent by-laws designed to stop any invasion of sex shops — but too late to halt Adults Only.

The police, however, have tried. In April, 1991, police forces in 14 municipalities, acting on instructions from the Ontario Provincial Police anti-pornography unit, raided 22 Adults Only stores across the province and seized 10 tapes from each. Despite the film board's approval of the videos, Jorgensen was convicted on charges of distributing obscene material in Hamilton and Scarborough. He has appealed both decisions. Courts in some other municipalities acquitted him, some police forces dropped the charges, and a few cities are awaiting the outcomes of the appeal before deciding whether to proceed. Jorgensen is also facing a charge in Winnipeg based on a police seizure of nine tapes in June, 1992.

From Jorgensen's perspective, the charges amount to little more than police harassment. "The police don't agree with the film board guidelines," he says. "They wanted enough cases before the courts to get some sort of precedent on obscenity. The governments can't get the police and the film boards to agree on what's obscene and what's not. So they say, 'Let's charge somebody, let the court decide.' It's just an abuse of the system and a waste of the taxpayers' money." Det. StaffSgt. Robert Matthews, director of the Ontario Provincial Police anti-pornography unit, Project P, says that police have laid charges because the courts, rather than film boards, should be the ultimate arbiter of what is — or is not — obscene.[8]

As of 1994 AOV had 86 outlets in five provinces and had about 400 employees. About one-third of these employees were university graduates. The company was contemplating expanding to the Maritimes with a long range goal of a coast-to-coast chain with 100 to 120 outlets. There were also plans to expand the product line to include lingerie and rubber products.

In order to develop and enhance AOV's national image and help connect AOV stores in different regions to a common goal, the following mission statement was developed:

Our mission is to provide excellence in customer service by encouraging the entrepreneurial spirit throughout the organization while displaying our values of fairness, honesty and mutual respect, enabling all stakeholders to achieve continuing growth and success.

SOCIAL IMPACT AND ACCEPTABILITY OF ADULT VIDEOS

There was a wide divergence of view about the social impact of adult videos. Some individuals and groups linked these videos directly to violence against and/or abuse of women and children, and cited various research studies to justify their claims. Robert Payne, who was once chairman of the OFRB, questioned such links as follows:

The increase in rapes and sexual assaults is true but why link them to pornography any more than we would link them to, I suppose, all the perpetrators probably at one time or another drank milk?[9]

Jorgensen explained his position on the social impact of his products as follows:

When I first got into the business, I was concerned about the views of people who were dead set against a business like this. At the time, I had never even seen an adult film; it was something I had never thought about. So I researched it in Saskatoon and found that all the material contained information to support either side — the conclusion seemed to depend on what you wanted to see. I found one individual who did a study of the studies and found it was like making pastry...the end result depended on the ingredients you put in...in other words, the evidence is not conclusive.

A member of one interest group responded to Jorgensen's position as follows:

The evidence may not be overwhelming but there is enough of it to justify concern. The tobacco industry will tell you that the link between smoking and getting cancer is not 100 percent definitive. Not all who smoke get cancer, but enough do to warrant strong anti-smoking laws. Similarly, not all men who watch pornographic films will sexually abuse women and children, but enough will to warrant strict regulations of pornography...(we) would like to see a ban on all sexually explicit material that is not for artistic purposes.[10]

To justify such a ban, points such as the following were made:

- Pornographic films reduce the beauty of sexual intimacy to the level of a spectator sport where there is no love and dignity involved.
- Men become addicted to pornography. It tears lives apart and destroys families.
- Young people are the most frequent consumers of sexually explicit material. (One study found 37 percent of young people between the ages of 12 and 17 watched sexually explicit videos at least once a month. The same study also found that college students displayed an "unbelievable" acceptance of rape myths and violence against women including tolerance for forced sexual intercourse with a woman who is drunk or sexually experienced). Teenagers who view adult videos will grow up with a distorted view of sexuality since the videos are their only form of sex education.

Jorgensen responded to calls for a ban as follows:

A ban would serve only to create a black underground market resulting in no restrictions in the nature of the films distributed. You would see all kinds of violent films. There would also be no restrictions on the age of the films' viewers. Currently, under the Ontario Theatres Act, video retailers are permitted to sell or rent sexually explicit films only to people 18 years of age and older, a regulation that AOV vigorously upholds. AOV store clerks ask for identification if a patron's age is in doubt and furthermore AOV goes beyond the Theatres Act by ensuring employees working in the stores are at least 18 years old. Overall, adult videos should be treated like tobacco and alcohol — beer and wine should not be sold in convenience stores and similarly adult videos should not be distributed in convenience stores and regular video outlets. Often their clerks are high school students who are not even 18 years old, are inexperienced and can let the adult product get into the wrong hands. (It was estimated 90 percent of regular video stores handled adult videos.)

Some regular video owners felt the attention should be focused on violent not sexually explicit videos. One owner noted:

Various churches and individuals have targeted adult videos as a moral evil. The groups have missed the mark. The censorship board (OFRB) has taken the violence out of the adult videos... It's the action/adventure and horror films that show violence against women and the degradation the groups want stamped out. Many of these are rated PG13 which makes them available to anyone over the age of 13 — with parental guidance. We get more complaints about the regular movies than we do about anything else.[11]

The diversity of views about the social impact of adult videos was reflected in reaction to AOV. Jorgensen noted:

> I've had women come in the door or write letters thanking me for saving their marriages. They say — "He's watching movies and he's not out running around anymore." At the same time, I have letters from special interest groups condemning me for destroying the world.[12]

Public opinion was mixed on the social impact of adult videos and the need for government regulation. (see Exhibit 2). Furthermore, changing government regulation continued to create different kinds of threats and opportunities not only in Canada but in other countries. For example, a British entrepreneur established a satellite service in Britain called Red Hot Dutch involving adult movies banned in Britain but approved under Holland's liberal laws. The service could be offered following a new European Community (EC) television directive in 1991 stating that any program approved by one EC country is automatically legal in all the others. (The entrepreneur's wife was apparently opposed to the service.)

THE CITY OF CAMBRIDGE

In the fall of 1993, the City of Cambridge Council referred to the Administration Committee of Council the matter of citizen complaints about local variety stores renting adult videos and allowing full public display of the containers of these videos which depicted explicit sexual acts. The Administration Committee, consisting of the mayor (Jane Brewer) plus four out of the ten city councillors, requested that the City Clerk report on the possibility of enacting an adult entertainment and adult video by-law similar to the by-law in nearby Burlington. The St. Ambrose Catholic Women's League advocated the Burlington by-law since it was "the strongest and most inclusive" of existing municipal by-laws. Under the Municipal Act, municipalities in Ontario did not have the authority to prohibit outright adult videos but only to licence, regulate, govern, classify, and inspect establishments renting or selling adult videos.

In January, 1994, David Calder, the Deputy City Clerk of the City of Cambridge presented a report to the Administration Committee which noted that "it appears that the City of Burlington by-law is achieving success in terms of its regulatory aims (although) there is currently a court challenge to the by-law by one adult video store owner." Despite the court challenge, Calder's report proposed a by-law modelled after the Burlington by-law. The Administration Committee accepted the proposal and the Council then passed the by-law which required the licensing of any establishment selling/renting adult videos with a licensing fee dependent on the percentage of adult videos. Video stores with no adult videos would not require any licence. A "Class A" establishment where more than 10 percent of the tapes are adult videos would have an annual fee of $850, while a "Class B" establishment where 10 percent or less of the tapes are adult videos would have a fee of $39.10 (the actual cost of issuing a business licence). Other stipulations were that "Class A" establishments had to ensure that all persons had to be at least 18 years old to enter the outlet and to purchase, rent or trade an adult video, and signage would have to indicate this restriction. "Class B" establishments (e.g., variety stores) had to keep adult videos from public view. There was to be a limit of four "Class A" establishments, and any "Class A" outlets closed could not be reopened. There would be an individual penalty of up to $25 000 and a corporate penalty of up to $50 000 for contravention of the by-law.

In response to the new by-law the legal counsel for AOV, which had two of the four "Class A" stores in Cambridge at the time, wrote the following in a letter to the City of Cambridge:

> we are involved in litigation challenging these by-laws in several municipalities....Our client...has regulated itself in a manner that we feel meets most of the goals that your municipality is trying to achieve...we certainly welcome communities such as Cambridge that are willing to sit down with us, along with the opposition groups, to create legislation that, within the confines of the jurisdiction that is allowed to municipalities, appropriately and fairly regulates this industry...

Gary Normore, owner of a "Class B" Cambridge video store expressed the concern in a letter that the licensing fee would have to increase to cover the costs of enforcing the by-law. Normore also noted the "irony" that limiting "Class A" stores will double their value overnight. While some "Class B" store owners indicated they needed adult videos to make their stores viable, for Normore the adult video segment did not make or break his business. (Normore's mother was a member of the Catholic Women's League and encouraged her son not to sell or rent adult videos. However, Normore decided not to give up this segment of the business which represented 10-15 percent of his revenues).

In regard to the concerns raised, the City created a roundtable panel which met in March, 1994 to provide advice on the by-law. The City invited those parties which had previously made presentations to either the Council or Administration Committee. Those participating in the roundtable included Calder (facilitator), Normore, Jorgensen of AOV and his counsel, a representative of the St. Ambrose Catholic Women's League, and another woman who described herself as "a victim of sexual abuse which was fuelled by pornography." It became clear to Calder following a "lively discussion" that there was no compromise position that would satisfy all parties. At the meeting, the representatives of AOV stated that the by-law was unfair and discriminatory under the Charter of Rights and Freedoms, and the city should simply prohibit the sale or rental of videos not approved by the OFRB and have one license fee for all stores carrying adult videos. The woman who described herself as "a victim of sexual abuse" recommended a dramatic increase in the fees to provide for more enforcement officers. The highest fee to date was $2500 in Niagara Falls.

Following the roundtable, Calder prepared a report in May, 1994 to the Administration Committee which recommended the following changes to the existing by-law: (*i*) eliminate the two classes of video stores ("It is questionable if two classes of activity can be created if the activity is basically the same for each class"), (*ii*) remove the restriction on the number of adult video stores ("The existing by-law would eventually eliminate any adult video store currently known as a 'Class A' video store. The municipality has the authority to limit the number but as the City solicitor states, the number authorized should be more than one to avoid any allegations that a monopoly has been established"), (*iii*) replace the dual fee structure with a "reasonable" licence fee which is not intended to prohibit or limit an activity ("A reasonable fee of perhaps $50.00 would encourage store owners to get licensed and become aware of the regulations... perhaps the penalty for contravention of the by-law could be higher rather than a high licence fee"), (*iv*) define an adult sex video using the OFRB guidelines (The current definition could include a wide selection of mainstream movies). The report noted these changes would accomplish "Council's main objective to get adult sex videos out of the view of the general public" and "a new by-law would also reduce the chance of a court challenge and any complications that a challenge would raise." The City

Solicitor supported the proposed changes to the by-law. In reflecting on what had happened, Calder was surprised that the initial problem of adult videos in convenience stores had turned into an attack on AOV.

The report from Calder presented the Cambridge Council with the following options in addition to the proposed changes to the existing by-law:

i.   keep the existing by-law in force making the current licence fees payable June 1, 1994.

ii. create a regulatory by-law similar to that of the adult magazine by-law, i.e., no licensing scheme but regulations (e.g., covers of adult videos must be placed behind an opaque screen, adult videos must be in a separate room).

iii. petition the Premier of Ontario to give municipalities the authority to prohibit adult sex videos in their respective municipalities.
The report concluded as follows:

> The Clerk's Department is not satisfied with By-Law 33-94 in its current form. Although the moral issue of adult sex videos is in the forefront of any discussion, the best staff can do is make suggestions for regulating an existing activity. Staff are of the opinion that a sound regulatory by-law will be successful in ensuring that adult sex videos are out of public view. To do any more than this will require the assistance of other levels of government. Therefore, it is staffs recommendation that the existing by-law be replaced with a by-law with changes as noted in this report.

The Administration Committee now had to decide what to do, taking into account Calder's report, the mission and vision of the City (see Exhibits 3 and 4), and the situation in other municipalities. For example, the City of Burlington Council indicated it would be fighting the challenge of its by-law but if the costs of the challenge were high, it was not clear if the defense would continue. In any case, adult videos were available in variety stores in full public view in several municipalities including Niagara Falls, Burlington, Scarborough, Mississauga, and Hamilton. Metropolitan Toronto had not acted on this matter.

EXHIBIT 1

"We have no absolute rights among us. The rights of each man, in our state of society, end precisely at the point where they encroach upon the rights of others."– *Sir Wilfrid Laurier*

Canadians enjoy the fundamental right to choose.

At Adult's Only Video, we recognize we're not for everyone, so if you don't wish to shop at our stores – you don't have to.

For those of you who do choose us as your entertainment choice we promise quality selection and friendly service.

It's a Matter of Choice!

Over 84 Locations across Canada. Check the Yellow Pages.

EXHIBIT 2   Toronto Star Poll

		Yes	No
The government should censor:	Movies	60	40
	Videos	60	40
	Magazines	58	42
	Books	48	52
Provincial film review boards should only have the right to classify or rate movies		60	40

	Agree	Disagree	No Opinion
Viewing pornography can help some couples with sex problems	40	55	5
Availability of pornography leads to increased violence toward women	59	39	2
Viewing pornography can contribute to better, more satisfying sexual relations between married couples	35	58	7
Pornography leads to greater sexual promiscuity	50	45	5
Pornography contributes to family breakdowns	40	56	4

Source: *Toronto Star*, Sept. 8, 1986
Note: Poll of 1000 Canadians across Canada, accurate to within 3.2 percentage points 19 times out of 20.

EXHIBIT 3   Mission Statement

The mission of the Corporation of the City of Cambridge is to foster and maintain, within the limits of its powers, a democratic, healthy, and secure community, using available resources to address the needs of its citizens, by providing, promoting, and maintaining appropriate and essential legislation.

EXHIBIT 4   Our Vision of Cambridge in the 21st Century

Cambridge celebrates the uniqueness of its communities and is united by its heritage, rivers and common future. Cambridge residents and visitors enjoy the natural environment, safe, clean, and caring neighbourhoods and ample cultural and recreational opportunities. Cambridge, as a community of opportunity, encourages business growth, entrepreneurial spirit, strong leadership, and civic pride.

NOTES

1. *Macleans* "The King of Porn," (October 11, 1993), 54.

2. *ibid*.

3. *Record*, June 26, 1993.

4. *Record*, July 2, 1993.

5. *Record,* June 26, 1993.

6. William Marshall and Sylvia Barrett, *Criminal Neglect: Why Sex Offenders Go Free*, (Toronto: Doubleday Canada, 1991), see chapter titled "The Link of Pornography."

7. *Record*, May 22, 1993, A2.

8. *Macleans*, "The King of Porn," 54.

9. "Naked and Uncensored, A Counterfeit Love Story," a program of the Evangelical Fellowship of Canada.

10. *The Daily Mercury*, "X-Rated Videos," May 9, 1992, 5.

11. *Cambridge Times*, January 30, 1994.

12. *Macleans*, "The King of Porn," 56.

6

ELECTROHOME AND THE ONTARIO GAMING INDUSTRY

In the spring of 1992, Electrohome, a well established Ontario company, had to decide whether it would venture away from its strategic direction to pursue an opportunity in the Ontario gaming industry. This case provides some background on Electrohome, the Ontario government's decision to legalize casino gambling and some of the arguments for and against Electrohome pursuing the opportunity in the Ontario gaming industry.

HISTORY OF ELECTROHOME

John Pollock was the third generation in his family to direct Electrohome. A.B. Pollock founded the firm in 1907 to produce Canada's first hornless phonograph. By the end of World War II, the firm was experiencing a period of steady growth. In 1950, Electrohome was able to gain electronics technology through a licensing agreement with RCA. Electrohome then used this knowledge to establish a policy of generating technologies in-house.

In the mid-1970s, 80 percent of Electrohome's sales were associated with television manufacturing. However, the company was finding it increasingly difficult to compete in this business because of lower priced, foreign — especially Japanese — competition, and furthermore the government planned to reduce its 15% tariff on imports. While most Canadian television manufacturers had exited the market, conceding to the cost advantage of the large Japanese firms, Electrohome decided to remain in the market. The company used tax incentives to develop new features for the television such as automatic fine tuning. Nevertheless, it was to be a losing battle. Pollock approached the Department of Industry, Trade, and Commerce (DITC) with a proposal for a $20 million research grant. Although he was able to use DITC grants in the past to expand Electrohome's engineering department, this time Pollock's request was turned down. The DITC criticized Electrohome's sales and profit forecasts, stating that Electrohome's problems could not be corrected by a research and development grant.[1]

As a result of the problems in the television industry, Electrohome was forced to reduce its 3000 person workforce by one-third. Members of the International Union of Electrical Workers reacted to the lay-offs by demonstrating on Parliament Hill. They were determined to convince the government that the increasing foreign competition and the declining Canadian import tariffs were harmful to the Canadian television industry and their jobs. The DITC was pressured by this group as well as the Canadian television industry, its workers and Electrohome to address these issues. A study was commissioned on the industry, which prompted the government to implement a five-year duty remission scheme which provided three provisions: (*i*) agreement not to lower tariffs below 15%; (*ii*) allowance for Third World countries to export duty-free into Canada; and (*iii*) permission for some Canadian manufacturers to import foreign-made televisions duty-free. Despite this scheme the foreign competitors advantage remained. In 1977, Electrohome posted its third consecutive year of losses — $11 million over a three-year period. Because of Electrohome's poor financial position, the Royal Bank considered calling in a $25 million demand loan. However, Electrohome had some influence, since John Pollock's father Carl sat on the bank's Board of Directors. It was decided to bring in a financial controls expert for a short period to help manage the company.

In 1977, Electrohome requested the DITC to assist the company in obtaining further loans from the bank to restructure the company. The Enterprise Development Board (EDB) agreed to guarantee 90% of the $25 million short-term loan which was restructured into a 15-year-long term note. As conditions of receiving the guarantee, a representative of EDB was appointed to the board, and the government retained the option of purchasing a certain amount of Electrohome's treasury stock until December 31, 1992.

By 1979, Electrohome's sales and profit levels showed substantial increases, due to the sudden emergence of a new market. The popularity of arcade video games provided a demand for Electrohome's video display screens. In 1980, the firm's financial situation had stabilized. Sales had increased 200% over a three-year period, enabling Electrohome to pay down the majority of the guaranteed loan. As a result, the bank's and government's control were eliminated. In response to these events, Pollock stated:

> The video boom bailed us out in the short run, but we had to make some very basic decisions about our future and we had to recognize that in electronics one simply cannot try to live behind protective barriers.[2]

The life cycle of the video arcade market was short, as was Electrohome's success. By 1982, strong Japanese and US competition and a saturated market pushed Electrohome into a poor position. Its inventory levels had become excessive and Electrohome's operations were again losing money.

During the remainder of the 1980s, Electrohome restructured away from consumer goods such as televisions and furniture, toward television broadcasting and electronic based visual communication products. Two Edmonton radio stations, the motor assembly division, a circuit manufacturing company, and a metal stamping business were sold. As well, pending CRTC approval, a Kitchener-Waterloo radio station was to be sold. Overall,

Pollock believed the company's limited size and distinct competencies directed the company away from the globally competitive consumer market industries and away from a diversification strategy.

As of 1992, Electrohome had two distinct business groups: electronicbased visual communication products and television broadcasting (see Exhibit 1). Electrohome's Electronics Group was split between Display Systems, Projection Systems, and a circuit board manufacturing business. Display Systems manufactured high quality video monitors targeted at the financial, medical, and process control industries. The Division sold customized products in small volumes for specific applications. This approach was very different from the mass produced commodity design offered by the Japanese competitors. This division would be responsible for products manufactured for the Ontario gaming industry. Display Systems' revenues increased in 1992 partially as a result of a supply agreement with Microvitec PLC, which had transferred to the U.K. the portion of the manufacturing and design previously sourced in Japan. This agreement provided Electrohome greater influence over design and more flexible, shorter lead times in the manufacturing of its products. Electrohome's Projection Systems Division produced medium to high resolution data/graphics equipment that displayed images on projection screens.

The Communications Group consisted of two CTV network television stations: CKCO-TV in Kitchener, Ontario and CFRN-TV in Edmonton, Alberta. During 1992, Electrohome attempted to gain a larger share of government-allocated resources for private television.

While Electrohome did not have a long-term plan to enter the Ontario gaming industry in 1992 it was clear that the industry offered a possible opportunity for the company. The remainder of this case will provide some background on the gaming industry and provide an assessment of the opportunity facing Electrohome.

BACKGROUND ON THE GAMING INDUSTRY

Before 1970, the only form of gaming permitted in Canada was pari-mutual track betting. New legislation in 1970 permitted other forms of gaming, which fell equally under federal and provincial authority. Due to problems interpreting the Criminal Code's meaning, a number of revisions were made in 1985. These amendments gave exclusive power to the provinces, and provided clear guidelines on the types of allowable games.

Lotteries and other games of chance such as bingos, raffles, break-open ticket schemes, and any pool system of betting on multiple sporting events or athletic contests could be legalized by the provinces. Also permitted under the Criminal Code were casinos consisting of blackjack, roulette, sicbo, wheel of fortune, as well as slot machines. Section 207 of the Criminal Code stated that these lottery schemes could be created by the province or licensed by charitable or religious organizations, or by a board of a fair or exhibition. Prohibited by the Criminal Code were dice games, three card monte, and punch boards. The popular US casino games "craps" and single event sports betting were not allowed in Canada. Exhibit 2 outlines the permitted gambling activities allowed in each province in the spring of 1992.

CASINO GAMBLING IN ONTARIO

With the deficit reaching $13 billion, the incentive to gain extra revenues had motivated the Ontario government to introduce casino gambling. Contrary to Bob Rae's prior comments regarding gambling ("it plays on greed"), the Ontario government's April 30, 1992 budget announced the introduction of casino gambling. At a press conference, the Minister of Consumer and Commercial Relations, Marilyn Churley, said, "our goals are straightforward: to create jobs, stimulate tourism, spur economic development and generate revenues." The initial casino project could generate $140 million in tax revenues annually. Also, there were potentially 2500 jobs that could be created. Churley's news release stated that both the public and private sectors would be involved in the project, and the casino business would be 100 percent government owned. Casino management companies would be chosen to run the casinos, however, the government had strict regulations for every aspect of establishing and operating the casinos. The government gave no indication whether it would favour casino management bids which included Ontario content.

The Ontario government planned to install slot machines in its new casino. The slot machine was the most popular gaming device and was used exclusively in casinos. A slot machine was a single game of chance that required a players to insert coins into the machine and then either push a button or pull a lever. If the player won, money was immediately dropped from the slot machine into the tray. The approximate selling price for a slot machine was $7000.

Another popular gaming device was the video lottery terminal (VLT) which sold for approximately $6000. VLTs were slot machines customized for licensed establishments and operated through a computer network. They were electronic machines, without an arm, and did not pay out cash winnings on the spot. The player was issued credits that were increased when the player won and subtracted when the player lost. When the player was finished, any remaining credits were displayed on a printed ticket that was redeemable for cash from the owner of that location. Winnings paid back to players of VLTs were relatively high — 80% to 93% of the money inserted into the machines, compared to 50% for traditional lotteries. A centralized control system linked all the VLTs into a single network making it possible to easily monitor many locations throughout the province. As a result, the risk of crime was reduced, government control was maintained and taxes were accurately collected.

Electrohome's initial revenue potential for the Ontario slot machine market was small for the following reasons: (*i*) there was to be only one casino initially (although a total of eight were planned); (*ii*) the government intended to use at least two vendors for 1500 to 2000 slot machines in each casino; (*iii*) Electrohome would have to split the revenues at least two ways, assuming it established a licensing agreement with one of the gaming products manufacturers. Nevertheless, the initial casino volume could be used as a stepping stone to the next seven proposed casinos and the potential video lottery terminal (VLT) market. In any case, if Electrohome became a supplier beyond the first or second casino and moved into VLTs, it would have to lease additional space. The capital requirements for further expansion were modest (estimated to be $100 000) and a large skilled labour force was readily available because of corporate downsizing in the area.

Even though the Ontario government did not consider a VLT market in its initial gambling plans, some observers were convinced the government would be attracted to the tremendous tax revenues available. A VLT market could generate $285 million in tax revenues annually along with 1000 jobs in the hospitality sector and 480 jobs in manufacturing.

326 Business and Government in Canada

EXPERIENCES IN OTHER PROVINCES

As of 1992, the status of gaming in each province varied widely. At the time of the Ontario casino announcement, it was reported that Quebec would introduce a casino the following January and the Quebec Finance Minister was recommending the establishment of a VLT network in Quebec. Manitoba had been operating a VLT network for two years, and BC, Alberta, and Saskatchewan were assessing the opportunity. In the Maritimes, gaming was regulated by the Atlantic Lottery Corporation (ALC). Before 1990, there were many privately-operated video poker machines which were commonly located in convenience stores and bars throughout the Maritimes. In 1990, the ALC required the stores and bars to switch to ALC lottery products (e.g., 6-49 and Scratch and Win). The ALC threatened to remove their 6-49 machines from any store continuing to operate video poker machines.

In 1992, there was pressure on the Nova Scotia government to remove the 2500 VLTs that were located in convenience stores. This pressure was the result of an increase in theft and compulsive gambling that was blamed on VLT accessibility. It was estimated that removing the VLTs would reduce the province's annual revenue significantly from the current level of $53 million and decrease the number of VLTs in the province to 1000. Store owners would likely oppose such action, because they collected $24 000 a year from each machine.

New Brunswick was facing the same public outcry over VLTs in convenience stores as Nova Scotia. However, New Brunswick government officials indicated that the province desperately needed the $33 million that the 3200 VLTs generated in tax revenues. In P.E.I. $20 million was spent on VLTs annually. Due to strong public opposition the government considered restricting play to between 11 a.m. and midnight, prohibiting operations on Sundays, Christmas, and Good Friday, requiring users to be a minimum age of 18 years of age and requiring an electronic display warning against the potential dangers of gambling.

Overall, potential VLT markets in 1992 were estimated to be: Ontario – 45 000; Quebec – 35 000; Manitoba – 6000; Maritime provinces – 5000.

REACTION TO GAMING EXPANSION IN ONTARIO

The possibility of a legalized VLT market in Ontario sparked interest from many groups including the Ontario Lottery Corporation (OLC), the Ontario Jockey Club (OJC), the Fireman's Association, the Liquor Control Board, the Ministry of Consumer and Commercial Relations, and the Ministry of Tourism.

The Association of Bingo Hall Owners of Ontario commissioned Insight Research Canada to poll the Ontario public regarding the new casino project. The study indicated that 77% of those polled had heard of the project, and "Ontarians are deeply divided on the issue of gambling casinos in Ontario — 49% are for the project while 45% are against it."[3] However, those opposed to it were more inclined to strongly hold their views (30%), compared to those in favour (17%). Exhibit 3 outlines the opinions of those polled with respect to their party affiliation and geographic location.

Support for the casino project was strongest among students at 63%, blue collar workers at 58%, Irish descent at 57%, and Catholics 56%. The most common reason for supporting the project was the revenue generated for the government, while the most common reason for disapproving was "gambling harms people."

Some organizations felt threatened by casino gambling. For example, the horse racing industry and Ontario farmers formed the Ontario Agriculture and Horse Racing Coalition to fight casino gambling. The horse racing industry feared it would cost them millions of dollars because gambling money would be diverted to casinos. As a result Ontario farmers would lose part of their $350 million in revenues generated from grain, straw, and feed sold to the horse racing industry. Bingo halls were in the same position as the Ontario Jockey Club (OJC), which operated Ontario horse racing. However, both groups could prosper if VLTs were placed in their bingo halls and race tracks.

Organizations such as the Interfaith Social Assistance Coalition, the Council of Reformed Churches, Groundwork — For A Just World and many other groups resisted gambling from a moral perspective. Some of the arguments presented by those opposed to gambling were:

- Organized crime is rooted in gambling. It seems difficult to separate the criminal element from the gaming industry. As a result, additional monitoring and policing costs would be required.

- Gambling puts an unfair tax on the poor. Pam Greenberg stated in a report on problem gambling "Not Quite the Pot of Gold," the typical person who had a gambling problem was likely to be female, low income or minority and a loner addicted to playing the lottery.

- There are additional social costs that are created by casinos. Compulsive gambling has been described as a disease that is similar to alcoholism. There are increased costs related to an increase in the number of people who require benefits resulting from addictions to gambling. The Detroit Casino Commission reported that the larger the casino industry, the greater the number of homeless, unemployed, and those dependent on government assistance.

- There would be a problem with teenagers gambling. In a New Jersey study, 3000 students were polled: 90% said they had gambled in the past year and 30% stated that they had gambled in the past week. The US National Committee of Problem Gambling reported that teenage compulsive/pathological gambling rate is 4-6% (6% of those that gamble become addicted), which is three times higher than the adult rate.

- The government has overestimated the revenue that will be generated. Not only will the novelty wear off in a few years, but the influx of money to gambling revenues will be extracted from other tax revenue sources. Also, bingos, charities, and race tracks will suffer due to the introduction of gambling.

- The government will become dependent on these gambling revenues. Howard Shaffer, the director of Harvard's Medical School, stated, "It is not just gamblers who are addicted to gambling, the governments are too. Governments try to balance fiscal problems on the backs of gamblers. Communities that legalize gambling risk sacrificing a diversified economy."

- It was expected that not all NDP MPPs would support the government's decision to legalize casinos, and one MPP argued the following: (*i*) the NDP government did not speak of gambling during its campaign platform; therefore, it could be argued it did not have a mandate to change its policy; (*ii*) assuming the government's function is to enhance the human spirit, gambling should not be promoted by the government, since it is built on greed and the concept of something for nothing, which devalues a community and the human spirit.

ELECTROHOME'S DECISION

There were a number of arguments for and against Electrohome's possible entry into the Ontario gaming industry. Arguments supporting the opportunity included:

i.   As an Ontario based company with an excellent reputation and unionized employees, Electrohome could become the Ontario government's preferred supplier for slot machines and VLTs. Furthermore, the government could promote the jobs created in Ontario for unionized employees as another advantage of introducing casino gambling.

ii.   There was the possibility of establishing a cooperative arrangement, such as a licensing agreement, with one of the many gaming products manufacturers. In fact, Electrohome's past experience with licensing agreements (RCA in 1950, and Microvitec PLC in the 1980s) had proven successful in terms of profits, new technologies and new markets. The major manufacturers expected to bid on Ontario casino slot machine contracts were Bally Gaming, IGT, and Slots R Us from the US, and Spielo Manufacturing from New Brunswick. Bally was a Las Vegas based company with hotel and casino operations across the world, and VLT machines in the Montana, South Dakota, and Eastern Canada markets. From 1983 to 1990, it was the exclusive contractor of VLTs and slot machines to the US Military — the single largest buyer of such equipment in the world. Recently, Bally consolidated its operations by constructing a new 150 000 square foot manufacturing and management center in Las Vegas. IGT was the largest gaming company in the world with manufacturing facilities throughout the world, including a Winnipeg plant. IGT had experience lobbying governments in several countries. Like Bally Gaming, IGT possessed VLT technology capable of monitoring the function of machines and tracking the play of customers. IGT's computer network capabilities included information systems for accounting, maintenance, marketing, operations, and security. Spielo manufacturing was operated in Moncton, New Brunswick by a young entrepreneur, Jon Manship. His first shipment was in 1991 to the Atlantic Canada market and by the spring of 1992 he had sold 4000 units.

iii.   Given Electrohome's erratic financial performance in the past (see Exhibit 4), it was important to find projects that could provide consistently strong profits. The VLT markets in Canada were expected to be large. It was difficult to estimate the financial returns at this point in the development of the project, but Electrohome's profits could range between $5 and $20 million, depending on such factors as market share, gross margin, and possibly the terms of a cooperative arrangement with one of the gaming products manufacturers.

Arguments against Electrohome pursuing the opportunity in the Ontario gaming industry included:

i.   Strategically, Electrohome's direction had been focused towards well defined businesses trying to strengthen its long term stability. The Display Systems Division was known for its high reliability to design, customization in modest volumes, and a high level of engineering support. This sophisticated job shop was currently not known for the manufacturing efficiency required for the assembly of mass produced products, such as slot machines. In fact, the company had abandoned contract manufacturing in 1986, because it was too competitive.

ii. The Ontario gaming opportunity was similar to the arcade boom in the 1980s. Both offered a highly profitable, but short-lived opportunity. The VLT market in Canada would likely be saturated in approximately four years.

iii. Electrohome lacked experience dealing with government as a customer. As a result, the company would be completely dependent on the advice and actions of external consultants in order to exploit this new market opportunity. Furthermore, Electrohome lacked experience dealing with government relations consultants.

iv. The government could decide to forego a VLT market, because of negative public opinion.

v. The government may not be able to give preference to Ontario firms, because of the pending NAFTA agreement.

vi. Even if Electrohome gained an advantage in receiving contracts in Ontario, this did not assure the company had advantages in other provinces. In fact, some provinces clearly required provincial content forcing US manufacturers to conduct some final assembly in the province.

vii. As well as the ethical concerns associated with gambling, Electrohome's excellent reputation could be negatively affected by the actions of interest groups strongly opposed to gambling. Electrohome was proud of its relationship with its community and employees. It used its broadcasting capabilities to promote local charities and donated time and money. As evidence of its concern for its employees and local community, Electrohome searched for a company that would retain the employees when it sold its furniture division.

THE NEXT STEP

Pollock sat in his office with a copy of the Ontario government's news release, announcing the introduction of casino gambling. He wondered how to respond to this opportunity in light of Electrohome's long-term strategy.

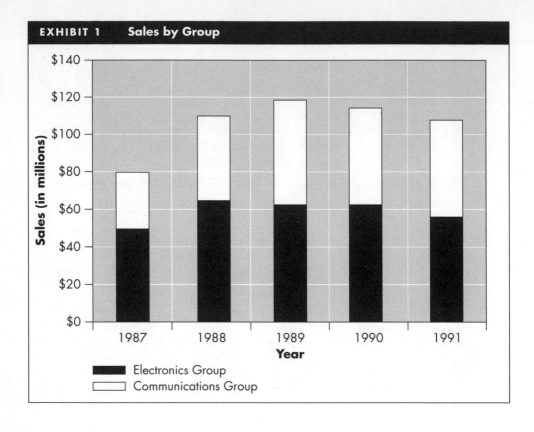

EXHIBIT 1   Sales by Group

EXHIBIT 2   Canadian Gaming at a Glance

Province or Territory	Lottery												Parimutuels					Off-track				
	Bingo	Card rooms	Casinos	Pull-tabs	Slot machines	Sports betting	Instant	Lotto	Numbers/cards	Keno	Passives	VLTs	Greyhound	Jai-alai	Harness	Quarter horse	Thoroughbred	Interprovincial intertrack	Intraprovincial intertrack	OTB, race/sportsbooks	Telephone betting	Teletheaters
Alberta	●		●	●		●	●	●	●		●				●	●	●	△	*		●	△
British Columbia	●		●	●	●	●	●	●	●	●	●				●	●	●	△	●		●	✖
Manitoba	●		●	●	●	●	●	●	●		●	*			●	●	●	●	△		●	*
New Brunswick	●					□	●	●	●	●	●	●			●			△	△	●	△	✖
Newfoundland	●		●			□	●	●	●	●	●	●			●			△	△	△	△	✖
Northwest Territories	●		●			●	●	●	●		●				△	△	△	△	△	△	△	△
Nova Scotia	●		●			□	●	●		●	●	●			●	□	△	△	□		●	✖
Ontario	●		●			△	●	●	●	●	●				●	●	●	△	●		□	△
Prince Edward Island	●		●			□	●	●	●	●	●	●			●			△	△	△	△	✖
Québec	●					●	●	●	●	●	●				●			△	□	△	□	✖
Saskatchewan	●		●	●		●	●	●	●		●				●	●	●	●	●		△	△
Yukon Territory	●	●				●	●	●	●		●				△	△	△	△	△	△	△	△

Explanation of symbols:

● legal and operative
* implemented since July 1990
△ authorized but not yet implemented
□ permitted by law and previously operative
✖ requires provincial approval

Source: Gaming & Wagering Business, Sept/Oct. Issue., 1990.

EXHIBIT 3	Results of the Poll		
PARTY AFFILIATION		**FOR**	**AGAINST**
P.C.		50%	50%
LIBERAL		49%	51%
NDP		43%	57%
LOCATION		**FOR**	**AGAINST**
CENTRAL		55%	37%
NORTH		55%	39%
SOUTH WEST		51%	44%
METRO BELT		46%	50%
METRO TORONTO		45%	49%
EASTERN		45%	47%

EXHIBIT 4	Net Income (before extraordinary items)

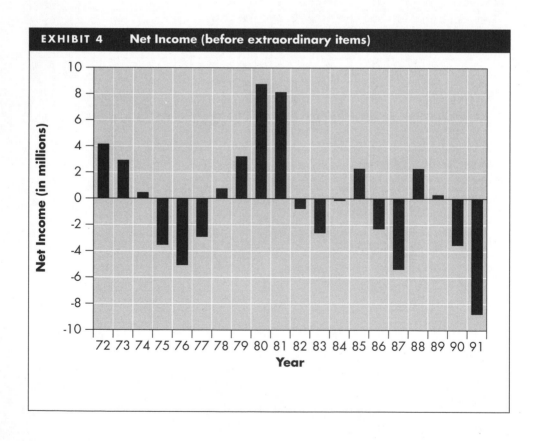

NOTES

1. Allen Morrison, and Harold Crookell, "Electrohome A1," University of Western Ontario, 1985, 5.

2. Allen Morrison and Harold Crookell, "Electrohome (B1)," University of Western Ontario, 1985, 6.

3. *The Toronto Star*, April 22, 1992, A1.

PRIVATIZING EDMONTON TELEPHONES CORPORATION

In November, 1994 the Board of Directors of Edmonton Telephones Corporation (ED TEL), the largest independent telephone company in Canada, had to decide on the next move in the negotiations which were taking place with TELUS Corporation. TELUS had made an offer to acquire ED TEL and the Board now had to determine its response to the offer. This case will provide information on the events leading to the decision facing the ED TEL Board.

BACKGROUND ON RELATIONSHIP BETWEEN ED TEL AND TELUS

ED TEL was a part of the long-standing Canadian telecommunications success. It was formed in 1893, more than a decade before Alberta became a province. Edmonton's telephone system was initiated by a private entrepreneur and purchased by the City in 1905 for $17 000. There were about 500 subscribers and a need for rapid growth. The City was better able than the individual to finance the needed system growth.

By the end of 1994, ED TEL had grown into a full-services telecommunications operation with nearly 400 000 access lines, over 2000 employees, a revenue base of $300 million and cost-based capital assets of nearly three-quarters of a billion dollars. ED TEL was an urban regional economic entity with services boundaries that were contiguous with those of the City of Edmonton. It was a large corporation in the context of the Edmonton region.

TELUS Corp. entirely surrounded the Edmonton region and served the rest of the province of Alberta. TELUS was about four times as large as ED TEL. TELUS was previously known as Alberta Government Telephones (AGT). When AGT was privatized in 1990 the name changed to TELUS.

The relationship between AGT and ED TEL had been that of disputes resulting in animosity between the two organizations. Interface between the two telephone companies was unavoidable so that long-distance and allied telephone services could be available to Edmonton and so AGT could access the highly profitable long-distance revenues. Edmonton was about one-third of the population and thus market of Alberta. There were several disputes, but two major ones stood out.

The first major source of dispute concerned boundaries. Each time Edmonton expanded by annexation, an issue arose regarding who should provide service to customers in the new area. Annexed area would be AGT service area taken into the city, so ED TEL claimed the right to provide telephone service. In 1971 the newly-elected provincial government forced AGT to accede a disputed area to ED TEL. The second major source of contention was the issue of long-distance revenue sharing. Edmonton felt entitled to a share of such revenues, but AGT countered that it alone carried the burden of providing essential but uneconomic telephone service to rural areas. The boundary issue was a major one in Edmonton during the 1971 election; the new government settled both matters by legislation which made telephone boundaries contiguous with the city boundary. The legislation also clarified that Edmonton would neither receive long-distance revenue shares nor have responsibility for cross-subsidy of rural service.

The 1970s legislation was imposed rather than mutually agreed with Edmonton, so the revenue-sharing dispute simmered on and exploded in the 1980s. The Miller Commission[1] was established by the province, and new legislation resulted in specified revenue sharing from the long-distance pot. Edmonton never thought it enough, and AGT continued to believe it was wrong. In 1992 competition was permitted by CRTC decision. ED TEL's long-distance revenues were significant, about 20% of the revenue base, but a manageable portion of the business that would be exposed to competition. AGT/TELUS was much more vulnerable to new competition because 80% of its revenue base was from the long distance source in 1990, falling to 70% by 1994. An indirect result was that the strategic value of ED TEL, to TELUS, was enhanced. A merged and rationalized company would be less vulnerable to competition and also be a stronger competitor itself.

KEY EVENTS AT ED TEL

In 1990, a major change took place for ED TEL. By City Council decision, the governance was changed from a city department to corporate governance with an arms-length board; an 11-person board was established, including the President/Chief Executive Officer (CEO). A policy option, which was to put the company up for sale, was rejected. Agreements were developed with the city-shareholder which included rate-of-return regulation and other payments to the City of Edmonton. The new status became a three-dimensional relationship of ED TEL to the city. The city represented the shareholders that are the citizens. Second, ED TEL's regulator was the city. Third, Edmonton was the regional economic development host.

Major regulatory changes, some driven by technology advances, began affecting ED TEL business commencing in 1992 when the long-distance market was opened to competition. The Board of Directors began to consider ownership alternatives. Another major regulatory change occurred in April, 1994, with a Supreme Court decision that in the future the CRTC and not the City would be regulator and CRTC rules would apply. With these regulatory changes, the City of Edmonton would lose customary revenues from ED TEL, yet it would need to make major new financial investments. Edmonton had to consider whether continued ownership of its telephone company was in the best interests of its citizens.

ED TEL was an important revenue source to its city-owner. The amount had grown gradually to nearly $40 million per year, revenue that would otherwise have had to come from elsewhere unless public services were to be curtailed. The CRTC regulatory changes would trim about $15 million off that revenue flow; CRTC policies would impose lower limits on rate of return, disallow certain payments, and require an improved equity/debt financial structure. Edmonton would lose significant city revenues for 1995 and beyond.

Like nearly all governments in Canada, the City of Edmonton was already in a difficult fiscal position. ED TEL's strategic planning called for investments of about a billion dollars over the next five to eight years, not evenly distributed; about half of this large amount was incremental due to technological convergence[2] and competitive multimedia investment requirements. As owner of ED TEL, the city would need to fund the necessary investments; for efficient financing, a major portion must be financed with equity. Higher-risk business required proportionately higher equity/debt ratios. Even if regulation was steady-state (not shifting from the city to federal CRTC), it would be very difficult for the city-owner to impose sufficiently higher property tax levels to meet the ownership risks and responsibilities of funding future ED TEL expansion and technological adaptation. In fact, as noted earlier, regulation was changing and the annual revenue-flow would decrease. Hence, property taxes would need to be raised even more.

OWNERSHIP OPTIONS

With the various regulatory changes, the ED TEL Board decided to pursue alternative ownership options. This section of the case reviews the background for these options.

1. City Department — city ownership and operation.

For 85 years Edmonton's telephone system was handled as a city public works department; the telephone system was a monopoly, with evolving ancillary businesses such as Yellow Pages. In 1989 the City decided to retain ownership but shifted operations to a newly-established corporate governance board. The thrust of the Council decision, not unanimously agreed, was that business operations were impeded by a decision-making system that was relatively slow and often log-jammed by other problems of a large modern-day civic government. If Edmonton were to choose this ownership option in 1994, the telephone company would revert to its pre-1990 situation.

2. City Corporation — city ownership but corporate governance.

This had been the policy in place since 1990. After nearly five years of experience, business operations had stabilized. However, dramatic external changes had occurred. The city-to-CRTC regulator change would have exceedingly major impact on the flow of funds from ED TEL to its city shareholder, at least a $15 million decrement on a base of about $40 million per year. There were three sources of impact: allowable rate of return, allowable master agreement "alimony" payments, and net revenue return allocation from Yellow Pages. The bottom-line result was that unless an alternate solution could be found, the city revenue decrement would need to be made up from property tax increases. This was not a happy prospect, and without much scope for phasing. Concurrently (in the coming few years) substantial and expeditious business investments would be necessary by the owner, complicated by the reality that many of these investments contained significant risks. Investment of public funds generally was risk-averse and slow. The combined regulatory impact and business investment requirement created a tenuous situation for the ED TEL city-owner. Continued city ownership would have required revenues (increases in city taxes) due to regulatory impact **and** investment monies (further increases in city taxes) to fund ownership responsibilities facilitating competitive actions in the rapidly changing marketplace. The grim outlook of this analysis motivated a search for policy options on behalf of the owner.

3. Privatization by Buy-out — ED TEL purchase/takeover.

While there could be other potential purchasers of ED TEL, the most likely source was TELUS. It had initiated purchase discussions with ED TEL in mid-1992; after separate and respective valuations analyses, the price positions were widely variant and the matter was dropped. The prospect of a deal was hampered by long-standing animosity between the two telephone companies. Inasmuch as the ED TEL board was dissatisfied with the price offer, no recommendation was taken to the city-shareholder-owner. The differing price expectations is explained as follows: economic valuation of business operations = X; value of economic synergies = Y; strategic value = Z. The separate and independent ED TEL and TELUS valuations of X were similar ($325-350 million) — thus not a source of dispute. ED TEL valuation of [Y + Z] was significant ($75-100 million); the TELUS position was that both Y and Z were zero. TELUS held firm to that position through 1992, so there was not a basis for detailed negotiation nor for continued discussion of privatization-via-acquisition. Had there been agreement that [Y + Z] was non-zero and substantial, a sharing of these values potentially might have been negotiated. When it became known in 1994 that ED TEL was pursuing option 4 below, TELUS expressed an interest in renewed discussions with ED TEL; these discussions took place within the pursuit of that option.

4. Privatization by IPO — investor purchase.

The Initial Public Offering (IPO) privatization option was pursued actively by ED TEL after the failure to reach a deal with TELUS. During 1994 ED TEL engaged corporate and consulting analysis and advice including investment banking, regulatory affairs, and corporate law. Applicable business concepts, ownership duality and risk-as-a-commodity, were relevant to the decision. Early in the process, City Council was advised of ED TEL board actions and reasons. Investment banking analysis indicated an ED TEL market value of $425-475 million; the city's independent advice concurred with that of ED TEL. To redress the debt/equity ratio required by new CRTC regulation, $25-35 million of this amount would be needed. The residual of about $400 million would become available to the City of Edmonton. The market value included the impact of Revenue Canada tax rulings and negotiable CRTC regulatory transition arrangements. By fall 1994 the ED TEL preliminary prospectus (see Appendix 1) had been developed and approved by the Board of Directors. In the fall of 1994 a market exposure exercise was to be undertaken; the potential for shares purchases would be afforded to investors directly or indirectly through major fiduciary institutions, pension funds, insurance companies, and others in the marketplace that manage the savings of Canadians. ED TEL shares investments would be offered. Corporations and companies, whether within the telecommunications sector or not, had the same opportunity to respond to the ED TEL prospectus. The expected decision period, based on price from the market, was November 1994. The final decision prerogative was the jurisdiction of Edmonton City Council.

DECISION PROCESS ISSUES

Privatization of ED TEL was a very difficult decision for Edmonton. The telephone company was a large regional economic entity and had an important parallel history to the city itself. Some citizens and their representatives felt that City Council made a long-term commitment to ownership in conjunction with the 1989 decision to form a corporate governance board beginning in 1990. Thus there was a significant feeling that privatization involved policy reversal rather than fresh policy determination. Four major decision process issues were apparent, as follows:

(i) Plebiscite. The 1989 decision included a City By-Law stating that 100% ownership would be retained; thus privatization could only take place by replacing that By-Law. Some members of City Council and a segment of the citizenry felt very strongly that such a decision should be made by public plebiscite rather than by Council itself. A citizens group, "Friends of ED TEL," was formed to challenge the privatization proposal and to resist it both legally and politically. A citizen petition was mounted in an effort to force a plebiscite onto the city, citing both legal and moral grounds. Investment banking advice had been that IPO marketing would be seriously jeopardized by an outstanding court case. A court decision struck down the legal argument, and a higher court decision upheld that decision. Leave for a Supreme Court of Canada appeal was requested, but denied. That concluded the issue.

(ii) Public Participation. ED TEL proposed to City Council that extensive public information sessions be held prior to any decisions. Council agreed, but also wished to hold a public hearing in Council Chambers after the public information sessions had been completed. Three regional (within Edmonton) public information sessions were held in early June 1994 culminating with a televised public information session. ED TEL paid the costs for these sessions. Later in June the City Council public hearing was held.

Throughout this period ED TEL was invited to meet with business, community, and special interest groups. There were numerous such meetings including public affairs staff, senior managers, and Board members. Concurrently, a public survey by the University of Alberta Population Research Laboratory was commissioned by ED TEL. The survey plumbed opinion as to privatization, allied constraints, and how the potential monies should be handled.

The public participation process thus had three components. These included group-invited meetings with ED TEL, public information sessions held by ED TEL, and a public hearing conducted by City Council. While disagreements remained on matters of policy, it appears that the public felt the opportunities for involvement and input were extensive.

(iii) Partitioning. Complex decisions can become impossible if a circularity evolves where no logical sequence can be followed. Opponents to a decision may enjoy success by fostering such circularity. That is a sound strategy where there is a high likelihood of losing an issue on its substantive merits. Proponents of a decision may enhance the probability of success by a countervailing strategy. In a case such as ED TEL privatization the decision circularity can be, "How can you decide without knowing the price?" and yet, "How can a price be determined in the absence of substantive agreement?" Complex decisions are facilitated by partitioning the larger decision into a sequence of linked but smaller decisions. The partitioning could be along the lines of sequential decisions "in principle," "constraints," and "price." That is, if constraints (e.g., regional economic development) can be agreed and the price is sufficient, would City Council agree to sell? If a proposal is not agreed in principle, there is no point in taking the time and resources to develop the essential details. Ultimately, in June 1994, following the public participation process, City Council made the "in principle" decision to privatize ED TEL. Seven of thirteen Council members were open to the privatization option, six (including the Mayor) were opposed. City Council's rules were important because a tie vote was deemed to be a loss, and a further rule stipulated that an issue may return to the agenda within a year only if 75% of Council voted to permit it.

(iv) Potential Sale Proceeds. The ED TEL proposal for privatization was for the City of Edmonton to handle the proceeds as they see fit. The public opinion survey revealed two unexpected major results. The first result was weaker-than-expected citizen resistance to the telephone company privatization. While certain persons and groups continued to hold strong feelings against it, the view seemed not to be generally shared. This result was confirmed by limited interest in the public information sessions and the public hearing. Strong views were expressed by a few — generally the same few citizens were attracted to each public participation opportunity. Mirroring the citizen response, the minority of City Council continued vigorously to resist the privatization proposal.

The other surprise was that citizens expressed strong concern about how the city would handle the money. Some of the reaction was highly cynical. Many who were asked if there should be a plebiscite on the sale of ED TEL, instead responded that there should be a plebiscite restricting what City Council could do with the expected $400 million proceeds. The City of Edmonton, with expertise and advice from their finance department, held the prerogative on this matter. A by-law could be prepared and passed which would constrain spending actions of the city, possibly similar to policies for financial management of endowments.

IPO PRIVATIZATION OPTION

Edmonton may have been willing to "supply" its corporate assets and its risks to the Canadian investment marketplace, but would there be sufficient "demand" in that Canadian marketplace for the property ownership including its attendant risks? That important question was posed to a leading Canadian investment banking firm, Nesbitt Burns. In turn, that firm engaged additional advice from a leading American firm, Goldman Sachs. The fundamental basis for the answer depends on whether there are investment funds (that manage savings of Canadians for longer-term gains) that need more risk; attendant to the risk profile is the prospect for larger future gains, especially capital gains, in funds' value. A factor in the analysis was Canadian tax law wherein preferred tax treatment was allowable only if a threshold proportion of the fund's investments was Canadian. ED TEL would constitute a new Canadian investment opportunity.

An *un*constrained IPO is strongest in the investment marketplace. Nevertheless, an offsetting consideration would be to harness ED TEL to maximum advantage in its regional economic development. A set of constraints was proposed to protect economic opportunities for the City of Edmonton. Each constraint imposed would result in (at least marginally) lower share prices. Many constraint options (and sub-options) were considered, and several were rejected. The following IPO privatization constraints were attached as "downside" protection for Edmonton:

i. The ED TEL head office would remain in Edmonton;

ii. The Board majority would be from Edmonton;

iii. Edmontonians would have a priority opportunity to purchase shares;

iv. ED TEL employees would have a priority opportunity to purchase shares; and

v. No single purchaser could acquire over 15% Common Shares ownership.

Two major potential constraints merit comment. One was the possibility that the City of Edmonton could insist on continuing as a partial owner. Respecting the advice of investment bankers and the ED TEL Board, that share value would be harmed by such a move, City Council agreed to an "all or nothing" decision with the result that 100% of the shares would be offered to investors. Another constraint proposed by the ED TEL Board was a Golden Warrant offer to the city for "upside" protection. The Warrant would have provided that after a specified period in the future, and if the share prices increased by a certain multiple, then the city, as former owner, would receive a block of shares. The City did not take up this offer. Apparently they saw the potential reward as being too distant in the future and, as previously mentioned, because of the Warrant's potential to act as a price constraint.

Privatization of ED TEL would generate a stronger investor price because of built-up potential tax credits so long as the purchaser (IPO or buy-out) was subject to corporate income tax. As a Crown Corporation (of the City of Edmonton), the company was in a non-taxable position. Certain tax credits could be available to private-sector purchasers that were taxable; the preferable tax position "capitalized" into economic value and share prices. In addition, the Industry Canada Minister and Federal Cabinet agreed on an Order-In-Council to ease ED TEL's transition to CRTC regulations. This move increased the attractiveness of the acquisition to a potential purchaser. In particular, a rate of return above the industry average was allowed by the Order-In-Council, and only a part of ED TEL's Yellow Pages business would be used in determining ED TEL's allowed rate of return. Both the tax credit and regulatory transition factors were applicable to either an IPO or buy-out/takeover privatization option so long as the purchaser was taxable under Canadian law.

An issue vital to either the IPO or purchase/takeover options was the unfunded pension liability of ED TEL. As a municipal government entity, ED TEL was included in the Alberta Local Authorities Pension Plan (LAPP) system. Like virtually all government pension plans in Canada, there was not full-fundedness at ED TEL, but instead a government guarantee, i.e, future payout provisions were guaranteed by the Alberta government. Privatization of ED

TEL meant leaving LAPP and the liabilities had to go somewhere or be covered. During the summer of 1994, representations to the Alberta government resulted in the passing of an Order-In-Council such that the Alberta government accepted the pension liability. As a result, go-forward pensions by a new private owner of ED TEL could begin without past liabilities being transferred. Without the Order-In-Council, the City of Edmonton would have to accept a lower price for ED TEL to compensate for the Alberta government liability. The Order-In-Council was passed without difficulty because the Alberta government understood the issue from having passed a similar Order-In-Council when AGT was privatized in 1990. Moreover, the government was philosophically in favour of privatization.

TELUS PRIVATIZATION OPTION

During the summer of 1994, pursuant to the June 1994 public meetings, ED TEL intentions of IPO privatization became widely known to the Canadian business community. A parameter of the public disclosure was that ED TEL expected to raise $425-$475 million in the Canadian investment marketplace. As a result of positive market response, TELUS began to reconsider its previous position. Informal inquiries were initiated by TELUS, but ED TEL held firm to the position that only public information about ED TEL could be disclosed prior to the public release of the Prospectus. Meanwhile the newly-hired President of TELUS arrived on November 1, 1994, only days after the public release of the ED TEL Prospectus.

TELUS expeditiously reconsidered its 1992 offer; it already had extensive information about ED TEL, and had begun additional work. Once the Prospectus had been issued, ED TEL was free to cooperate with TELUS (excepting strategic planning information, in case a deal was not consummated) so that TELUS could decide whether to bid anew. At TELUS' request, the IPO privatization option was suspended for a short time period, so there could be a determination of whether TELUS would decide to make a firm offer. By mid-November 1994, TELUS had made a new offer of $465 million, matching the IPO market evaluation.

In addition to the cash payment and the assumption of ED TEL debt ($170 million), TELUS offered several other commitments to Edmonton:

i. ED TEL would maintain its identity as an operating subsidiary of TELUS; ED TEL would continue to have its own Board of Directors (the majority of whom shall be from Edmonton).

ii. TELUS and ED TEL Head Offices and Head Office Operations would continue to be in Edmonton within specified time and circumstances.[3]

iii. The Chief Operating Officer (COO) for ED TEL would be appointed by its own Board.

iv. Two additional Edmontonians would be appointed to the TELUS Board.

v. No ED TEL lay-offs for a year, and subject to earning its regulated rate of return, no lay-offs for an additional three years.

vi. Subject to CRTC decisions, rates in Edmonton would continue to be determined independently.

vii. TELUS would expand its research and development investments commitments ($12 million in 1995) in Edmonton.

viii. ED TEL employees would have a special one-time opportunity to purchase TELUS shares, and access to the existing employee share purchase plan of TELUS.

ix. ED TEL pensions would be kept whole.

x. The respective Mobility (Cellular) companies would merge immediately.

Timing was a barrier for the TELUS option. All major merger/takeover transactions in Canada were subject to the Competition Act. In 1986 Parliament legislated that applicable portions of the law would be under the Civil Code rather than the Criminal Code; thus the law now provided for Competition Bureau prior-review of such major potential transactions. Procedural processes, including timing, precluded a Competition Bureau decision by the end of the calendar year. However, the Revenue Canada tax ruling contemplated an IPO privatization and was to expire on December 31, 1994. This was extended to March 31 in relation to the TELUS offer, and to May 31, 1995 if an IPO was to be undertaken. Another major federal Government decision was necessary. The CRTC transition (regulatory) arrangements also contemplated an IPO, but Industry Canada initiated a new Order-In-Council for the same time extension and to permit a similar regulatory transition under a TELUS-purchase privatization. The Revenue Canada and CRTC regulatory transition provisions allowed time for the Competition Bureau to do its work. A ruling from the Competition Bureau was forthcoming at the end of February, 1995.

THE NEXT MOVE

The ED TEL Board now had to decide what to do about the TELUS offer. It could advise Edmonton City Council (the final decision maker) to accept the offer, or renegotiate with TELUS or reject the TELUS offer in favour of some other option such as an IPO privatization.

Confidential Information Memorandum

This document is confidential and has been prepared for the internal use of banking and selling group members only. Under no circumstances are its contents to be communicated to the public or the press. Securities legislation in all provinces prohibits such distribution. This memorandum should be read in conjunction with the preliminary prospectus dated October 27, 1994. The information contained herein, while obtained from sources which we believe to be reliable, is not guaranteed as to accuracy or completeness. This memorandum is for information purposes only and does not constitute an offer to sell or a solicitation to buy the securities referred to herein.

Initial Public Offering   **October 28, 1994**

and Secondary Offering

ED TEL Inc.
$520 000 000 - $540 000 000
40 million Common Shares
$13.00 to $13.50 per Common Share

Investment Highlights

- Unique and Favourable Regulatory Environment
- Strong Earnings Performance
- Positioned for Competition
- Mobility Services Growth
- Commitment to Multimedia Opportunities
- Pure Telecommunications Investment

Schedule of Information Meetings

City	Date	Time	Place
Edmonton	Thursday, November 24th	7:30 a.m.	Hotel Macdonald, Empire Ballroom
Calgary	Thursday, November 24th	12:15 p.m.	Calgary Convention Centre, Macleod Hall C
Vancouver	Friday, November 25th	12:15 p.m.	Pan Pacific Hotel, Crystal Pavilion B & C
Winnipeg	Monday, November 28th	7:30 a.m.	Westin Hotel, West Ballroom
Toronto	Tuesday, November 29th	4:15 p.m.	Crowne Plaza, Ballroom A
Montreal	Wednesday, November 30th	12:15 p.m.	Le Westin Mont-Royal, Salon Printemps

NESBITT BURNS INC.

WOOD GUNDY INC.   SCOTIAMCLEOD INC.   GOLDMAN SACHS CANADA

GORDON CAPITAL CORPORATION	MIDLAND WALWYN CAPITAL INC.	RICHARDSON GREENSHIELDS OF CANADA LIMITED	TORONTO DOMINION SECURITIES INC.
FIRST MARATHON SECURITIES LIMITED	GOEPEL SHIELDS & PARTNERS INC.	LEVESQUE BEAUBIEN GEOFFRION INC.	PETERS & CO. LIMITED

FIRSTENERGY CAPITAL CORP.

(For list of contacts please see back page)

Summary of the Offering

Issuer:	ED TEL Inc.
Issue:	Initial Public Offering and Secondary Offering of 40 000 000 Common Shares.
Treasury Offering:	Approximately 2.5 million Common Shares
Secondary Offering:	Approximately 37.5 million Common Shares
Amount:	$520 000 000 to $540 000 000
Offering Price:	$13.00 to $13.50 per Common Share
Dividends:	ED TEL expects to pay quarterly dividends based on a payout ratio of approximately 60% of net income resulting in an anticipated initial annual yield in the range of 5.75% to 6.00%.
Use of Proceeds:	The net proceeds to ED TEL from the Common Shares offered in the Treasury Offering will be used for capital expenditures and on-going working capital requirements. ED TEL will not receive any part of the proceeds from the sale of Common Shares under the Secondary Offering.
Selling Shareholder:	The City of Edmonton will be disposing of its entire Common Share position in ED TEL. The City has retained special voting rights in certain limited events through a special share.
Restrictions on Ownership and Voting:	For a five year period, no person or group of associated persons may hold, as beneficial owners, more than 15% of the outstanding Common Shares. Beneficial share ownership, in aggregate, by non-residents of Canada will be limited to 20% of the outstanding Common Shares.
Priority Allocation:	Common Shares will be offered to all purchasers at the Offering Price. ED TEL residential telephone subscribers are entitled to purchase, in priority to all other purchasers, not less than 25 Common Shares nor more than 100 Common Shares per residential access line. Any ED TEL employee is further entitled to purchase additional Common Shares subject to the minimum and maximum mentioned above. The priority allocation period is expected to end on November 25, 1994.
Eligibility:	Eligible under usual statutes as well as for RRSP's, RRIF's, and DPSP's.
Listing:	As a condition of closing, the Common Shares will be listed on The Toronto Stock Exchange, the Montreal Exchange and the Alberta Stock Exchange.
Timing:	Pricing expected the week of December 5, 1994. Closing expected the week of December 19, 1994.

The Company

ED TEL provides a full range of integrated telecommunications services and products to residential and business customers, primarily in Edmonton, through its three operating subsidiaries. The local exchange operation represents the majority of ED TEL's telecommunications operations.

ED TEL Communications Inc.

- operates the local exchange.
- has over 400 000 network access lines as at September 30, 1994.
- offers local telecommunications services to residences and businesses.
- offers a full range of enhanced services to businesses and residential customers.
- is interconnected with long distance networks and markets long distance service packages.
- offers a full range of data services and products, including local area networks, Frame Relay services and ISDN services.

ED TEL Mobility Inc.

- has 30 383 cellular subscribers as at July 31, 1994.
- offers a full range of enhanced services and long distance packages to cellular customers.
- is a shareholder in Mobility Canada which provides roaming coverage over an area covering approximately 80% of the population in Canada and the United States.
- has 6 765 paging units in service as at July 31, 1994.
- offers private mobile services.

ED TEL Directory Inc.

- sells, produces and distributes advertising services and products through mediums such as:
  — white pages
  — *Yellow Pages*™
  — *Asian Pages*™
  — *Talking Community Pages*™
  — street and address directory
  — Centrex directory
- ED TEL's Directory's *Yellow Pages*™ directory has over 2 000 pages and over 30 000 advertisers, and is the largest in Canada based on pages of paid advertising.
- member of Canadian Yellow Pages Service (CANYPS) and Yellow Page Publishers Association (YPPA).

Investment Highlights

Unique and Favourable Regulatory Environment

ED TEL Communications Inc., ED TEL's local exchange operation, is regulated by the Canadian Radio-television and Telecommunications Commission (the "CRTC") under the directive (the "Directive") covering a transitional period from the data of reorganization until October 25, 1998. Highlights of the Directive are as follows:

High Allowable Rate of Return
Rate of return range on common equity of 11.5% - 13.5%. This will represent the highest allowable rate of return for any publicly traded Canadian telephone company.

Shareholder Entitlements
The Directive permits ED TEL Communications to earn income in excess of the regulated rate of return of 11.5% to 13.5% as a result of the additional tax deductions available to ED TEL created by a reorganization of ED TEL. These additional tax deductions allow ED TEL Communications a higher revenue, and therefore higher income, than would otherwise be allowed in a year under the rate of return regulation by an amount estimated to be in excess of $17.2 million per year during the term of the Directive.

Directory Profit
The Directive also provides for the partial integrality of ED TEL Directory to the local exchange operations carried on by ED TEL Communications. This provides ED TEL Directory with the opportunity to earn net income for the benefit of ETI shareholders which will not be included in ED TEL Communication's calculation of its regulated rate of return. This partial integrality of ED TEL's directory operations to its local exchange operations is a unique feature as compared to other CRTC regulated telecommunications companies, whose directory operations are generally treated as being fully integral to their local exchange operations.

Strong Earnings Performance

Since incorporation in 1990, ED TEL has experienced a steady growth in net income and has earned in excess of its maximum allowable return on equity. This has been achieved without the need for local rate increases since 1990.

As part of the reorganization, all subsidy payments and user fees paid by ED TEL to the City have been eliminated. These payments will represent approximately $24.0 million of expenses in 1994. The termination of these payments represent a major component of the increased profitability for ED TEL going forward. These expense savings will be partially offset by property and business taxes payable as a private company.

ED TEL's strong historic earnings performance and the reorganization will support strong future earnings as shown in the selected financial data below:

Investment Highlights Continued

	Actual 1991	Actual 1992	Pro forma 1993	Pro forma Seven Months Ended July 31 1994	Forecast 1995
Operating Revenue (000's)	$277 882	$288 120	$309 047	$183 887	$329 800
Annual Growth Rate	3.1%	3.7%	7.3%	2.7%[1]	3.9%
Income from Continuing Operations (000's)	$20 430	$23 124	$45 411	$32 181	$50 900
Return on Equity from Continuing Operations	**15.5%**	**16.8%**	**25.9%**	—	—

Note:
(1) Calculated using 1994 12 month ETC forecast revenues.

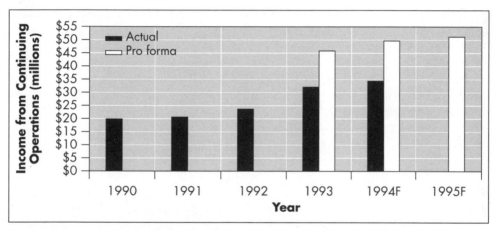

Note: 1994 pro forma income is calculated using the 12 month 1994 ETC income from continuing operations forecast plus user fees, subsidy payments and provision for rate stabilization for 1994 less pro forma income taxes and pro forma property and business taxes annualized from the 7 months ended July 31, 1994.

Positioned for Competition

Although competition has to date been very limited in ED TEL's local exchange market, ED TEL is well positioned for any future competition given the following:

- *Low Rates* — ED TEL's basic residential and business rates are among the lowest in Canada.

- *Focused Urban Market* — ED TEL serves a concentrated urban area allowing for greater operating efficiencies.

- *Low Long Distance Exposure* — ED TEL is less vulnerable to long distance competition for two reasons. ED TEL's contribution from long distance revenues accounted for only 21% of its total corporate revenues for 1993, as compared to the average of approximately 50% for other publicly traded Canadian telephone companies. Secondly, ED TEL receives an interconnection charge for all long distance calls regardless of carrier.

Investment Highlights Continued

- *Relationship with TELUS/AGT* — The Company has entered into a series of agreements with TELUS/AGT which cover long distance settlement payments, TELUS/AGT's access to ED TEL's local exchange network, long distance package marketing commissions and other mutually beneficial business opportunities.

- *Value Added Services* — ED TEL has continued to increase penetration rates of enhanced services to both residential and business customers. As of July 31, 1994, enhanced services revenue represented 34% of total business network service revenue and 16% of total residential network service revenue.

- *Customer Satisfaction* — ED TEL's semi-annual customer service surveys have revealed that there is approximately a 90% satisfaction rate among ED TEL customers based on level of service. This satisfaction level, coupled with ED TEL's local reputation, will support ED TEL's introduction of new competitive services.

- *Technologically Advanced Networks* — ED TEL has developed one of the most modern local telecommunications networks in North America. ED TEL's local wireline network is currently 96% digitally switched, with 100% digitalization scheduled to be achieved by October 31, 1994. In addition, this network includes over 600 km of high capacity fibre optic cable, accessible by all of ED TEL's key business customers. ED TEL's cellular network is 100% digital. Digital technology allows ED TEL to offer high margin enhanced services, such as Custom Calling Features, Call Management Services and Voice Messaging, to its cellular and local customers.

- *Financing for Growth* — The Treasury Offering will supply funds that will support future growth of ED TEL and provide the company with a strong balance sheet.

Mobility Services Growth

ED TEL Mobility's digital cellular coverage area encompasses a population base of over 735 000 with 30 383 ED TEL cellular customers as at July 31, 1994. The following table illustrates the dramatic growth ED TEL Mobility has experienced since 1990:

	July 31 1994	1993	December 31 1992	1991	1990
ED TEL Cellular Customers	30 383	25 465	19 011	12 707	7 927
Annual Growth Rate	33.1%(1)	33.9%	49.6%	60.3%	—
ED TEL Mobility Revenues (000's)	$15 539	$20 908	$18 973	$14 175	$12 053
Annual Growth Rate	27.4%(1)	10.2%	33.8%	17.6%	—
Estimated Company Cellular Penetration	4.1%	3.5%	2.6%	1.8%	1.1%

Note: (1) Annualized

Investment Highlights Continued

Commitment to Multimedia Opportunities

ED TEL recognizes the importance of new services and products as a means for future growth. The development of multimedia services, such as home banking, home shopping and video on demand, is being closely tracked and studied by ED TEL. In addition, ED TEL is conducting a number of technology trials and aimed at building expertise for the introduction of multimedia services and products. These services and products will be offered to ED TEL customers as technology and customer demand lead to proven profitability.

Pure Telecommunications Investment

ED TEL Communications contributes approximately 80% of ED TEL's revenues. Other operations are in closely related fields such as cellular and paging (ED TEL Mobility) as well as directory publishing (ED TEL Directory).

ED TEL's strategy is to focus exclusively on its telecommunications business and to provide a full range of services and products within that sector. Through increased penetration rates for existing enhanced services and the introduction of new enhanced services, ED TEL will continue to develop expertise and critical infrastructure necessary to provide additional new services and products in the future, thus maintaining ED TEL's network leadership position.

CRTC Decision 94-19

CRTC Decision 94-19, released September 16, 1994, fundamentally changes the future regulatory framework for the telecommunications industry in various ways. Decision 94-19 was directed expressly at certain Stentor members and does not specifically apply to independent telephone companies such as ED TEL. However, ED TEL expects that the following general principles contained in Decision 94-19 will be applied to the telecommunications industry as a whole:

- the opportunity for telephone companies to enter new services such as multimedia and transactional services as both network service carriers and content providers.

- the replacement of rate of return regulation with price cap regulation over time. The regulation of prices charged for services rather than the earnings of the telephone companies will provide efficient companies with greater earnings upside potential.

- the splitting of telecommunications operations into utility and competitive segments with the utility segment subject to price cap regulation in the future.

- the reduction of long distance subsidization of local telephone service through rate rebalancing.

During the term of the Directive the CRTC must comply with the provisions of the Directive in respect of the regulation of ED TEL, however, ED TEL's long term strategy is consistent with the principles of Decision 94-19.

Selected Consolidated Financial Information

Income Statement Data

(000's)	Forcast Year Ending December 31 1995	Pro forma Seven Months Ended July 31 1994	Proforma Year Ended December 31 1993	Seven Months Ended July 31 1994	Seven Months Ended July 31 1993	Year Ended December 31 1993	Year Ended December 31 1992	Year Ended December 31 1991
		(unaudited)	(unaudited)	(unaudited)				
Revenue	$329 800	$183 887	$309 047	$183 887	$170 531	$309 047	$288 120	$277 882
Expenses	259 000	140 258	244 464	147 985	140 883	252 884	245 727	233 369
Income from Operations	70 800	43 629	64 583	35 902	29 648	56 163	42 393	44 513
Interest expense, net	15 700	9 161	16 152	10 036	10 358	17 652	19 102	18 755
Provision for rate stabilization	—	—	—	2 200	2 638	6 462	167	5 328
Provision for income tax	4 200	2 287	3 020	—	—	—	—	—
Income from Continuing Operations	$50 900	$32 181	$45 411	$23 666	$16 652	$32 049	$23 124	$20 430

Balance Sheet Data

(000's)	Pro forma as at July 31 1994	As at July 31 1994	Year Ended December 31 1993	Year Ended December 31 1992
	(unaudited)	(unaudited)		
Capital assets	$382 104	$382 104	$383 393	$368 381
Total assets	481 309	455 694	460 468	439 039
Long-term debt, including current portion	187 554	187 554	197 980	191 428
Reserve for rate stabilization	—	2 200	18 089	11 627
Shareholders' equity	203 714	173 714	148 486	140 413

Selected Consolidated Financial Information Continued

Key Operating Statistics

	July 31	Year Ended December 31			
Statistics/As at	1994	1993	1992	1991	1990
Network access lines	395 373[1]	399 716	394 720	391 129	379 918
Full time employees	2 006	2 041	2 026	2 009	1 958
Annual revenue per employee	n.a.	$151 400	$142 200	$138 300	$137 700
Cellular customers	30 383	25 465	19 011	12 707	7 927
Percentage of lines digitally switched	96%[2]	92%	82%	81%	63%
Residential enhanced	16%	14%	11%	7%	6%
Business enhanced service revenue as a % of total business network service revenue	34%	30%	28%	26%	15%

Notes:
(1) 400 245 network access lines as at September 30, 1994.
(2) 100% digitally switched as at October 31, 1994

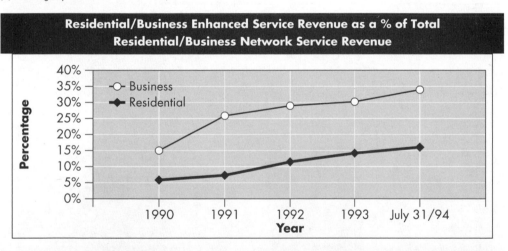

Residential/Business Enhanced Service Revenue as a % of Total Residential/Business Network Service Revenue

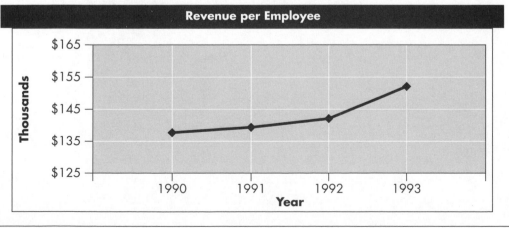

Revenue per Employee

Selected Consolidated Financial Information Continued

Income by Subsidiary

(000's)	Forecast Income Year Ending December 31 1995	Pro forma Income Seven Months Ending July 31 1994	Pro forma Forecast Income Year Ending December 31 1993
	(unaudited)	(unaudited)	(unaudited)
ED TEL Mobility	$4 200	$1 944	$544
ED TEL Directory	9 800	6 749	7 546
ED TEL Communications	41 100	25 775	40 341
Income before provision for income tax	55 100	34 468	48 431
Provision for income tax	4 200	2 287	3 020
Consolidated income from continuing operations	$50 900	$32 181	$45 411

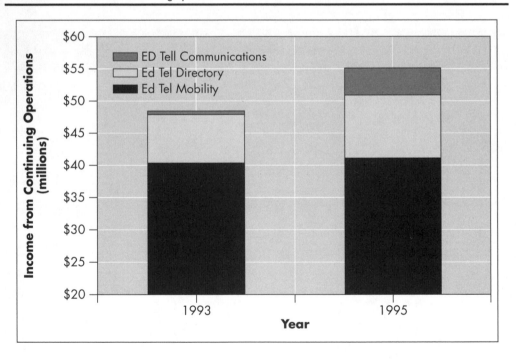

Comparable Information

Comparative Pricing

The table below illustrates the attractive pricing of this issue compared to other publicly traded Canadian telephone companies:

Company	Current Price	Dividend	1995F E.P.S. [1]	P/E Ratio	Yield
	(10/27/94)				
BCE	$46.750	$2.68	$3.86	11.4	5.7%
B.C. Tel	$24.875	$1.24	$1.99	12.5	5.0%
Bruncor	$23.625	$1.28	$1.90	12.4	5.4%
Island Tel	$23.000	$1.20	$1.99	11.6	5.2%
Maritime Tel	$24.125	$1.28	$2.04	11.8	5.3%
NewTel	$20.625	$1.36	$2.00	10.3	6.6%
Quebec Tel	$19.000	$1.24	$1.81	10.5	6.5%
TELUS	$16.625	$0.92	$1.62	<u>10.3</u>	<u>5.5%</u>
Average				**11.4**	**5.7%**
ED TEL	$13.000	$0.78	$1.27[2]	10.2	6.0%
	13.250	$0.78	$1.27	$10.4	5.9%
	13.500	$0.78	$1.27	$10.6	5.8%

Notes:
(1) Forecast supplied by IBES October 20, 1994.
(2) Forecast January 1, 1995 to December 31, 1995.

For Information Contact:

NESBITT BURNS INC.

Investment Banking		*Syndication*	
Rob Wonnacott	(403) 260-9369	Paul Allison	(416) 359-4357
Shane Fildes	(403) 260-9317	Wayne Huhtanen	(416) 359-6566
WOOD GUNDY INC.		SCOTIAMCLEOD INC.	
Douglas G. Cunningham	(416) 594-7476	James Mahony	(403) 298-4066
GOLDMAN SACHS CANADA		GORDON CAPITAL CORPORATION	
David Gluskin	(416) 343-8840	Gerald C. Throop	(416) 868-5392
MIDLAND WALWYN CAPITAL INC.		RICHARDSON GREENSHIELDS OF CANADA LIMITED	
Peter A. Myers	(403) 231-7301	Kevin B. McLachlan	(403) 266-9603
TORONTO DOMINION SECURITIES INC.		FIRST MARATHON SECURITIES LIMITED	
Wendy A. Leaney	(416) 982-2631	C. Michael Stuart	(403) 290-0809
GOEPEL SHIELDS & PARTNERS INC.		LEVESQUE BEAUBIEN GEOFFRION INC.	
J. Graham Weir	(403) 297-0439	John McCormick	(403) 531-8420
PETERS & CO. LIMITED		FIRST ENERGY CAPITAL CORP.	
Bruce A. Fiell	(403) 261-2228	Mark T. Phipps	(403) 262-0600

NOTES

This case was written by Allan A. Warrack, University of Alberta, with the assistance of Mark. C. Baetz, Wilfred Laurier University. © Copyright, 1996. University of Alberta and Wilfred Laurier University. Distributed through the LAURIER INSTITUTE, School of Business and Economics, Wilfrid Laurier University, Waterloo, Ontario, Canada, N2L 3C5. No part of this case may be reproduced, stored in a retrieval system, or transmitted in any form or by any means — electronic, mechanical, photocopying, recording, or otherwise — without the permission of The Laurier Institute, School of Business and Economics, Wilfrid Laurier University.

1. Justice Tevie Miller of the Court of Queen's Bench, later Associate Chief Justice.

2. Convergence is the merging of broadcast, telecommunications and computer sectors.

3. When privatized in 1990, TELUS agreed not to move its head office from Edmonton for five years without provincial government concurrence. As a result, beginning in 1996, TELUS was free to move its head office and if ED TEL was privatized by an IPO, TELUS was virtually certain to move from Edmonton to Calgary because it was TELUS's biggest market by far. In addition to the significant economic impact, losing the TELUS head office to Calgary would be a monumental psychological blow to Edmonton. Its sensitivity had become acute due to losses of other head offices to Calgary, especially Interprovincial Pipelines Ltd. (IPL) and Shaw Cable. Most major companies headquartered in Alberta were in Calgary.

PROTECTED AREAS AND THE MINING INDUSTRY IN CANADA

In 1994, various representatives of the Land Access Issue Group (LAIG) were gathering for a meeting as part of a multi-stakeholder consultative process known as the Whitehorse Mining Initiative (WMI). In this meeting, the participants were attempting to resolve a major area of disagreement concerning an issue which had caused a virtual impasse in the discussions. The issue involved the protection of representative samples of natural regions and critical wildlife habitats in Canada. This case will review the background for the creation of the WMI and the perspectives of the key participants in the process.

BACKGROUND EVENTS

In September 1992, in Whitehorse, Yukon, at the annual conference of mines ministers of the various governments in Canada, the Mining Association of Canada (MAC) presented a proposal on behalf of its member companies and provincial and territorial mining associations/chambers. Recognizing the need for the mining industry "to earn the trust of Canadians and to prove that it can operate in an environmentally sensitive and sustainable fashion," the MAC proposed the creation of a multi-stakeholder process to develop a common vision and strategic plan for the minerals and metals industry in Canada. The proposal was loosely modelled on the Canada Forest Accord, which had been signed by various stakeholders in the forest industry in 1992 and provided strategic priorities to guide the policies and actions of Canada's forest communities over the next five years.[1] Although the proposal may have surprised government officials, the concerns of the industry about the uncertain socio-political regulatory environment in Canada was a familiar theme from previous annual meetings of mines ministers.

The ministers agreed to the proposal and named the ensuing process the Whitehorse Mining Initiative (WMI). The following five sectors of society agreed to participate in the process: the mining industry, federal/provincial governments, labour unions, Aboriginal peoples, and the environmental community. It was agreed the process would conclude no later than the annual meeting of mines ministers in the fall of 1994. The federal government agreed to assume one-third of the costs, the ten provincial and two territorial governments assumed another third (split according to the ratio of their mineral production), and the Mining Association of Canada assumed the remaining third.

The WMI was to be spearheaded by a Leadership Council composed of all the mines ministers in Canada, top officials of mining and processing companies, leaders of national Aboriginal organizations, labour unions, and environmental organizations, and independent individuals drawn mainly from the academic field. The Leadership Council was to be coordinated and supported by a Working Group, composed of assistant deputy ministers and other senior bureaucrats from a range of ministries and departments, upper management officials in mining and processing companies, heads of industry associations, and key representatives from the Aboriginal, labour, and environmental communities.

Four multi-stakeholder "Issue Groups" were formed to prepare a report addressing the four main issue areas identified as being important to the mining industry. The four areas chosen were (*i*) land access, (*ii*) environmental management and regulations, (*iii*) finance and taxation, and (*iv*) workplace/workforce/community. In addressing their main issue area, each group was to discuss all stakeholder concerns, try to identify common ground, and then work towards agreement on the means to resolve any stakeholder concerns. There were no guidelines given about whether Issue Group participants were speaking on behalf of their respective organizations. After reviewing the Issue Group Reports, the Leadership Council was expected to produce its own report to be known as a "Leadership Accord." The Accord was to be a document which leaders of all WMI constituencies would support and endorse at the mines ministers meeting in the fall of 1994. The Leadership Council was not expected necessarily to endorse the Issue Group reports. A secretariat was created to help coordinate and support the various groups formed in the WMI.

Over the summer and fall of 1993, the Issue Groups began their deliberations. Among the four Issue Groups, the most contentious issue causing a virtual impasse occurred in the Land Access Issue Group (LAIG). The issue involved the protection from mineral exploration and development of representative samples of natural regions and critical wildlife habitats in Canada. The different perspectives of each of the key participants on this issue are described in the next section of this case and in Exhibit 1.

PERSPECTIVES OF KEY PARTICIPANTS

1. Federal/Provincial/Territorial Governments

In November, 1992 the federal, provincial, and territorial Ministers of Environment, Parks, and Wildlife endorsed the "Tri-Council Statement of Commitment to Complete Canada's Networks of Protected Areas." The Statement was also endorsed by Canada's (federal/provincial/territorial) Forests Ministers and representatives of the four national Aboriginal organizations. The five commitments in the Statement were:

i.   complete Canada's networks of protected areas representative of Canada's land-based natural regions by the year 2000 and accelerate the protection of areas representative of Canada's marine natural regions (422 "natural regions" which recognized broad-scale changes in climate and landforms had been identified in Canada; the concept of preserving representative samples of each of Canada's natural regions within a protected areas network was central to the Tri-Council Statement and the Canadian Wilderness Charter—see Exhibit 2; the notion of setting aside representative protected areas was first suggested in 1982 at the Third World Congress on National Parks).

ii. accelerate the identification and protection of Canada's critical wildlife habitat.

iii. adopt frameworks, strategies, and timeframes for the completion of the protected areas networks.

iv. continue to cooperate in the protection of ecosystems, landscapes, and wildlife habitat.

v.   ensure that protected areas are integral components of all sustainable development strategies.

The premises of the five commitments were identified as follows:

- Canada's natural heritage — its wildlands, waters, and wildlife — unites and defines us all as Canadians.

- Canada has a special global responsibility to protect its natural heritage given that:

— Canada is steward of almost 20% of the planet's wilderness (excluding Antarctica), 20% of its fresh water, and 24% of its remaining wetlands

— Canada is one of the few nations that still has an opportunity to represent its natural regions and features, and to conserve its critical wildlife habitat.

- Protected areas have scientific, educational, inspirational, and recreational values for humankind and contribute to sustainable development.

- Protected areas are essential to Canada's environmental health, biological diversity, and ecological processes.

- The ecological health of protected areas is affected by the quality of the surrounding environment.

- The opportunities to protect Canada's natural regions and wildlife habitat are quickly being foreclosed.

- Canada's natural heritage should be safeguarded through a variety of protected areas, including national and provincial parks, ecological reserves, wildlife management areas, and migratory bird sanctuaries.

- Protected areas must be complemented by sound public and private stewardship of all of Canada's lands.

- Aboriginal peoples have a significant and unique role in the protection of Canada's natural heritage.

- The protection of Canada's natural heritage cannot be achieved by any one government or agency.

- Canadians want to be involved in decisions affecting protected areas.

The Tri-Council Statement was the political response to public support for the Canadian Wilderness Charter, the foundation of the Endangered Spaces campaign launched by the World Wildlife Fund Canada in 1989. The goal of the Endangered Spaces Campaign was to achieve the representation of each of Canada's 422 natural regions within a defined protected areas network and the Campaign put a target date for government programs. As of the end of 1993, 32 of the 422 regions were fully represented, 52 were moderately represented, 112 were partially represented, and 226 had little or no representation at all. In total, 4.9 percent of land in Canada had been set aside as "protected areas" where mining was prohibited. Another 1.6 percent was closed, temporarily or permanently, to mineral exploration and development for a variety of reasons, e.g., aboriginal land claims, urban development, roads, railways. Because the federal, provincial, and territorial governments had publicly committed to completing its own network of protected areas, it was expected that at least 12 percent of Canada would eventually be closed to mineral exploration and development. The 12 percent guideline appeared not only in the Endangered Spaces Campaign, but also was echoed in the federal government Green Plan in 1990 and in the unanimous resolution of the House of Commons in 1991.

Different governments were moving at different speeds on completing the protected areas network for their jurisdiction. None of the governments had target dates for completing their network, although most governments had developed a map of natural regions to guide their actions. The overall goal was to protect an area representing the range of elements (i.e., habitats, species, or other natural features) found in that natural region. However, lack of cooperation among governments in defining the natural regions meant that the same natural features could be represented twice within the protected area networks on both sides of a political boundary.

2. Mining Industry

The mining industry had a number of concerns about the completion of Canada's protected areas network. First, there were uncertainties about what areas will be withdrawn or restricted, the size of these areas, and how adjacent areas will be managed. Second, industry's ability to plan its exploration and development activities would be inhibited because of the uncertainty of the time for completing the identification, publicizing, and final selection of protected areas candidate sites. Third, decisions on protected areas may be made without enough information concerning the mineral resource potential of these areas. This last concern was based on the following premises: inadequate government geological mapping, inadequate industry mineral exploration, the limitations of geological deposit models, inadequate techniques used by government geologists and planners for assessing mineral potential, the on-going challenge of measuring the mineral potential of an area because of new uses for minerals, changing technologies for mineral exploration and extraction, and changing world prices.

Another overall concern of the mining industry related to mineral tenure. Because of the costs and risks associated with exploration, potentially involving decades of effort, the industry required a system of secure mineral tenure whereby explorers had clear "title" to deposits found and a concomitant exclusive right to proceed to the mining stage if all regulatory requirements were met. These rights provided the incentive for organizations to commit funds to mineral exploration. Without such rights, the chain of motivation would break down. However, there were increasingly differing views on the nature of "mineral rights" and "mineral tenure." Some lawyers considered "mineral tenure" to be a "property right" giving clear title upon the staking of mineral claims, while others considered "mineral tenure" to be in the nature of a contract or licence, not a property right. Regardless of this debate, the international community had historically regarded Canada's secure systems of mineral tenure as a major attraction for investment.

During the meetings of the LAIG, it became apparent that there were deep divisions even in the mining industry on the issue of protected areas. Some of the division could be attributed to the fact that some companies in the industry were involved in all or some of the various mining stages, i.e., mineral exploration, mining, smelting, refining and semifabrication, while other companies were only involved in exploration. The potentially divergent interests within the industry accounted for the fact that there was more than one industry association. While the Mining Association of Canada (MAC) members accounted for the vast majority of Canada's output of metals and major industrial materials, there was also the Prospectors and Developers Association of Canada (PDAC), whose members were deeply involved in exploration. A few companies were members of both associations. As might be expected, PDAC members tended to be more opposed than MAC members to the concept of protected areas prohibiting mineral exploration. Company size tended to affect positions taken. The larger companies had the ability to explore anywhere in the world, while the smaller prospecting companies in Canada were tied to Canada and could lose their livelihood depending on the regulatory restrictions.

Another source of conflict within the industry concerned the use of resource assessments in planning protected areas. Mineral resource assessments are tools which have been used by companies for planning exploration strategies, and they have also been used by some government agencies for locating parks away from high-potential ground. One industry faction (those most familiar with government processes) endorsed the use of resource assessments in planning protected areas and wished to see their use expanded, notably by including industry's knowledge base in the assessments. This was seen as a means for industry to justify its involvement in protected area decisions and thereby providing some insurance of not being frozen out altogether in these decisions. The other industry faction (consisting of highly technical explorationists) strenuously objected to this position, pointing out that resource assessments have severe limitations. This faction noted that resource assessments can be totally invalidated by the relatively frequent occurrence of a new geological theory and as a result, industry should not be a party to use an inadequate tool for locking up land in perpetuity. This group argued strongly for movable boundaries around protected areas, a demand which had not been accepted at all by environmentalists and governments.

3. Aboriginal Community

Historically, mineral development proceeded in Canada without the consent or involvement of the Aboriginal community.[2] Furthermore, there were other instances where the community did consent to development but derived none of the benefits. However, with the settlement of land claims, Aboriginal communities obtained authority over lands and resources including the right to decide whether to develop its mineral resources.

Pending the settlement of land claims, special agreements (e.g., Memoranda of Understanding) were sometimes established between Aboriginal and non-Aboriginal governments for defining how mineral (and other) development would take place on Aboriginal land before, during and after land-claims settlements. In addition, agreements were also created between Aboriginal governments and mining companies covering such areas as employment and training, contracting opportunities, and environmental protection. With regard to the completion of Canada's protected areas networks, the Aboriginal groups were concerned that there be full consultation of the Aboriginal community in the process used to complete the networks. They also sought assurances that traditional hunting and gathering activities would be permitted in protected areas. Some aboriginal groups recognized and welcomed the development/employment potential of mining while others were more sceptical.

4. Environmental Sector

The environmental groups had the following concerns about the completion of Canada's protected areas networks: (*i*) leading up to WMI, industry representatives were quite adamant in their opposition to protected areas and there was slow progress of governments in getting candidate areas on the table and in establishing the protected areas; (*ii*) in parts of Canada, mineral staking was preempting protected areas plans and as a result, potential candidate areas may be lost to development; (*iii*) compromises may occur on protected area boundaries to accommodate other interests; (*iv*) provincial governments may change their protected area policies to allow resource development in some protected areas; (*v*) resource development may be incompatible on lands adjacent to protected areas, i.e., adjacent lands played an important role as buffer zones to be regulated more intensively.

On the issue of mineral tenure, environmental groups were particularly concerned about the parts of Canada (seven provinces, Yukon and Northwest Territories) with a "free entry" tenure system. (Only PEI, Nova Scotia and Alberta used a "discretionary" tenure system). The "free entry" system was developed in Europe in the 1500s and played a role in later legislation in the 1800s encouraging opening up new land for settlement and development. Under "free entry," rights were given to enter and access mineral lands, locate and stake a claim without consultation, and profit from the extraction of mineral resources in the claimed area. Environmental groups were concerned that "free entry" gave precedence to minerals over other kinds of resource development and/or protection based on the premise that minerals are rare, unpredictable and unmovable.

With regard to this "special status" of mining, environmental groups had at least two concerns: (*i*) the habitats of many threatened and endangered species are at least as rare as mineral deposits, are no more movable, and are much more subject to irreparable damage than mineral deposits; (*ii*) mineral exploration is extensive in its reach into the back country, and contributed significantly to a legacy of access roads and waste across remote areas of Canada. (In response to criticisms of past environmental impacts, the industry noted that significant steps has been taken to operate in a more environmentally responsible manner through better technology, new technical practices, and better management.) Overall, environmental groups were concerned that the "free entry" system did not appear to enable governments to attach environmental conditions to mineral permits. On the issue of compensation for mineral rights, the environmental group's general position was that governments could refund out of pocket expenses if a park was established before the mining permit was approved, and compensation should only be considered if a working mine was expropriated.

ATTEMPTING TO REACH CONSENSUS

After several meetings of the LAIG it was becoming clear that the issue of protected areas was a major area of disagreement threatening the outcome of the process. The environmental sector representatives were adamant that the mining industry support the concept that each of Canada's 422 natural regions should have a representative area free of industrial development. As noted earlier the industry was deeply divided on this issue. A facilitator (Daniel Johnston) was hired to assist the Issue Group. (See Exhibit 3 for a list of LAIG members).

A possible way to resolve the impasse was for the participants to negotiate using other issues where there were opposing positions. For example, the environmental sector representatives took the position that there should be flexibility and government discretion over mineral tenure, i.e., under certain conditions the government should be able to take any valid mineral claims and leases without compensation. However, such flexibility was an anathema to the mining industry (as noted earlier). Furthermore, when a mineral tenure was cancelled, the industry believed that compensation must be paid in a timely fashion based on technical and economic estimates of foregone market value, not simply the costs incurred. Environmental groups disputed this.

Two other controversial issues were: (*i*) whether to allow mining everywhere outside "core" protected areas (and, if so, under what conditions); and (*ii*) which parties should be given access to the decision-making process for protected areas. On the first issue, representatives of the environmental sector were quite reluctant to endorse mining in all areas outside "core" protected areas such as wildlife sanctuaries. On the issue of access to the decision-making processes, both the environmental and mining industry representatives tended to support access for everyone.

Underlying the LAIG discussions was a highly controversial proposed mine located at Windy Craggy Mountain situated in a remote area in northwestern British Columbia near the borders of Alaska and the Yukon Territory. Geddes Resources Inc. hoped to develop the potentially large deposit of primarily copper with by-products of cobalt, silver, and gold. Geddes estimated the value of the copper output to be US $15 billion. With the exhaustion of ore reserves and subsequent closure of other Canadian copper mines, along with a significant depletion of known, easily accessible economic deposits in Canada, the industry was looking for new mines such as Windy Craggy to fill the gap. Furthermore, there had been an overall downturn in mining exploration in Canada in the early 1990s, while large investments were made in developing countries as a result of government reforms, attractive investment incentives and unexplored, more easily exploitable mineral potential. Nevertheless, in the case of Windy Craggy, Geddes faced significant opposition to its plans from a network of North American environment groups who had various concerns such as the earthquake safety of the tailings dams, the potential damage to fisheries stocks caused by acid mine drainage, and how the project might impact the largest eagle sanctuary in the world, and one of the world's densest grizzly bear habitats. There was also significant opposition from US interests. For example, an American river rafting operator opposed the proposed transportation corridor along the "last best river in North America." Vice Presidential candidate Al Gore entered the debate, hoping publicly that Canadian government authorities would reject the mine. Geddes planned a number of actions to minimize environmental damage such as flying in staff rather than using the roadway running through the river valley. An analysis of the interests of the various stakeholders is presented in Exhibit 4.

Controversy on the Windy Craggy project escalated for several months, leading the BC government to ask its Commission on Resources and Environment (CORE) to recommend a solution. CORE identified 86 potential sources of environmental risk and concluded that the World Heritage Convention would drive American interests to ensure that there was no prospect of damage to salmon habitat and other marine life, and that under the current plan, this assurance was not possible. CORE advised the government to consider having six months of public hearings.

In June 1993, the BC government announced its rejection of the Geddes' proposal, deciding that the ecological value of the area outweighed its potential mineral value and on that basis designated the area as a "protected area." It later became a World Heritage site. One analyst attributed the outcome in part to the failure by Geddes to appreciate the importance of public opinion which "was formed almost exclusively on the basis of what the institutionalized environmental lobby said about the project."[3] This analyst noted: "Attempts by Geddes to get its story out were made only after it was apparent that the project was experiencing difficulties."[4]

For several reasons the mining industry was angered by the outcome of the Windy Craggy project. First, the industry generally believed that the BC government's decision was based purely on political grounds rather than scientific grounds. For example, there was a suggestion that the decision was "quid pro quo" to the environmental lobby for decisions made allowing logging of old growth forest in Clayoquot Sound, on Vancouver Island.[5] Second, the industry felt there was a breach of due process when the government suspended review of the project under the Mine Development Assessment Process. Turning over the issue to the newly-instituted, untested CORE process was seen as a change in the rules in that the assessment of the project did not take place under the purview of an environmental review panel. Third, industry believed that the government acted in bad faith when it introduced a controversial bill denying the right to compensation for the exploration costs and potential earnings lost of the industry stakeholders. This bill was introduced following the government decision to reject the project. Even though the BC government was under no legal obligation to pay compensation, the industry felt the government was treating the industry unfairly. Finally, the industry was concerned that a large part of the area surrounding the proposed project was thought to contain extensive mineral wealth, and 20 companies, including Geddes Resources, held mineral claims in the area.

The Windy Craggy project outcome added to the challenges of reaching consensus in the LAIG on the issue of protected areas. There was some feeling among the participants that the events surrounding the project should not be discussed since it was "too explosive an issue" and such a "sore point." On the other hand, there was also some feeling that it could be used as a basis for understanding how a better process could be achieved and there was a need to find a better way to deal with such conflicts, since it was seen by all sides as an example of a "bad process."

As the deadline for submitting a report approached, and as the other Issue Groups were reaching consensus (see Exhibit 5 for an example of principles/objectives established), the LAIG had to come to a decision about their impasse. Some alternatives were: (*i*) agree to disagree by submitting a report which described why the participants could not reach a consensus; (*ii*) negotiate consensus by involving a variety of issues; and (*iii*) do not submit any report on the basis that no consensus was possible on the key issues.

EXHIBIT 1   Stakeholder Statements at the WMI

Aboriginal groups see the WMI as an opportunity to 'seek widespread consultation, share information—particularly about the aspirations of Aboriginal peoples—and present key issues with all stakeholders.'

Labour representatives indicate that 'citizenship is what ultimately underpins labour's commitment to the process embodied in the WMI. Labour views its roles as "stakeholder" in broad social terms, although they are terms rooted in our primary role as representatives and advocates for the driller, driver, wordprocessor, and labour-technician...sharing the economic benefits means sharing the responsibilities.'

Environmental organizations believe that 'The situation of decreasing investment in mining, unresolved land claims between Aboriginal and federal and provincial governments, environmental degradation, and a vulnerable labour force, requires a comprehensive and coordinated response by Canadians. New partnerships must be forged to ensure international and domestic investment in an ecologically, socially, and economically sustainable mining sector.'

Industry bases its expectations on overcoming the current reality that 'the sector is poorly understood, is pursued by historical images, and faces a rapidly changing investment, environmental, and regulatory climate.' While the 'WMI will not solve every problem nor end future controversy, it can open avenues of dialogue, increase understanding and appreciation, and facilitate behaviour changes on all sides.'

Governments, in recognizing that every province and territory of the country benefits from mining, want to join with other stakeholders to assist the mining industry to fulfill its dual responsibility—to be a strong and growing economic contributor and to be a steward for the natural-resource wealth we all enjoy.

Source: Whitehorse Mining Initiative Secretariat, Workbook for Participants in the Whitehorse Mining Initiative Leadership Council Luncheon Meeting, September 14, 1993, Section 4—WMI Vision Statement, 23.

| EXHIBIT 2 | Canadian Wilderness Charter |

1. WHEREAS *humankind is but one of millions of species sharing the planet Earth and whereas the future of the Earth is severely threatened by the activities of this single species,* **2.** WHEREAS *our planet has already lost much of its former wilderness character, thereby endangering many species and ecosystems,* **3.** WHEREAS *Canadians still have the opportunity to complete a network of protected areas representing the biological diversity of our country,* **4.** WHEREAS *Canada's remaining wild places, be they land or water, merit protection for their inherent value,* **5.** WHEREAS *the protection of wilderness also meets an intrinsic human need for spiritual rekindling and artistic inspiration,* **6.** WHEREAS *Canada's once vast wilderness has deeply shaped the national identity and continues to profoundly influence how we view ourselves as Canadians.* **7.** WHEREAS *Canada's aboriginal peoples hold deep and direct ties to wilderness areas throughout Canada and seek to maintain options for traditional wilderness use,* **8.** WHEREAS *protected areas can serve a variety of purposes including: **a)** preserving a generic reservoir of wild plants and animals for future use and appreciation by citizens of Canada and the world, **b)** producing economic benefits from environmentally sensitive tourism, **c)** offering opportunities for research and environmental education,* **9.** WHEREAS *the opportunity to complete a national network of protected areas must be grasped and acted upon during the next ten years, or be lost,*

WE AGREE AND URGE:

1. THAT *governments, industries, environmental groups and individual Canadians commit themselves to a national effort to establish at least one representative protected area in each of the natural regions of Canada by the year 2000,* **2.** THAT *the total area thereby protected comprise at least 12% of the lands and waters of Canada as recommended in the World Commission on Environment and Development's report, Our Common Future,* **3.** THAT *public and private agencies at international, national, provincial, territorial and local levels rigorously monitor progress toward meeting these goals in Canada and ensure that they are fully achieved, and* **4.** THAT *federal, provincial and territorial government conservation agencies on behalf of all Canadians develop action plans by 1990 for achieving these goals by the year 2000.*

As of December 1993, the *Canadian Wilderness Charter* had been signed by more than 250 non-governmental organizations representing the environmental movement, organized religion, business and commerce, recreation and tourism, and naturalists.

EXHIBIT 3   Land Access Issue Group Members

Facilitator

Norman P. MacLeod
Envirotech

Provincial/Territorial

David Hopper
Land Use Planner
Department of Natural Resources
Province of Nova Scotia

Heather Robertson
Land Use Planner
Mineral Sector Analysis Branch
Mines and Minerals Division
Ministry of Northern Development and
Mines
Province of Ontario

Benoit Nadeau
Chargée Projet
Ministère de l'Énergie et des Ressources
Gouvernement du Québec

Paul L. Dean
Assistant Deputy Minister
Mineral Resource Management Branch
Department of Mines and Energy
Province of Newfoundland and Labrador

Graeme McLaren
Manager
Land Use Policy
Land Management & Policy Branch
Ministry of Energy, Mines & Petroleum
Resources
Province of British Columbia

Federal

Peter Hale
Senior Policy Adviser
Resource Management Division
Mineral Policy Sector
Department of Energy, Mines &
Resources
Government of Canada

Colleen Snipper
Director
Protected Areas Group
Environment Canada
Government of Canada

Aboriginals

Jerry Asp
Consultant

Darliea Dorey
Vice-President
Native Council of Canada

Paul Quassa
Nunaeut Beneficiary

Mike Paulette
Vice-President
Métis Nation

Industry

Bruce McKnight
Vice-President
Corporate Affairs
Westmin Resources Limited

Roger Wallis
Vice-President
Exploration
Billiton Metals Canada Inc.

Dennis Prince
Director
Exploration Services
Falconbridge Limited

Robert Keyes
Vice-President
Economics
The Mining Association of Canada

Michael Bourassa
Partner
Aird & Berlis

W.J. Wolfe
General Manager
Canadian Exploration
Cominco Limited

Labour

Bert Pereboom
Senior Program Officer
Business Branch
Research Department
United Steelworkers of America

Environment

Kevin McNamee
Director, Wildlands Program
Canadian Nature Federation

Howard Epstein
Board Member
Ecology Action Centre

Norma Wilson
Volunteer
Canadian Parks and Wilderness Society

Alan Young
Canadian Environmental Network

WMI Secretariat

Lois Hooge
Head
Whitehorse Mining Initiative Secretariat

Torsten Strom
Group Coordinator
Whitehorse Mining Initiative Secretariat

Other Participants

Tony Andrews
Managing Director
Prospectors and Developers Association
of Canada

Phil Fraser
Former Vice-President
Native Council of Canada

Edmond Gus
Consultant
Assembly of First Nations

Tom Hoefer
General Manager
NWT Chamber of Mines

Jim Johnston
Department of Canadian Heritage
Government of Canada

David Luff
Executive Director
Department of Energy
Government of Alberta

Hans Matthews
President
Canadian Aboriginal Minerals
Association

George Miller
President
Mining Association of Canada

Process Support

Daniel Johnston
Partner
Sutherland-Johnston-MacLean Barristers
& Solicitors

Torsten Strom
Issue Group Coordinator
WMI Secretariat

Lois Hooge
Head
WMI Secretariat

Wendy Wesley
Secretarial support
WMI Secretariat

Resource People

Frank Wilson
Co-ordinator
Planning System Review Project
Ministry of Natural Resources
Government of Ontario

Dana Richardson
Director
Municipal Planning Policy Branch
Ministry of Municipal Affairs and Planning
Government of Ontario

Wayne Wagner
Mineral Strategy Branch
Mining Sector
Department of Natural Resources
Government of Canada

Jim Johnston
Department of Canadian Heritage
Government of Canada

Lyn Anglin
Geological Survey of Canada
Department of Natural Resources
Government of Canada

Charles Jones
Resource Management Geologist
Department of Energy and Mines
Government of Manitoba

EXHIBIT 4 Stakeholders Concerns with the Windy Craggy Project Proposal

Stakeholder	Concerns
1. Alaska state agencies -Office of the Governor -House of Representatives -Department of Fish and Game -Department of Natural Resources -Department of Transport and Public Facilities -Alaska Industrial Development	Impacts on land and water habitats inadequately addressed Inadequate contingency plans for chemical and oil spills Acid mine drainage, water quality, and impact on wildlife Inadequate details on use of Haines Highway and Alaskan ports Impact of migrant workers on Alaskan services Impact of roads and public access on bald eagles and their habitat Inadequate opportunities for public involvement in review Seismic potential and stability of impoundment structures Impact on tourism All significant issues identified but not resolved
2. City of Haines, City of Yakutat Haines Borough	Support project for economic benefits subject to removal of environment constraints
3. City of Haines, Chamber of Commerce	Approve of project and use of port facilities subject to attention to environmental protection measures
4. Federal agencies -EPA -NOAA -National Parks -Department of Interior	Inadequate environmental baseline data Waste rock disposal Water quality and impact on fisheries Risk management: earthquakes and tailing pond failures Wilderness and recreational values Inadequate opportunity for public input in British Columbia

5. Environmentalists/ENGOs
    -Sierra Club
    -National Wildlife Federation
    -Wilderness Society
    -Wilderness Journeys
    -Lynn Canal Conservation Inc.
    -Tat International
    -Tatshenshini Wild
    -Western Canada Wilderness
    -Audubon Society
    -Canadian Nature Federation
    -American Rivers
    -International Rivers Network

    Acid rock drainage
    Inadequate opportunities for public
      involvement in review
    Water quality and impact on fisheries
    Natural hazards: earthquakes, failure of
      tailing ponds
    Wilderness and recreational values
    Impacts in the USA
    IJC not consulted sufficiently early in the
      review process

6. First Nations

    Land claim

    -Champaign-Aishihik Bank (Yukon)

    Impacts on water, fisheries and wildlife
    Employment benefits desirable

    -Tahtlan Band (BC)

    Impacts on water, fisheries and wildlife

    -Council for Yukon Indians
    -Alaska Native Brotherhood and
      Sisterhood

    Impacts on water, fisheries and wildlife
    Contingency plans for hazards

7. BC agencies
    Energy mines

    Open pit mining
    Waste rock disposal, and acid mine
      drainage
    Water treatment and management
    Reclamation (mine closure, revegetation,
      structural)

    -BC Environment

    Acid mine drainage
    Road impacts on wildlife
    Long-term integrity of tailing ponds

    -Parks

    Road impact on wilderness values
    Inadequate assessment of wilderness
      values

    -Lands and Parks

    Lack of land use decision prior to techni-
      cal evaluation
    Inadequate information on environmental
      protection
    Acid mine drainage

    -Forests

    Project's economic viability
    Access road hydrology
    Landscape analysis of all proposed work

| -Regional and Economic Development | Inadequate details on incremental work force build up |
| | Inadequate details on transport of inputs and products |

-Tourism

World heritage value of area underestimated

Roads and bridges compromise wilderness and scenic values

Acid rock drainage

Integrity of tailings pond

-Municipal Affairs
Recreation and Culture

No archaeological impact assessment of access road

Inadequate assessment of alternatives to road haulage

-Native Affairs

Impact on First Nations in BC, Yukon, and Alaska

Part of area subject of land claim

-Social Services

Residents of area require priority in job opportunities

-Advanced Education, Science and Technology

Company should recruit local people

. -Health

Road impacts on community watersheds

Storage and disposal facilities at camp sites

8. Yukon
Economic Development

Impacts on Alaska's economy

Impact on access road on local tourism

Impacts on water, and other transboundary resources

9. Federal
-Environment Canada

Inadequate information on environmental impacts

-Fisheries and Oceans
-Transport Canada
-Energy, Mines and Resources

Acid rock drainage

Water quality and impact on fisheries

Road impact on wilderness values

Earthquake hazards

Glacial hazards

Source: J.C. Day and J. Affum, "Windy Craggy: Institutions and Stakeholders," Resource Policy, 21: 1, pp. 21-26, 1995.

**EXHIBIT 5   Example of Principles/Objectives Established
in Another Issue Group[6]**

FINANCE AND TAXATION ISSUE GROUP PRINCIPLES

i. *Capital Formation*
    The mineral industry requires readily accessible investment capital from Canadian capital markets on a globally competitive basis.

ii. *Exploration Investment Capital*

    Canada must remain competitive in attracting exploration investment capital for domestic projects to maintain exploration levels, replenish reserves, and ensure continuing economic vitality and employment in Canada.

The Cost of Doing Business: Mining Taxes, Charges and Regulatory Compliance Costs

Our fiscal and regulatory regimes, which affect the cost to industry of finding and developing new mineral deposits in Canada, should be as simple as possible, pragmatic and fair, with a positive influence on Canada's mineral competitiveness.

Reclamation of Current and Future Mines

In order to have a sustainable mineral industry in Canada over the long term, current and future mine sites need to be managed and operated in an environmentally sound manner and fully reclaimed after operations cease, and progressively where possible.

For current and future mines, Canada's mineral industry, on a company-by-company basis, accepts the primary financial responsibility for preventing and cleaning up environmental disturbances that its activities cause.

Reclamation of Old Mine Sites

Old mine sites must be reclaimed beginning with those posing the greatest health/environmental risk.

Government Services

In recognition of the wealth-generating activity supported by mines and minerals departments, the means must be found to continue the provision of essential government services and products while maintaining the current standards of quality and expertise.

Aboriginal-Industry Business Relationships

Aboriginal peoples and communities should have the opportunity to fully participate in mineral development in Canada.

Legislation, policies, and agreements should encourage growth in Aboriginal-industry business relationships and the financing of mineral projects on reserves.

A fiscal regime should exist which is conducive to mineral industry activities by Aboriginal peoples.

Productive business relationships between Aboriginal peoples and the mineral industry will depend on mutual understanding and open lines of communication.

NOTES

This case was prepared by Professor Mark Baetz (Wilfrid Laurier University) as a basis for class discussion and not to illustrate either effective or ineffective management practices. Funding for the development of this case was provided by the National Management Education Project in Business and the Environment at the Schulich School of Business, York University, under the terms of a project funded by Ontario Hydro. Copyright © 1997 York University. All rights reserved. No part of this publication may be reproduced by any means without permission. For more information, reprint permission, or to order copies of this case study, call (416) 736-5809 or write to the Erivan K. Haub Program in Business and the Environment, Schulich School of Business, York University, 4700 Keele St., North York, Ontario, M3J 1P3.

1. The Canada Forest Accord was different from the WMI as follows: it was funded solely by the government, had a large secretariat, and stakeholders met in a few large open conference-type consultations instead of meeting repeatedly in smaller issue groups.

2. "Aboriginal community" includes Bands, Band Councils, designated Aboriginal organizations, and local or regional Aboriginal communities and their corporations.

3. George Hood, "Windy Craggy: An Analysis of Environmental Interest Groups and Mining Industry Approaches," *Resources Policy*, 21:1, (March 1995), 18.

4. *ibid*, 18, 19.

5. *ibid*, 18.

6. For purposes of the Issue Groups, a "principle" was defined as a "desirable situation which is not currently the norm," and "objective" was defined as "what needs to happen to address the situation described in the principle."

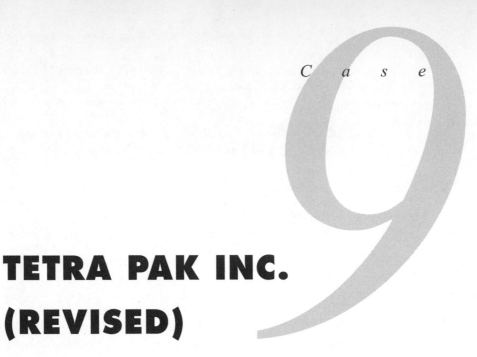

TETRA PAK INC. (REVISED)

In November, 1990, Tetra Pak Inc.'s Environmental Steering Committee, comprised of the President and CEO, the Vice-President Marketing/Environment, the Vice-President Finance, the Corporate Communications Manager, and the Manager Environmental Affairs, met to review the company's communications campaign which had been established during the previous fall. The members of the Committee wanted to determine the success of the year-long campaign and the direction the company should take in the future.

A year earlier, Tetra Pak Inc. (hereafter Tetra) of Aurora, Ontario had obtained consent from Head Office in Lausanne, Switzerland to pursue the possibility of recycling its drink boxes. This action was taken to respond to growing Canadian public concern about the contribution of non-recyclable, non-refillable packages to solid waste landfill sites. To address these concerns, Tetra hired a Manager of Environmental Affairs and, in conjunction with Superwood Ontario Limited, implemented a method of recycling juice boxes by mixing them with plastics to manufacture plastic lumber. Tetra also carried out an aggressive multi-faceted communications campaign, targeting the general public, Tetra customers, the government, and the media. Although the campaign attracted attention to the recyclability of juice boxes, its main objective was to highlight the benefits of the package and its minimal impact on the environment.

THE COMPANY

Tetra was a wholly-owned Canadian subsidiary within the Swedish-based Tetra Pak Group (hereafter TPG) which was founded in 1951 by Dr. Ruben Rausing, a Swedish scientist.

From a small Swedish company with one research facility in Sweden, TPG grew into a highly successful multinational corporation, based in Lausanne, Switzerland, selling its products in 108 countries around the world. Operations included specialized research facilities in seven countries and production plants in thirty countries. TPG had remained 100% family-owned since its inception and was managed by Dr. Rausing's sons. The company expected 1991 revenues of more than $5 billion from sales of about 60 billion cartons around the world.

In the late 1940s, Rausing travelled extensively to many of the developing nations of the world and was disturbed by the poverty and hunger he encountered. He dedicated himself to a vision of developing an ultra-efficient packaging system to make milk — nature's perfect food — more accessible. To do this he invented and perfected a strong, yet lightweight, leak-proof package, and made it aseptic, so that it would not require refrigeration. After years of experimentation and engineering, in 1969 he introduced the Tetra Brik Aseptic (TBA) box, which was lighter and more compact than existing containers, required fewer resources to manufacture and transport, and generated less waste after use. Thanks to TBA, room temperature milk could remain fresh long enough to reach people in countries where refrigerated transport and storage was scarce or, unavailable.

Dr. Rausing devised a package made from a laminate of three materials. He did this because by employing three materials he could choose them for certain properties, and also use a minimum amount of each material, thereby minimizing the effect upon the environment. The laminate was formed of paperboard, polyethylene, and aluminum foil (alufoil), in a ratio by weight of 75,20,5 (percentages). The paperboard gave the package strength and stiffness. The polyethylene was chosen for its inertness, thereby protecting the food, and protecting the paperboard from humidity; it also acted as an adhesive layer to bond the paper to the alufoil, and protected the printing/design. The alufoil acted as a barrier against transmission of gas (oxygen), bacteria, and light.

TPG obtained its first overseas patent in Canada in 1958, enjoying great success with its Canadian entry product, a single-serve coffee cream carton in the shape of a tetrahedron. In the mid-1970s, it set up a sales office near Toronto to increase its sales in Canada and later expanded to offices in Vancouver and Montreal. In 1985, the company decided to invest roughly $25 million in a state-of-the-art production facility in Aurora, Ontario just north of Toronto.

In terms of its administration, TPG was a lean organization. The President and CEO of the Canadian subsidiary reported to a senior executive in Switzerland. Tetra had extensive autonomy over its day-to-day operations, with the exception of major capital and operating expenditures. It employed approximately 240 employees across Canada. In Aurora, people were involved in technical service, production, research and development, and sales administration.

THE PRODUCT

TPG's sole business was the manufacture of packaging systems for liquid food products. Research efforts examining packaging for semi-solid food such as soup and cheese were under way. However, TPG did not intend to look beyond the food industry for packaging business. For example, it would not consider shampoos, bleaches, and motor oils.

The major product manufactured by TPG was the carton (commonly known as a juice box). The juice box maintained a high level of nutrition and flavour protection while ensuring safety to consumers. These benefits had persuaded many consumers to switch containers. For example, in September, 1986, the Institute of Cardiology in Montreal switched from cans to drink boxes for the fruit juice supplied to its new heart recipients. Juice boxes ensured maximum hygiene during the recovery period, and were considered easier and safer to use than cans. Furthermore, the TBA box was the only packing medium for soya milk, the cow's milk substitute preferred by vegetarians and others allergic to cow's milk.

Various independent studies confirmed the juice box's benefits, both as a product and for its impact on the environment (Exhibit 1). In 1989, aseptic packaging was hailed by the Institute of Food Technologists as "the most important food science innovation of the past 50 years."

PRODUCTION

The packaging cartons (both TBA and non-aseptic) were produced worldwide in seven sizes of varying shapes. Tetra manufactured 250 ml and 1 L boxes and was one of several plants supplying these sizes to TPG's worldwide markets. In late 1990, it was additionally assigned responsibility for the 125 ml carton. Sizes not produced in Canada were imported from plants in other countries to service Canadian customers.

Customers worked closely with Tetra to design the packaging artwork. Tetra then printed the design on offset printing presses. The printed paper was laminated with layers of polyethylene and a microthin layer of aluminum. End-products were then delivered to the customers as rolls of "laminated paper." Due to economies of scale, the minimum purchase order quantity had been set at 250 000 boxes.

The process of sterilizing the paper, filling the packages with liquid food and then folding the packages into boxes took place at the customers' premises. The juice box was aseptic because the product was sterilized with hydrogen peroxide and the sterilized liquid filling occurred with no air contact. The machines which performed this process cost approximately $1 million each and were leased to customers by Tetra. This allowed Tetra to ensure that regular maintenance was performed and that the high quality standards of the machines were maintained. In 1990, approximately 25 Canadian customers leased these machines. They sold surplus production time to an additional 50-60 customers whose volumes did not justify their own capital investment. Tetra's major customers were major juice and fruit beverage producers.

Tetra had always operated under stringent internal environmental policies. The company purchased its raw materials (paper, foil, polyethylene granules, and ink) from suppliers which it believed utilized the "best available technology" to minimize their impact on the environment. Tetra used non-solvent organic inks which were cured by electron beam in the offset printing process, again to minimize emissions to the atmosphere.

SALES

Tetra dominated the drink box industry in Canada, with a major share of the approximately one billion carton annual market. Combibloc Inc. was the only other supplier of juice boxes in Canada.

Tetra faced significant secondary competition from glass bottles, cans, gable-top cartons, plastic bottles, polyethylene pouches, and plastic jugs. In 1990, respective shares of these container suppliers for the ready-to-serve juice/drink and nectar market were estimated to be: (*i*) juice boxes, 35%; (*ii*) glass bottles, 15%; (*iii*) gable-top cartons, 15%; (*iv*) plastic bottles, 15%; (*v*) cans, 15%; and (*vi*) other, 5%.

EVENTS LEADING UP TO NOVEMBER, 1989

TPG had not felt a need to actively pursue the possibility of recycling its juice boxes. To a great extent, this view was influenced by the fact that incineration for energy recovery (electricity and steam heat) was a widely accepted method of solid waste disposal in Europe. Fifty to seventy per cent of solid waste in Sweden, France, and Germany was incinerated. Landfill sites were not a viable alternative given the population density of European countries.

In Canada, however, incineration was causing growing concern. For example, a 35-40 year old incinerator plant in Toronto closed down in 1988 as a result of public outcry against its smoke and other toxic emissions. In this instance, the plant was old and had not been well maintained. New incineration facilities, such as Victoria Hospital's Energy from Waste Plant in London, Ontario, employed sophisticated equipment and stringent emission control technologies. Nonetheless, the public image of incinerators had already been irreversibly damaged by earlier events (Exhibit 2).

Furthermore, the public was increasingly concerned about capacity problems at landfill sites, which were attributed to one-way packaging materials. Between 1991 and 1994, Ontario faced the loss of about 45 percent of its annual landfill capacity. Pollution Probe and other environmental organizations, which echoed "green movements" in Germany, Austria, and Belgium, advocated the use of refillable containers over one-way containers and recycling over incineration. However, such groups did not always take a consistent position. For example, in 1988, Pollution Probe in the U.K. issued the original "Green Consumer Guide" stating that Tetra Pak cartons were closepacking, light, and save space and therefore economize on fuel in transport. Pollution Probe in Canada issued a Canadian version in 1989 listing "5 BAD PACKAGES," with Tetra Pak heading the list. When this discrepancy was pointed out to Pollution Probe in Canada they responded that the two organizations were separate and distinct.

The slogan "reduce, reuse, and recycle" was well advertised via radio and newspaper. Notwithstanding the many benefits of the juice box, it became a prime target for environmentalists. Elementary school teachers wrote to parents, asking them not to include juice boxes in their children's lunches. This posed a serious threat to the survival of Tetra. Consequently, Tetra felt strong pressures to respond.

Given the movement towards recycling in Canada, the executives of the company felt that, until juice boxes could be recycled, it would not be possible to effectively convince the Canadian public that Tetra cartons were "environmentally benign." An innovative recycling approach (which involved recycling mixed plastic waste to produce durable synthetic lumber material) developed by Advanced Recycling Technology Ltd. of Belgium had been available since 1987. Patents to the technology and the equipment had subsequently been transferred to Superwood International (based in Dublin, Ireland), who, in turn, had licensed Superwood franchisees around the world. Superwood Ontario Limited of Mississauga, Ontario, obtained its licence in 1989. Tetra, working closely with Superwood International in Ireland, determined that juice boxes, as well as the wrap and straws, could be used as a raw material for this plastic lumber. The juice boxes blended well into the process, and physical testing showed that the incorporation of the paper and aluminum fibres gave the lumber improved strength and stiffness.

Given this development, Tetra requested approval from its head office to sanction the possibility of recycling its products. Approval to "do whatever was deemed necessary" was granted in November, 1989. Tetra initially provided a $1 million loan and technical assistance to Superwood Ontario Ltd., which opened its doors on June 1, 1990. The Ontario and federal government each provided about $200 000 in grants to Superwood. The grants were made available by the Waste Reduction Branch of the Ontario Ministry of the Environment under the Industrial Waste Diversion Program and the federal Department of Industry, Science, and Technology under a program to encourage new recycling technologies. Second, Tetra began an expensive, multifaceted communications campaign to promote its carton's recyclability and minimal environmental impact. In the longer term, some Tetra managers hoped to convince relevant stakeholders that incineration of its packages to create energy was the optimal waste management solution so that recycling would be unnecessary as in many other countries.

Superwood Ontario Limited

Superwood was the result of an innovative plastic extrusion technology. The process combined mixed plastic waste from consumer and industrial sources to produce plastic lumber which could replace wood in a variety of useful applications. At full capacity, Superwood Ontario Limited could process over 3200 (metric) tonnes of mixed plastic and juice boxes per year.

Superwood was a strong, durable, and waterproof material which could be used to produce a variety of products, including picnic tables, park benches, curb stops, planter boxes, and retaining walls. Several Toronto-area pools had adopted Superwood for benches and storage areas. A mall in Scarborough planned to use 400 curb stops (48 benches and approximately 100 planter boxes) manufactured from Superwood. If acceptance of Superwood continued to grow, environmental concerns regarding juice boxes might be reduced. However, the markets for such recycled products were undeveloped and only a maximum of 15 percent of the volume of the final product contained Tetra materials. The company was working to find a production technology which would incorporate a higher degree of its own material.

Municipal Collection

Of the 27 million tonnes of solid waste produced by Canadians, less than 12 000 tonnes consisted of juice boxes. Because of this low volume, Tetra could not be expected to operate a collection system for its cartons. Instead, the company had to convince municipalities, who were legally responsible for solid waste management, to include juice boxes as part of the plastic stream in their Blue Box programs. The rough breakdown of recyclable materials collected in 1990 was: newspapers, 75%; glass, 10%; steel, 10%; and PET/plastics, 5%.

The Blue Box collection system had been created under the auspices of a unique business-government cooperative arrangement. In 1985, Ontario Multi-Material Recycling

Inc. (OMMRI), an association of the soft drink industry and its container and container material suppliers reached an agreement with the Ontario government whereby the costs of the Blue Box program would be shared and non-refillable containers would be permitted using an initial sales ratio of 60/40 non-refillable to refillable. The ratio would change to 70/30 when a 50% recycling ratio was achieved. Over the period 1986 to 1989, the costs of the Blue Box program were shared as follows: (*i*) OMMRI: one-third of capital costs and some of the promotional costs (OMMRI contributed $20 million over the four-year period); (*ii*) provincial government: one-third of capital costs and a declining ratio of operating costs (from 50 percent to zero); (*iii*) municipalities: one-third of capital costs and operating costs not covered by the province. In 1989, the Blue Box system was acclaimed by the United Nations Environment Program and the Ontario Ministry of the Environment, the Recycling Council of Ontario, and OMMRI were jointly presented with the UN's Environment Award. In the spring of 1990, because of provincial government desires to broaden private sector involvement in waste reduction activities a new agreement was reached involving more industry groups to expand the Blue Box program. Under the new agreement, six industry sectors agreed to provide $45 million over the five years, 1990 to 1994, to help fund the system which had a mandate to extend the Blue Box network to reach 80 percent of Ontario households and expand the range of materials collected. Pollution Probe estimated that the soft drink industry saved up to $80 million annually using non-refillable containers.[1] However, there was some concern that if provincial governments did not continue to subsidize the Blue Box program, the municipalities would pull out of the program.

It was difficult to sell municipalities on the idea of collecting juice boxes as part of the Blue Box program. Many did not have the ability to sort or bale the materials nor the capacity to warehouse them once collected. Others simply expressed no interest in the concept. Several municipalities were also reassessing their existing recycling programs. Superwood had three arguments to use in attempting to include juice boxes in municipal recycling programs: (*i*) significant volumes of materials are diverted from landfills; (*ii*) no sorting of plastics into different types and sorts is necessary; and (*iii*) a guaranteed market exists since Superwood would sign a contract to buy all their baled post-consumer waste at $60/tonne for a specified period of time.

Tetra's first success with the Blue Box program occurred in Markham, Ontario. In June, 1990, coinciding with the opening of Superwood, the Town of Markham announced that it would start a pilot program to include all mixed plastics and, for the first time in the world, juice boxes. Only those boxes bearing the triangular "Tetra Pak" logo would be accepted. In light of the success of the pilot, the municipality was collecting juice boxes from over 40 000 Markham homes by the fall of 1990. The municipality of Lindsay, Ontario followed in early October, 1990.

THE ECOLOGO

In 1988, the federal government announced a new environmental labelling program to help consumers recognize products deemed least harmful to the environment. A black and white maple leaf, made of three intertwined doves, known as the "EcoLogo" was the government's "environmental seal of approval." A sixteen-member Environmental Choice Board was created to decide whether to give EcoLogos for various product categories and if so, to establish criteria for deciding if an applicant could be licensed (for three years) to use the

EcoLogo. The Canadian Standards Association administered the testing. The program was patterned after similar efforts in other countries, particularly the Blue Angel symbol developed in Germany in the late 1970s.

Soon after the EcoLogo program was announced, Tetra made inquiries about using the EcoLogo. Government officials were impressed with the energy efficiency and reduction characteristics of Tetra's product, but stated that politically, granting permission to use the logo would not be appropriate, since the product could not be recycled. However, Superwood was given permission to use the EcoLogo. By the fall of 1990, 26 products had won the right to display the logo, but it was expected that many more products would be approved. The federal government planned a multi-million dollar advertising program to give such products a marketing advantage over competitors.

MANAGER-ENVIRONMENTAL AFFAIRS

In addition to the efforts described above, Tetra's President created a new position, Manager Environmental Affairs, in January, 1990. The individual hired for the position, Dr. Abe Kabayama, had a Ph.D. in physical chemistry and relevant work experience in the US and Canada in the management of environmental affairs and government relations. He reported to the Vice-President, Marketing/ Environment, and was given full authority by the Environmental Steering Committee to deal with issues within his mandate. Kabayama's responsibilities included: (*i*) researching new technologies to validate the company's sustainable development efforts; (*ii*) establishing internal recycling programs; (*iii*) developing markets for recycled materials; (*iv*) reducing plant emissions and energy consumption; (*v*) responding to concerns of a technical nature from the public, government, etc.; and (*vi*) persuading municipalities to expand their Blue Box collections to included mixed plastics and juice boxes. Kabayama was enthusiastic about the Tetra Pak organization because of the environmental record of the company's products.

A NATIONAL PACKAGING PROTOCOL

In 1989, in response to demands from consumer groups, environmentalists, and various levels of government, the Canadian Council of Ministers of the Environment (federal and provincial ministers of the environment) decided to explore the feasibility of developing national policies aimed at reducing the amount of waste entering landfill sites. A Task Force was commissioned, composed of representatives from all relevant stakeholder groups, including the packaging industry, to develop a set of "guiding principles" for eliminating landfill waste.

During the Task Force consultations, Tetra strongly recommended that before any further policy development occurred, more research should be conducted to determine the relative environmental impacts of various disposable, recyclable, and refillable containers. Tetra also made the following points:

i. A "waste efficiency audit" of different packaging systems should be conducted to examine the amount of material used (weight, volume) to deliver an equivalent amount of product. For example, a European study found that a 1 litre Tetra Pak aseptic carton generated 27 grams of waste, as compared to 338 grams for an equivalent volume nonrefillable glass container.

ii. An "environmental impact audit" should be conducted to examine the amount of raw materials, water, and energy consumed in producing different types of packages, as well as the amount of pollution created.

iii. Municipal officials in Ontario were concerned that the 25% interim and 50% final reduction goals of the Ontario government for landfill waste, to be achieved by 1992 and 2000 respectively, were too ambitious and unrealistic, particularly because of the negative stance the provincial government had taken toward municipal incineration. The provincial government provided little financial support to municipalities to meet the reduction targets and to help fund programs like blue box collection. As a result, the municipalities were pushing for the return of a bottle deposit system and a ban on all non-reusable or non-recyclable packages. However, retailers and packaging companies were generally opposed to any form of deposit system.

iv. A voluntary set of guidelines, incorporating a monitoring mechanism to ensure reduction targets were met, would be preferred to government-imposed regulations.

Overall, Tetra recommended that reduction be established as the first priority of any waste management strategy. While recycling should be viewed as an important component to reduce the volume of waste diverted to landfills, Tetra felt the packaging industry should be encouraged to develop new technologies and preserve existing ones (such as the aseptic carton) which achieved reductions in the amount of inputs used to produce packaging material.

The final text for the "National Packaging Protocol" was endorsed in early 1990. The Protocol was based on the "3R Hierarchy:" Reduce, Reuse, and Recycle. Recovery options, such as energy from waste (EFW) and incineration were not encompassed or envisioned in the Protocol. The adoption of a 3R Hierarchy placed companies like Tetra at a severe disadvantage, since aseptic containers were not reusable or easily recyclable, and they could not further reduce the volume of raw material inputs used in manufacturing the container, since such reductions had been incorporated into the original package design. Specific "across the board" waste reduction targets were established in the Protocol as follows: Packaging sent for disposal shall be cut to at least 80% of the 1988 level by the end of 1992, 65% of the 1988 level by the end of 1996 and 50% of the 1988 level by the end of 2000.

An independent auditor determined the appropriate 1988 base figure for each type of packing material sent to landfills to monitor compliance with these targets. The initial base figure for Tetra was set at 12 000 tonnes.[2] Given the relatively light weight of the aseptic carton, this 1988 base figure for Tetra was extremely low for the number of litres distributed by that amount of packaging material, even when compared to packages that could be recycled (Exhibit 3). Tetra was concerned that its own base figure of 12 000 tonnes would have to be reduced by 50 percent, but learned from the Packaging Task Force that the 50 percent reduction target was intended to be an "across the board" target rather than a target applied equally to each product. In any case, compliance with the targets was entirely voluntary, although various levels of government throughout Canada threatened to implement regulations, and even ban products or increase taxes if specified reductions were not achieved voluntarily.

While the National Packaging Protocol could conceivably ensure a consistent approach to regulations for packaging across Canada, different provinces were in fact considering different regulatory approaches. Some provinces were inclined to adopt deposit refillable systems, where industry would be told what to do, while other provinces were considering a "product stewardship model" involving industry self-regulation. Some observers considered the product stewardship model more mature, because industry would be responsible for regulating itself, but also more dangerous given the challenges of enforcement and the uncertainty about what financial and other commitments would be made by each company.

OTHER TETRA PAK INITIATIVES

Tetra Pak addressed the issue of minimizing the environmental impact of the company's products through a number of initiatives:

i. In Canada, the company provided financial and technical assistance to Superwood. However, in 1990, the amount of waste diverted to the three plastic lumber companies operating in Canada was small (representing a total of 2000 tonnes per annum) and synthetic wood, being new to Canada, had a very small market.

ii. Pilot programs began on a limited scale in the US, Germany and Spain to "repulp" used Tetra Pak cartons. Repulping was a recycling process commonly employed in paper mills whereby waste paper was shredded, mixed with water in a pulper and then remanufactured into new paper. Tetra Pak cartons could be repulped in a normal repulping unit outfitted with screens to remove aluminum and polyethylene particles. These particles could then be recycled along with waste plastics into plastic lumber.

iii. In 1990, a pilot project had been launched in Germany to produce chipboard composed entirely of aseptic carton waste. The end product had many of the physical properties of wood and, because of the plastic content, could be thermoformed by placing it in a mold and applying heat. To be economically viable, a chipboard plant required a reliable feedstock supply of approximately 100 000 tonnes per year, which far exceeded the amount of drinking carton waste generated in the Canadian market (12 000 tonnes per annum).

iv. Tetra explored a number of extrusion applications. In the extrusion process, aseptic cartons were shredded, heated, and, in some instances, mixed with other inputs to produce a number of different products. Using extrusion, fuel pellets could be produced from cartons to be burned in industrial boilers and cement kilns. These pellets were cheaper than coal and burned cleanly, but tended to cause uneven temperature levels and slagging in boilers, hindering market development efforts. Pallet spacers could also be made using extrusion technology. These spacers were widely used by a variety of industrial firms, including Tetra Pak. However, the end product was heavier than conventional wood pallets.

v. Tetra Pak signed a development contract with BTI of Germany to refine a method of manufacturing low density rigid board using drink cartons. These boards could be used in products such as wallboard and acoustic panels.

vi. Tetra dramatically reduced the volumes of its own plant waste.

vii. In Canada, Tetra funded research to explore the development of other processes which could use aseptic carton waste. These included the use of cartons to replace wood chips in the manufacture of medium density fibreboard (used extensively in the construction and furniture industries).

THE 1990 COMMUNICATIONS CAMPAIGN

Tetra structured its 1990 communications campaign around three major target groups: the general public, the company's customers and suppliers, and various levels of government. The overall objectives were to change the perception that laminated plastics could not be recycled and to reinforce the environmental advantage of juice boxes in terms of reductions in waste, energy consumption, and use of raw materials.

General Public

For years, school boards had encouraged students to make nutritious lunch choices in packages that did not break and were safe to use. Juice and milk in Tetra Pak drink boxes seemed to be an obvious choice for many families. However, teachers and parents had developed a negative impression of juice boxes based upon misinformation about their "environmental impact."

To kick off the awareness campaign, Tetra worked with a major advertising agency to develop a full page print ad (Exhibit 4) which appeared in newspapers within Eastern Canada in August and September, 1990. The ad stated that the juice box was "a package of environmental solutions" and highlighted reduction of waste, raw materials, air pollution, and energy, as well as the carton's recyclability. Similar advertisements appeared in *Chatelaine*, *Canadian Living* and *Macleans* magazines and in several teachers' journals.

With the assistance of a major British Columbia-based advertising firm, Tetra also developed a full colour newspaper insert titled "The Juice Box Story," which appeared in all dailies and some weeklies across Canada during the fall of 1990. Tetra Pak's "very efficient package" (combining the best technology and materials, minimal energy use, minimal landfill impact, and recyclability) was emphasized. Flyers were also distributed to residents whenever their city or municipality began to accept drink boxes in their Blue Box program.

Customers and Suppliers

Tetra took a different approach with its business partners. The company felt it was crucial that its customers and suppliers understood that Tetra was taking a proactive role in managing issues of sustainable development. In early October, 1990, Tetra developed the following "Ten Point Program" for its customers and suppliers: (*i*) Theme: "Good for you, good for the earth," (*ii*) Publicity, (*iii*) Advertising (consumer/trade), (*iv*) In-store campaign ("shelf talkers"), (*v*) Consumer promotions, (*vi*) Educators' program (school kits), (*vii*) Recycling (Superwood), (*viii*) Government relations, (*ix*) Cooperative programs, (*x*) Establishment of the Canadian Beverage Box Council (an association of aseptic packagers, i.e., Tetra, Combibloc and their customers).

By November, the program had been communicated via presentations by senior management to Tetra's major customers. Feedback was positive, with the general message being "we're glad you're doing something." Tetra also encouraged its customers to be proactive by including "environmental messages" as part of their package design. The company's interaction with its suppliers was still at a preliminary stage.

Government

During his previous work, the Manager of Environmental Affairs had established excellent connections with federal and provincial government officials and various committees across Canada He maintained regular contact with these organizations in his new role at Tetra. For example, Tetra had enjoyed a strong relationship with the Ontario Liberal government, actively participating in committees such as the Ontario Recycling Advisory Council which represented various business and environmental groups and municipalities. In 1990, a senior manager of Tetra also joined the Board of Directors of OMMRI.

The company recognized the importance of continuous communication with government groups. Recent experiences in the United States had demonstrated the costs of not communicating adequately with government. In particular, the State of Maine passed legislation in 1989 which banned the sale of any beverage in aseptic cartons. The ban in Maine occurred because the aseptic packaging industry did not have, at that time, a system for monitoring legislation being introduced and considered in the federal, state, and municipal legislative bodies. The Maine Legislature had set up an Environment Committee in 1987 to study ways and means of reducing the solid waste stream. One of the solutions studied was to establish a beverage container deposit system under which all beverages, with the exception of milk, would carry a deposit. Moreover, only containers which satisfied one of three criteria (refillability, recyclability, or biodegradability) would be permitted. All other containers would be banned, i.e., could not be sold in the state. The pertinent legislation was passed in September, 1989, and was slated to come into effect on September 1, 1990. (Milk, health food, and concentrates could still be sold in TBA.)

With the 1989 passage of the law banning aseptic cartons, Tetra Pak and Combibloc immediately formed the Aseptic Packaging Council (APC), to monitor all relevant legislation and/or regulations, to provide information and communication, and to research and implement recycling initiatives across the nation. The Environment Committee in Maine held hearings on January 23, 1990 to listen to arguments related to the ban on aseptic packaging. The APC argued that TBA should be allowed into the Maine deposit system because it was compostable and recyclable into synthetic lumber or chipboard. Opponents argued that the aseptic container industry had not expressed concern about the solid waste problem until the ban was passed, and that the law should be allowed to operate before any changes were considered. After the hearings, Maine decided to retain the ban on the juice box.

Many other states introduced or considered the adoption of legislation similar to the Maine legislation, but the APC national government relations program was successful in side-tracking such initiatives. However, in Maine, the APC failed to have the ban temporarily lifted to facilitate an APC-sponsored pilot-recycling program.

As in the United States, Tetra saw the regulatory environment in Canada as both fluid and complex. The company hired a government relations consulting firm to keep the company informed about what was happening at both the federal and provincial government levels, since each province had to be viewed as a "separate challenge." The consulting firm was not hired to lobby on Tetra's behalf, but to gather information about what options the governments were considering, the individuals involved and their backgrounds, and the "key influences" on each government. The consulting firm also provided Tetra with an objective view of the issues, and periodically gave advice to the company about possible alliances.

To assist Tetra in communicating its message to governments in Canada, a 12-minute video entitled: "A Balanced Environment" was developed with the help of a major public relations firm (see Exhibit 5). The show was initially used in a presentation to the British Columbia government which was considering deposit legislation. Tetra planned to use the show in similar presentations to other provincial governments, the federal government, and a variety of other groups in the educational and recycling fields.

Tetra also developed another 12 minute video entitled: "A Box Called Tyler" to educate students about the possible recyclability of the juice box in response to the increasing trend towards "garbageless lunch" programs. In these programs, students were discouraged from bringing non-reusable and non-recyclable packages for lunch. In addition to the video, the company initiated a pilot school recycling program to collect Tetra packages from the school board in the Region of York north of Toronto. Student committees were formed to take responsibility for collecting the packages and Tetra took responsibility for providing the necessary equipment and collecting and delivering the packages to Superwood for recycling. From this program, the company hoped to gain information about the costs, logistics and attitudes of school boards, teachers and children. The Environmental Committee of the Toronto School Board reviewed the program and decided not to participate.

In general, Tetra's approach was "to make itself very available" to participate in packaging or environment-related events or conferences. The company's attitude was that these presented opportunities to communicate accurate messages about the environmental impact of juice boxes.

NOVEMBER 1990

In November, 1990, one year after the initiation of their communications campaign, the Environmental Steering Committee decided to review their progress to date. The Committee's general feeling was that the communications campaign was "good, but not good enough" and therefore, members considered changes Tetra could make.

Tetra had received some encouraging feedback regarding the newspaper advertisements and inserts. A toll-free telephone number was established to handle inquiries from the public regarding information in Tetra advertisements. Over 2000 calls were recorded, more than 85% of them positive. However, many people had the perception that Tetra was promoting recyclability, even though the company knew that its product was not being recycled in many municipalities. They complained that the claims meant little to them until their communities began to accept juice boxes as part of their local Blue Box programs. Tetra's explanations that municipalities determined which materials would be recycled, and that they were often slow to implement collection programs, seemed to fall on deaf ears.

During pre-election speeches, the newly-elected NDP government in the province of Ontario had pledged to ban the use of juice boxes (Exhibit 6). The Environmental Steering Committee was uncertain about the impact this would have on the company's business, as policies had not yet been established regarding environmental issues. However, the company was concerned about the role the new government might play in helping or hindering its activities.

EXHIBIT 1

The Inside Story

Outside and in, Tetra Brik cartons were designed to ensure optimum flavour and nutrition protection for a variety of liquid foods, and to use minimal amounts of materials and energy.

The end result is a unique package that reduces demands on the environment.

- Most Tetra Brik paper comes from forests where the growth rate is greater than the fell rate. A renewable resource, paper composes 75 percent of Tetra Brik cartons and uses little or no chlorine in the bleaching process.

- Tetra Brik paper uses 1.5 times less water in the manufacturing process than refillable glass bottles, and 2.5 times less than nonrefillable glass bottles.

- A micro-thin layer of aluminum, about five percent of the total, provides an impenetrable barrier against air, light and bacteria.

- There's less aluminum in a Tetra Brik carton than the lightest of any screw-on bottle cap.

- The small amount of aluminum in a Tetra Brik carton saves more energy than is required to make it, because it allows liquid food to be shipped and stored without refrigeration.

- Pure, food grade polyethylene plastic makes up 20 percent of all Tetra Brik cartons. In all, Tetra Brik cartons seal in the best food quality possible.

A Clean-Air Approach to Packaging

- Manufacturing Tetra Brik cartons creates less air and water pollution than most other kinds of packaging.

- Tetra Brik users indicate that these cartons require half the energy costs to manufacture and deliver products to market than other packaging.

- Tetra Brik cartons comprise less than three percent of the total weight of the product. A

1-litre glass bottle comprises 30 percent or more of the product's total weight.

- In June 1989, The Institute of Food Technologists in the United States recognized aseptic innovation in the past 50 years. The reasons cited were outstanding levels of nutrition and flavour protection, and consumer safety.

Going the Distance for Less

- Less than two standard semi-trailers can transport a million unfilled 1-litre Tetra Brik cartons. 52 semi-trailers are needed to haul a million unfilled litre-size glass jars or bottles.

- Filled Tetra Brik cartons take up 30 percent less energy to ship than glass bottles.

- Tetra Brik cartons produce 12 times less waste than glass bottles for equal product shipments (taking into account Canada's 25 percent recycling rate for glass bottles).

Tetra Brik Cartons are Recyclable

- Tetra Pak packaging recycles into many useful products including shoe soles, mats and a durable lumber substitute called "Superwood".

- In June, 1990 Tetra Brik cartons were collected for the first time in curbside Blue Box containers in Markham, Ontario.

- Tetra Pak plans to extend recycling programs for drinking boxes into Vancouver and Montreal by the end of 1990, and eventually across all of Canada.

Already, Tetra Pak is minimizing its effect on the environment by greatly reducing its environmental demands during manufacturing and shipping.

Now that it is recyclable, this modern packaging miracle will come full circle in meeting consumers' needs and those of the environment.

**EXHIBIT 2   NDP Facing 'Environment Test' from
Anti-Pollution Activists**

NDP
Transition to Power
11 days to Oct. 1

Pollution Probe says the first 18 months of Rae government will indicate how much is going to be done.

By Gordon Sanderson and Rob McKenzie

The London Free Press   Sept. 20, 1990

TORONTO—Pollution Probe has set a tough timetable for the new NDP government to deliver on its promise of an environmental cleanup.

"We're looking at the first 18 months as a real test of how much is going to be done," the coalition's Janine Ferretti said Wednesday at Queen's Park. "We will fight for the adoption of the new government's environmental blueprint for Ontario."

Incinerator Ban: Among other things, the watchdog group is calling for an immediate ban on new garbage incinerators and, within a year, a plan to shut down existing incinerators, including Victoria Hospital's three-year old, $32 million energy-from-waste plant, where the bulk of London's household garbage is burned.

Hospital spokesman John Finney said the incinerator is equipped with "state-of-the-art pollution control equipment" and complies with strict rules on pollution. He said it also reduces the hospital's energy bill, freeing up dollars for health care.

Last December, Westminster (nearby London) sued the hospital and London because the city was dumping fly ash from the incinerator at a city-owned landfill in Westminster. Federal tests indicated excesses of toxic metals such as cadmium and lead in the ash.

The hospital stopped dumping the ash in March and began shipping it to a waste company near Sarnia. Westminster dropped the portion of its suit against the hospital and is "not actively pursuing" the portion against the city, says Mayor Dave Murray.

Ban Supported: Ferretti said Pollution Probe was encouraged by Rae's responses during the election campaign to a questionnaire on the environment.

Rae supported an immediate ban on municipal garbage incineration and endorsed the view that incinerators undermine efforts to reduce waste. (The Liberal government ended the dumping of incinerator fly ash in municipal landfills as of September 1).

EXHIBIT 3   Over 500 000 Tonnes of Landfill Saved

- Between 1982 and 1989 inclusive, Tetra Pak sold packaging for a total of approximately 1.6 billion litres of liquid food, using 62 000 tonnes of packaging material (all of which went to landfill).

- If the same volume had been sold in 1.36-L and 284-ml steel cans, the net landfill would have been about 130 000 tonnes (with 50% recycling included in the calculations).

- If the same volume had been sold in 1-L and 284-ml glass bottles, total landfill would have been about 625 000 tonnes (with 25% recycling included in the calculations).

- The difference in landfill additions between Tetra Pak packaging and glass (563 000 tonnes) is roughly equal to the total amount of landfill produced annually by a city the size of Ottawa.

- Had the same 1.6 billion litres been sold in refillable bottles, making thirteen round trips (the average in Europe is seven), the amount of landfill produced by glass bottles would have been about the same as that produced by beverage boxes, but with the added disadvantage of more fossil fuels used in transporting these heavy containers back and forth and more energy used in heating wash water.

These are the assumptions upon which the above comparisons were made:

Weights		TBA[1] Volume (1982–1989 inclusive)	
1-L TBA carton	31.4g	784 million litres	(1-L family size)
1-L glass bottle	400g	<u>853.5 million litres</u>	(250-ml single serve)
1.36-L steel can	166g	1637.5 million litres total	
250-ml TBA carton	11g		
294-ml glass bottle	173g		
284-ml steel can	55g		

Recycling Rates (national average)

TBA:	0% (TBA recycling began in 1990)
Glass:	25%
Steel:	50%

[1] TBA refers to Tetra Brik Aseptic cartons.

EXHIBIT 4

THIS IS AN ENVIRONMENTAL SOLUTION

The beverage box is a package of environmental solutions.

Reduce Waste. A beverage box is 97% beverage, only 3% packaging. Litre for litre, that's ten times less packaging than glass bottles: ten times less waste.

Reduced Raw Materials. Beverage boxes use less raw materials than glass bottles. And 75% of those raw materials come from renewable resources.

Reduced Air Pollution. Unfilled beverage boxes are light weight and are shipped in compact rolls. A million empty ones can be carried in 2 semi-trailers, compared to 50 *semi-trailers* for that many one-litre glass bottles.

Reduced Energy. Filled beverage boxes are compact and fit together like building blocks with no wasted space, saving energy when storing and shipping them.

Recycling. Beverage boxes can be recycled. Students in York Region deposit them in recycling bins at 102 schools. Markham and Lindsay include beverage boxes in their municipal Blue Box programs. Tetra Pak is working to get other municipalities involved right across Canada.

The Right Choice. Beverage boxes reduce waste, reduce energy use, and conserve resources. They're one of the most healthy and nutritious packages ever invented according to the Institute of Food Technologies.

Beverage boxes are an environmental solution. For your family and for your future.

A box of solutions

For more facts on beverage packaging and the environment, call 1-800-263-2228 or write Tetra Pak Inc., 200 Vandorf Road, Aurora, Ontario L4G 3G8

EXHIBIT 5   **COMMUNICATION VIDEO: "A BALANCED ENVIRONMENT"**

"All of us are in a balancing act between what consumers want and what the environment can take; between what we produce and what we are left with. All packaging is very much under the microscope from an environmental point of view and there is a lot of misinformation out there in the marketplace. We don't have a crisis we have an opportunity to get a head start on what we throw away. We must reduce by taking less out of the environment when a product is made and when economically and environmentally feasible we must recycle by putting less back in the environment when the product is consumed. So consumers like to focus on recycle but we've got to be sure that in fostering recycling we don't defeat source reduction. Reduce and recycle — for a truly balanced environment we must strive to do both."

The next segment of the video described the composition of the Tetra Pak aseptic carton.

In the next segment of the video different individuals representing the Institute of Food Technologists, National Research Council, American Management Association, and Tetra Pak commented on the benefits of the Tetra Pak (Tetra) carton. An "Environmental Summary" concluded this segment of the video by flashing the following four points: (*i*) "No hot water washing/detergents." (The viewer was expected to be aware that reusing glass bottles required hot water washing — which required energy and the use of detergents — which created water pollution; however, the Tetra Pak carton was never, and could never be refilled primarily because health authorities prohibited refilling packages consisting of semi-permeable materials, such as paper, wood and plastic); (*ii*) "Less aluminum—than screw-on caps." (This point was meant to address concerns that aluminum should not be thrown away but should be recycled). (*iii*) "Lower energy consumption." (The video noted: "The environmental impact of any package is fundamentally in the areas of energy use, non-renewable resource use, and solid waste creation. When you reduce the weight of a package you reduce the energy required because you reduce the materials"); (*iv*) "Reduced fuel and exhaust emissions." (The video noted: "52 semi-transport trailers are needed to transport 1 million empty glass or metal containers. Tetra Pak cartons are shipped in compact rolls. One million cartons require less than two semi-trailers reducing fuel consumption and exhaust emissions by over 26 times). The end of this segment of the video noted: "Tetra Pak environmental policy sums up these facts and figures: To provide <u>cost effective</u> packaging systems for liquid food that maximize product <u>quality and safety</u> and simultaneously <u>minimize effects on the environment</u>" (underlined words were emphasized).

The final segment of the video dealt with the recycling issue and noted the following:

"As consumers we all make choices about the products we consume and their waste. When that waste is an empty Tetra Pak carton we have two choices: throw it out or recycle it. In either case, because the carton is made with less material in the beginning, there is less waste. The first and best way of dealing with solid waste is to not create it at all — what is called source reduction....litre for litre Tetra Pak cartons produce as little as one-tenth the landfill produced by today's glass bottles and that's after subtracting the bottles that are recycled. Caps and labels off glass bottles are not usually recycled and even they can weigh up to one-third of the whole aseptic package...if we achieved our goal of source reduction to a very high degree, recycling would essentially disappear because there wouldn't be enough material around to recycle."

The segment concluded by describing how Tetra Pak cartons were being recycled into "excellent" particle board and synthetic lumber. It was noted that "the first production plant is in Germany," and "Blue Box collection of Tetra cartons has already begun in parts of southern Ontario and Tetra is working to expand this across Canada..A study by the Grocery Products Manufacturers of Canada states that almost seven of ten Canadians are willing to participate in a curbside recycling program."

The video concluded as follows: "Because it reduces and is now recyclable, we're convinced the Tetra brik aseptic package is a responsible and environmentally sound package. We will cooperate with government, industry partners, and consumers to make it even better. That's our commitment to a world insisting on healthy products and a healthy environment."

| EXHIBIT 6 | NDP'S PROMISE TO OUTLAW BEVERAGE BOXES 'SHOCKING' |

By John Fox, Financial Post, September 18, 1990

The pre-election pledge of a senior Ontario, New Democrat to ban the use of boxes as beverage containers because they are difficult to recycle is "shocking and shortsighted," says a spokesman for **Tetra Pak Inc.,** the product's maker.

Ruth Grier, a senior NDP MPP rumored to be headed for the environment portfolio in premier-elect Bob Rae's cabinet, promised the ban during a public debate in Toronto a week before her party's election win.

Many environmentalists don't like the containers — used to package everything from wine to milk shakes — because they are not reusable and contain a combination of plastic, paper and aluminum that makes them hard to recycle.

A spokesman for Grier said she would have no comment on the fate of the boxes until after a cabinet has been appointed.

Jaan Koel, a spokesman for the Aurora, Ont. company Tetra Pak, a wholly-owned subsidiary of Swiss-based Tetra Pak Rausing SA, said Grier's opposition to drinking boxes is based on "purely a surface evaluation of the situation" and not on "solid, factual information."

He said the company, with sales of 920 million boxes a year in Canada worth $100 million — and 35% to 40% of sales in Ontario — is launching a recycling program in Linsday, Ont. and Markham, Ont. in October. Householders will be asked to separate drinking boxes and other plastics from their blue boxes for collection and sale to Superwood Ontario Ltd. of Mississauga, Ont., which will turn them into plastic lumber.

Superwood is also in negotiations with recycling officials in Vancouver and Montreal. Koel said it may take several years to expand the program to the entire Ontario blue box system.

In the meantime, critics of the drinking boxes ignore their environmental and economic advantage, he said.

He said the light-weight packages offer huge savings in transportation costs and the environmental impacts of burning fossil fuels. For example, two million empty drinking boxes can be shipped in two tractor trailers. The same number of empty glass or metal containers would require 52 trucks, Koel said.

Because they are more compact than bottles or cans, he added, they also contribute less to the province's overflowing garbage dumps.

NOTES

This case was prepared by Jennifer McNaughton and Fred Chan under the supervision of John S. Hulland of the Western Business School and by Mark Baetz, with the assistance of Peter Kelly, both of Wilfrid Laurier University. This case was prepared primarily from public sources. Certain information in the case may have been disguised to protect confidentiality. This case was prepared as a basis for class discussion rather than to illustrate effective or ineffective handling of an administrative situation. Copyright 1992 © University of Western Ontario and Wilfrid Laurier University 04/92. (Revised 09/97). Distributed through the LAURIER INSTITUTE, School of Business and Economics, Wilfrid Laurier University, Waterloo, Ontario, Canada, N2L 3C5. No part of this case may be reproduced, stored in a retrieval system, or transmitted in any form or by any means — electronic, mechanical, photocopying, recording, or otherwise — without the permission of The Laurier Institute, School of Business and Economics, Wilfrid Laurier University.

1. *Financial Times of Canada*, February 3, 1992, 1.
2. Disguised figure to protect confidentiality.

10

UNIROYAL CHEMICAL IN ELMIRA

In January, 1990, the top management group at Uniroyal Chemical Ltd. in Elmira, Ontario was attempting to determine their next move. The company had just been hit with an unprecedented emergency directive by the Ontario Ministry of the Environment (MOE) forcing the company to lay off employees. This was the first time an MOE directive resulted in lay-offs.

HISTORICAL OVERVIEW

In 1941, Naugatuck Chemical, a division of Dominion Rubber Company, the Canadian subsidiary of United States Rubber Co., bought an abandoned Elmira, Ontario plant to manufacture chemicals for stabilizing explosives. In 1945, Naugatuck began making pesticides such as weedkiller 2,4-D, and the insecticide DDT. While Naugatuck provided economic benefits to Elmira there were also some costs. One resident who moved near the plant in 1951 noted:

> The first thing you noticed was the smell. There were nights you'd wake up in bed choking... but you accepted it...Naugatuck had saved the town and had given jobs.

The corporate name of the Elmira operations changed with changes in ownership. As of 1990, the Elmira operation was named Uniroyal Chemical Ltd. (hereafter Uniroyal) and was a wholly-owned subsidiary of US-based Uniroyal Chemical Company, Inc. (UCCI).

Some of the products produced at the plant in Elmira proved to be controversial. DDT was ultimately banned, and Agent Orange containing herbicides 2,4-D and 2,4,5-T was used in the Vietnam war, but the U.S. army discontinued its use following concerns about dioxin, an impurity associated with 2,4-D and 2,4,5-T. In 1978, Vietnam veterans launched a class action suit claiming subsequent cancer, fetal abnormalities and skin diseases linked to dioxin. Dow Chemical Co., which had also produced Agent Orange ultimately paid $180 million (US) to veterans after evidence in court revealed company knowledge of dioxin's hazards prior to sales to the US army.

UNIROYAL AS A RESPONSIBLE CORPORATE CITIZEN

As of 1990, Uniroyal's Elmira plant was generating sales of about $115 million, with 260 hourly and 107 salaried employees. Another 50 Uniroyal employees worked at a lab in Guelph, and 50 more in sales, marketing and service offices in Montreal, Calgary, and Elmira. The Elmira plant which manufactured specialty chemicals for the rubber and agricultural industries represented the second largest of eight plants in UCCI which had facilities in the United States, Canada, Brazil, Europe, and Taiwan as well as joint ventures in Mexico and Argentina. In 1990 Uniroyal represented the largest employer and taxpayer in Elmira, a town of 7300 people.

Uniroyal management saw quality as a key part of the company's strategy. In November, 1989, Uniroyal won the silver medal in the quality category of the federal awards program, Canada Awards for Business Excellence. While Uniroyal management and employees were pleased with the 1989 award, 11 Elmira residents wrote the federal government to question the award given the "chemical pollution" from the company. Bob Verdun, the editor of *The Independent*, Elmira's only newspaper wrote: "It certainly has not mattered to the government of Canada that Uniroyal has caused serious pollution of air, water and land in the process of 'meeting the needs of the marketplace...'" In media interviews, Ruck noted the following about the company's environmental record: "Uniroyal has always complied with the requirements of the law of the land that were in effect, as well as the state of technology at any point in time." Furthermore, Uniroyal management considered the company to be one of the most environmentally responsible companies in Canada and the Elmira plant to be a world-class facility. The company had spent $20 million on modernization and $11 million on environmental cleanup activities from 1984 to 1990.

Walter Ruck had been general manager of the Elmira operation since 1985. The 47-year-old American moved to Elmira from the Connecticut headquarters and resided in nearby Waterloo. Under Ruck, Uniroyal's sales from the Elmira operation increased by forty-five percent although employment was lower than five years before. Ruck believed Uniroyal was a responsible corporate citizen and felt a good public image was important in order to maintain employee morale, attract employees, retain and attract customers, and retain the confidence of investors. The company was committed to the "Responsible Care" program, a set of stringent operating codes of practice recently developed by the Canadian Chemical Producers' Association, to which Uniroyal belonged. In addition, Uniroyal placed ads in the local media to publicize productivity and innovation awards for workers, and to honour long-time plant employees. The company also gave $10 000 to a local park, sponsored local sports groups, offered repeatedly to meet with citizens' groups, and made its staff and firefighting equipment available to the local volunteer fire department.

PROTECTING THE ENVIRONMENT: THE EARLY YEARS

Naugatuck's first production manager recognized that company wastes should not be dumped directly into the Canagagigue Creek, located beside the plant. Therefore, the company purchased farmland across the creek for pits and open-air lagoons so that solid and liquid wastes would go through a settling process before entering the creek. The lagoons worked like above-ground "septic tanks," permitting some settling of materials as liquids seeped into the sand-gravel-clay mixture in the ground. In the 1950s, Naugatuck responded to new government guidelines and began burying wastes in steel drums on the site.

In 1963, Uniroyal became the first company in Ontario to cooperate with a municipality in providing funding (one-third of the capital costs) and technology for a sewage treatment plant (STP) to serve both the company and the town. The STP would minimize the hazards of dumping untreated wastewater and raw municipal sewage into the Canagagigue Creek. Cattle had died after drinking water from the creek and Uniroyal and the Ontario Water Resources Commission (OWRC) predecessor to the MOE, compensated the farmers for this loss. In 1969, the company changed the procedures for disposing of its wastes. Under the supervision of the OWRC, Uniroyal excavated old barrels containing chemical wastes and placed them in two pits which were lined with plastic.

In 1978, MOE put pressure on Uniroyal to improve the quality of the effluent sent to the STP. In December, 1978, the MOE approved a plant expansion by Uniroyal conditional on the waste quality improving. Negotiations in 1979 with Waterloo regional government (hereafter the Region), owner of the STP and the MOE, operator of the STP, resulted in the company contributing $184 000 to an expansion of the STP and spending more than $4 million on waste treatment equipment on the Uniroyal site. The company continued to pay one-third of the operating cost of the STP.

WATER AND AIR CONTAMINATION: CONCERNS OF THE 1980S

An aquifer (a gravel formation containing groundwater) was under the Uniroyal plant site, and was part of the same aquifer providing Elmira with its municipal water supply. Following MOE concern about possible contamination of Elmira's water supply, Uniroyal dug wells on its site. MOE tests of the water in 1981 found chemicals at low concentrations. More test wells were dug on the site and at one point low levels of dioxin were detected and efforts were begun to find the source of the chemicals. Possible sources were the covered pits and buried barrels that had not been unearthed. Further testing of the wells by the MOE on and around Uniroyal's site revealed that the chemicals were moving very slowly, if at all. Nevertheless, many people in Elmira were distressed about the potential threat to the drinking water supply.

Uniroyal's off-site waste disposal was becoming more costly and less available, and as a result in 1981 the company installed the world's first WETOX ("Wet Air Oxidation") system to convert toxic wastes into material which could be handled by a conventional STP. Federal grants under the Enterprise Development program covered $200 000 of the system's $1.3 million cost because the facility was state-of-the-art. The Ontario Research Foundation, then the research arm of the Ontario Ministry of Industry and Tourism, developed the technological refinements for the new system which reduced the volume of off-site waste disposal by 25 percent, saving the company $300 000/year in disposal costs.

During 1982, two new advisory committees were created that would affect Uniroyal. One committee, known as the Citizens' Environmental Advisory Committee (CEAC) was an ad-hoc committee of Woolwich Township Council. By this time, Elmira and St. Jacobs, along with surrounding hamlets became the Township of Woolwich following the establishment of regional governments in the 1970s. Murray Haight, a professor of environmental studies at the University of Waterloo and resident of Elmira who chaired CEAC since its inception described the origins of CEAC as follows:

> Recognizing the need for citizen involvement, the MOE called a public meeting with Uniroyal to indicate to the community that there was a problem with contamination of the groundwater. (A consultant retained by Uniroyal told the meeting that the constant pull of the production wells at the north and south end of Elmira which supplied the town with its drinking water had lowered the water table by 12 feet and caused contaminants at the surface of the Uniroyal site to move down into the municipal aquifer). Uniroyal was proposing to address the problem by constructing and operating containment wells (to act as a counter-pull and prevent contamination from reaching the municipal wells). For the people at the meeting, it became clear that not only was there a groundwater problem but the more important pressing issue was air contamination. It was felt that whenever the winds were in the right conditions, people were expected to breathe air containing contaminants they did not understand. The feeling was "enough is enough, this has got to stop." It was decided that a group should be formed to deal with these issues and the message went back to both the MOE and Township that there was a desire and willingness of individuals to get involved to see conditions improve.

The MOE decided that a citizens committee would lack credibility if formed by the MOE so Ken Seiling an Elmira resident who was Township Mayor put the issue before the Township Council which decided to create CEAC. Haight described the functioning of CEAC as follows:

> It is a unique citizens group unlike anything anywhere. CEAC consists of two council members and four to eight citizen volunteers appointed by Council. The membership of the committee has been balanced including business people so that there is understanding of how industry works as well as concern about the consequences of industrial activity. As a committee of Council, CEAC has a political base which gives it political manoeuvrability. This is important since unfortunately a lot of these issues have to be dealt with in a political forum. CEAC does not need to raise funds. Its objective is to consult with Uniroyal on various environmental issues and report to Council. A newsletter to Elmira residents helps to ensure communication between CEAC and the community.

From the beginning, Haight, as chair of CEAC took a non-confrontational stance with Uniroyal, which set the tone for a good working relationship between CEAC and Uniroyal.

The other advisory committee affecting Uniroyal was formed by the MOE and was known as the Technical Advisory Committee (TAC). It consisted of representatives from the Region (representing the engineering and health departments), Grand River Conservation Authority (responsible for the condition of the Grand River), MOE (including staff from the district office, west central region and experts from the Toronto operations), Uniroyal, the Township of Woolwich, and CEAC. Haight was the CEAC representative on TAC. Both TAC and CEAC typically met once a month.

At the time of forming CEAC and TAC, there was considerable confusion about the terms of reference of these committees. It was agreed that the main function of TAC was to advise the MOE about all abatement matters concerning Uniroyal, to keep the involved agencies informed, and to serve as a forum for discussion and for technical input on all activities.

One of the first issues to be considered by both TAC and CEAC was the operation of containment wells the company had constructed to prevent contaminated groundwater from migrating off the company's property. On this issue, some members of both TAC and CEAC were opposed to the operation of the wells having received advice from faculty and graduate students at the University of Waterloo Institute for Groundwater Research who concluded that operating the wells would accelerate the contamination problem by drawing down contaminants from sources on the surface. There was also a major concern about how to properly treat the pumped contaminated water prior to discharge to the creek. However, the MOE's own hydrogeologist, the Region, and Bob Verdun of *The Independent* all supported operating the wells. Verdun noted, "if the wells don't work positively the results will be easy to measure." In a memo, an MOE director told the assistant deputy minister that "it is our opinion that it is imperative to arrest any potential for off property migration of chemicals in the deep municipal aquifer...the purge wells are necessary to remove or halt the spread of contaminants now in the deep aquifer...the pumps must go into operation." Nevertheless, the MOE was concerned that CEAC and TAC members would resign if the wells were operated, thereby attracting considerable negative publicity, so the MOE "took a gamble" and decided to refuse Uniroyal permission to operate the wells.

Another noteworthy event unusual for Uniroyal took place in 1982 when Uniroyal was fined for violating environmental regulations. The company failed to report a spill of wastewater resulting from an operator error. As a result, the company was fined $2500 and the company disciplined the operator.

In 1983, the general manager of the Uniroyal Chemical Division pointed out that the company had so far spent $7 million on pollution control and that environmental operating costs at Elmira were the highest per pound of products produced in all of the company's facilities throughout the world. This manager noted: "If we could get more funding from the government bodies, it would ease the pain." Also in 1983, the MOE turned down a suggestion by Uniroyal to reduce the size of TAC by eliminating the CEAC representative and designating a committee member to brief CEAC.

In 1984, when the Region upgraded and expanded the Elmira STP, Uniroyal paid approximately $1 million of the $3.8 million capital costs. At the time of the STP expansion, the MOE also issued a control order, an enforcement instrument under the Environmental Protection Act. The order required Uniroyal to undertake a comprehensive hydrogeologic research and monitoring program, construction of new test wells, and study and implementation of remedial measures for the buried pits and open-air lagoons.

In 1985, following investigations carried out as part of the 1984 control order Uniroyal began to excavate over 1600 drums of buried toxic waste. It was found that the buried drums contained traces of dioxin, DDT herbicides, arsenic, and cyanide. However the dioxin levels (i.e., 0.009 parts per billion [ppb] to 7.2 ppb) were well within the MOE standard guidelines of the time (1000 ppb).

Another environmental problem facing Uniroyal in the 1980s concerned air emissions. While MOE had been receiving odour complaints about the plant for years, the number had risen by 1984. The company responded in the summer of 1984 by shutting down processes that caused smells when winds blew towards town. Production was stopped on 33 days that summer, resulting in "considerable" losses, but complaints dropped dramatically. By early 1985 Uniroyal had spent $100 000 on equipment to reduce emissions. Haight of CEAC noted that the company has made "a giant step forward in cleaning up the air." He further noted: "Why did they do this when they didn't have to? I like to think our group is influential enough that when issues are raised the company takes action." The company also took voluntary action when it followed a new worldwide company policy and spent $5 million to replace its five open-air lagoons with four above ground storage tanks. This action reduced some of the odours and prevented the wastewater from leaking or flooding into the Canagagigue Creek.

The buried drum excavation proved particularly difficult and costly. After several delays, the project ended in late 1987, and the bill was around $1 million, well over the $500 000 initial estimate. A well known environmental group, Pollution Probe, complimented the community and company for working together on the excavation project.

THE INCINERATOR PROJECT

Tricil of Sarnia was the only company in Canada able to handle certain Uniroyal wastes. Tricil's incinerator burned liquids from the plant that could not be sent to the STP, and had handled the contents of the buried drums. In order to eliminate Uniroyal's dependence on Tricil and reduce trucking and operating costs, the company decided to investigate building their own liquid waste incinerator on the site. The company approached MOE officials on the project, and received approval in principle in October, 1987, to build an $800 000 gas-fired incinerator.

In June 1988, an MOE official informed Haight of CEAC about the plans for the incinerator, but Haight decided to keep the plans confidential after being told by the MOE official that "the project would never fly." At a later meeting in January, 1989, involving Uniroyal and CEAC, Uniroyal was questioned by CEAC about the incinerator plans, and CEAC was surprised to learn that the project was proceeding. This January meeting was the first time that Uniroyal was aware that CEAC had known since June, 1988 about the incinerator plans. When Uniroyal provided more details about the incinerator project to CEAC in April, 1989, CEAC decided to inform Township Council which reacted immediately by writing the MOE expressing concerns about air pollution and asking to be included in the process. Township Mayor Bob Waters led a delegation to Uniroyal with a similar message. Because emissions could affect surrounding areas, the Region was involved, and the now Region chair Ken Seiling, wrote MOE Minister, Jim Bradley.

On May 15, 1989, Uniroyal publicly announced its incinerator plans, with the MOE adding the requirement of public hearings under the Environmental Assessment Act. After receiving the letter from the Township Council, the MOE official noted: "The company could have proceeded without public hearings, but the MOE used its discretionary powers to bump up the project to ensure greater scrutiny." The "bump up" procedure was both a result of growing public pressure and a shift in provincial policy designating facilities that burn liquid wastes under the Environmental Assessment (EA) Act.

Both Uniroyal and the MOE were criticized for the handling of the process related to the incinerator. CEAC members criticized Uniroyal for issuing an information pamphlet stating that the company had "volunteered" to be "bumped up" for greater scrutiny under the EA Act. The MOE was criticized for negotiating with Uniroyal in secret on such a sensitive matter as air pollution. Ministry officials responded that there was an unintended breakdown in communications with local bodies; one official noted that "the incinerator wasn't a secret, we just hadn't informed them."

Public opposition to the incinerator was evident from the outset. Informal local meetings held to discuss the plans were so well attended and concern so high that an environmental group, APT Environment (Assuring Protection for Tomorrow's Environment) was formed in August, 1989. Two of the founders of APT Environment (hereafter APT) who resigned from CEAC felt that CEAC had become too much a part of the local power structure and too complacent and cautious to be openly critical of Uniroyal's activities having been instructed not to comment publicly on the incinerator plans.

While Councillors did not openly oppose the incinerator plans, they insisted that Uniroyal prove that all alternatives had been explored, and had acted accordingly. They wrote Bradley requesting that Environmental Assessment hearings on the project be held, and hired an environmental lawyer to guide their efforts.

During this period, CEAC was critical of other actions involving Uniroyal. The consultant for a $1 million groundwater contamination research project funded by the MOE, federal government and Uniroyal was given approval by Uniroyal to begin research on the plant's aquifer but certain MOE officials were not informed. In addition, new equipment was installed with the MOE's approval, but without the appropriate environmental monitoring program. Both situations were rectified following criticism by CEAC.

Air emissions became a problem again in 1989. Haight described the summer of 1989 as "one of the stinkiest summers." One discharge required the refinishing of about 50 cars near the plant. While Uniroyal did not immediately report the discharge to the MOE on the grounds that it was technically not a leak, the local media publicized the event. As a result of this publicity, the MOE conducted a one-week investigation and no charges were laid by the MOE. In response to the odour problems, the company installed new machinery, kept a closer eye on monitoring the processing operation responsible for the odour problem and offered public plant tours.

THE NDMA PROBLEM IN ELMIRA

While Uniroyal and the town were preparing for the hearings concerning the incinerator, another issue surfaced that quickly captured the town's attention. On November 10, 1989, the Region shut down two of the municipal wells serving Elmira and St. Jacobs (a village just south of Elmira) after the water surveillance program instituted by the MOE found levels of the chemical Nnitroso dimethylamine (NDMA) in the wells as high as 40 ppb, far above the US EPA guideline of 0.014 ppb. The MOE labs were among the most sophisticated in Canada, and seen by some as best able to detect NDMA. Staff were assigned to conduct the testing of scores of water samples, each of which took 30 hours to analyze under rigorous conditions. At the urging of CEAC's chair, the company shelved its plans for the incinerator until the NDMA situation was resolved.

Following the discovery of NDMA in the Elmira wells, the MOE decided to establish an interim drinking water guideline for NDMA of 0.014 ppb, the same as the U.S. EPA. This guideline was somewhat impractical at the time given that detection levels for NDMA were only about 0.01 ppb; at 0.014 ppb NDMA increased the risk of cancer by 0.001% (1 in 100 000) in a 70 kg man if he drank two litres of the water each day for about 70 years. Agriculture Canada knew that NDMA and other nitrosamines were in the preservatives in food but considered it acceptable at levels much higher than found in Elmira's water.

There was confusion about how NDMA formed. Some studies indicated that it may form whenever nitrates react with acid, so a bacon-and-tomato sandwich would be a source of the chemical. It was also produced when fertilizers broke down, and during the beer malting process. Therefore it could well be produced naturally as well as man-made.

Since there were no guidelines in Canada at the time of the detection in Elmira and the health risks were unclear given conflicting expert opinion about these risks, the Region chose to "err on the side of safety" and closed the Elmira wells. It issued public statements about the hazard involved, and tried to calm fears by "putting the risk in context:" water contamination levels were compared to concentrations found in beer, vegetables, bacon, and other products. Private well-owners in the south end of Elmira had their wells tested and those with NDMA were advised to use alternate water supplies.

Faced with a decrease in supply, the Region asked Uniroyal and other industries to curtail their water consumption. Uniroyal was the largest user in town, accounting for two-thirds of water consumption in both Elmira and St. Jacobs. The company complied with the request and cut its water intake by over 50 percent resulting in the reduction of some manufacturing activities.

UNIROYAL AND NDMA

In the late 1970s, the MOE tested for NDMA at the Uniroyal site and found none in the effluent but levels of 1100 parts per million in the lagoons. As a result, Uniroyal changed its production process and informed the MOE it had eliminated NDMA from its process. In 1987 and 1988 the MOE detected NDMA in the Elmira STP and in June 1988 NDMA was detected at 34 ppb in groundwater just off the Uniroyal site. These detections were kept secret by the MOE because it was concluded the chemical would not move quickly to pose a threat to Elmira's water supply. (Uniroyal later learned about these detections). In November 1989, following the Elmira wells shutdown, the MOE tested to ensure Uniroyal was not causing the contamination. The results of these tests had shown no detection. It therefore came as a surprise when the chemical was found on December 7 in two monitoring wells near the plant site, and again on December 18 in effluent from Uniroyal to the STP (at 2000 ppb) and at 50 ppb out of the STP into Canagagigue Creek. Furthermore, nine wells in Kitchener along the Grand River were closed after traces of NDMA were found in the river and in three of the nine wells. (The Canagagigue Creek flows into the Grand River which served as a drinking water supply for several communities including Cayuga, Six Nations Indian Reserve, and Brantford, see map — Exhibit 1.)

After the effluent discovery on December 18, the company cooperated with MOE experts and shut down processes that could form NDMA as a by-product. On December 20, Uniroyal released a statement acknowledging that MOE tests show that the company is a possible source of NDMA in the municipal aquifer. One week after the suspected processes were shut down, contamination levels in the wastewater going to and from the STP fell sharply, confirming that the plant was a source of the chemical.

Following a misunderstanding between the MOE and Uniroyal, the MOE issued an emergency directive on December 30 placing a limit of 0.5 ppb in NDMA discharges from the Elmira STP. The misunderstanding related to the Christmas break. On December 20, Uniroyal announced it was shutting down those facilities that could be the potential source of the effluent problem until the water contamination problem was resolved; in addition the company indicated that the plant would close for the Christmas holidays. MOE officials assumed that the company would be closed until after New Year's. On December 28, Steven Salbach, acting director of the MOE west-central region, was "greatly disturbed" to learn that the plant had been reopened and wastewater was being sent to the STP. (Salbach was acting for Boris Boyko who was on a special assignment at the time. Boyko was quite familiar with Uniroyal managers and the Uniroyal site, having been the MOE director interacting with Uniroyal for many years). Ruck informed Salbach that the discharges to the STP had always continued over plant shutdown periods in order to maintain a high level of efficiency at the STP. Ruck also indicated surprise to Salbach that he was not aware of the continual discharges because the MOE operated the STP and was certainly knowledgeable about the discharge levels from Uniroyal to the STP. Nevertheless, Salbach decided he could not trust Uniroyal which was discharging NDMA waste "with no clear understanding of the consequences," and a legal course was chosen. Ruck described it as a perfectly understandable misunderstanding. He noted:

> We said we would shut down for Christmas and we did, from about Dec. 21 to the 25th or 26th. Being civil servants, they thought that meant until after New Year's.

The MOE directive forced Uniroyal to reduce its manufacturing production by 50 percent.

RESPONDING TO THE EMERGENCY DIRECTIVE

Uniroyal managers were shocked by the MOE directive for a number of reasons:

i.   NDMA was not on the list of 140 priority pollutants identified by government agencies in Canada and the United States as chemicals to be measured for and eliminated first out of any system. (In fact, prior to November, 1989, Ruck had never even heard of NDMA).

ii.   There were no regulatory restrictions on NDMA concentrations in the discharges from other STPs in Ontario and Uniroyal suspected that other companies were discharging NDMA at even higher concentrations than Uniroyal. When asked why Uniroyal was singled out, MOE officials responded that the MOE was responding to the media coverage (described in one media report as "the hottest issue in the province").

iii.   The levels of NDMA detected in 1989 (said to be 2000 ppb in discharges to the STP) were dramatically lower than in 1979 (200 000 ppb).

iv.   Uniroyal questioned the reliability of the MOE's analytical testing and sampling methods.

v.   Prior to this directive, Uniroyal had been able to negotiate with the MOE and not face unilateral action. It appeared that the only reason for the order was because of the misunderstanding with Salbach about when the plant would reopen after the Christmas holiday shutdown.

vi.   Restrictions on Uniroyal's ability to discharge its wastewater could require a change in products at the plant. (Some products generated more wastewater than others). Furthermore, it was not possible to shut down all sources of water reaching Uniroyal's wastewater system since chemical storage areas and process building roofs drained rainwater and melted snow into the treatment system. As a result, the company could be forced to ship wastewater by rail cars and tanker trucks to disposal facilities in Ohio and New Jersey, since there were no such facilities available in Canada.

vii. In order to overturn the directive, Uniroyal would have to file an appeal with the Environmental Appeal Board which had the power to question the directive, amend it or substitute it with a new notice. However, the appeal process could take a long time, given the technical complexities involved. It could also require large legal fees for the parties involved. In the meantime, about 17 employees would continue to be laid off with more lay-offs likely unless the plant returned to full production.

viii. Uniroyal considered the limit of 0.5 ppb in NDMA discharges to be arbitrary, unreasonable and unjustifiable on either an environmental or technological basis. There were no generally agreed-upon guidelines for NDMA. Overall, Uniroyal found the regulatory environment to be frustrating and unfair. One Uniroyal manager noted:

> Compared with the United States, few items are regulated in Ontario. (The MOE had regulations on fewer than 500 substances while there were more than 600 000 in use in various industries at any one time). Furthermore, there are sometimes different rules for different companies. Specifically, Uniroyal Chemical is the only company in the province of Ontario that must meet NDMA discharge regulations. Any other individual or industry can dump as much NDMA as they wish into their wastewater.

THE NEXT MOVE

In determining Uniroyal's next move, there were a number of factors which could be considered as follows:

i. It was not clear who would bear financial responsibility for cleaning up Elmira's contaminated drinking-water supply (which could cost $40-60 million) and for providing alternative water supplies to the town of Elmira (which could cost $30 million). Uniroyal felt the MOE should accept substantial responsibility for several reasons including; (a) the MOE had been on record for more than a decade as saying it would protect the municipal water supply; (b) the MOE refused Uniroyal permission to operate containment wells that would have contained contamination on-site.

ii. There were many Uniroyal employees who were angry and frustrated by the government's move. One employee noted:

> Uniroyal is being centred out as the polluter of something that's been there millions of years. Rotten leaves cause NDMA for God's sake. They put it in food, in beer, in smoked food products...You have to drink three gallons of water a day for fifty years and you might stand a chance of getting cancer.

iii. Relations between the media and the company had been quite strained at times. When a television reporter attempted, unannounced, in December 1989, to film on camera an interview with Uniroyal's manager of manufacturing, the reporter was asked to leave. Earlier in 1989, after being "misrepresented and misquoted" in *Independent* articles, Ruck wrote Verdun to say that "in the future, in order to ensure accurate representation, I will respond only in writing to written questions proposed by your staff, or in one-on-one, face-to-face, discussions."

iv. The Region with responsibility for water supply had assembled a team of consultants to which MOE staff were assigned. The Region chair, Seiling, was disturbed by the MOE's obvious failure to protect the water supply. Seiling noted:

> The last time we went through this we had various experts in the Ministry telling us what was being done, and how we were being protected. I have certainly become much more skeptical this time around. I am not prepared to accept assurances at their face value regardless of where they come from. This is one of the reasons that we are, as a Region, adopting a little more independence in trying to verify as best we can what information comes to us.

The Region wanted to be involved in any discussions or negotiations between the MOE and Uniroyal.

In the context of these factors, the company could make any or all of the following moves:

i. Devote more resources to the public affairs function such as by retaining a public affairs consultant and/or creating a public affairs department. (There was no such department at the time).

ii. Call a press conference to explain the company's position.

iii. Conduct a public opinion poll (e.g., to determine public perception of the company and responsibility for the cleanup).

iv. File an appeal of the MOE directive with the Environmental Appeal Board.

EXHIBIT 1 **Map of Relevant Area**

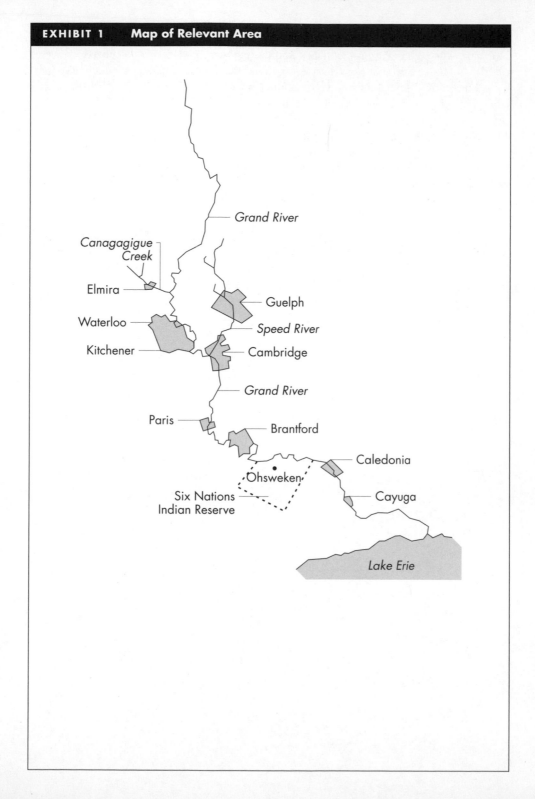

NOTES

This case was prepared from published sources by Mark C. Baetz with the assistance of Charles Scott as a basis for class discussion, rather than to illustrate either effective or ineffective handling of an administrative situation. Copyright © Mark C. Baetz, Wilfrid Laurier University. Revised 11/94. Distributed through the LAURIER INSTITUTE, School of Business and Economics, Wilfrid Laurier University, Waterloo, Ontario, Canada, N2L 3C5. No part of this case may be reproduced, stored in a retrieval system, or transmitted in any form or by any means — electronic, mechanical, photocopying, recording, or otherwise — without the permission of The Laurier Institute, School of Business and Economics, Wilfrid Laurier University.

11

ONTARIO HYDRO AND THE MATTAGAMI PROJECT

PART I: THE MATTAGAMI COMPLEX

A. The Challenge

It was December 1991, and Debbie Smith sat quietly in her chair reflecting on the task that faced her. Debbie was the recently appointed Manager of Aboriginal and Northern Affairs, a senior level management position which had just been established by Ontario Hydro. The work of the committee for which she was responsible had finally been completed. It was now her task to prepare and present a final report to the Board of the corporation. She had set aside a day without interruption to develop a presentation strategy that would identify clearly for the Board the nature and significance of the decision that Ontario Hydro faced. It was not the size of the project that was crucial in this case, though the project was not inconsiderable — a four dam redevelopment project along the Mattagami River in Northern Ontario. Rather, the final report she would put to the Board would be the first major test of the new environmental and ethical policies of the corporation, policies that she knew were destined to change in dramatic ways the corporation's understanding of its environmental and social responsibilities.

Integrating the policy changes into the strategic planning process had been a challenge for senior management. But management had been a part of the evolution of those policies and had had ample opportunity to develop an understanding of their implications for strategic planning as well as day-to-day operations. The Board had not had the same immersion experience. They had approved the new directions and indeed had participated in their articulation, yet they had not been working with them intensively since their formulation. Debbie knew that her first challenge was to present the final report in a way that allowed the Board members the opportunity to retrace the reasons for the changes in corporate policy and their application to development strategy.

Debbie knew that the redevelopment project, known as the Mattagami Complex, was only a small part of an extensive operation. Ontario Hydro was currently one of Canada's largest corporations generating annual revenues of over $7 billion and holding assets of over $43 billion. It was now the largest electric utility in North America. The corporation employed approximately 30 000 people and served over 3 million retail customers. Ontario Hydro was able to produce the required power through a combination of nuclear, fossil, and hydro-electric sources. Nuclear generating stations were supplying just over half of the total system energy requirements, while fossil-fuelled generation and hydroelectric stations each contributed approximately one-quarter of the remaining power. In terms of hydroelectric power, over 65 generating stations were producing approximately 34 million megawatt-hours of energy a year.

Despite its tremendous growth over the years, the Crown corporation had continued to struggle in making energy development decisions that were acceptable to all of its stake-holders. In this case, the decision regarded not only whether to proceed with the extension of four hydroelectric dams along the Mattagami River in northeastern Ontario, but how to proceed. The project had gone through an environmental assessment. Subsequent public evaluation of that assessment had raised a number of significant issues for the corporation. Ontario Hydro's historical approach to making development decisions based on least cost planning was clearly under attack. Indeed, the new environmental and ethical policies now in place had been developed as a response to what in retrospect were now acknowledged by the corporation to be well-founded criticisms. The challenge was now to apply these new poli-cies creatively and constructively to the situation at hand.

Having examined the issues the Board would have to discuss; Debbie made her first decision. She would first review the case and remind the Board of the weaknesses inherent in Ontario Hydro's historical approach to hydroelectric generation. She would then review the position that had been set out in the environmental assessment prepared by manage-ment for public discussion. The position taken by management had reflected what Ontario Hydro officials, guiding the process, had identified as the interests of the project's key stakeholders. The public response to the environmental assessment had been positive with one exception: the Aboriginal reaction had been bitterly critical.

In response to the corporation's environmental assessment a First Nation coalition devel-oped a counterproposal that they submitted directly to the Ontario government. A crucial period of discussion and negotiation had followed which led to the creation of a working group — 50% of whose members came from the Native community. This group had been assigned the task of attempting to build a consensus on the proposed development. Debbie and her committee at Ontario Hydro had been deeply involved in that process. Indeed, their recom-mendations were built around the proposals created by the working group that the govern-ment had established.

It was now Debbie's task to write a report that would draw the Board into a discussion that would help them to understand the recommendations they would then have to evaluate. She knew that to accomplish this goal she would have to review both the facts of the case and the limitations of the corporation's historical approach to the development of hydroelectric generating stations. Without an understanding of that history, a balanced evaluation of the Report's recommendations would not be possible. She would then have to review the Mattagami Complex proposal, the Aboriginal reaction to it, their counterproposal and the nature and results of the involvement of the Ontario government.

With this plan to guide her, Debbie began to review the facts of the case[1] before setting out to write her report.

B. The Mattagami River Area

i. *Geography*

The Mattagami River is one of several rivers draining the Moose River Basin, an area of approximately 108 000 km^2; a region larger than Ireland (Exhibit 1). The Mattagami river itself is 491 km long and drains a subbasin area of 41 672 km^2. The river flows in a northerly direction and empties into the Moose River 96 km upstream from James Bay.

The Mattagami River runs through the Pre-Cambrian Shield and the Hudson Bay Lowlands. Vegetation in the vicinity of the hydroelectric stations along the river consists mainly of boreal forests. Downstream from the dams, the boreal forest of the Canadian Shield transforms into the Hudson Bay Lowlands where poor climate and drainage retards tree growth. The basin's wildlife population includes: moose, bear, beaver, fox, otter, and numerous species of birds, amphibians, and fish.

ii. *The Local Inhabitants*

The non-Native population in the Moose River Basin numbers approximately 80 000, with over half of these people living in Timmins. The area most directly affected by the hydroelectric development supports a non-Native population of approximately 17 000 and includes the communities of: Kapuskasing (10 850), Smooth Rock Falls (2100), Moonbeam (1250), Val RitaHarty (1200), Fauquier-Strickland (815), and Opasatika (400).

The Aboriginal population in the Basin and along the James Bay coast numbers approximately 10 000. Some live in isolated communities, and others live close to, or within, urban centres. The two largest Aboriginal communities are Moosonee and Moose Factory Island, which are located 5 km apart at the mouth of the Moose River. Of the 1500 residents living in Moosonee, approximately 900 are of Aboriginal descent. Approximately 2200 Aboriginal inhabitants live on Moose Factory Island.

The political organization of the Aboriginal communities living in the Moose River Basin is complex. The majority of Aboriginals are members of recognized First Nations and are represented by different Tribal Councils. However, other Aboriginals are not members of recognized First Nations and are considered "non-status" Aboriginals.

There are nine Cree and Ojibway First Nations in the Basin. Six of these First Nations (Wagoshig, Matachewan, Mattagami, Brunswick House, Chapleau Ojibway, and Chapleau Cree) are members of the Wabun Tribal Council and are located in the southern end of the Basin. The other three First Nations in the Basin (New Post, Moose Factory, and Mocreebec) are members of the Mushkegowuk Tribal Council. The New Post First Nation is located in the southern end of the Basin near Cochrane. The Moose Factory and Mocreebec First Nations are located in the northern end of the Basin, on Moose Factory Island along the James Bay coast.

All the First Nations involved in this discussion, with the exception of the Mocreebec, are among the 46 First Nations covered by Treaty #9, signed in 1905 and are represented by the Nishnawbe-Aski Nation (NAN) which was founded in 1973. The Mocreebec First Nation is a special case as it is not recognized as a band by the federal government, does not have a reserve, and does not receive federal government payments.

C. The Origins of the Mattagami Complex Redevelopment Proposal

i. Early Development in the Moose River Basin

Though human activity in the Moose River Basin dates back 2500 to 5000 years, the first European trading post was not established until 1776 in Moose Factory by the Hudson Bay Company. In the early 1900s, railway lines opened up portions of the Basin to agricultural settlement, mining, and lumbering. Between 1911 and 1932, a total of nine private hydro-electric developments were established on the Mattagami and Abitibi rivers to supply power to the new industries. One such development was the Smoky Falls Station on the Mattagami River (described below). During the 1930s, the Hydro-Electric Power Commission of Ontario (the precursor to Ontario Hydro) purchased a number of these private generating systems in order to increase the Commission's hydroelectric capacity.

Early mining and lumbering development in the Moose River Basin provided some benefits to the Aboriginal people, such as casual or wage labour and easier access to traditional hunting grounds in some cases. However, there were profound negative consequences as well which included: the loss of lands and resources used for traditional harvesting, exposure to infectious disease, and other related social problems.

The early hydroelectric projects also had significant environmental and social consequences. Among the outcomes: aboriginal lands were partially flooded; graves and campsites disappeared; traditional lifestyles were disrupted by construction; the incursion of hunters and fishers resulted in a growing non-Native population, improved access by roads and railway transportation facilitated development; and fish and wildlife habitats were polluted and destroyed.

Available evidence suggests that only very limited attempts to mitigate the damaging effects of development had been undertaken. The attitudes of developers had been dominated by a simple belief in the benefits of development and the economic opportunities it provided.

ii. The Smoky Falls Generating Station

In 1922, the "model" town of Kapuskasing was built around the creation of a pulp and paper mill. The mill was operated by the Spruce Falls Power and Paper Corporation (SFPP) owned by Kimberly Clark and *The New York Times*. The plant had been established to provide a reliable supply of newsprint for the newspaper. Over 700 people were hired to operate the pulp and paper plant while another 3500 were employed to fell the wood. At that time it took almost two days' production and 225 acres of forest to make the Sunday Edition of *The New York Times*.

In 1928, the SFPP constructed the Smoky Falls Generating Station on the Mattagami River for the principal purpose of supplying power to their plant in Kapuskasing. The Smoky

Falls Station was one of the earliest hydroelectric power stations in the Moose River Basin on the Mattagami River. The building of the station replaced a natural waterfall having a drop of approximately 80 feet. The plant was operated as a "run-of-river" or "base-load" station (see Appendix A). Electrical power was transmitted via an 80 km 115kV transmission line from the Smoky Falls Station directly to SFPP's mill in Kapuskasing 24 hours a day.

The development of the Smoky Falls Station caused some environmental damage. Aboriginal reports indicate that a spawning ground upriver from the dam was destroyed as fish access to it was blocked. Noise from the plant's operations was reported to have caused wildlife to move away from what had been a traditional trapping area. Native hunters reported a deterioration in the quality of the fish, geese, and ducks. However, as the station was a "run-of-river" operation flooding and erosion damage was not extensive.

Despite the environmental problems, access to an inexpensive electrical supply played a crucial role in ensuring the economic viability of the SFPP Corporation leading in turn to growth and stability for the town of Kapuskasing.

iii. The 1960s Development

In order to increase its hydroelectric production, Ontario Hydro constructed several facilities on the Mattagami River in the 1960s: the Little Long Station (1963), Harmon Station (1965), and Kipling Station (1966). The Little Long Station is upstream from the Smoky Falls Station, while the Harmon and Kipling Stations are both downstream. The stations are between 60 to 100 km north of Kapuskasing. Beginning in 1963, a small trout stream known as Adam Creek was used to divert excess water around the hydroelectric stations. The three stations and Adam Creek became known as the Mattagami Complex.

The three new stations, Little Long, Harmon, and Kipling, were built with a quite different function from the Smoky Falls Station. The Smoky Falls Station was designed as a base load station to provide a continuous supply of energy to the SFPP mill in Kapuskasing. The other three stations were to be "peaking" stations, operating for approximately five hours per day. These stations were designed to provide electrical power only during the periods of peak electrical demand from Ontario Hydro's consumers.

The functioning of each of the four dams depends on the build up and subsequent release of a headpond through the dam structure. The headponds for each station differ in size, the largest being Little Long (7167 ha), followed by Harmon (251 ha), Smoky Falls (213 ha), and Kipling (141 ha). By agreement with SFPP, Ontario Hydro discharges sufficient water from the Little Long Station to restore the Smoky Falls' headpond to its full level each day. Due to the different operating patterns between Smoky Falls and the other three stations, the headpond water levels of the four stations fluctuate daily up to three metres.

As mentioned above, the Adam Creek Diversion was an important element of the Mattagami Complex. The 37 km long creek extends from the mouth of the Little Long headpond, 2.5 km east of the Little Long Station, and runs back into the Mattagami River 17 km downstream of the Kipling Station. A control structure (or spillway) was constructed at the mouth of the creek as a means of rerouting excess water around the four generating stations along the Mattagami River. Each time water flows exceed 541 m^3/s, the creek is used to bypass excess water around the generating stations. The most extensive use of Adam Creek occurs with winter runoff from mid-April to the end of June. At this time of year the volume of water flowing down the creek is similar to that which flows over Niagara Falls.

The use of the creek as a spillway had profound environmental consequences. At one time, Adam Creek was a tiny trout creek that a person could literally jump across. Over the intervening 30 years, the small creek was transformed into a wide river channel by the erosion of approximately 27 million cubic metres of soil resulting from the increased water flow. The eroded banks at the mouth of the creek grew to be twenty to thirty metres high with pools of water varying in depth from two to six metres. As a result, the creek has changed to the point where it is hardly recognizable to local Cree residents.

iv. Impacts of 1960s Development

Hydroelectric developments along the Mattagami River in the 1960s had certain positive consequences for the Aboriginal people. Some Native people benefited economically as they were hired to work on the construction of the dams. In addition, though not a direct consequence of the dams on the Mattagami, the towns of Moose Factory and Moosonee were finally connected to the Ontario power grid in 1973, alleviating the need to use diesel generators to produce electricity.

On the negative side, construction and use of the Mattagami Complex resulted in damaging environmental and social impacts as reported by the Native people affected.[2] Aboriginal witness statements collected during the Demand/Supply Plan Environmental Assessment hearings indicated that the dams had had a deleterious impact on the wildlife in the Basin. Population declines in a number of bird species were observed including: owls, woodpeckers, songbirds, grouse, and chickadees. Cree hunters also observed a decline in the number of geese. The decline was partly attributed to the decreased availability of underwater food for the geese to eat resulting from mud and silt deposits caused by the dams. According to Cree Elders, the dams have made the river so polluted that geese and ducks have become too contaminated to eat.

Elders have also observed major declines in otter, mink, and fox populations. Noise from the dams' generators is said to have driven wildlife away. Other animal populations such as caribou, white tailed deer, and moose appear to have declined. Herbicide spraying along Ontario Hydro transmission lines is reported by Natives and their elders to have adversely affected moose and other animals that eat the sprayed berry plants.

The flooding of plant communities and feed beds caused by the release of water has resulted in less food for beavers. This has caused a reduction in beaver populations in river banks. Beavers have drowned or frozen to death in their lodges as a result of releases of winter water creating additional layers of ice. The quality of beaver, muskrat, and otter fur is reported to have deteriorated.

Natives have observed that downriver from the Mattagami dams there has been a decline in the number of fish and fish habitat, as well as the discovery of sick fish, all resulting in a net loss of fisheries. These environmental effects have also extended upriver above the dams where traditional fisheries have been lost and important spawning beds flooded or silted over. Native people report that all of this has resulted from the unnaturally low and fluctuating water levels caused by the operation of the dams.

The dams also have had significant direct and indirect social impacts on the Native population. Water quality deterioration has made the rivers unsuitable as a source of drinking water. Individuals who swam in the Moose River near Moose Factory sometimes developed skin infections. Families ceased washing clothes in the Moose River.

The flooding caused by the operation of the dams destroyed a number of historic Cree settlement sites, historic portages, fur trade sites, and cemeteries. Oral histories record an Elder as complaining:

> A number of cemeteries where my people were buried are now beneath the Little Long Dam reservoir. We can't visit them anymore because they are underwater.

In order to construct the dams, roads were built which created additional pressures on the traditional Aboriginal way of life. The improved access for non-Native hunters generated additional competition between subsistence and sport hunters. The roads allowed increased access by game wardens causing increased incidents of harassment for Natives in their practice of subsistence fishing and hunting. The access roads were also used to expand logging activities into new areas. The logging companies' use of clearcutting was detrimental to fur-bearing mammals and fish, and thus created difficulties for Cree families pursuing subsistence trapping.

Travel problems were caused by the dams releasing an unnatural cycle of water. For Native users the river was their highway, yet the fluctuating river levels made boat travel difficult or impossible. Above the dams, former rapids, islands, and portages were flooded making navigation confusing for travellers. The construction and use of the dams created dangerous travel conditions because of tree stumps in the flooded areas, flooded traditional camp sites, and flooded travel routes. During the summer the unnaturally low water levels made the river too dry for travel. During the winter, the river ice broke up much earlier thus shortening the late-winter travel period and hindering the ability of the Cree people to reach trapping grounds.

According to Aboriginal sources, Aboriginal communities were not consulted about the planning or construction of the Hydro dams. Neither is there evidence of serious efforts at mitigation nor compensation for the social, economic, or heritage impacts resulting from the construction and operation of the dams.

v. *Ontario Hydro's 25 Year Demand/Supply Plan*

By 1984, Ontario Hydro was predicting that new electrical power options were going to be required as electricity demand increases of 60 to 200 percent by the year 2014 were projected. In response to these forecasts and to ensure a sufficient energy supply to meet Ontario's future needs, Ontario Hydro developed what became known as the 25 year Demand/Supply Plan (DSP).

The DSP consisted primarily of the rehabilitation and development of hydraulic, nuclear, and fossil generating stations. As part of the DSP, Ontario Hydro stated that it wanted to proceed with twelve hydraulic projects in the Moose River Basin: six new dams, five extensions of existing dams, and the redevelopment of one dam. In December 1989, Ontario Hydro submitted its plans to the Ontario Ministry of the Environment. An Environmental Assessment Hearing commenced shortly afterwards. As one small part of the hydraulic component of the DSP, Ontario Hydro submitted an Environmental Assessment for the Mattagami Complex in November 1990. The Environmental Assessment examined the extension of three hydroelectric stations on the Mattagami River (Little Long, Harmon, and Kipling) and the redevelopment of the Smoky Falls Station (still owned at that time by the SFPP corporation).

vi. Ontario Hydro's Mattagami Complex Proposal

Ontario Hydro's Mattagami Complex proposal was developed as a means to increase the hydroelectric generation capacity on the Mattagami River. The existing four-station Complex produced 450 MW of power (Little Long [2 units x 61 MW], Smoky Falls [4 units x 14 MW], Harmon [2 units x 68 MW], and Kipling [2 units x 68 MW]). The proposal called for the addition of one unit to the Little Long (61 MW), Harmon (68 MW), and Kipling (68 MW) generating stations, and the construction of a new (3 units x 80 MW) power station adjacent to the existing Smoky Falls Station. The current Smoky Falls Station would be retired. The redevelopment would provide an additional 381 MW of capacity to help meet Ontario's peak electrical requirements. A new 230 KV transmission line would be built between the Smoky Falls and Little Long Stations stretching 7 km. It would replace the existing 110 KV transmission line between Smoky Falls and Kapuskasing. The small community of workers currently living at Smoky Falls would be relocated to Kapuskasing as the dam would be operated remotely.

The major benefit of the project was that it would provide for the sequential or "in-step" operation of the four hydroelectric plants. Currently, this was impossible, as the Smoky Falls Station was a "base load" station operating continuously, while the other three operated only five hours a day as "peaking" stations (see Appendix A). In-step operation could only take place when the plants had similar discharge capacities and generated electricity for the same period of time each day. By retiring the current station at Smoky Falls and building a "peaking" station in its place the hydraulic potential of the river could be maximized.

vii. Sale of the Smoky Falls Station to Ontario Hydro

By early 1991, SFPP had determined that it was no longer in their financial interests to continue operating their mill in Kapuskasing as it had produced dismal profits since 1986. Following an unsuccessful attempt to sell the mill, SFPP began to prepare to shut down most of its operations. The loss of SFPP would have turned Kapuskasing into a ghost town. Approximately 1200 direct jobs and 6200 indirect jobs in a town of about 11 000 people would have been lost. A political crisis erupted placing pressure on the Ontario government to intervene.

In August 1991, as a result of the Ontario government's intervention, the majority of the shares in the SFPP corporation were sold by Kimberly Clark and *The New York Times* to SFPP's employees. As part of the buy-out arrangements, the Smoky Falls Generating Station was to be sold to Ontario Hydro. The purchase price for the station included an immediate payment by Ontario Hydro of $140 million to Kimberly Clark and *The New York Times* plus a $34 million cash payment to help finance upgrading the mill. Ontario Hydro would also provide the mill with 10 years of free power. Ontario Hydro only agreed to purchase the Smoky Falls Station, on the condition that the environmental assessment to redevelop the site was approved by the Ontario government. Without such redevelopment, the site was considered useless to Ontario Hydro. The Ontario government agreed to pay Ontario Hydro $247 million if the environmental assessment was not approved.

D. Reassessing the Planning Process

A number of issues surfaced as a result of Ontario Hydro's decision to redevelop the Mattagami Complex. Previous hydroelectric development had left a serious residue of anger and resentment on the part of the Aboriginal communities negatively affected. It was clear that overcoming this resentment would require significant changes in planning and project implementation than what had occurred in the past.

For much of the century, Ontario Hydro's study and exploitation of the hydraulic potential of the great rivers draining the Canadian Shield had been governed by its mandate: "to provide a reliable supply of electrical power and energy to the people of Ontario at the lowest feasible long-term costs." To fulfill this mandate, dams were constructed on northern rivers that altered in environmentally significant ways the flow of rivers so as to create huge new reservoirs. Such reservoirs were needed to ensure reliable energy that could be produced over long time periods in response to fluctuating demand. The resulting energy was delivered at a relatively low monetary cost and considerable economic benefit to the residents of Ontario. However, the developments imposed substantial costs on Native communities in the absence of meaningful consultation and counterveiling benefits recognizable as such by those affected.

The legacy of these developments was reflected in an acute sense of grievance which now dominated discussion of Northern Ontario resource use. It was reflected as well in substantial environmental problems that now confronted Native and non-Native communities in the North. These problems were all mirrored in the Mattagami Complex debate.

In Debbie's view, it was crucial that the Board realize the nature of these problems if they were to understand subsequent events as they unfolded as well as the committee's final recommendations.

PART II: RECONCEPTUALIZING THE PLANNING PROCESS

The task that now faced Debbie was to explain clearly to the Board the new principles underlying project planning for the Mattagami Complex and how they might affect the decision making process. Some decision-making tools, the mandate and the principle of "least cost planning" for instance, remained as important considerations. Ontario Hydro's mandate stated that the corporation must: "provide a reliable supply of electrical power and energy to the people of Ontario, at the lowest long-term feasible cost." The proposed redevelopment of the Mattagami Complex had much to recommend it in light of this mandate. If realized, the redeveloped complex would allow the utility to extract substantially more of the energy potential of the river with positive financial benefits when measured against the direct costs of the project. Proceeding with the project was clearly consistent with the mandate and the principle of "least cost planning."

However, two crucial changes had been made with respect to how projects were to be evaluated at Ontario Hydro. The first had been forced by legislation. Ontario Hydro was now required to take into account the *Environmental Assessment Act* (R.S.O. 1980, c.140).[3] This legislation had as its stated aim "the betterment of the people of Ontario by providing for the protection, conservation and wise management in Ontario of the environment" (s.2). The environment was defined to include the natural environment as well as "the social, economic and cultural conditions that influence the life of man or a community" [s.1(c)][4]. This Act modified in significant ways the regulatory setting in which energy planning, on the part of Ontario Hydro, now had to take place. For example, the corporation was now required by law to take into account costs that historically it had externalized thereby passing them onto the public at large.

This aforementioned change was clearly of importance in evaluating the proposed development. However, of even greater significance was the policy decision taken by the corporation to endorse the principle of sustainable development in its planning and project activities.[5] Senior management had concluded that commitment to sustainable development required four things that:

i.   *All direct costs associated with the project were to be internalized in the planning process.* This meant that regardless of what the law might say on the subject Ontario Hydro's planners had to identify who was likely to be negatively impacted by a project, what the nature of that impact would be, and then to build the costs of those impacts into the cost/benefit analysis used to assess the viability of the project.

ii. *Social and environmental impacts were to be included in the cost/benefit calculations.* That is that the impact on people as well as on the natural environment would have to be assessed. Project planning had to consider the costs and benefits of environmental protection and conservation, regional economic stability, recreation, health, heritage protection, and Aboriginal concerns.

iii. *Future as well as present social and environmental costs and benefits had to be factored into the analysis.* This element takes into consideration that the desire to meet the energy needs of present generations cannot compromise the ability of future generations to meet theirs.

iv. *Generally, it is preferable that those who bear the risks of a project also share equitably in the benefits.*

Consideration of these four principles led internally to a new planning and environmental assessment process for Ontario Hydro. The corporation's new guidelines formulated to allow Ontario Hydro *to meet the electrical power needs of the province in the most sustainable or least unsustainable manner* could be summarized as follows:

- Integrating environmental, social and economic costs in all cost calculations;
- Informing and consulting with the public in identifying benefits and costs;
- Mitigating all adverse impacts where economically feasible;
- Substituting offsetting benefits for losses where economically feasible for all residual impacts; and
- Compensating fairly for all adverse residual impacts, where mitigation or substitution was not possible.

A. Assessing the Mattagami Project Under the New Planning Guidelines

The above changes had a significant impact on strategic planning. They required, among other things, that Ontario Hydro identify and consult with project stakeholders. Research revealed the existence of both primary stakeholders, those likely to be directly affected by the project and secondary stakeholders, those for whom any impacts were likely to be more indirect who would be impacted by the project.

i. *Primary Stakeholders*

Ontario Hydro, the Aboriginal communities of Moosonee and Moose Factory, the Ontario government, the Spruce Falls Pulp and Paper Corporation, and the town of Kapuskasing were identified as primary stakeholders in the process.

Ontario Hydro's stake was based on the desire to produce more cost effective and efficient energy from the Mattagami River than was presently the case. Also, at stake for the corporation, were relationships with northern Ontario's Aboriginal populations. Although the 1960s hydroelectric development had generated large revenues for Ontario Hydro, it had also caused a great deal of environmental damage. This situation led to a great deal of mistrust on the part of the Aboriginal community toward the corporation. That mistrust was now a significant obstacle in effectively involving the Aboriginal communities in the new planning process.

The *Aboriginal communities living in Moosonee and Moose Factory* had been most affected by previous development. They had suffered more than other Aboriginal communities in the Basin as a result of being located downstream from the Mattagami Complex. These Aboriginal communities still relied heavily on traditional resource harvesting activities both for commerce and food. Research available to the corporation indicated that one third of the Native population continued to be directly involved with fishing and hunting. Approximately 50% of the protein consumed by native residents of Moose Factory was obtained from the wild.

Thus, the Aboriginal communities were a critical primary stakeholder in the project. Their oral culture was replete with stories about the negative environmental impacts of previous development upon hunting, fishing, trapping, gathering wild plants, and other traditional pursuits. They were concerned that further development would accelerate the destruction of their way of life. As one Aboriginal stated:

> I think and wish that the building of the dams had never happened, because here and now we are already losing a lot of our culture and our ways of life. Those dams would end our culture. They would break the Circle of Life.

The Aboriginal First Nations were concerned about the planning process, resource development, the cumulative effects of development in the basin as a whole, and compensation for damage done by past development. The Aboriginals were as a consequence now making self-government a critical issue. Furthermore, they had decided that given their distinct status as original inhabitants, negotiations must be on a government-to-government basis.

The provincial government and its ministries were also primary stakeholders. The government was ultimately responsible for the environmental assessment process and would inevitably be held politically accountable for the resolution of the conflict. As well, the Ontario government had agreed to pay Ontario Hydro $247 million if the Environmental Assessment of the proposed redevelopment of the entire Mattagami Complex did not obtain project approval. Issues for the government were: job creation, energy production, Aboriginal self-government, and past grievances. Two ministries were principally responsible for overseeing the approval process, the Ontario Ministry of the Environment and Energy and the Ontario Ministry of Natural Resources.

The Spruce Falls Pulp and Paper Corporation was also directly affected. If the development did not proceed the result might well be higher energy costs for the corporation which ultimately might make the company's products less competitive in the marketplace. If the project did proceed, SFPP would switch from exclusive use of the Smoky Falls Generating Station to drawing power from the Ontario Hydro Bulk Energy System. This would result in a more reliable energy supply for the corporation, less downtime from poor energy supply and lower operating costs as a result of not having to operate and maintain the generating station and the community of workers that lived there, as well as receiving free power from Ontario Hydro for 10 years.

If the SFPP were to close, *the entire community of Kapuskasing* with a population approximately 10 840 people would be in jeopardy as SFPP employed around 30% of the community's work force. As well, 52% of the shares of SFPP were now owned by the pulp and paper company's employees. A further 9% of the shares were held by area residents. Many of the employees had invested their life savings into the future of the corporation.

SFPP also provided significant indirect economic benefits to the community in Kapuskasing. Many of the approximately 358 businesses, the majority of which were quite small, provided services directly or indirectly to SFPP or its employees. If SFPP were shut down, so would the vast majority of these businesses.

Alternately there would be a positive economic benefit for Kapuskasing from the proposed development. Up to 2035 person years of direct project employment would be made available to qualified people over the five year construction period, resulting in a peak labour force of 650 workers. As well, approximately 250 indirect jobs would be generated. Local businesses would benefit from direct project purchases of goods and services. Kapuskasing could experience additional net revenues of between $25 000 to $35 000 per year during the construction period as a result of additional property taxes and provincial grants.

It was clear, therefore, that the town of Kapuskasing was also a primary stakeholder in the project.

ii. Secondary Stakeholders

Identified secondary stakeholders included: other municipalities in the area, labour groups, independent power producers, tourist operators, and environmental groups.

The municipalities likely to be indirectly affected by the project included the *towns* or the *residents* of Smooth Rock Falls, Val Rita-Harty, Moonbeam, and Fauquier. These communities were primarily concerned with promoting economic growth and stability. New hydroelectric development would provide additional jobs and training, and some stimulation in spending. In the past they had benefited from Ontario Hydro development, through job creation and indirectly through access to cheaper electric power. The communities had expressed environmental concerns and had indicated that they would be opposed to development that would result in further deterioration. However, since they had been assured by Ontario Hydro that this was unlikely, they wanted the hydroelectric development to be approved.

Labour groups such as the International Union of Operating Engineers and the Labourers' International Union of North America, had been and would continue to be directly affected by hydroelectric development. Future construction would result in increased direct and indirect employment opportunities for their members.

There were several *independent power producers* in the Basin. These proponents of non-utility generation (NUGs) were concerned about economic opportunities for power development. The resolution of the conflict would establish conditions for further development and would therefore affect their ability to negotiate with Ontario Hydro and the Aboriginals for approval of future projects. They were represented by the Independent Power Producers' Society of Ontario (IPPSO).

Tourist operators would also be impacted. For example, if wildlife were harmed, hunting and fishing outfitters would be negatively affected. On the other hand, any development that improved access would benefit those same outfitters, as well operators of snowmobile tours, motel operators, and so on.

Environmental groups such as the Coalition of Environmental Groups, Energy Probe, and Northwatch were concerned about the hydroelectric development. Their main apprehension was over the cumulative effects of the development, now and in the future.

B. Project Assessment

Ontario Hydro's own assessment had led to the conclusion that tested against its historical criteria the Mattagami proposal represented a lowest cost development option for the corporation. Management had also concluded that the planning criteria that had evolved from the corporation's understanding of what was required by the Environmental Assessment Act and its commitment to sustainable development constituted a fair basis for responding to the concerns of all those likely to benefit or suffer as a result of the development. The redevelopment would allow a more efficient and productive use of the hydraulic potential of the river. The construction phase would benefit local communities economically through the creation of employment and related purchasing of goods and services. Permitting the redevelopment would justify the purchase of the Smoky Falls Station from the Spruce Falls Pulp and Paper Corporation saving tax dollars and strengthening the economic viability of the mill and consequently the town of Kapuskasing. Equally important in light of their commitment to sustainable development, these economic benefits would be accompanied by potential for certain environmental improvements. Ontario Hydro indicated that the planned redevelopment would have little deleterious impact on soil, vegetation, wildlife, and aquatic habitat. The Project would however lead to a reduction in shoreline erosion in headponds, downstream erosion in Adam Creek, and in the passage of fish through the Adam Creek control structure, all of which pointed in the direction of environmental remediation.

Ontario Hydro was aware that some negative environmental impacts would result from the redevelopment that it was proposing. However, it was publicly committed to mitigating those impacts where possible. For example, although there would be additional angling and hunting pressure on fish and wildlife populations from the construction workforce, the corporation had proposed measures to both restrict and discourage excessive hunting and angling activities during the construction period. Although the peaking operations would increase the water level fluctuation downstream of the Kipling Station, Ontario Hydro was proposing to maintain minimal water levels to prevent the dewatering of aquatic habitat. A new spawning habitat would be created in the Smoky Falls' tailrace[6] (see Appendix A) to compensate for the loss of spawning grounds as a result of the redevelopment. Ontario Hydro's environmental assessment also acknowledged that there would be some residual impacts for which compensation would be required. For example, Ontario Hydro was proposing to "co-operate with trappers to identify yields before the project and compensate financial losses resulting from project activities." Ontario Hydro also offered to compensate for impacts on Aboriginal harvesting activities. Through its environmental assessment Ontario Hydro had publicly stated both that it would:

> ...seek to provide fair compensation for all subsistence users and licensed trappers in the project area for any losses that may result from the undertaking. With their co-operation, funding will be provided to area First Nations to define both pre- and post-development levels of Aboriginal harvesting.

And that:

> ...Should impacts be identified, options such as financial compensation, replacement of losses in kind (e.g., provision of fish, fowl, etc. from other sources) or other equivalent impact management measures (e.g., to establish new trap lines, relocate cabins, etc.) will be offered.

The commitment to inform and consult was reflected in "public information and feedback" which "were the cornerstones of the public involvement program for the Mattagami River Extensions Environmental Assessment Study." Although its relationship with the Nishnawbe-Aski First Nations was acknowledged as strained,[7] attempts were being made to rectify the situation including the appointment of a Corporate Aboriginal Affairs Coordinator.

Finally, Ontario Hydro had undertaken to deal with the grievances to which the earlier developments on the river had given rise. However, it had rejected the view that settling those grievances was, or should be, an element in any environmental assessment carried out under the *Environmental Assessment Act*. Its views in this matter had been sustained against legal challenges.

Almost certainly, given the new environmental philosophy of the corporation and the public commitments that were entailed, the Board would be surprised and upset to learn that the Aboriginal communities affected continued to be angrily opposed to the development as proposed by the corporation. Debbie understood clearly that explaining why this was the case would be an important component of her presentation.

PART III: AN ABORIGINAL COUNTERPROPOSAL

Debbie's next task would be to carefully review the First Nations' response to Ontario Hydro's proposed redevelopment of the Mattagami Complex. That response had three components. First was a commitment to sustainable development that the Native People's Circle on Environment and Development (established to bring an Aboriginal perspective to the Ontario Round Table on Environment and Economy) suggested had always been a guiding concept for Native people. This commitment, they went on to say, was reflected in the Native view that "the land and its resources be preserved for the benefit of past, present, and future generations."

As with Ontario Hydro, sustainability for the Aboriginal people was closely linked to economic well-being. This apparent agreement, however, masked important differences.

Randy Kapashesit, Chief of the Mocreebec First Nation, had underlined these differences in pointing out that:

> Ontario Hydro's notion of economic development is not supportive of the kind of economy that is reflective of our own culture, values, traditions and environment.

Underlying these distinct perspectives were different ways of assessing the impacts of hydraulic development on the land. For Ontario Hydro, the land was a resource to be used. From a Native perspective, the land was something deserving great respect, a source of cultural, aesthetic, spiritual as well as economic value. The land was seen as possessing great value in its own right. Its health was viewed as directly linked to human well-being. From an Aboriginal perspective, sustainability was impossible in the absence of respect for the land. The implications of these two perspectives for dealing with the concept of sustainability were striking. For Ontario Hydro, impacts were discussed with a view to replacing losses with equivalent substitutes and failing that providing financial compensation, however, these same impacts were seen by the Aboriginal people as affecting their capacity to sustain a way of life.

The second component in the First Nations' response was the insistence that historical grievances associated with past development be addressed as a condition of future development. This view is captured succinctly by Chief Kapashesit in a statement to the Environmental Assessment Board created to evaluate Ontario Hydro's 25-year Demand/Supply Plan. As he put it:

> Justice requires that...past grievances be settled before future projects are even considered. It is immoral for Ontario Hydro to be talking about future projects when they have not entered into settlements to compensate for the damage they inflicted by past projects.

For the First Nations involved, sustainable development had a historical dimension that they were not prepared to ignore.

The third component of the Aboriginal position on the proposed Mattagami Complex extensions was the demand that there should be no further development until the rights of the First Nation communities to self-government had been recognized. Recognition was to include control over the development of natural resources in areas of Native jurisdiction. The logic behind this demand stemmed directly from the importance of preserving the traditional native way of life and sustainability, and the consistent failure to date on the part of those developing the North to respect values of central importance to the Native communities affected by change. Aboriginal control over the land and its use would ensure that future development was appropriately responsive to those values.

PART IV: THE ONTARIO GOVERNMENT'S OPTION

Debbie knew that historically Ontario Hydro had been closely linked to the Government of Ontario. For example, the Board's Chair and CEO were appointed by the premier of the province. At the same time, the corporation had always tried to operate on business principles at arms length from the government. Hence taking the Board through an evaluation of the results of what was essentially a government inspired initiative in which the corporation had played only a supporting role would certainly be difficult. Debbie decided to set her explanation in the context of the government's substantial financial, economic, and political interest in resolving the conflict that emerged in response to the Mattagami Complex proposal.

The government's response to the conflict was to create a consultative process designed to lead to a consensus on redevelopment. In response to a report it commissioned in July 1991, the provincial government attempted to facilitate problem solving in two distinct ways. Both were designed to resolve the conflict over the Mattagami Complex Proposal fairly while laying the framework for constructive resolution of the longer term resource use planning issues. The process reflected the view that there could be no adequate resolution of the problems without addressing both the economic interests of the non-Native stakeholders and Aboriginal concerns about the right to equitable participation on their part in resource development and resource management.

First, the Ontario government proposed the creation of a "technical group" with a mandate to review "how the design and/or operation of the [Mattagami Complex] Project could be modified to achieve the primary objective of environmental enhancement as well as the production of energy." The government proposed that the group have four members: two appointed by the government and two by the Moose River and the New Post First Nations. The government also committed itself to providing the financial and technical resources the group would need to assess the Mattagami Complex project, as well as consult broadly and report their findings to the government and the elected chiefs and councils of the New Post, Moose Factory, and Mocreebec First Nations. In addition, the technical group's mandate was to make recommendations on any issues of concern identified in the consultative process. In proposing the committee, the Minister implied a willingness to be guided in his decisions on the project in the event that a consensus report that was able to win First Nation support was forthcoming.

Secondly, the government proposed the collection of data establishing the existing biophysical, social, cultural, and economic environmental conditions in the Moose River Basin. This data could then be used to establish a baseline against which the cumulative impacts of resource development in the basin could be measured. The government proposed that "traditional knowledge" as well as scientific data be included in the database.

In calling for a baseline data study, the government was responding to a fundamental Native environmental concern, namely, that the environment should be looked at holistically. In responding to resource development proposals, Native spokespeople argued that what matters is not the aggregate environmental impact of any particular development looked at in isolation but the cumulative impact of resource development in the Moose River Basin looked at as a whole. Native groups also argued that cumulative impacts could only be calculated against pre-established environmental bench-marks. Identifying bench-marks for the Moose River Basin before further development was approved was therefore a fundamental demand which the government hoped in this way to satisfy.

PART V: THE RECOMMENDATIONS

If she succeeded in her goal of explaining the evolution of management thinking, Debbie knew the Board would be in a position to determine the fate of the Mattagami project. Her final task was now to set out the committee's analysis and recommendation to the Board. She had an afternoon to complete this most crucial part of her task. She sat down to write.

EXHIBIT 1   Map of Relevant Area

Source: Ontario Hydro, Environmental Assessment Summary (1991), "Hydroelectric Generating Station Extensions, Mattagami River."

APPENDIX A Components of a Hydroelectric Generating Station

The main components of a hydroelectric generating station are the dam or diversion weir, the powerhouse, and the water passages. The dam or diversion weir directs the flowing water into a canal or turbine inlet. The water then passes through a turbine, causing it to spin with enough force to create electricity in a generator. The water is then returned to the river via a tailrace channel. When the supply of water exceeds the plant's capacity, it is redirected around the station via a sluiceway.

There are two main types of generating stations. The first type is a "run-of-river" or "base load" operation which harnesses the natural flow of the river. The power output of such a plant fluctuates with the stream flow and operates 24 hours a day. The second type of station is known as a "peaking" operation. Unlike a base load station, a dam is used to build up a reservoir of water or "headpond". During periods of peak power demand, the water is released through the turbines of the power station. As a result, both headpond, and downstream water levels fluctuate greatly each day which can cause downstream flooding and the erosion of river banks.

Both types of operation require an electrical transmission system to transport the electricity to the bulk electrical system. The electrical transmission system consists of transformers at each generating station, and overhead transmission lines that must be kept clear of brush and trees, a task that is accomplished through the use of herbicides and in other ways.

SOURCES

The information presented in the case comes from the following sources.

Adams, T. 1992. "Witness Statement." *DSP Environmental Assessment Hearing*, Exhibit #855, December.

Allen, G. 1991. "Ontario Backs Mill Buy-out Plan." *The Globe and Mail*, June 20, A4.

Bennett, Kearon. 1992. "Small Hydro Research Summary Report." *Appendix G, DSP Environmental Assessment Hearing*, Exhibit #926, November.

Cheena, G. 1992. "Witness Statement." Ontario Hydro. DSP Environmental Assessment Hearing, Exhibit #883, December.

Conway, T. 1992. "Impacts of Prior Development." DSP Environmental Assessment Hearing, Exhibit #890, December.

DeLauney, D. 1992. "Report of the Provincial Representative: Moose River Basin Consultations." Report prepared for the Ministry of Natural Resources, April.

Environmental Assessment Act, R.S.O. 1980, c.140.

Environmental Assessment Act, R.S.O. 1990, c.E.18.

ESSA (Environmental and Social Systems Analysts Ltd.). 1992. "Hypotheses of Effects of Development in the Moose River Basin Workshop Summary — Final Report." DSP Environmental Assessment Hearing, Exhibit #719, March.

Faries, B. 1992. "Witness Statement." DSP Environmental Assessment Hearing, Exhibit #876, December.

Fowlie, L. 1991. "Town That Refused To Die." *Financial Post*, December 2830, 16.

Jones, I. 1992. "Witness Statement." DSP Environmental Assessment Hearing, Exhibit #950, December.

Kapashesit, R. 1992. "Evidence in Chief." DSP Environmental Assessment Hearing, Exhibit #1019, December.

Keir, A. 1992. "Socio-Economic Impact Assessment: Reference Document of Hydroelectric Generating Station Extensions Mattagami River." Prepared for Ontario Hydro Corporate Relations Branch, Vols. 1 and 2, January.

Linklater, M. 1992. "Witness Statement." DSP Environmental Assessment Hearing, Exhibit #877, December, 1992.

MacDonald, R. 1992. "Witness Statement." DSP Environmental Assessment Hearing, Exhibit #852, December, 1992.

Mackie, R. 1991. "Can't Afford Mill Bailout, Premier Says." *The Globe and Mail*. July 15, A8.

Morrison, J. 1992. "Colonization, Resource Extraction and Hydroelectric Development in the Moose River Basin: A Preliminary History of the Implications For Aboriginal People." DSP Environmental Assessment Hearing, Exhibit #869, November.

Mugiskan, Chief W. 1992. "Witness Statement." DSP Environmental Assessment Hearing, Exhibit #866, December.

Nation K., and Noble K. 1991. "U.S. Firm Rejects Newsprint Mill Deal." *The Globe and Mail*, June 29, B1 and B4.

"Native People's Circle on Environmental and Development." 1992. Report prepared for the Ontario Round Table on Environment and Economy.

Noble, K. 1991. "Kapuskasing Deal Best For Everybody." *The Globe and Mail*, August 15, B1 and 4.

Ontario Hydro. 1989a. *Demand/Supply Plan Report*, DSP Environmental Assessment Hearing, Exhibit #3, December.

Ontario Hydro. 1989b. *Demand Supply Plan Environmental Analysis*. DSP Environmental Assessment Hearing, Exhibit #4, December.

Ontario Hydro. 1990. *Environmental Assessment: Hydroelectric Generating Station Extensions Mattagami River*, October.

Ontario Hydro. 1991a. *Annual Report.*

Ontario Hydro. 1991b. *The Gifts of Nature.* May.

Ontario Hydro. 1991c. *Environmental Assessment Summary: Hydroelectric Generating Station Extensions Mattagami River*, February.

Ontario Hydro. 1993. *Report of the Task Force on Sustainable Energy Development: A Strategy For Sustainable Energy Development and Use For Ontario Hydro*, October 18.

Ontario Ministry of Natural Resources. 1993a. "Draft Terms of Reference/Work Plan for the Technical Group." July 28.

Ontario Ministry of Natural Resources. 1993b. "Moose River Basin Baseline Data Collection Project, Background Report." August.

Philp, M. 1991. "Spruce Falls Mill May Close." *The Globe and Mail*. March 20, B3.

Roderique, J. 1992. "Witness Statement." DSP Environmental Assessment Hearing, Exhibit #875, December.

Sears, S.K., and Paterson, M. 1991. "Integrated Ecosystem Based Planning for Hydroelectric Generation Development in a Remote Northern Ontario River Basin." DSP Environmental Assessment Hearing, Exhibit #382, May.

Submission Letters. 1992. Review of Environmental Assessment for the Proposed Hydroelectric Generating Station Extensions on the Mattagami River. Ministry of the Environment, Environmental Assessment Branch.

Sutherland, J. 1992. "Witness Statement." DSP Environmental Assessment Hearing, Exhibit #873, December.

Sutherland, P. 1992. "Witness Statement." DSP Environmental Assessment Hearing, Exhibit #874, December.

NOTES

Funding support for this research was provided by the Social Sciences and Humanities Research Council (Strategic Grants Program), York University's National Management Education Project in Business and the Environment, and York University's Schulich School of Business Small Research Grants Program. Funding for the development of this and other case studies examining Canadian business and environment issues was generously provided to the National Management Education Project in Business and the Environment by Ontario Hydro. This case was prepared by Mark Schwartz (PhD candidate) and Professor Wesley Cross, York University as the basis for class discussion and not to illustrate either effective or ineffective management practices. Copyright © 1997 York University. All rights reserved. No part of this publication may be reproduced by any means without permission. For more information, reprint permission or to order copies of this case study, call (416) 736-5809 or write to the Erivan K. Haub Program in Business and the Environment, Schulich School of Business, York University, 4700 Keele St., North York, Ontario, M3J 1P3.

This case study is a product of an interdisciplinary environmental ethics research project studying four situations involving the use or extraction of natural resources in Ontario and northern British Columbia. The authors wish to acknowledge the contribution of: Maria Radford who did much of the original document research; David Pearson, a project coin-vestigator, Ralph Wheeler (Ministry of Natural Resources) and Mario Durepos (Ontario Hydro) who are project partners; Paul Wilkinson and Associates; the Ontario Aboriginal Research Coalition, created to direct research into the effects on Ontario's First Nations of Ontario Hydro's 25-Year Plan, who financed the collection of oral histories assembled to which we refer in a number of places; Chief Ernest Beck and David Fletcher of the Moose Factory First Nation, Chief Randy Kapashesit of the Mocreebec First Nation, and John Turner of the Mushkegowuk Tribal Council who provided guidance and site visit assistance and Ontario Hydro who arranged a site visit to the Mattagami Complex. Without the assistance of all of these people, this research would not have been possible. Also acting as coinvestigators for the project involved in other aspects of the research were John Lewko and Craig Summers (Laurentian University).

1. The account that follows is based on Ontario Hydro's Environmental Assessment, Aboriginal Witness Statements (Adams, Conway, Roderique, J. Sutherland, P. Sutherland), and an exhibit by J. Morrison used during the Demand/ Supply Plan Environmental Assessment Hearing.

2. See Aboriginal Witness Statements, DSP Environmental Assessment Hearing, Exhibits: 829886, 947951, 10181019.

3. Presently the *Environmental Assessment Act* R.S.O. 1990, c.E.18.

4. More specifically, the *Environmental Assessment Act* defines the environment to include:

   i) air, land or water,

   ii) plant and animal life, including man,

   iii) the social, economic and cultural conditions that influence the life of man or a community,

   iv) any building, structure, machine or other device or thing made by man, *v)* any solid, liquid, gas, odour, heat, sound, vibration, or radiation resulting directly or indirectly from the activities of man, or

vi) any part or combination of the foregoing and the interrelationships between any two or more or them. (Revised Statutes of Ontario, 1980, s.1(c))

5. Note, in 1993 Ontario Hydro announced a new mandate namely:

    To recommend an overall corporate strategy that will enable Ontario Hydro to become the world leader in the pursuit of more sustainable forms of energy production, development and use, in response to Agenda 21; to help Ontario achieve a more innovative, energy efficient and internationally competitive economy by applying the principles of sustainable development. (Ontario Hydro Report, p.vii)

6. A tailrace is a channel which carries away water which has passed through the generating station.

7. The First Nations in the Moose River Basin refused to cooperate with Ontario Hydro's environmental assessment.

Index

United States Rubber Co., 394
Unitel, 75
Unity, National, 196
University of Waterloo Institute
 for Groundwater Research,
 398
Upper Canada, 90. See also
 Ontario
Upper Lakes Shipping Ltd., 25
Urban development, 359
Uruguay Round, General
 Agreement on Tariffs and
 Trade (1986-94), 212

Val Rita-Hardy, Ontario, 409, 418
Valhalla Society, 267
Value Added Tax (VAT), 56, 172
Van Horne, William, 17
Van Horne Institute, 112
Vancouver Board of Trade, 273
Vancouver Sun, 263, 274
Varity Corporation, 198
Verdun, Bob, 395, 398, 403
Vertical integration, 9
VIA Rail, 106, 121
Victoria Hospital, London,
 Ontario, 377
Victory Aircraft Ltd., 107
Video Lottery Terminals (VLTs),
 96, 325, 328, 329
Visible hand, 3, 44, 52, 115
Volatile organic compounds
 (VOCs), 283

Wabun Tribal Council, 409
Wagoshig First Nation, 409
War of 1812, 15
Ward Max, 161, 294
Wardair, 77, 292, 301
War Supplies Ltd., 107
War-time Housing Ltd., 107
War-time Oils Ltd., 107
Washington (state), 283
Waste Management Act, British
 Columbia, 280
Water-based paints, 283
Waters, Bob, 399
Waterloo Regional Police, 311-
 312
West Germany, 32, 35, 45
West Publishing, 77
Westar Mining, 296
Western Europe, 63
Western Canada Wilderness
 Committee (WCWC), 265,
 266-267, 268

Westfair Foods Ltd., 75
Weston Bakeries Ltd., 75
Weston, W. Galen, 75
Weston family, 75
WETOX ("Wet Air Oxidation")
 system, 396
White, Bob, 203
White Farm Equipment, 198
White paper, 201
White Paper on Employment and
 Income, 1948, 21
White Paper on Employment and
 Reconstruction, 1945, 20
Whitehorse Mining Initiative
 (WMI), 356-357, 361
 Leadership council, 357
 stakeholder statements, 364
William M. Mercer Ltd., 249
Wilson, Michael, 22, 172
Windy Craggy Mountain mine,
 362-363
 stakeholder concerns, 369-
 371
Winnipeg Hydro, 121
Woolwich Township Council,
 397
Workers' Compensation Board,
 50
World Bank, 211, 229
World Economic Forum and
 International Institute for
 Management Development,
 30
World economy, 27-30
World Heritage Convention, 363
World Trade Organization
 (WTO), 155, 156, 211, 212,
 213
World War II, 20
World Wildlife Fund Canada,
 359

Xerox Canada Inc., 81

York Region, Ontario, 385

Zellers, 75